Katharine
Annals of an Immigrant Family
1866-1964

by
DAVID SCHLICHTING

▪ ▪ ▪

translations by
Merlin Schlichting

▪ ▪ ▪

copyediting by
Melanne Schlichting

Memoir Books
Chico, California

Dedicated

to my mother

Doris Lafere Schlichting
1919-2019

Katharine: Annals of an Immigrant Family, 1866-1964
Copyright ©2024 by David Schlichting
ISBN: 978-1-937748-40-1
Library of Congress Control Number: 2025902031

First Edition

All rights reserved. No portion of this book may be used for any AI purposes, reproduced, or reprinted in any manner whatsoever (except in reviews) that is in violation of copyright restrictions without written permission.

Cover background:	"Beige mulberry textured paper" by rawpixel.com on Freepik.com
Cover photographs:	Katharine Hinderer surrounded by family, 1945, detail (front cover)
	Gottlieb and Katharine Hinderer, 1940s (back cover, top)
	Katharine Hinderer, 1960 (back cover, bottom)

Layout/design by Josie Reifschneider-Smith, Heidelberg Graphics

Printed by Memoir Books, *an Imprint of Heidelberg Graphics*
Chico, California 95926
Heidelberggraphics@gmail.com

Contents

Acknowledgments ix
Introduction xi

Part I—From Wuerttemberg to Minnesota

Chapter 1: The Old Country 1
    Family Beginnings 1
    Germany the Nation—First Steps 2
    Germany the Nation—Failed Attempts 3
    Turning Point 5
    A Nation In Its Youth 7
    Downward Spiral 7

Chapter 2: The Weller and Hinderer Families 11
    Alfdorf and St. Stephan Church 11
    Sophie Weller and Johannes Hinderer 15
    Wuerttemberg Farms 17
    The Weller Family of Alfdorf 17
    Alfdorf – Then and Now 19
    The Hinderer Family of Brend 21
    Brend – Then and Now 22

Chapter 3: The Deininger and Heinz Families 29
    Gehren and Kaisersbach 29
    The Protestant Church of Kaisersbach 31
    Johann <u>Gottlieb</u> Deininger and Karoline Heinz 33
    The Current Residents of the Gehren Property 36
    The Gehren Property 38
    The Heinz Family of Gehren 41
    The Heinz Family Book of Sermons 44
    Wuerttemberg Citizenship and Marriage Practices 48

Chapter 4: Passage to America 53
    By the Numbers 54
    Why They Left Wuerttemberg 56
    Why They Chose America 57
    The Means of Travel 59
    Katharine and Gottlieb – How They Met 60
    Leaving Home 61
    Across the Ocean 63
    Arrival in America 64
    Their Destination 66

Chapter 5: Washtenaw County Michigan 69

Michigan 69
Tracking the Michigan Family 70
Rosine (Weller) Koeder's Family 71
Michael Weller's Family 78
Sophie (Weller) Hinderer's Family 82
The Michigan Hinderer Family – The Children of Johannes and Sophie 85
Johann (John) Georg Hinderer 85
Christine Catharine Hinderer 86
Gottlob Hinderer 89
August Hinderer 92
Michigan and Minnesota 93
Was It Michigan or Iowa? 94

Chapter 6: The Iowa Hinderers 95

Iowa Beginnings 95
Settling Iowa - The Milwaukee Road 97
Postville, St. Paul Lutheran Church, and Two Hinderer Families 101
Gottfried Hinderer b. 1857 and Rosine Nise 102
Gottlieb and Katharine Hinderer 109
Katharine's Hymnal 114
The 1890s – Ruin and Recovery 114

Chapter 7: Minnesota—Land For Sale 119

Indian Land – The Minnesota Story 120
The Sioux on the Great Plains 122
Water Is What Matters 123
Yellow Medicine and Lac Qui Parle Counties 125
Canby and the Winona & St. Peter Railroad Company 127

Part II

Introduction 137
Storytellers 137

John Hinderer

Doris Schlichting

George, Mabel, and Bob Monson

Maurine (Krug) Gjovig

Leonard Krug, Bette (Krug) Weber, and Florence (Krug) Rousseau

Don Engstrand and Norma (Engstrand) Sandrock

Emma Swenson

Chapter 8: A Farm on the Prairie 139
- Minnesota Arrival - 1898 139
- The Sod House 140
- Their Land Purchase 142
- Building Their House – Room by Room 145
- First Things First – Farm Necessities 150
- Outbuildings and Utilities 152
- Transportation 154
- Farm Crops 155
- Farm Animals 158
- Family Recipes 161

Chapter 9: The Hinderer Farm: Through the Years 165
- A Working Family 165
- Food and Necessities 172
- Church Attendance 175
- District 66 School 175
- High School 178
- Leisure Time 179
- Depression Followed by Wars 185
- After the War 186
- Family Recipes 191

Chapter 10: The Monson Family 193
- Tena Hinderer 193
- John Monson's Family 196
- Kanabec County 196
- Tena and John 202
- Life on Tena and John's Farm 203
- George, Mabel, and Bob 206
- The Later Years 209
- Family Recipes 210

Chapter 11: The Illinois Krug Family 213
- The Krug Immigrants - Adults 214
- Krug Immigrants - Children 216
- <u>Johann</u> Konrad Krug (#4) & Anna <u>Margaret</u> (Margaretha) Elizabeth Schaller (#5) 219
- Hansen Immigrants 220
- Perschnick Immigrants 220
- <u>Andrew</u> Hansen (#6) and <u>Mary</u> Perschnick (#7) 224
- Martin Krug (#1) and His Parents – <u>John</u> George Krug (#2) & Anna Hansen (#3) 224
- Nels Hansen 227

    Nels Hansen and Anna (Hansen) Krug 228
    The Two Hansen Families Move to Minnesota 228

Chapter 12: Sophie and Martin Krug 233

    Sophie Hinderer 234
    Martin Krug 235
    Sophie Hinderer Meets Martin Krug 236
    Sophie and Martin – Early Times 237
    Family Complications 239
    Sophie and Martin – Family Years 239
    Sophie Krug's Death and the Aftermath 242
    A Perspective 244

Chapter 13: Emma Hinderer, Ralph Lafere, and Doris Lafere 245

    1918 – A Dangerous World 245
    At Home in America – Women's Suffrage and Prohibition 246
    Emma and Her Hinderer Family 248
    Emma and Ralph Lafere 249
    Sioux Falls, South Dakota 251
    Emma on the Farm; 1919-1926 253
    Ralph Lafere – After Sioux Falls 253
    Using DNA to Search for Ancestors 257

Chapter 14: Emma Lafere and Martin Krug 259

    Doris – Her Childhood 259
    1926 259
    The Rental Farms 262
    A Complicated Family 263
    The Parents 264
    Farm Stories – Recollections of Childhood 266
    Martin Krug and Prohibition 271
    The Death of Martin Krug 272
    After Martin Krug's Death 273

Chapter 15: Emma Krug—Single Parent 275

    Emma Krug's Canby Homes 275
    Emma's Children – Leaving Home 278
    Family Stories – the Hinderers 289
    Family Stories – Emma 292
    More Children's Stories 294
    Emma – The Later Years 299
    Family Recipes 300

Chapter 16: Mary and Albert Engstrand 303

John Engstrand – the Early Years 304
John Engstrand and Anna Johnson – Family Years 305
Arthur Engstrand – Dutiful Farmer and Civic Leader 310
Mary Hinderer 311
Albert Engstrand 312
Albert Engstrand and Mary Hinderer 314
Life on the Engstrand Farm 321
The Engstrand's Farmhouse 324
School Days 325
Their Separate Ways 326
Arthur, Mary, and the Engstrand Farm – The Later Years 329
Family Recipes 330

Chapter 17: Our Greatest Generation—Hinderer Family Members in World War II 333

Four Hinderer Men 333
Johnny Krug, U.S. Navy 333
John Hinderer, Pvt. U.S. Army 341
Don Engstrand, Lt. U.S. Army Air Corps 355
Bill Gjovig, U.S. Navy 365
On Reflection 373

Chapter 18: Katharine—A Tribute 379

Appendix A: Ancestor Families 383

Introduction 383
Ancestors of Gottlieb Hinderer (1866-1951) 384
Ancestors of Katharine Deininger Hinderer (1872-1964) 386

Appendix B: A Tour of St. Stephan Church, Aldorf 389

The Tour Begins: Historic Aldorf and Its People 389
St. Stephan Church of Aldorf 389

Appendix C: Family Recipes 395

Katharine Hinderer 396
Martha Hinderer 398
Tene Monson 399
Emma Krug 401
Mary Engstrand 406

Index 407

Acknowledgments

The author acknowledges and thanks those who contributed their time and skills to the composition of this book. The home team for *Katharine* was identical to those who worked on the previous family story, *Hinrich*. First, my brother Merlin Schlichting worked through all of the original German documents. This meant word-by-word translations from the original script into modern German and then into English. His work provided the factual foundation for the early chapters.

Those same early chapters were enriched by a 2019 tour of the southwestern part of Germany native to this family. Merlin, my son Ryan Schlichting, and I shared this delightful experience. The pictures, the new acquaintances, the tours, the historical documents, the wonderfully warm personal welcomes, and even the home-cooked meals all encouraged the completion of this book. Merlin's language fluency was essential to gaining this life experience. Ryan's sketches and thoughts also made their way into the early chapters. Thank you, Merlin and Ryan.

Merlin and his wife Jill Schlichting contributed their editor's skills to proofread the chapters and offer both corrections and suggestions. Their observations improved the narrative allowing easier comprehension by readers, most of whom will not be familiar with the story. Thank you for your time and work so essential to the story-telling process.

As with the prior family story about Hinrich Schlichting, my wife Melanne Schlichting worked as copyeditor on every page of this book. She had the task of reading through and refining the many drafts of each chapter. As someone not familiar with the story, she identified the confusing elements in the narrative and suggested how those could be made clearer. As a critical reader of both fiction and non-fiction, she set the standard for what makes a story read well. To Melanne, my thanks and my love.

This home team laboriously worked through the narrative and also reviewed the many pictures, illustrations, diagrams, and family trees. They made *Katharine* more accurate, more readable, and ready for publishing.

My gratitude, as well, to the professionals, now friends, at Heidelberg Graphics. Their skills created pages that have both balance and visual appeal. Larry Jackson has worked with inexperienced authors for many years. As *Katharine* neared the home stretch, Larry promised to see this book through to the finish, one way or another. Thank you Larry, and my best wishes to you in your retirement. A welcome and thanks to Josie Reifschneider-Smith who now continues the work of this quintessential local business. It was Josie who labored through the page layout and final editing. She forged the draft documents together into this family story. Her contagious enthusiasm, skill, and encouragement guided the work to completion.

Historical information was sourced variably from online digitized data and from archives. In particular, the chapter on Hinderer family members in World War II required outside assistance. The Eisenhower Presidential Library copied dozens of pages that traced John Hinderer's army unit from their U.S. base through the European war theater. My thanks to Bill Beigel, who found original military documents for both Don Engstrand and Bill Gjovig. These documents allowed me to write with certainty about these two young men during the war years.

Thanks also to the professionals at Ancestry ProGenealogists. Their original research and expertise allowed me to compose what had previously been a blank page regarding Doris (Lafere) Schlichting's paternal ancestry. It was a delicate subject, but thanks to their work, this new information can be presented and discussed with certainty.

Although they are no longer here to thank, the contribution of the many storytellers requires acknowledgement. These members of the Hinderer family were at the heart of the stories retold in *Katharine*. Their love for this family shone through the many hours of taped recordings they provided. Their stories were at times difficult and even emotional for them to retell. More often, however, the stories were accompanied by a smile and a laugh. By any measure, this is also their story, and I believe they would have taken pride in it.

Finally, I wish to acknowledge my fellow descendants of this Hinderer family. Some of you contributed photos, memories, and tangible mementos from this family. Not one of you held back in your generosity. These are the elements that make families and family stories so special. Your recognition of the value of writing *Katharine* kept me working toward a completion that we can pass along to our descendants.

David Schlichting

Introduction

THE HINDERER FAMILY

The composition of *Katharine* began in 2019. The storyline follows the lives of the author's maternal great grandparents, Katharine Deininger and Gottlieb Hinderer. They were born in southwestern Germany and emigrated to America in the late 1800s. They raised their children on farms in the Midwest where they both lived long and productive lives.

Interviews of family members were used to develop much of the story told in *Katharine*. These "storytellers" offered a window into the day-to-day lives of the Hinderer family during the first half of the 20th century.

The first section of the book is arranged chronologically. The German birth families of Katharine and Gottlieb are discussed as well as the circumstances of their meeting. Historical information allows an understanding of daily life in late 19th century Germany. In their homeland, they were young, poor, and unlikely to become a successful farm family. Their solution was to leave their birth families and Germany behind. In the early 1890s, they were part of a great wave of European humanity responding to the promise of land ownership in America.

The narrative follows the couple through their early life on Iowa rental farms where their first five children were born. They saved money until they were able to purchase farmland in southwestern Minnesota. The Hinderers and other immigrants like them took advantage of large-scale U.S. government land sales. Both skill and hard labor were needed to successfully navigate those early years of farm ownership.

The second section of the book explores the lives of Katharine and Gottlieb's children. These chapters are arranged in the children's birth order. In this second section, the "storytellers" provide the central narrative with their personal recollections of family life. Historical information has been added to the stories told by these children. This allows readers an opportunity to understand these family members within the context of 20th century America.

Two world wars separated by the worst depression since the 1890s provided the historical backdrop to the children's lives. As they grew into adulthood, the risks they took, and the decisions they made are discussed. These Hinderer children were a part of what would later be called "The Greatest Generation."

The World War II combat experience of four Hinderer men is detailed in one chapter. Their military service was never a topic discussed at family gatherings or reunions. Nevertheless, their original combat records reveal the dangers they survived and the deep patriotism of that era. This chapter has been written to honor these four men who risked their lives to preserve the nation Katharine and Gottlieb chose as their own.

In its conclusion, this family story is a tribute to the author's great grandmother, Katharine Hinderer. She was the cornerstone personality that shaped and bonded this family. A tribute to her is detailed in the final chapter.

THE BOOK

Chapters are organized in a predictable format. Each chapter begins with a historical timeline listing dates discussed in that chapter. The dates of family events are mixed with more general historical dates.

Numbered endnotes are listed following each chapter. They document source material and offer more detailed explanations not included in the narrative. The endnotes are also used to reference the GPS coordinates of locations listed in the story. A mapping program such as Google Maps is an easy way to view these locations in modern times.

Several chapters conclude with a reference to Appendix C, which contains a collection of family recipes. For those who decide to recreate these dishes, a word of caution is in order. The recipes are reprinted as they were originally written. They have not been tested using modern ingredients. Consider it a cooking adventure, and you will not be disappointed.

The text is augmented with numerous photos, illustrations, historical documents, and charts. These are positioned within the narrative to both explain and authenticate the topics being discussed.

Three appendices and an index follow the narrative chapters:

- Appendix A expands the two charts listing Katharine and Gottlieb's ancestors. Introductory remarks explain how these charts have been constructed.

- Appendix B describes a 2019 tour of St. Stephan church in Alfdorf.

- Appendix C is a collection of family recipes.

The narrative includes some speculative elements. The author takes full responsibility for the speculations made and the conclusions drawn.

Part I

From Wuerttemberg to Minnesota

Chapter 1

The Old Country

Timeline

1787 – U.S. Constitution signed

1797 – Napoleon I invaded German lands

1804 – Lewis and Clark explored the western U.S.

1815 – Napoleon I defeated – the German Confederation formed

1834 – McCormick introduced a mechanical grain cutter

1848 – Failed German Revolution led to emigration

1860-1865 – U.S. Civil War curbed immigration

1864 – Prussia controlled northern German lands

1866 – Gottlieb Hinderer was born in Alfdorf

1866 – Prussia defeated Austria

1871 – Prussia defeated France

1871 – The German Empire was formed

1872 – Katharine Deininger was born in Gehren

1873 – Worldwide depression

1879 – Edison invented the light bulb

1880s – Peak German inflow into the U.S.

1890 – Kaiser Wilhelm II ousted Chancellor Bismarck

1891 – Katharine and Gottlieb emigrated to America

1893 – Another worldwide depression

1898 – Spanish-American War

1901 – McKinley assassinated - Theodore Roosevelt became president

1914 – World War I began

Family Beginnings

Brend, Alfdorf, and Kaisersbach are neighboring communities in the picturesque Swabian region of southwestern Germany. Today, they have populations of several hundred to a few thousand citizens. In the mid-1800s when Gottlieb Hinderer and Katharine Deininger were born, they had fewer citizens, and travel between them was by foot or hoof.

The terrain in this part of Germany has rolling hills. Towns and villages are only a mile or two apart, separated by forested land and grassy fields. Even today, communities are connected by walking paths, winding roadways, and shared churches.

From the hilltop village of Brend, the Hinderer family could hear the tolling bells of St. Stephan Church in nearby Alfdorf. Johannes Hinderer first met Sophie Weller in St. Stephan Church. In 1865 they were married in the same church. Sophie's father, Jacob Weller, was a farmer and their family lived in Alfdorf. Johannes's father, Gottfried Hinderer, was also a farmer and their family lived in Brend. St. Stephan Church was the link that brought the Weller and Hinderer families together. Johannes and Sophie's son, Gottlieb, was born a year later in the fall of 1866.

Six years later in 1872, Johann Deininger and Karoline Heinz registered the birth of their first daughter, Katharine. They were also farmers. They lived in a small country house built on a hairpin roadway turn near the town of Kaisersbach. Like Alfdorf, Kaisersbach had its own Protestant church, and Katharine's birth was properly entered into that church's records.

For centuries, poor farmers lived in small towns and villages. Their homes sheltered both family

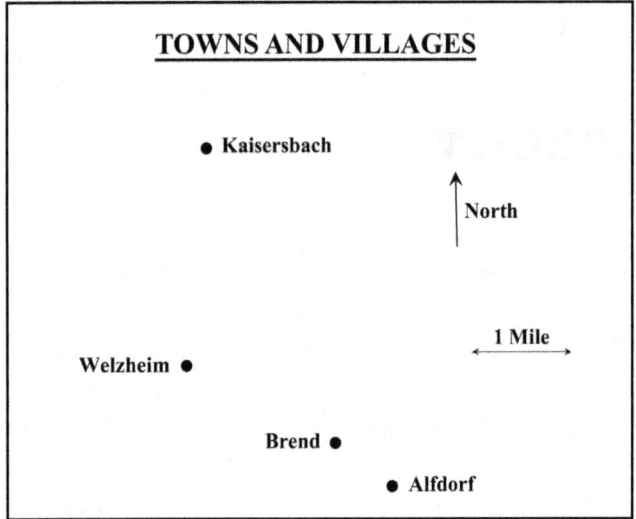

The local villages and towns were close to one another. Source: Illustration by author.

and livestock. On hillside slopes, the farmers lived on the second level above their animals. Where the land was nearly flat, the families lived in cottage-sized homes with a common wall between them and their livestock. Land parcels were generally small, a few acres at most. The animals they raised and the gardens they planted fed their family year-round. Most days, the adults and older children worked away from home on farm tracts owned by aristocratic families or the church. Their farm income and their home food supply depended on good weather and a healthy working family. Insufficient tillable land, crop failures, injuries, infectious diseases, and a rigid social structure locked them into generations of poverty.

German-speaking lands are ancient, occupied for centuries by a series of tribal groups and societies long before Europeans came to the Americas. As a unified nation, however, Germany is nearly 100 years younger than the United States of America. The birth of Gottlieb and Katharine, in 1866 and 1872 respectively, straddled the official formation of the German Empire in 1871.

This is the story of Katharine and Gottlieb, their birth families, their emigration, and the expansion of their family in America. Their story is framed by the history of their homeland, the turbulent times in which they were raised, and the American nation they chose as their own.

Germany the Nation—First Steps

The story begins in the near-landlocked center of continental Europe. In the early 1800s, today's Germany was a collection of sovereign states, cities, and church-controlled tracts. For centuries, this collection was known as the Holy Roman Empire. The spoken languages were Germanic, but the many dialects stifled communication. The name Holy Roman Empire implied there was a central government, but this was not the case. Regional governing bodies held the real authority, and their policies determined the rules for the common folk. It was the last remnant of feudal times when a few aristocratic families and the church held land ownership and authority over the commoners. Each regional prince or governing body made decisions with the primary goal of maintaining their own power and wealth. French writer Voltaire observed that the Holy Roman Empire was neither holy nor Roman. The absence of a strong central government made the notion of an empire more wishful thinking than reality.

By 1800, much of Europe had already formed nations with controlling central governments. Waterways were the travel routes for conducting trade and thereby accumulating wealth. Countries with expansive oceanic borders and developed waterway networks had a trade advantage. They tended to mature into sovereign nations earlier than the landlocked midlands. England, France, Spain, Sweden, and the Netherlands were already nations with central governments. Most of these governments were monarchies, but constitutional changes were trending toward greater involvement by the entire citizenry. The central power structure of these true nations gave them an advantage over the separate states, cities, and church-controlled tracts of the Holy Roman Empire.

The Swabian (in German, Schwäbisch) home of these ancestral families was part of the Kingdom of Wuerttemberg in what is now southwestern Germany. In 1800, it was the southwestern edge of the Holy Roman Empire. Empire armies were based east of Wuerttemberg (also spelled Württemberg) in what is now Austria. In those early years of the 19th century, the Holy Roman Empire was under attack from the east and the west. From the east, the Ottoman Turks invaded and eventually occupied part of what is now Austria. From the west, the armies of Napoleon I of France invaded both Wuerttemberg and the Germanic states to the north. From 1800 to 1815, Wuerttemberg was a battleground state.

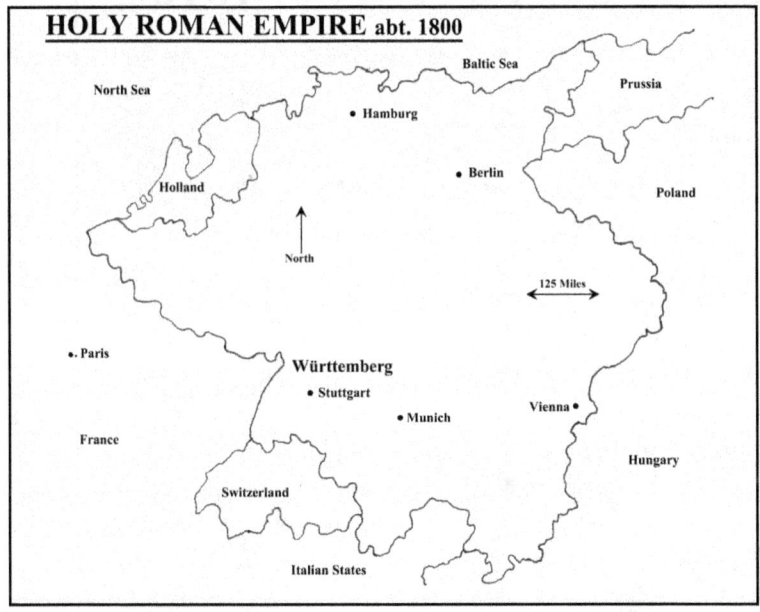

The Holy Roman Empire in about 1800 included most of central Europe. Source: Illustration by author.

The rulers of the Kingdom of Wuerttemberg had for centuries been aligned with the Holy Roman Empire based in Austria. After 1800, French army victories demanded a new consideration. Wuerttemberg's leaders performed a balancing act, siding with whichever army was then in control. Most often, this was the French. Napoleon I rewarded his aligned Wuerttemberg leaders by expanding their land holdings. Allegiance to France continued until 1815 when Napoleon I's armies were defeated throughout Europe. This dampened French influence and reoriented Wuerttemberg's leaders toward their Germanic neighbors to the north and east.

The balance of power inside Wuerttemberg was even more complex. There was a state authority, generally a prince, but his power base was precarious. Hundreds of small towns and villages established their own borders, laws, a system of courts, and trade networks. If the prince of Wuerttemberg demanded unpopular changes, the local authorities might choose to align with a different prince or form a new state of their own. The result was a countryside dotted with constantly realigning small power centers. From the top down, both Wuerttemberg and the Holy Roman Empire were fragmented and vulnerable to attack.

Germany the Nation— Failed Attempts

In 1815, the separate German states established a political structure called the German Confederation of 1815. It was somewhat like today's European Union. It consisted of 35 monarchies and four city-states, all independently governed. Ostensibly, forming the Confederation would lead to reduced trade barriers and greater prosperity. The goal of the regional leaders, however, was to keep their separate power centers intact. In the end, it failed. Confederation states were still without the military protection of a strong central power. As before, commoners had no voice in the ruling governments.

Across the Atlantic Ocean, the United States was emerging as a new form of democratic governance. Their democracy balanced power between three governing bodies with all citizens given a voice through representative elections. After winning independence from England, it took over ten years for Americans to hammer out a governing constitution. Nevertheless, this new democracy had held together. With successful alternative examples of governance on both sides of the Atlantic, the German Confederation of 1815 was out of touch with the times.

By the mid-1800s, the Industrial Revolution was in full swing throughout the Western World. Commercial transportation by waterways was replaced by railway systems powered by steam locomotives. Newly constructed urban factories attracted workers from farms and villages. In poor families, property was generally passed on to children. As the population increased, the acreage available to one farmer became progressively smaller. With insufficient land to sustain a family, moving into a town and working in a factory was appealing to sons and daughters of poor farmers.

Factories were a new idea. Regulations aimed at protecting workers were still in the future. Working parents and their children often toiled side by side. The living quarters in factory towns and cities were

The failed German Confederation of 1815 was a loose affiliation of independent states. Source: "Europe 1815 After the Congress of Vienna" (Alexander Altenhof, April 14, 2017, CC BY-SA 4.0), accessed January 2021, https://commons.wikimedia.org/wiki/file:europe_1815_map_en.png#file. Edited by author.

polluted ghettos lacking sanitation. For factory workers, there was little hope of earning their way to a more prosperous life.

The more educated people in the Confederation were better off economically, but also discontent. Their progressive ideals of democratic governance posed a threat to the local princes. In addition, weather-caused crop failures in the late 1840s threatened both the commoners and the educated populace. By mid-century, the German Confederation of 1815 was ripe for change.

The resulting German Revolution of 1848 was an attempt to establish a democratic German nation. In the end, it failed to produce a centralized nation, but it did stimulate the first large-scale emigration of Germans to America. Wuerttemberg did not experience violent riots during the 1848 revolution, but it did suffer a loss of population due to emigration. The revolution also sparked the rise of local organizations called Vereine. These were clubs organized for personal pursuits such as supporting sports teams. However, a Vereine also provided a meeting place for city dwellers and villagers alike. Here they could voice complaints and discuss new visions for political change.

Importantly, the states of the original German Confederation of 1815 did not share power and influence equally. Two states, Prussia in the north and Austria in the south, dominated. Each had its own well-equipped army, and each made separate alliances to promote their own gain. Austria was the seat of the historical Habsburg monarchy with stronger ties to Rome and traditional Catholicism. Prussia was predominantly Protestant and was ruled by its own succession of ambitious monarchs. Prussian armies conquered lands from the Baltic countries and parts of Russia westward through Poland, Pomerania, and into the northern states of the German Confederation.

Turning Point

The decade of the 1860s was a turning point. In 1864, the Prussian state fostered a strategic alliance with the Austrian state to push the neighboring Danes northward. Their combined armies defeated the Danes and annexed the battleground states of Schleswig and Holstein under Prussian control.

Less than two years later, Prussian political strategist Otto von Bismarck plotted to extend his control. He used a disagreement about governing Schleswig and Holstein as an excuse to challenge Austria for control of the entire German Confederation. The ensuing Seven Weeks War of 1866 was decisive. Prussian forces quickly defeated their former ally Austria and its aligned states. The victorious Prussians could now control the entire German Confederation. The defeated Austrians became the separate nation of Austria.

1866 was also the birth year of Gottlieb Hinderer. His home state of Wuerttemberg was aligned with the Austrians during the Seven Weeks War of 1866. With the defeat of the Austrians, the three southern states of Wuerttemberg, Baden, and Bavaria were pressured to acquiesce to the Prussians.

The lingering French influence in the three southern German states was Chancellor Bismarck's next target. The Franco-Prussian War of 1870 played perfectly into his hands. Prussian armies defeated Napoleon III of France, ending the era of French influence. The post-war negotiations brought the three southern states into the tightening grip of Prussian control.

The German Empire of 1871, sometimes called the Second Reich, established a central government dominated by the Prussians. Unification of the separate states required negotiations and diplomacy, but a single German nation had finally been formed. It was almost 100 years after Americans had declared their independence from England. Katharine Deininger was born in 1872, one year after Germany became a nation.

In America, the decade of the 1860s was a turning point as well. The unresolved issue of slavery had reached a crisis point. The economy of the South depended on slave labor while the more industrialized North sided with Abolitionists

The states of Prussia and Austria dominated the Confederation, and after 1866, Prussia was in control. Source: "Europe 1867" (Alexander Altenhof, April 14, 2017, CC BY-SA 4.0), accessed January 2021, https://commons.wikimedia.org/wiki/File:Europe_1867_map_en.png. Edited by author.

against slavery. The 1860 election of Abraham Lincoln led to the secession of southern states and the American Civil War. On both sides of the Atlantic, warfare was the theme of this decade.

The American war brought immigration to a near standstill. It effectively closed the main escape route for a German populace embroiled in the three wars of the decade. Robert E. Lee's surrender to Ulysses S. Grant in April 1865 ended the American Civil War. It also reopened America's door to immigration. From 1870 to the end of the century, large-scale emigration from central Europe to America was the order of the day.

The events of the 19th century played out somewhat differently in Gottlieb and Katharine's Swabian region of Wuerttemberg. In the early 1800s, *La Grande Armée* ("The Grand Army") of Napoleon I occupied the countryside. They engaged in destructive battles against the Austrian army. Both armies lived off the land. This meant they required local farmers to quarter and feed their soldiers, the support personnel, and the armies' livestock. Even worse, Napoleon I conscripted thousands of Wuerttemberg's young men and deployed them as French soldiers. Some were sent as far away as Russia.

During and after the years of the German Confederation of 1815, Wuerttemberg commoners were mainly farmers. They were poorer than commoners in the more industrialized German states to the north. They embraced the Industrial Revolution, but their factories were small and located in towns rather than urban cities. Even the building of railway lines trailed railroad expansion in the northern states. The agriculture-based economy of Wuerttemberg persisted after the formation of the German Empire in 1871. At the end of the century, most of the people still lived in small towns and villages rather than urban centers. It is not surprising that the ancestors of both Gottlieb and Katharine were poor farmers living in Wuerttemberg's small towns and villages.

A Nation In Its Youth

The military and political brilliance of Prussian Chancellor Otto von Bismarck did not ensure a smooth beginning for the German Empire. 1873 was the beginning of what in Europe would be known as the Long Depression. In Germany, it lasted from 1873 until 1879. In other European nations, it persisted for more than a decade. In England and on the continent, financial markets collapsed, banks failed, and currency values plummeted.

The Long Depression in Europe also had an American component. Economic expansion after the American Civil War fueled wild speculation in railway companies beyond solvency. The result, known in America as the Panic of 1873, produced a collapse of American markets, bank failures and civil unrest. Furthermore, the German Empire ended the use of silver coins, and this had a damaging effect on the American economy. Silver ore had been mined in the western U.S. and exported to Germany for minting their coins. Germany's decision meant the U.S. silver export market disappeared. It was an early example of economic globalization and worldwide depression. Until the 1930s, the Panic of 1873 was the "Great Depression" American citizens would recall.

Compared to other European nations, Germany emerged from the Long Depression more quickly and with broader economic vigor. Chancellor Bismarck was the strategist behind both domestic and international policies. He deftly established strategic alliances with European continental powers, thereby preventing warfare for nearly twenty years. This break from constant treasury-draining wars allowed the German economy to recover.

At home, Bismarck manipulated squabbling political and religious partisans. He was able to prevent any one of them from threatening the central authority of the German Empire. It was a chess game both at home and abroad, and Bismarck was the master.

The early years of the German Empire saw enlightened reforms. These included a provision for children's education and a welfare system for workers suffering from sickness or accidents. Even old age and disability supports were enacted. Social support systems had the effect of increasing worker productivity. They also stifled the appeal of rising socialist movements spreading across Europe. However, as the economy improved, Bismarck's domestic policies tended to increase the control of the central government.

The end of Bismarck's remarkable leadership tenure came from within Germany. An initial series of compliant monarchs ended with the ascent of 29-year-old Wilhelm II as Kaiser. Bismarck's intricate alliances were at odds with Wilhelm II's openly expansionist goals. His egotistical and bombastic personality demanded unwavering allegiance. His devotion was to his army, not his people. He saw his authority as absolute, and to many Germans he became a cult figure. Kaiser Wilhelm II stated it bluntly: "There is only one master in the Reich and that is I; I shall tolerate no other."[1] After a series of heated arguments, he demanded and received Bismarck's resignation in 1890. It was one year before Gottlieb Hinderer and Katharine Deininger emigrated to America.

Downward Spiral

During the last decade of the 1800s, the Western World began a downward spiral. It would eventually lead to the massive carnage of World War I. It was

By 1878, the German Empire was a true nation. Source: "Europe 1878" (Alexander Altenhof, April 14, 2017, CC BY-SA 4.0), accessed January 2021, https://commons.wikimedia.org/wiki/File:Europe_1878_map_en.png. Edited by author.

an era of nationalistic fervor, intolerance, and expansion-minded militarism.

In Germany, Kaiser Wilhelm II's belief in his personal superiority helped foster a sense of national destiny. His notion of the presumed genetic superiority of one group or nation was not new. It perversely claimed that the economic success of a nation was due to superior genetics rather than a balance of government control and personal freedoms. The same idea was used again in 1930s Germany. In both cases, genetic superiority was promoted by a despotic ruler wishing to ensure continuation of his own personal power.

In England, the last vestiges of the aristocratic ruling class slowly faded into a more representative government. In Russia, Tsar Alexander II was assassinated in 1881. The remaining Russian royal family members were murdered by Bolsheviks early in the next century. Anarchy movements throughout the Western World threatened all political structures. Anarchists believed that land ownership was the underlying evil in society. It was a self-defeating idealism that offered no room for compromise, and no practical way to govern a nation.

In America, now a century old, settlers spanned the continent. There was no unclaimed western land to act as a safety valve for a restless population. The youthful American democracy aspired to become a dominant influence in international politics. This era was called the "Gilded Age." New industrial giants such as Rockefeller in oil, Carnegie in steel, Vanderbilt and Gould in railroads, and J.P. Morgan in finance created controlling monopolies.

Their opponents were political machines, corrupt unions, and "yellow" journalism publications. It took the unstoppable energy of Theodore Roosevelt's "Square Deal" presidency of 1901 to begin the political journey toward achieving a balance between these powerful combatants.

World War I was the black hole that would capture nations of the Western World. Toward the end of the 19th century there was a universal sense that a great conflict was coming, and nothing could be done to stop it. Land wars had always been the way neighboring nations settled disagreements and satisfied the power lust of their rulers. The promises of change made by a new generation of political leaders had not been fulfilled. Old monarchies were dying, but there was a vacuum of peaceful governing systems waiting in the wings. And at that time, there was no worldwide body offering diplomatic solutions to disputes between nations.

This was the turbulent world that Gottlieb Hinderer and Katharine Deininger entered. They were the children of poor farmers in a rural region of their German homeland. Their country and their families were people rich, but land poor. It was a sobering beginning for their lives together.

Notes

1. Barbara W. Tuchman, *The Proud Tower: A Portrait of the World Before the War, 1890-1914* (New York: Random House, 2014), 268.

Katharine

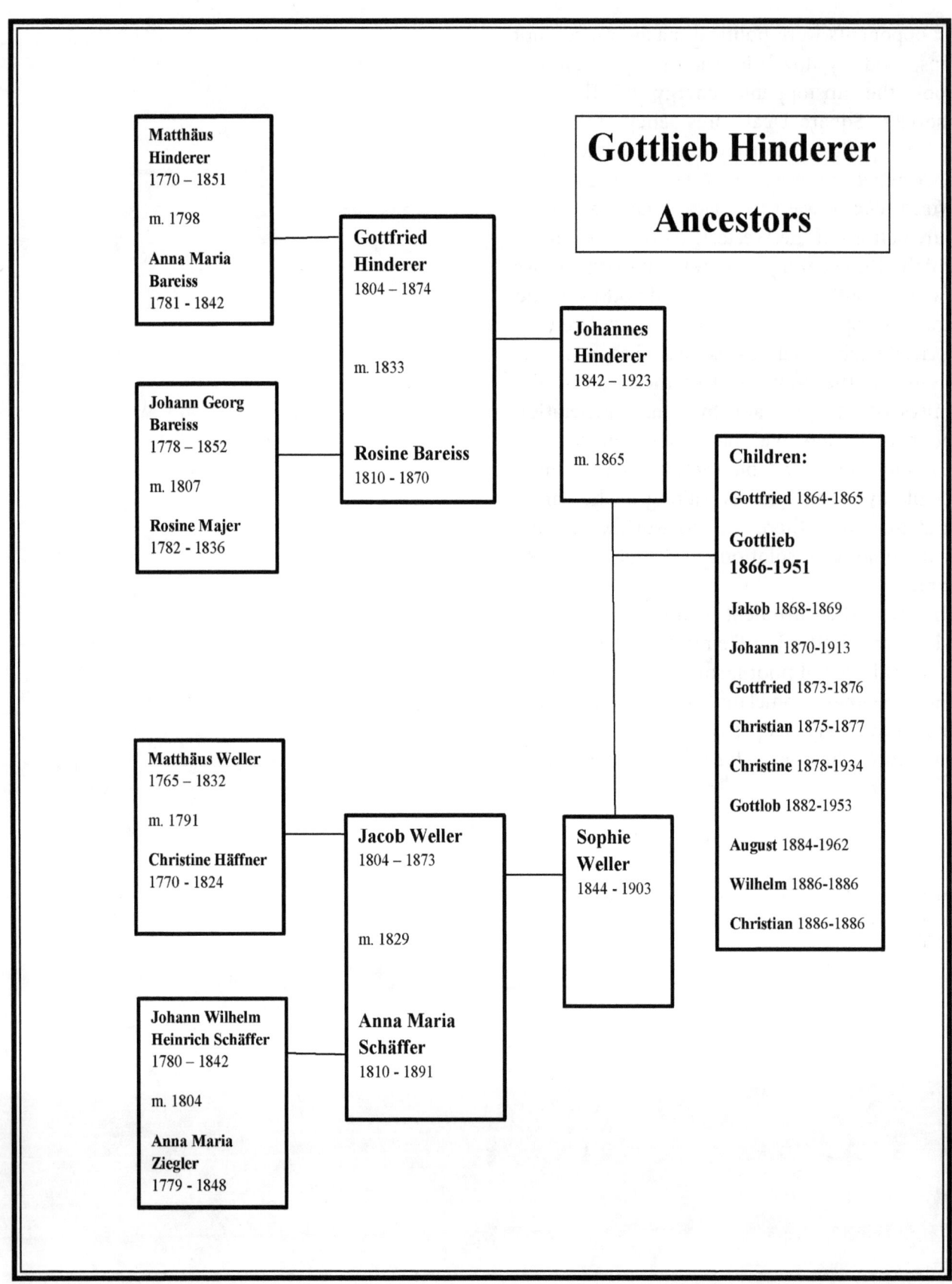

Chapter 2

The Weller and Hinderer Families

Timeline

1143 – The town of Alfdorf was first described
1297 – An Alfdorf chapel was first described
1517 – The Protestant Reformation challenged the papacy
1628 – Baron vom Holst became patron of St. Stephan Church
1660s – The Hinderers lived in Brend
1700s – The Wellers lived in Alfdorf
1787 – The U.S. Constitution was signed
1800 – Wuerttemberg aligned with Napoleon I
1842 – Johannes Hinderer was born in Brend
1844 – Sophie Weller was born in Alfdorf
1852 – Sophie's sister Rosine emigrated to Michigan
1861-1865 – U.S. Civil War curbed immigration
1864 – Sophie's brother Michael emigrated to Michigan
1865 – Johannes Hinderer married Sophie Weller
1866 – Gottlieb Hinderer was born in Alfdorf
1866 – Prussia defeated Austria and allied Wuerttemberg
1869 – The U.S. transcontinental railroad was completed
1871 – Wuerttemberg joined the German Empire
1872 – Katharine Deininger was born in Gehren
1873 – Worldwide depression
1890 – Kaiser Wilhelm II ousted Chancellor Bismarck
1890 – The U.S. life expectancy was 45 years
1891 – Gottlieb and Katharine emigrated to Iowa
1895 – Johannes, Sophie, and children emigrated to Michigan
1914 – World War I began

Alfdorf and St. Stephan Church

In the Swabian region of Wuerttemberg, towns and villages were located on higher ground atop rolling hills. Homes were built within these settlements rather than scattered about the countryside. Towns and villages provided merchant services, neighborly social exchange, and protection from destructive raiders.

The densely forested countryside was an ideal source of lumber for early settlers, and millworks were a common business. Over time, much of the forested land was cleared and converted into farmland.

Regional churches were built in larger towns and were attended by both commoners and noble families. Surrounding villages were populated by commoners, mostly peasant farmers. This was the relationship between the town of Alfdorf[1] and the neighboring village of Brend.[2] Alfdorf had the regional church and a larger population. Brend was a nearby village, home to a few farm families.

The town of Alfdorf is first named in monastery records from 1143. By that time, the Roman Empire was more than 500 years past its zenith, and no longer a power in Europe. Christianity had split into eastern and western factions. The western faction, based in Rome, launched multiple crusades meant to retake the Holy Land from Muslims. At the time of the crusades, papal authority was absolute, and separation of church and state did not exist. Alfdorf and the surrounding midlands of Western Europe fell under the authority of the Roman Catholic Church and its aligned nobility.

The advent of Protestantism in the early 1500s challenged the Roman Catholic alignment of the Alfdorf church. After 100 years of changing

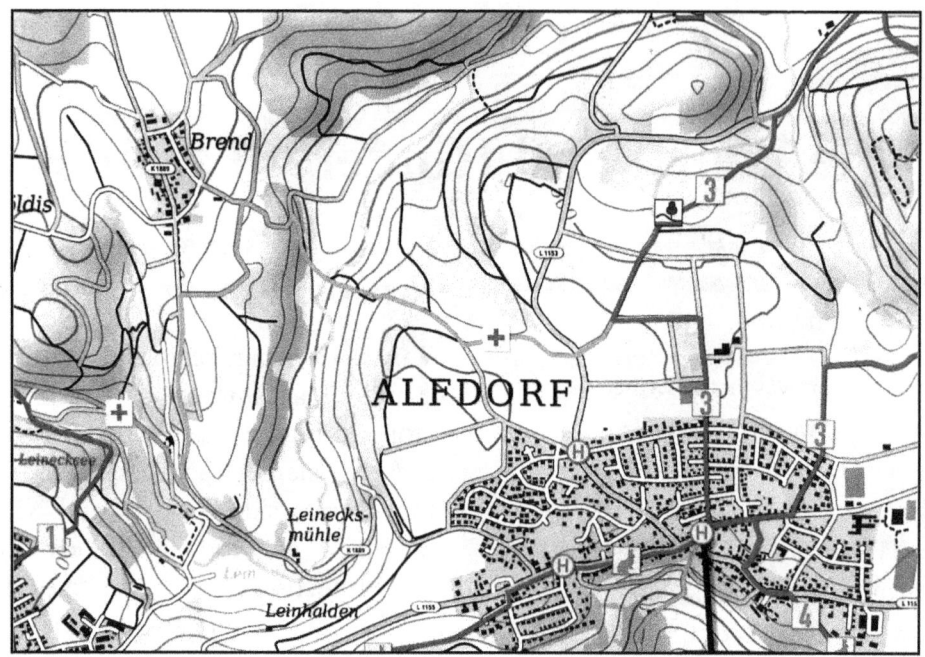

The town of Alfdorf and village of Brend are about a mile apart. Source: Topo map on a street sign in Welzheim, Germany. Photographed and edited by author.

Alfdorf sits atop a hill. The St. Stephan Church bell tower is near the right edge of this photo. Source: Photographed and edited by author.

allegiance, Protestant control was permanently established. In Alfdorf and throughout Wuerttemberg, towns had only a single church. Once Alfdorf aligned with Protestantism, the church, the nobility, and the religious practice of the commoners was strictly Protestant.

Initially, two Protestant noble families controlled the area, which included Alfdorf. This division of authority created conflict in town governance. In 1628, however, Baron Georg Friedrich vom Holtz[3] became the patron of St. Stephan Church[4] (*Stephanuskirche*). Over time, this patron family increased their influence in Alfdorf and the surrounding lands. The linkage of the vom Holtz family and St. Stephan Church of Alfdorf continued throughout the 19th century.

When a noble family became the patron of a church, they were given privilege, authority, and responsibility. Privilege included civil governance of the town, a separate room in the church for patron family members, and a private burial plot in the cemetery. Authority meant they alone selected the pastor to lead the congregation and controlled the church expenditures. Responsibility meant the patron family paid for the maintenance and, if needed, replacement of church buildings. Patronage committed future generations of that noble family to the welfare of that parish. Today, many of the churches built in the era of patronage have kept the separate interior rooms and private burial plots reserved for patron family members.

St. Stephan Church continued for centuries as the central focus of religion in Alfdorf. Over time, the building itself underwent several small-scale renovations as authorized by the patron family. About the time of the American Revolution in the 1770s, the vom Holtz patrons decided to replace the entire church building. They engaged a respected Wuerttemberg builder who designed the new St. Stephan Church with an unusual architecture.

The new church was built in a transverse design, meaning the entrance was along one long wall. Inside, the altar and elevated pulpit were centered on the opposite north long wall. The pews were arranged in a semicircle facing the altar. The intent was to focus the parishioner's attention on the altar

The main entrance of St. Stephan Church is midway along the southern long wall. Source: Photographed and edited by author.

Katharine

The St. Stephan Church altar and elevated pulpit are centered on the long north wall opposite the main entrance. The pews are arranged in a semicircle facing the altar. Source: Photographed and edited by author.

This St. Stephan Church memorial board honors soldiers who died during WWI. Their home villages are listed. The family names include both Weller and Hinderer. Source: Photographed and edited by author.

and the pastor. The old bell tower on the west end of the building was broadened and elevated to balance its size with the larger church.

The capacity of the rebuilt church was greater than needed for the citizens of Alfdorf. St. Stephan Church was meant to be a regional church. It was where families from Alfdorf and the surrounding villages would gather for worship.

The new church was designed with a walled-off private room on the loge level above the main entrance. Only the patron vom Holtz family was permitted in this room. When the church was built, it was also the only room with a source of heat. The private room offered the patron family an unobstructed view of the altar and pulpit. St. Stephan Church stands today as it appeared when built 240 years ago. The interior has been modernized, but the transverse design and private patron's room with its ancient woodburning stove remain.

Today, the church's white-washed interior walls display pastel-painted biblical scenes. Wall-mounted memorial boards list the names of church members killed in 20th century wars. The memorial boards have subtitles identifying the villages where those members lived.

Sophie Weller and Johannes Hinderer

In the mid-1800s, the Weller and Hinderer families were both members of St. Stephan Church in Alfdorf. The Wellers lived in Alfdorf while the Hinderer home was in the nearby village of Brend. In Wuerttemberg, each church kept official records of its members. One type of record was called a family table or family group record. Family tables displayed three generations: the husband and wife, their parents, and their children. It was a cumulative record summarizing one couple's history together. Family tables vary in the quality of the writing and also the details they record. For example, a parent's home village may be recorded, but whether they still lived in that village or had moved in with a younger family member may not be noted. The St. Stephan Church record for Johannes Hinderer and Sophie Weller is a typical family table.

The family table for Johannes and Sophie states that both the Hinderer and Weller men listed on the left page were farmers. On the right page, the first child named Gottfried and then another son Gottlieb were born in Alfdorf. All the later children were born in Brend. At that time, births took place at home. Consequently, the location of a birth was where the mother was living. The conclusion drawn is that Sophie and probably Johannes lived in Alfdorf with Sophie's parents for several years. After Gottlieb was born in 1866, they left Alfdorf and joined the Hinderer family living in Brend. Of the eleven children born to Sophie and Johannes, only five lived past their early childhood years.

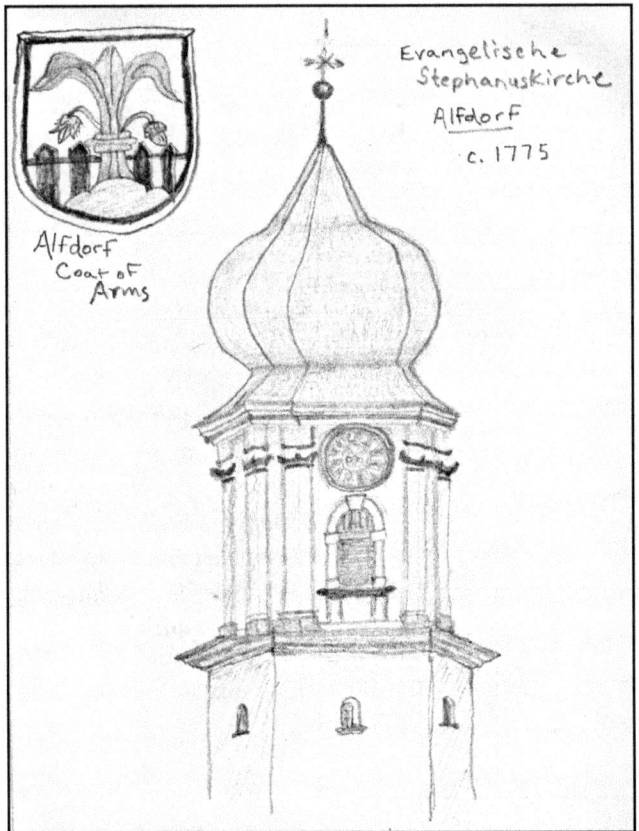

A pencil sketching of the rebuilt bell tower of St. Stephan Church. Source: Ryan Schlichting, October 2019. Edited by author.

Katharine

The family table for Johannes Hinderer and Sophie Weller. The husband and wife are listed in the upper section of the left page with their parents beneath. Their children, including Gottlieb, are on the right page. Source: "Württemberg, Germany, Family Tables, 1550-1985" online database (Lehi, UT: Ancestry.com, 2016), accessed November 2020.

Family Table for Johannes Hinderer and Sophie (Weller) Hinderer

Place, Day, and Year of Birth	House Father	Place, Day, and Year of Marriage	House Mother	Place, Day, and Year of Birth
Brend, 20 August 1842	Hinderer, Johannes Farmer in Brend	Alfdorf 3 Sept. 1865	Sophie	Alfdorf, 9 Mar 1844
Father >	Gottfried Hinderer, Farmer in Brend (II, 117)		Jacob Weller, Farmer in Alfdorf (I, 395)	< Father
Mother >	(5) Rosine née Bareiss		(7) Anna Marie née Schäfer	< Mother

No.	Names of Children	Birth	Confirmation or First Communion	Marriage	Death
1	Gottfried	Alfdorf 23 Nov 1864	--	--	10 July 1865
2	**Gottlieb**	Alfdorf 15 Sept. 1866	Alfdorf, 1880	--	--
3	Jakob	Brend 9 Aug 1868	--	--	9 April 1869
4	Johann Georg	Brend 19 Jan. 1870	Alfdorf, 1884	--	--
5	Gottfried	Brend, 31 Jan. 1873	--	--	20 Jan. 1876
6	Christian Carl	Brend, 23 Sept. 1875	--	--	2 Sept. 1877
7	Christine Catharine	Brend, 12 May 1878	Alfd. 1892	--	--
8	Gottlob	Brend, 12 Jul. 1882, Bapt. 24 July	--	--	--
9	August	Brend, 23 Oct. 1884, Bapt. 31 Oct.	--	--	--
10	Wilhelm Twins:	Brend, 11 Apr. 1886, Bapt.12 Apr.	--	--	24 Apr. 1886
11	Christian				19 Apr. 1886

The English translation of the family table for Johannes Hinderer and Sophie Weller. Source: Compiled and translated by Merlin Schlichting. Edited by author.

WUERTTEMBERG FARMS

In Wuerttemberg, grown children did not move great distances from where their parents lived. Rather than selling to a stranger, home and property were inherited by children. In most areas of Wuerttemberg, property was evenly inherited by all the children or at least by the sons. In the Alfdorf region, however, it was more common for the oldest son to inherit all the property. The trade-off was that the parents remained living with the son who inherited the home. The oldest son's family fared well, but his siblings had to look elsewhere for farmland and a home. During the 19th century, the population of Wuerttemberg nearly quadrupled. Regardless of the local inheritance practice, farmable acreage per person decreased with each succeeding generation.

There were dozens of districts in the Kingdom of Wuerttemberg, and each contained towns and villages with strong local autonomy. A farmer was legally bound to comply with the regulations in his own jurisdiction. Towns and villages appointed networks of citizen committees to conduct surveillance and report regulatory deviations. Community courts decreed judgements on farmers who broke local rules. Membership in these regulatory groups was prized. Court and committee members were the controlling town elite.

The regulations were exhaustive. Rules stated how much land a farmer could own or lease, and which crop was to be planted on each parcel. Rules controlled the date the farmer planted and harvested each crop, and the sequence of yearly crop rotation. Permission to raise large animals for food was also regulated. Hay and fodder crops were in limited supply during the cold winter months. There was not sufficient feed for all farmers to over-winter large animals. The solution was to allow only the higher-ranking farmers to keep large animals through the winter.

The sale of farmland and transfer of leasing rights was also subject to committee approval. A farmer wanting to purchase or lease land could be rejected on grounds of his religion or political affiliation. Candidates considered too poor or of a lower social rank might also be rejected. The community-run committees would not accept anyone who might become a financial burden to the town residents. In general, committees favored local candidates. This reduced the threat of outsiders gaining a foothold and threatening their authority. Enterprising farmers were not allowed to acquire more land and thereby become more prosperous. The end result was most farmers worked small tracts of land and remained poor. In Wuerttemberg, this intricate web of control lasted well past the middle 1800s.[5]

The majority of Wuerttemberg farmers were tenants on land owned by a nobleman or the church. Community regulations dictated how these tenants paid their rent. During most of the 1800s, payments were made in crop shares, not cash. Each farmer owed between a quarter and a third of their crops as rent. They paid the crop shares to several authorities: the landowner, the church, and the local community. Toward the end of the 1800s, rental payments were more commonly made in cash.

As the per capita farmland dwindled, it became impossible for farming alone to support a family. To survive, farm families were forced to add other skills or sell another service. Farming became a part time vocation.

In Wuerttemberg, modernization of farm methods and farmer prosperity lagged behind the German states in the north. The priority for the landowner, the church, and the community was to perpetuate their income flow. They accomplished this by endorsing the old inheritance practices, encouraging exhaustive community regulations, and limiting land ownership.

THE WELLER FAMILY OF ALFDORF

Sophie Weller grew up with her parents and siblings near the center of Alfdorf. The family tables for her paternal Weller ancestors can be traced back

Katharine

Jacob Weller and Anna Maria Schäffer

Married 12 May 1829 in Alfdorf:

    Jacob Weller – b. 25 Nov 1804 in Alfdorf; d. 22 Apr 1873, age 68, in Wuerttemberg

    Anna Maria Schäffer – b. 16 Mar 1810 in Rehnenmuehle; d. 15 Jan 1891, age 80, in Wuerttemberg

Children:

    Rosine – b. 2 Feb 1830; emigrated 1852; d. 13 May 1909, age 79, in Michigan

    Stillborn – b. 2 Aug 1833

    Michael – b. 17 Apr 1838; emigrated 1864; d. 5 Sep 1905, age 67, in Michigan

    Anna Marie – b. 15 Sep 1841; d. 15 Nov 1895, age 53, in Wuerttemberg

Twin daughters b. 9 Mar 1844:

Sophie – m. 3 Sep 1865 in Alfdorf to Johannes Hinderer; emigrated 1895; d. 9 Dec 1903, age 59, in Michigan

    Katherine – d. 1 Dec 1892, age 48, in Wuerttemberg

    Jakob – b. 29 Apr 1846; d. 21 Dec 1846, age 8 months, in Alfdorf

    Anna Marie – b. 23 Sep 1849; d. 28 Sep 1849, age 5 days, in Alfdorf

---

The family of Jacob Weller and Anna Maria Schäffer included twin daughters Sophie and Katherine, b. 1844. Sophie and two older siblings, Rosine and Michael, emigrated to Michigan. Source: Compiled by author; translated by Merlin Schlichting.

to her great grandfather, Johann Jakob Weller, born in 1724. These family tables are all from Alfdorf, indicating the Wellers had been residents of the Alfdorf community for many years.

Sophie's parents, Jacob Weller and Anna Maria Schäffer, were married in 1829. Jacob and his father's ancestors were all described as farmers. Anna Maria's family came from Rehnenmuehle, a small village east of Alfdorf.

Jacob and Anna Maria Weller had five children who reached adulthood. The oldest was Rosine, followed by an only son Michael, and then Anna Marie, named after her mother. Following these three single births, twins Sophie and Katherine were born in 1844. Two children were born after Sophie and Katherine, but they both died in infancy. The high childhood mortality rate meant that Sophie and her twin sister Katherine grew up as the youngest of five children in the Weller household.

Sophie Weller's birth family played a key role in the emigration story of both the Wellers and the Hinderers. In 1851 when Sophie was seven, her oldest sister Rosine married Ulrich Köther (at times spelled Koether, Kother, Koeder, or Kader). The family table for Rosine and Ulrich indicated their first child was born in 1849 and lived only a few days. Next, a son Friederich was born in Alfdorf in 1851. Most likely, Rosine, her husband Ulrich, and their son Friederich lived in Sophie's parent's home. In the spring of 1852, Rosine, Ulrich, and their son emigrated to America and settled in the state of Michigan. Rosine was the first member of the Weller and Hinderer families to emigrate to America.

Rosine's departure in 1852 left 14-year-old Michael as the oldest Weller child still living in Alfdorf. Sister Anna Marie was 11, and twins Sophie and Katherine were seven. This family group remained unchanged for over a decade. It was during this time that Sophie would have met her future husband Johannes Hinderer at St. Stephan Church in Alfdorf.

In 1864 when Sophie was twenty, her older brother Michael followed the path of Rosine and emigrated to Michigan. As will be seen later, bachelor Michael lived with Rosine and Ulrich's growing Michigan family. Michael Weller was the only son to survive childhood. His emigration ended the succession of Weller farmers living in Alfdorf.

Sophie and Johannes Hinderer's first child was born in Alfdorf late in 1864. This child, named Gottfried, lived for less than one year. Their second child, Gottlieb Hinderer, was born in September 1866, also in Alfdorf. Most likely, Sophie's first two children were born in the Weller home. In this family, daughters and their future husbands had children while living with maternal parents. This was a recurring family pattern in Wuerttemberg.

Thirty years later in 1895, Sophie, her husband Johannes Hinderer, and three of their children emigrated to Michigan. By the end of the 1800s, three of the five Weller siblings were living near each other in Washtenaw County, Michigan: Rosine, Michael, and Sophie. Sophie's parents remained in Germany, as did her twin sister Katherine and older sister Anna Marie.

ALFDORF – THEN AND NOW

The Alfdorf of Sophie's youth can be better understood thanks to an old map retrieved from the town archives. This map dates from 1831, only two years after Sophie's parents were married. It was originally hand drawn using pen and ink.

The old map identifies the town center as an intersection of streets, which in those days would have been simple cart paths. The oldest buildings, near the town center, housed merchants and family homes. One street angles toward the upper left of the 1831 map. Today, it is named *Schützenstrasse*. Poor families lived along this street rather than near the town center. During the years of changing political alliances, destructive raiders attacked towns controlled by their rivals. The homes of poor families on the perimeter of Alfdorf were the first to suffer. They acted as a buffer and an early warning for the merchants and wealthier families living near the center of Alfdorf.

The first 1831 (upper) map shows detailed narrow strips of land extending in parallel lines away from the streets. These lines indicate how land parcels were divided. Adjacent parcels might be worked by different farmers or by the same family. A single strip of land served two purposes. Small gardens were planted near the houses to grow produce for families. The more distant ground was planted in crops regulated by the citizen committees described earlier.

An enlarged view of the 1831 (lower) map identifies the intersection at the town center, and St. Stephan Church which is faintly numbered 183. Land ownership documents were used to trace the location of the Weller home.[6] On this enlarged map, their home is faintly numbered 44. By today's measure, the Weller family lived about a city block from both the town center and St. Stephan Church.

The location of the Weller home near the center of Alfdorf has economic implications. It suggests that the many generations of this family were more prosperous than the poorer families living along the *Schützenstrasse* on the outskirts of town.

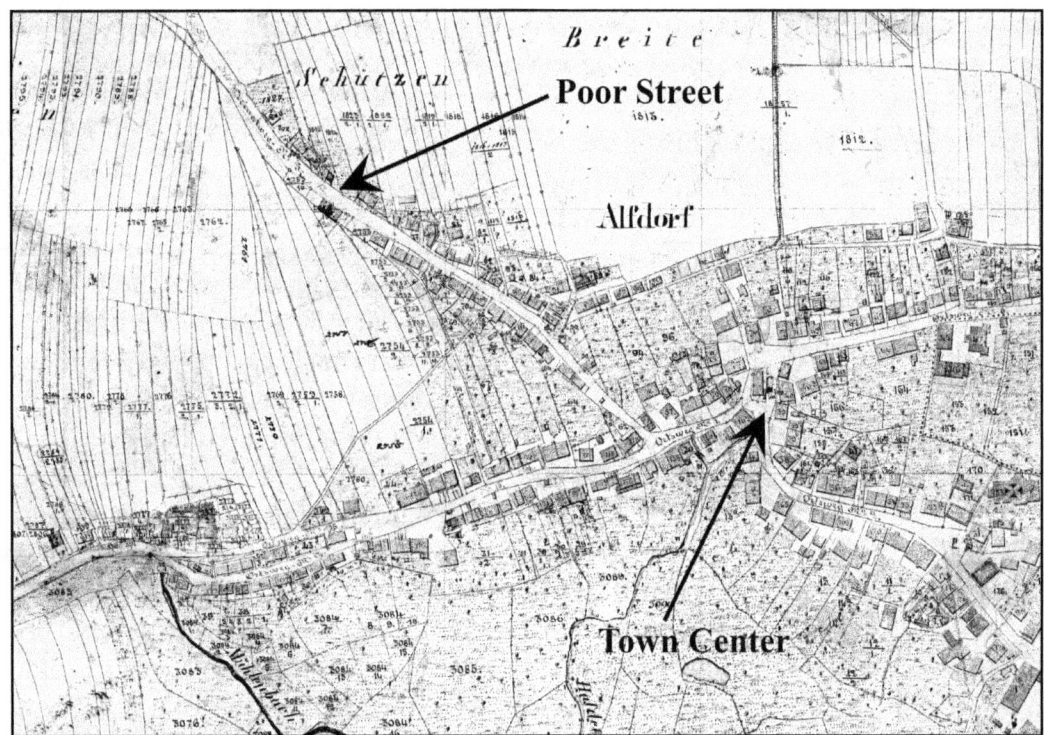

The 1831 map of Alfdorf with numbered buildings and streets. The town center and the street housing poor families are identified. Source: Alfdorf city records office, courtesy of Rolf Schön. Edited by author.

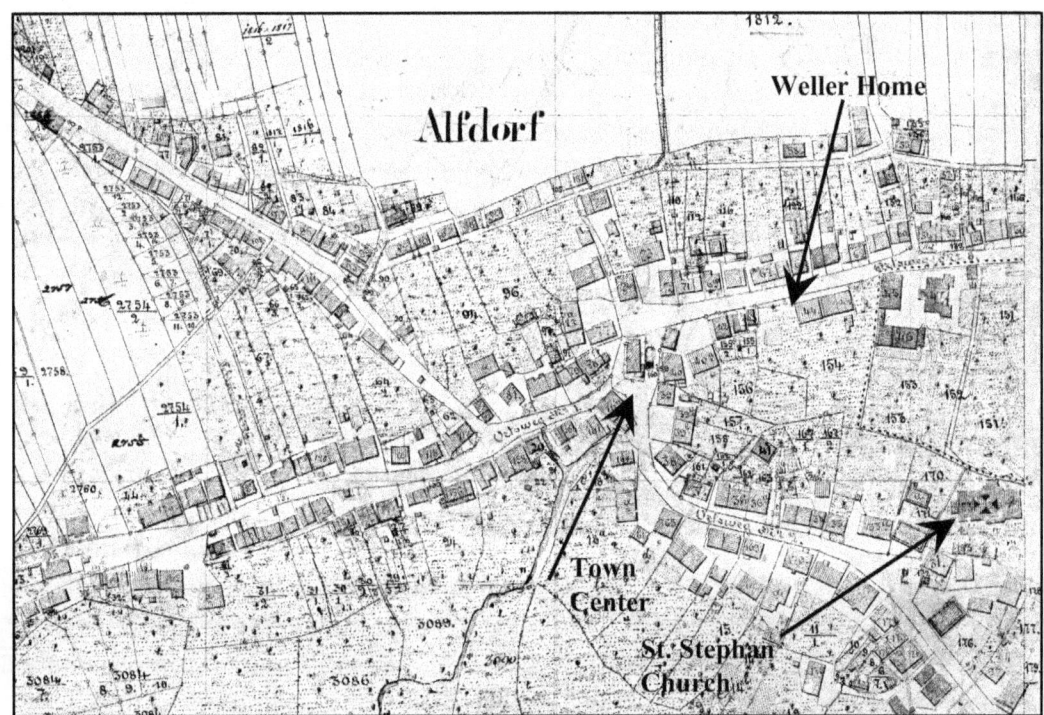

An enlarged view of the 1831 map shows St. Stephan Church and the Weller home. Source: Alfdorf city records office, courtesy of Rolf Schön. Edited by author.

Looking north toward the town center in today's Alfdorf. Source: Photo by author, October 2019.

Today, Alfdorf is a town with over 7,000 residents. The streets have been paved and widened. Modern buildings have been constructed at the edge of town. Many local residents are employed here by manufacturing and technology businesses. The street names seen on the 1831 map have been changed, but many of the older buildings near the town center remain.

The Weller house where Sophie was born has been replaced by a modern home. St. Stephan Church remains, however, as it was in Sophie's youth.

THE HINDERER FAMILY OF BREND

There are over 150 terms in the old German language that translate into one English word: farmer.[7] The old German words identified whether the farmer had inherited the land, and if he owned or leased the property. The particular word implied the size of the property and if it included a house or possibly only a cottage. It also indicated how he came to own the land, or if a lease could be passed on to his heirs. Using different words had a densely stratifying effect. The single word told everyone where in the social hierarchy a farmer ranked. In general, the lowest ranked farmers had the fewest rights and the most obligations. It was a hair-splitting vocabulary designed to communicate rank within the large population of farmers.

In 1833, Johannes Hinderer's father, Gottfried, married Rosina Bareiss. Rosina was the daughter of an attorney living in the nearby village of Heldiss (or *Höldis*). This village is located less than a mile west of Brend. Like Brend, Heldiss came within the region served by St. Stephan Church of Alfdorf. Johannes's father Gottfried Hinderer likely met his future wife Rosina through their attendance at St. Stephan Church in Alfdorf.

> **Gottfried Hinderer and Rosina Bareiss**
>
> **Married 4 Jun 1833 in Alfdorf:**
>
> **Gottfried Hinderer** – b.15 Oct 1804 in Brend; d. 21 Nov 1874, age 70, in Brend
>
> **Rosina Bareiss** – b. 23 Nov 1810 in Heldiss; d. 22 May 1870, age 59, in Brend
>
> **Children:**
>
> **Stillborn** – b. 29 Oct 1835
>
> **Katharina** – b. 11 Dec 1836; m. 12 Jan 1858; d. date and place unknown
>
> **Luise Marie** – b. 27 Jul 1838; d. 25 Oct 1883, age 45, place unknown
>
> **Johannes – b. 20 Aug 1842 in Brend; m. 3 Sep 1865 in Alfdorf to Sophie Weller; d. 18 Aug 1923, age 81, in Michigan**
>
> **Eva** – b. 21 Mar 1845; d. 10 May 1846, age 1 year, in Brend
>
> **Gottfried** – b. 14 Nov 1847; m. 13 Jul 1869; d. 4 Nov 1918, age 71, place unknown
>
> **Rosine** – b. 7 Apr 1850; d. 26 Mar 1851, age 1 year, in Brend
>
> **Johann Georg** – b. 26 Apr 1851; d. 12 Sep 1851, age 5 months, in Brend
>
> **Matthaeus** – b. 19 May 1855; d. 22 Apr 1866, age 10, in Brend

The children of Gottfried Hinderer and Rosina Bareiss included Johannes, the oldest surviving son. Johannes emigrated to Michigan with his wife Sophie and three of their children in 1895. Source: Compiled by author; translated by Merlin Schlichting, 2019; additional dates by David Schlichting, 2020.

The family table for Gottfried Hinderer and Rosina Bareiss is notable for the same high rate of childhood mortality seen in the Weller family. Of their nine children, only four lived into adulthood, and Johannes was their oldest son. Father Gottfried Hinderer, born in 1804, had also been an oldest son. The local custom of the oldest son inheriting the home property prevailed for generations in this Hinderer family.

The family table for Johannes and Sophie Hinderer recorded that Johannes was a farmer (Bauer) residing in Brend. Similarly, family tables for both his father Gottfried and grandfather Matthäus indicated they were farmers living in Brend. As early as 1660, Hinderer ancestors were recorded as farmers with homes in Brend.

What is not known is the acreage these Hinderer generations farmed, or the precise location of their crop land. Daily travel to their fields would have been by foot or horseback. Most likely, the fields they farmed were near their home, tucked against the outskirts of Brend.

In summary, the Hinderers of Brend were typical farmers for their time. For generations, they farmed the land, lived in the same home, and passed along ownership of their home to the oldest son.

BREND – THEN AND NOW

The regional archive for Brend has preserved an old map of this village.[8] Like the map of Alfdorf,

The Weller and Hinderer Families

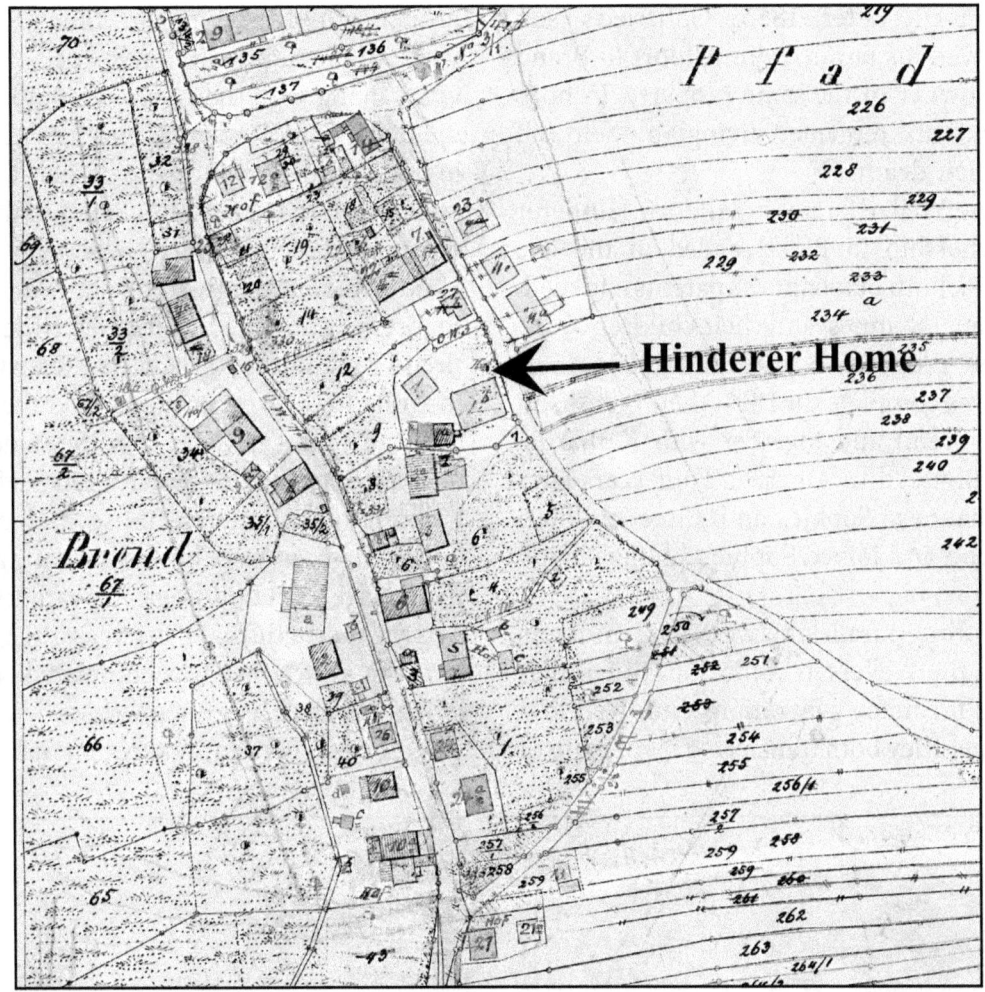

The 1831 map of Brend. The buildings and streets are numbered, and the Hinderer home is identified. Source: Regional records office, courtesy of Rolf Schön. Edited by author.

the map of Brend was hand drawn with pen and ink in 1831. Johannes Hinderer was born in 1842. The old map shows the layout of Brend as it was in Johannes's youth.

The old map identifies homes, land parcels, and streets by numbers rather than by names. In 1831, Brend was a small residential village with homes lining two parallel streets. By today's measure, the entire length of those two streets was, at most, two city blocks. As in Alfdorf, the narrow strips of farmland are all numbered and extend outward from the residential streets. Ownership records were used to identify the building site where the Hinderer family lived for generations.[9]

The old map shows three buildings on the Hinderer property in Brend. One would have been the family's house and another a barn. The house was farthest from the street and is faintly numbered "1" on the map. The largest structure, likely the barn, was closest to the street and is numbered "1b." As noted in Chapter 1, barns were built near streets so animal waste could be easily carted off to fertilize fields. The purpose of the third building is unknown.

Recall that when parents gave ownership of their property to a son, they remained living with the son's family. In 1833, Gottfried Hinderer took ownership of the Brend property from his father

Matthäus. Shortly after 1866, Gottfried's son Johannes moved his family from Alfdorf to Brend and became owner of the same property. In both cases, the parents remained living in their old home until their death.

As with the Weller family in Alfdorf, Hinderer property ownership in Brend ended in the late 1800s. By 1875, both of Johannes's parents had died, leaving Sophie, Johannes, and their children alone on the Brend property. By the mid-1880s, their own family was complete. In 1891, their oldest son Gottlieb left Brend and together with Katharine Deininger emigrated to America. Four years later in 1895, Johannes, Sophie, and three children departed Brend and joined Sophie's siblings living in Michigan.

There are strong parallels between the Hinderers in Brend and the Wellers in Alfdorf. Both families were farmers for many generations and lived in a town or village. They both transferred ownership of property to oldest sons, but the parents remained living in the home. Daughters began their families while living with their parents. Both families were members of St. Stephan Church in Alfdorf. Finally, in both families, ownership of their historic homes ended with the generation living in the late 1800s.

Archival records track ownership of the former Hinderer home in Brend into modern times. Before he emigrated, Johannes Hinderer sold the Brend buildings to Friedrich Kiefer who was also identified as a farmer. Shortly after the beginning of the 20th century, Kiefer sold the same property to Gottfried Stecher. In the early 1900s a fire destroyed the original Hinderer house and barn. A new house and barn were built, so what stand today are the replacement buildings. A weathervane atop the current house displays the year 1912, possibly the year the new house was completed. The residents living there today are named Müller, and descend from the Stecher family through marriage.

The current house and barn on the former Hinderer property in Brend. Source: Photographed and edited by author.

A house across the street from the former Hinderer property displays the old half-timbered building style. Source: Photographed and edited by author.

From Brend, a pathway still leads to Alfdorf, a 30-minute walk away. Source: Photographed and edited by author.

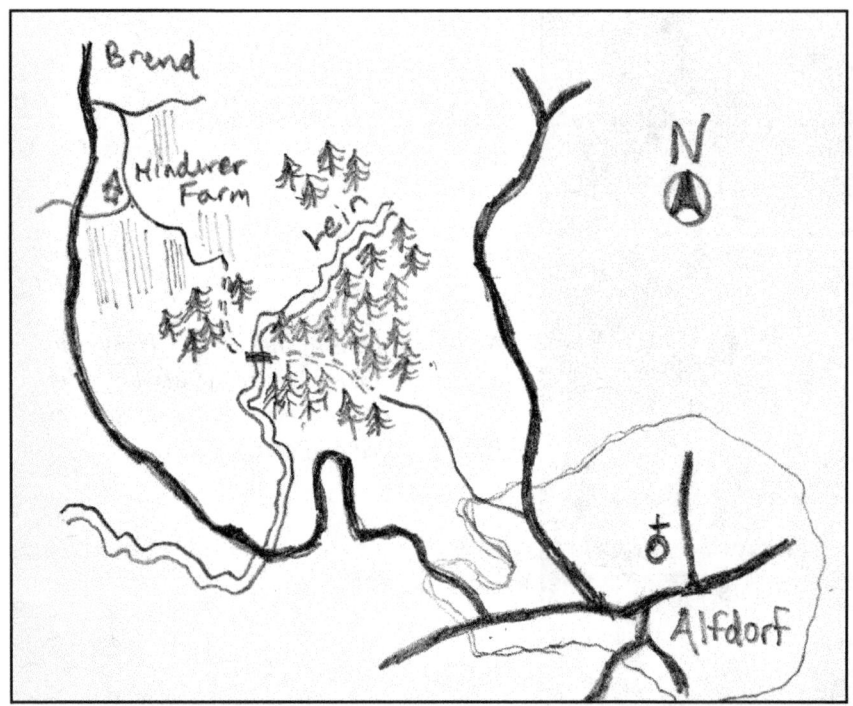

A pencil sketching of the footpath between Brend and Alfdorf. Source: Illustration by Ryan Schlichting; edited by author.

"There is a footpath that leads from Brend to Alfdorf. The Pastor in Alfdorf called it a church path, as it would have been the way people from Brend would walk to get to church in Alfdorf. I decided to walk it. It is a beautiful trail. On either end on the hillsides, it goes through fields and apple orchards. The middle section goes through a forest through the center of which runs the River Lein. A little footbridge allows you to cross it. The forest was dark, damp, and full of moss and mushrooms. Right out of a Brothers Grimm fairytale. I took a few rocks from both the fields of the Hinderer farm and the church path knowing our ancestors used both as part of their daily lives." Ryan Schlichting, October 2019

Today, the street where the Hinderer property was located has a name: Hintere Gasse. The current house is numbered 27. Hintere Gasse translates roughly as "lane behind the main street." The roadway itself has a modern surface, but remains very narrow with buildings only a step or two from the pavement. Most village homes are more modern than those on the former Hinderer property. Nevertheless, a few older homes still display the half-timbered construction used by German builders for centuries.[10]

In the 21st century, Brend remains a small village with two parallel streets, neither more than two blocks long. From the former Hinderer property, the view toward the southeast shows rolling farmland and a distant forest. If you take a thirty-minute walk along the fields and through that forest, you will glimpse Alfdorf atop the next hillside.

Notes

1. To locate Alfdorf, in Google Maps insert coordinates 48.843803, 9.718935 in the search box and click the search button.

2. To locate Brend, in Google Maps insert coordinates 48.855305, 9.693206 in the search box and click the search button.

3. "Vom" is a conjunction of "Von dem," so the name might at one time have been "von dem Holtz," but it came to be known better by the shortened form, "vom Holtz."

According to a timeline chart in Alfdorf's city hall, Georg Friederich vom Holtz bought the lower castle (Unteres Schloss) in 1628. The upper castle (Oberes Schloss) belonged to another member of the nobility. This essentially divided the town between two families.

"vom Holtz" was/is the name of a noble family and is very old. The timeline indicated that descendants still own some of the town's property.

The explanation for "vom" was supplied by Merlin Schlichting and is gratefully acknowledged.

4. To locate St. Stephan Church, in Google Maps insert coordinates 48.843209, 9.721781 in the search box and click the search button.

5. S. Ogilvie, M. Küpker, and J. Maegraith, "Community Characteristics and Demographic Development: Three Württemberg Communities, 1558-1914" (Cambridge Working Papers in Economics 0910, Faculty of Economics, University of Cambridge, 2009), 65-71, https://sheilaghogilvie.com/wp-content/uploads/publications/cwpe0910.pdf.

6. To locate the Weller home, in Google Maps insert coordinates 48.844168, 9.720173 in the search box and click the search button.

7. Baerbel K. Johnson, "Life on the Farm: Understanding Your German Peasant Ancestors" (International German Genealogy Conference [IGGC], Sacramento, CA, June 15-17, 2019), 68-71.

8. The research work and scans supplied by Rolf Schön are gratefully acknowledged.

9. To find the Hinderer home, in Google Maps insert coordinates 48.855888, 9.693148 in the search box and click the search button.

10. Half-timbered construction uses intersecting wood beams with masonry filling the spaces between beams. It is less expensive than all brick construction and the masonry preserves the wood. It has become symbolic of old German buildings. Today, historic buildings in town centers have been rebuilt using the same method.

Katharine

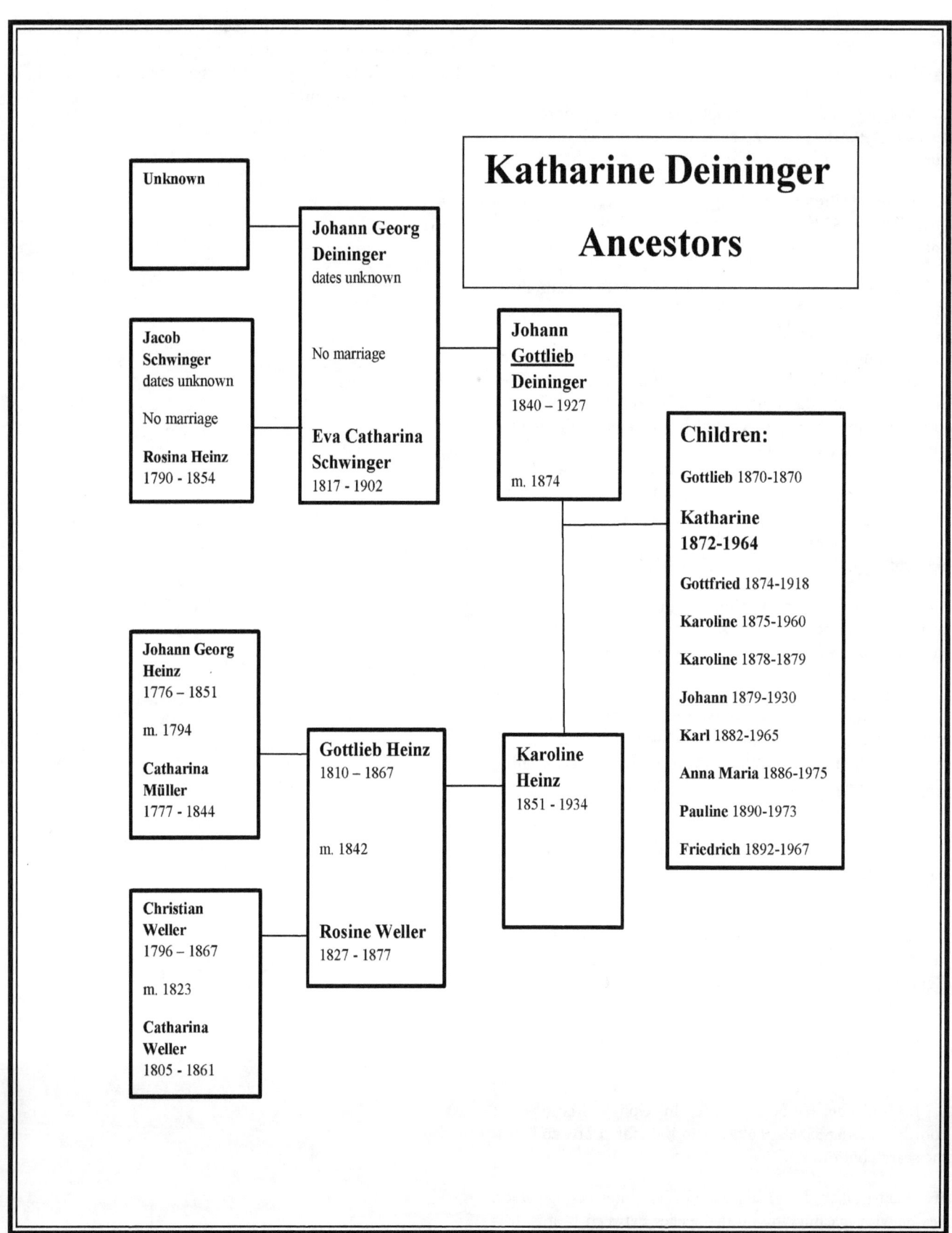

Chapter 3

The Deininger and Heinz Families

Timeline

1787 – The U.S. Constitution was signed

1815 – Napoleon I was defeated - the German Confederation was formed

1840 – Johann Gottlieb Deininger was born in Huettenbuehl

1851 – Karoline Heinz was born in Gebenweiler

1861-1865 – The U.S. Civil War curbed immigration

1866 – Gottlieb Hinderer was born in Alfdorf

1866 – Prussia defeated Austria and allied Wuerttemberg

1869 – The Kaisersbach church was dedicated

1871 – Wuerttemberg joined the German Empire

1872 – Katharine Deininger was born in Gehren

1873 – Worldwide economic depression

1890 – Kaiser Wilhelm II ousted Chancellor Bismarck

1891 – Katharine and Gottlieb emigrated to America

1914 – World War I began

Gehren and Kaisersbach

Traveling northward from Alfdorf and Brend, the landscape gives way to idyllic farms along winding country roadways. The rolling pastures and tillable land are similar, but the villages are smaller, and the patchwork of forests more expansive.

Katharine Deininger was born in the hamlet of Gehren.[1] It is a cluster of a half-dozen homes centered on a U-shaped pivot along a narrow country road. Long strips of gardens fan outward from the roadway painting the landscape many shades of green. Apple trees grow in the yards of homes, near the edge of forests, and dotting the pastureland.

Records from the late 1800s refer to this hamlet as Gebenweilergehren. The lengthy name distinguished it from the village of Gebenweiler[2] located a half mile to the west. More recently, this long name has been officially abbreviated to Gehren.

Records from early in the 1800s simply identify the entire region as Gebenweiler. A person said to be born in Gebenweiler back then, may have been born in either Gebenweiler or Gehren.

The town of Kaisersbach[3] is located a mile northwest of Gehren along another winding roadway. Kaisersbach is a larger town with numerous homes and many small businesses. There are merchant shops, a few restaurants, a post office and, importantly, a regional Protestant church. This church serves the people of Kaisersbach as well as those living in Gehren, Gebenweiler, and a handful of other small villages.

A 2019 photo of the narrow roadway, the homes, and outbuildings composing the tiny hamlet of Gehren. Source: Photographed and edited by author.

The Gehren home where the Deininger and Heinz descendants live today. Source: Photographed and edited by author (2019).

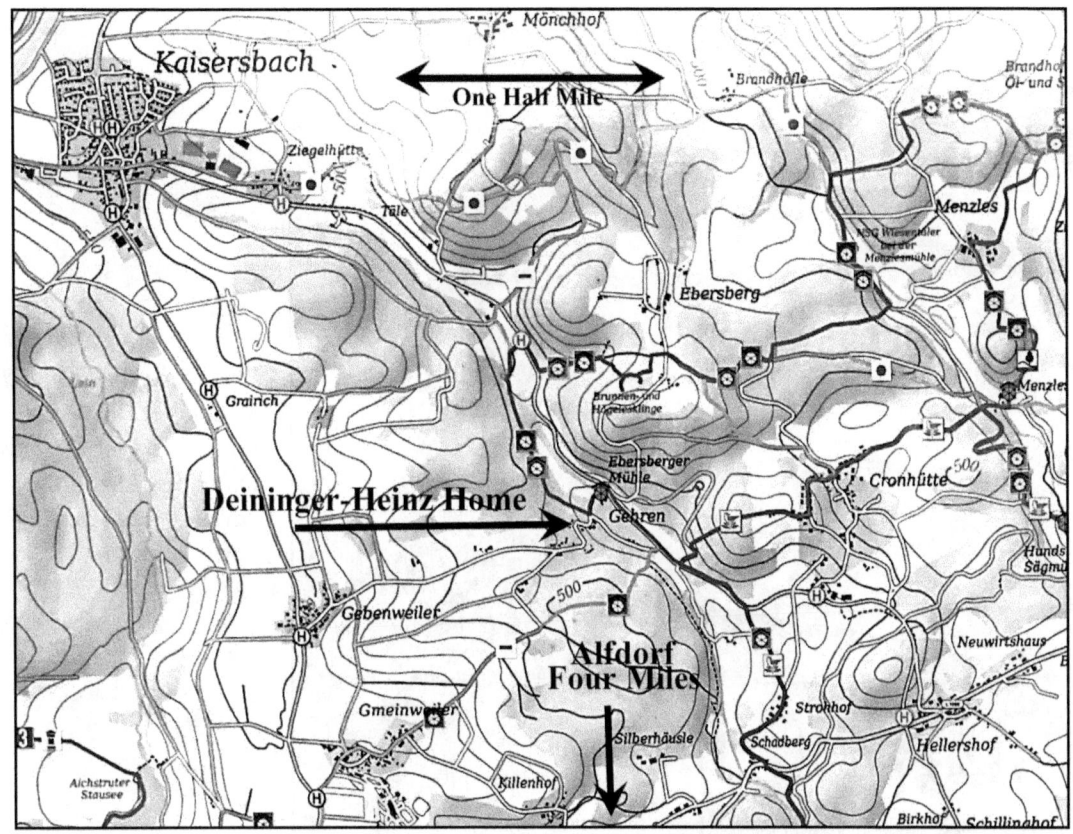

The town of Kaisersbach, the village of Gebenweiler, and the tiny collection of homes known as Gehren. Source: Topo map on a street sign in Welzheim Germany. Photographed and edited by author.

THE PROTESTANT CHURCH OF KAISERSBACH

The church in Kaisersbach did not become the regional parish for Gehren until the second half of the 19th century. This church is officially named *Evangelische Kirche Kaisersbach*, which translates as Protestant Church of Kaisersbach.[4] The church was dedicated in 1869.

Before 1869, people living in Kaisersbach and nearby villages like Gehren were assigned to a church in Welzheim. This was a considerably larger town more than three miles south of Kaisersbach.

In the 1850s, Kaisersbach civil and church officials petitioned the then-reigning Prince of Wuerttemberg. They wished to build a new regional church in their own town. Church records from those years provide insight into public works methods when Wuerttemberg was an independent kingdom.

Although petitions to build a new church began as early as 1855, this proposal had vocal critics. Some Kaisersbach citizens who owned businesses in Welzheim spoke out against a new church. They feared severing ties with the Welzheim church would damage their businesses. Other critics complained about losing their prestigious seating in the Welzheim church. They feared that in a new Kaisersbach church, they might be assigned seating next to lower-status commoners. These examples reveal how controlled church attendance had become. The location of your home dictated where you must attend church. In addition, church seating was by assignment. Parishioners pridefully guarded their privileged seating because it reflected their status in the community.

The Protestant Church of Kaisersbach was built on a promontory of land which today is surrounded by paved streets. Source: Photo by author, 2019.

In spite of the critics, funding for a new church was eventually approved. The ranking Kaisersbach religious and civil authorities sent a letter to the Prince of Wuerttemberg thanking him for financing the construction. The gratuitous language of their letter reveals how the absolute authority of the Prince of Wuerttemberg was acknowledged. It also makes clear that the state, not local citizens, paid for the church construction:

Your Royal Majesty has, on the 27th of this month, displayed a graciousness of the highest order in granting approval for the founding of a congregation within the parish district of Kaisersbach, along with a gracious gift on the 1st of this month of the most generous sum of 500 Gulden from your private funds. For this, we, in the name of the newly formed congregation, express our most reverent thanks to your majesty, along with the wish that, as your Royal Majesty has graciously vouchsafed the welfare of the congregation through many gracious deeds, Almighty God would grant perpetual blessing upon your Royal Majesty and your entire house.

We remain, with deepest reverence to your Royal Majesty and in most submissive and loyal obedience.

Signed: (The city pastor, the mayor, and parish council members)[5]

Construction milestones and setbacks were chronicled in the Kaisersbach church records. In 1864, the first pastor was officially assigned, and a residence was built for him. This pastor's residence was also financed entirely by the state, not the local parishioners. Construction of the church itself began in 1866 but was quickly suspended due to the outbreak of war between Prussia and Austria. In that war, Wuerttemberg was aligned with Austria against the victorious Prussians. In spite of being on the losing side, Wuerttemberg was able to negotiate an agreeable peace treaty with the Prussians. In early 1867, new bids for the church construction were received, a groundbreaking ceremony was held, and the work renewed. In 1869, the construction was completed and the church was officially dedicated.

The completion of the Protestant Church of Kaisersbach fits into the timeline of German history. It also fits into the story of the Deininger and Heinz families. Two years after the 1869 church dedication, the Prussian-dominated German Empire of 1871 was formally established. A year later, Katharine Deininger was born in nearby Gehren. Her birth was duly recorded in the register of the new Protestant Church of Kaisersbach.

JOHANN GOTTLIEB DEININGER AND KAROLINE HEINZ

Katharine Deininger's parents lived in the village of Gehren. Like the Weller family described in Chapter 2, her parents did not marry for several years after their first child was born. Katharine's oldest brother, Gottlieb, was born and died in 1870. Katharine was the second child, born in October 1872. Her parents then married in January of 1874. Their remaining children were born between March 1874 and February 1892. The family table for this couple records that eight of their ten children lived into adulthood.

Katharine's father's middle name, Gottlieb, is underlined in this family table. The underlined name is the name he was known by. In the early and middle 1800s, an infant boy sometimes had two given names, such as Johann Gottlieb. Johann, when followed by another given name, was often a symbolic religious name. The name listed second, in this case Gottlieb, was his *Rufname*, the name he was known by. In many church records, the *Rufname* is underlined.

The family table for Katharine's parents is a complex document with a wealth of additional information. Mainly, it records the typical three generations: the primary couple, their parents, and their children. Additionally, this family table contains information about several later generations.

The family table indicates it was Katharine's mother's Heinz family who lived on the Gehren property. Like the Wellers in Alfdorf, Katharine's parents lived with her mother's birth family during their early years together. Her parents then married and remained together the rest of their lives.

Katharine's father, Johann Gottlieb Deininger, was from Huettenbuehl[6] (also spelled *Hüttenbühl*). He worked as a day-laborer in Gebenweiler. The collection of homes known as Huettenbuehl is located two miles southeast of Gehren. Most likely, Johann Gottlieb Deininger met Karoline Heinz when he worked as a day-laborer. His work might

This grainy image of Katharine's mother Karoline (Heinz) Deininger b. 1851, is labeled "Grandma Deininger, 80th birthday" (1931). Source: From the author's collection, originally from the Hinderer Minnesota home. Edited by author.

Katharine

The family table of Katharine Deininger's birth family. This is the original German document. Source: Ev.-Luth. Church Archive Stuttgart, Parish Register 1577, Vol. 7, Family Records Kaisersbach. Edited by author.

Family Table for
Johann Gottlieb Deininger and Karoline Heinz

p. 524 (*in original register*)　　　**Gebenweiler.gehren** (*page heading in original register*)

Birth	House Father	Marriage	House Mother	Birth
Hüttenbühl 13 May 1840	Johann Gottlieb Deininger, resident of Hüttenbühl, day-laborer in Gebenweiler, Lutheran, died 22 Feb. 1927	Kaisersbach 25 January 1874	Karoline Heinz, Lutheran, died [Gebenweiler] Gehren, 11 July 1934	Gebenweiler 16 December 1851
Father >	Johann Georg Deininger		Gottlieb Heinz, r[esident] and f[armer] in Gebenweiler	< Father
Mother >	Eva Katharine Schwinger of Hüttenbühl, unmarried		Rosine née Weller (Reference) I 494	< Mother

No.	Names of Children	Birth / Baptism	Confirmation	Marriage	Death
1. *before marriage*	Gottlieb	Gebenweiler 12 Sept. 1870	--	--	27 Sept. 1870
2.	**Katharine**	14 Oct. 1872	Kaisersbach 11 Apr 1886	to North America, 12 Dec. 1891	
3. *in marriage*	Gottfried	18 March 1874	22 April 1888 Kaisersbach	--	Gebenw.Gehren 2 July 1918
4.	Karoline Christine ª	25 Dec. 1875 in Kaisersbach	7 April 1889	30 Aug 1910 in Kaisersbach to farmer Christian Joos of Menzles	
5.	Karoline	1 Mar. 1878 in Gbnwlr / 3 Mar. 1878, Ksrsb.	--	--	22 March 1879
6.	Johann Christian	21 Dec. 1879 in Gbn.gehren / 25 Dec, Ksrsb.	16 Apr. 1893	10 Oct 1918 in Korb near Waiblingen to Karoline Merkle	7 March 1930 in Waiblingen
7.	Karl	20 Feb 1882 in GebGehr / 24 Feb Ksrsb.	12 Apr 1896	7 Apr 1911 to Pauline Karol[ina] Bretzger, resident of Cannstatt	--
8.	Anna Maria ᵇ˒ᶜ	5 Nov 1886 / 7 Nov Ksrsb.	1 April 1900	--	Gebenweilergehren 18 Sept. 1975
9.	Pauline	8 June 1890 / 12 June 1890	10 April 1904	--	Gebenweilergehren 23 Jan. 1973
10.	Friedrich	9 Feb 1892 / 14 Feb 1892	1 April 1906	... 27 Nov 1926 with Emma Schloz of Waiblingen	
a	Anna Maria (illegitimate child of Karoline Christine)	Gebenw.Gehren 8 Dec 1909	Kaisersbach 19 Dec 1909		
b	Christine Luise (illegitimate child of Anna Maria)	20 July 1910 / 31 July 1910	6 April 1924	20 Mar 1933 in Cannstatt to Gotthelf Frey, ...resident in...	
c	Christian Ludwig (illegitimate child of Anna Maria)	7 July 1913 / 13 July 1913			

The English translation of the family table of Katharine Deininger's birth family. See text for notable information. Primary Source: Ev.-Luth. Church Archive Stuttgart, Parish Register 1577, Vol. 7, Family Records Kaisersbach. Translated by Merlin Schlichting.

Katharine

An undated photo of Karl Deininger b. 1882, younger brother of Katharine Deininger. The photo was likely taken between 1900 and 1910. Karl later served in WWI and suffered the loss of a leg in battle. Source: From the author's collection, originally from the Hinderer Minnesota home. Edited by author.

have been in the village of Gebenweiler, or possibly in Gehren itself.

The topmost section of the family table indicated that Johann Gottlieb was born outside of marriage. Unfortunately, Johann Gottlieb's father, Johann Georg Deininger, could not be traced back into earlier generations. His mother, Eva Catharine Schwinger, never married Johann Georg Deininger. Eva Catharine was also born outside of marriage.

The topic of Wuerttemberg marriage practices during the 1800s is discussed later in this chapter.

In the lower children's section of the family table, the record for Katharine and her siblings contains more valuable detail. For Katharine, the date of her emigration to America is correctly recorded (on a separate page) as 12 Dec. 1891. Her younger siblings are numbered 3 through 10. Each child occupies a line running left to right. For each child, the archivist who compiled the family table added any lifetime events they discovered.

This family table also lists children from later generations. They are labeled with lower-case letters "a," "b," and "c" in the English version. Of the eight siblings who lived past childhood, Katharine was the only one who left Wuerttemberg.

The birth of Katharine Deininger and her siblings spanned more than two decades. In fact, Katharine emigrated to America in December 1891, a few months before her youngest sibling, Fritz (Friedrich), was born. This means a complete family photo could not have been taken. However, mother Karoline and a few of Katharine's youngest siblings were photographed during the 1900s.

THE CURRENT RESIDENTS OF THE GEHREN PROPERTY

The family now residing on the ancestral Gehren property descend from Katharine Deininger's sister Marie (Anna Maria). This sister was numbered 8 in the family table. Marie did not marry but had two children including a daughter named Christine Luise (b. 1910). As previously noted, the underlined name, in this case Luise, was the name she was known by.

In the original family table, the section with more recent generations of children is marginally legible. In addition, much of the recent family lineage information comes from family members, not source documents. Nevertheless, the church records and family statements allow tracking the Gehren property ownership forward in time.

The three youngest siblings of Katharine Deininger: Left to Right: Marie (Anna Maria) b.1886, Pauline b.1890, and Fritz (Friedrich) b.1892. This 1967 photo was taken in their Gehren home. Source: Merlin Schlichting, edited by author.

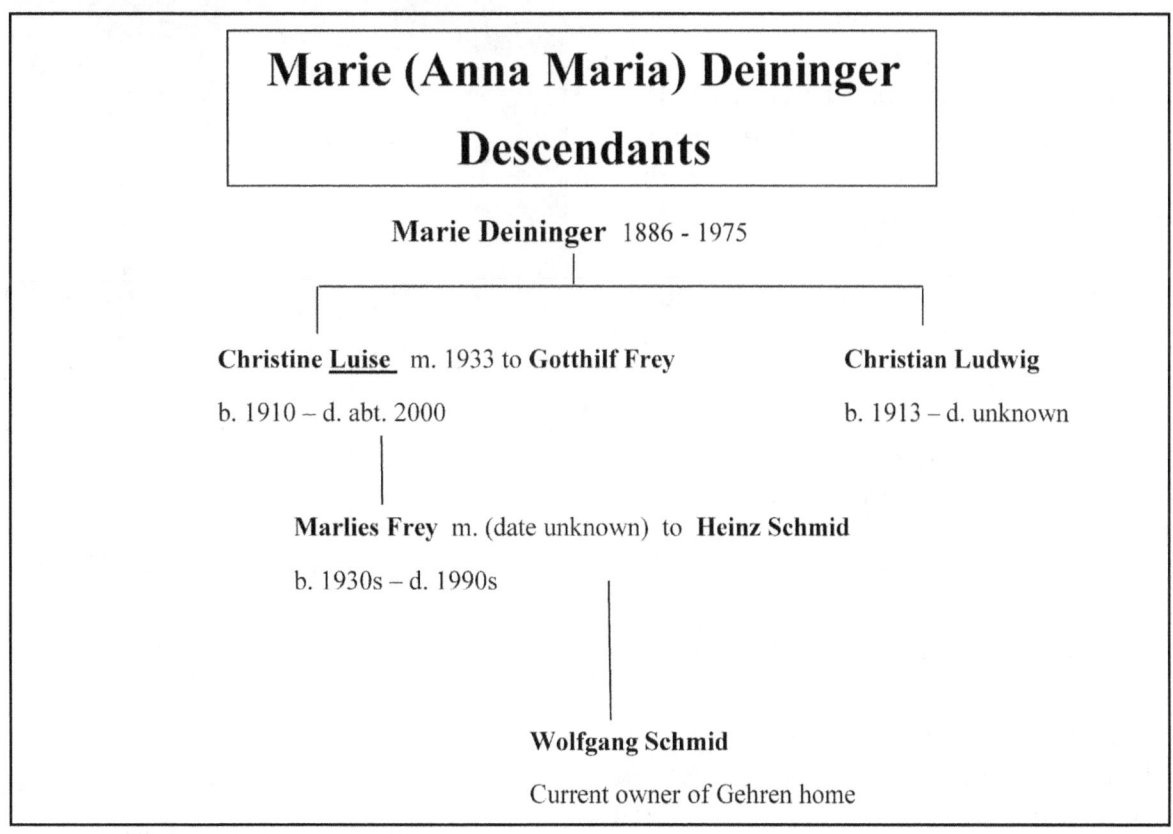

An illustration of the descendants of Marie (Anna Maria) Deininger. Source: Information supplied by family members. Illustration by author.

The family table stated that Marie's daughter Luise married Gotthilf Frey in 1933. Gotthilf was, by family story, killed in WWII. Luise and Gotthilf had one child, a daughter named Marlies.

Marlies Frey married Heinz Schmid and together they had one son, Wolfgang Schmid. Marlies died in the 1990s followed by her husband Heinz a few years later. Their son Wolfgang, his wife Ursula, and their two adult sons now live on the Gehren property.

In October 2019, Merlin, David, and Ryan Schlichting made an unannounced visit to this family. We were received warmly and even invited back to enjoy a home-cooked meal. A traditional meal was prepared by Ursula: goulash and "made-from-scratch" spaetzle.

One additional document helps to explain the ownership history of the Gehren property. Parents Johann Gottlieb Deininger and Karoline (Heinz) Deininger prepared a will. They sent a copy to their daughter Katharine who was by then living in America. The will was dated December 1922 when Johann Gottlieb was 82 and Karoline was 71. It stated that Katharine's youngest sister Pauline had, for some years, contributed housekeeping and farm work on the Gehren property with no compensation. The parents decided that Pauline should inherit that property. The will additionally stipulated that Pauline's unmarried sister (Marie) could continue to live in their Gehren home so long as she remained unmarried. The parents also willed money to their granddaughter Luise, the daughter of Marie.

Pauline died in 1973 at the age of 83. At that time, her older sister Marie was still living in the Gehren home. Marie died two years later in 1975. When Pauline died, the family story is that she willed the house and property to her sister Marie's granddaughter Marlies. By that time, Marlies was married to Heinz Schmid. Years later, Marlies and Heinz Schmid's only child, Wolfgang, inherited the ancestral Gehren property from his parents.

THE GEHREN PROPERTY

Today we saw the site of the old Deininger farm. The original house is gone now. The owner, Wolfgang, is a distant relative and showed us an old picture of the house. Amazingly, he brought out a very old book which was the family Bible (Book of Sermons) handed down through the generations. Family member names are written on the front pages including my great great grandmother, Katharine Deininger, who was the one to emigrate to America with Gottlieb Hinderer.

Like most farms in the area, the Deininger farmhouse is surrounded by green fields. Downhill from the house is a forest that, if you hike down through it, will bring you to a creek called Blinde Rot (Blind Red), which eventually runs into the River Lein. Wolfgang has a large garden bed in the field where he is growing mostly cruciferous vegetables. Alongside that bed was a field of mustard which he uses for a cover crop; he calls it green manure. There is a section of forest, northwest of the house, that Wolfgang is responsible for, but it is also where they get their firewood. They had rabbits, goats, and chickens.

— Ryan Schlichting
October 6, 2019

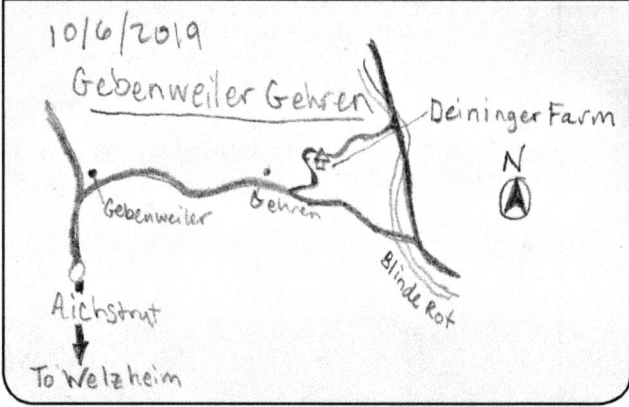

A pencil sketch of the Gehren countryside drawn by Ryan Schlichting. Source: Ryan Schlichting, October 6, 2019, Edited by author.

The family garden stretches downhill toward the forest and the creek named Blinde Rot. Fall vegetables are growing on the left and a cover crop, Wolfgang's "green manure," is on the right. Source: Photographed and edited by author.

Katharine Deininger was born in a traditional 1800s Wuerttemberg house. The house combined both family and livestock in a single building. The part of the house where the family lived was small with a single front doorway. The animals were separately sheltered, but under the same roof. The animal quarters had a separate doorway. The slope of the hillside meant the animal doorway was at a level below the family entrance. A 1977 photo shows a VW bus parked next to the livestock doorway at the back corner of the house. Katharine was born in this house in 1872. This means the house was more than 100 years old at the time of this 1977 photo.

Two aerial photos of the Gehren property contrast the house of Katharine's era with today's house built in 1998. The aerial photo of the older house is undated, but it is likely from the late 1970s. In this photo the house shutters are opened, and the animal doorway is seen in the lower right corner of the building. There are several other buildings tightly compressed into the tip of the narrow roadway turn.

The aerial photo of today's house built in 1998 was taken from about the same angle. The position of the house inside the tight roadway turn is the same. The house itself has been completely rebuilt with the lower livestock area replaced by a basement.

When did Katharine Deininger's ancestors first live in the old Gehren house? The family table for her parents states they lived in Gehren when her older brother Gottlieb was born in 1870. It is also clear that it was her mother's Heinz family who were the earlier residents of Gebenweiler. Her father Johann Gottlieb was from Huettenbuehl. The church records from before 1870 identify the family residence as Gebenweiler, not Gebenweilergehren

A 1977 photograph of Katharine Deininger's birth home. The window shutters are closed in the family section of the house. This view of the back of the house shows the animal entrance near the lower right corner. Source: Merlin Schlichting. Edited by David Schlichting.

A late 1970s aerial photo of the old house and nearby buildings. The family area window shutters are open as is the animal doorway. Note that the buildings are constructed close together inside the tight roadway turn. Source: Access to the original photo courtesy of Wolfgang Schmid. Photographed and edited by author.

A 2018 aerial photo of the current house built in 1998. Note that the livestock quarters have been replaced by a basement. Source: Access to the original photo courtesy of Wolfgang Schmid. Photographed and edited by author.

or Gehren. The Heinz family may well have lived in the same Gehren house, but the church record is inexact. Unlike Alfdorf and Brend, no property ownership maps were found from Gebenweiler or Gehren.

A pragmatic approach is to consider historic use of the term "Gebenweiler" to mean the half-mile area which includes both Gehren and the village of Gebenweiler. Using this approach, Katharine Deininger's direct line was tracked back into earlier generations. The family's location in Gebenweiler is documented as early as 1787. Back then, one of her direct ancestors, Johann Georg Weller, was a farmer in Gebenweiler. However, his descendants did not all remain in Gebenweiler. Instead, they moved away from Gebenweiler to neighboring villages. This is not surprising in light of the discussion in Chapter 2 regarding land inheritance. There was only so much land available and most children had to look elsewhere to find enough farmland to support their own family.

A continuous Heinz family presence in Gebenweiler began with Katharine Deininger's maternal grandfather Gottlieb Heinz. In an 1827 document, he was described as a recently arrived farmer in Gebenweiler. This means the Heinz family has been continuously located in Gebenweiler, and likely in Gehren itself, since 1827.

THE HEINZ FAMILY OF GEHREN

The family table for Katharine Deininger's maternal grandparents, Gottlieb Heinz and Rosine Weller, included the usual three generations. The upper section of the table described the primary couple, Gottlieb Heinz and Rosine Weller. Gottlieb Heinz was born in 1810 and died in 1867. Rosine Weller was born in 1827 and died in 1877. They were married in Welzheim in 1842. Recall that the Kaisersbach church was not completed until 1869. At the time of their 1842 marriage, Welzheim was still the regional church for people living in Gehren.

This primary couple was remarkable for several reasons. Their age difference, 17 years, was very uncommon. Even more unusual, husband Gottlieb was a godparent for his future wife when she was

Katharine

The family table for Gottlieb Heinz and Rosine Weller. Katharine Deininger's mother, Karoline Heinz, is child #5. See text for comments. Source: Ev.-Luth. Church Archive Stuttgart, Parish Register 1577, Vol. 7, Family Records Kaisersbach. Edited by author.

Family Table for
Gottlieb Heinz and Rosine Weller

p. 494 (*in original parish register*)   **Gebenweiler**

Birth	Father	Marriage	Mother	Birth
3 August 1810	Heinz, Gottlieb, resident and farmer. Died 1 June 1867	Welzheim 19 June 1842	Rosine Weller. Died 25 Dec 1877	3 May 1827
His Father--	Johann Georg Heinz, farmer in Kaisersbach	Christian Weller, farmer in Strohhof		--Her Father
His Mother--	Catharina née Mueller	Catharina née Weller		--Her Mother

Children

Register No.	Children's Names	Birth	Confirmation	Marriage	Death
1	Johann Georg	2 Aug 1844	...	...	27 Feb 1845
2	Anna Maria	5 Jan 1846	Kaisersbach 22 Apr 1860	23 Jun 1868 to Joh. Dahlecker, Gebenweiler	19 Jul 1930
3	Catharine Rosine	1 Oct 1847	...	...	17 June 1860
4	Christina	20 Jan 1849	...	...	23 Jan 1851
5	**Caroline**[1]	**16 Dec 1851**	**23 Apr 1865**	**25 Jan 1874 in Kaisersbach to Johann Gottlieb Deininger, day laborer in Gebenweiler**	**11 Jul 1934**
6	Johann Gottlieb	18 Jun 1854	...	...	30 Nov 1854
7	Johann Gottfried	7 Apr 1856, Gebenweiler	3 Apr 1870	19 Jun 1890 to Marie Bareiss	26 Oct 1936
8 and 9	Johann Georg Georg Carl	18 Apr 1859 18 Apr 1859	... ...	... ...	6 May 1859 11 May 1859
10	Friederich	3 Aug 1860	19 Apr 1874	emigrated to Sandusky, Ohio in Sept. 1882	
11	Karl August	1 Jun 1866	18 Apr 1880	emigrated to Sandusky, Ohio 13 May 1883	

[1] In this family table, Karoline's name was spelled "Caroline."

An English translation of the family table for Gottlieb Heinz and Rosine Weller. Katharine Deininger's mother, Karoline Heinz, is child #5. In this family table, her given name was spelled "Caroline." Note the emigration of two younger brothers in the early 1880s. Source: Ev.-Luth. Church Archive Stuttgart, Parish Register 1577, Vol. 7, Family Records Kaisersbach. Translation by Merlin Schlichting. Editing by David Schlichting.

baptized in 1827. It was the baptism document that stated Gottlieb was a recently arrived farmer living in Gebenweiler. Adding to the unique features of this couple, Rosine was only fifteen years old when she married Gottlieb.

In the middle parent's section of the family table, Gottlieb Heinz's father was listed as a farmer in Kaisersbach. Rosine Weller's parents lived in the hamlet of Strohhof, less than a mile southeast of Gehren. This means neither of their parents were living in Gebenweiler or Gehren. It was Gottlieb and Rosine who began the continuous family presence in Gebenweiler, and probably Gehren.

The lower section of the table lists the primary couple's children in the order of their birth. There were eleven children, all born after Gottlieb and Rosine's marriage in 1842. Of these eleven children, only five lived into their adult years.

Katharine Deininger's mother Karoline is child number 5. Her birth date is noted and her marriage to Johann Gottlieb Deininger is documented near the right edge of her entry line. In addition, an "X" precedes her name referring to a footnote at the bottom of the page. The footnote is partially visible as the lowest entry on the original family table. This footnote documents the birth of Karoline's first two children (Gottlieb and then Katharine) prior to her marriage to Johann Gottlieb Deininger.

Children 10 and 11 are Friederich and Karl August Heinz. Their entries state they both emigrated to Sandusky, Ohio. Friederich left in 1882 when he was 22. Karl August followed in 1883, less than a month before his 17th birthday. These two brothers were uncles to Katharine Deininger. Their emigration to America was nearly ten years before Katharine Deininger left Wuerttemberg.

A consideration of the childhood years of Katharine Deininger brings into focus the family life she experienced. She was born and grew up in the old Gehren house. Quite likely, her mother Karoline's birth family lived in the same house. Her youngest uncle, Karl August, was only six years old when Katharine was born in 1872. In turn, Katharine would have been a ten-year-old girl when Karl August emigrated in 1883. This connection between overlapping generations meant Katharine grew up familiar with the experience of family emigration.

THE HEINZ FAMILY BOOK OF SERMONS

The current owner of the Gehren property, Wolfgang Schmid, is the keeper of an old book from his Heinz family's past. Rather than a family Bible, it is a book of sermons designed for a family to use in their home.[7]

This particular book of sermons was printed in 1841. It has a heavy leather-surfaced front and back covering, with chronologically ordered pages of sermons in between. For families in Gehren and nearby villages, attending church in either Weltzheim or later in Kaisersbach was not always possible. A popular alternative during the mid-1800s was for a family with strong religious beliefs to own a book of sermons, one for each Sunday and each holy day. On the days they were unable to attend a church service, they could worship at home, in part, by reading the sermon for that day.

The book of sermons owned by the Heinz family is not of particular importance except for three hand-written pages inside the front cover. Each of the three pages is focused on a different person or family. Each page also has a unique handwriting style. The authors are not identified, but the pages were almost certainly written by three different family members.

The first handwritten page was a dedication to Gottlieb Heinz, Karoline's father. The script used has a calligraphy-like flourish. The dedication page was dated 1843, two years after the book of sermons was published. The dedication page identified this particular book as a part of the Heinz family's religious life.

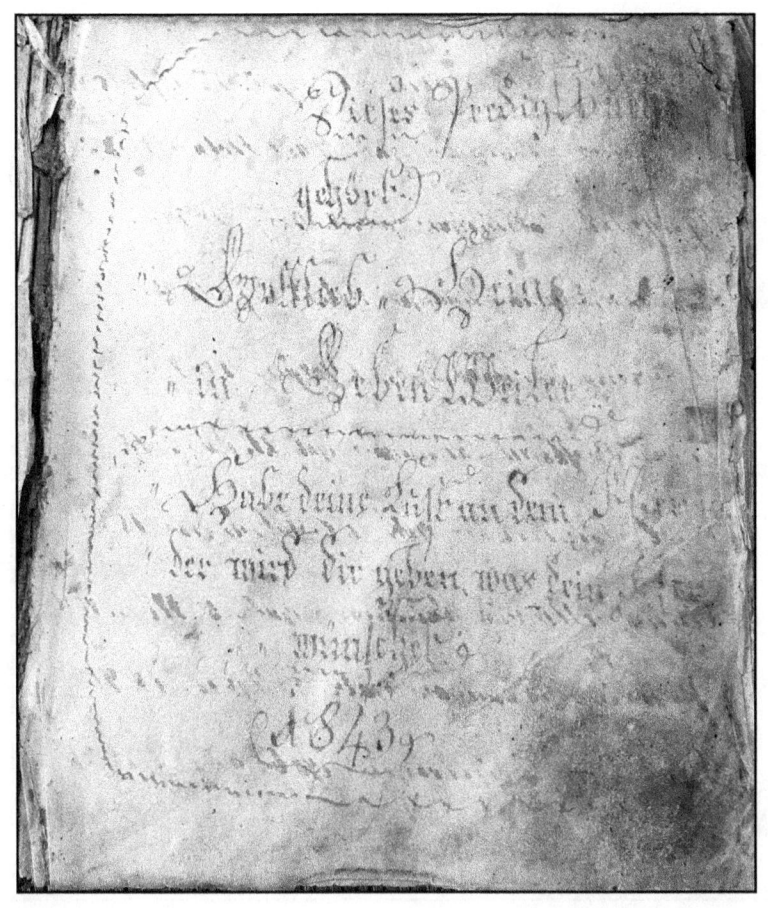

The Heinz book of sermons was dedicated to Gottlieb Heinz b. 1810. See text for the translation. The dedication page was dated 1843. Source: Access courtesy of Wolfgang Schmid. Translated by Merlin Schlichting. Photographed and edited by author.

The English translation of the dedication page reads:

> This Book of Sermons
> Belongs to
> **Gottlieb Heinz**
> in Geben Weiler
> Be joyful in the Lord.
> He will grant you the desires
> of your heart.
> 1843

The second handwritten page in chronological order contained a listing of the children of Gottlieb Heinz b. 1810, and his wife Rosine (Weller) Heinz. The top line on this page included the name Johann Georg Heinz followed by a birth date: 3 August. The year is not entirely legible but was most likely 1844. This was the name and birth date (the actual birth date was 2 August) of Gottlieb and Rosine's first child, who died when he was only six months old.

After the opening paragraph, there was a listing of their next ten children in the order of their birth. Katharine Deininger's mother, Karoline Heinz, was the fourth child down this list, and was written in darker ink. Her birth date was written as 15 December 1851 (the church record stated it was 16 December 1851). On this page, the spelling of her given name was *Charoline*. Overall, the page is a tribute to all the children of Gottlieb and Rosine Heinz, but it especially honors their first child, Johann Georg, who died so young. As with the other pages, the author of this page was not identified.

The final handwritten page was another list of children arranged in birth order. This page was a simple listing with no introduction, no explanation, and no named author. Nevertheless, it is easily recognized. It was a listing of Katharine Deininger and her siblings arranged by birthdate.

Katharine

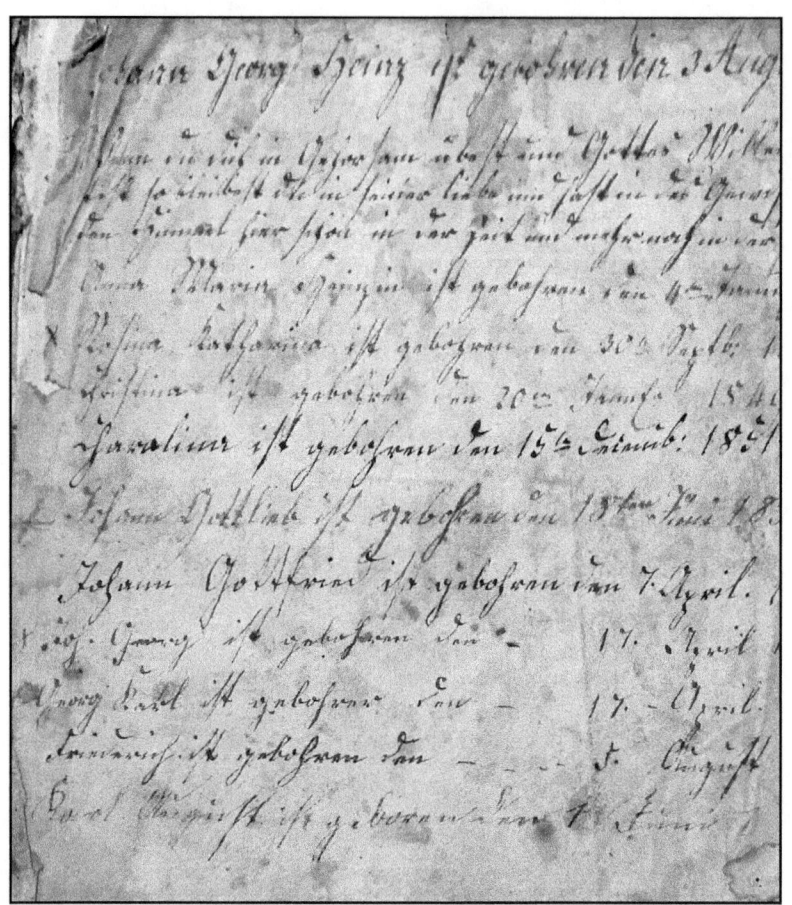

This page honored the eleven children of Gottlieb and Rosine (Weller) Heinz, with a special honor given to their first child Johann Georg who died at six months of age. Daughter Karoline b. 1851, the mother of Katharine Deininger, is the fourth child down. See text for comments. Source: Access courtesy of Wolfgang Schmid. Translated by Merlin Schlichting. Photographed and edited by author.

Book of Sermons
Children of Gottlieb Heinz and Rosine (Weller) Heinz

Johann Georg Heinz was born the 3rd of August 184_ (last digit illegible)

If you practice obedience and hold faithfully to God's will, you remain in his love and possess the heavenly victory of conscience now in this life and still more in eternity.

Anna Maria Heinzin, born 4 January 1846	Johann Gottfried was born 7 April 1856
Rosina Katharina, born 30 September 1847	Joh(ann) Georg was born 17 April 1859
Christina was born 20 January 1849	Georg Karl was born 17 April 1859
Charolina was born 15 December 1851	Friederich was born 5 August 1860
Johann Gottlieb was born 18 June 1854	Karl August was born 7 June 1866

Note: This page of the Book of Sermons listed the children of Gottlieb Heinz and Rosine (Weller) Heinz. The name of Katharine Deininger's mother Karoline was spelled "Charolina."

The English translation of this page. The topmost line honored their first child. The long list included all other children of Gottlieb Heinz and Rosine (Weller) Heinz. Their daughter Karoline b. 1851, the mother of Katharine Deininger, is the fourth child down the list. Source: Access courtesy of Wolfgang Schmid. Translated by Merlin Schlichting.

The Deininger and Heinz Families

This page listed the children of Johann Gottlieb Deininger and Karoline (Heinz) Deininger. It included Katharine Deininger, listed second, b. 14 October 1872. Source: Access courtesy of Wolfgang Schmid. Photographed and edited by author.

Book of Sermons
Untitled Page

(Children of Johann Gottlieb Deininger and Karoline Heinz)

Gottlieb Deininger born 12 Sept. 1870

Katharina Deininger born 14 October 1872

Gottfried Deininger born 18 March 1874

Christina Karolina Deininger born 25 Dec. 1875

Karoline Deininger born 1 March 1878

Johann Christian Deininger born 21 Dec. 1879

Karl Deininger born 20 February 1882

Anna Maria Deininger born 5 Nov. 1886

Paulina Deininger born 8 Jun. 1890

Friedrich Deininger born 9 Feb. 1892

The English translation of the Book of Sermons page that listed the children of Johann Gottlieb Deininger and Karoline (Heinz) Deininger. Source: Translation by author.

Katherine was the second child, born 14 October 1872. The year is not entirely legible but can be inferred. The writing style is once again unique. All children, including Katharine's youngest brother Fritz (Friedrich) b. 1892 were included. This means the author could not have been Katharine, who emigrated to America in 1891. Most likely, Katharine's mother Karoline (Heinz) Deininger proudly added this list of her own children to the Heinz family Book of Sermons.

WUERTTEMBERG CITIZENSHIP AND MARRIAGE PRACTICES

Marriage rules and practices in the 1800s differed from what is common today. The Weller family of Alfdorf included examples of marriage occurring years after a couple began living together and having children. Daughters, their chosen partners, and their children lived for several years in the daughter's parents' home. After a few years, the daughters married their chosen partner and had additional children. Eventually, these daughters and their new families moved away.

In Gehren, Katharine Deininger's parents similarly had children, including Katharine, before they married and then had additional children. In this instance, the new family did not move away from their ancestral family home. Katharine's paternal Deininger line included examples of illegitimacy and births outside of marriage. In some cases, the parents never married. The question arises whether this variety of family structures was due to personal choice, societal pressures, or some other circumstance.

Granting permission for a couple to marry was intricately linked to the rules for citizenship. To understand family structures, the rules for citizenship must first be examined.

In the United States, our policy has been that citizenship is granted by simply being born in this country. The same is true for our neighbors in Canada and Mexico. In fact, most countries in the Western Hemisphere use place of birth as the measure for granting citizenship. This practice is known by the Latin term *jus soli*. It means the soil (place) of your birth is what makes you a citizen. Although common in the Western Hemisphere, it is not the most common practice worldwide.

Rather than the place where you were born, most countries today and in the past have used some form of *jus sanguinis*. This means one or both parent's nationality (your blood line) determines your citizenship. The variations are many and often complex, but in practice, children born within a country are not automatically citizens of that country. Over time, countries have tended to modify citizenship rules to address problems caused by unwanted immigration. Nevertheless, most countries in the world continue to use some form of *jus sanguinis* to determine citizenship.

Prior to the late 19th century, German states regulated who could and who could not become a full citizen. It was not automatically granted simply by birth. Rural Wuerttemberg, with intricate community controls, enforced arbitrary rules regarding citizenship. For example, citizenship could be denied because of inadequate financial means to support yourself and your family. The town and village courts did not offer citizenship to residents who might become a financial burden to their community.

Permission to marry was also regulated by local community courts and the church. A citizen was more likely to be granted permission to marry than a non-citizen. Marriage might eventually be permitted for non-citizens, but both bride and groom had to prove their value to the community. Unlike today, marriage was not an easily granted license authorizing life together as a couple. Marriage was a controlled privilege only given to couples able to contribute economically to the fabric of local society.

One method of controlling marriage among commoners was to have a public reading of a couple's intention to marry. This was known as the "banns of marriage." This practice dates back hundreds of years, but in the 1800s it meant that the intention to marry must first be announced in sequential church services. A reading of the banns was an opportunity for any community member to object to the marriage and, in theory, subsequent childbearing. Today, a public reading of intention to marry may seem odd or old fashioned. However, it remains in many religious and civil ceremonies in the form of statements such as: "speak now or forever hold your peace."

In Wuerttemberg, the granting of marriage permits was codified into both local and state law. Permits were only granted to local couples who passed community scrutiny. A couple newly arriving in a town and claiming to already possess a state-issued marriage permit could be forced to display the permit or face expulsion. Even if such a permit were valid, the community could petition the state to rescind that permit. State regulations in mid-1800s Wuerttemberg were designed to preserve the ability of community courts to control permission to marry.[8]

During most of the 1800s, the Weller, Hinderer, Deininger, and Heinz families lived under these rules for citizenship and marriage. For a young couple lacking financial means, marriage rejection by the banns or a community court could be avoided by living with parents. If the parents paid the cost of housing and childbearing, the community was at no financial risk.

The ancestor couples described in Chapters 2 and 3 did not leave written explanations for why they lived with their parents. Nevertheless, it was a simple solution to a common dilemma. For a young couple back then, living with parents would not have seemed out of the ordinary. Instead, it was a way for them to live together, start a family, and not violate community rules.

For couples who never married, their specific reasons are similarly unknown. Perhaps marriage was not financially possible, or perhaps the children were the product of a liaison. Personal relationships were not so different back then, and effective birth control was more than a century in the future.

Restriction of marriage permits also had the indirect effect of reducing the number of children born to commoners. A woman's life expectancy was shorter in the 19th century. This was due to untreatable infectious diseases and the morbidity and mortality of childbirth. A delay of marriage often meant fewer childbearing years for a woman.

Penalties for ignoring marriage regulations were severe. A woman having children out of wedlock ran the risk of being expelled by a local community court. Then as now, enforcement of local rules varied greatly. This was the nature of local governance. Community courts could overlook transgressions, and local officials could be coerced or bribed. Nevertheless, the degree of life control faced by commoners was extreme.

After the formation of the German Empire in 1871, Chancellor Bismarck "liberalized" the rules for marriage. Control of marriage was taken away from the church and the community courts and was assumed by the central German government. This shift of authority provided benefits to Chancellor Bismarck. He eliminated local power centers, standardized the process of marriage throughout the Empire, and gained accurate census information. The new marriage records became a database for future taxation and military conscription.

Chapter 2 recounted the use of a hair-splitting vocabulary to place every farmer on a hierarchy of social rank. Citizenship and marriage rules similarly split the populace into multiple ranks. Even in small villages, local statutes created a myriad of civil offices. Citizens holding an office gained status and power. The effect was to create a finely stratified society, often with one citizen pitted against the other. For most of the 19th century, the monied nobility and the religious hierarchy controlled the purse strings. The advent of the German Empire in 1871 shifted control to the central government but did not lead to an easier life for commoners.

From farming practices to citizenship and marriage, Wuerttemberg residents in the 1800s were controlled by rules. Rank in a community was the critical factor, and a parent's rank dictated their children's opportunities. The economic future for young Wuerttemberg couples did not align with Thomas Jefferson's radical statement in the American Declaration of Independence: "all men are created equal." It is not surprising that many Wuerttemberg residents, particularly poor young adults, were drawn across the Atlantic Ocean to find a better life.

> When day comes we step out of the shade,
>   aflame and unafraid.
> The new dawn blooms as we free it.
> For there is always light,
>   if only we're brave enough to see it,
>   if only we're brave enough to be it.[9]

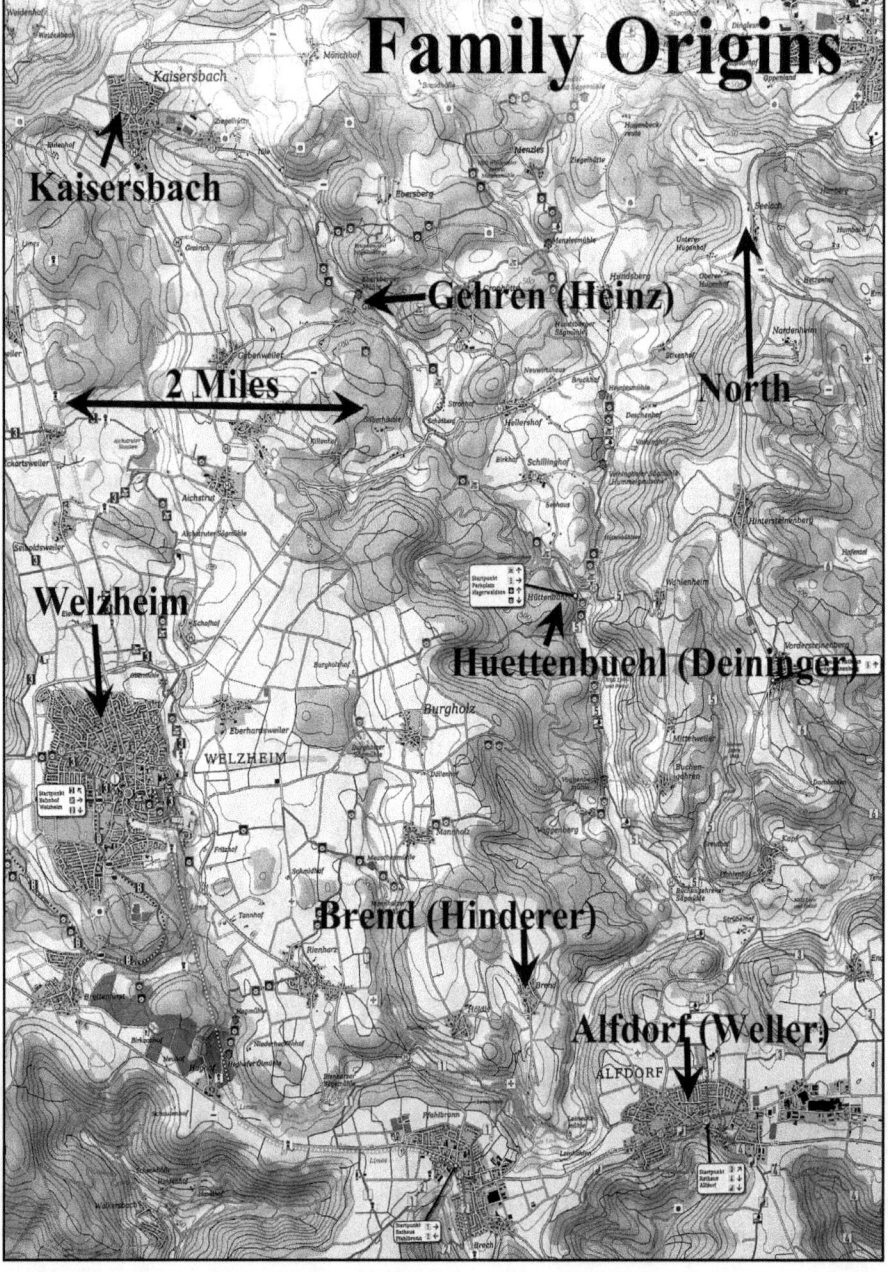

Wuerttemberg town and village origins of the four ancestor families. The mileage scale is approximate. Source: A 2019 photo of a street sign in Welzheim. Photographed and edited by author.

Notes

1. To locate Gehren, in Google Maps insert coordinates 48.913972, 9.668781 in the search box and click search.

2. To locate Gebenweiler, in Google Maps insert coordinates 48.910042, 9.650742 in the search box and click search.

3. To locate Kaisersbach, in Google Maps insert coordinates 48.929620, 9.639558 in the search box and click search.

4. To locate the Kaisersbach church, in Google Maps insert coordinates 48.929190, 9.639891 in the search box and click search.

5. Document courtesy of Pastor Frank Lutz. Translation by Merlin Schlichting

6. To locate the Huettenbuehl area, in Google Maps insert coordinates 48.892781, 9.700998 in the search box and click search.

7. The information about the historical use of these sermon books is offered by Merlin Schlichting.

8. S. Ogilvie, M. Küpker, and J. Maegraith, "Community Characteristics and Demographic Development: Three Württemberg Communities, 1558-1914" (Cambridge Working Papers in Economics 0910, Faculty of Economics, University of Cambridge, 2009), 65-71, https://sheilaghogilvie.com/wp-content/uploads/publications/cwpe0910.pdf.

9. Excerpted from *The Hill We Climb* by Amanda Gorman, Youth Poet Laureate of the United States, January 2021.

A 2019 image of the current Gehren family members. Left and right are Merlin and David Schlichting. Between them are son Max Schmid, father Wolfgang Schmid and mother Ursula Schmid. A second son was away from home. Source: photographed by Ryan Schlichting and edited by author.

Chapter 4

Passage to America

Timeline

1852 – Sophie Weller's sister emigrated to Michigan

1862 – The Homestead Act offered farmland to settlers

1865 – The U.S. Civil War ended; Lincoln was assassinated

1866 – Gottlieb Hinderer was born in Alfdorf

1869 – The U.S. transcontinental railroad was completed

1871 – The German Empire was formed

1872 – Katharine Deininger was born in Gehren

1882 – Gottfried Hinderer emigrated to Iowa

1880s – The peak of German emigration to the U.S.

1890 – The final Battle of the American Indian Wars

1891 – Gottlieb and Katharine emigrated to America

1893 – The Panic of 1893 led to economic depression

1895 – Johannes and Sophie Hinderer emigrated to Michigan

1898 – The Spanish-American War

1914 – World War I began

Symbols are important, and reminders of the essence of this country are very important. ...it is good to have a great statue in the [New York] harbor that says: this is why we came and let us not forget it.

~ Mario Cuomo[1]

• • • • • • •

On the evening of December 23, 1891, the westbound steamship *Havel* moved slowly from the Atlantic Ocean through the Verrazano Narrows into New York harbor. The weather was reportedly mild for December, with a bank of fog hanging over the distant Manhattan skyline.

Once inside New York harbor, the bow of the *Havel* turned slowly to starboard and headed toward its final destination—the Barge Office in Battery Park at the southern tip of Manhattan Island. Along the port side, the silhouette of the five-year-old Statue of Liberty came slowly into view. It was massive and unlike any monument previously constructed. By daylight, the 300 copper plates that formed her skin showed a dull green patina that would define the statue's future appearance. A few hundred yards beyond Lady Liberty, the *Havel* passed the newly completed brick walls of the Ellis Island immigration center. One week later, on January 1, 1892, Ellis Island opened its doors as the primary immigrant screening facility in America.

The trans-Atlantic voyage of the *Havel* began nine days earlier in the bustling North Sea port of Bremen, Germany. In Bremen, 615 passengers boarded the steamer. The following day, another 87 passengers came aboard in Southampton, England.

Aboard the *Havel*, 236 of the passengers were in first and second-class cabins. Many of them were Americans returning home. Other cabins were booked by Europeans on vacation, and a few held immigrants who could afford a private cabin.

The remaining 466 passengers were crowded into bunk beds in the steerage levels below the cabins. The *Havel* made many such voyages. Transporting immigrants to America was a profitable business and the *Havel* was one of the many "work-horse" steamers.

Gottlieb Hinderer and Katharine Deininger were among the men, women, and children crowded into the steerage levels of the *Havel*. For them, the statue with the uplifted torch was neither a welcome home symbol nor the beginning of a vacation. As immigrants, they had little money, no property, and spoke no English. To them, the Statue of Liberty was a symbol of hope. They were now on an unchangeable course into an unknowable future.

By the Numbers

Arguably, all humans living in the Western Hemisphere could be said to have immigrant origins. Native Americans likely arrived by way of a land bridge between Siberia and Alaska during the last ice age. Europeans sailed westward thousands of years later. The ancestors of all American societies came from somewhere else.

For Europeans, ocean travel was the only route to North America. A successful passage required a blend of craftmanship, the science of navigation and finance. European enclaves in the Western Hemisphere included Scandinavian fishing colonies in Greenland, Spanish gold seekers in Florida and the Caribbean, French fur traders on Canadian waterways, and English settlements along the American east coast. Each European group amounted to a trickle of humanity. They had to overcome the physical elements of ocean travel and the resistance of an already-peopled continent.

Each European settlement required enough time to gain a foothold. Some early settlements failed, leaving behind tools and building remnants, which would be discovered later by archeologists. The surviving European colonies slowly expanded westward. Spanish colonies were located along the southern Atlantic seaboard, the Caribbean, and Central America. French colonies were on the northern U.S. Atlantic seaboard and in Canada. English colonies grew along the mid-Atlantic seaboard between the Spanish and the French.

The gradual pace of immigration changed during the 19th century. German immigration statistics are an example of this change. Between 1820 and 1900, over 5 million Germans emigrated to America.[2] In 1860, the population of the United States was 30 million. The arrival of 5 million Germans in a country with only 30 million residents had a profound impact. Wuerttemberg, the homeland of Katharine and Gottlieb, was the origin of the greatest number of German immigrants.

The Germans were not the only immigrants arriving in the mid-1800s. Irish immigration peaked between 1840 and 1860. The Irish were fleeing from overpopulation and famine in their homeland. The peak of Scandinavian immigration did not come until the decade of the 1880s, coinciding with the peak decade of German arrivals.[3] Near the end of the 19th century, it was Italy, Greece, and Austria-Hungary that led the list of European immigrant origins. Throughout the 50 years following the American Civil War, one in every seven adults in America was foreign born.[4] The languages spoken by the new arrivals changed from decade to decade, but the pace of immigration was relentless.

Not all of these immigrants became permanent residents of the United States. Emigration from the United States back to Europe is more difficult to assess, and was not officially recorded until the early 1900s. Overall, the largest U.S. immigrant demographic was single young men. Like their fellow immigrants, an estimated one third of these young men crossed back to Europe one or many times.

Some young men had no intention of becoming permanent residents of America. They worked for months or years in America, and then used their savings to buy property in their European homeland. Others were called "birds of passage,"

```
OUTGOING STEAMERS.
            TO-DAY.
                                          Mails      Vessel
Vessel.    Line.     For                  close.     sails.
Assyrian, Allan-State, Glasgow............    10     a m
Rugia, Hamb-Amer, Hamburg..............       12     m
Claribel, Atlas, Kingston, &c........... 1 p m  3    p m
Ravensdale, H & C Am, Kingston, &c....10 a m 12      m
Smeaton Tower, NY&PR, Porto Rico..... 3 p m  5       p m
B Yglesias, Span Trans, Havana, &c...... 8 a m 10    a m
Southwold, NY& Cuba, Havana.......... 1 p m  3       p m
Rowena, Clyde, Port au Prince, &c........ 1 p m  3   p m

        SATURDAY, DEC. 26.
Etruria, Cunard, Liverpool...............10:30 a m  2 p m
Ethiopia, Anchor, Glasgow................12      m  2 p m
Veendam, Neth-Amer, Rotterdam........12      m  2 p m
La Gascogne, Fr Trans, Havre.......... 8:30 a m 12   m
Yucatan, NY & Cuba, Havana............11     a m  1  p m

        TUESDAY, DEC. 29.
Wisconsin, Guion, Liverpool..................       4 p m
Moravia, Hamb-Amer, Hamburg...........              7 a m
Havel, NG Lloyd, Bremen via South'pton,11 a m  2    p m


        SHIPPING NEWS.

PORT OF NEW-YORK.....WEDNESDAY, DEC. 23, 1891.
               ARRIVED.
    Steamer Italy (Br), Goudie, Liverpool Dec 5, with mdse to
F W J Hurst. Arrived at the Bar at 0 a m.
    Steamer Ethiopia (Br), Wilson, Glasgow Dec 10, Moville 11,
with mdse and passengers to Henderson Bros. Arrived at the
Bar at 5.15 a m.
    Steamer Bellagio (Br), Blacklock, Glasgow Dec 5, in ballast
to Henderson Bros. Arrived at the Bar at 0 p m. 22.
    Steamer Parthian (Br), Thompson, Shields Nov 30, in bal-
last to Miller, Bull & Co.
    Steamer Havel (Ger), Jungst, Bremen Dec 14, Southampton
15, with mdse and passengers to Oelrichs & Co.
    Steamer Volmer (Dan), Heinzelman, Troon Dec 4, in ballast
to Funch, Edye & Co.
```

The *Havel* departed Bremen, Germany on December 14, 1891 and arrived in New York on December 23, 1891. A return voyage to Bremen was scheduled for December 29, 1891. Source: New-York Tribune, December 24, 1891, p. 12, accessed May 2021, www.Newspapers.com. Edited by author.

meaning they were migrant workers in America. These young men made the trans-Atlantic voyage year after year. The most common pattern was for a migrant worker to arrive each spring when work was plentiful and return to their homeland in the fall.[5] The expanding American economy offered them a financial opportunity not available in Europe

Immigration stories are accompanied by popular myths.[6] One myth is that most immigrants were escaping religious persecution or conscription into European armies. This was true for a few, but their numbers were small.

A second myth is that all immigrants were impoverished. The majority did cross the Atlantic Ocean in the least-expensive steerage levels of the ships. However, passenger manifests typically included dozens and occasionally a few hundred immigrants in second and first-class cabins.

Stowaways did not slip undetected into America. Crew members of each ship carefully screened passenger documents before leaving their home port. Once all passengers were aboard, the ship's crew created a passenger manifest before leaving port. At American ports of entry, no passenger was allowed to disembark if their name was not on the manifest.

Undoubtedly, some passengers lied about their personal information. In the 19th century, a passport was not required to disembark at American ports. False information could easily slip past American port officials. For their part, the shipping companies cared only that their passengers would be allowed to enter the U.S. The reason was financial. If American port officials denied entry, the shipping company had to return the passenger to their European port of departure at the company's expense.

Some families claim their European surnames were altered by American agents at Ellis Island or other ports of entry. This rarely happened. Immigration agents at American ports were fluent in the native language of the ship's country of origin.

In fact, about one third of agents were themselves immigrants. If an appropriate interpreter was not available at the time of their arrival, the immigrant was detained at the port of entry until a native language speaker was found. Surnames did get changed, but the change was made by the immigrants after they arrived in America.

Finally, America was not a "melting pot" in the sense of immigrants quickly bonding into a shared identity with those already living here. Almost all immigrants had either family contacts or financial sponsors in America. The Americans exchanged letters with the prospective immigrant describing the best route to their destination. When immigrants arrived at their destination, they were in familiar company. The family members or sponsors spoke their native language and taught them how to get by in this country. Enclaves of Europeans, all comfortably speaking their native language, were the norm in 19th century America. This was particularly true for German-speaking groups. Assimilation of Germans into American society took several generations.

Why They Left Wuerttemberg

The ancestor families of Gottlieb Hinderer and Katharine Deininger were all commoners, either farmers or day laborers. In their families, there was no threat of military conscription, no intellectual suppression, and no experience of religious persecution. Family members who emigrated had personal reasons for leaving their German homeland.

The reasons these immigrants left Germany have been previously discussed. Generations of Wuerttemberg families faced a progressive decline in their economic prospects. Children lacked the opportunity experienced by their parents. With each generation, they faced both reduced per-capita farmland and rigid rules governing farm practices. Community courts strictly controlled citizenship and permission to marry. For single men and young couples, it was this economic and social pressure that pushed them to leave their homeland.

By 1890, members of both Gottlieb's and Katharine's families had left Wuerttemberg and emigrated to America. Most of these relatives lived in Michigan and two brothers were in Ohio. One family, who will be discussed later, was already living in Iowa. Although it was a daunting endeavor for Gottlieb and Katharine, members of both of their families had already paved a pathway to America.

German immigrants, in particular, demonstrated "momentum" or "chain" migration. These terms reflect individuals or earlier immigrant families who attract other members of their family to follow in their footsteps.

After the mid-1800s, there were regions throughout the American Midwest where German was the most common spoken language. City dwellers from Germany migrated to the "German Triangle" in the American Midwest. This was the description given to Cincinnati, Milwaukee, and St. Louis. In these cities and within this triangle, German-speaking enclaves lived, worked, worshipped, and celebrated holidays as they had done for centuries in Germany. For new immigrants, chain migration meant that once they settled in America, they could comfortably lead a social life similar to what they had always experienced in the old country.

Why They Chose America

The push to leave Wuerttemberg was accompanied by a "pull" that attracted fully 90% of German emigrants to choose America as their destination.[7] At first, this may seem surprising. The pivotal events of 19th century American history were not attractive. The century began with the War of 1812 and ended with the Spanish American War. At mid-point, the fledgling republic nearly self-destructed in a civil war over slavery and secession of states from the union. The country's earliest known inhabitants were referred to as savages. Their tribes were subjected to displacement from their homeland, governmental treachery, and wars of annihilation. Two presidents were assassinated in the 1800s, and major depressions in 1873 and 1893 drove the economy downward. Nevertheless, the Germans and other Europeans came with the hope of a better life in America.

An important fact about Gottlieb and Katharine is that they arrived in 1891, late in the century. The two presidential assassinations, Lincoln in 1865 and Garfield in 1881, had resulted in an orderly succession of governmental authority. Episodes of economic depression were followed by new federal regulations and economic expansion. In the American Civil War, the principal of national unity defeated fragmentation, and slavery was abolished. The final battle of the Indian Wars occurred in 1890 at Wounded Knee in South Dakota. By 1891, all battles taking place on American soil were over, and the resilience of the 100-year-old republic was established.

Most German immigrants in the 19th century settled in American cities. The immigrants in Gottlieb's and Katharine's family lines, however, were from farming families. With farming skills in their background, the availability of farmland in America was a key attraction.

In earlier centuries, American lands were populated from east to west by a rich mixture of Indian tribal societies. At first contact, European diseases like smallpox decimated the native tribes along the Atlantic coast of America. As settlements of Europeans expanded westward, the surviving tribal groups were forced westward as well. Tribes that were historic enemies were increasingly compressed against one another. Clashes between these tribes and against the expanding settler colonies were inevitable.

The cultural history of most Indian tribes did not prepare them for their new locations in North America. For example, Eastern tribes had lived for centuries in forested settlements. They did not have the cultural knowledge of how to survive in the treeless Midwest prairie grasslands or the semi-arid Great Plains.

By the mid-19th century, the policy of the U.S. government became focused on confining tribes to reservations. The policy had two goals. The first goal was to remove the tribes from the farmable or gold-containing land desired by Americans. For example, gold was discovered in the Appalachian Mountains of Georgia in 1828. Cherokee tribes had lived in these mountains for centuries. The government's solution was to march thousands of indigenous Cherokees along the "Trail of Tears" to an Oklahoma reservation. A second governmental goal was to allow settlers to travel safely to western states. In 1848, gold was discovered at John Sutter's sawmill on the American River in California. This discovery brought a rush of humanity to the West. Many "49ers" had to traverse half of the continent to seek their fortune. Confinement of tribes within reservations allowed a safer passage for Americans caravanning to California and Oregon.

The United States government wanted the newly vacated tribal lands repopulated quickly. During the mid to late 1800s, the Pacific Railroad Act[8] issued land grants and right-of-way bonds to railroad companies. The railroad companies used this governmental largesse to extend their rail lines westward. The companies were also allowed to sell any land not needed for their tracks to the general public. This land had been given to them freely, but they could sell any unused land for company profit. Once rail transportation was in place, settlers and merchants eagerly followed. In the end, almost 10 percent of the land owned by the United States government became the property of railroad companies.

The Homestead Act of 1862 "sold" former Indian tribal land to individual settlers. It began as a campaign promise of the 1860 Republican presidential candidate, Abraham Lincoln. Similar to the Pacific Railroad Acts, the goal of the Homestead Act was to encourage settlers to move west. Former tribal land was offered at virtually no cost in parcels of 160 acres. Civil War veterans were also eligible for Homestead Act land. A deeply indebted United States government reduced its payroll debt to soldiers by offering them land. In sum, the former tribal land had become a prized commodity. The United States government wanted it settled, while the immigrants and soldiers wanted to own it.

The Homestead Act of 1862 was widely abused by speculators using paid agents to buy land which could be profitably resold. "Manifest Destiny" was their motto. Manifest destiny was the proclamation that European-Americans were destined by "Divine Providence" to expand with the railroad lines from coast to coast. A companion slogan aimed at farmers was "rain follows the plow." All a farmer had to do was plow over the native prairie grass, and rain would fall. At first, this prediction seemed true.

Farming in the mid-1800s depended entirely on natural rainfall. The decade of the 1870s experienced above average rainfall, particularly in the Midwest and on the semi-arid Great Plains. It seemed as if the farmer's plow had changed the climate: rain did follow the plow. Unfortunately, the decades of the 1880s and the 1890s saw the climate revert first to average rainfall, and then outright drought. Farm crops in the Midwest and on the Great Plains dried up. The sodbuster's plow created clouds of blowing dirt on this now-arid land. Boom towns became ghost towns. The speculators were enriched and settlers went broke.[9]

The promise offered by the Homestead Act of 1862 did encourage emigration from Europe to America as well as the migration of Easterners to the Midwest and the Great Plains. For a few, it was the ticket to financial success. For the majority, it brought misery and eventual bankruptcy.

Finally, during the second half of the 19th century, promotional advertising was widely used to "pull" Germans to America. Germans and other Northern Europeans were stereotyped as hard workers, whether in urban factories or on farmlands. Privately owned businesses and governmental agencies sought to attract this productive labor force to the U.S.

In Germany, pamphlets, newspapers, and German-speaking agents promoted America. Books printed in German told them what to expect in America and how to travel once they arrived. Railroad companies and land speculators offered free tickets to visit new frontier communities. The advertising was typically outrageous. American land was said to offer unparalleled productivity, streams with pure-flowing water, and a climate that could cure all ills.

Agencies representing American state governments also advertised heavily. In Minnesota, a Board of Immigration was created to attract settlers to the upper Midwest. The Board sent pamphlets to Germany and other northern European countries, all written in their native language. The pamphlets described Homestead Act land as being nearly free, but sure to be worth hundreds of dollars after only five years. You could pay a pittance, make a few improvements, and then resell it for a profit. Frontier states like Minnesota also advertised in American states farther east. The frontier states wanted settlers, and did not care if they were newly arrived immigrants or earlier immigrants looking for a better life in the booming Midwest.[10]

THE MEANS OF TRAVEL

The Industrial Revolution dramatically changed the means of travel during the 19th century. Early in the century, long distance travel was by paid passage on rivers and canals. Short distance travel was either on foot or by horseback. Steam-powered railroad locomotives, first introduced in the early 1800s, revolutionized the means of travel. In Germany, the first rail lines were laid in the industrialized midlands. These areas had both industrial products and a population requiring transportation. German rail lines extended mainly north to south carrying merchandise and people between the midlands and North Sea port cities.

After the mid-1800s, even rural Wuerttemberg with its forests and rolling hills was traversed by rail lines. By 1890, both Germany and America were a maze of railroad lines. It was these railways that carried most immigrants from Wuerttemberg to North Sea ports of embarkation, and from the American east coast to their Midwest destinations.

Katharine and Gottlieb left their Wuerttemberg homeland from the North Sea port city of Bremen. Hamburg and Bremen were the two most heavily trafficked German ports of embarkation during the 19th century. Both cities are located on rivers several miles upstream from the foul-weather-prone North Sea. Bremen[11] is on the Weser River and Hamburg[12] is on the Elbe River. A third port city on the North Sea was Bremerhaven. It is located at the mouth of the Weser River downstream from Bremen. The attraction of Bremerhaven to the shipping companies was that it could accommodate the larger steamers that dominated shipping toward the end of the century.

Katharine and Gottlieb traveled in steerage, known to Germans as *Zwischendeck*. This translates literally as "between decks." During the earlier years of sailing vessels, steerage was located between the upper deck cabins and the lower cargo hold. When steamers took over, the number of deck levels increased, but steerage was still located between the upper cabins and the lower cargo level.

Passengers in steerage were required to supply their own eating utensils, bed linens and a mattress if they wished to have one. Food was included in the fare they paid, but the quality was poor and the supply limited. Most passengers brought as much food as possible from home.

During the Atlantic crossing, life aboard the ships was mostly boring. Shipping companies learned it was best to enforce strict daily routines, thereby keeping the passengers busy.[13] One family representative was assigned to retrieve meals for all of their family and could distribute the food as they wished. As the business of immigration matured during the century, rules protecting passengers became more commonplace. One such regulation assessed the shipping company a $10 fee for any onboard death during the voyage. Shipping companies competed with one another for passengers. Improving steerage conditions helped grow their reputation and their business.

Until the mid-19th century, sailing vessels were the means of crossing the Atlantic Ocean. The voyage on a sailing ship was far more dangerous than on the later steamers. The danger was due to a sailing ship's dependence on favorable weather, and because navigation measurement was inaccurate. Storms on the North Atlantic destroyed some sailing vessels. More often, the storms extended the transit time to the point of near starvation for the passengers. The average Atlantic Ocean transit time for sailing ships was four to 12 weeks.

Latitude, how far north or south of the equator you were, had been accurately measured for centuries by the use of a sextant. Measurement of longitude, how far from Europe you had sailed, required development of an accurate measure of time. Solutions were sought for centuries, but measurement of longitude at sea was unreliable until near the end of the 19th century. The inaccuracy of measuring longitude led to poor decisions aboard sailing vessels. If a storm caused damage to the sailing ship, the captain could not determine if it would be faster to attempt a return to Europe or continue toward America.

By the mid-19th century, sailing ships were being replaced by steam-powered vessels. With "steamers," weather was no longer a factor. Not all sailing ships braved a North Atlantic crossing during stormy winter months. Steamers, however, produced a steady flow of immigrants throughout the calendar year. With steamers, the average transit time plummeted. By the 1890s, steamers crossed the Atlantic Ocean in about 12 days. The price of the voyage was affordable for most commoners. Steerage fare on a steamer cost slightly less than a month's salary for a skilled laborer like a carpenter.[14]

As the vessels changed during the 19th century, so did the travel routes. In the days of sailing ships, most German emigrants were taken to America by an "indirect" route. They left their German port of embarkation and sailed first to Hull, a town on the eastern coast of England. From Hull, trains carried the German emigrants to Liverpool, a large port city along the western English coast. Liverpool acted as a passenger reshuffling port. Sailing ships from many European countries brought passengers to Liverpool. A reshuffled mix of passengers then boarded a second sailing ship for the much longer trans-Atlantic voyage to America.

When steamships took over the German immigrant routes, the train ride across England offered no financial advantage to shipping companies. The sharply reduced Atlantic Ocean transit time meant more money could be made by completing frequent roundtrips. Steamers still made short stopovers at English and Irish ports, but the purpose was to maximize their passenger load.

KATHARINE AND GOTTLIEB – HOW THEY MET

Some events surrounding Katharine and Gottlieb's emigration are clearly identified on official documents, but others are not. Family stories help to fill in the knowledge gaps, but they are less reliable. Katharine and Gottlieb left no written or oral history of why they made the choices they did. To the best of our knowledge, no family member recorded or asked them how they met and why they left Germany.

According to family story, Katharine Deininger worked as a domestic helper for the Johannes and Sophie Hinderer family in Brend, Germany. Recall that Johannes and Sophie began their life together living with Sophie's parents in Alfdorf. Their first two children, including Gottlieb, were born in

Alfdorf. Their family table states that their third child was born in Brend in 1868. This confirms that by 1868, they had moved away from Sophie's parents in Alfdorf and taken residence with the parents of Johannes Hinderer in Brend. From 1868 until their 1895 emigration, Johannes and Sophie lived in the ancestral Hinderer home in Brend. In this case, the family story of Katharine working in Brend is consistent with the known facts about where Gottlieb's family lived.

In October 1890, Katharine Deininger turned 18 years old. Chapter 3 described how her birth family lived for years with her Heinz grandparent's family in their ancestral Gehren home. By 1890, Katharine was one of seven siblings living in that home. Her Heinz grandparents had died, but both of her parents and one of her mother's brothers also lived in the Gehren home. This means there were ten people living in the small Gehren home.

There is no record or story of when Katharine began working for the Hinderers in Brend, or if that was her first job as a domestic helper. Daughters frequently worked away from their family home and most often as domestic helpers. This aided the daughter's family because there was one less mouth to feed back at home, and she could send any meager salary home to help her parents. In Wuerttemberg, daughters rarely inherited family farms. Sending them to other communities introduced them to new families, and possibly a future spouse. This was the reality for young women at that time.

Leaving Home

The steamer *Havel* carrying Katharine and Gottlieb left Bremen, Germany on December 14, 1891. Most likely, the couple left their Wuerttemberg home at least a week prior to that departure date. By rail, they would have first traveled west from Brend to the Wuerttemberg capital city of Stuttgart. From Stuttgart, main railroad lines extended northward to port cities on the North Sea. By 1891, these railroad routes were heavily used by travelers and for transporting merchandise.

The state of Wuerttemberg kept records of residents intending to emigrate. Anyone wanting official state permission to emigrate could apply. Although there was no obligation for emigrants to apply, a permission document might allow easier entrance into their destination country. Receiving official permission to emigrate required weeks or more to process. This means that those who are registered in the Wuerttemberg files had made plans to emigrate well ahead of their departure. Neither

The Havel *was built in 1890. She had 3 masts, 2 funnels, and could carry up to 826 passengers. Source: "New York Port, Ship Images, 1851-1891" (Lehi, UT: Ancestry.com), accessed May 2021. Edited by author.*

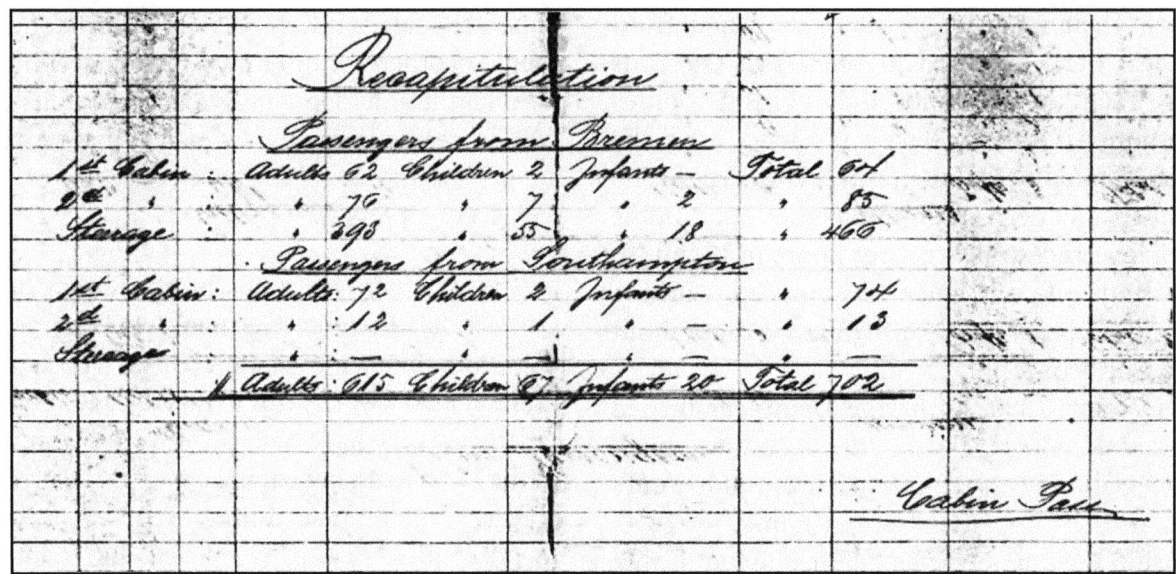

A summary of passengers aboard the Havel. *The 87 who boarded in Southampton all occupied the more expensive cabin compartments. Source: "New York, U.S., Arriving Passenger and Crew Lists (including Castle Garden and Ellis Island), 1820-1957" online database (Provo, UT: Ancestry.com, 2010), accessed May 2021. Edited by author.*

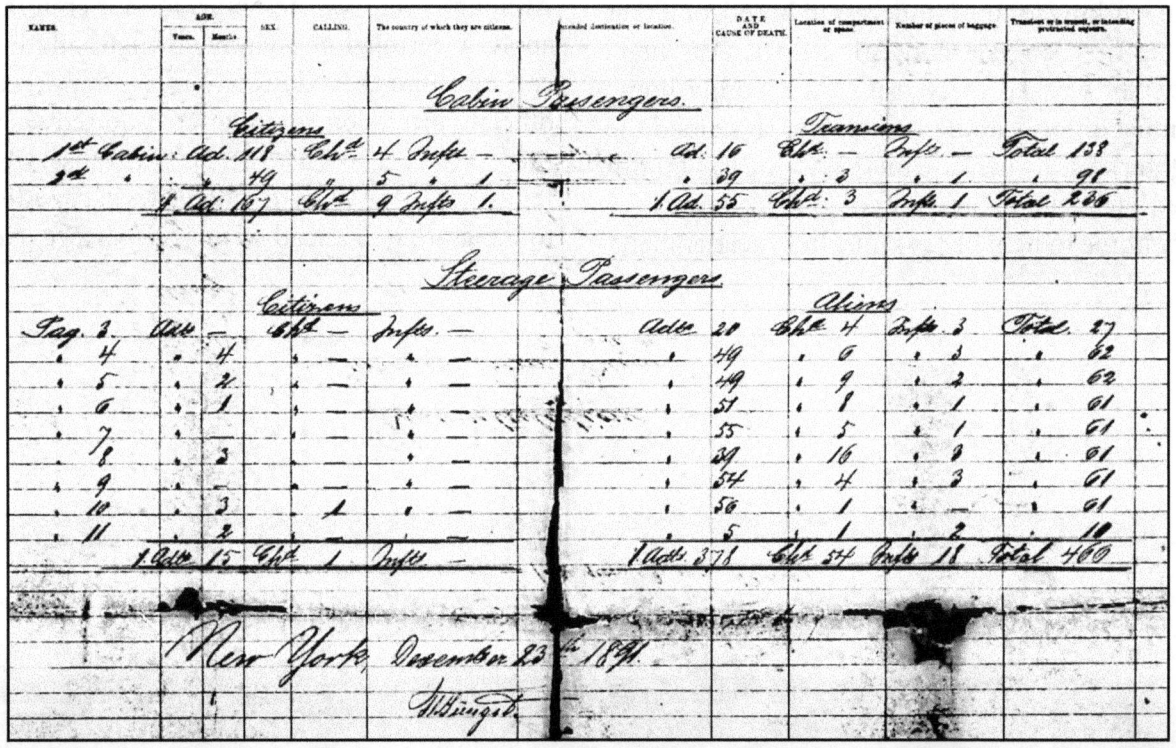

This second passenger summary reflects cabins occupied by both citizens and visitors, while steerage passengers were nearly all immigrants planning to remain in America. Source: "New York, U.S., Arriving Passenger and Crew Lists (including Castle Garden and Ellis Island), 1820-1957" online database (Provo, UT: Ancestry.com, 2010), accessed May 2021. Edited by author.

Gottlieb Hinderer nor Katharine Deininger was entered into the Wuerttemberg Emigration Index. This suggests their departure was not a long-standing plan.

Across the Ocean

The passenger manifest of the *Havel's* voyage on December 14, 1891, included a summary of passengers boarding in Bremen, and passengers who boarded the next day in Southampton, England. This summary specified their onboard location, in cabins or in steerage. The summary also divided passengers by age category: adults, children, and infants. It should be noted that the onboard location of the Bremen passengers was both in cabins and in steerage. Those who boarded in England all paid for the more expensive cabins.

The passenger manifest of this voyage of the *Havel* included a second summarization as well. This summary also divided passengers into those in cabins and those traveling in steerage. However, it added additional detail. Cabin passengers were divided into subcategories of "citizens" such as Americans returning home or "transiens" (transients), those visiting America. Steerage passengers were divided into "citizens" or "aliens." In the language of manifests, alien meant a foreign-born passenger. Not unexpectedly, nearly all passengers who traveled in steerage were listed as aliens.

The broader observation is the large number of passengers, 702, on this one steamer. In 1891, New York was the largest U.S. entry point for immigrants, but not the only one. With multiple steamers arriving daily at multiple entry points, the scale of immigration to America can be fully appreciated.

On the passenger manifest for this voyage of the *Havel*, Gottlieb Hinderer and Katharine Deininger were listed on separate pages. Families and couples traveling together were always listed together, one after the other, on a ship's manifest. Gottlieb and Katharine's separate page listings means they chose to travel and be recorded as individuals, not as a couple.

Gottlieb's entry is better preserved than Katharine's. He is listed on page 4 of the manifest as passenger 206. His age is correctly listed as 25 and his occupation is laborer. His origin is incorrectly recorded as Austria. His intended destination is recorded as Michigan. Recall that his mother Sophie's older siblings already lived in Michigan. In other columns, his entry stated he intended to have a "protracted sojourn." The meaning was that he, like every other steerage passenger on this page, did not plan to return to Germany. The error of naming Austria as his home could have been a misunderstanding by the crew member, or a deliberate deception on Gottlieb's part.

Katharine Deininger's entry on the manifest is nearly illegible. She is found on page 7 of the

The wooden trunk believed to accompany Gottlieb Hinderer. The visible writing translates as: Gottlieb Hinderer from Bremen to New York. The lowest line is faded and illegible. Source: Access courtesy of Sharon Halverson. Photographed and edited by author.

Katharine

manifest, passenger 389. Her name is spelled "Catha Deininger." She is listed as a 20-year-old female. Her true age was 19. Any statements about her occupation, her place of origin, and her destination are no longer visible.

Arrival in America

Prior to 1855, there were no official immigrant entry points in the United States and no federal regulation of immigrant entry. Immigration rules were deemed to be the province of individual states. In 1855, the city of New York opened an entry point at Castle Garden located at the southern tip of Manhattan Island. It was a city and state-run facility without federal involvement. In the view of the federal government, immigration was to be encouraged and so it went unregulated.

In April 1890, the federal government took control of immigration. Rather than use Castle Garden, they temporarily used the nearby Barge Office in Battery Park. The Barge Office was used until a new entry facility on Ellis Island opened in January 1892.[15] By chance, Gottlieb and Katharine emigrated to America during those months when the Barge Office was the official New York point of entry.

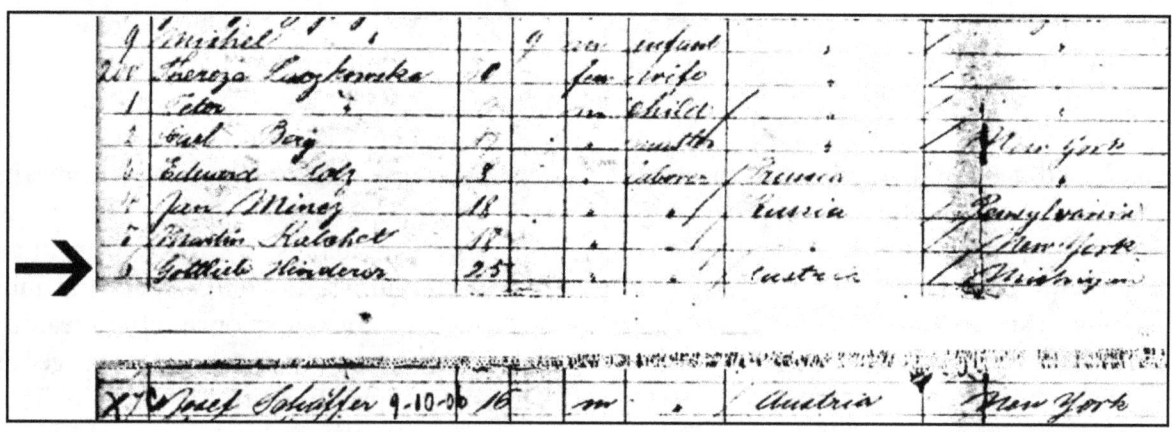

Gottlieb Hinderer is numbered 206 on the passenger manifest of the Havel. His age is correct but his birthplace is incorrectly listed as Austria. His destination is Michigan. See text for details. Source: "New York, U.S., Arriving Passenger and Crew Lists (including Castle Garden and Ellis Island), 1820-1957" online database (Provo, UT: Ancestry.com, 2010), accessed May 2021. Edited by author.

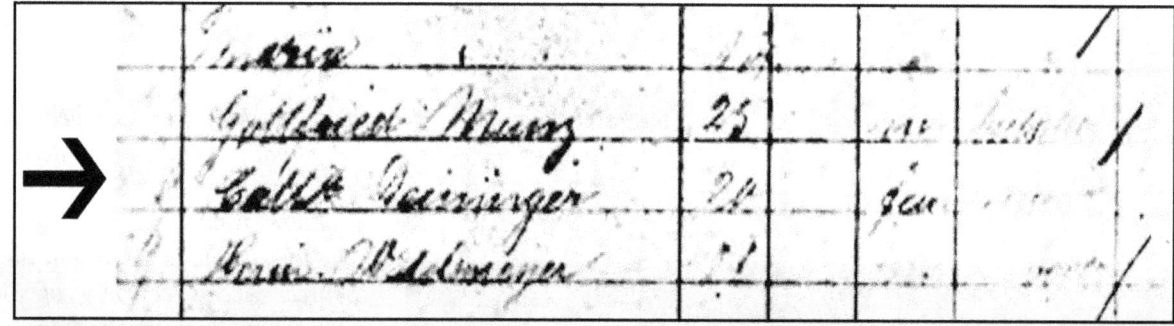

Katharine Deininger is passenger 389 on the passenger manifest of the Havel. Her listed age of 20 is incorrect. Her real age was 19. The remaining information is not visible. Source: "New York, U.S., Arriving Passenger and Crew Lists (including Castle Garden and Ellis Island), 1820-1957" online database (Provo, UT: Ancestry.com, 2010), accessed May 2021. Edited by author.

Passage to America

This is an 1865 image of the Barge Office in Battery Park at the southern tip of Manhattan Island. Gottlieb and Katharine processed through this building in December 1891. Source: "Barge Office at the Battery New York City. New York Battery Park, ca. 1865" (New York, NY: George Stacy Publisher), accessed May 2021, https://www.loc.gov/item/2017645395/. Edited by author.

Katharine

Their Destination

The next step in the immigration story of Gottlieb and Katharine is speculative. Gottlieb's passenger manifest record stated he intended to go to Michigan. Travel by rail to Michigan would have been easily accomplished. However, the first document listing Gottlieb and Katharine in America was recorded in Iowa. Possibly they first made a short visit to Michigan, but no record of this has been discovered.

Intriguing information comes by way of Gottlieb's sister Christine Catharine Hinderer. Christine accompanied her parents Johannes and Sophie Hinderer when they emigrated from Wuerttemberg to Michigan in 1895. When her family arrived in New York, Christine was two days shy of her 17th birthday. In Michigan, Christine eventually married and had a daughter named Elsa. The story passed down from Christine to Elsa was that her oldest brother Gottlieb had a serious disagreement with his parents while they all still lived in Brend. Christine did not reveal the nature of that disagreement. This story of a serious disagreement with his parents and the absence of an entry in the Wuerttemberg Emigration Index suggests that Gottlieb and Katharine made a hurried decision to emigrate.

On February 2, 1892, the names of Gottlieb Hinderer and Katharine Deininger are recorded on a legal document in Allamakee County, Iowa. This was only six weeks after their arrival in New York harbor. The Allamakee County record date strongly suggests that Iowa was their true destination. For nearly another decade, all documents for Gottlieb and Katharine originate from this same area in the northeastern corner of Iowa where they began their life in America.

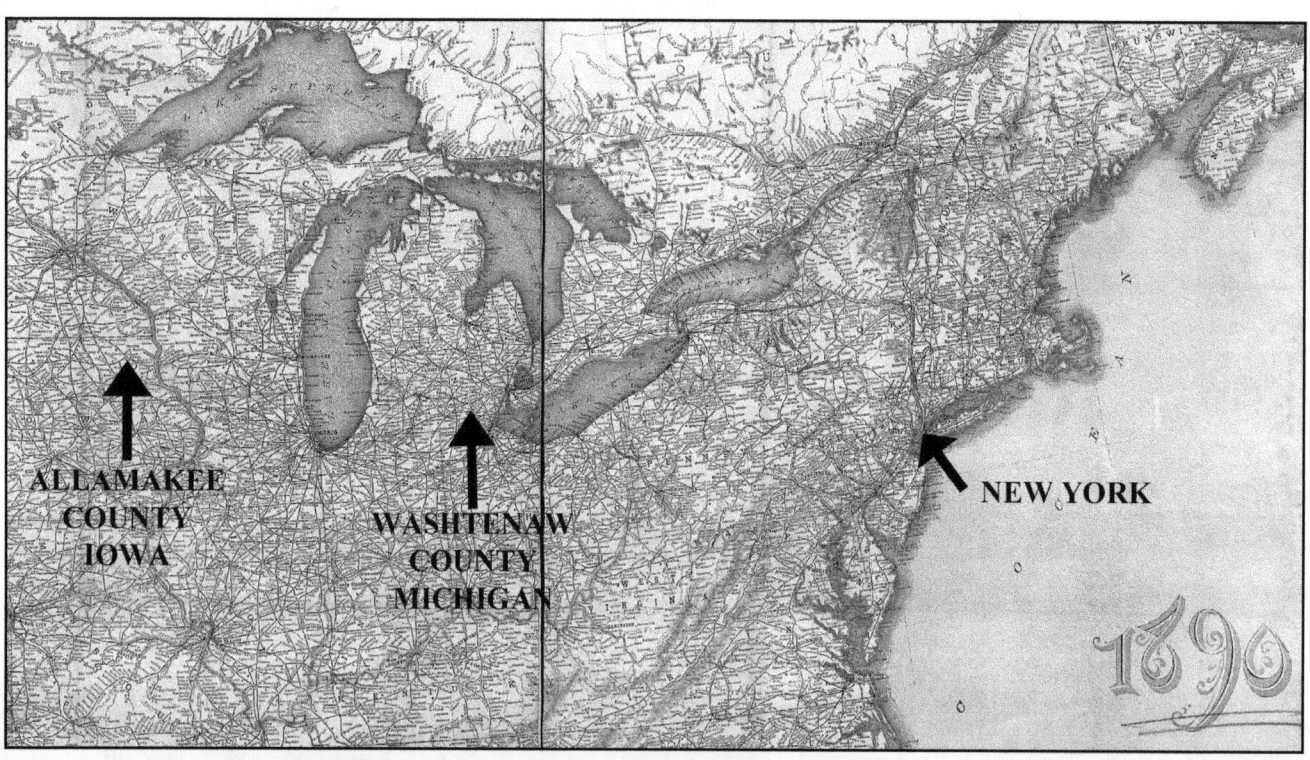

This 1890 map of U.S. railroads shows a myriad of rail lines from New York to Michigan and Iowa. Source: Matthews, Northrup & Co.'s, "Official Railroad Map of the United States, Dominion of Canada and Mexico Perfected to Date from Latest Authentic Sources," scale ca. 1:4,300,000, 82 x 136 cm (Buffalo, NY: Matthews-Northrup & Co.'s, 1890), Library of Congress, accessed May 2021, https://www.loc.gov/item/gm71000843/. Edited by author.

Notes

1. Mario Cuomo, first generation American and former governor of New York.

2. United States Department of Homeland Security, *Yearbook of Immigration Statistics: 2008* (Washington, D.C.: U.S. Department of Homeland Security, Office of Immigration Statistics, 2009), accessed May 2021, https://www.dhs.gov/ohss/topics/immigration/yearbook/2008.

3. Roger Daniels, *Coming to America: A History of Immigration and Ethnicity in American Life*, 2nd ed. (New York: HarperCollins, 2002), 128-84.

4. Ibid., 125.

5. Dick Eastman, "What They Never Told You About Immigration," Eastman's Online Genealogy Newsletter, Plus Edition, November 17, 2016. (https://eogn.com/)

6. Ibid.

7. "Immigrations and Relocation in U.S. History: German," Library of Congress, accessed May 2021, https://www.loc.gov/classroom-materials/immigration/german/.

8. "The Pacific Railroad Act of 1862 (12 Stat. 489)," U.S. National Archives, accessed May 2021, https://www.archives.gov/milestone-documents/pacific-railway-act.

9. Wallace Stegner, *Beyond the Hundredth Meridian: John Wesley Powell and the Second Opening of the West* (Boston: Houghton Mifflin, 1954), 215–23.

10. Annette Burke Lyttle, "How Advertising Brought Our German-Speaking Ancestors to the Midwest" (International German Genealogy Conference [IGGC], Sacramento, CA, June 15-17, 2019): 40-44.

11. To locate Bremen, in Google Maps insert coordinates 53.099854, 8.764503 in the search box and click search.

12. To locate Hamburg, in Google Maps insert coordinates 53.540948, 9.927816 in the search box and click search.

13. Sacramento German Genealogy Society [SGGS], "They Traveled in Steerage," *Der Blumenbaum*, 22, no. 2 (2004): 65-67.

14. Wolfgang Grams, "Hurra wir fahren nach Amerika II: Travel Patterns During the Age of Steam" (International German Genealogy Conference [IGGC], Sacramento, CA, June 15-17, 2019): 218-221.

15. "So All Immigrants Came Through Ellis Island, Right?" My Genealogy Hound/Hearthstone Legacy Publications, accessed May 2021, https://www.mygenealogyhound.com/genealogy-articles/ellis-island-castle-garden-barge-office-immigration-history.htm.

Chapter 5

Washtenaw County, Michigan

Timeline

Early 1820s – First European settlers in Washtenaw County

1826 – The Washtenaw County boundary was drawn

1852 – Rosine Weller emigrated to Washtenaw County

1864 – Michael Weller emigrated to Washtenaw County

1865 – The U.S. Civil War ended; Lincoln assassinated

1866 – Gottlieb Hinderer was born in Alfdorf

1871 – The German Empire was formed

1872 – Katharine Deininger was born in Gehren

1880s – The Peak of German emigration to the U.S.

1891 – Gottlieb and Katharine emigrated to America

1895 – Johannes and Sophie Hinderer emigrated to Washtenaw County

1898 – The Spanish-American War

1903 – Sophie (Weller) Hinderer died

1905 – Michael Weller died

1909 – Rosine (Weller/Koeder) Haug died

1914 – World War I began

1923 – Johannes Hinderer died

MICHIGAN

The northward recession of glaciers following the last ice age left the lower peninsula of Michigan a jigsaw puzzle of rocks, gravel, swamps, lakes, and open land. Taken together, this mix of former glacial debris is called "drift." The immense weight of those glaciers scoured out what had been ancient riverbeds. These deep impressions became the five Great Lakes of the upper Midwest.[1] The retreating glaciers also left behind smaller meltwater lakes seasonally composed of both water and ice. As the climate continued to warm, the meltwater lakes diminished in size until they were dry.

Much of the earth's finite water is a balance between the vast stores in the oceans and a smaller amount held as continental fresh-water lakes, snow, and ice. The cold temperatures of the last ice age locked more ice atop continents, leaving less water in oceans. When the sea level dropped, a land bridge was exposed between today's Siberia and Alaska. This land bridge was the route used by groups of humans who migrated from Asia to North America. The tribal societies expanded southward into today's United States. Here the tribes prospered due to the warmer climates, forested lands, and the abundance of food sources. The Ojibwe, a descendant tribe, once occupied the lower peninsula of Michigan. They gave it the name "Michigan," which in their language meant "large water." It was a fitting name for the lower peninsula. Lakes Michigan, Huron, and Erie make up three of its four borders.

In the 1700s, fur trading settlements and protective forts were built by the French along the shoreline of lakes Erie and Huron. After the

French were defeated in the French and Indian War of 1763, the British controlled these outposts near Detroit. Twenty years later, the treaty ending the successful American Revolution ceded control of this entire "Northwest Territory" to the United States. It included what is now Ohio, Indiana, and Michigan.

Despite the long history of European activity on the Great Lakes, the interior of Michigan's lower peninsula was largely unknown to settlers in the early 1800s. Most settlers were farmers, and they chose to avoid this rugged area of glacial drift. The more easily farmable land in Ohio and Indiana was better suited to their way of life.

Washtenaw County[2] is located in the southeastern corner of Michigan's lower peninsula. It lies immediately west of Wayne County and the city of Detroit. The first frontier cabins were built there in the early 1820s. County boundary lines were drawn in 1822, but it was not until 1826 that Washtenaw County was officially recognized by the Michigan Territorial Legislature.[3] The first roadway traversing the county was surveyed in 1826. It was intended to connect the city of Detroit with the growing population center in Chicago on the western shore of Lake Michigan. This dirt roadway passed through the Washtenaw County village of Saline, just south of the larger town of Ann Arbor. Saline is about five miles east of where the Weller family members settled a few decades later.

In the 1820s, both Americans and Europeans were actively recruited by federal and state governments to move to Michigan's lower peninsula. New roadways and railroad lines were built to encourage this settlement. For the most part, the strategy worked. In 1820, there were no European citizens recorded living in the county. Ten years later, Washtenaw County had a population of over 4,000, and in 1850 it was almost 30,000.[4]

In the early 1820s, most Washtenaw County land was purchased by American citizens already living along the eastern seaboard. These "Yankee" owners often resold their land a few years later when a handsome profit could be made. By the 1830s however, most land buyers were German immigrants arriving in eastern port cities. Brochures that advertised Michigan land were distributed to immigrants at the east coast ports of arrival. As noted in Chapter 4, this was a common and successful technique. What followed was an example of "chain" migration. After the first German settlers came, they encouraged their homeland friends and family to join them in Michigan.

From the 1830s on, most of the German immigrants who settled southwest of Ann Arbor came from Wuerttemberg. They included Swabian families from what is known as the Rems Valley region of Wuerttemberg.[5] The Rems Valley includes the towns of Alfdorf, Brend, Gehren, and Kaisersbach. It was the homeland of the ancestor families discussed in Chapters 2 and 3. The flow of Wuerttemberg immigrants into Washtenaw County peaked in the decades of the 1850s and 1860s.[6] By the end of the century, the immigrant surge from Wuerttemberg was over.

Tracking the Michigan Family

The first family member to arrive in Washtenaw County was Rosine (Weller) Koeder. According to their German family table, Rosine, her husband Ulrich, and their son Friederich emigrated in the spring of 1852. Rosine's younger brother Michael was the next to emigrate, followed by her sister Sophie (Weller) and husband Johannes Hinderer in 1895. These three Weller siblings settled near one another in Washtenaw County Michigan.

Apart from the Weller siblings in Michigan, another family ancestor emigrated to Iowa in the second half of the 19th century. This ancestor was related to Gottlieb Hinderer through his father's Hinderer family. His role in the story of Gottlieb and Katharine will be discussed in Chapter 6. The three Weller families in Michigan and the one Hinderer family in Iowa were all related to Gottlieb Hinderer.

Washtenaw County, Michigan

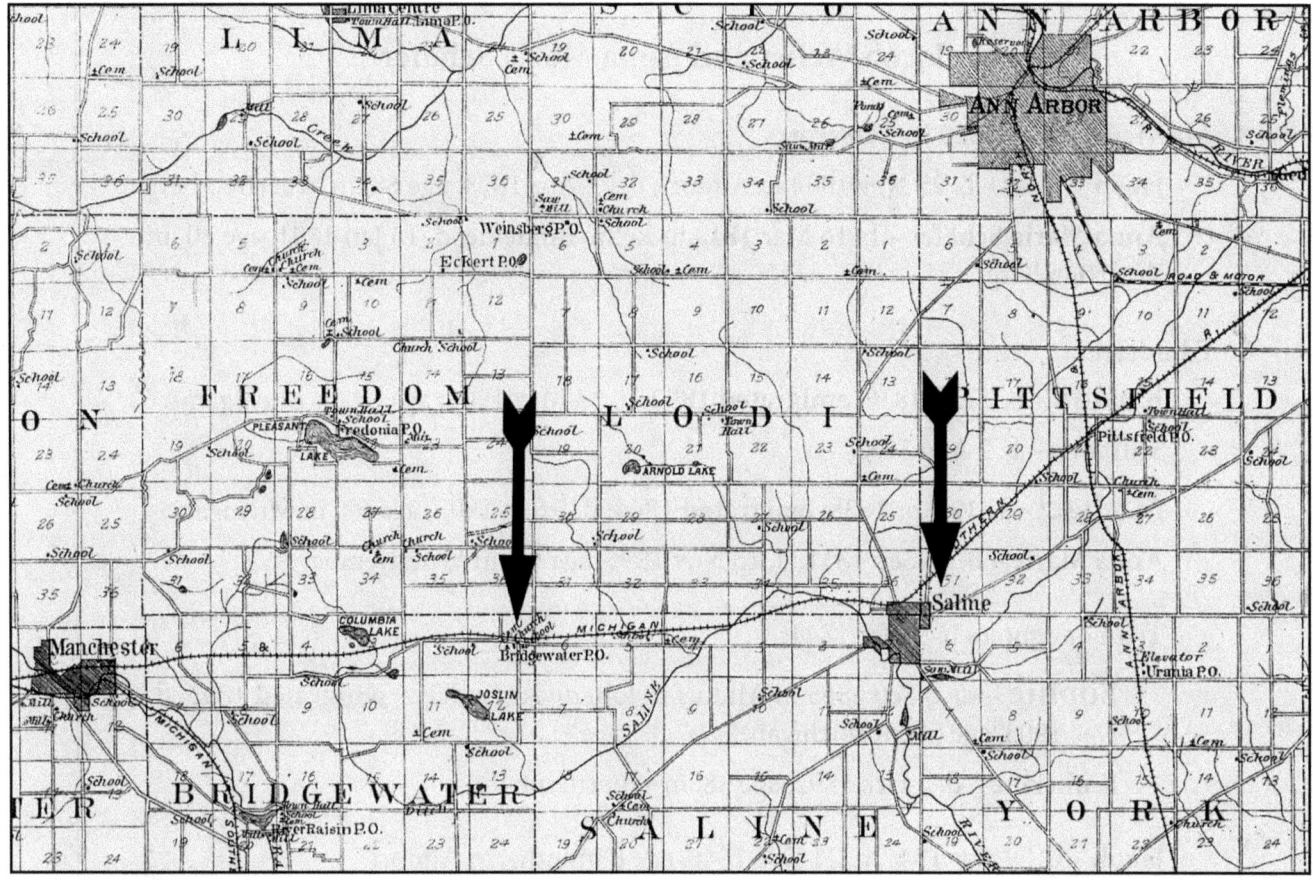

An 1895 Map of Washtenaw County. Townships were named (ex. LODI). Each township had 36 numbered sections, and each section was one mile square. Weller family members settled west of the town of Saline near the village of Bridgewater in sections 1 and 12 of Bridgewater Township, and section 6 of Saline Township. Source: Geo. A. Ogle & Co. Standard Atlas of Washtenaw County, Michigan: Chicago: Geo. A. Ogle & Co, 1895. Map. https://www.loc.gov/item/2007633240/ (Accessed June2021). Edited by author

Katharine Deininger had two uncles from her mother's Heinz family who emigrated to Ohio as young adults. There is no known history of contact between Katharine and those Ohio uncles.

Rosine (Weller) Koeder's Family

Rosine was the oldest child in the Weller family described in Chapter 2. Her father was a local farmer, and their home was near the center of Alfdorf, a short walk from St. Stephan Church. Ulrich Koeder[7] was six years older than Rosine. His family also lived in Alfdorf and likely attended St. Stephan Church. Generations of Koeder men were identified as local farmers living in Alfdorf. Like Rosine, Ulrich Koeder was the oldest child in his birth family.

In Alfdorf, Ulrich and Rosine's first child was born in 1849. She was named Anna Maria after Rosine's mother, but she lived only a few days. Their second child, Friederich,[8] was born in 1851. Ulrich and Rosine were married a few months after Friederich's birth. As noted earlier, marriage after the birth of one or several children was a common Wuerttemberg practice at that time.

The German family table for Ulrich and Rosine is helpful because it documents their departure from Alfdorf. The exact date is not given, but a notation following Ulrich's name states they departed for America in the spring of 1852.

Katharine

> ### Jacob Weller and Anna Maria Schäfer
>
> **Married 12 May 1829 in Täferrot:**
>
> **Jacob Weller** – b. 25 Nov 1804 in Alfdorf; d. 22 Apr 1873, age 68, in Wuerttemberg
>
> **Anna Maria Schäfer** – b. 16 Mar 1810 in Rehnenmuehle; d. 15 Jan 1891, age 80, in Wuerttemberg
>
> **Children:**
>
> **Rosine** – b. 2 Feb 1830; <u>emigrated 1852</u>; d. 13 May 1909, age 79, in Michigan
>
> **Stillborn** – b. 2 Aug 1833
>
> **Michael** – b. 17 Apr 1838; <u>emigrated 1864</u>; d. 5 Sep 1905, age 67, in Michigan
>
> **Anna Marie** – b. 15 Sep 1841; d. 15 Nov 1895, age 53, in Wuerttemberg
>
> **Twin daughters** b. 9 Mar 1844:
>
> **Sophie** – m. 3 Sep 1865 in Alfdorf to Johannes Hinderer; <u>emigrated 1895</u>; d. 9 Dec 1903, age 59, in Michigan
>
> **Katherine** – d. 1 Dec 1892, age 48, in Wuerttemberg
>
> **Jakob** – b. 29 Apr 1846; d. 21 Dec 1846, age 8 months, in Alfdorf
>
> **Anna Marie** – b. 23 Sep 1849; d. 28 Sep 1849, age 5 days, in Alfdorf

A translation of the family table for the Wellers of Alfdorf. Children Rosine, Michael, and Sophie emigrated to Michigan in the order of their birth. Source: Translation by Merlin Schlichting as edited by the author.

Ulrich, Rosine, and Friederich Koeder have not been found in a passenger listing. Nevertheless, in 1852 their passage across the Atlantic Ocean would have been either by sailing ship or an early steamer. Sailing ships made the voyage in four to twelve weeks while the early steamers were able to cut that time in half. The reason Ulrich and Rosine emigrated is also unknown. Ulrich was the oldest son in his family and could have become the next generation of Koeder farmers living in Alfdorf. Nevertheless, he left that heritage behind and emigrated to a frontier region of America only recently occupied by Europeans.

While neither Ulrich nor Rosine left written information about their lives in Michigan, they can be tracked by historical documents such as census records and plat maps. A federal census has been conducted every decade from the late 1700s until today. Except for 1890,[9] census records from the mid-1800s through the early 1900s are generally available.

Census records must be interpreted with some caution. They are considered a "derivative" document. This means that although they were constructed close to the same time as the original data was gathered, they were still transcribed and therefore not the original. Census takers relied on verbal information which they wrote down on note pads and later transcribed onto formal census pages. The people living in these frontier

Birth	Father	Marriage	Mother	Birth
Alfdorf	Ulrich Kother	in Alfdorf	Rosine	Alfdorf
29 Mar 1824	To America in the spring of 1852	7 May 1851		2 Feb 1830

This portion of the family table for Ulrich and Rosine included their vital dates and their departure for America. An English translation has been added at the bottom. Source: "Württemberg, Germany, Family Tables, 1550-1985" online database (Lehi, UT: Ancestry.com, 2016), accessed June 2021. Translation by Merlin Schlichting and edited by author.

states were often foreign born and spoke minimal English. Names on the census records are often spelled phonetically and unintended transcription errors did occur.

Plat maps were constructed by county land offices to record ownership and boundaries of land parcels. They were not regularly constructed and only a few have been preserved. Plat maps were derived from county records of land ownership. Each plat map depicts land ownership as of a specific date. Plat maps are considered "secondary" documents because their information was extracted from many hundreds of land purchase and sale records. This task was tedious and very time-consuming. The resulting plat maps were complex, hand-printed illustrations. Both spelling errors and location errors occurred on plat maps.

Ulrich and Rosine emigrated in 1852. Four years later, the plat map of 1856 was drawn. This 1856 plat map documents their ownership of 80 acres in section 12 of Bridgewater Township, Washtenaw County, Michigan. Bridgewater Township has 36 numbered sections with each section measuring one mile square. On this 1856 map, their name is recorded as "C. Koeder," A roadway runs north to south along the eastern edge of their property. The two black squares along the roadway identify the location of homes or other buildings on their property.

Four years after the 1856 Plat Map was published, the 1860 Federal Census was conducted. This census was conducted during an historic time in America. In 1860, Abraham Lincoln was elected president and the southern states seceded

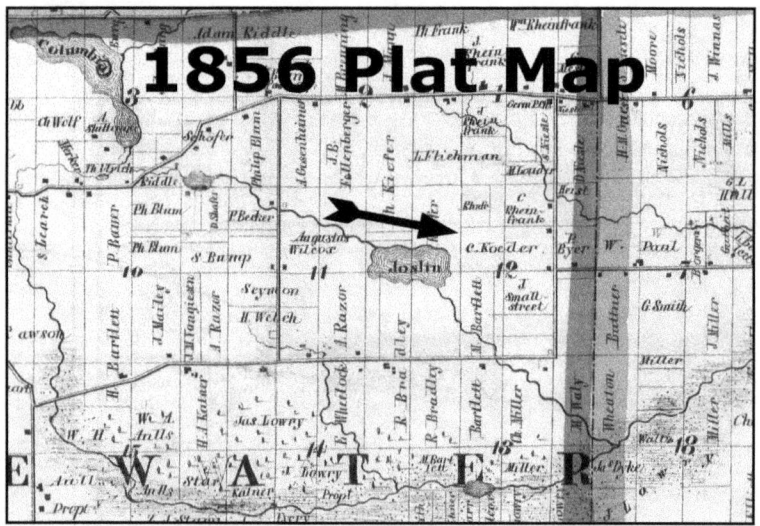

A small part of the 1856 plat map for Washtenaw County. The Koeders lived in section 12 of Bridgewater Township. See text for details. Source: Gustavus R. Bechler and E. Wenig, "Map of Washtenaw County, Michigan: From Actual Surveys," 109 x 122 cm (Philadelphia: Bechler, Wenig & Co, 1856), Library of Congress, accessed June 2021, https://www.loc.gov/item/2012593013/. Edited by author.

from the Union. The American Civil War began with the bombardment of Fort Sumpter the next year. Although the nation seemed on the verge of collapse, the 1860 census takers made their way through the farmland of rural Michigan.

Ulrich and Rosine were interviewed in late June for the 1860 census. By this date, their nine-year-old immigrant son Friederich had three younger sisters. To this census taker, the name Ulrich sounded like "Oderick" and Koeder became "Koter." Of the three girls, the oldest was "Rosina," named after her mother. Ulrich's vocation was "F," likely a shorthand for farmer. He owned real property valued at $1400 and personal property worth $600. The far-right column correctly noted that Ulrich, Rosine, and Friederich were born in Wuerttemberg, while the three girls were born in Michigan. Considering the language barrier, this census is quite accurate.

Another plat map was published in 1864, the final full year of the American Civil War. This map detailed the same 80-acre parcel of land, now recorded as owned by "U. Kader." The buildings and nearby roadways appear the same as drawn on the prior plat map.

The 1870 Federal Census considerably expanded the knowledge of this family. In this census, Ulrich "Kader" was 46 years old, and the value of his real property had increased to $7,000. His family had also increased. Since the 1860 census, he and Rosine had had two more daughters followed by two sons, a total of eight children at home.

The 1860 Federal Census documented Ulrich and Rosine with four children and real property worth $1400. Considering the language barrier, the census record was quite accurate. See text for other details. Source: "1860 United States Federal Census" online database (Provo, UT: Ancestry.com, 2009), accessed June 2021. Images reproduced by FamilySearch.. Edited by author.

Washtenaw County, Michigan

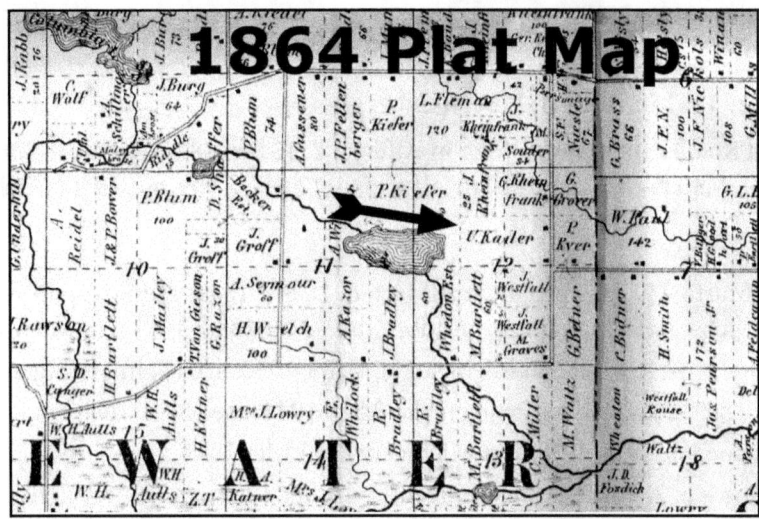

The 1864 plat map noted U. (Ulrich) Kader owned the same 80 acres seen on the 1856 plat map. Source: Gustavus R. Bechler and E. Wenig, "Map of the Counties of Washtenaw and Lenawee, Michigan," 143 x 143 cm (Philadelphia: Samuel Geil Publisher, 1864), Library of Congress, accessed June 2021, https://www.loc.gov/item/2012593163/. Edited by author.

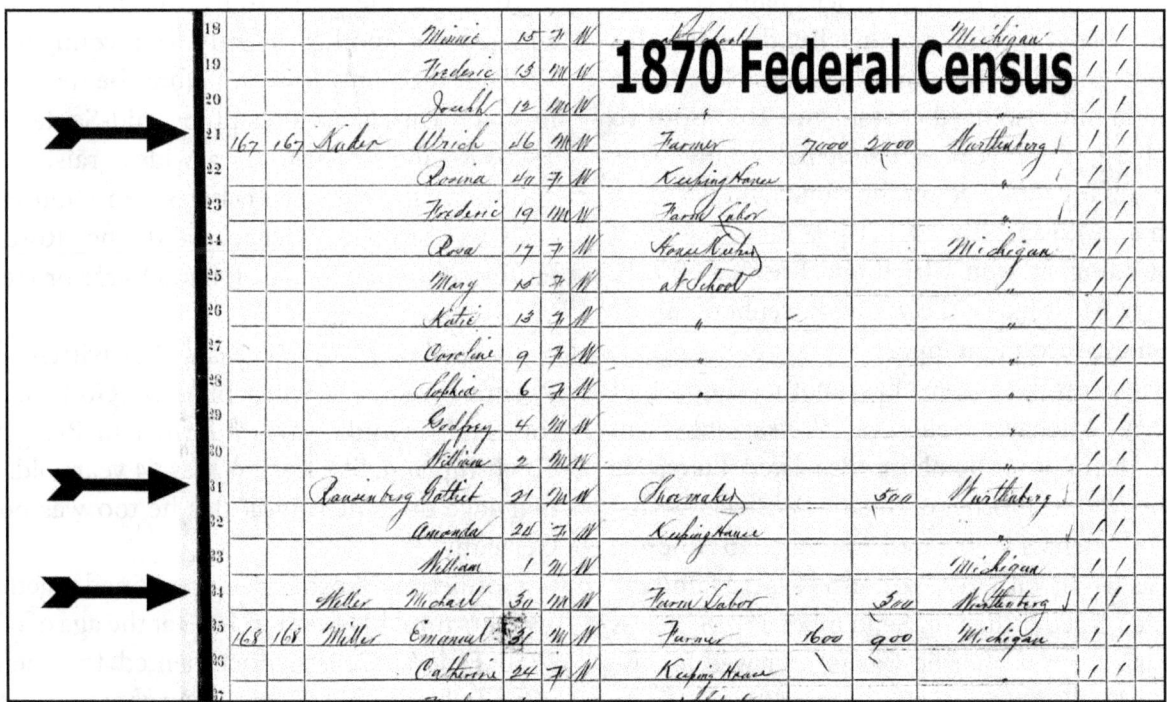

The 1870 Federal Census documented that Ulrich and Rosine had eight children. A second family named Rosenberg as well as Rosine's brother Michael Weller also lived on their property. See text for details. Source: "1870 United States Federal Census" online database (Provo, UT: Ancestry.com, 2009), access June 2021. Images reproduced by FamilySearch. Edited by author.

Rosine Weller and Ulrich Koeder

Married - 7 May 1851 in Alfdorf, Wuerttemberg:

Ulrich Koeder – b. 29 Mar 1824 in Alfdorf; d. 13 Sep 1870, age 46, in Michigan
Rosine Weller – b. 2 Feb 1830 in Alfdorf; d. 13 May 1909, age 79, in Michigan

Children:

Anna Maria – b. 23 Sep 1849 in Alfdorf; d. 28 Sep 1849, age 5 days, in Alfdorf
Friederich – b. 15 Mar 1851 in Alfdorf; d. 11 Mar 1888, age 37, in Michigan
Rosine – b. 30 Apr 1853 in Michigan; d. 7 Apr 1940, age 87, in Michigan
Mary – b. 9 Oct 1855 in Michigan; d. 13 Sep 1944, age 88, in Michigan
Catharine – b. 12 Nov 1857 in Michigan; d. 11 Mar 1944, age 86, in Michigan
Caroline – b. 27 Jul 1861 in Michigan; d. 26 Apr 1928, age 66, in Michigan
Sophia – b. 13 Sep 1863 in Michigan; d. 1 Dec 1928, age 65, in Michigan
Godfrey – b. Mar 1866 in Michigan; d. 1959, age 93, in Michigan
William – b. 1868 in Michigan; d. 6 Sep 1870, age 2, in Michigan

The family of Rosine (Weller) and Ulrich Koeder. Source: Compilation by author.

The column to the left of Ulrich's name contains the number 167. All persons listed under this number resided at this single location. Note that a second family also lived at residence 167. Gottlieb Rosenberg, a 21-year-old shoemaker, his wife, and an infant son lived on the same land parcel as Ulrich and Rosine. The earlier plat maps recorded two building sites on Ulrich and Rosine's 80-acre property. Most likely, the young Rosenberg family lived in the second building.

Finally, residence 167 has another important addition. Michael Weller, a 30-year-old farm laborer from Wuerttemberg also lived there. He was the Alfdorf brother of Rosine (Weller) Koeder. By 1870, Michael Weller had emigrated to America and was living with his older sister's large family.

Ulrich Koeder died on September 13, 1870, less than two months after he was interviewed for the 1870 Federal Census. A Michigan death certificate has not been found for him. The cause of his death, at age 46, is unknown. He is buried in St. John's Lutheran Church Cemetery in Bridgewater Township, Washtenaw County, Michigan.

At about the same time, Ulrich's wife Rosine suffered yet another tragedy. Her youngest child William died only a week before the death of her husband Ulrich. As a result, by mid-September of 1870, Rosine Koeder was a widow raising seven children. She, along with her seven children, her younger brother Michael, and the Rosenberg family continued to live on her 80-acre property in Washtenaw County.

In April of 1874, four years after Ulrich's death, Rosine (Weller) Koeder married Gottlieb Haug (or Hauk). Gottlieb was a farmer in Bridgewater Township and, like Rosine, was 44 years old. Their marriage document indicates he too was born in Germany.

Gottlieb and Rosine Haug remained together for 18 years until his death in 1892 at the age of 62. The 1880 Federal Census documented the members of their household. Rosine's surname was spelled Haug. Gottlieb's given name was incorrectly recorded as "Gaudelope." Rosine's 14-year-old son by her marriage to Ulrich Koeder, Godfrey "Kader," was living with them. An unrelated 21-year-old

On April 16, 1874, Rosine (Weller) Koeder married Gottlieb Haug (Hauk), a German-born farmer. They both lived in Bridgewater Township. Source: "Michigan, U.S., Marriage Records, 1867-1952" online database (Provo, UT: Ancestry, 2015), accessed June 2021. Edited by author.

1880 Federal Census

The 1880 Federal Census recorded Rosine living with her second husband Gottlieb (Gaudelope is incorrect) Haug. Rosine's 14-year-old son Godfrey Kader and a 21-year-old farm worker lived with them. See text for other details. Source: "1880 United States Federal Census" online database (Lehi, UT: Ancestry.com), accessed June 2021. Edited by author.

farm hand also lived with them. Rosine's brother Michael and the Rosenberg family no longer lived on this property.

A final plat map, this one from 1896, displayed the same 80-acre parcel of land owned by Rosine or "Rosina" Haug. However, by 1896 Rosine had purchased another 50 acres, thus increasing her parcel to 130 acres. Her son Godfrey "Kader," owned a separate 50 acres bordering her property on the south side. Rosine's property had only a single building site on this 1896 plat map. Son Godfrey Kader's 50-acre property also had a single building site. By 1896, the intersection of the roads north of Rosine's property was officially named Bridgewater.

Rosine died on May 13, 1909, in Saline Township, not Bridgewater Township. Her death location suggests she was no longer living at home on her farm. At the time of her death, she was 79 years old and had been a widow, for a second time,

The 1896 Plat Map of Washtenaw County showed that Rosine Haug owned 130 acres of land, and her son Godfrey Kader owned 50 acres nearby. The road intersection north of their property was officially named Bridgewater. Source: "M. M. Dickson & Co's Township and Sectional Pocket Map of Washtenaw County, Michigan," 63 x 79 cm (Ann Arbor, MI: M. M. Dickson & Co, 1896), Library of Congress, accessed June 2021, https://www.loc.gov/item/02024899/. Edited by author.

since 1892. Her death certificate stated she died of "Old Age."

Rosine was the first of the Weller siblings to emigrate to America. She established her home in the frontier farmland of Washtenaw County Michigan. She survived two husbands and paved a pathway, first for her younger brother Michael Weller, and later for her younger sister Sophie (Weller) Hinderer.

Michael Weller's Family

Like his sisters Rosine and Sophie, Michael Weller was born and raised in Alfdorf and grew up attending St. Stephan Church. As the only son who lived to adulthood, Michael stood to inherit the farming practice of his father and grandfather. Michael was 14 when his older sister Rosine emigrated to America with her husband and their child. Years later and for unknown reasons, Michael gave up his Alfdorf farm inheritance and joined his sister Rosine in Michigan.

The best match for Michael Weller's passenger listing stated he emigrated to America in 1864. This was unusual timing because it was the last full year of the American Civil War. Immigration rates dropped off precipitously during the Civil War and then climbed once the war ended in April 1865.

Michael's likely passenger listing identified him as a 26-year-old farmer. He emigrated aboard the sailing ship *Arnold Boninger*, arriving in New York on February 16, 1864. He traveled alone, one of 155 passengers on this sailing vessel. His passage was also unique among the Weller siblings because the *Arnold Boninger* departed from Le Havre, France. Alfdorf, in the Rems Valley of Wuerttemberg, is due east of Le Havre France. The distance between Alfdorf and Le Havre is almost the same as between Alfdorf

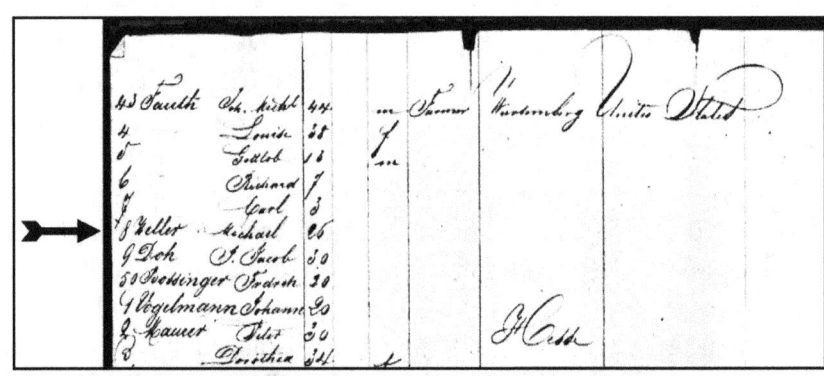

The passenger list from the February 1864 voyage of the Arnold Boninger *included 26-year-old farmer Michael Weller from Wuerttemberg. See text for other details. Source: "Year: 1864; Arrival: New York, New York" (Microfilm Serial: M237, 1820-1897; Microfilm Roll 237; Line: 6; List Number: 10), accessed June 2021 (Provo, UT: Ancestry). Edited by author.*

and the northern German port cities of Bremen and Hamburg. The use of this French port city was not unusual for Wuerttemberg emigrants.

On this voyage, the *Arnold Boninger* carried passengers of several nationalities: German, Swiss, French, and Italian. The duration of the Atlantic passage was not stated, but anywhere from four to twelve weeks would have been typical. The arrival document noted that of the 155 adult passengers, one young woman had died during the voyage.

Michael's mode of travel from New York to Michigan was undocumented. However, plat maps show that by 1864, several east to west railroad lines extended through Washtenaw County. One railroad line passed through the town of Ypsilanti, 20 miles east of his sister Rosine's home. From the Ypsilanti railway station, the old roadway from Detroit to Chicago would have taken Michael to within a mile of Rosine's farm.

The previously shown 1870 Federal Census documented Michael Weller living with his sister's family and working as a farm laborer. On that census page, of the 15 adults listed, all but two were born in Germany and most of these Germans were from Wuerttemberg. Although "Yankees" from the American east coast first settled this part of Michigan's lower peninsula, by 1870, most land near the Wellers was now owned by Wuerttemberg-born farmers.

On April 27, 1874, Michael Weller married Elizabeth Brenner, also an immigrant from Wuerttemberg. Elizabeth was born in the village of Egenhausen, southwest of Stuttgart. She was born and baptized on July 12, 1843, making her five years younger than Michael. Elizabeth Brenner arrived in New York on Nov. 25, 1871, aboard the steamer S.S. *Donau*. Her passenger list entry indicated she traveled alone.

A Washtenaw County Directory dated 1878 published a listing for a Michael Weller living in Bridgewater Township. This directory stated that Michael Weller owned 32 acres of land in section 1 of Bridgewater Township.

The 1880 Federal Census was conducted six years after Michael and Elizabeth's marriage. By this time, Michael and Elizabeth had three daughters and one son. Like his sister Rosine, Michael's family lived in Bridgewater Township. They were listed as residence number 40. Their oldest daughter was Mary, followed by Anna, and then three-year-old Rosa. Their youngest child was one-year-old Gottlieb, incorrectly spelled "Godeloupe" on the census. Each of the entries listed the correct place of birth in the far-right column: Wuerttemberg Germany for the parents and Michigan for all four children. A final household resident was listed as "servant," a term used broadly in census documents for anyone working for the family.

The 1896 plat map identified the Bridgewater Township location of Michael and Elizabeth's 32-acre farm. It was in section 1, in the extreme northeastern corner of Bridgewater Township, west of the town of Bridgewater. A railway line cut through their property and the building site is located next to the roadway. By 1896, Michael's older sister Rosine was remarried to Gottlieb Haug. Rosine and Gottlieb's property can be seen on the map, a half mile south of Michael and Elizabeth's 32 acres.

The 1900 Federal Census was the final document with Michael (Mike) and Elizabeth Weller listed together. They were still living on their 32-acre Bridgewater Township farm. The three daughters and one son listed on the 1880 census were no longer living at home. However, an additional son, 12-year-old Theodore Carl Weller, was listed and was away from home attending school.

Ten years later, the 1910 Federal Census added yet another son, Fred. Although Fred was born in 1882, he was not listed on the 1900 census when he would have been 18. This means that in 1900, Fred lived away from home, but then returned home and was counted in the 1910 census. Tracking through subsequent census documents indicates that the three sons of Michael and Elizabeth: Gottlieb, Fred, and Theodore, remained bachelors their entire lives.

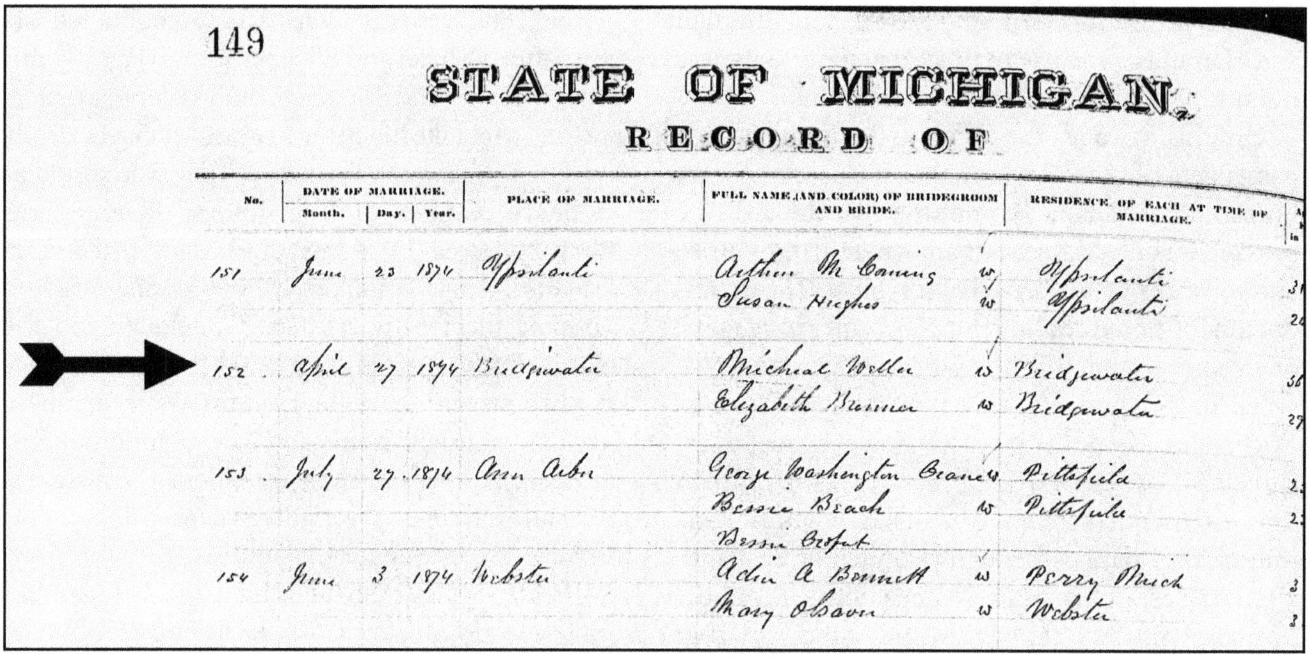

149

STATE OF MICHIGAN.

RECORD OF

No.	Date of Marriage. Month.	Day.	Year.	Place of Marriage.	Full Name (and Color) of Bridegroom and Bride.		Residence of Each at Time of Marriage.
151	June	23	1874	Ypsilanti	Arthur McCanning	w	Ypsilanti
					Susan Hughes	w	Ypsilanti
152	April	27	1874	Bridgewater	Michael Weller	w	Bridgewater
					Elizabeth Brenner	w	Bridgewater
153	July	27	1874	Ann Arbor	George Washington Graner	w	Pittsfield
					Bessie Beach	w	Pittsfield
					Bessie Brofort		
154	June	3	1874	Webster	Adin A Bennett	w	Perry Mich
					Mary Olsson	w	Webster

The 1874 marriage record of Michael Weller and Elizabeth Brenner in Bridgewater Township. Source: "Michigan, U.S., Marriage Records, 1867-1952" online database (Provo, UT: Ancestry.com, 2015), accessed June 2021. Edited by author.

Michael Weller and Elizabeth Brenner

Married - 27 Apr 1874 in Bridgewater Township, Washtenaw County, Michigan:

Michael Weller – b. 17 Apr 1838 in Alfdorf; d. 5 Sep 1905, age 67, in Michigan

Elizabeth Brenner – b. 12 Jul 1843 in Egenhausen, Germany; d. 7 Mar 1919, age 75, in Michigan

Children:

Mary – b. 22 Mar 1872 in Michigan; d. 5 Sep 1960, age 88, in Michigan

Anna – b. abt. 1875 in Michigan; d. after 1930

Rosa – b. 4 Dec 1876 in Michigan; d. 28 Jun 1922, age 45, in Michigan

Gottlieb – b. 15 Mar 1879 in Michigan; d. 23 Dec 1943, age 64, in Michigan

Fred – b. 15 Oct 1882 in Michigan; d. 1964, age 82, in Michigan

Theodore Carl – b. 20 Aug 1887 in Michigan; d. 20 Apr 1954, age 66, in Michigan

The family of Michael and Elizabeth Weller. Source: Compiled by author.

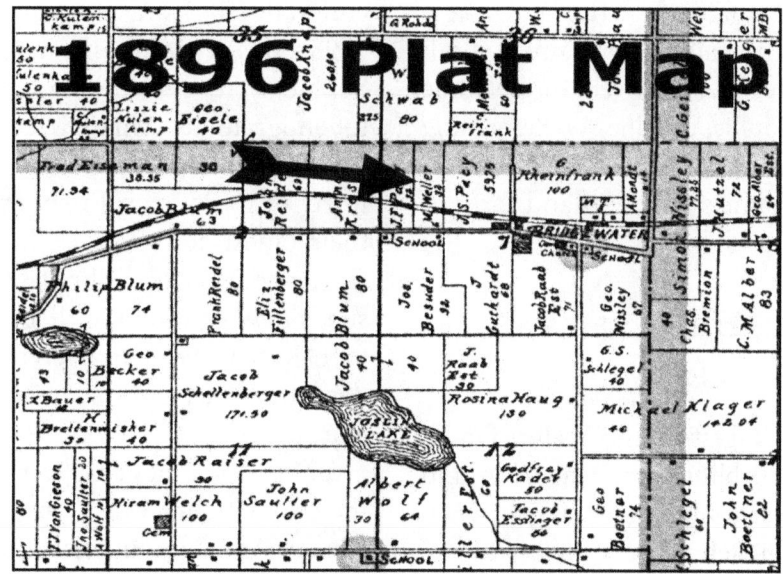

The 1880 Federal Census included the growing family of Michael and Elizabeth Weller, plus a live-in domestic. See text for additional details. Source: "1880 United States Federal Census" online database (Lehi, UT: Ancestry.com), accessed June 2021. Edited by author.

The 1896 Plat Map identified the 32 acres (arrow) owned by Michael and Elizabeth Weller. See text for other details. Source: "M. M. Dickson & Co's Township and Sectional Pocket Map of Washtenaw County, Michigan," 63 x 79 cm (Ann Arbor, MI: M. M. Dickson & Co, 1896), Library of Congress, accessed June 2021, https://www.loc.gov/item/02024899/. Edited by author.

The 1900 Federal Census listed "Mike" and Elizabeth Weller still living in Bridgewater Township. Their youngest son Theodore Carl, age 12, was away at school. See text for additional details. Source: "1900 United States Federal Census" online database (Provo, UT: Ancestry.com, 2004), accessed June 2024. Edited by author.

Michael Weller died on September 5, 1905. On his death certificate, his residence was recorded as Bridgewater Township, suggesting he died at home. He was 67 years old. The cause of his death was listed as valvular disease of the heart.

After Michael's death, his widow Elizabeth continued to live in Bridgewater Township. At the time of the 1910 Federal Census, Elizabeth was living with two of her sons, Gottlieb and Fred. She died at home on March 7, 1919, at the age of 75.

Michael and Elizabeth Weller lived in Bridgewater Township during their entire adult lives in America. Their six children were born and raised on a 32-acre farm near the land where Michael's sister Rosine raised her family. Both Michael and his sister Rosine lived to welcome their younger sister Sophie, the final Weller sibling who emigrated to America. She arrived in 1895 with her husband Johannes Hinderer and three of their children.

Sophie (Weller) Hinderer's Family

Sophie was the youngest of the Weller family immigrants. Like her siblings, she was born and raised in Alfdorf. She was only seven years old when her oldest sister Rosine left Alfdorf for Michigan. She was twenty when her only brother Michael emigrated. When Michael left in 1864, Sophie and Johannes Hinderer were already a couple living in Alfdorf, most likely with Sophie's parents. Their first son Gottfried was born that year but died in infancy. Their second son Gottlieb was born in the fall of 1866. After Gottlieb's birth, the family moved to Brend, living with husband Johannes Hinderer's parents.

There is one intriguing piece of information regarding Sophie and Johannes. In 1865, while they still lived in Alfdorf and before their son Gottlieb was born, the Wuerttemberg Immigration Index recorded an application by Johannes Hinderer to emigrate. They did not leave Wuerttemberg until 1895, 30 years later. This means that Johannes and Sophie were considering and possibly planning to emigrate to America early in their married life. Why they did not leave Brend for those thirty years is open to speculation. Nevertheless, their oldest son Gottlieb likely grew up hearing family conversation about moving to America. It sheds new light on Gottlieb's decision to emigrate with Katharine Deininger in 1891. Perhaps their departure was not as precipitous as it had first appeared.

Before Johannes and Sophie emigrated in 1895, they sold their Brend property to an unrelated farmer. As a consequence, they left Wuerttemberg

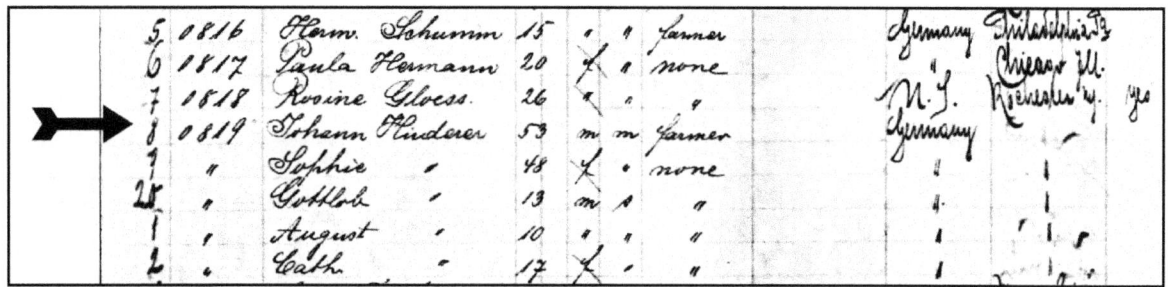

The steamer Saale arrived in New York on May 10, 1895, with the family of Johannes (Johann) and Sophie Hinderer. Ticket 819 included parents Johannes and Sophie plus children Cath. (Christine Catharine) age 17, Gottlob age 13, and August age 10. Their son John Georg did not travel with them. Their oldest son, Gottlieb, was already living in Iowa. Source: "New York, U.S., Arriving Passenger and Crew Lists (including Castle Garden and Ellis Island), 1820-1957" online database (Provo, UT: Ancestry.com, 2010), accessed June 2021. Edited by author.

with the money earned from the sale of their property.

Sophie's mother, Anna Maria Weller, had died in Alfdorf in 1891. Anna Maria was the last surviving parent of either Johannes or Sophie in Wuerttemberg. Furthermore, by 1895 all but one sibling of both Sophie and Johannes had also died. In sum, by 1895 Johannes and Sophie had no remaining ties with their Brend property, and only two immediate family members still living in Brend and Alfdorf.

Johannes and Sophie Hinderer's family emigrated at three separate times over the course of several years. Their oldest son Gottlieb, together with Katharine Deininger, arrived in America in December 1891. Johannes and Sophie Hinderer with their three youngest children crossed the Atlantic Ocean aboard the steamer *Saale* in 1895. They are listed as a family among the many hundreds of other steerage passengers. Their second-oldest son John Georg did not travel with them aboard the *Saale*. His emigration will be discussed later.

The *Saale* was a typical passenger ship designed to carry immigrants from Europe to America. It was owned by the North German Lloyd line and began service in 1886. The *Saale* carried a maximum of 1,240 passengers. Like the other passenger ships, nearly all of them traveled in steerage.

The steamer *Saale* with Johannes, Sophie, and children Christine, Gottlob, and August Hinderer, arrived in New York on May 10, 1895. The date they departed from Bremen was not stated, but it would have been one of the last few days in April of that year. As was usual, the *Saale* first stopped at Southampton, England where it boarded a few additional passengers prior to crossing the ocean.

When they arrived in May 1895, the Ellis Island Immigration Center had been the primary immigrant receiving point for over three years. The Hinderers and other steerage passengers would have first entered the main building on Ellis Island. Steerage passengers were all screened for their mental and physical health. Passengers able to afford a cabin were allowed entry into the U.S. without screening.

Inside the main building, steerage passengers first climbed a stairway to the second floor where they lined up before immigration officers. This stairway was their first medical test and was meant to reveal physical disabilities. Those unable to climb the stairs were shuttled to a separate waiting area for a more careful evaluation of their suitability for entry. If they were denied entry for any reason, their only option was to reboard and return to Germany. A child who failed a test also had to return to Germany. Parents had to decide which one of them would return to their homeland with the child.

German immigrants who passed the stairway test were met by officers fluent in their language. Their entry paperwork was reviewed, and a cursory physical exam performed prior to releasing them into the country. It may have made them anxious and uncomfortable, but with the large number of passengers aboard these steamers, their fate was determined quickly. The immigration center also included a facility for medical treatment or temporary observation. Immigrants diagnosed with common chronic illnesses such as tuberculosis were not allowed entry.

Like Sophie's two older siblings, her own family's travel route to Michigan was not documented. By 1895, a complex network of railway lines linked the eastern seaboard to Michigan and the Midwest. The transcontinental railway had been completed over 25 years earlier, so American citizens and immigrants had many options for railroad transportation across the entire continent.

The 1896 plat map of Washtenaw County was published one year following the Hinderer family's arrival. This map confirmed that Johannes and Sophie were financially able to buy 187 acres of land west of the town of Saline, near the village of Bridgewater. The money they earned from the sale of their Brend property was quickly reinvested in Michigan farmland. Although their farm was

Katharine

in Saline Township, it was immediately adjacent to Bridgewater Township. Today, the location of their farm is 7640 Austin Rd., Saline, Michigan.[10]

A closer view of their property identified the 1896 owner as John "Handerer" with a quarter section (160 acres) located south of a roadway and 27 acres north of the roadway. A railroad track, indicated by a dashed line, cut across this northern part of the property. The village of Bridgewater was less than one mile west of their farm.

A wider view of this 1896 plat map reveals the proximity of the three Weller siblings. This image measures only three miles from the left to the right edge. At the end of the 19th century, the three Weller siblings owned land within two miles of one another.

Sophie and Johannes were living on their Saline Township farm at the time of the 1900 Federal Census. They were living alone at this time, five years after they left Brend. All four of their immigrant children in Michigan had left home.

Sophie Hinderer died on December 9, 1903, eight years after arriving in Michigan. She was 59 years old. Family information is that she lived with chronic asthma for many years. She reportedly said the best she ever felt was during the voyage across the Atlantic. This would make sense for someone with allergies and asthma. She died while still a resident of Saline Township, suggesting her death was at home.

Despite the family story of chronic asthma, Sophie's death certificate stated she died of chronic nephritis, a term used for long-standing kidney disease. She also had dropsy, an old-fashioned word meaning fluid accumulation. Her dropsy may have been due to the chronic kidney disease.

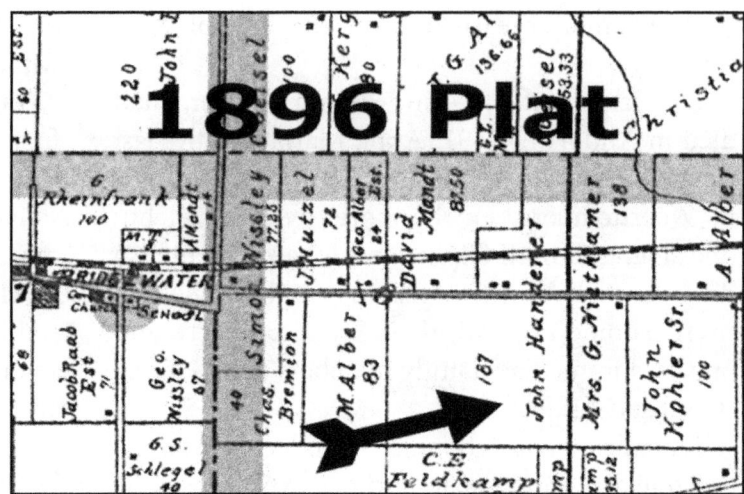

One year after immigration, Johannes Hinderer (John Handerer) owned 187 acres of land in section 6 of Saline Township less than one mile east of the village of Bridgewater. See text for added details. Source: "M. M. Dickson & Co's Township and Sectional Pocket Map of Washtenaw County, Michigan," 63 x 79 cm (Ann Arbor, MI: M. M. Dickson & Co, 1896), Library of Congress, accessed June 2021, https://www.loc.gov/item/02024899/. Edited by author.

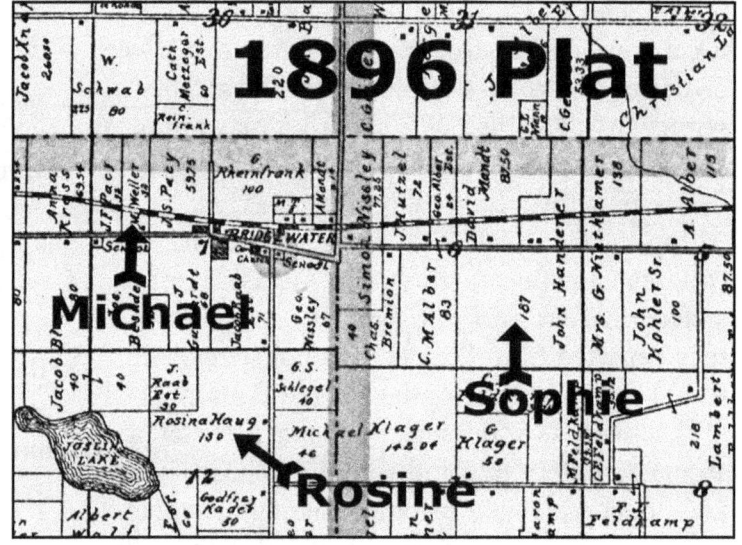

The 1896 plat map includes the properties owned by Rosine (Weller) Haug, Michael Weller, and Sophie (Weller) Hinderer. They lived within two miles of one another. Source: "M. M. Dickson & Co's Township and Sectional Pocket Map of Washtenaw County, Michigan," 63 x 79 cm (Ann Arbor, MI: M. M. Dickson & Co, 1896), Library of Congress, accessed June 2021, https://www.loc.gov/item/02024899/. Edited by author.

The Michigan Hinderer Family – The Children of Johannes and Sophie

Katharine Hinderer eventually formed close ties with her husband Gottlieb's siblings in Michigan. An exchange of letters began as early as the late 1890s. This was after Gottlieb and Katharine had left Iowa and were living in Minnesota. From Minnesota, Katharine, or "Kate" as some Michigan relatives referred to her, exchanged letters with Gottlieb's extended family in Michigan. By the mid-1900s, snapshot photos show Gottlieb's Michigan relatives vacationing in Minnesota.

Early on, Gottlieb was less communicative with his birth family than his wife Katharine. The first evidence of him visiting his Michigan family was in the 1920s when his father Johannes died. Perhaps that event opened the door to renew a relationship with his sister Christine and brothers Gottlob and August.

Johann (John) Georg Hinderer

The historical record is sketchy for this son of Johannes and Sophie. He was the oldest child who emigrated to Michigan. The family table from Germany indicated he was born in Brend in 1870. He was four years younger than his brother Gottlieb (b. 1866) and eight years older than his sister Christine Catharine (b. 1878). He was not listed with his parents and younger siblings aboard the Saale when they arrived in 1895.

Passenger list searches have revealed several possible matches for John Georg's trans-Atlantic passage, but none fit him perfectly. A single laborer named John Hinderer, was also listed in the

---

Sophie Weller and Johannes Hinderer

Married – 3 Sep 1865 in Alfdorf, Wuerttemberg:

Johannes Hinderer – b. 20 Aug 1842 in Brend; d. 18 Aug 1923, age 81, in Michigan
Sophie Weller – b. 9 Mar 1844 in Alfdorf; d. 9 Dec 1903, age 59, in Michigan

Children:

Gottfried – b. 23 Dec 1864 in Alfdorf; d. 10 Jul 1865, age 7 months, in Alfdorf
Gottlieb – b. 15 Sep 1866 in Alfdorf; d. 25 Aug 1951, age 85, in Minnesota
Jakob – b. 9 Aug 1868 in Brend; d. 9 Apr 1869, age 8 months, in Brend
Johann Georg – b. 19 Jan 1870 in Brend; d. 2 May 1913, age 43, in Michigan
Gottfried – b 31 Jan 1873 in Brend; d. 20 Jan 1876, age 3, in Brend
Christian Carl – b. 23 Sep 1875 in Brend; d. 2 Sep 1877, age 2, in Brend
Christine Catharine – b. 12 May 1878 in Brend; d. 28 Jun 1934, age 56, in Michigan
Gottlob – b. 12 Jul 1882 in Brend; d. 8 Mar 1953, age 70, in Michigan
August – b. 23 Oct 1884 in Brend; d. 24 May 1962, age 77, in Michigan
Twins Christian & Wilhelm – b. 11 Apr 1886 in Brend. Christian d. 19 Apr 1886, age 8 days, in Brend & Wilhelm d. 24 Apr 1886, age 13 days, in Brend

---

The family of Sophie (Weller) and Johannes Hinderer. Family members who emigrated to America are in bold type. Source: Compiled by author.

1900 Federal Census for Bridgewater Township, Washtenaw County, but this man's age does not match John Georg. In the end, John Georg's year of emigration and location in 1900 are both uncertain.

The first confirmed listing for John Georg was the 1910 Federal Census. In 1910, he was living in Saline Township with the family of his younger brother Gottlob. The census stated he did odd jobs on the farm. This census also claimed his emigration year was 1888, seven years before his parent's emigration in 1895. Record searches have failed to confirm this earlier emigration date.

A photo of the three Michigan brothers with their father is dated *circa* 1908. It is an image of the four Hinderer men in front of a barn. Each man is holding a team of horses. The location was not recorded, but it was likely the original home of Johannes and Sophie in Saline Township. The men are posed dressed in suits, not their everyday work clothes.

John Georg Hinderer died on May 2, 1913, age 43, as the result of a farm accident. His Michigan death record stated he was run over by a piece of farm equipment, suffering fatal injuries. He had never been married and had no children.

Christine Catharine Hinderer

Christine Catharine Hinderer was the third child of Johannes and Sophie to reach adulthood. She married William Weber on January 16, 1900. She was 21 years old, and he was 25. Both newlyweds were Swabian immigrants from the Rems Valley in Wuerttemberg. Their story is enriched by recollections passed down through their youngest daughter Elsa Edna who in turn passed them on to her daughter.

The family story is that William and Christine went to the same school while growing up in Wuerttemberg. Christine was born and grew up in Brend. She, with her family, attended St. Stephan Church in Alfdorf. It is likely she attended a public school in the area. For children as well as adults, transportation between Wuerttemberg villages was either on foot or by horse. If Christine and William attended a school together, the school had to be close to Brend.

William (or *Wilhelm*) Weber was born September 28, 1874. He grew up in the village of Breitenfürst[11] located three miles west of Brend. William's father, Johann Georg Weber was a farmer who lived in

The three Michigan brothers: Left to Right - Gottlob, August, and John Georg, with their father Johannes on the far right, ca. 1908. Source: From the author's collection; edited by author.

Breitenfürst. Their German family table identified his mother as Maria Funk. The proximity of Brend and Breitenfürst makes the family story of William and Christine attending school together plausible. The Weber family table indicated that William was the fifth of ten children. His entry line in this record also stated that he emigrated to America in 1891.

William's mother Maria died when she was 40 years old, less than two months after her 10th child was born. Her death left William's father with 10 children between the ages of two months and 23 years. The family table also indicated his father did not remarry. William's inheritance would not have been substantive because he was the fifth of 10 children. As the decade of the 1890s began, William's birth family was facing a near-hopeless future.

The family story continued that William was subject to conscription into German military service when he turned 18 in the year 1892. To avoid this, he decided to emigrate to America before his 18th birthday.

William's 1891 emigration record documents his arrival in America. William Weber is a common German name. Identifying a young man with this name traveling alone has a significant potential for error. However, the passenger list record for William was unusually detailed, enabling certainty that this was the young man who later married Christine Hinderer.

William was listed as Wilh. (an abbreviation for Wilhelm) Weber. He arrived in New York on August 29, 1891, about a year before his 18th birthday, aboard the steamer *Columbia*. The ship departed from Hamburg with a stop at Southampton England to add passengers. Wilh. Weber's origin was documented as Wuerttemberg and more exactly as Breitenfürst. His destination was Michigan. This unusually detailed passenger record allows certainty that this was William's passage.

The family story continued that William's emigration was sponsored by a Michigan woman related to an acquaintance of his in Wuerttemberg. Specific details are lacking, but the idea of sponsorship was common for single immigrants, both men and women. In William's case, he owed labor to his sponsor in exchange for room and board. Immigrant women usually owed their American sponsor domestic duties like housekeeping or help with child rearing. The immigrant's typical goal was to save enough money to fulfill the obligation to their sponsor and then be free to acquire their own property or to start their own family in America.

William worked for farmers near the villages of Clinton and Tecumseh in neighboring Lenawee County, Michigan. These villages are about 10 miles southwest of the Johannes and Sophie Hinderer farm in Washtenaw County. During winter months, he reportedly attended a district school to learn English.

In Michigan, marriages were not only recorded in local churches or civil offices, but also in a chronological summary for the entire county. This countywide summary is a "secondary" record, meaning it was compiled long after the marriage

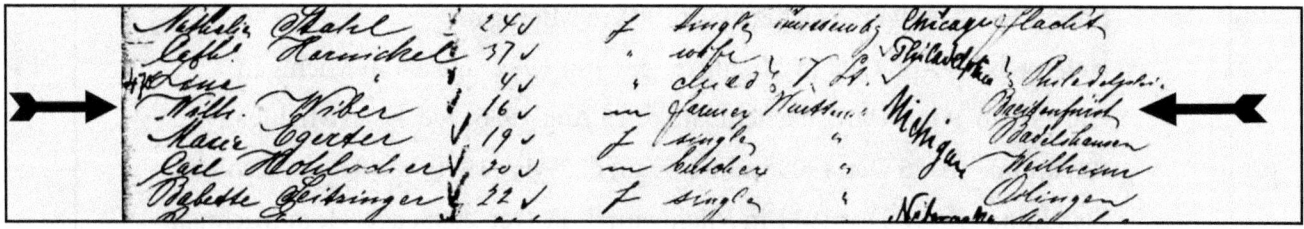

The passenger listing for Wilh. (William) Weber from Breitenfürst, Wuerttemberg. His destination was Michigan. The steamer Columbia *arrived in New York on August 29, 1891. Source: "New York, U.S., Arriving Passenger and Crew Lists (including Castle Garden and Ellis Island), 1820-1957" online database (Provo, UT: Ancestry.com, 2010), accessed June 2021. Edited by author.*

The middle marriage entry was for Wm. Weber and "Christina Henderer." The marriage date on the far right was January 16, 1900. William's father's given name "Geo" for Georg is correct. His mother's maiden name Barreis should have been Funk. Source: "Michigan, U.S., Marriage Records, 1867-1952" online database (Provo, UT: Ancestry.com, 2015), accessed June 2021. Edited by author.

took place. Because it is "secondary," it has a greater chance of containing transcription errors.

The 1900 Michigan marriage summary for William and Christine was mostly accurate. Christine's father's given name was transcribed as John (Johannes), and her mother's birth surname as Weller. Both names were correct. William's father's given name was listed as Geo (Georg) which is also correct. His mother's maiden name was recorded as Barreis on the marriage record rather than Funk. The reason for this apparent error is unknown. Two Wuerttemberg documents: his parent's family table and the record of William's birth and baptism confirmed that his mother's birth surname was Funk.

Christine and William's story continued with their 1903 purchase of a farm in Lodi Township, Washtenaw County. Their farm was located at

---

Christine Hinderer and William Weber

Married – 16 Jan 1900 in Washtenaw County, Michigan:

> **William Weber** – b. 28 Sep 1874 in Breitenfürst; d. 18 Sep 1936, age 62, in Michigan
>
> **Christine Hinderer** – b. 12 May 1878 in Brend; d. 28 Jun 1934, age 56, in Michigan

Children:

> **Alfred** – b. 14 Oct 1900 in Michigan; d. 24 Apr 1957, age 56, in Michigan
>
> **Edwin E.** – b. 1904 in Michigan; d. 1904 in Michigan
>
> **Helen** – b. 16 Apr 1905 in Michigan; d. 1 Jun 1992, age 87, in Michigan
>
> **Harold** – b. 9 Jun 1907 in Michigan; d. 15 Aug 1936, age 29, in Michigan
>
> **Raymond** – b. 26 Dec 1908 in Michigan; d. 2 May 1990, age 81, in Michigan
>
> **Elsa Edna** – b. 18 Dec 1911 in Michigan; d. 11 Dec 2005, age 94, in Michigan
>
> **Unnamed infant** – b. 1913 in Michigan; d. 1913 in Michigan

The family of Christine Catharine Hinderer and William Weber. Source: Compiled by author.

6665 West Ellsworth Road,[12] four miles west of the city of Ann Arbor and about five miles north of Christine's parents, Sophie and Johannes Hinderer in Saline Township.

Christine and William lived their entire married lives on their farm in Lodi Township. They had seven children, and five of these survived into adulthood. Christine died in 1934 and William died two years later in 1936. Their home provided a reunion site for family gatherings, with snapshots taken in the early 1940s showing generations of their family joined by the extended family members of Christine's siblings, Gottlob and August.

Gottlob Hinderer

Twelve-year-old Gottlob Hinderer arrived in America with his parents and siblings aboard the steamer Saale. He was four years younger than his sister Christine and two years older than his brother August.

Gottlob would have spoken a distinctly Swabian dialect of his native German language. Most immigrant children attended district schools where they were taught English, sometimes as a routine subject and sometimes as the only language allowed in school. Regardless, Gottlob grew up speaking his native Swabian German at home while learning English at school. It was a bilingual language pattern followed repeatedly by immigrant children.

As with the other members of this Hinderer family, there are no diaries or journals to document Gottlob's early years in Michigan. However, there are several photographs and census records from his early life.

A professional photograph was taken of Gottlob and his younger brother August. The photo was undated but was likely taken in the late 1890s or 1900. Gottlob would have been 17 or 18, and August 15 or 16. In this photo, older brother Gottlob is seated.

August (standing) and Gottlob Hinderer ca. 1900. See text. Source: Author's collection. Edited by author.

The next documented event for Gottlob was his marriage to Rosa (or Rosie) Bareis on December 21, 1904. The compiled chronological list of Washtenaw County marriages was the source of this information. Gottlob's family information was correctly recorded. His father was named John (Johannes) and his mother's maiden name was Weller.

Rosa's line on this "secondary" marriage record is problematic. It states that her father's given name was Conrad. Presumably, his surname, like Rosa's, was Bareis. Her mother's maiden name was also recorded as Bareis. It is possible but unlikely that both her father and mother had the same surname. Alternatively, Rosa may have decided to use her mother's surname as her own. Finally, this may simply be a transcription error in the compiled record.

Later census documents all stated that Rosa emigrated to America in 1900 and one census stated she came from Wuerttemberg, Germany. Her stated birth year varied between the census documents but was most commonly listed as 1885. Despite these clues, neither her German birth record nor her immigration passenger listing has been identified with certainty.

Another family photo shows Gottlob and Rosa as a young couple. The photo is not dated, but was taken around the year of their marriage, 1904. On the back of the photo, the original owner of the photo wrote "Gottlob and Rosa." On other photos of this couple, she was also referred to as Rosa. Family members knew her as Rosa rather than Rosie.

Gottlob and Rosa lived on a farm in Saline Township until they retired and moved to the city of Ann Arbor. Six years after their marriage, the 1910 census listed their family with three daughters. This census stated Gottlob owned his farm but carried a mortgage. His younger brother, 26-year-old August, lived on the same property and was said to be Gottlob's partner in farming. His older brother John (John Georg) also lived with him doing odd jobs. Finally, 23-year-old Clara Waltz lived with this extended Hinderer family and worked as a "servant," most likely meaning she did domestic chores.

A photo of Gottlob's family is dated *circa* 1908. Gottlob is seated on the left and his wife Rosa is seated on the right. Between them are their first two children, Edna and Elmer. The 1908 date is based on the estimated age of son Elmer in the photo. Standing behind the family, left to right, are brothers August and John Georg Hinderer, their maid Clara Waltz, and father Johannes Hinderer. The house in the background was likely Gottlob's home in Saline Township.

By the time of the 1920 census, Gottlob and Rosa's family had expanded to include six children. Brothers August and John Georg were absent from the household in 1920. Gottlob's older brother John Georg had died in a farming accident in 1913.

A photo of Gottlob and Rosa (Rosie) Hinderer taken at about the time of their marriage in 1904. Source: Author's collection. Edited by author.

A circa 1908 photo of Gottlob and his wife Rosa seated, and children Elmer and Edna between them. Standing (left to right) are August and John Georg Hinderer, domestic helper Clara Waltz, and father Johannes Hinderer. Source: From the author's collection; edited by author.

Gottlob Hinderer and Rosa Bareis

Married – 21 Dec 1904 in Washtenaw County, Michigan:

Gottlob Hinderer – b. 12 Jul 1882 in Brend; d. 8 Mar 1953, age 70, in Michigan

Rosa Bareis – b. abt. 1885 in Wuerttemberg; d. 26 Aug 1954, abt. age 69, in Michigan

Children:

Edna Lydia – b. 9 Oct 1905 in Michigan; d. 4 Jan 1922, age 16, in Michigan

Elmer – b. 3 Aug 1907 in Michigan; d. 12 Mar 1973, age 65, in Michigan

Clara D. – b. 11 Feb 1909 in Michigan; d. 18 Nov 2001, age 92, in Michigan

Louise A. – b. 10 Jan 1912 in Michigan; d. 28 Sep 2001, age 89, in Michigan

Ottilde – b. 7 Dec 1914 in Michigan; d. 1 Apr 1996, age 81, in Michigan

Loren August – b. 27 Oct 1920 in Michigan; d. 14 Jun 1974, age 53, in Michigan

Lillian – b. 3 Sep 1923 in Michigan; d. 26 Dec 2012, age 89, in Michigan

The family of Gottlob Hinderer and Rosa Bareis. Source: Compiled by author.

Katharine

Gottlob's younger brother August had married and by 1920 was living elsewhere. Gottlob's father, John (Johannes), still lived with Gottlob and Rosa. Another person, Albert C. Bareis, also lived with Gottlob and Rosa. The census states Albert was Gottlob's brother-in-law, suggesting he was Rosa's brother. Despite this clue about the Bareis family, documents discovered from Albert's birth family recorded no older sister named Rosa. In the end, their relationship and the details of Rosa's birth family remain uncertain.

The next two census documents from 1930 and 1940 continued to list Gottlob and Rosa. In both records, they lived on their farm in Saline Township. By 1940, only their two youngest children were still living with them.

When Gottlob and Rosa retired from farming, they moved into the town of Ann Arbor. Gottlob died there in 1953, and Rosa died about a year later.

August Hinderer

August was the youngest child of Johannes and Sophie Hinderer who survived to adulthood. There were younger twin brothers born in 1886, but they died in infancy. August was born in Brend in October 1884, which meant he was 10 years old when he emigrated aboard the *Saale* in May of 1895.

After arriving in Washtenaw County, August did not remain on his parent's farm for long. In

A snapshot of August and Tina Hinderer dated 1941. It was taken during a visit to Minnesota. Source: Photo by Martha Hinderer as edited by author.

1900 when he was 15 years old, he was listed as a boarder and farm laborer working for another family in Saline Township. By the time of the next census in 1910, he lived with his brother Gottlob's family and was recorded as being Gottlob's farming partner.

The Michigan marriage registry listed August Hinderer and Tina Walz married in Lodi Township on December 21, 1910. Tina's parents were George Walz and Katherine Rouse. August's parent's names were correct. Source: "Michigan, U.S., Marriage Records, 1867-1952" online database (Provo, UT: Ancestry.com, 2015), accessed June 2021. Edited by author.

In December 1910, a few months after the census, August married 19-year-old Tina Walz. Tina was born and raised in Lodi Township, Washtenaw County. Lodi Township is adjacent to and north of Saline Township. This means her home was only a few miles north of the Hinderer farm in Saline Township. August and Tina's farm was located on West Waters Road in Lodi Township.[13]

August and Tina's only child, Walter, was born February 1, 1912. Federal census records for 1920, 1930, and 1940 all list August, Tina, and Walter Hinderer living together on their Lodi Township farm. Walter did not marry and did not have children.

August's wife Tina died January 15, 1944, on their Lodi Township farm. Her death certificate stated an episode of flu was followed by pneumonia. She was 52 years old. August later retired from farming and, like his brother Gottlob, moved to Ann Arbor where he died in 1962. Interestingly, their gravestone spells Tina's given name as "Tema" rather than Tina. August and Tina's son Walter died in 1977, at the age of 65.

MICHIGAN AND MINNESOTA

The rift between Gottlieb Hinderer and the Michigan Hinderer family ended in 1923, after his father Johannes died. By this time, Gottlieb, Katharine, and their grown children had lived in Minnesota for over two decades. According to the family story, Gottlieb would not visit his extended family in Michigan until after the death of Johannes in 1923. A snapshot photo of the three living brothers was taken at the time of Gottlieb's first Michigan visit.

In a later photograph dated 1941, Gottlieb and his wife Katharine were pictured standing in front

A snapshot photo of the Hinderer brothers in Michigan ca. 1923. Left to right – August, Gottlieb, and Gottlob. Source: From the author's collection; edited by author.

of the home of a Michigan relative. This photo confirmed at least one Michigan visit for Gottlieb and Katharine together.

Photos taken in the late 1930s, early 1940s and early 1950s showed members of Michigan families visiting Gottlieb and Katharine's farm in Minnesota. Gottlieb's youngest brother August Hinderer and his wife Tina are pictured in Minnesota in the early 1940s. Elsa (Weber), the youngest child of Gottlieb's only sister Christine, was photographed in Minnesota with her husband Carl Brenner. The photos of Elsa's family are from the 1940s and 1950s. Taken together, these photos document that by the mid-1900s, the extended Hinderer families in Michigan and Minnesota had renewed their mutual friendships.

Was It Michigan or Iowa?

The 1891 passenger listing for Gottlieb Hinderer stated that Michigan was his destination in America. The story of the Michigan Weller and Hinderer families has been retold in this chapter without knowing if Gottlieb Hinderer and Katharine Deininger ever traveled through Michigan in 1891.

Gottlieb and Katharine arrived in America in late December 1891. About six weeks later they were living in Iowa. This short timeline dictates that if they did pass through Washtenaw County Michigan, it was a temporary layover. Their destination was the northeastern corner of Iowa where yet another Hinderer relative had already settled. The story of Gottlieb and Katharine's life in Iowa is the subject of the next chapter.

Notes

1. Reed Wicander and James S. Monroe, *Historical Geology: Evolution of Earth & Life Through Time* (Boston: Cengage Learning, 2016), 351-59.

2. To locate Washtenaw County, in Google Maps insert coordinates 42.254810, -83.835370 in the search box and click search.

3. *History of Washtenaw County Michigan* (Chicago: Cas. C. Chapman, 1881), 123-25.

4. Ibid., 595.

5. Dale R. Herter, and Terry Stollsteimer, "A History of German Settlers in Washtenaw County 1830-1930," January 2007 (updated January 2009): 15. Rootsweb.com, accessed June 2021, http://sites.rootsweb.com/~miwashte/washtenawgermansettlerhistory.pdf.

6. Ibid., 21.

7. In German documents, this surname may be spelled Köder or Köther. American documents variably spell it Koether, Kother, Koeder, and Kader.

8. His name is sometimes spelled Frederick or Fredrick.

9. Most records from the 1890 federal census were destroyed by a fire.

10. To locate this farm, in Google Maps insert coordinates 42.160665, -83.877619 in the search box and click search.

11. To locate Breitenfürst, in Google Maps insert coordinates 48.857142, 9.624124 in the search box and click search.

12. To locate this farm, in Google Maps insert coordinates 42.226083, -83.859592 in the search box and click search.

13. In Google Maps insert coordinates 42.241874, -83.834164 in the search box and click search. This locates West Waters Road, not the exact farm site.

Chapter 6

The Iowa Hinderers

Timeline

1803 – The Louisiana Purchase

1815 – The U.S. controlled the Mississippi River

1832 – The Blackhawk Indian War

1846 – Iowa became the 29th state

1855 – Rosine Nise was born in Alfdorf

1857 – Gottfried Hinderer was born in Cronhütte

1857 – The first railroad reached the Mississippi River

1865 – The U.S. Civil War ended; Lincoln assassinated

1866 – Gottlieb Hinderer was born in Alfdorf

1872 – Katharine Deininger was born in Gehren

1882 – Gottfried Hinderer emigrated to Iowa

1883 – Rosine Nise and child emigrated to Iowa

1883 – Gottfried Hinderer married Rosine Nise

1890 – The final Battle of the American Indian Wars

1891 – Gottlieb and Katharine emigrated to the U.S.

1892 – Gottlieb and Katharine were married in Iowa

1893 – The Panic of 1893

1892-1898 – Five children were born to Gottlieb and Katharine in Iowa

1898 – The Spanish-American War

1899 – Gottlieb and Katharine bought Minnesota land

1914 – World War I began

Iowa Beginnings

The topography of the far northeastern corner of Iowa is unlike the rest of the state. Instead of flat terrain covered by rich prairie soil, the northeastern corner has a thin soil layer resting atop limestone. Creeks and rivers have cut rugged valleys through the limestone layers as they drain toward the Mississippi River. Together with southeastern Minnesota and southwestern Wisconsin, this corner of Iowa is part of the "driftless" area. Driftless means it did not have an overlying glacial covering at the peak of the last ice age, about 14,000 years ago. This unique area contains limestone caves as well as both animals and plants found nowhere else in Iowa. Plateaus within the driftless area allow farming, but the soil is less productive than the deep loam of the prairie land farther west.

Prior to 1803, the western border of the United States was the Mississippi River. The 1803 Louisiana Purchase included what is now Iowa and nearly doubled the size of the United States. That same year, Lewis and Clark set course from St. Louis, Missouri traveling by boat up the Missouri River. Their voyage of discovery navigated through the section of the river that later became the western border of Iowa. The land between the Missouri and Mississippi rivers was unsettled in 1803 and was known simply as "Indian Territory."

At the time of the Louisiana Purchase, the western part of Iowa along the Missouri River was occupied by Sioux tribal groups. The nomadic Sioux had lived and hunted in this area for centuries.

On the eastern side of the future state, multiple Indian tribes were forced to live along the Mississippi River in uneasy proximity to one another. The tribes included the Winnebago, the Sauk, the Fox, and the Potawatomi. These tribes were not native to the area near the Mississippi River. They were granted this land by treaty with the U.S. because of the relentless westward expansion of settlers. Their original homelands had been located around the Great Lakes as far east as the St. Lawrence River in Canada.

After 1803, the U.S. owned territory on both sides of the Mississippi River. Nevertheless, the government chose not to forcibly remove the British military from their Mississippi River fortifications. The continued British presence meant the U.S. owned the river but did not control traffic on the river. This decision proved costly during the War of 1812.

Prairie du Chien, Wisconsin,[1] an old French fur-trading town on the river, was the site of the British river fortification at the outbreak of the War of 1812. During the war, American forces sailed upriver from St. Louis on two separate forays trying to force the British out. Both American military engagements failed. Nevertheless, when the war ended in 1815, the terms of the peace treaty gave full control of the river to the Americans.

The American military presence on the river proved useful a decade later. In the 1820s and early 1830s, Indian tribes still lived on the land on both sides of the Mississippi River. By this time, settlers were moving onto this land, which had been granted to the tribes by earlier treaties. The U.S. government requested meetings with the tribes living throughout Iowa. The meetings were billed as a way to keep peace between the tribes, including the Sioux in the west and north. The negotiated settlement had nothing to do with tribal rivalries. The Prairie du Chien treaties of 1825 through 1830 ended tribal control of the land near the Mississippi River. A few Indian leaders argued and later fought battles against this final loss of

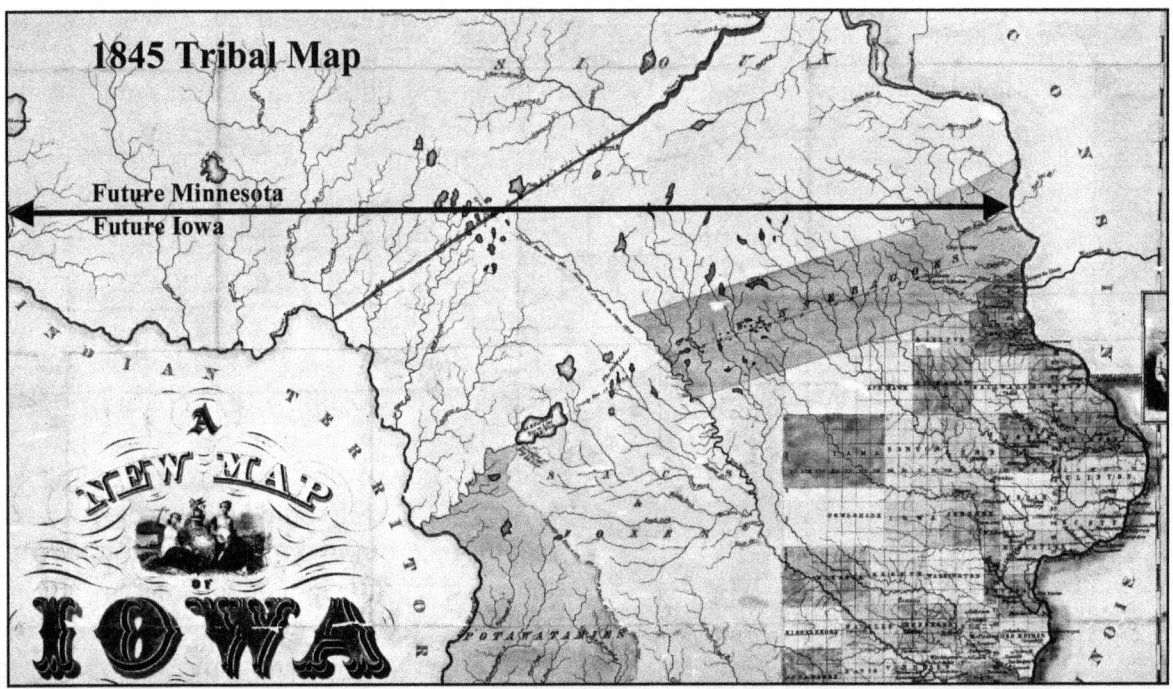

This 1845 map names a few counties along the Mississippi River. It also names Indian tribes from the eastern U.S. that had been granted land along the Mississippi. Sioux tribes occupied "Indian Territory" in the west and north. Source: "A New Map of Iowa: Accompanied with Notes by W. Barrows," 46 x 58 cm (Cincinnati: Doolittle & Munson, 1845) Library of Congress, access July 2021, https://www.loc.gov/item/2007626856/. Edited by author.

their Iowa and Illinois land, but in the end, their efforts failed.[2]

The relentless westward displacement of Indian groups came to a final resolution when the U.S. government initiated the policy of forcing tribes to live on reservations. By this process, the eastern Iowa and Illinois tribes were moved even farther west onto the Great Plains. Their new reservations were carefully located on government-owned land considered undesirable to settlers.

Iowa followed a pathway to statehood that had been laid out years earlier by the U.S. Congress. When the population of a defined area reached 5,000, residents were allowed to apply for territory status and elect a legislature. When the population reached 60,000, they could apply to become a state.[3] In 1834, Iowa was a part of Michigan Territory. In 1836, Michigan applied to become a state but did not want to include the far western Iowa lands. The solution was to remove Iowa from Michigan Territory and add it to the nearby Wisconsin Territory. By this process, Iowa remained part of a territory and in the queue for later statehood.

Achieving statehood was more complicated. At that time, the greatest issue in the U.S. Congress was maintaining a balance between states that allowed slave ownership with those that did not. Iowans did not own slaves, so gaining statehood required the admission of another state where slavery was allowed. Florida was admitted as a slave-owning state in 1845, thus opening the door for a new state from the North. Iowa statehood followed in December 1846.

Settling Iowa - The Milwaukee Road

Prairie du Chien, Wisconsin, played a pivotal role in settling the four northeastern counties of Iowa. It is located on the Wisconsin side of the Mississippi River near where the Wisconsin River empties into the Mississippi. This location meant Prairie du Chien received both river and overland traffic. Settlers and commodities came to Prairie du Chien from Minnesota, inland Wisconsin, and the rapidly growing cities of Milwaukee and Chicago on the western shore of Lake Michigan. Across the Mississippi River, the small towns of McGregor and Marquette, Iowa, welcomed the traffic crossing the river from Prairie du Chien. The merchants in these towns sold supplies to westbound settlers who continued on their journey into the four counties of northeastern Iowa. Twenty miles or a day's journey from the river, the town of Postville, Iowa, was a second stopping point for travelers.

During the mid-1800s, expanding railroads became the primary means of transportation. Trains replaced the barge traffic on rivers and the horse-drawn wagons traveling overland. In April 1857, a railroad line was completed between Milwaukee on the western shore of Lake Michigan and Prairie du Chien on the Wisconsin side of the Mississippi River. It was the first successful linkage of a Great Lakes port city and the upper Mississippi River.

In northeastern Iowa, what was later known as the "Milwaukee Road" was the key railroad builder. The first section from Milwaukee west was originally named the "Wisconsin and Mississippi Railroad." This name followed the common pattern of naming a railway line according to its place of origin and its terminus.

Expansion of the Milwaukee Road westward was accomplished in two ways. Usually, the parent company itself laid the new tracks. When the opportunity arose, however, the parent company also bought and used short railway sections previously built by smaller companies.

In the earliest years, railway travelers arriving in Prairie du Chien boarded river barges or ferryboats to cross the Mississippi River into Iowa. Once in Iowa, they had to continue their journey by horse or on foot.

By 1865, the Milwaukee Road had begun construction of rail lines on the Iowa side of the Mississippi River. The new tracks angled northwest

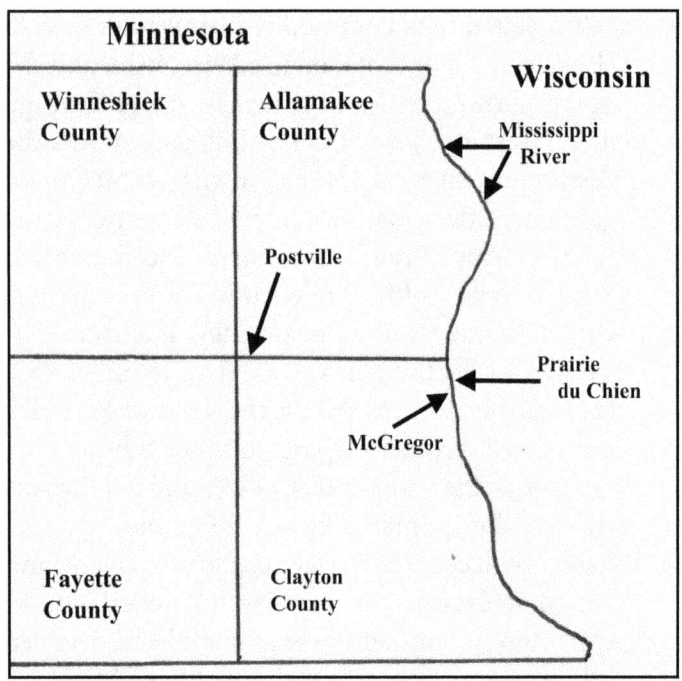

An illustration of the location of key early settlements in northeastern Iowa. The distance between Prairie du Chien, Wisconsin, and Postville, Iowa, is about 20 miles. Source: Illustration by author.

This 1855 map showed the Prairie du Chien terminus of the Wisconsin and Mississippi Railroad. There were no railroad tracks on the Iowa side. Westward travel in Iowa was by horse or on foot. Note that several names are misspelled. Source: "Map of Iowa Exhibiting the Townships, Cities, Villages Post Offices, Railroads, Common Roads & Other Improvements," (Cincinnati: Edward Mendenhall Publisher, 1855), Library of Congress, accessed July 2021, https://www.loc.gov/item/98688478/. Edited by author.

through Postville, Iowa, and continued toward Minnesota.

The Milwaukee Road provided transportation in both directions. It was used for moving settlers and supplies west and wheat or other farm crops east. The eastbound crops were destined for port cities on Lake Michigan. From there, the farm products could be shipped to mills and distribution centers around the Great Lakes.

The greatest bottleneck for this particular rail line was crossing the Mississippi River. By 1865, barges had been designed that were capable of carrying entire train cars. The trains were disassembled on one side of the river and the individual cars rolled onto barges with embedded railroad tracks. The barges were pulled across the river by a cable, and the train cars were then reassembled on the opposite side.

An 1865 map indicated that railway tracks had been completed from McGregor, Iowa, on the river to beyond Postville, Iowa, 20 miles to the west. The dashed line beyond Postville indicated that the extension of the tracks toward Minnesota was still under construction. At this same time, a different railroad company, the Minnesota Central, was laying railroad tracks southward from St. Paul, Minnesota, toward the Iowa border. In 1867, the Milwaukee Road purchased the Minnesota Central. The merged company was renamed the Milwaukee and St. Paul Railway.

In November of 1867, the new tracks from St. Paul and from Iowa connected in Austin, Minnesota,[4] near the Iowa border. For the first time, there was a continuous railway line from Milwaukee, Wisconsin, on Lake Michigan through Prairie du Chien and northeastern Iowa to St. Paul, Minnesota.

This same railway company completed another connection from Milwaukee, Wisconsin, south to Chicago, Illinois. This extension required yet

This 1865 map indicated completion of railway tracks from McGregor, Iowa, to beyond Postville. The extension into Minnesota, shown as a dashed line, was still under construction. Source: "Map Showing the Line of the Milwaukee & St. Paul Railroad and Its Western and North Western Connections," scale 1:1,250,000, 37 x 54 cm (New York: G. W. & C. B. Coulton & Co., 1865), Library of Congress, accessed July 2021, https://www.loc.gov/item/98688715/. Edited by author.

Katharine

another name change: the Chicago, Milwaukee, and St. Paul Railway, or as it was more commonly known, the "Milwaukee Road."

In 1874, the first railway bridge across the northern Mississippi River was built at Prairie du Chien, Wisconsin.[5] The bridge was located where an island in the center of the Mississippi divided the river into two main channels. This allowed bridge construction in two connected sections east and west of the center island. Each of the two sections included a hinged length of tracks built atop floating pontoons. The flow of the river opened the hinged pontoon sections allowing boats to pass on the river. A cable then pulled each floating section of track back into its original position allowing trains to pass over the river. The fixed sections of the bridge were constructed as railroad trestles built on permanent pilings. The so-called pile-pontoon bridge was used successfully for decades. Cross-river traffic was now faster than the old barge system, although train speed was limited to seven miles per hour.

A map from 1892, the same year Gottlieb Hinderer and Katharine Deininger arrived in Iowa, displayed the railroad system they would have used. In 1892, their Iowa contacts were already settled near Postville at the intersection of the four northeastern counties of Iowa. When Gottlieb and Katharine arrived, railroads crisscrossed the state of Iowa including the four counties in the northeastern corner. The pile-pontoon bridge across the Mississippi River had been in service for nearly 20 years. This transportation infrastructure provided reliably scheduled passenger traffic from Milwaukee and Chicago on Lake Michigan to both Iowa and Minnesota.

When Katharine and Gottlieb arrived in Iowa, a continuous railroad line crossed the Mississippi River at Prairie du Chien and then angled northwestward through Postville, Iowa, and on, via Austin, Minnesota, to St. Paul. It was named the Chicago, Milwaukee, and St. Paul R.R. Source: North West Publishing Co., "Plat Book of Chickasaw County, Iowa: Drawn from Actual Surveys & County Records" (Philadelphia: F. Bourquin, 1892), Library of Congress, accessed July 2021, https://www.loc.gov/item/2008622189/. Edited by author.

Postville, St. Paul Lutheran Church, and Two Hinderer Families

The border lines of the four counties in Iowa's northeastern corner changed several times in the 1830s and 1840s. By 1849, both Allamakee County in the far northeastern corner and Clayton County to its south were defined by their modern borders. By 1851, the boundaries of all four counties were permanently defined.

Postville, Iowa,[6] is located near the intersection of the four counties. Most of the town lies within Allamakee County, but a few buildings on the south side of the town are technically in Clayton County.

Postville's first occupant and the town namesake was a tradesman named Joel Post. In January 1849, Mr. Post was appointed to the honorary position of postmaster of Postville. Unfortunately, Mr. Post never learned of his appointment because he died before the news reached Postville five days later.[7] The anecdotal story of Mr. Post's unfulfilled appointment illustrates the slow pace of frontier communication in mid-1800s Iowa.

As a farming and trade community, Postville grew steadily, but slowly, during the second half of the 19th century. The population did not exceed 1,000 until the federal census of 1920.[8] The completion of the railway line through Postville in the 1860s added accessibility but did not produce a population "boom."

In 1871, the first German Lutheran Church was constructed in Postville. It was a small plain-looking rectangular wooden building. In the 1880s, the growing congregation began construction of a larger church, which was completed in 1891. The new 1891 church was officially named St. Paul's Evangelical Lutheran Church. A dedication service with 600 people in attendance[9] was held in November of 1891, one month before Gottlieb

An 1890s photo of St. Paul's Evangelical Lutheran Church, Postville Iowa. The church parsonage is on the right. This was the appearance of the church when the Hinderer families attended services. Source: St. Paul Lutheran Church. Scanned with permission and edited by author.

Hinderer and Katharine Deininger arrived in America.[10] Today, this same church is simply named St. Paul Lutheran Church.[11]

In the more than 125 years since its dedication, St. Paul Lutheran Church has continued to archive its original registry records. Births, baptisms, and marriages dating back to the 1890s are available for viewing. Two Hinderer families attended St. Paul Lutheran Church during the 1890s. The registry books include the birth and baptism of children from both of these families.

Investigation of deed purchase and sales records indicated neither Hinderer family owned land in Iowa. Their names do not appear in the county buy/sell records for the years they lived in Iowa. The conclusion is that they were either laborers working for a landowner, or they rented the land they farmed. In either case, plat maps showing land ownership would not display their names. As a result, only census and church records can be used to identify where the two families lived.

A 2015 photo of St. Paul Lutheran Church. The original brick façade has been replaced by stone. Source: Photo by author.

Counties in Iowa and other states are subdivided into townships. In turn, most townships are subdivided into sections with each section measuring one mile square. This rule of thumb is generally true, but oddly shaped borders make exceptions common. For example, the eastern border of both Allamakee County and Clayton County is the Mississippi River. The townships and sections along the river are not square due to the irregular course of the river.

The 1892 Iowa map helps visualize the two townships where the Hinderer families lived. With Postville centered near the intersection of the four counties, Clayton County lies southeast of the intersection. Within Clayton County, Grand Meadow is the name of the township at the intersection. Fayette County lies southwest of the intersection. Within Fayette County, Clermont is the township at the intersection. The records indicate the Hinderer families only lived in Grand Meadow Township of Clayton County and Clermont Township of Fayette County. These are adjacent townships in separate counties. Their homes were within a few miles of Postville and also within a few miles of one another.

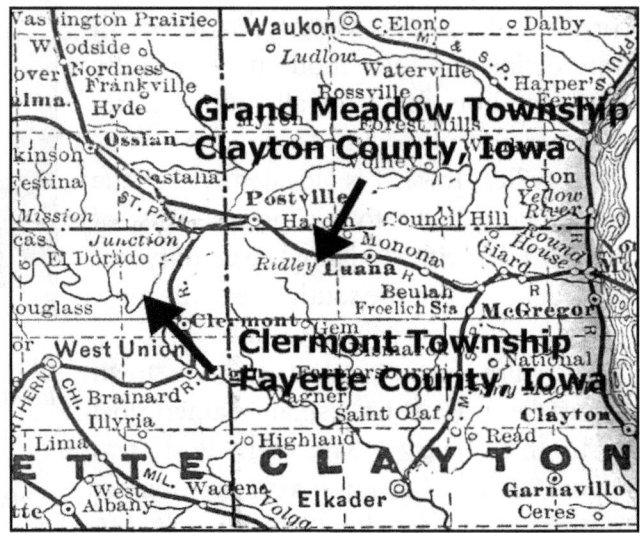

The 1892 map shows Postville, Iowa, at the intersection of four counties. The Hinderer families lived in either Grand Meadow Township of Clayton County or Clermont Township of Fayette County. Source: North West Publishing Co., "Plat Book of Chickasaw County, Iowa: Drawn from Actual Surveys & County Records" (Philadelphia: F. Bourquin, 1892), Library of Congress, accessed July 2021, https://www.loc.gov/item/2008622189/. Edited by author.

Gottfried Hinderer b. 1857 and Rosine Nise

Gottfried Hinderer was Gottlieb and Katharine's contact person in Iowa. Gottfried was Gottlieb's first cousin, once (one generation) removed. Their relationship to one another is best understood from a family chart. In the late 1800s, the given name Gottfried was extremely popular and often used generation after generation. The confusion caused by the repetitive use of this name is lessened by adding the birth year after the name. For example:

Gottlieb and Katharine's contact in Iowa was Gottfried Hinderer b.1857.

Gottfried Hinderer's father, Christian, was the younger brother of Gottlieb's grandfather Gottfried b.1804. Brothers Christian and Gottfried b.1804, along with another five siblings, were all born in Brend and attended church in Alfdorf. The older brother, Gottfried b.1804, continued to live in Brend, but the younger brother Christian moved to a nearby village when he married.

Christian Hinderer's wife Rosina Weller was from the village of Cronhütte[12] located less than five miles north of Brend. Christian and Rosina were married in 1842 and remained residents

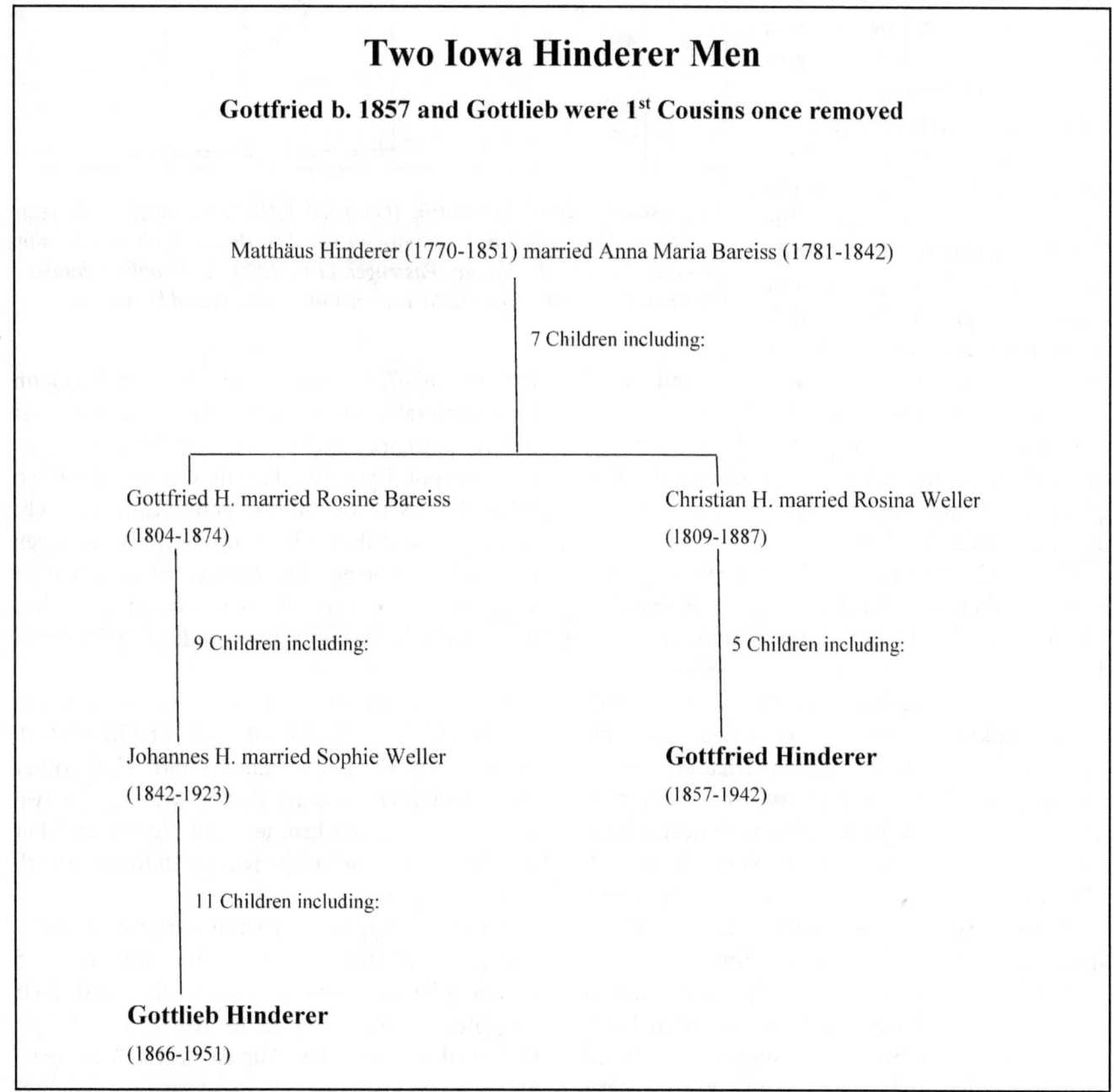

A family chart illustrating the relationship between Gottlieb Hinderer and Gottfried Hinderer b.1857. They were 1st cousins, once (one generation) removed. Source: Illustration by author.

of Cronhütte their entire lives. Christian was described as a Söldner. This word meant he owned a small plot of land, possibly only a garden. It was Christian and Rosina Hinderer's son Gottfried b.1857 who later became Gottlieb and Katharine's contact person in Iowa. He was the fourth of Christian and Rosina's five children, all born in Cronhütte, Wuerttemberg.

Although Gottfried b.1857 was born in Cronhütte, he would have known and visited his father Christian's birth family still living in Brend. It was most likely through his family link to Brend that he met his future wife, Rosine Nise.[13] Rosine was born and raised in Alfdorf. Her family, like the Hinderers from Brend, would have attended St. Stephen Church in Alfdorf. St. Stephen Church was the likely meeting place for Rosine Nise of Alfdorf and Gottfried Hinderer from Cronhütte.

Gottfried Hinderer b.1857 and Rosine Nise lived together several years before being married. In fact, they did not marry until later when they lived in Iowa. Their first child, a daughter named Carolina Rosina was born in Alfdorf in June 1880.

For unknown reasons, Gottfried Hinderer b.1857 decided to emigrate to America. He arrived in Baltimore aboard the ship *America* on October 18, 1882. He traveled alone. His wife Rosine Nise and daughter Carolina Rosina remained in Alfdorf. The couple's second child, a son named Gottfried Carl, was born in Alfdorf on October 28, 1882, 10 days after his father's arrival in Baltimore.

Within months, possibly weeks, of his arrival in America, Gottfried b.1857 was living in Iowa. The certitude of his action suggests Gottfried also had a personal contact in this northeastern corner of Iowa. The best candidate for his contact was his wife Rosine's younger brother Johann (or

The passenger listing for Gottfr. (Gottfried b.1857) Hinderer, a 26-year-old laborer. He arrived in Baltimore on October 18, 1882, aboard the ship America. Source: "Baltimore, Passenger Lists, 1820-1964" online database (Provo, UT: Ancestry.com, 2006), accessed July 2021. Edited by author.

John b. 1858). Census records state that Johann Nise emigrated to Iowa in 1881, about a year before Gottfried. Additionally, an 1896 plat map of Clermont Township, Fayette County identified John Nise as owner of 160 acres. Unfortunately, passenger records for Johann Nise have not been found. Nevertheless, the balance of information suggests that Rosine's brother Johann (or John) Nise was the Iowa contact person for Gottfried and Rosine.

In early February 1883, Gottfried and Rosine's second child, son Gottfried Carl, died in Alfdorf. He was less than four months old. Their other child, daughter Carolina Rosine, was almost two years old when her brother died. Rosine and her daughter were most likely living with Rosine's birth family in Alfdorf.

Although they lived apart in separate countries and had lost their second child, Gottfried and Rosine Hinderer had a plan. Rosine and their daughter would emigrate to America and join Gottfried in Iowa. On August 4, 1883, 28-year-old Rosine Nise and her two-year-old daughter Carolina Rosine arrived in New York harbor aboard the steamship *Neckar*. It was less than one

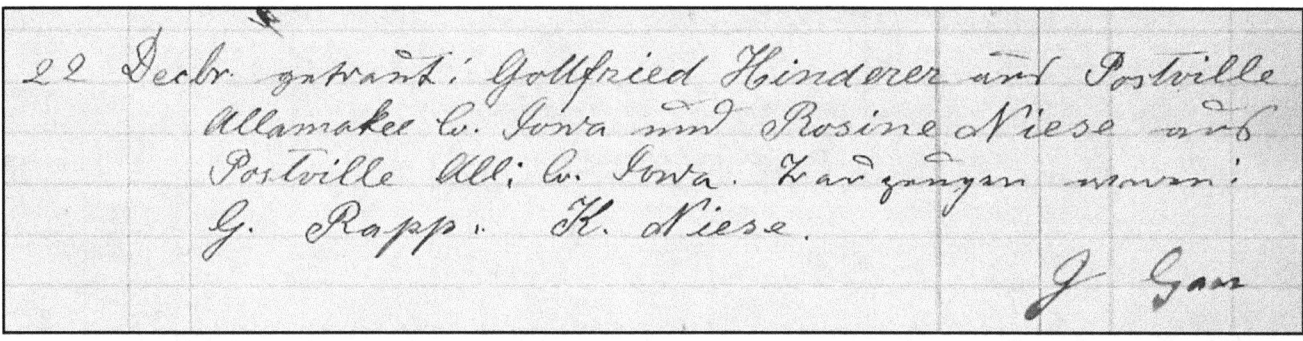

St. Paul Lutheran Church recorded the marriage of Gottfried Hinderer and Rosina Niese (Nise) on December 22, 1883. Both were said to be from Postville. Witness K. Niese (Nise) may have been Rosina's younger sister Carolina, a fellow passenger aboard the Neckar. Carolina is sometimes spelled Karolina. Source: St. Paul Lutheran Church registry. Photographed and edited by author.

year after Gottfried's arrival and six months after the death of their infant son. Rosine's 24-year-old younger sister traveled with them aboard the *Neckar*. This sister was also named Carolina and journeyed with Rosine and two-year-old Carolina Rosina to northeastern Iowa.[14]

On December 22, 1883, a little over four months after Rosine's arrival, Iowa state records document the marriage of Rosine Nise and Gottfried Hinderer. Their marriage took place in Postville, in Allamakee County. In this record, Gottfried was listed as a farmer from Postville. Their marriage was also recorded in the registry of St. Paul Lutheran Church of Postville.

Two years later, the 1885 Iowa state census identified Gottfried and Rosine living less than three miles south of Postville in Grand Meadow Township, Clayton County. There were no new children at the time of this census, but the household did include a domestic helper or "servant" in the language of the census. Rosine was recorded as "Rosa" on this census. Gottfried was listed as a laborer meaning he worked for someone else and did not own land. This 1885 Iowa census stated exactly where Gottfried and Rosine lived: the southeast quarter of section 17 in Grand Meadow Township, Clayton County, Iowa.

A plat map of Grand Meadow Township in Clayton County was printed at almost the same time as this 1885 Iowa Census. Each section in Grand Meadow township is numbered and is one mile square. Section 17 begins two miles south of Postville and extends south another mile. Gottfried's name is not found in section 17. This confirms that Gottfried Hinderer was not a landowner. The owner of the southeast quarter of section 17 where the family lived was Mr. William Larrabee.

The 1885 Iowa State Census identified Gottfried and Rosa (Rosine) together with their daughter Caroline and a domestic helper. Gottfried was a laborer and the family lived in the southwest quarter of Section 17, Grand Meadow Township, Clayton County. Source: "Iowa, U.S., State Census Collection, 1836-1925" online database (Provo, UT: Ancestry.com, 2007), accessed July 2021. Edited by author.

Katharine

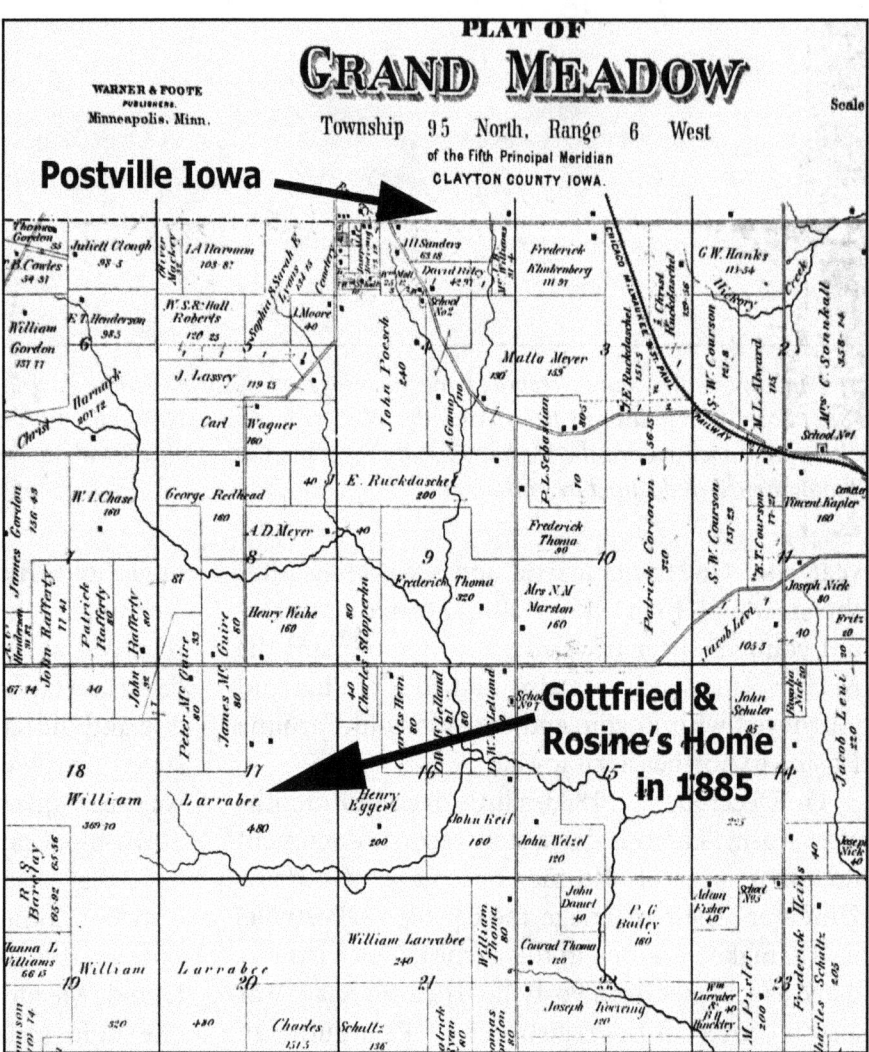

In 1885, Gottfried, Rosine, and daughter Carolina Hinderer lived on land owned by William Larrabee in section 17. Each numbered section is one mile square. Postville was between two and three miles north of their home. Source: "Iowa, U.S., State Census Collection, 1836-1925" online database (Provo, UT: Ancestry.com, 2007), accessed July 2021. Edited by author.

Ida Christine Pauline Hinderer was born in March of 1885 and baptized in July that year. The church record confirmed that in 1885, Gottfried and Rosine lived in Grand Meadow Township, Clayton County. Source: St. Paul Lutherna Church records. Photographed and edited by author.

Gottfried and Rosine's first child born in Iowa was named Ida. She was born in March 1885 and baptized in July that same year. Her baptismal entry in the St. Paul Lutheran Church registry confirms the family's location in 1885: Grand Meadow township of Clayton County.

In June 1887, two years after Ida's birth, another daughter was born to Gottfried and Rosine. Emma Christine Elisa's birth record in the St. Paul Lutheran Church registry stated the family now lived in Clermont Township. As was noted earlier, Clermont and Grand Meadow are adjacent townships in separate counties. Taken together, these documents indicate that between March 1885 and June 1887, Gottfried and Rosine moved their family a few miles west to Clermont Township in Fayette County. Clermont Township was also the location of the farm owned by Rosine's brother, Johann Nise.

By the time Gottlieb and Katharine Hinderer arrived in 1892, cousin Gottfried and his growing family had already moved to Clermont Township. The records show that Gottlieb and Katharine first lived in Grand Meadow Township, Clayton County. Having lived there only a few years earlier, cousin Gottfried likely helped the two new arrivals find housing and work in Grand Meadow Township.

An unusual twist in the story of Gottfried and Rosine concerns the spelling of their surname. Gottfried Hinderer became a naturalized citizen of the United States on November 1, 1886.[15] The record of his citizenship was unremarkable except his surname was spelled "Henderer" rather than Hinderer. Subsequent documents repeated this new spelling, suggesting the surname change was intentional. Furthermore, from 1900 on, all census documents indicate Gottfried and Rosine's surname was further shortened to "Hender." Records for their unmarried children dated after 1900 also list their surnames as Hender. The reason they changed their surname from Hinderer to Henderer and then Hender is unknown.

Gottfried and Rosine had seven children. Their last five children were all born in Iowa with the youngest, Henry, born in 1898. The 1900 U.S. Census found them still living in Clermont Township, Fayette County, Iowa.

The story of Gottfried and Rosine has one final twist. The 1910 U.S. Census listed them and their three youngest children living in Clay County in northwestern Minnesota. The exact date and reason for the move from Iowa to Minnesota is unknown.

In the 1910 census, Gottfried, Rosine, and their two youngest sons lived on a farm in Elmwood Township, Clay County, Minnesota.[16] As was the case in Iowa, Gottfried was listed as a farmer who rented his land. Their youngest daughter Lena Catherine, or "Katie," was also living in Elmwood Township. She was working as a domestic helper in the home of a family living near Gottfried and Rosine. The surname of all of the family members continued to be listed as Hender.

The "Henders" of Minnesota lived the remainder of their lives in Clay County. In the 1920 U.S. Census, Gottfried, Rosine, and their two sons still resided on a farm in Elmwood Township. By the time of this census, their daughter Katie had married Clarence Tebelman and had one son who was less than a year old.

Rosine Hender (Hinderer) died in September of 1922 in Clay County, Minnesota. Six years later in 1928, daughter Katie Tebelman became a widow due to the accidental death of her husband Clarence. The death of Clarence left Katie with three young sons to raise on her own. By the time of the 1930 U.S. Census, widow Katie Tebelman, her three sons, and her 73-year-old father Gottfried all lived in one household. They resided in the city of Barnesville, also in Clay County, Minnesota. By the time of the 1940 census, Katie's oldest son Donald had left home. Her two younger sons and her 82-year-old father still lived with her in Barnesville. Gottfried Hender (Hinderer) died on April 20, 1942, in Barnesville, Minnesota, at the age of 84. He is buried in Rosemound Cemetery, Barnesville, Minnesota.[17]

Gottfried Hinderer (later Hender) and Rosine Nise

Married 22 Dec 1883 in Postville, Iowa:

Gottfried Hinderer – b. 21 Aug 1857 in Cronhütte Wuerttemberg; d. 20 Apr 1942 in Barnesville, Clay County, MN.

Rosine Nise – b. 10 Jul 1855 in Alfdorf; d. 3 Sep 1922 in Clay County MN

Children:

Carolina Rosina – b. 16 Jun 1880 in Alfdorf; m. 14 Feb 1903 in Iowa; d. 4 May 1964 in Iowa

Gottfried Carl – b. 28 Oct 1882 in Alfdorf; d. 8 Feb 1883 in Alfdorf

Ida Christine Pauline – b. Mar 1885 in Iowa; d. 6 Jul 1927 in Clay County, MN

Emma Christine Elisa – b. 14 Jun 1887 in Iowa; d. 19 Apr 1966 in Iowa

Johann Karl Georg – b. 10 Jul 1890 in Iowa; d. 15 Jan 1960 in Clay County, MN

Catharine (Katie) Lena – b. 3 Nov 1893 in Iowa; m. in MN; d. Dec 1978 in Clay County, MN

Henry – b. Jul 1898 in Iowa; m. 18 Aug 1934 in MN; d. 21 Aug 1964 in Clay County, MN

The family of Gottfried and Rosine Hinderer (later Hender). The parents and four of their children had moved to Minnesota sometime between 1900 and 1910. Source: Compiled by author.

The 1910 U.S. Census listed Gottfried, Rosine, and two sons in Elmwood Township, Clay County, Minnesota. Their 16-year-old daughter "Katie" Hender was working as a domestic helper for their neighbors, the McCabes. Source: "1910 United States Federal Census" online database (Lehi, UT: Ancestry.com, 2006, accessed July 2021. Edited by author.

Gottlieb and Katharine Hinderer

Gottlieb and Katharine arrived in New York on December 23, 1891. Their journey to Iowa followed quickly. The first document locating them in Iowa was the county recording of their Postville, Iowa, marriage on February 5, 1892. Their arrival in Iowa may have been weeks or even a month earlier. The same marriage date, February 5, 1892, was recorded in the compiled marriage records for the state of Iowa.

A different date is written on a church marriage certificate. This second certificate was completed by a representative of St. Paul Lutheran Church in Postville, Iowa. Careful inspection of the church certificate reveals it has been altered. It falsely lists their marriage date as February 26, 1891. This marriage date is not possible because on that date, Gottlieb and Katharine had not yet arrived in America. The author of and reason for the falsification is open to speculation. The salient information is that the civil marriage record and the state compilation contain their true marriage date: February 5, 1892.

Like his cousin Gottfried, Gottlieb did not own land in Iowa. He either worked as a laborer on farms owned by others, or he rented farmland. Therefore, plat maps did not contain his name. His family's location can only be determined by census and church records.

Beginning in 1880, Iowa law required that counties keep vital records. The vital records included births, marriages, and deaths. However, county offices did not have the means to monitor citizens and enforce this regulation. In 2015, a search of both Clayton and Fayette County records failed to find civil birth records for any of Gottlieb and Katharine Hinderer's children. Once again, church and census records together with secondary records were the only resources available to document the children's birth dates and their location in Iowa.

Gottlieb and Katharine had seven children. The older children, four girls and one boy, were born in Iowa. Twins Martha and John were born after the family left Iowa and moved to Minnesota.

Christine (Christina or Tena) Katharine Hinderer was born on April 23, 1892, in Grand Meadow Township, Clayton County, Iowa. For most of her life, she was known to family and friends as Tena. The St. Paul Lutheran Church registry recorded Tena's baptism on August 28, 1892.

The county record of Gottlieb and Katharine's marriage had two parts. The upper half granted them a license to be married. The lower half documented their marriage on Feb. 5, 1892. Two different officials signed these two documents. The spelling of Gottlieb and Katharine's names varies. Source: County records for Allamakee County Iowa, Waukon, Iowa. Scanned with permission and edited by author.

This church certificate of marriage has been falsified. Both the "26" date and the "1891" year were added after scratching out original numbers. Source: From the author's collection.

Tena's birth in April of 1892 opens up speculation concerning the rift between her father Gottlieb and his father Johannes. Her birth date means that while living in Brend, Gottlieb and the family's domestic helper, Katharine Deininger, were a couple. This relationship would have occurred in the late summer and fall of 1891, and possibly earlier. At that time, Gottlieb's parents Johannes and Sophie were already planning to emigrate to Michigan. Katharine's pregnancy may have contributed to the contention between Gottlieb and his father.

Carl Jacob Hinderer was born on February 9, 1894. Like his older sister Tena, Carl was born in Grand Meadow Township, Clayton County, Iowa. He was baptized on August 26, 1894. Carl's second cousin, the daughter of Gottfried and Rosine Hinderer, was baptized on the same day.

The 1895 Iowa state census confirmed the family composition after Carl's baptism in late August 1894. The census did not list Sophie who was born in November 1895. The census page is not dated, but most census recordings are taken early in the year or mid-year. Although the census page is of poor quality, the Hinderer family names are visible. At the time of the 1895 census, Gottlieb and Katharine still lived in Grand Meadow Township, Clayton County.

Sophie Karoline Hinderer was born November 15, 1895 but was not baptized until October 9, 1897, nearly two years later. For unknown reasons, Gottlieb and Katharine delayed Sophie's baptism until after the birth of their fourth child, Emma. The baptism of these two sisters was listed in the order of their birth in the St. Paul Lutheran Church registry.

Emma Anna Hinderer was born February 10, 1897. The baptismal entry for the two sisters stated they were both born in Clermont Township (Fayette County). The older sister, Sophie Karoline, was born there in November 1895. As noted above, the 1895 Iowa state census taken in early or mid-1895 indicated the family still lived in Clayton County. The conclusion drawn is that Gottlieb and Katharine moved their family from Clayton

Gottlieb Hinderer and Katharine Deininger

Married 5 Feb 1892 in Postville, Iowa:

Gottlieb Hinderer – b. 15 Sep 1866 in Alfdorf; d. 25 Aug 1951 in Canby, Minnesota
Katharine Deininger – b. 14 Oct 1872 in Gehren; d. 19 Mar 1964 in Lac qui Parle Co., Minnesota

Children:

Christine (Christina or Tena) Katharine – b. 23 Apr 1892 in Clayton Co., Iowa; d. 10 May 1991 in Kanabec Co., Minnesota
Carl Jacob – b. 9 Feb 1894 in Clayton Co., Iowa; d. 29 Jan 1979 in Madison, Lac qui Parle Co., Minnesota
Sophie Karoline – b. 15 Nov 1895 in Fayette Co. Iowa; d. 25 Mar 1926 in Canby, Minnesota
Emma Anna – b. 10 Feb 1897 in Fayette Co., Iowa; d. 8 Oct 1990 in Canby, Minnesota
Maria (Mary) Clara Caroline – b. 12 May 1898 in Fayette Co., Iowa; d. 10 Jun 1981 in Dawson, Minnesota

Twins – b. 26 Dec 1906 in Lac qui Parle Co., Minnesota:

Martha Rosa Elizabeth – d. 19 Jul 2003 in Canby, Minnesota
John William David – d. 6 Apr 2003 in Canby, Minnesota

The family of Gottlieb and Katharine Hinderer with birth and death dates, and locations. Source: Compiled by author.

1895 Iowa Census
Grand Meadow Township, Clayton County

This low resolution image identified the Hinderer family in early 1895. They lived in Grand Meadow Township, Clayton County, Iowa. Source: "Iowa State Census, 1895" online database with images, Clayton image 374 of 1001; citing State Historical Society, Des Moines, FamilySearch, accessed August 2021, https://familysearch.org/ark:/61903/3:1:S3HT-6XMJ-S7?cc=1803957&wc=M612-2MS%3A145598201. Edited by author.

Katharine

> **Baptism - Tena Hinderer**
>
> Aug. 28. Christine Katharine <u>Hinderer</u>, born
> 23 Apr. '92, daughter of Gottlieb Hinderer and
> Catharine (born as) Deininger, Grand Meadow,
> Witness or sponsor: Christine Wegner.

The baptismal entry for Christine (Christina or Tena) Katharine Hinderer in the St. Paul Lutheran Church registry. Tena was born April 23, 1892, in Grand Meadow Township, Clayton County, Iowa. Source: St. Paul Lutheran Church registry. Photographed and edited by author.

> **Baptism - Carl Hinderer**
>
> Aug. 26. Carl Jacob <u>Hinderer</u>, son of Gottlieb
> Hinderer and Catharina (born as) Deininger,
> Witness or sponsor: Carl Wegner, Jacob Meyer.

Carl Jacob Hinderer was born February 9, 1894, and baptized August 26, 1894. Source: St. Paul Lutheran Church registry. Photographed and edited by author.

> **Baptisms - Sophie Karoline and Emma Anna**

The birth order listing for the October 9, 1897 baptisms of sisters Sophie Karoline and Emma Anna. Their birth dates and the location of their births (Clermont Township) were also stated. The witnesses or sponsors are in the far right column. Source: St. Paul Lutheran Church registry. Photographed and edited by author.

Timelines

Gottfried and Rosine	Gottlieb and Katharine
Oct 1882 Gottfried arrived in Iowa	
Aug 1883 Rosine arrived in Iowa	
Dec 1883 Married in Postville Iowa	
1885 Lived in Grand Meadow twp.	
1887 Lived in Clermont twp.	
	Dec 1891 Arrived in America
1885-1898 Five children born in Iowa	Feb 1892 Married in Postville Iowa
	Apr 1892 Tena born in Grand Meadow twp
	1894-1898 Four children born in Iowa
1900 Changed name to Hender. Still lived in Clermont twp. Iowa	1899 Lived in Minnesota
	1906 Twin children born in Minnesota
1910 Lived in Clay Co. Minnesota	
1922 Death of Rosine in Minnesota	
1942 Death of Gottfried in Minnesota	
	1951 Death of Gottlieb in Minnesota
	1964 Death of Katharine in Minnesota

Timelines for the Hinderer families in Iowa and then Minnesota. Gottfried arrived in Iowa earlier and remained living there longer. Eventually, both families moved to Minnesota. Source: Compiled by author.

County, Iowa, to Fayette County in mid-1895 before Sophie's birth that November.

Gottfried and Rosine Hinderer's family had made the same move from Clayton to Fayette County about ten years earlier. They did not move to Minnesota until after 1900. This means that for several years after 1895, the families of cousins Gottfried and Gottlieb both lived in Clermont Township, Fayette County, Iowa.

Maria (Mary) Clara Caroline Hinderer was born May 12, 1898, in Clermont Township, Fayette County, Iowa. Mary's birth record was not found in the St. Paul Lutheran Church registry in Postville, Iowa. It would have been unusual, but not unheard of, for parents to baptize all but one child. Mary's birth information was obtained from later Minnesota records that included her birth date and location.

The milestone events of the two Hinderer families are more easily understood when they are placed side by side in a timeline. Gottfried arrived in Iowa before Gottlieb and remained in Iowa after Gottlieb and Katharine moved to Minnesota.

Katharine's Hymnal

Gottlieb and Katharine did not arrive in America with many possessions. The wooden trunk displayed in Chapter 4 likely contained nearly all of their clothing and the few personal items they treasured. One such personal item was Katharine's hymnal. The hymnal was probably given to Katharine by her parents when she was confirmed in the Kaisersbach church in 1886. The hymnal was published in Stuttgart, the capital city of Wuerttemberg, one year before her confirmation.

After Katharine's death, her hymnal was passed along to her youngest son John Hinderer. John did not marry or have children of his own. When he was elderly, John passed the hymnal along to a nephew, Merlin Schlichting, who understood and spoke the language. Inside the front cover, the hymnal had a single hand-written page that Merlin was able to translate. This page was written by Katharine in a now-abandoned German writing style known as Kurrent. This writing style used letter characters that are not used in modern German or English writing.[18]

Chapter 3 discussed the Heinz family book of sermons. That book had several hand-written pages honoring several generations of Heinz family children. Katharine and her siblings were listed on a page that was most certainly written by her mother, Karoline Heinz.

Katharine followed her mother's example by charting the births of her own children in her hymnal. Katharine began with her own name followed by her children's names and birthdates. The two children born later in Minnesota are not on the page. This suggests the names in the hymnal were written during the years Katharine lived in Iowa: from Tena's birth in 1892 through Mary's birth in 1898.

The 1890s – Ruin and Recovery

During the years Gottlieb and Katharine lived in Iowa, important events changed the entire country. The decade of the 1890s was the height of the "gilded age" when monopolistic companies controlled entire industries. For their shrewd business success, a handful of tycoons gathered vast family fortunes. It was not until after the turn of the century that government regulation restored competition and economic balance.

The Panic of 1893 was an economic depression that damaged the lives of all citizens, including newly arrived immigrants. The decade of the 1880s had been a boom time for the upper Midwest and particularly the Dakotas in the northern part of the Great Plains. Railroads built new lines and settlers rushed in to populate these former Sioux Indian lands. When the 1893 depression began, banks, railroads, and markets collapsed, leaving settlers without cash or credit. Thousands of settlers fled from the Dakotas, but a few had no choice but to remain. They were too poor to move. Popular verses sung by these poor Dakotans went: "We

The Iowa Hinderers

The title page of Katharine's hymnal printed in 1885 in Stuttgart, Wuerttemberg. It is titled "Gesangbuch" which translates as hymnal. Source: Merlin Schlichting; edited by author.

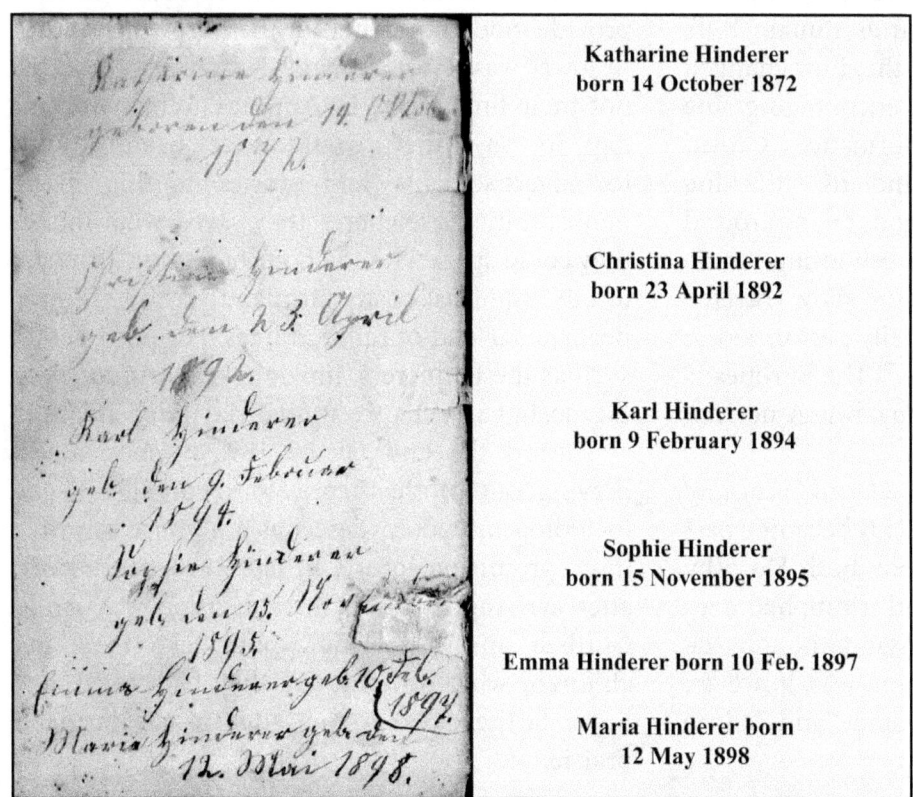

Katharine Hinderer
born 14 October 1872

Christina Hinderer
born 23 April 1892

Karl Hinderer
born 9 February 1894

Sophie Hinderer
born 15 November 1895

Emma Hinderer born 10 Feb. 1897

Maria Hinderer born
12 May 1898

Katharine used a blank hymnal page to list her own birth and the births of her five children born in Iowa. Source: Merlin Schlichting. Edited and translated by author.

do not live, we only stay; We are too poor to get away."[19]

The immediate cause of the Panic of 1893 was over-leveraged railroad companies that could not make payments to their lender banks, which in turn failed. Investors in American stocks began a run on gold. The precious metal was seen as a safer haven for their investment money than the failing railroad companies and banks.

Blame for this depression can also be placed on a contrary Mother Nature. Devastating drought in the late 1880s and early 1890s brought hardship throughout the Midwest: "In God we trusted, in Kansas we busted" went another saying. The native, more water-conserving, grasslands of the Great Plains had been plowed under, exposing bare dirt. The dirt quickly dried out and became clouds of choking dust. By 1892, the belief in an endless western frontier was gone, and with it the dreams of farmers and small town businessmen alike.

For some, the reality of widespread poverty was softened by escapism through drama and books. Fantasies of a western frontier were played out in the dramatic enactments known as Buffalo Bill's Wild West Show. Over the years, the show changed the featured scenes, thereby encouraging the audience to attend repeated performances. Crowd favorites included heartless Indians attacking settler cabins and buckboard wagons racing around the arena. A buckskin-clad sharpshooting Annie Oakley delighted the audience. The show traveled throughout America and eventually performed in England and continental Europe.[20] The Europeans were also captivated by the fiction of the American frontier.

L. Frank Baum's book *The Wonderful Wizard of Oz* was published in 1900 and quickly became a best seller. His imaginary tornado took both Dorothy and readers to a land where good triumphed over evil. The story was set in Kansas although the author had never been there. Baum was, however, personally familiar with bankruptcy and failure because he had suffered through the Dakota land bust.

In real life, caring for infants and children was frightening. Young mothers lived in fear their babies would not survive their first months and childhood years. Immigrant parents had no child-rearing experience and often no family nearby to consult when their children became ill. Communication by letter with their Wuerttemberg parents took at least a week in each direction. Cholera and other diarrheal illnesses commonly killed infants. Typhoid fever caused by contaminated well water killed both young and old. Consumption (tuberculosis) was the most common cause of death in young adults.[21] Most families lost one or several of their children before they reached adulthood. The average lifespan for someone born in 1890s America was about 50 years.

Having arrived in 1891, Gottlieb and Katharine experienced the 1893 depression firsthand. They had taken the risk of leaving Wuerttemberg with nothing of monetary value. The depression years of the early 1890s meant endless work was required to provide food and shelter for their growing family.

Iowa was Gottlieb and Katharine's first but not their final home in America. While working day to day, they would have been attuned to advertisements and stories touting grand opportunities elsewhere. They saved what money they could spare with the hope of finding farmland to buy. The least costly farmland was often found near the far end of railroad lines. For poor people such as the Hinderers, moving was seen not as an escape, but as a chance at financial independence.

Toward the end of the 1890s, America was moving out of the depression. For all citizens, including the poor, there was a glimpse toward a more promising future. In late 1898, seven years after arriving in Iowa, their decision was made. Gottlieb and Katharine would take their five children, what little money they had saved, and move farther west to the edge of the farmable prairie.

Notes

1. To locate Prairie du Chien, in Google Maps insert coordinates 43.046653, -91.138005 in the search box and click the search button.

2. The Blackhawk War of 1832 was an example of futile wars against takeover of Indian land by the U.S.

3. "The Path to Statehood," Iowa Pathways, Iowa PBS, accessed July 2021, https://www.iowapbs.org/iowapathways/mypath/path-statehood.

4. To locate Austin, in Google Maps insert coordinates 43.668007, -92.974082 in the search box and click the search button.

5. Wikipedia, s.v. "Pile-Pontoon Railroad Bridge," last modified May 31, 2024, 01:00 (UTC), https://en.wikipedia.org/wiki/Pile%E2%80%93Pontoon_Railroad_Bridge.

6. To locate Postville, in Google Maps insert coordinates 43.082246, -91.568075 in the search box and click the search button.

7. W. E. Alexander, *History of Winneshiek and Allamakee Counties, Iowa* (Sioux City, IA: Western Publishing, 1882), 408.

8. Wikipedia, s.v. "Postville, Iowa," last modified July 1, 2021, 02:51 (UTC), https://en.wikipedia.org/w/index.php?title=Postville,_Iowa&oldid=1031339766.

9. This robust number of attendees meant nearly the entire town was present.

10. "St. Paul's Evangelical Lutheran Church," IA Gen Web Project, accessed July 2021, http://iagenweb.org/allamakee/church/stpaul_hx.htm.

11. To locate the church, in Google Maps insert coordinates 43.082361, -91.567632 in the search box and click the search button.

12. To locate Cronhütte, in Google Maps insert coordinates 48.915660, 9.686817 in the search box and click the search button.

13. Rosina's surname is also spelled, Niess, Nice or Niss.

14. The page that listed these three people as passengers on the *Neckar* is extremely dark and could not be acceptably edited for display.

15. "U.S. Naturalization Record Indexes, 1791-1992" (online database) *Ancestry.com* (Provo, UT: Ancestry.com, 2010), accessed July 2021. Indexed in World Archives Project.

16. To locate Elmwood Township, Clay County, Minnesota, in Google Maps insert coordinates 46.761157, -96.610680 in the search box and click the search button.

17. To locate Rosemound Cemetery, in Google Maps insert coordinates 46.654230, -96.442380 in the search box and click the search button.

18. The information and provenance regarding Katharine's hymnal was provided by Merlin Schlichting

19. Caroline Fraser, *Prairie Fires—The American Dreams of Laura Ingalls Wilder* (New York: Henry Holt, 2017), 168.

20. Sarah J. Blackstone, *Buckskins, Bullets and Business, A History of Buffalo Bill's Wild West* (Westport CT: Greenwood Press, 1954), 1-9.

21. Thomas Goetz, *The Remedy* (New York: Gotham Books, 2014), 91.

Chapter 7

Minnesota — Land For Sale

Timeline

1849 – Minnesota became a Territory

1858 – Minnesota became the 32nd State

1862 – The Dakota Sioux were expelled from Minnesota

1865 – The American Civil War ended; Lincoln assassinated

1867 – John Wesley Powell explored the Grand Canyon

1869 – The first transcontinental railroad was completed

1869 – The first settler colony arrived in Lac qui Parle County

1870 – First settlers built homes in Canby

1871 – Yellow Medicine and Lac qui Parle counties were defined

1873–1878 – Locusts destroyed crops

1876 – The town of Canby was platted by the railroad

1876 – The Battle of the Little Bighorn

1888 – John Lund opened his land business in Canby

1890 – The Canby population was 470

1890 – The Wounded Knee Massacre ended the Indian Wars

1892 – Gottlieb and Katharine were married in Iowa

1893 – Fire destroyed Canby businesses

1898 – Gottlieb and Katharine arrived in Canby

This chapter describes the land that became Yellow Medicine and Lac qui Parle counties. It provides an understanding of the terrain, and the history of Indian and settler societies that lived in this part of southwestern Minnesota.

In the early 1840s, a Swiss geologist named Jean Louis Agassiz pieced together the glacial history of the borderlands between Minnesota and the Dakotas. He proposed that thousands of years earlier, a mass of glacial ice covered these borderlands. The glacier expanded northward covering all of mid-continental Canada.

By 14,000 BC, this mass of glacial ice extended as far south as today's Lac qui Parle County, Minnesota. Another lobe of glacial ice covered eastern Minnesota as far south as the Twin Cities.

By 12,000 BC, the climate had warmed, and most of Minnesota was free of ice. In western Minnesota, a meltwater lake replaced the glacial ice mass. This meltwater lake has been named Lake Agassiz to honor the geologist who helped describe it.

The natural drainage of Lake Agassiz was northward toward Hudson Bay. However, solid glacial ice still blocked that exit. The southernmost part of Lake Agassiz was periodically ice-free.[1] When the melting ice and debris at the south end of Lake Agassiz gave way, the lake's meltwater burst out as a torrential river. This river was called the Glacial River Warren. Its extreme flow volume carved out today's Minnesota River valley. At times of peak flow, the Glacial River Warren carried a larger volume of water than any river in North America today. Like today's Minnesota River, it eventually joined the Mississippi River and flowed south into the Gulf of Mexico.[2]

Today, the Minnesota River originates at the southern tip of Big Stone Lake near Ortonville,

Minnesota.³ This river continues in a southeastward direction as a series of small lakes. The final lake in the series is Lac qui Parle, "the lake that speaks." These gentle waterways are a trickle compared to their ice age parent—the Glacial River Warren.

You can still see a raised plateau of land that extends southward from Big Stone Lake. It is elevated a few hundred feet above the surrounding prairie. This plateau, called the Buffalo Ridge, is a remnant from the last ice age. When the ice dam at the southern end of Lake Agassiz burst open, mud, rocks, and boulders were forced southward by the water. Over time, these layers of flushed out solid material created this raised plateau. The Buffalo Ridge extends more than a hundred miles south, as far as the northwest corner of Iowa.

The southern part of Lake Agassiz and the Glacial River Warren outflow. Source: "Map Showing the Areas of Lake Agassiz and of the Upper Laurentian Lakes," in Warren Upham, The Glacial Lake Agassiz. Monographs of the U.S. Geological Survey, Vol. XXV (Washington, D.C.: GPO, 1895), plate III. Edited by author.

Indian Land – The Minnesota Story

In the early 1800s, there were two rival Indian tribes in Minnesota: the Sioux and the Ojibwe.⁴ The Ojibwe lived in northern Minnesota, southern Canada, Wisconsin, and around the Great Lakes. They spoke an Algonquian language that originated in Canada and the eastern U.S. They were a woodland society with a lifestyle based on hunting and trapping. The Ojibwe were particularly noted for their use of birch bark canoes and the cultivation of wild rice.

The Sioux tribal groups lived on the Great Plains and in Minnesota. They all spoke a Siouan language. The Sioux tribes on the Great Plains rode horses introduced by earlier Spanish explorers. Their lifestyle was centered on the buffalo herds. These Great Plains Sioux were known as the Lakota or Teton Sioux.

A separate Sioux tribal group lived in Minnesota and was known as the Dakota or Santee Sioux. These Minnesota Sioux had a woodland lifestyle more akin to the Ojibwe than the Lakota Sioux on the Great Plains. The Minnesota Sioux hunted and fished in the same waterways as the Ojibwe. The Minnesota and Mississippi rivers were transportation highways for both tribes. Rivalry over control of these waterways caused conflicts between the two tribes for hundreds of years.

The arrival of land-hungry settlers added yet another group competing for the use of Minnesota waterways and land.[5]

When settlers pushed into Minnesota early in the 19th century, there was no governmental body that regulated or recorded land ownership. Fort Snelling, at the juncture of the Minnesota and Mississippi rivers, was the only official U.S. government outpost. When these early settlers built cabins, cleared land, and began farming, they did not own the land. Technically, they were squatters on what the U.S. government termed "Indian land."

The root of the conflict between Indian and settler cultures was the concept of land ownership. Settlers, with their European origins, followed the idea of owning land with defined borders and rights. Indian cultures had no concept of owning land. They often competed and fought with one another for control of land. However, no individual Indian or tribal group had a document stating they owned a specific parcel of land. To these Indian tribes, land was simply a natural occurrence, like sunshine or rain.

After Minnesota achieved territorial status in 1849, the relationship between Indian and settler cultures in Minnesota rapidly deteriorated. The arrival of settlers restricted the hunting lifestyle of the Minnesota Sioux. They were forced to rely more heavily on trapping beaver and trading the pelts for food or cash. The pelts were in great demand to make fur hats for fashionable Europeans. By the mid-1800s, however, fur hats had declined in popularity. Although the market demand for beaver pelts dwindled, the Indians still needed food and cash. The local traders provided these necessities by extending credit to the Indians. By 1851, the Dakota Sioux in Minnesota were deeply in debt to the local traders.

In a series of treaties with the U.S. Government, the Dakota Sioux chiefs agreed to give up the rights to their fertile prairie lands in southern Minnesota. In exchange, the tribes received a cash payment of twelve cents an acre and were promised an annual stipend from the government. The treaties also restricted Sioux families to a narrow strip of land extending ten miles on either side of the Minnesota River. These treaties began the downward slide of Dakota Sioux culture in Minnesota. Economic necessity had forced the Sioux leaders to accept the Western concept of land ownership. Selling their tribal land implied they had originally owned it. Now, however, nearly all of their land belonged to the U.S. Government.

The former tribal land was quickly resold to eager settlers. By 1852, one year after the final treaty was signed, an estimated 20,000 new settlers arrived in Minnesota. During this same brief time, St. Paul grew from several hundred residents to 8,000.[6] The U.S. Census Bureau recorded the 1850 population of Minnesota at 6,077, all living in the southeastern corner. By 1860, a decade later and nine years after the treaty was signed, the Minnesota population was over 172,000. It was a 28-fold increase in one decade.[7]

Minnesota achieved statehood in 1858, two years before the U.S. presidential race of 1860. Abraham Lincoln's 1860 election was quickly followed by passage of the Homestead Act of 1862. This legislation promised 160 acres of government-owned land virtually free to new settlers. The only requirement was to live on the land for five years and begin farming. The Homestead Act of 1862 added to the Minnesota land rush.

President Lincoln did not witness the impact of the Homestead Act on the Dakota Sioux or the rush of settlers to Minnesota. The secession of southern states and early battles of the American Civil War required his attention. In 1862, his Union Army was losing the war.

In the early 1860s, Minnesota was the western edge of frontier settlements in the Midwest. The new state contributed troops in support of the Union Army. The attention of the country, however, was focused on the bloody Civil War battles. This anonymity of the Minnesota frontier ended with the Dakota War of 1862.

Although the 1851 treaty with the U.S. government promised them a yearly stipend, by 1862, the Dakota Sioux in Minnesota faced a crisis.

The annual cash stipend promised to them was no longer distributed to tribal members. Instead, the U.S. Bureau of Indian Affairs sent the cash payments to local traders. The logic behind this was that the Indians owed money to the traders, so the government money should be paid directly to these traders. This left the Sioux with no cash. Furthermore, the 20-mile-wide strip of tribal land along the Minnesota River did not provide enough game or wild rice to feed their families. New settlers were now living outside the boundaries of tribal territory. These recent settlers were not squatters. They owned their land and did not tolerate intrusions by Indians looking for game. In short, the Minnesota Dakota Sioux lacked cash to buy food and did not own enough land on which to grow or hunt for food. Their families were starving.

In August of 1862, a small band of young Dakota Sioux killed five settlers. Within weeks, other attacks on settlers occurred as far away as the Red River Valley in northwestern Minnesota. Within a month, Union troops were diverted from the Civil War and dispatched to end the Minnesota bloodshed. When the military forces arrived, the Dakota Sioux were quickly outnumbered and outgunned. In the end, an unknown number of Sioux and hundreds of settlers died.

After the fighting was over, the Indians were held accountable for their attacks. A military tribunal held in the fall of 1862 sentenced 303 Indians to death. President Lincoln reviewed the tribunal records and commuted the death sentence of all but 38 Indians. These 38 were hanged "en masse" in Mankato, Minnesota, in December 1862. Historically, it is still the largest mass execution in the history of the United States.

As a result of the 1862 War, the U.S. government expelled the Dakota Sioux from their narrow strip of land along the Minnesota River. This meant they were left with no remaining tribal land in Minnesota. Over subsequent years, tribal members returned and lived in scattered locations around the state. Nevertheless, 1862 was the end of the Dakota Sioux as a tribal society in Minnesota.

The 1862 banishment of the Dakota Sioux opened all of southwestern Minnesota to settlement. This included the land that later became Yellow Medicine and Lac qui Parle counties. Overall, in a span of only 15 years, the entire Minnesota homeland of the Dakota Sioux had been converted into land available for settlement.

THE SIOUX ON THE GREAT PLAINS

In the Dakota Territory west of the Minnesota border, the Indian vs. settler saga occurred later but had a similar outcome. Here, the Lakota Sioux were living on a vast tract of treaty-negotiated land extending from the Missouri River west to the Wyoming border. It included the Black Hills of South Dakota, considered by the U.S. government to be of little value for settlement. This assumption changed in 1874 when gold was discovered in the Black Hills. Thousands of miners illegally trespassed onto the Lakota land seeking their fortune in gold. The U.S. government did nothing to prohibit this illegal invasion.

By 1876, violent encounters between the illegal miners and the Lakota Sioux were commonplace. As had happened in Minnesota, federal troops were ordered to intervene and put an end to the violence. In June of 1876, subordinate army officer George Armstrong Custer led a battalion of 265 soldiers to their death. He recklessly attacked Chief Sitting Bull and 2,500 combined Sioux and Cheyenne warriors. Now known as the Battle of the Little Bighorn, this victory for Sitting Bull and the Lakota Sioux was short-lived. Although the Lakota were defending their rightful territory, they were ultimately forced to surrender their homeland to the U.S. military.

A few bands of Lakota Sioux warriors refused to surrender and escaped into Canada. Over the next decade, these warriors made sporadic forays south into the Dakotas, but they were never able to recapture their homeland.

Clashes between bands of Lakota Sioux and settlers ended in 1890. In late December, the U.S.

Cavalry massacred two hundred Lakota Sioux men, women, and children near Wounded Knee Creek in southwestern South Dakota. Like the Minnesota Sioux, the Lakota Sioux on the Great Plains lost their tribal lands.

The mass movement of settlers into the Dakota Territory did not wait for the final episode at Wounded Knee. By 1880, the U.S. government declared ownership of former Lakota Sioux land in the Dakota Territory. Tracts of this land were then given to railroad companies in exchange for laying track across Dakota. It was the standard formula: build railroad tracks first, and homesteading settlers would soon follow.

WATER IS WHAT MATTERS

The landscape and climate of the western part of the Dakota Territory was not like the tall-grass prairie land of Minnesota and Iowa. Instead, the western two thirds of Dakota Territory was part of the semi-arid Great Plains. The railroad companies, the politicians, and the land speculators chose to ignore this difference. For them, it was about political dealing and making money from land sales.

The U.S. Government debated how to divide the land in western Dakota Territory. Naturalist John Wesley Powell provided a voice of reason in this debate. His professional credentials were solid. By 1867, Powell had achieved scientific prominence by exploring and mapping the cavernous reaches of the Grand Canyon of the Colorado River. Importantly, he was also well versed in recorded annual rainfall amounts from throughout the Midwest and the West.

This was the era prior to mechanized water pumping, so rainfall was the only source of water for crops. Powell pointed out that the western part of the Dakota Territory was subject to drying winds and years of severe drought. In 1877, Powell delivered a speech to an audience of scientists arguing against selling Dakota land to homesteaders. He said the Dakotas and much of the West should only be used for large plots of grazing land.[8] Powell predicted that small homestead farms would fail. The politicians and land speculators dismissed Powell and his prediction as lacking "vision."

Traditionally, wheat was the primary cash crop grown on early Midwest farms. In the eastern U.S., farmers grew a "soft" wheat, which was readily milled into flour. In the Midwest, however, farmers could grow only "hard" wheat varieties. In the late 1870s, a new milling process was engineered that milled the "hard" Midwestern wheat into a marketable commodity. New railroad lines across the Dakotas could transport the wheat to milling companies in St. Paul, Milwaukee, and Chicago.

By the late 1870s, three accomplishments set the stage for expansion across the Dakotas. First, former Lakota Sioux land was available for settlement. Second, railroad companies had begun laying track westward on government-granted land. Finally, hard wheat from Midwest farms was a marketable commodity. What was needed were homesteaders.

Speculators wildly promoted the Dakota lands with fictitious claims of abundant waterways and uniformly fertile soil awaiting the homesteader's plow. The inflow of new settlers was dramatic. In 1870, the settler population of today's South Dakota was estimated to be 11-12,000. By 1880, the population was 98,000. Five years later in 1885, it was 263,000. During the 15 years, from 1870 to 1885, railroad track miles in South Dakota increased from zero to 2,456, and the number of towns grew from 6 to 213.[9]

Between 1878 and 1880, the earliest settlers followed the new railroad lines and homesteaded the more productive eastern third of the Dakotas. In the fall of 1880, the vagaries of winter weather on the prairie caught these first settlers by surprise. From October of 1880 through the early summer of 1881, relentless snowstorms enveloped the Dakotas and western Minnesota.

The early settlers on the edge of the frontier depended entirely on the railroads to deliver supplies, including their food. By mid-winter 1880, supply trains could not pass through the deep snowdrifts. Railroad companies hired crews from nearby towns to hand-shovel the snow off the tracks. Their handwork was only effective until the next storm buried the track under drifted snow. In the end, these early Dakota families were marooned with no trains to bring them food or supplies.

In the eastern Dakota town of De Smet, the birth family of Laura Ingalls Wilder narrowly survived the 1880 winter. They shared their thin-walled wooden home with another family. The story of their near starvation was the basis of Wilder's fictional work *The Long Winter* written later in her life.

Ten miles east of the Dakota border, the snowstorms of 1880 isolated the frontier village of Canby, Minnesota. Canby's main street was covered by 10 to 15 feet of snow. Residents exited two-story buildings by crawling out of upper story windows directly onto snowbanks. Some residents dug into snowbanks hoping to find wooden fence posts. The posts could be cut and used as fuel to heat their homes. Yellow Medicine County historian Arthur Rose wrote in 1914: "There never was a winter to compare with this one [1880] in duration, continued severity, depth of snow, and damage to property."[10] Snowmelt in the early summer of 1881 caused historic flooding of the Minnesota River. It was reminiscent of the outburst events of the Glacial River Warren.

After the notorious winter of 1880-1881, railway construction continued westward covering the entire Dakota Territory. These new railway lines brought eager farmers to the western part of the Dakotas. What the government, the railroads, and the new farmers on the Great Plains could not control, however, was rainfall.

The 100th Meridian was the approximate dividing line cutting through the Dakotas. Meridians are imaginary lines extending from the North Pole to the South Pole. Dakota land located east of the 100th Meridian was farmable except during years of severe drought. Land located west of the 100th Meridian received insufficient reliable rainfall to raise crops. The 100th Meridian was an artificial line, but it was a useful guide to successful farming without irrigation.

The principal of the 100th Meridian was proposed during the time preceding mechanical water pumping. John Wesley Powell could not have foreseen the invention of mechanical water pumps. At first, these new mechanical systems were thought to be the solution to unreliable rainfall west of the 100th Meridian.

Windmills were the first mechanical systems to pump water. For small farmers, they became affordable late in the 19th century. Across the Dakotas, windmills pumped groundwater for families and livestock. However, windmills could not pump sufficient water to irrigate large fields of cropland.

In the early 20th century, the development of engine-powered pumps changed irrigation practices once again. Engine power gave farmers access to a deep underground water source: the Ogallala aquifer. This vast aquifer of fresh water extended from South Dakota southward into Texas and New Mexico.

The ability to pump water from the Ogallala aquifer ultimately lead to the invention of center-pivot irrigation systems. Introduced in the 1950s, these rotating wheels of water pipelines distributed Ogallala water over the farmland surface. With center-pivot systems, the semi-arid Great Plains became dotted with 100-acre circles of green cropland.

The miracle of green cropland in a near-desert did not last long. By the 1980s, so much water had been pumped from the Ogallala aquifer that wells in South Dakota and Texas were going dry. The Ogallala aquifer's recharge rate using surface rainfall is exceedingly slow, in some areas only a few one-hundredths of an inch per year. Because of over-drafting the aquifer, the prediction of naturalist John Wesley Powell 100 years earlier reemerged as a truth: successful farming in semi-arid land has a short life expectancy.

Yellow Medicine and Lac Qui Parle Counties

When Minnesota achieved statehood in 1858, Yellow Medicine and Lac qui Parle County lands were part of larger territorial counties. At first, they both belonged to Blue Earth County, then later to Brown County, and in 1865 both became part of Redwood County. It was not until 1871 that Yellow Medicine and Lac qui Parle county lands achieved official county status with modern boundary lines.[11]

In the summer of 1869, a wagon train with twenty-two Norwegian families caravanned from Iowa to Minnesota in search of cheap land. They came from Fayette and Winneshiek counties in northeastern Iowa. Known as the Jacobson party, these pioneer families traveled in canvas-covered wagons, drawn by oxen. They followed rough trails, and when necessary forged new pathways overland. They passed through Austin, Minnesota, and then the small village of Mankato, located at a sharp bend along the Minnesota River. Thirty miles upstream from Mankato, they rendezvoused with members of their scouting party at Ft. Ridgley.[12] From the fort, the wagon train continued upstream along the south bank of the Minnesota River until they reached the lake known as Lac qui Parle. There they found land with enough timber to build cabins prior to the onset of winter storms. These twenty-two families from northeastern Iowa formed the first colony of settlers in Lac qui Parle County, Minnesota.[13] Their 1869 journey was thirty years before Gottlieb and Katharine Hinderer arrived in Canby, Minnesota.

Lac qui Parle, "the lake that speaks," was the name that was given to the county's namesake lake by the French explorer Nicollet. This mile wide and ten-mile-long lake is actually a widening of the Minnesota River. The oral history of the native Indians described the echoing sound of waves as they broke against shoreline rocks during storms. To them, it was as if the lake were "speaking."[14]

Yellow Medicine County's name came from the root of a plant growing along the shore of the Yellow Medicine River. The native Sioux used this root for medicinal purposes. Translated into English, the Dakota Sioux spoken word for this root was "Yellow Medicine."

In both counties, settlement began in the east near the Minnesota River and proceeded westward toward the Dakota border. Three years after the Dakota War of 1862, the first settlers arrived in the eastern part of what became Yellow Medicine County. The Canby area in western Yellow Medicine County did not record any settler residents until 1870. The Jacobson party arrived in eastern Lac qui Parle County in 1869.

Although both counties were officially recognized in 1871, the location of both county seats changed over time. County seat designation was coveted by newly organized villages. It assured a reliable business base for the town regardless of economic cycles. In both counties, the villages that were home to the first few settlers simply declared themselves to be the county seat. In both counties however, these first villages eventually lost out to towns that experienced a more robust population growth.

In Lac qui Parle County, a band of Norwegians led by "King Jake," a Jacobson brother from the original Jacobson party, hijacked the county seat building. On a wintery November night in 1886, they physically moved the county office building from tiny Lac qui Parle City to their own town, Madison. Madison's rival villages, Lac qui Parle City and nearby Dawson, were left empty-handed.[15] In Yellow Medicine County, Granite Falls ultimately secured county seat designation after prolonged political squabbling with rival towns.

Towns and villages captured the greatest attention of historians who recorded early growth in the two counties. However, the majority of

In 1886, Madison resident "King Jake" Jacobson and a band of Norwegians hijacked the Lac qui Parle County building from Lac qui Parle City to Madison. "King Jake" Jacobson is standing on top of the building holding the American flag. Source: Access to this image courtesy of the Lac qui Parle County History Center. Photographed and edited by author.

early settler families lived solitary lives on farms scattered across the open prairie. These farmers built shanty homes for their families and straw barns for their animals. The natural landscape in both counties was part of the tall grass prairie, and nearly all of this land was suitable for farming. The new settlers were quick to plow the land and plant crops. At that time, sowing and harvesting was done manually. Any farming "implements" they owned were mechanically simple, and were powered by horses, mules, or oxen.

The successful early farmers struck a fine balance between the types of crops they planted. Corn and grass crops were meant to feed farm animals. Their animals provided settler families with food: milk, meat, and eggs. The key was to plant only enough corn and hay to feed their animals. All remaining tillable land was planted in wheat. A small amount of the harvested wheat was kept as seed for the next spring. Another small portion was milled into flour used to bake goods for the family. All remaining wheat was a cash crop sold at market price. The sale money was needed to buy dry goods and farm supplies.

Every successful farmer planted a large family garden. The gardens supplied fresh produce during the summer and fall. Gardens also produced root crops that were preserved in earthen cellars. Potatoes and root vegetables sustained families during the long Minnesota winters.

Many farmers in southwestern Minnesota lost the struggle for financial survival between the years 1873 and 1878. The problem began in June of 1873 when a dark cloud was first seen over the summer sky. It moved slowly, eventually blanketing the countryside. The cloud was a swarm of locusts so thick their combined weight broke tree branches, and their bodies were stacked up to a foot thick on the ground. Farmers fired guns and tried burning the insects, but nothing drove them off. The locusts moved on only when they had consumed every green plant in sight.

Some farmers reckoned that the June 1873 locust swarm was a fluke of nature. Unfortunately, this was not the case. What the settlers did not understand was that the locust swarms had laid their eggs in the fields, ready to repeat the cycle the following year.

The summer of 1875 witnessed the largest swarm of locusts ever recorded in human history. It eventually moved over every state from Texas to the Dakotas, and into Saskatchewan, Canada. The main swarm was estimated to be 110 miles wide, 1,800 miles long and up to a quarter mile thick.[16]

Settlers' plans for golden fields of wheat and bountiful gardens vanished.

After 1875, the crop destruction by locusts gradually declined. The reason for the decline was unknown. Some speculated it was due to greater rainfall in the spring and summer. Others theorized an unknown parasite had infected the locust eggs and prevented them from hatching. Regardless, the geographic pattern of infestation became patchy, so fewer farmers were affected. By 1878, five years after it began, the plague of locusts ended. In Yellow Medicine and Lac qui Parle counties, the locust years financially ruined many of the earliest settlers. The dollar value of farmland and the number of land sales sharply declined.

Canby and the Winona & St. Peter Railroad Company

In 1872, John Swenson attached a storefront to his claim shanty on the prairie land of western Yellow Medicine County. His plan was to become a merchant and sell supplies to fellow settlers. Swenson's tiny storefront was the first business in what would become the town of Canby, Minnesota.

Two years later in 1874, the enterprising Swenson suggested his store could also serve as a post office. Establishing a new post office required that the town have a name, and Swenson again took the lead. He suggested "Canby" in honor of recently deceased General Edward Canby. The general had been killed during the Modoc Indian Wars in Northern California. At the time of its official naming, Canby was a one-building one-man town.[17]

In 1872, the same year that Swenson established his storefront, the Winona & St. Peter Railroad Company[18] finished laying tracks as far west as Marshall, Minnesota.[19] Marshall is located thirty miles southeast of Canby in neighboring Lyon County.

A year later in 1873, the same railroad company laid tracks through western Yellow Medicine County, passing within hailing distance of John Swenson's Canby storefront. The railroad company's goal was to extend their tracks into the Dakotas. Watertown, South Dakota, was meant to be the next station along their extension westward.

In 1873, land along the tracks between Marshall and Canby was sparsely populated by homesteading families. There was insufficient freight and passenger traffic to justify a regularly scheduled train. For three years after its construction, the only rail traffic beyond Marshall was an engine and an empty caboose. This "train" ran once each Saturday without freight or passengers. The reason for this odd schedule was bureaucratic. At that time, the U.S. government required that railroads receiving free land grants were to have at least one scheduled train run each week. The engine and empty caboose allowed the Winona & St. Peter to achieve regulatory compliance.[20]

The storefront built by John Swenson in 1872. When built, it was the only business in Canby, and Swenson was the only resident. Source: Arthur P. Rose, "An Illustrated History of Yellow Medicine County, Minnesota (Marshall, MN: Northern History Publishing), 108, accessed October 2021, https://www.familysearch.org/library/books/records/item/791078-an-illustrated-history-of-yellow-medicine-county-minnesota. Edited by author.

Katharine

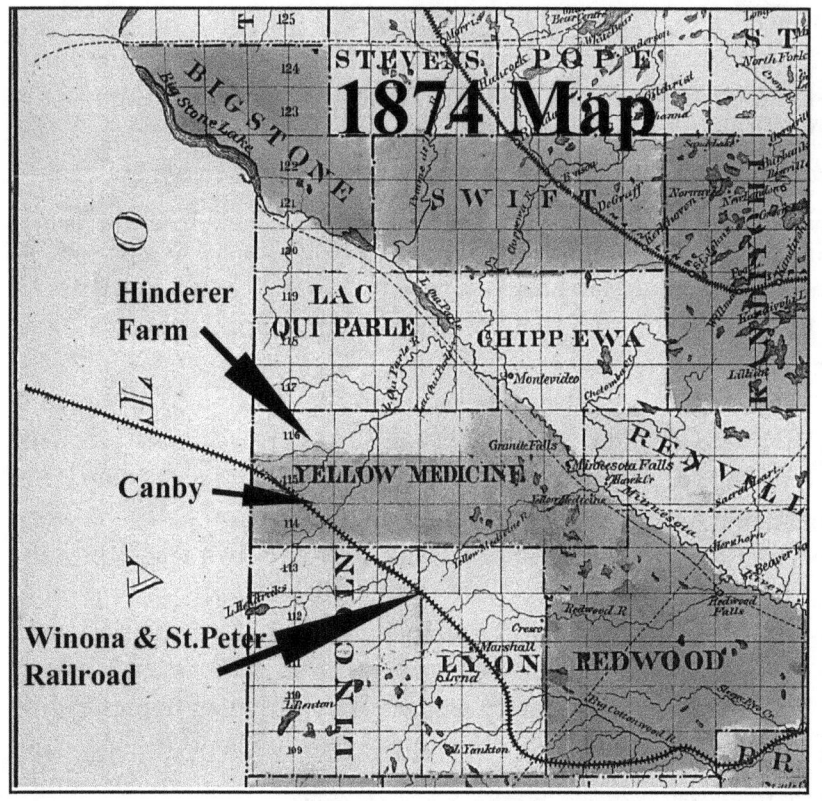

This 1874 map included the new Winona & St. Peter track from Marshall, MN through Yellow Medicine County and on into Dakota Territory. Arrows identify the location of Canby and the future Hinderer farm. Source: "Township and Railroad Map of Minnesota Published for the Legislative Manual" (St. Paul, MN: A. J. Reed, Lithograph, 1874), Library of Congress, accessed September 27, 2021, https://www.loc.gov/item/98688501/. Edited by author.

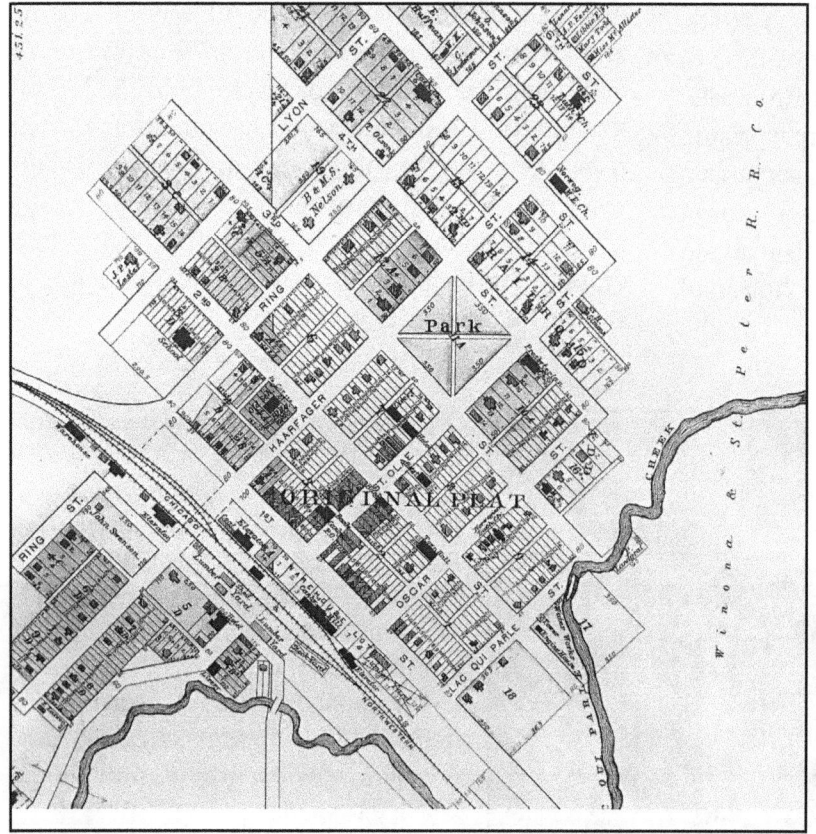

This 1900 plat map of Canby included the railroad tracks and parallel streets dead-ending at the tracks. The original 1876 street names remained the same in 1900 and even today. Source: Image access courtesy of the Canby Depot Museum. Photographed and edited by author.

The interconnection of government land policy, railroad companies, and settlers held true in western Minnesota as elsewhere. The U.S. government declared ownership of Sioux land in Minnesota after the 1862 war. Government land grants were issued to railroad companies if they laid track westward. The railroads laid the track, built towns, and sold the excess land to settlers. Profit from the land sales enriched the railroad's shareholders and financed laying more track. It was a system that expanded railroads, built towns, and populated the land.

In the second half of the 1800s, railroads controlled the location of towns. They also mapped the layout, called platting, of new towns along their lines. Towns were focal points where settler farmers could buy merchandise and also ship out their harvests. Canby, like most railroad towns, was conceived and platted by the railroad that ran through it. For Canby, that railroad was the Winona & St. Peter Railroad Company.

Railroad towns like Canby were laid out in a T-shape with a small number of parallel streets dead-ending at the railroad tracks. Canby's original 1876 plat map included familiar street names that ended at the railroad tracks: Ring, Haarfager, St. Olaf, Oscar, and Lac qui Parle. The cross streets running parallel to the tracks were named using a number sequence. First Street was usually the street nearest the railroad tracks.

Lots in Canby were sold by the Winona & St. Peter railroad to any interested party. A provision of the sale was that a building or home must be under construction within six months of purchase. By December of 1876, the same year Canby was platted, new merchants had arrived. They purchased lots and began construction. By the end of 1877, John Swenson's store and post office had been joined by businesses selling dry goods, groceries, hardware, furniture, lumber, and farm supplies. The village of Canby was thriving. Early Canby had a distinctly Scandinavian populace. A journalist from Granite Falls in eastern Yellow Medicine County later quipped: "The population here [in Canby] is all Norwegian except four Germans and one American."[21]

Canby was incorporated as a village in 1879, one year after the last locust plague. By 1881, Canby had the appearance of a typical frontier town. Hotels, saloons, a bank, and other businesses had been added to the merchant buildings "downtown." Beyond these downtown businesses, merchants and town workers bought lots and built homes for their families. Churches and schools soon followed.

The growth of Canby during the 1880s was accompanied by a renewed interest in nearby farmland. After the years of locust swarms and the brutal winter of 1880-1881, settlers were again attracted to the area. As farm production improved, the market value of farms and unplowed prairie land increased.

John Lund was a prominent figure in the history of Canby. He also played a key role in the 1898 Hinderer land acquisition. Lund arrived with his parents in 1876, the same year the Winona & St. Peter railroad platted out the town. His father built a general merchandise store, becoming one of the first businessmen in Canby.

In 1888 at the age of twenty, John Lund married a local girl and opened his Canby land-brokerage business. He soon became the most well-known land agent in the area. In 1889, one year after opening his business, "Land Lund" brokered the sale of over 60,000 acres of land. The local newspaper wrote: "It [he] has done more to build up Canby and the area and the country at large than can be described in words."[22]

In Yellow Medicine County as elsewhere, the U.S. government transferred the ownership of odd-numbered sections of prairie land to the railroad company. These "land grant" sections included parcels up to twenty miles on either side of the actual railroad tracks. Railroad companies like the Winona & St. Peter created internal departments tasked with selling this excess land. Independent agents like John Lund made their living linking the railroad company land sellers with the arriving settlers looking for land to buy.

CANBY AT TWO YEARS OLD. Canby became an incorporated village in 1879 by a legislative act. On March 8, the first village officers were elected. They included John Swenson, president; Gustave Erickson, E. P. LeSuer, and John P. Arnott, trustees; H. C. Westby, recorder; O. N. Lund, treasurer; John Moor, justice; and L. C. Mosier, constable. This picture is believed to have been taken in 1881 when Canby was two years old from the top of

This 1881 panorama (above and to the right) and its original caption captured the frontier-town look of two-year-old Canby. Businesses lined the main street with homes in the distance. Source: Image access courtesy of the Canby Depot Museum. Photographed and edited by author.

For the most part, new families arrived in Canby by train. John Lund personally greeted these prospective buyers at the Canby station. He dressed outlandishly like a uniformed bandleader and blew a cornet to gain attention to his sales pitch. He hired local horse and rig owners to transport the prospective buyers to his Canby business office. These same temporary assistants then drove Lund's clients out into the countryside to view parcels of available land.

Lund's circus-like tactics worked. Within a few years, he had opened land sales offices in South Dakota, North Dakota, and Iowa. In 1891, he began construction of a palatial Victorian-style mansion on the corner of St. Olaf and Fourth in Canby.[23]

In the mid-1890s, Lund's interests expanded into politics. By 1898, the year the Hinderers arrived, he was the mayor of Canby. After the turn of the century, he sold his mansion in Canby and moved his land business headquarters to the Twin Cities. By 1905, he had been elected to the Minnesota legislature and was considered a front-running candidate for governor.

Lund's legendary climb to fame in Minnesota ended in 1908. During that year he suffered a deep depression following the death of his wife in the Twin Cities. His anguish was compounded by a disastrous land deal that left this former millionaire bankrupt. In April of 1908, he took his own life at the age of forty.[24]

The 1890s witnessed another pivotal event in the history of Canby. On the evening of September 8, 1893, a man refueling a kerosene lantern inside a meat market ignited a wind-swept firestorm that raged through downtown Canby. The town had no water delivery system to put out the fire. The destruction of Canby's downtown was near total; every store along the main business street was lost.

The resilient Canby business community began to rebuild immediately after the fire. The conflagration had served notice that wooden buildings built one against another were an invitation to destruction by fire. Within months, reconstruction of downtown businesses had begun using fireproof bricks and stone. Temporary wooden structures were permitted only if they were to be soon replaced by fireproof materials. By the second year following the fire, nearly the entire business district had been rebuilt.[25]

the Winona and St. Peter Railroad wind pump tower. It was presented to the Canby Open Hand Lodge 65 of the Independent Order of Odd Fellows by Judge Ole Hartwick, a renowned Yellow Medicine County figure who began learning law under John P. Arnott while serving as recorder, marshal, and deputy sheriff in Canby. In 1886, he was elected clerk of the court, taking office on January 1, 1887. Judge Hartwick died in 1945.

Looking west over Canby's business district following the 1893 fire. The large building standing in the right background was a schoolhouse. Source: Image access courtesy of the Canby Depot Museum. Photographed and edited by author.

Looking east over Canby's business district. Residents of Canby inspect the destruction caused by the 1893 fire. Source: Image access courtesy of the Canby Depot Museum. Photographed and edited by author.

This postcard image from the early 1900s looks northward along St. Olaf Avenue, now Highway 75. The brick and stone construction is evident. Note that the street is unpaved. Both horse-drawn and motorized vehicles were in use. Source: From the John Hinderer postcard collection. Edited by author.

The family of Gottlieb and Katharine Hinderer moved from northeastern Iowa to Canby, Minnesota in 1898. It was 35 years after the Sioux had been banished from Minnesota and eight years after the final battle of the Indian Wars on the Great Plains. By this time, the village of Canby was nearly 20 years old. The town's downtown businesses had been rebuilt after the destructive fire five years earlier. By any measure, it was a time of optimism and opportunity. By 1898, competing railroads crisscrossed the western Minnesota and Dakota countryside. With clear evidence of prosperity all around, time was growing short for settlers wanting to purchase cheap railroad land.

Notes

1. To locate the southern extent of what was once Lake Agassiz, in Google Maps insert coordinates 45.375302, -96.520844 in the search box and click the search button.

2. Guy Gibbon, *Archaeology of Minnesota: The Prehistory of the Upper Mississippi River Region* (Minneapolis: The University of Minnesota Press, 2012), 45.

3. To locate Ortonville, in Google Maps insert coordinates 45.304276, -96.445395 in the search box and click the search button.

4. There are several acceptable spellings for Ojibwe. This tribal group is also referred to as the Chippewa.

5. David Schlichting, *Hinrich: Annals of an Immigrant Family, 1866-1913* (Chico, CA: Memoir Books, 2015), 70.

6. Ray Allen Billington, *Westward Expansion: A History of the American Frontier*, 6th ed. (Albuquerque: University of New Mexico Press, 2001), 122.

7. J. A. Wheelock and William B. Dana, "Progress of Population in Minnesota" (*Merchants' Magazine and Commercial Review*, August 1982), Northern Illinois University Digital Library, accessed June 2024, https://digital.lib.niu.edu/islandora/object/niu-twain%3A10922.

8. Caroline Fraser, *Prairie Fires—The American Dreams of Laura Ingalls Wilder* (New York: Henry Holt, 2017), 94-99.

9. James Fredrick Hamburg, *The Influence of Railroads Upon the Process and Patterns of Settlement in South Dakota* (New York: Arno Press, 1981), 4.

10. Arthur P. Rose, *An Illustrated History of Yellow Medicine County Minnesota* (Marshall MN: Northern History Publishing, 1914), 123.

11. Rose, *An Illustrated History*, 87.

12. To locate Ft. Ridgley, in Google Maps insert coordinates 44.454424, -94.734653 in the search box and click the search button.

13. L. R. Moyer and O. G. Dale, *Chippewa and Lac qui Parle Counties Minnesota—Their People, Industries and Institutions, Volume 1* (Indianapolis, IN: B. F. Bowen & Company, 1916), 411-15.

14. Lac qui Parle County, Minnesota: http://genealogytrails.com/minn/lacquiparle/history_county.html. Accessed October, 2021.

15. For the story of "King Jake" Jacob Jacobson, see Curt Brown, "'King Jake,' Norwegian-born Minnesotan, Reigned in Lac qui Parle," *Star Tribune*, July 8, 2018, 5:37 p.m., CDT, https://www.startribune.com/king-jake-norwegian-born-minnesotan-reigned-in-lac-qui-parle/433354283/. Accessed November 22, 2021.

16. Fraser, *Prairie Fires*, 70-77.

17. "Town History—Canby," Genealogy Trails, accessed October 2021, http://genealogytrails.com/minn/yellowmedicine/history_towncanby.html.

18. The Winona and St. Peter Railroad Company later became a part of the Chicago & Northwestern System.

19. To locate Marshall, Minnesota, in Google Maps insert coordinates 44.448250, -95.783344 in the search box and click the search button.

20. Rose, *An Illustrated History*, 108.

21. Ibid., 191.

22. *Canby News*, August 18, 1893.

23. The house stands today at St. Olaf (Highway 75) and Fourth St. It is known as the Lund-Hoel House and is operated as a historical museum of Canby and the surrounding region.

24. The story of John Lund, his house, and his place in Canby history is retold in the museum booklet: *Centennial Celebration History Booklet, 1891–1991* compiled by MECCA, the historical agency operating the Lund-Hoel House Museum.

25. Carl and Amy Narvestad, *A History of Yellow Medicine County, Minnesota: 1872–1972* (Granite Falls, MN: Yellow Medicine County Historical Society, 1972), 315-16.

Part II

The Minnesota-Born Family
(In Birth Order)

NAME	BIRTH	MOTHER
John Hinderer	Dec. 1906	Katharine
Doris Lafere	Apr. 1919	Emma
Johnny Krug	Aug. 1919	Sophie
Ray Engstrand	May 1920	Mary
William Krug	May 1922	Sophie
Don Engstrand	Jul. 1922	Mary
Norma Engstrand	Aug. 1924	Mary
Maurine Krug	Jan. 1925	Sophie
George Monson	Oct. 1926	Tena
Ruth Engstrand	Nov. 1927	Mary
Deloris Krug	Apr. 1928	Emma
Leonard Krug	Aug. 1929	Emma
Mabel Monson	Aug. 1929	Tena
Bette Krug	May 1931	Emma
Florence Krug	Dec. 1932	Emma
Jeanette Krug	May 1934	Emma
Bob Monson	Sep. 1934	Tena

Storytellers

INTRODUCTION

This second section follows the life of the Hinderer family after they arrived in Minnesota and settled on their Lac qui Parle County farm.

The story begins with their purchase of unplowed prairie land. It continues through the early years when the Hinderer children were living at home and contributing their labor to the well-being of the family. It then traces the lives of these children. Four daughters left the home farm to begin their own families. The remaining three siblings lived on the home farm nearly their entire lives.

As in earlier chapters, documents and images are used to authenticate the information that is presented. In addition, this second section benefits from the recollections of family members and others who had direct experience with the Hinderer family. In each case, these "storytellers" graciously provided their many recollections, adding personal memories to the family story.

The interviews were conducted between the years 2000 and 2005. The transcripts of the interviews were validated by each storyteller.

Much of the Minnesota Hinderer story was either inspired by, or depended entirely on, these family storytellers. The second section begins with brief profiles of the storytellers, including their connection to the Hinderer family.

THE STORYTELLERS

John Hinderer. John and his twin sister Martha were born in Minnesota in late December 1906. They were the youngest of Gottlieb and Katharine's seven children. John was interviewed in 2000 when he lived at Sylvan Place, a senior living facility in Canby, Minnesota. His sharp memory brought into focus the early family details and the chronology of events during the first half of the 1900s. John's contributions are essential to the Hinderer story.

Doris Schlichting. Doris (Lafere) Schlichting was born in 1919, the first child of Emma Hinderer. When Emma's first husband, Ralph Lafere, abandoned them, Emma and infant Doris returned home to the Hinderer farm. Doris was raised by her Hinderer grandparents until her middle teens when she moved to Canby and attended high school. Her window of time on the farm made her a witness to pivotal family events. She recalled the death of her Aunt Sophie and the subsequent marriage of her mother Emma to Sophie's widower husband, Martin Krug. As the oldest member of a new generation, Doris was both a family member and an observer of this complex mixture of siblings, half siblings, and cousins.

George, Mabel, and Bob Monson. These three children of Tena Hinderer and John Monson all provided interviews or written recollections. The stories told to them by their mother Tena revealed the extraordinary hardship of her early life on the Hinderer farm. Their father John Monson's years of farming the rocky terrain of Kanabec County, Minnesota meant a lifetime of hard labor for him as well. They composed a tightly knit family of five, and their stories reflect this devotion to one another.

Maurine (Krug) Gjovig. Maurine was the only child of Sophie Hinderer and Martin Krug who was interviewed. She was the youngest of Sophie's three surviving children. After her mother's death, Maurine and her two siblings, Johnny and William, became part of the extended family of Martin Krug and his second wife, Emma (Hinderer) Lafere. Maurine's touching stories expand the personal information concerning Martin Krug. Martin's marriage to sisters Sophie and Emma meant all of his children were raised together as a single family.

Leonard Krug, Bette (Krug) Weber, and Florence (Krug) Rousseau. Leonard, Bette and Florence were Emma's children by her marriage to Martin Krug. It was the second marriage for both Emma and Martin. As will be described, Emma's children remained unusually close to their Hinderer grandparents. They were regular Sunday visitors to the farm. After Martin Krug's death, the Hinderers frequently brought food and supplies to Emma in Canby. Their stories illustrate the close bond between these two families.

Don Engstrand and Norma (Engstrand) Sandrock. Don and Norma were two of Mary (Hinderer) Engstrand's four children. They were raised on a farm near the village of Dawson, Minnesota, ten miles from the Hinderer farm. The stories from their home farm were repeatedly mixed with the stories of Sunday visits to the Hinderers, or the Hinderers visiting the Engstrands. The Engstrand farm was one of the first to be homesteaded in Providence township, Lac qui Parle County. Their lineage added Swedish ancestry to the Hinderer story. As a family, they personally experienced the tragic consequences of World War I. Their view of the Hinderer family contributes to our appreciation of how families survived through hardships, both natural and human caused.

Emma Swenson. This extraordinary lady was interviewed as she neared her 100th birthday. At the time, she lived alone and was nearly blind, but her memory was vivid. Emma was the younger half-sister of Martin Krug. After Martin's first wife Sophie (Hinderer) died, Emma Swenson helped care for Martin and Sophie's three children. Later when Martin and his second wife Emma (Hinderer) had children, Emma Swenson moved in with the growing family to help with daily chores. Emma Swenson was opinionated, blunt, and delightful in describing the Hinderer and Krug families.

Chapter 8

A Farm on the Prairie

Timeline

1870 – Settlers built the first homes in Canby

1873–1878 – Locusts destroyed crops

1890 – The Canby population was 470

1892 – Gottlieb and Katharine were married in Iowa

1893 – Fire destroyed Canby businesses

1898 – The Hinderers arrived in Minnesota

1898 – The Hinderers over-wintered in a sod house

1899 – The Hinderers purchased 120 acres

1899 – The Hinderers built a two-room house

1905 – A kitchen was added to their house

1906 – John and Martha Hinderer were born

1912 – The Hinderers added 40 acres to their farm

1914 – A new barn was built

1914 – WWI began.

1917 – The U.S. entered WWI

1919 – Emma and her infant returned to the farm

1919–1933 – Prohibition enforced in the U.S.

1920 – A porch was added to the farmhouse

1925 – A new kitchen and mudroom were added

1929 – The Great Depression began

1936 – John Hinderer bought his first tractor

1939 – WWII began in Europe

1948 – Electricity was installed on the Hinderer farm

1951 – Gottlieb Hinderer died

Minnesota Arrival - 1898

Gottlieb and Katharine Hinderer did not leave a diary or travelogue revealing details of their move from Iowa to Minnesota. Nevertheless, the timing of their move can be determined from dated documents and from what they later told their son, John Hinderer.

John and his twin sister Martha were born in 1906, eight years after their family left Iowa. John was interviewed in 2000 and commented on a broad range of personal and family memories. John was told by his parents that the family moved from Iowa to Minnesota in 1898.

Civil records document that the Hinderer's fifth child, Mary, was born in Fayette County, Iowa, in May of 1898. In early February 1899, less than nine months later, Gottlieb and Katharine signed a document to purchase land in Minnesota. John's statement that the family arrived in 1898 fits within this time frame. The Hinderers moved to Minnesota in the summer or fall of 1898 before winter snowstorms began.

John believed his father made more than one trip from Iowa to Minnesota. He suggested Gottlieb may have first traveled alone by train to scout out land purchase opportunities near Canby. He also theorized his father made at least one later train trip to bring his Iowa farm animals to the family's new home in Minnesota. Both ideas are plausible. Railroad companies extended free train passage to settlers. It was meant to attract new families and ease the transport of their possessions, including livestock.

Gottlieb and Katharine purchased unplowed prairie land. Katharine later described it bluntly, "there was not even a single tree or bush on the property, not one." Before settlers arrived, the prairie in Lac qui Parle County had few naturally growing trees. The trees and bushes that were there grew along creeks and streams. One reason for the lack of trees in the open countryside was prairie fires. Before settlers arrived, Indians deliberately set seasonal fires to encourage regrowth of prairie grasses. The fresh grass was an attraction to grazing animals like deer and bison, food staples for the Indians. Prairie fires were also caused by summer lightning storms common in the Midwest. The end result was a nearly treeless landscape and little wood for building homes.

The U.S. Census conducted in June 1900 identified the Hinderers in Minnesota. This census was conducted 18 months after their arrival in Minnesota. The family was living in Freeland Township, Lac qui Parle County. Gottlieb was 33 years old and Katharine, listed as "Catarina," was 28.[1] Their five children ranged from Mary, age two, to the oldest child Christina, age eight. All five children had been born in Iowa. Both parents had been born in Germany. Coincidentally, the census taker who recorded this census page was John Engstrand. He was two-year-old Mary Hinderer's future father-in-law.

The Sod House

There is a time gap between the Hinderer's Minnesota arrival late in 1898 and their purchase of farmland in 1899. Their family of seven required temporary living quarters during those months. John and others in the family were told that the Hinderers first lived in a sod house located near the land they purchased. John was told that other families had lived in the same sod house prior to the Hinderers. The sod house was located in what is now the front yard of a farm a half-mile north of the Hinderer's home.[2] The farm with the sod house was also the location of the District 66 schoolhouse where the Hinderer children later received their limited formal education.

The Hinderers likely moved into the sod house in the fall of 1898. Before they could move out of the sod house, they had to build a shelter on their newly purchased land. Building a livable shelter took time and warmer weather. The earliest opportunity to begin house construction would have been in the spring or summer of 1899. This

The June 1900 U.S. Census identified 33-year-old Gottlieb, his wife "Catarina," and their five children ages 2-8. They lived in Freeland Township, Lac qui Parle County, Minnesota. All five children had been born in Iowa. Source: "Year: 1900; Census Place: Freeland, Lac Qui Parle, Minnesota" (Family History Library Microfilm: 1240772; Page 10; Enumeration District: 0126), accessed November 2021. Edited by author.

The sod house where the Hinderers and other families lived was in the front yard of a farm a half mile north of the Hinderer farm. Today, this farm's address is 1131 205th Ave. North. Source: Photography and editing by author.

means the Hinderer family of seven spent most of one year in the sod house, including one entire winter.

Sod houses, also called soddies, bring to mind sentimental thoughts of pioneer America. In fact, most sod houses consisted of only a single room with a single entrance doorway. Some soddies had one or two windows, but many had no windows. Inside most soddies, the walls were simply dirt. Furnishings were sparse, and a small stove inside the house provided both heat and a cooking surface.

In hilly terrain, sod houses were dug into a steep hillside with the "roof" consisting of the natural hillside grass and dirt. A doorway was cut into the down-sloping face of the hillside. The dirt inside was carefully dug out and replaced by timbers supporting the weight of the surface soil and grass. A hole was dug through the "roof" to vent smoke. Windows might be added on either side of the door for lighting. More often, the only opening was the doorway.

The sod house used by the Hinderers was on flat terrain. Without a hillside to dig into, the walls of their soddie were built with sod bricks. These bricks were thick rectangular-shaped cutouts of prairie grass and dirt. The sod bricks were staggered one atop the other like brick walls today. An opening for the door and possibly a window required a sturdy "header" timber with more sod bricks stacked above the header. Finally, the roof was constructed using timber for posts and support beams. Above the support beams, more sod bricks formed the roof. Like their hillside counterparts, free-standing sod houses were most often a single room with one door and sometimes one window.

In a 1957 letter, Katharine described their sod house: ". . . it was part sod. There were several steps down into the house so windows were half below the ground." Her description indicates that their sod house was partly an underground cellar and partly sod bricks above ground level. It had several windows which were located at about ground level.

Sod houses had a few good qualities. Most of the construction material was readily at hand: dirt and grass. Timber for support beams was not abundant on the prairie, so timber availability influenced the size of the house. A door was required, but windows were optional and expensive. Windows also diminished one key benefit of a sod house: their ability to moderate Midwest temperature extremes. On hot and humid summer days, sod houses remained cool inside. In wintertime, they remained naturally warmer than uninsulated wood-framed houses. If a stove fire was maintained during the winter, the temperature inside the soddy remained above freezing. With few trees on the prairie, firewood was often unavailable. Corncobs, "twists" of dried grasses, and dried animal dung were alternative fuels.

The many problems of sod houses are easy to imagine. They were dark, damp, smoky, and cold for much of the year. Bugs and vermin were always present in the roof and in the sod walls. Heavy snowfall improved the insulating effect of the sod roof but required careful attention. A plugged roof vent might lead to smoke and deadly fumes accumulating inside the sod house. Summer rains meant water, mud, and insects dripping from the ceiling. The inside floor of a sod house was simply dirt, so a leaky roof turned the floors into mud. For the Hinderer family of seven, cooking meals and washing clothes through one entire winter must have been a severe test.

Their Land Purchase

Gottlieb and Katharine Hinderer purchased two diagonally separated parcels of land in Freeland Township[3] near the southern border of Lac qui Parle County. Added together, their two parcels totaled 120 acres. The purchase price was $1000. Of the 120 acres, 40 acres were in section 35 of Freeland Township. They built their house and outbuildings in the northeastern corner of this 40-acre parcel. The remaining 80 acres were in section 25 diagonally across a roadway intersection from the 40 acres.[4] They bought both land parcels from the Winona & St. Peter Railroad Company. Their land had been given to this railroad company as a land grant from the U.S. Government.

This ca. 1880 free-standing sod house was located seven miles east of Madison in Lac qui Parle County. Note the layered sod walls, one door, and one window. Source: Minneapolis StarTribune, *September 9, 2017, accessed November 15, 2021. Edited by author.*

A Farm on the Prairie

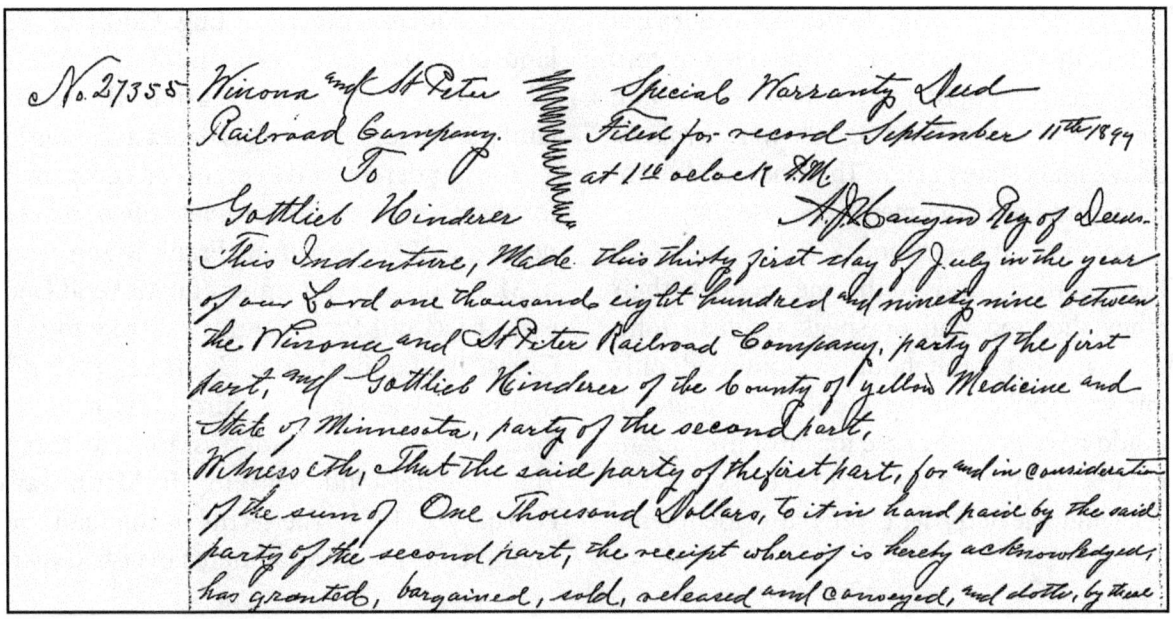

A section of the July 31, 1899 purchase agreement was between the Winona and St. Peter Railroad Company and Gottlieb Hinderer. The purchase price of the 120 acres was $1000. Source: Lac qui Parle County Recorder's Office. Edited by author.

The two Hinderer parcels fulfilled the U.S. government's rules for a railroad company to sell to settlers. First, the land had to be within 20 miles of the actual railroad tracks. With the Winona & St. Peter tracks running through the town of Canby, the Hinderer property was well inside that limit. Second, the land grant sections had to be alternating rather than adjacent to one another.[5] Sections 25 and 35 were alternating sections. A plat map helps visualize how the two Hinderer parcels connected at the corner of alternating sections 25 and 35.

The 40-acre parcel of land in section 35, including the building site, was gently rolling terrain. The 80-acre parcel diagonally northeast from the building site was nearly flat. The Hinderer farmland was like most of the prairie land in Yellow Medicine and Lac qui Parle counties. With skill and hard work, it was suitable for growing crops and grazing livestock.

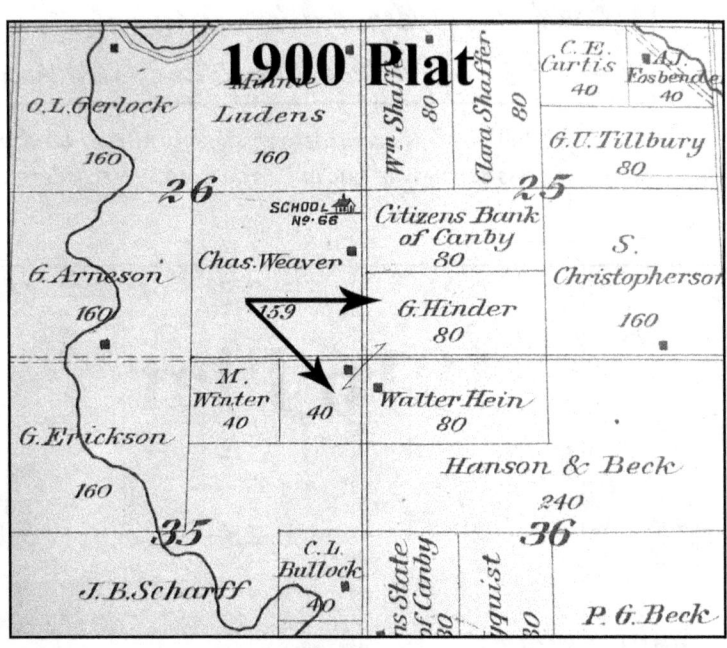

This plat map from 1900 included Gottlieb Hinder (Hinderer) owner of 80 acres in section 25, and 40 acres diagonally across an intersection in section 35. These are alternating, not adjacent, sections. The black square near the intersection is the location of their buildings in section 35. Note District 66 school a half mile north. Source: Image access courtesy of Lac qui Parle County Museum. Photographed and edited by author.

Katharine

Although land agent John Lund's name does not appear on any document, John Hinderer was told that his parents bought their 120 acres through Mr. Lund. Back then, land agents were brokers, like today's real estate agents. Their names did not appear on purchase documents because they were not a party in the transaction.

When Gottlieb and Katharine bought their land, they did not read or speak English. John Hinderer said that throughout his childhood, only German was spoken in the Hinderer household. This would have been the case for most immigrant land buyers. They were unable to understand the complex language of the land-purchase documents they signed.

Two documents regarding Gottlieb's original land purchase have been discovered. The first is a loan to Gottlieb and Katharine. The second, the land purchase document, is dated five months later.

The Hinderers paid the railroad company $1,000 for their 120 acres. To complete the purchase, they needed a $750 loan from Frank Mann who lived in McLeod County, Minnesota. McLeod County is east of Lac qui Parle County halfway to the Twin Cities. It is unlikely the Hinderers ever met Mr. Mann. He was simply a third-party lender whose loan allowed the Hinderers to buy their land. The Hinderer's indenture to Mr. Mann was dated February 1, 1899. The terms of the loan included multiple payment installments over five years with

The July 1899 purchase contract reassigned the two land parcels from Aron J Lind to Gottlieb Hinderer. Source: Access courtesy of Lac qui Parle County Recorder's Office. Edited by author.

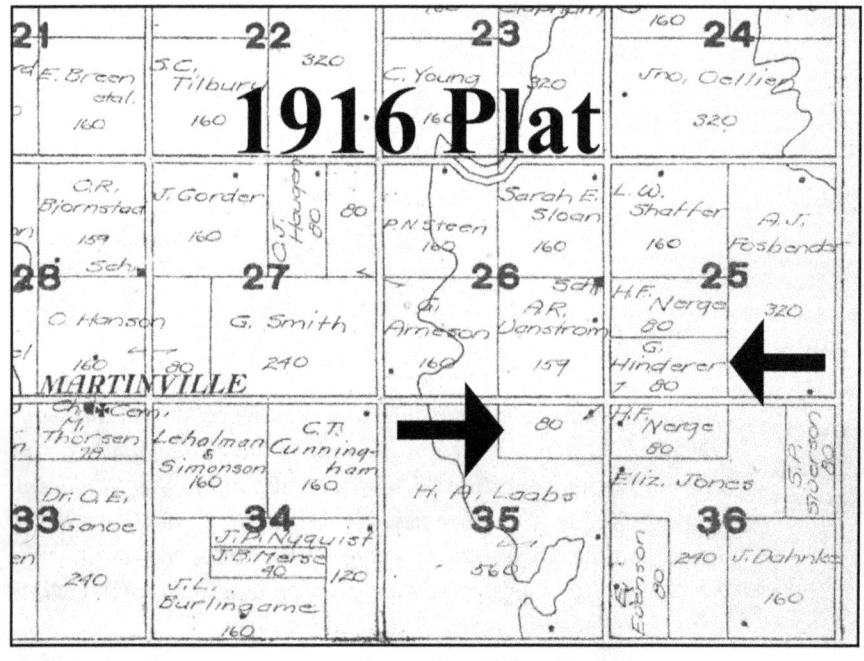

After their 1912 purchase of another 40 acres in section 35, Gottlieb and Katharine owned two 80 acre parcels located diagonally across an intersection. Their house and outbuildings were in the northeast corner of section 35. Source: Image access courtesy of Lac qui Parle County Museum. Photographed and edited by author.

interest charges added. The source of the $250 balance the Hinderers owed the railroad is not stated. Most likely, they paid this balance with their own cash savings.

Gottlieb's purchase contract with the Winona & St. Peter Railroad Company was dated July 1, 1899, five months after the loan contract. The purchase agreement included another complicating element. It stated that the Hinderer land was previously contracted by the railroad to a Canby farmer named Aron J. Lind. It went on to state that the contract with Mr. Lind had now been "assigned" to Gottlieb Hinderer. The full meaning of this statement was not explained. In some manner, the railroad's contractual obligation to Mr. Lind was satisfied, so the land could then be sold to Gottlieb.

Taken together, these two documents reveal an unusually complex transaction. It would have required an experienced land agent like John Lund to broker the deal. First, he had to secure a loan from a private lender. Second, he had to convince Mr. Aron J. Lind to release his contractual right to the land. He then had to connect the railroad company with the new buyer. Finally, he had to convince the German-speaking Hinderers that the price was fair, and the transaction legal.

Gottlieb and Katharine added another 40 acres to their farm in 1912. This parcel was immediately west of the 40 acres in section 35 where their buildings were located. After this second land purchase, they owned 160 acres composed of two 80-acre parcels diagonally separated by a roadway intersection. John said he thought this added 40 acres was owned by a family named Arneson. However, the purchase document indicated a husband and wife named Schram previously owned the land. Gottlieb paid $1,900 for this final 40-acre parcel. Thirteen years earlier, he had paid only $1,000 for the 120 acres he bought from the railroad company. In this short time, land prices had increased sharply. A plat map drawn in 1916 illustrated their ownership of the complete 160 acres.

Building Their House – Room by Room

John Hinderer revealed that his father Gottlieb was not a skilled carpenter. This explains why, over the years, their family home and outbuildings were constructed by hired local carpenters. Gottlieb and his family contributed their labor rather than carpentry and construction expertise.

The Hinderer farmhouse was built in stages. The overriding reason for this piecemeal house construction was financial. The Hinderers borrowed most of the money required for their 1899 land purchase. They likely had little money remaining to build their house. During the next 25 years, they added rooms to the house when they had enough cash to do so.

Photographs indicate there were five construction stages between 1899 and 1925. The stages can be summarized as follows: the first construction in 1899 satisfied the critical need to find a shelter other than the sod house. This first shelter consisted of one room downstairs with one bedroom above. The second stage added a combined kitchen and dining room downstairs, plus a second bedroom upstairs. Next, a third downstairs room and upstairs bedroom were added. Fourth, an enclosed porch was attached to the south side of the house. Finally, an enlarged kitchen and a new entry mudroom completed the house.

Both John Hinderer and his niece, Doris (Lafere) Schlichting,[6] were told that the first section of the house was a two-story structure. It consisted of a single room downstairs with a single room above. John estimated that the footprint of this structure was 14 by 16 feet. In later years, this first downstairs room became the living room. The first upstairs room was the family's only bedroom. After living in the sod house, even this 14 by 16-foot two-story shelter was an improvement. The foundation supporting the structure was simply fieldstones.

Katharine

A root cellar was dug beneath the first downstairs room. As John and Doris noted, this was not a true basement. It was simply a dugout storage cellar with dirt walls and floor. The entry to the root cellar was along the east side of the house. A photo circa 1912 shows the cellar entry doors behind the seated family.

A photo circa 1912 shows the Hinderer family eating melon. Left to Right: Carl, Emma, John, Mary, Martha, and Katharine. The arrow identifies the entrance to the original root cellar. Source: Photo courtesy of Becci Fischer. Edited by author.

John said the next downstairs room to be built was a combined kitchen and dining area. This addition was constructed around 1905. A second bedroom was added above this room. For those who visited the farmhouse in the mid-1900s, this first kitchen was eventually used as the Hinderer's dining room.

The next addition similarly consisted of a downstairs room and an upstairs bedroom. It was joined to the north side of the first room (future living room). The result was a comfortable arrangement of downstairs living, dining, and kitchen areas plus three bedrooms upstairs. Two photos illustrate the appearance of the house between 1912 and 1913 (p. 147).

A third photo (p. 148) provides a broader view of the house and outbuildings. This photo was taken between 1917 and 1920. The barn built in 1914 is in the background. The house consisted of three downstairs rooms with the entry stoop leading directly into the combined kitchen and dining area. The original root cellar entry is visible on the east side of the house. A well with a pump is located across the driveway from the house.

The next addition was a porch that spanned the entire south side of the house. It included a new entrance door with steps leading down to the driveway. Glass windows with screens provided ventilation during warm summer weather. The porch was used seasonally as sleeping quarters for both John and his older brother Carl. Adding this room had the effect of buffering the main house from southern winds and winter storms. Above this porch, a second-story open deck was trimmed with a wooden railing. A doorway from one of the upstairs bedrooms allowed access onto the deck.

Two photos show this addition. One photo included Martha with her niece, Emma's daughter Doris Lafere. The photo with Doris was taken around 1924. This means the addition was built between 1919 and 1924. When the porch was added, the fieldstone house foundation was replaced by concrete blocks.

The fifth and final addition to the house produced a greatly enlarged kitchen area with a new entryway through a mudroom. This addition completed the outward appearance of the house seen in family photos taken after 1930. Only minor internal changes were later made to accommodate the addition of indoor plumbing.

A Farm on the Prairie

A photo circa 1912 with the construction stages numbered. The camera is aimed northwest. Note that the house entrance was into the combined kitchen and dining area, not the first room built. Irregular fieldstones form the foundation. Left to right rear: Tena, Mary, Sophie, Carl, and Emma. Front: John, Katharine, Martha and Gottlieb. Source: The Doris Schlichting collection. Edited by author.

A photo circa 1913 with the construction stages numbered. The camera is aimed northeast. The water storage cistern was covered by a boulder. Note that roof-mounted lightning rods had been added. The family members left to right are Sophie, Mary, Tena, John, Emma, Martha, and Katharine. Source: Photo courtesy of Becci Fischer. Edited by author.

This photo of the Hinderer farm was taken between 1917 and 1920. The camera is aimed west. Note the new barn built in 1914. The house entryway leads directly into the dining area. The original root cellar door is at ground level along the east face of the house. Gottlieb's hand-dug well used for potable water is across the driveway from the house. Source: From the Doris Schlichting collection. Edited by author.

The mudroom served as a buffer between the heated part of the house and the outside elements. Outdoor boots were removed and left on the mudroom floor. Dirty overalls, coats, and winter jackets were hung from hooks in the mudroom. Over the years, several generations of clothes washing machines were kept in one corner of this room. A bushel basket filled with corncobs sat near the kitchen entry. The corncobs were used to fire the cookstove in Katharine's new kitchen. This basket was replenished daily from the nearby "cob shed" located at the end of a short sidewalk. As the name implies, the cob shed was filled with corncobs left over from last year's harvest. At first, corncobs were the main cookstove fuel. In later years, split wood was also stashed in the bushel basket. The split wood came from storm-downed trees on the Hinderer property or hauled home from a neighbor's land. Finally, the mudroom contained a "slop" bucket for the hogs. Cooking waste, leftover skim milk, vegetables peels, and fruit discards filled the slop bucket. Each day, Gottlieb carried this bucket to the hog barn and poured it into a long feeding trough.

Emma Hinderer's daughter Bette (Krug) Weber recalled that the Hinderer house was unlike most farmhouses in one respect. Because of the mudroom and Katharine's strict rules, the inside rooms, including the kitchen, "never smelled like a barn."

When it was completed, the new kitchen was Katharine's domain and the hub of activity in the house. Family and visitors entered the house through the mudroom and then into the new kitchen. The centerpiece of Katharine's kitchen was a heavy all-metal cookstove. It came equipped with surface burners and a great oven. A refillable water tank was attached to the back of the cookstove. As the fire chamber inside the stove heated, the water in the tank heated as well. This tank was the source

This photo includes the porch addition with a deck above. The camera is aimed north. Note that the entry to the house was through the porch. A large boulder covered the cistern opening and several downspouts directed rainwater into a storage barrel. Source: From the Doris Schlichting collection. Edited by author.

This circa 1924 photo shows Martha and her niece Doris Lafere. At the time of this photo, the entry mudroom and enlarged kitchen had not yet been built. Concrete blocks have replaced the original fieldstone foundation of the house. Source: From the Doris Schlichting collection. Edited by author.

of hot water for handwashing, baths, and washing clothes. Water meant for cooking and for drinking was pumped daily from the hand-dug well across the driveway from the house. The cookstove with its all-metal chimney was the only heat source necessary in the new kitchen.

A cabinet next to the cookstove served as a prep table for cooking. It had an attached metal-surfaced shelf and a kerosene lamp mounted on one side. This single lamp was the only light in the cooking area. Opposite the cookstove, the kitchen table with chairs sat against the wall. At mealtime, the table was pulled out so the entire family could be seated around it. If hog butchering was forced indoors due to bad weather, the kitchen table served double duty as a meat-cutting surface. A second kerosene lamp was mounted on the wall above the kitchen table. On winter evenings, the two kerosene lamps were the only light source in the new kitchen. John had a low opinion of these early kerosene lamps. He said, "if you got ten feet away, you couldn't find them."

First Things First – Farm Necessities

Water. Water, both for drinking and washing, was an immediate requirement. John was told that a cistern was dug at the same time the first section of the house was constructed. Cisterns stored rainwater, or "soft" water as John called it, in a cave-like underground space. Cistern water was used for all domestic purposes except cooking and drinking. Mainly, it was heated in the cookstove water tank. As noted earlier, this hot water was then used for taking baths and for washing clothes, dishes, and hands. The house photos from the early 1900s show an elaborate system for collecting rainwater and directing it into a storage barrel which was later emptied into the cistern.

During the winter, John said he shoveled snow into their cistern to replenish their "soft" water supply. He said only a small amount of snow was shoveled at one time. This allowed the snow to melt in the cistern rather than remain frozen underground. If a cistern went dry before spring rains arrived, water could be hauled from a neighbor's farm and emptied into the cistern. Alternatively, water could be purchased from a vendor and emptied into a farm's cistern.

The new kitchen and mudroom added by the Hinderers was built over their cistern. These overhead rooms insulated the cistern and prevented winter freezing. Until the mudroom and new kitchen were added, a large boulder covered the opening to the cistern.

Only well water was used for cooking and drinking. Wells on farms were dug by hand and covered with boards. The boards supported the heavy hand pump and kept children from falling into the well. John remembered his father digging the well across the driveway from the house. John was born in 1906, seven years after the Hinderers moved onto their farm. This means either Gottlieb dug an earlier well before John was born, or he purchased potable water from a vendor.

John recalled that a neighbor helped his father dig the well across the driveway by the house.[7] John said Gottlieb did the difficult hand shoveling down in the well. He filled buckets with dirt and the neighbor used a rope to lift the buckets and empty out the dirt. John said his father dug down to a large rock, which he managed to dislodge. When the rock moved, water rose upward. As John described it, Gottlieb "hit a vein." The naturally-flowing water filled the well part way toward the ground surface. John's recollection was that when it was completed, this well measured 24 feet deep by 4 feet wide. Gottlieb capped the well with thick wooden planks and mounted a metal hand pump atop the boards. When the old wooden planks rotted, Gottlieb topped the well with concrete tiles. Years later, a small gasoline-powered engine replaced the hand pump. When electricity was added to the farm in 1948, an electric motor replaced the gasoline engine.

In John's memory, Gottlieb's hand-dug well by their house produced the best drinking water on the property. The water pumped from this well was hard and always tasted good.[8] There was no rust and no particulate material. John said you could set out a glass of water from that well, and it always remained clear.

Whether on purpose or by chance, Gottlieb dug this well by the house in a safe location. Infectious diseases and sanitation were only beginning to be understood in the late 19th and early 20th centuries. Earlier, many farm family members were sickened or died from typhoid fever. This bacterial disease was typically due to contamination of wells by animal waste. The usual triggering event was a rainstorm that created contaminated surface water that flowed into a well. Gottlieb's hand-dug well was located on higher ground and some distance from where he kept his animals. This source of good-tasting drinking water was never a cause of illness in his family.

The Hinderers eventually added indoor plumbing to their home. This included a large sink with a water faucet in the kitchen, just past the mudroom. A full bathroom was added on the opposite side of the kitchen next to the stairway leading upstairs to the bedrooms. There was never an upstairs bathroom.

Despite the new water faucet at the kitchen sink, drinking water was still pumped each morning from Gottlieb's hand-dug well across the driveway. One of the "boys," Carl or John, pumped the water into a white enamel bucket. The bucket was carried into the kitchen and placed on one side of the kitchen sink. A ladle always sat next to the bucket. Adults and children alike dipped the ladle into the bucket and drank the tasty hard water. Guests might choose to use glasses or cups filled from the faucet, but the family always used the enamel bucket and ladle to drink water.

A second well was machine-drilled near the hog shed after the 1914 barn was built. John said this well was considerably deeper than Gottlieb's hand-dug well by the house. A company from New Ulm, Minnesota drilled this second well using an engine-powered auger. According to John, the water from this deeper well was more brackish and never as tasty as the water from the older well by the house. The Hinderers used both wells. The well near the barns provided water for the animals while Gottlieb's hand-dug well by the house was the source of drinking water for the family.

The 80 acres across the intersection from the house was used initially as a pasture for the Hinderer cattle. This eighty-acre pasture did not have a well. John recalled that each day, the cattle had to be driven across the roadway intersection to drink from a water tank in the barnyard. In the 1920s, the Hinderers decided to dig a third

This is the hand pump first mounted on the well across the driveway from the Hinderer house. It was eventually powered by a small gasoline engine and later by an electric motor. This hand pump is now located in the garden of Anne and Craig Felix on their farm in Northern California. Anne Felix is a great-great granddaughter of Katharine and Gottlieb. Source: Photographed and edited by author.

well so the animals had access to drinking water on the 80-acre pasture. Doris (Lafere) Schlichting recalled this well-digging adventure from her early childhood. Doris said a neighbor, Mr. Honeyman, was hired as a water dowser (also called water divining or witching) to locate underground water. She said she and her Uncle Carl accompanied Mr. Honeyman who used a Y-shaped stick while he walked around the pasture. He claimed that when the stick was over water, it would bend. Later, when the stick did bend, Doris thought Mr. Honeyman was just teasing her. To prove this was not a trick, Mr. Honeyman told Doris to hold the stick. She said she did not know what to expect, but then the stick began to bend in her hands. She said this scared her and she immediately dropped the stick and ran home.

John said this third well on their property was dug near where Mr. Honeyman's stick began to bend. He added that it always produced sufficient water for the cattle. In fact, John said that in the fall after particularly rainy summers, water flowed continuously from the well without pumping.[9]

Heat. Minnesota winters required heat in the farmhouse. The Hinderer farmhouse never had "central" heating with ducts and registers. Instead, individual room heaters were installed in the downstairs living and dining rooms. Upstairs bedrooms were heated by means of small grill-like openings cut between upper and lower story rooms. The openings could be adjusted to control the upward heat flow into the bedrooms. As has been noted, Katharine's cookstove was the only heat source required in her new kitchen.

Food Storage. Prior to electric refrigeration, food storage required an underground cellar. Over the years, the Hinderers dug two root cellars and eventually a true basement. The first root cellar on the east side of the house has been described. The second root cellar was dug near the corn crib and hog barn. There was a second vegetable garden area north of the corn crib, so this was a handy location for the second root cellar.

When the new kitchen was added, a stairway leading down to a complete basement was also built. The stairway was located between Katharine's new kitchen and the dining room. This true basement was used to preserve root crops harvested from the summer garden. It was also a cool storage area for preserving cuts of meat after winter butchering. The original cistern was located directly under the new kitchen. A hand pump was used to draw the cistern water from the basement to the upstairs kitchen so it could be heated in the cookstove water tank.

Outbuildings and Utilities

Outbuildings. While the Hinderers were building the first section of their house in 1899, they also built shelters for their animals. They first built a wood-framed barn John called the horse barn. Against one end of the horse barn, Gottlieb added a straw barn. The straw barn used grasses or straw to form walls. A few wooden beams supported the roof, which was also straw-covered. Like sod houses, straw barns were better insulated than their wood-framed counterparts. John fondly remembered Gottlieb's straw barn. He said that on cold winter days, the straw barn was always warmer than the wood-framed horse barn.

An aerial photo from the 1950s illustrated the location of the farm buildings. In this photo, the horse barn and attached straw barn have been replaced by a metal machine shed. Gottlieb's hog barn is partly hidden behind the 1914 barn. The house is complete although the new kitchen and mudroom are hidden from view. A short walkway leads from the house to the cob shed. In the 1950s, the corncob-fired cookstove was still the only heat source for the kitchen.

The chicken coop was tended daily, in earlier years by Katharine and later by her youngest daughter Martha. There were two vegetable garden areas. One was east of the house near the roadway. The second was near the hog barn to the right (north) of the corn crib. Gottlieb's well across the driveway from the house can be seen in the photo.

A Farm on the Prairie

An aerial photo from about 1950 included the Hinderer farmhouse and outbuildings. See text for details. Source: From the Doris Schlichting collections. Edited by author.

By the 1950s, it was powered by an electric motor, but was still being used for the family's drinking water.

Lighting. John's low opinion of their old kerosene lanterns changed when newer "Aladdin" kerosene lamps became available. These lamps burned a more refined grade of kerosene. They also added a glowing mantle above the wick, so their illumination was considerably brighter. Although Aladdin lamps and their fuel were more expensive than kerosene lanterns, a single Aladdin lamp could illuminate an entire room.[10]

Electricity. Across America in the 1930s and 1940s, farms upgraded their energy source by linking up to rural electrical systems. Once the roadway poles, wires and transformers were in place, farm homes and outbuildings could tap into the electricity. There was considerable expense to this conversion. Houses and outbuildings all needed remodeling to safely accommodate the wiring. The Hinderer farm did not add electricity until 1948. Like most modernizing decisions on their farm, John took the lead in adding electricity. By 1948, he had returned home from his overseas duty in WWII and was eager to update their farm.

Telephones. Telephone systems presented less of an installation challenge than electricity. Telegraph and later telephone line systems were widely in place in the U.S. by the late 1800s. They required a lower power source and most farm families only needed one wall-mounted telephone. Doris recalled that by the early 1920s, the Hinderers already had a telephone.

Norma (Engstrand) Sandrock said the Engstrand farm near Dawson had a telephone shortly after the Hinderers. She said all rural phones were "party" rather than private lines. Each family's telephone had a ring code consisting of long and short rings. For the Engstrands, their code was three short rings. Party line members knew the ring codes for the other families sharing the line. Nosey neighbors could lift their receiver and listen in to any conversation. If you heard a click during your conversation, a neighbor was likely listening.

Norma said the Engstrands and Hinderers would visit one another about every other week, almost always on a Sunday. She said that although both families had telephones, their visits were never discussed or scheduled. Norma's mother Mary would say: "I think the folks are coming." (Mary would always call the Hinderers "the folks.") The surprising thing, Norma said, was that Mary was usually right.

Transportation

Horsepower. When the Hinderers first moved onto their property, they along with their neighbors did not own an automobile. Travel was always by horse-drawn wagon. The few dirt roads that had been constructed were impassable much of the year. John said that if his father Gottlieb went to town, he drove his horse team straight overland. There were no fences or roadside ditches in his way. In favorable weather, he hitched his horses to a box wagon. In winter, travel to town was unusual, but their horse-drawn sleigh would serve the same purpose. Usually, Gottlieb carried harvested wheat to flour mills in either Canby or Madison. He left home in the early morning so that he, along with the milled flour and any store-bought supplies, was home by dark.

Doris recalled that she normally walked the half-mile north to District 66 school. On stormy winter days, her Uncle Carl would hitch the horses to their sleigh and give her a welcome ride. Even after the Engstrands and Hinderers had automobiles, Doris said that winter visits were usually by horse-drawn sleigh. Early automobiles could not pass through snow as easily as a horse-drawn sleigh. To keep passengers warm, wooden-handled flat irons were first heated on top of the cookstove. The hot irons were then placed on the floor of the sleigh surrounded and covered by bricks. Passengers sat over these warm bricks and covered themselves with heavy blankets. Doris said Katharine and her mother Emma made these blankets. In her memory, the sleigh ride between the two farms was brisk but comfortable due to the hot irons and blankets.

The Hinderers kept one team of horses as late as the 1950s. The previously displayed aerial photo from the 1950s shows a white and a dark horse on the far left. These two horses, Dick and Barney, were purchased from an unrelated neighbor, also named Hinderer. Dick was larger and more animated than Barney. Together, they were a gentle team that remained on the Hinderer farm well beyond their working years.

When company visited the farm, John occasionally hitched Dick and Barney to an empty hay wagon. He invited the children to ride along on a neighborhood tour over the gravel roads. A lucky grandnephew or grandniece might be standing in the front of the wagon next to John. The best part of the ride was when John handed the reins over and said, "you drive us home."

Of course, Dick and Barney were entirely capable of finding the way home on their own. Nevertheless, for children born after the day of draft horses, holding the reins of these large work animals was the highlight of their day.

Automobiles. According to John, the Hinderer's first automobile was a 1917 Ford Model T. As Henry Ford said, his "tin lizzie" or "flivver" came in "any color as long as it was black." In 1917, a Model T sold for $500. Over 750,000 Americans bought one.[11] The Hinderer's Model T had a top with side curtains that kept out some of the summer dust and winter cold. However, John's recollection was guarded: "I'll tell you, in the winter you would [want to] have a heavy coat on and some boots too."

In the 1920s, country roads were poorly constructed and not maintained most of the year. With poor road conditions, John said the automobile trip to Canby might take well over an hour or even two.

A Farm on the Prairie

The Hinderer's Aladdin Lamp, now located in the home of Merlin and Jill Schlichting. The mantle is inside the base of the glass chimney. When lit, the mantle glowed white hot, illuminating an entire room. Source: Image courtesy of Merlin Schlichting. Edited by author.

This pre-1920 telephone was sold by Montgomery Ward Co. for about $12. The crank on the right created an electrical current that signaled the operator. The ring bells alerted the receiving party. The receiver on the left was lifted free and both parties spoke into their center microphones. Source: Phone courtesy of Barbara Wolhart. Photographed and edited by author.

John recalled one occasion when he, his sisters Martha and Emma, and brother Carl traveled to a neighbor's home in their Model T. He said these neighbors were Swabian Germans like the Hinderers. The husband played the accordion and all the kids had fun dancing to his tunes. Late that night while driving home, the Hinderer siblings had to cross a creek. Bridge construction forced driver Carl to make a detour into the surrounding fields. John said it was dark, and when those old Fords slowed down, their lights dimmed to almost nothing. Carl's detour took the Model T directly over a construction pile driver he couldn't see, bending the car's rear axle. They were all forced to walk home, and they didn't get there until two in the morning. It was scary at the time, but John said it later made a good story that they all laughed about.

The Hinderer's second auto was a 1926 Dodge Brothers touring car. It had a more powerful four-cylinder engine. John said the larger wooden-spoked wheels allowed it to motor through snow in the wintertime. In his estimation, it was a big improvement over the Model T.

Farm Crops

The Hinderers, like other farmers of the time, plowed over the prairie soil and planted wheat and corn. Some of the harvested wheat was saved as seed for the next year. Other wheat was taken to a flour mill in town. The mill would grind the wheat for home baking or breakfast cereal. Any extra wheat was sold for cash. The corn was used to feed their animals. Both corn and wheat were essential for making it through the winter and surviving financially until the next harvest.

Wheat. By the late 1800s, wheat farming had progressed from all hand labor to the use of machinery. Each decade brought a new cycle of farm implements. Machinery advertisements promised to improve productivity and reduce labor costs. Each farmer had to weigh the cost of the new implement against the labor expense it might save. He also had to estimate how long the machinery would last until it was succeeded by an even better implement. Farming had become a more complicated and financially risky business.

Farmers no longer walked the fields hand-casting wheat seed. The fields were first prepared by horse-drawn tilling equipment to plow and break up the prairie soil. The same horse teams then pulled seed drills or wagons with mechanized seed spreaders back and forth, evenly seeding the fields. At harvest time, the hand scythe had been replaced by horse-drawn binders that cut and tied the wheat into bundles. The tied bundles were then stacked by hand into shocks for drying.

The dried wheat shocks were pitchforked onto open-sided wagons and driven home to a waiting threshing machine. Steam engines powered the threshing machines. These engines were attached to the threshing machine by a long revolving belt. Wheat straw, grain hulls, and chaff were blown from the thresher onto piles. The grain meant to be sold was collected in cloth sacks. The grain kept for next year's seed or milling was loaded into a box wagon and then hand-shoveled into the farmer's granary.

Wheat for the Hinderer's home use was hauled to Canby or Madison and milled in two different ways. Wheat for baked bread, cakes or other desserts was first hulled and then finely ground. Wheat meant for hot breakfast cereal was ground more coarsely and included some hulls. John called this cereal "farina" which he compared to today's Cream of Wheat except it was darker colored and coarser. John liked the hot farina breakfast cereal. He said, "if you added some sugar or honey, it was even better."

Threshing wheat was a hot and dirty job, but neighbors did the work together. They formed "threshing crews" that moved from farm to farm during the heat of summer. One steam engine and one threshing machine could serve a half-dozen farms. Decades later, combines, also called harvesters, replaced threshing machines and their crews. The combines or harvesters merged the entire process of cutting and threshing grains into one machine.

Corn. Land preparation for a corn crop was the same as for wheat. However, planting the corn presented a greater challenge to farmers. Corn was planted in long straight rows extending across the fields. Early on, farmers walked their fields with hand-planting tools. The tool was plunged into the soil at regular intervals, and the kernels released under the surface. Corn rows had to be as wide apart as a horse's hips, 40 to 42 inches, to allow later passage of horse-drawn cultivators.

The first horse-drawn mechanical corn planters required a guide wire stretched from one end of the row to the other. The wire usually had knots every 40 to 42 inches, which triggered the seed kernels to drop. The result was a "cross-checked" field of corn with plants spaced equally apart in two directions. Cross-checked corn permitted cultivation in two directions and thus fewer weeds.

The greatest challenge with a corn crop was the fall harvest. Ears of corn did not harden to maturity until late fall after a frost. In some years, this would be after the first winter snow. With or without snow, it was cold and hard work.

Throughout the early 1900s, the Hinderers harvested their corn by hand. Adult and children pickers walked side by side along corn rows twisting the hardened ear of corn away from the husk and cornstalk.

Most corn pickers wore a glove-like corn husking "peg" on one hand. An experienced picker using a husking peg could quickly strip the husk from the ear and break the ear from the stalk in one motion.[12] A horse-drawn wagon slowly followed the line of pickers through the field. When the wagon was full, it was pulled back to the farmyard. There, the ears of corn were shoveled into the corncrib for drying out over winter. The next spring, the ears of corn were "shelled" either by hand or by using a hand-cranked device. The result was shelled corn to feed the animals and corncobs to fuel the kitchen cookstove.

During their childhood years, Carl and his sisters harvested corn by hand. The Hinderer's first corn crop was likely harvested in the fall of 1899. Tena, the oldest Hinderer child, was seven years old that fall. From age seven until she left home as a 12-year-old, she helped in the fields. Tena described harvesting corn to her oldest son George Monson:

We children always helped pick corn in the fall. To keep our feet from freezing, we wrapped them in gunny sacks when we walked the cornfields.[13]

The Hinderer children's schooling often fell victim to fieldwork, particularly during corn harvest. For these older Hinderer children, rewards and treats were few. When twins John and Martha were born on the day after Christmas in 1906, the older children were told that the twins were their Christmas present.

Flax. Like other local farmers, the Hinderers grew fields of flax from time to time. This minor crop was always sold for cash. Flax fields were easily recognizable when the grain was in bloom. Summer breezes and sky-blue flowers gave the appearance of waves of blue water moving through the field. The long straight flax stems were used to manufacture linen cloth. Compressed flax seeds produced linseed oil which was used as a wood preservative.

Hay. Every farmer had fields devoted to hay production. Grasses and legumes fed livestock during the winter when frozen pastures were hidden under a blanket of snow. The grasses were the least expensive type of hay to plant, but they also carried less nutritional value than legumes, such as alfalfa and clover. In addition, these two common legumes benefitted the soil by replenishing nitrogen.

Hay was cut and allowed to dry in the field. Complete drying was essential for safety. Wet hay stacked in the field or in a barn might begin to compost, producing enough heat to ignite and burn.

Hand or horse-drawn rakes gathered the dry hay in the fields. In the earlier years, the hay was stacked by hand around the fields. During the

A 1937 photo shows John Hinderer standing on a load of tied wheat bundles. Note that the wagon wheels are metal. Source: From the Doris Schlichting collection. Edited by author.

Another 1937 photo shows John Hinderer forking the grain bundles into the threshing machine. The straw was blown onto a pile on the left and the grain filled a partially hidden horse-drawn box wagon. This threshing machine was branded "Yellow Fellow." The steam engine powering the threshing machine was hidden behind John's hay wagon. Source: From the Doris Schlichting collection. Edited by author.

winter months, the farmer hauled the hay from field to home as it was needed to feed his livestock.

After the Hinderer's 1914 barn was built, their dried hay was forked onto a wagon, taken home, and then lifted by rope and pulley into the barn's haymow. Haystacks in fields were no longer necessary. The haymow was always located on a second level of the barn, above where the animals were housed. During winter months, a filled haymow provided food for the animals. Like the Hinderer's old straw barn, it also insulated the animals from the cold.

Fertilizer. Farm productivity required rich soil. The freshly plowed native prairie grass contained enough nitrogen to nourish the crops for several years. However, corn in particular soon required an added source of nitrogen. A horse-drawn manure spreader provided the solution. Before commercial fertilizers were available, animal manure enriched farmer's cornfields. The horse-drawn manure spreaders used a wheel-driven mechanism to slowly move the manure toward the rear of the "honey wagon." Rotating beaters then spread the nitrogen-rich waste behind the spreader.

John recalled that when his niece Doris Lafere was a young child in the early 1920s, she loved to be outdoors. In the spring of the year, John and his older brother Carl always cleaned the winter accumulation of manure and straw out of the cattle barn. John said it took four horses to pull their manure spreader when it was fully loaded. He said his niece Doris waited in the warm kitchen until the spreader was filled. Wrapped in a heavy coat, Doris then ran outside to claim a seat aboard the rig, hanging on with both hands. John said it didn't matter how cold it was, or how bad it smelled, she wanted to ride.

Farm Animals

Horses. Early in the 20th century, draft horses provided the power for most farmers, including the Hinderers. John believed his father made a second train journey from Iowa to Minnesota.

His purpose was to bring the animals he owned in Iowa to his Minnesota farm. Undoubtedly, any draft horses he owned would have been included in this trainload. In the early 1900s, the Hinderers owned as many as six draft horses.

In his interview, John related several stories about horse-drawn implements. He described one incident involving a horse-drawn triple-box wagon. These wagons had horses hitched to an undercarriage. The undercarriage assembly included the hitch itself, wheels, axles, and the support frame. Several types of "boxes" such as a wooden grain box or open hay wagon could be seated atop the undercarriage. Whether empty or loaded, only the weight of the boxes held them onto the undercarriage.

Before a bridge was built across the creek west of the Hinderer farm, horses and wagons simply drove across the creek through the water. One spring, a neighbor farmer had a narrow escape. While crossing in the creek, the high water from spring snowmelt lifted his wooden wagon box away from the undercarriage and the horses. The wagon box began to float downstream with the farmer still holding the reins. John said the box was "like a boat." Sensibly, the farmer quickly drove the horses forward and then dropped the reins. The horses pulled the undercarriage onto the shore while the farmer and the wagon box were rescued downstream.

John said that when he was old enough to do fieldwork, his father no longer worked in the fields. "The boys," Carl and John, worked the horses in the fields while Gottlieb tended the animals at home, particularly his hogs. An exception occurred when it was time to cultivate corn. The Hinderers owned three single-row horse-drawn cultivators. This allowed all three men to cultivate cornfields. Each cultivator required two horses.[14] The horses walked in the spaces between rows while the cultivator straddled the corn row. Depending on the cultivator type, the farmer either walked behind or sat on top of the implement. Cultivating a cornfield, even with three men using six horses, took many hours.

In addition to their own land, the Hinderers planted corn on rental land west of their farm. John said this rental venture did not last long. It took too much time to drive the horse teams and cultivators to these distant fields.

Horses to Tractors. John bought his first tractor in 1936. It was a John Deere two-cylinder, model B, quaintly called a "Johnny putt-putt." It had metal-lugged all-steel rear wheels and a hand clutch. The model B was first manufactured in 1935. At the time, it was the latest in small farm tractors. Rubber rear tires were available, but John's model B had the original steel wheels.

John said he bought the tractor on his own, without consulting Gottlieb or his older brother Carl. It was a way for him to modernize the farm and avoid any argument. John's model B came with a plow and a disc. John and Carl rebuilt the hitches of their horse-drawn field implements so either horses or the new tractor could pull the equipment.

The conversion from draft horse to tractor power was slow, and for some of the older farmers, too much to accept. John said that for years both his father and Carl preferred to use the horse-drawn cultivators. Carl ultimately converted to using the tractor-mounted cultivator, but John said that Gottlieb wanted none of it.

Hogs. Nearly all immigrant German farmers raised hogs. It was a practice carried over from the old country. The Hinderers, like most German farm families, raised hogs destined for their own dinner table. When they could afford the feed, they raised additional hogs and sold them for cash.

Butchering hogs was done at home, mainly in the winter when there was little field work. The Hinderers had a concrete smokehouse located up the hill near their hog barn. Some cuts of the butchered hog were smoked for longer preservation. The smoked meat could even be buried in a granary or corncrib where the cold winter temperature aided preservation. Incidentally, the Hinderer

Katharine

John Hinderer used this small pocket "ledger" to track the identification of the Hinderer hogs. Source: From the John Hinderer collection. Edited by author.

A photo from the early 1940s included Jeanette Krug seated on the metal water pipe with Bob Monson leaning against the pipe and Florence Krug kneeling. The small wooden chilling tank for cream cans is on the right. The pump is out of view to the left and the large cattle watering tank is out of view to the right. Source: From the Doris Schlichting collection. Edited by author.

smokehouse served as a tornado shelter during threatening summer storms.

In his later years, Gottlieb turned over the hog-raising chores to John. By the late 1940s, John had returned home from his duties in WWII and had taken over management of their farm. John used a small pocket journal to track the identification of the hogs. By this time, John was raising most of the hogs for cash sale rather than the family dinner table. Tracking hogs for litter size, growth rate, and freedom from diseases translated into a higher profit.

Cattle. In the early 1900s, the Hinderer cattle were used for milk production. Milk from cows provided protein for the growing children. However, the milk was never consumed at home as whole milk. A hand-cranked milk separator spun the fresh whole milk until it separated into cream and skim milk. The cream was stored in heavy metal cans and sold to the local creamery. The family drank the skim milk. If there was excess skim milk, it was added to the "slop" bucket for the hogs.

Gottlieb's hand-dug well across the driveway from the house provided the cold water used to chill the metal cream cans. A metal pipe carried the cold water from the pump to a small wooden tank. The pipe then continued from the small tank to a cattle watering tank in the barnyard. Cream cans were kept cool in the small tank until the creamery truck picked them up daily. After the 1930s, most of the Hinderer milk cows were replaced by beef cattle meant for cash sale.

Chickens. Chickens were always present on the Hinderer farm. The aerial farm photo shown earlier included the Hinderer chicken house a short distance north and west of the house. Eggs and chicken meat were a source of dietary protein for the family. In the early years, Katharine, like most farm wives, cared for the hens. Later, the chickens were Martha's responsibility. It was a pattern repeated on most Minnesota farms in the early 1900s. The women tended the chickens and the garden, while the men cared for the larger animals and worked in the fields.

Dogs and Cats. Like most farmers, the Hinderers kept one or two dogs and a half-dozen cats on their farm. Their dogs and cats were always kept outside. Dogs were useful during the fall pheasant hunting season, but they also had a more serious role to play. They alerted the family to unfamiliar vehicles entering the driveway and kept the farm free from critters like raccoons and skunks. The cats also had a specific purpose. They controlled the rodent population in the barn, the granary, and the corncrib.

Family Recipes

Katharine's recipes (Appendix C) are reproduced as recalled or recorded by family members. Some ingredients may not be readily available today. Although the quantity may seem too large, the food was often meant to feed a large working family. For those willing to try their hand at cooking, smaller quantities are suggested as a starting point.

■ ■ ■

Notes

1. In her native German language, Katharine pronounced her given name cah-tah-REE-nah. The census taker recorded her name exactly as it was pronounced.

2. To locate this farm, in Google Maps insert coordinates 44.824308, -96.235956 in the search box and click the search button.

3. The citizens wanted to name their township "Freedom," but that name had already been used. Freeland was their second choice.

4. To locate the intersection, in Google Maps insert coordinates 44.820010, -96.235593 in the search box and click the search button. This pinpoints the roadway intersection between the two parcels of Hinderer-owned land.

5. A section of land measures one mile square.

6. Doris was born in 1919. Together with her mother Emma (Hinderer) Lafere, she moved to the Hinderer farm in the summer of 1919. She spent her entire childhood on

the Hinderer farm, raised by her grandmother Katharine Hinderer. Her birth surname is variably spelled Lafere, LaFere or La Fere.

7. To locate this well, in Google Maps insert coordinates 44.819178, -96.236471 in the search box and click the search button.

8. Hard water refers to increased mineral content, mainly calcium, in the water. Underground water flows through calcium-containing rock leaching out some of the minerals. Hard water is generally considered more tasty than softened water which lacks minerals.

9. John's description fits what is called an "artesian" water source. Underground water is so close to the surface that when the water table is high, water flows out onto the surface without pumping.

10. Aladdin lamps with special chimneys, mantles, and highly refined kerosene can still be purchased in some "old fashioned" hardware stores and online. Older Coleman-style camp lanterns also gain brightness by using a mantle. These Coleman lanterns originally burned a different petroleum-based fuel known as white gas.

11. Wikipedia, s.v. "Ford Model T," last modified March 14, 2022, 20:29 (UTC), https://en.wikipedia.org/w/index.php?title=Ford_Model_T&oldid=1077160346.

12. Corn husking contests, often at county and state fairs, continue to be popular in some Midwest states.

13. A gunny sack is a large bag made of coarse natural material such as burlap or hemp. When filled with grain, a gunny sack weighs about 100 lbs. Today, grain sacks are usually made out of a synthetic material.

14. This particular story suggests the Hinderers owned six horses in the early 1920s when John was old enough to work in the fields.

Katharine

Hinderer Family Events

1891 – Katharine and Gottlieb arrived in the U.S.

1892 – Katharine and Gottlieb were married in Iowa

1892 – Christine (Tena) was born in Iowa

1894 – Carl was born in Iowa

1895 – Sophie was born in Iowa

1897 – Emma was born in Iowa

1898 – Mary was born in Iowa

1898 – The family moved to Minnesota

1899 – Prairie land was purchased; the first buildings were completed

1904 – Tena began working away from home

1906 – John and Martha were born on the Minnesota farm

1918, Jan. – Sophie married Martin Krug

1918, Sep. – Emma married Ralph Lafere

1919, May – Emma and her infant returned home

1919, Nov. – Mary married Albert Engstrand

1925, Nov. – Tena married John Monson

1926, Mar. – Sophie died

1926, Dec. – Emma married Martin Krug

1930 – Martha left home for Michigan

1935 – Martin Krug died

1940 – John was drafted and Martha returned home

1945 – John was discharged and returned home

1951 – Gottlieb died

1964 – Katharine died

The Hinderer family timeline chronicles the sequence of important family events. The years 1918 through 1935 witnessed many family changes. Source: Compiled by author.

Chapter 9

The Hinderer Farm: Through the Years

Timeline

1898 – The Hinderers arrived in Minnesota
1899 – The Hinderers purchased 120 acres
1904 – Tena began working away from home
1906 – Twins John and Martha were born
1912 – The Hinderers added 40 acres
1914 – A new barn was built
1917 – The U.S. entered WWI
1918, Jan. – Sophie married Martin Krug
1918, Sep. – Emma married Ralph Lafere
1918, Nov. – World War I ended
1919, May – Emma and her infant returned to the farm
1919, Nov. – Mary married Albert Engstrand
1925 – Tena married John Monson
1925 – The farmhouse was completed
1926, Mar. – Sophie (Hinderer) Krug died
1926, Dec. – Emma married Martin Krug
1929 – The Great Depression began
1935 – Martin Krug died; Emma moved into Canby
1939 – World War II began in Europe
1940 – John Hinderer registered for military service
1940 – Martha returned home from Michigan
1941, Dec. – The U.S. entered WWII
1945 – John was discharged and returned home
1945, Sep. – WWII ended
1951 – Gottlieb Hinderer died
1964 – Katharine Hinderer died
1989 – John Hinderer sold the farm

The Hinderers purchased their farm in Lac qui Parle County, Minnesota, in 1899. John Hinderer sold it in 1989, ninety years later. During the early years, the American-born Hinderer children worked alongside their German-born parents. Between 1904 and 1920, the older Hinderer daughters worked for other area families, adding their wages to their parent's farm earnings. By 1927, four Hinderer daughters had married and moved away from the family farm. Gottlieb, Katharine, and three unmarried siblings remained on the farm. These five Hinderers managed the farm for another 60 years. Through two world wars and the Great Depression, this farm family continued to harvest crops, tend their livestock, and share food with family members in need.

A Working Family

Gottlieb. During the first few years in Minnesota, Gottlieb Hinderer personally accomplished nearly all the field work and heavy chores on their farm. Gottlieb's oldest son Carl was only five years old when the first Minnesota crops were harvested in 1899. By the time his son John was born in late 1906, Carl was 12 and able to help his father work the teams of draft horses in the fields.

For the first 25 years on their farm, it was Gottlieb who decided the farming strategy, supervised the fieldwork, and directed the care of the animals. To be sure, his wife Katharine likely added her opinions, and his two sons provided their labor. However, the responsibility for farming success or failure rested solely on Gottlieb.

By the mid-1920s, John was old enough to join Carl working the teams of draft horses. With both sons doing fieldwork, Gottlieb's primary role shifted to work at home. His job was tending the large animals, particularly his hogs. According to John, his father enjoyed caring for the hogs. If the gardens required an extra hand, Gottlieb was also available to help Katharine grow the produce needed to feed the family.

John characterized his father as "not too bad to talk to, really. He had his work and did it without complaining." Younger generation family members agreed. Bette (Krug) Weber recalled Gottlieb as being quiet, but she cautioned that her memory of him was from later in his life. She said he spoke English well enough but conversed little with the rest of the family.

Florence (Krug) Rousseau recalled that after their heavy noon "dinner," her Grandma Hinderer (Katharine) and Aunt Martha always went upstairs to nap. This left young Florence alone with Gottlieb. Florence said she and her grandfather would sit together outside and just talk. Their talks were not about anything important, but she enjoyed these quiet conversations.

As time passed, Gottlieb trusted Florence enough to ask her to give him a shave. He sat outside on an old wooden chair in the front yard. Florence said she learned how to lather up his face using an old shaving mug and brush. The hard part was shaving his coarse whiskers with a straight-edge razor. She admitted she made a few nicks, but she said he never complained. Later in her life, Florence saved this razor as a memory of their times together.

Both Florence and her older brother Leonard Krug[1] said they got along well with their grandfather. However, they also both played pranks on him. Florence said she once locked Gottlieb inside his hog house, so he had to crawl out through the little door the pigs used. Leonard said he played the same trick on his grandfather. One time, when Gottlieb crawled out through the little door, he was cursing loudly in German and chased Leonard around the farmyard. Leonard said his grandfather finally became winded and gave up the chase. Florence and Leonard both said this hog house prank became something of a game between Gottlieb and his two grandchildren.

Katharine. By all accounts, Katharine controlled all household work duties. She also set rules for her children and grandchildren to follow. Physically, she was small and appeared frail, but her notion of duties and behavior was respected throughout the extended family.

Don Engstrand (son of Mary Hinderer) said his Grandma Hinderer "knew what was what in that family." Bette (Krug) Weber observed that Katharine's control was never talked about, and she did not give out verbal orders to the family. Nevertheless, everyone knew she was in charge. Katharine's daughter Tena told her own children that her mother could hold a conversation with anyone, including the men, on any number of subjects. Katharine was opinionated but fair. Her personal heavy workload and her generosity gave credence to the behavior she expected from other family members.

Katharine placed herself in charge of planting trees, including many apple trees. She was determined to correct the treeless landscape of their Minnesota farm. The apples were a delicious and pragmatic reminiscence from her childhood home in Gehren Germany. Within a few years, the apple trees provided fruit for eating fresh as well as for canning. During the drought years of the 1930s, the family hand-watered these trees. They carried buckets of water from the cistern to keep their apple trees alive and productive.

Katharine planted, maintained, and harvested a garden every summer. Garden produce was essential to feed her large family. Her first garden was east of the farmhouse extending from the house to the roadway. A second garden was later added west of the house near the corn crib. The Hinderer daughters living at home always helped Katharine tend the garden. As noted earlier, Gottlieb worked in the garden as well.

For most of her life, Katharine took responsibility for all aspects of food preparation. The Hinderer family ate their meals seated around the small table in the kitchen. If "company" were visiting, the large oak dinner table in the dining room was expanded to accommodate everyone. Katharine and Gottlieb sat at the kitchen end of the dining room table. With this seating arrangement, Katharine could easily carry the bowls of food from the kitchen to the dining room. In the 1940s and later, Martha took over more of the cooking responsibilities. Her dining room chair was next to Katharine's, so she too was near the kitchen and could help serve.

The schedule of meals served on the Hinderer farm was legendary. In the early morning, Katharine fired up the cookstove to make coffee (ground coffee beans boiled in water). The men would drink a cup before heading outside for their early morning chores. After the animals were cared for, the men washed up and sat down with the rest of the family for a full breakfast. When it was mid-morning, sandwiches were prepared and taken to the men working in the fields.[2] This was followed by a noon meal. They called this noon meal "dinner," and it was the largest meal of the day. Mid-afternoon meant more sandwiches carried to field workers. The evening chores of caring for the animals was followed by a sit-down "supper." This supper was a full meal but lighter than the noon dinner. A late evening dessert course prepared the family for their night's rest. Sayings like "early to bed and early to rise" or "she went to bed and got up with the chickens" were true to life on the Hinderer farm. "Sleeping in" simply did not happen.

The three regular meals plus two sandwich sessions and a final dessert course meant the Hinderer family consumed an enormous number of calories each day. Yet not one person in this family was obese or overweight. Their calorie consumption was burned each day by long hours of physical labor.

Cleaning duties were performed or supervised by Katharine. When her daughters were old enough, they were also tasked with these chores. This experience, together with caring for younger siblings, prepared the girls for work away from home as domestic helpers.

Spring cleaning was Katharine's annual airing-out of the heavy bedding. After the screen porch was built in the early 1920s, bedding was carried from the upstairs bedrooms onto the deck above the porch and draped over the railings. Katharine, and later Martha, beat the dust from the bedding and allowed it to freshen in the spring breezes.

Don Engstrand said he always admired Katharine who he, and most others, called Grandma Hinderer.[3] He said he had one vivid memory of his Grandma Hinderer. When she was very old and quite ill, Don and his mother Mary paid her a visit. Don said that although Katharine was failing, she told them that she "could not die now because the men were too busy." "You know," Don said, "she stayed alive until they weren't so busy and then she died." Don said he would never forget her consideration of family before herself, even when she was dying.

The Boys. Carl and John Hinderer were born 12 years apart, but their eventual work duties on the farm were the same. Older brother Carl never lived away from the farm. He was required to register for possible military service in June of 1917, two months after the U.S. entered World War I. Although Carl was 23 at the time, he was never drafted. Eighteen months later, that war ended. Carl was also required to register for possible military service in 1942, six months after the U.S. entered World War II. By this time, he was 48 years old, and his younger brother John had already been drafted into the Army. Although registered and eligible to serve in two world wars, Carl was never drafted into active military service.

From 1930 on, John's leadership role on the farm steadily increased. By the mid-1930s, he had assumed responsibility for modernizing their farming implements and methods. He was absent from the farm during World War II. When he returned home in 1945, he took full control of managing the farm.

Katharine

The personalities of the two Hinderer brothers have often been contrasted. Carl was older, less voluble, and less likely to engage with younger family members. His work ethic was never in question, but he was often likened to his less-talkative father, Gottlieb. John was more engaging, particularly with the younger generations of family members. Nieces and nephews from the extended Hinderer family all loved to be with Uncle John.

John disputed the stern characterization of his older brother. He recalled that in his own youth, Carl was his role model. He also pointed out that Carl was quite adept at having a good time. When the Hinderers visited neighbors and music was part of the evening, John said that Carl was the best dancer in the room. Nephew Leonard Krug agreed with John. He recalled that Carl and his sisters drove to barn dances as far away as Gary, South Dakota. These outings were largely due to Carl's enjoyment of dancing.

John recalled a visit to a family named Nagel who lived near the Norwegian Church west of the Hinderer farm. On this occasion, the entire Hinderer family traveled for an evening of fun. John said:

The old folks and us younger kids stayed there [at the Nagel's] *while the others* [including Carl] *went to a dance. By golly,[4] they didn't get back until about five in the morning, so we had a lot of time for chasing around all night. We kids were outside most of the time playing by moonlight.*

Leonard revealed another side of his Uncle Carl. When Leonard was a young boy, Carl told him that he once saw the infamous outlaw Jesse James casing a bank right in downtown Canby. Leonard said that at the time, it made a big impression on him. Unfortunately, the fact was that Jesse James was killed in 1882, twelve years before Carl was born. Clearly, Carl did have a sense of humor.

Twenty-three-year-old Carl Hinderer registered for military service shortly after the U.S. entered WWI. He did not serve on active duty. Source: "Year: 1910; Census Place: Freeland, Lac Qui Parle, Minnesota" (Family History Library Microfilm: 1374722; Roll: T624_709; Page: 7B; Enumeration District: 0065), accessed March 2022. Edited by author.

In later years, Carl and John generally took a night off during the week to drive into Canby. The trip to town included the purchase of necessities, but it was mainly a social visit. The two brothers rendezvoused with other farmers for a beer or two at a local Canby bar. Their personal beer choice was branded "Grain Belt."

Christine. "Tena" was the oldest daughter and therefore Katharine's primary helper. Her duties in the fields during corn harvest were previously described. Tena's many duties at home often meant a poor attendance record at the district school. In fact, she later told her children that she had fewer years of formal education than her mother Katharine. Tena's children George and Mabel Monson noted that despite her minimal schooling, their mother was surprisingly good at spelling and writing grammatically correct letters.

Tena told her children that she began working for neighboring farm families in 1904 when she was 12 years old. Like most girls working as domestic helpers, Tena lived with these families. Later, Tena worked for the family of a Dr. Tillish in Canby. She was particularly fond of this family.

In the early 1920s, Tena left the Canby area to work in Northfield, Minnesota. She worked in the laundry of a boarding house operated by the Odd Fellows. While working at the boarding house, she became friends with another employee, Ethel Monson. Ethel was the sister of Tena's future husband John Monson.

Sophie and Emma. Sisters Sophie and Emma were often documented together beginning with their first years in Iowa. Although they were born 15 months apart, they were baptized on the same day. On the Minnesota farm, Katharine required at least one daughter to help her at home. John recalled that older sister Sophie was more often assigned to these home duties. Younger sister Emma also worked at home, but John said she worked away from home for other families more often than Sophie. Doris (Lafere) Schlichting said that when her mother Emma was 16 or 17, she worked for Dr. Tillish in Canby. It was the same family that Emma's oldest sister Tena once worked for.

Mary. Mary was the fourth-born daughter in the family and was an infant when the Hinderers moved to Minnesota. This meant she was too young to do heavy field work like her older sisters. When twins John and Martha were born late in 1906, Mary was 8 years old. She told her children Don Engstrand and Norma (Engstrand) Sandrock that her primary work on the farm was sewing and caring

The 1910 U.S. Census was the only census listing the complete Hinderer family. Seventeen-year-old Christine was included even though she was working away from home. In another column, she was listed as a servant for a private family. All other children lived at home. Source: "Year: 1910; Census Place: Freeland, Lac Qui Parle, Minnesota" (FHL Microfilm: 1374722; Roll: T624_709; Page: 7B; Enumeration District: 0065), accessed March 2022. Edited by author.

Sisters Sophie (left) and Emma were confirmed together in 1911. Source: From the author's collection.

for John and Martha. Unlike her older siblings, Mary attended District 66 school on a regular basis and completed six grades. Coincidentally, one of her teachers at this school was Arthur Engstrand, Mary's future brother-in-law.

Martha. Martha and her twin brother John were linked to the Minnesota farm throughout their lives. The one exception for John was his time in the Army during World War II. For Martha, her time away from the farm was spent working in Michigan. She returned home to help her Minnesota family when her twin brother John was drafted in 1942. After 1942, Martha remained on the farm until it was sold out of the family.

Martha's oldest sister Tena had begun working away from home before Martha was born. Sisters Sophie and Emma often worked away from home while Martha was still a small child. Consequently, Martha's three oldest sisters were not a part of her childhood experience. Sister Mary cared for the twins Martha and John when they were small, but she too worked away from home before her marriage in 1919. The departure of the four oldest Hinderer daughters by 1918 meant 12-year-old Martha was the only daughter left to help Katharine at home. Martha's teen age years were sobered by the necessity of being her mother's primary assistant.

The exact date Martha moved to Michigan is uncertain, but photos and documents suggest it was in the late 1920s. John did not state the reason Martha moved to Michigan. He said she initially worked in a school dormitory in Ann Arbor. Hinderer relatives Elsa Brenner and her husband Carl were employed by the same school. After a short time, John said that Martha decided to work as a domestic helper for a family named Collins. The U.S. Census from April 1930 listed Martha working as a "servant" for the Collins family in Ann Arbor, Michigan. The Collins family owned a ladies' apparel store and had two young children. Martha took many photos of the Collins family while they vacationed at their lakeside home. John said Martha was quite fond of this family.

Doris. The 1930 U.S. Census stated that Katharine's household workload was aided by an 18-year-old married "servant." At the time, her 11-year-old granddaughter, Doris Lafere, was still living with the Hinderers. Doris's mother Emma had married widower Martin Krug in 1926 and lived on a nearby farm. The details of Emma's life will be discussed in later chapters.

From infancy through her mid-teen years, granddaughter Doris (Lafere) Schlichting lived on the Hinderer farm. By 1924, she had begun her schooling at the District 66 one-room schoolhouse a half-mile north of the farm. Unlike her Hinderer aunts and uncles, Doris was able to attend this school for eight full grades.

Doris recalled that her grandmother Katharine was the primary influence on her early life. In 1919, Emma had returned to the Hinderer farm with Doris. Emma soon began domestic work for other families. When this work began, she would

The Hinderer Farm: Through the Years

A studio photo of twins John and Martha Hinderer taken in about 1910. Source: From the author's collection.

The 1922 confirmation picture of John and Martha Hinderer. Source: From the author's collection.

live with these families. Doris, however, continued to live with Katharine and Gottlieb.

In late 1926, Emma married widower Martin Krug. Emma, Martin, and Martin's three children by Sophie lived on a rental farm located a mile from the Hinderer farm. Doris was able to visit her mother often, but she continued to live on the Hinderer farm. As a result of these family changes, Doris was raised almost entirely by her grandmother Katharine.

Doris recalled helping her grandmother Katharine with cleaning and cooking chores, mainly

The 1920 U.S. Census listed Carl, Martha, and John (Johnny) living on the Hinderer farm. Emma (Hinderer) Lafere had returned home with her infant daughter Doris. The other Hinderer sisters were no longer living at home. Source: "Year: 1920; Census Place: Freeland, Lac Qui Parle, Minnesota" (Family History Library Microfilm: Roll: T625_842; Page: 11A; Enumeration District: 91), accessed March 2022. Edited by author.

Katharine

1930 Census

The U.S. Census recorded in April 1930 listed Carl and John as the only Hinderer siblings still living on the farm. Martha had already moved to Michigan and Emma was no longer living on the farm (by 1930 she had married Martin Krug). Gottlieb and Katharine's granddaughter (incorrectly listed as Gottlieb's niece) Doris Lafere was living with her grandparents. An 18-year-old married "servant" also lived with the Hinderers. Source: "Year: 1930; Census Place: Freeland, Lac Qui Parle, Minnesota" (Family History Library Microfilm: 2340838; Page: 5A; Enumeration District: 0010), accessed March 2022. Edited by author.

during the early 1930s. By this time, Martha had left home to work in Michigan. Doris and a "servant" lady were Katharine's only assistants. These were the years of the Great Depression. Katharine's work ethic and frugal economics at home were lessons imprinted on her granddaughter Doris.

Food and Necessities

Fruits and Vegetables. Katharine's apple trees were more than 15 years old and fully productive by the early 1920s. These were the years when Doris recalled the daily use of apple products. She said she ate apples fresh, canned, and made into applesauce. Apple butter was spread over bread or buns instead of real butter. Doris said she ate so many apple products as a child that as an adult, she could not tolerate apple butter. Nothing from the harvested apples went to waste. Rotted fruit, apple cores, and peelings were all fed to Gottlieb's hogs.

Apples were not the only fruit trees on the farm. Doris recalled that the Hinderers had plum trees as well as peach trees, a rarity in Minnesota at that time. She said Gottlieb also copied his Michigan relatives by planting Concord grapes. They were grown to be eaten fresh. Seasonally, fresh rhubarb and strawberries were harvested from the gardens. These were transformed into desserts, jams, and sauces both on their own and mixed together. Green vegetables were harvested and eaten throughout the summer. Root crops were dug up in the fall and preserved for winter meals. The annual pattern was to grow and consume fresh fruits and vegetables during half of the year and to preserve them together with the root crops for winter meals.

Milk Products. As noted earlier, whole milk was separated into skim milk for family use and cream that was sold for cash. Doris recalled that the absence of cream and butter in her daily diet created a craving for rich cream. Her frequent walks to the farm where her mother Emma and Martin Krug lived offered a solution to this craving. Emma often prepared sliced home-baked bread covered with fresh cream and sugar as a special treat for Doris.

Butchered Pork. Pork products were a primary source of protein for the Hinderers. Their butchered hogs were processed into an array of meat products. Some cuts were smoked, others were preserved in serving-size portions, and trimmings were ground into homemade sausages.

Preserving serving-sized cuts in fat was a unique process used by families before refrigeration was commonplace. John recalled that the fat was first cut into chunks. It was then heated in a large pan on the kitchen cookstove until it melted. The scum or crust that formed on the surface of the hot fat was called "cracklings." It was skimmed away leaving clear liquid fat. This clear fat could then be used either to make lard or soap. The skimmed cracklings were not discarded. First, they were forced through a cloth-covered sausage stuffer. Any liquid fat was saved. The residual crackling solids were treasured as a bread topping by both Gottlieb and Carl.

The cut portions of meat, such as pork chops, were first fried in lard until they were partially cooked. This was called "fry-down meat." To preserve these cuts, they were stacked in layers inside a large crock. Liquid fat was added to each layer until the crock was filled with meat and fat. A final layer of liquid fat covered the surface of the meat. When the fat solidified, the meat could be preserved for months. The crocks filled with meat and solidified fat were always stored in the cool temperature of the underground basement or cellar.

Doris said hog butchering day was special for her. She didn't watch the actual butchering, but after walking home from school, Katharine had a treat waiting for her. The large crocks with cooling fat and meat would still be sitting on the kitchen stove. Her grandmother removed one pork chop and finished cooking it. She then gave the hot pork chop to Doris together with some fresh-baked bread. Doris said it was the most delicious meat she ever tasted.

No part of the butchered hog went to waste. The less meaty sections and organ meats were ground into sausages of several styles. One was called blood sausage and, according to Doris, it did contain some of the hog's blood. Katharine used a hand-cranked sausage stuffer to force the mix of ingredients into casings. Doris said the thoroughly cleaned casings were harvested from one specific part of the hog's intestine. She remembered Katharine using a knife to scrape the casing clean. She then rinsed them using lye soap. Loops of freshly stuffed sausage casings were tied off at both ends with a string. Next, they were strung on a wooden handle and carried down into the cool basement. After the sausage cured and hardened, one loop at a time was cut free from the wooden handle. At mealtime, the sausage was fried in lard on the cookstove.

Soap. On the Hinderer farm, the ancient craft of making soap went hand in hand with butchering. The two essential ingredients of soap were fat or oil and a caustic substance such as lye. Butchering hogs provided the fat, and concentrated lye could be purchased in town. The storytellers did not provide a specific Hinderer recipe for soap, but the process of making the soap was clearly recalled.

John said that soap making was best done outside. A large pan was heated atop an open wood fire. The pan was broad and had a flat bottom. It was perched on a circle of stones surrounding the fire. A metal flange was fashioned around the pan. This flange directed all the heat from the fire onto the bottom of the pan. Doris said the Hinderer soap pan was charred black from repeated use. After the fat destined for lard had been set aside, the remaining liquid fat was carried outside and poured into the soap pan. Lye was carefully added to the liquid fat. This was a dangerous step because any lye that splattered onto skin would cause a severe burn.[5] The lye and fat mix was stirred until the lye was entirely dissolved and evenly mixed with the fat. After hours of heating, the mix was allowed to cool and solidify overnight. In the morning John said that Katharine would cut the soap into bars. John noted that certain fatty areas of the hog produced a better-quality lard or soap. The general rule was that the clearer the liquefied fat, the better the lard or soap would look. John said that if bad winter weather prevented an outside fire, they could make a smaller batch of soap on the kitchen cookstove.

Washing Clothes. The Hinderers used cistern (collected rain) water combined with homemade soap for washing clothes. Prior to 1925, their standard practice was to use hot water, soap, a metal washtub, and a washboard. Both washing and rinsing required substantial arm strength.

In the late 1920s, Katharine purchased a series of mechanical washing machines. With no electricity until 1948, their first washing machines were hand operated. Doris said that Katharine first heated large copper tubs of cistern water on her cookstove. Then, in good weather, she carried them outside to the wash "machine." The first machine Doris recalled was a large washtub with a lever on the side that was pushed back and forth to agitate the clothes. Next, Katharine bought a unit with a manual wringer mounted on top of the tub. It was an improvement because it squeezed more of the water from the clothes. When it was not in use, the washing machine was stored in the mudroom.

In favorable weather, the washed clothing was hung out to dry on an outside clothesline. In poor weather, Katharine washed their clothes in the kitchen, and then dried them on wooden racks scattered around the kitchen.

Honey. Store-bought granular sugar was expensive and often unavailable. Molasses was available, but it had a strong flavor and was primarily used in small amounts for baking. Sorghum was slightly sweet and was also used by the Hinderers as a spreadable bread topping. Honey, however, was the sweetener most often used on the farm. It was available naturally, it was free except for supplies, and it required no special preservation.

John learned how to provide the honey for the family by capturing bee swarms. He learned the technique from a neighbor ironically named Julius Honeyman. Mr. Honeyman was traditionally called upon by area farmers when a bee swarm was seen in a tree or on a house.

John watched Mr. Honeyman's capture method and decided he could do it too. He purchased commercially built bee boxes with an inside chamber for the bees to live. Above the living space, there were removable racks of "supers" where the bees produced honeycomb and honey. John said that one healthy hive could produce up to four pounds of honey in a season.

Doris recalled that John cut out a section of protective netting that was shaped like a barrel. It was large enough to cover both John's head and shoulders and was tied loosely around his neck. He also tied off his shirtsleeves and his trouser cuffs with twine. To Doris, John's bee capture method was both fascinating and scary.

One summer day, Doris said that her grandmother Katharine heard the rumbling sound of bees swarming and spotted them in a tree outside her kitchen window. Katharine told Doris to signal John by banging metal pans together.[6] John came home from the field and put on his protective gear. He then took a clean hive and lifted it up until it was positioned directly under the teepee-shaped swarm. When he wiggled the branch of the tree, the swarm dropped into the hive and John had a new colony of healthy bees.

In those days, farmers planted fields of clover meant for either pasture or winter hay. John said that, in his opinion, the fields of white clover produced a finer-tasting honey than red clover. The honey produced by John's bees was like a bonus crop. The fields of clover fed both the cattle and the bees.

Store-Bought Goods. On occasion, Katharine accompanied Gottlieb on his all-day trips to Canby

---

SOAP

11 c of lard	1 can Lewis lye	½ c borax
9 c of water		1 c ammonia

Mix lye and lard and stir until lye is mixed well. Add borax and ammonia. Add water and stir 10 minutes. Place in empty fruit box lined with paper and clean cloth. After 2 or 3 hours cut into bars.

One of several soap recipes from a Lac qui Parle County church cookbook. In this recipe, the essential ingredients, fat (lard) and lye, were supplemented by borax and ammonia. Source: Providence Valley Lutheran Church Cookbook. Circa 1948. Edited by author.

in the horse-drawn wagon or the sleigh. She might buy molasses or sorghum while Gottlieb took their wheat to the local mill to be ground into flour and breakfast cereal. In the 1920s and later, the mills bagged the flour in sacks that had colorful patterns. The sacks looked almost like store-bought sewing material. Katharine reused these sacks to make aprons for herself and dresses for Doris. Katharine's main purpose in town, however, was to shop for ready-made clothing. Doris said that these purchases were mainly undergarments but might also include clothing that was too difficult or too time consuming to sew at home. The scale of store-bought food and ready-made clothing was small. For the most part, the Hinderer farm was self-sufficient.

Church Attendance

John said that the Hinderers first attended the Florida (township) Lutheran Church located a few miles west of the Hinderer farm. It was a Norwegian church, but the congregation allowed the Germans to have regular services in their own language. John said he was baptized at the Florida Lutheran Church.

John recalled one year when the Norwegians had a Christmas program on the night before the German service. John said "they left some candies there for us German kids to have. Of course, we ate it all." John added that at times the Hinderers attended the Antelope Baptist Church located southwest of the Hinderer farm. They only attended this church when there was a service in German. Katharine said the Baptists were really nice and if she wasn't a Lutheran, she probably would have been a Baptist. To Katharine, the character of the people mattered more than their theology.

By 1911, the Hinderers regularly attended Zacchaeus German Lutheran Church on Haarfager Avenue in Canby. This would be their regular congregation thereafter. Sophie and Emma Hinderer were confirmed in this church in 1911. Subsequent confirmations, weddings, and baptisms nearly all took place in this German Lutheran Church.[7]

District 66 School

The Hinderer children and granddaughter Doris Lafere all walked the half mile to District 66 school. When the first rooms of the farmhouse

An early 1900s image of Zacchaeus German Lutheran Church on Haarfager Avenue in Canby. By 1911, the Hinderers were members of this congregation. Source: Image access courtesy of the Canby Depot Museum. Photographed and edited by author.

were constructed in 1899, the Hinderer's oldest child Christine was seven years old and eligible to become a first grader. For the next 34 years, one or several of the Hinderer children, or their granddaughter, attended this school.

Like most farm families, the Hinderer children's school attendance followed seasonal cycles. When the family required manpower at home or in the fields, school attendance suffered. During the 34-year period, however, there was a gradual improvement in attendance. The children born first received the least schooling. The comments of oldest child Tena have been noted. Second child Carl often stayed home to help his father Gottlieb. The value of the education he missed was not lost on Carl, however. Later in his life, he served as chairman of the District 66 school board. By the time Mary Hinderer attended school, she was able to complete six grades. Twins John and Martha, and granddaughter Doris, completed all eight grades.

The Hinderer children and granddaughter Doris had to overcome a language barrier at school. Both John and Doris agreed that at home, they spoke nothing but German. At school, the teachers spoke only English. There is no record of how the older children overcame this problem, but they did. John said, "You know, kids learn pretty quick."

Doris recalled starting first grade when she was six years old. She loved her teacher, Amanda Anderson. Doris stated that when she began school, she did not speak a word of English. Her dedicated teacher stayed in the classroom with Doris during recess to teach her English. Doris said that later in her youth she decided she wanted to become a teacher like Miss Anderson.[8]

Teachers, including Amanda Anderson, usually spent weeknights boarding with families living near the school. Miss Anderson spent time during the school year living with the Hinderers.

John said he liked going to school, and it was not too hard for him. He described a geography test the students took in 7th grade as "easy." In 8th grade, he had to take a county-wide arithmetic test and it wasn't too hard either. However, John admitted "I was in a hurry or something and I made a couple of easy mistakes. I passed but didn't get such a good grade. John's entire class then went to another school for a different county-wide test. This time, there were arithmetic problems John hadn't ever studied. He said:

The District 66 schoolhouse burned for the second time in late 1955. During the 1955-1956 school year, Carl Hinderer was chairman of the school board. Source: Image access courtesy of the Lac qui Parle County Museum. Photographed and edited by author.

The Hinderer Farm: Through the Years

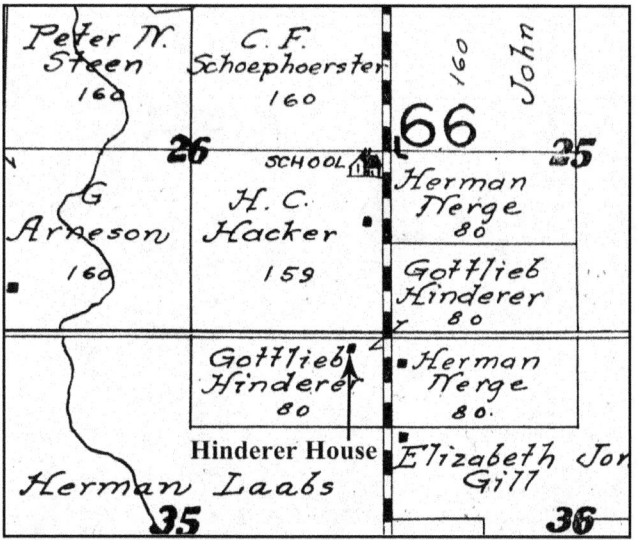

This detail from a 1929 plat map shows the Hinderer farm building site near a roadway intersection. District 66 school is in section 26 one half mile north of the Hinderers. Source: Image access courtesy of the Lac qui Parle County Museum. Photographed and edited by author.

I knew darned well I couldn't do it…my classmates didn't pass, but I think I got an 84, so I passed. There were thirteen of us taking the test, and I think just three of us boys passed.

Over the years, District 66 had many teachers, both young men and, more often, young women. These were not college graduates with bachelor's degrees. As late as 1940, teaching in a district elementary school required only one year of training after high school in what was called a normal school. Maurine (Krug) Gjovig was an example of this training process. She graduated from Canby High School and then spent the summer working away from home. She returned home that fall and attended one year of normal school in the same building as Canby High School. Maurine then taught in a district school east of Canby for two years.

One teacher, Lydia (Hennig) Bode, taught school in District 66 for two years from September 1936 through May 1938. Her own family lived in Canby, but when school was in session, her father drove her out to live with the Hinderers. Miss Hennig wrote a heartfelt reflection of her teaching years.

Miss Hennig described the District 66 schoolhouse as one of the better ones in Lac qui Parle County. The schoolhouse had a small porch attached to the east-facing entry. Surprisingly, this school also had a reed organ. Miss Hennig said she played the organ and taught the children songs, including Christmas songs.

The schoolhouse was heated by a jacketed stove that stood in one corner. It was the teacher's job to arrive early and light a fire in this stove. Later in the day, the older boys took turns bringing in wood and coal to keep the fire burning.

One day while cleaning ashes from the stove, Miss Hennig said that a cinder flew into her eye, temporarily blinding her. When the students arrived, she placed an older girl in charge of the class and walked the half mile south to the Hinderer farm. She said John Hinderer drove her to Canby where a doctor successfully removed the cinder.

Miss Hennig was upset that some of her students were not clean when they came to school. She said "[the boys] had evidence of what they ate for meals on the bib of their overalls." Sometimes a boy might have dirty hands and fingernails. In that case, Miss Hennig would ask the boy to leave his desk to wash his hands and clean his fingernails. She indicated that discipline was rarely a problem. Once, she was angry with a student and sent him home, but that was the only time it happened. Her greatest regret, she said, was despite her best efforts, some students never learned to read. Although her teaching experience was sometimes disheartening, there were also moments of achievement and satisfaction.

Miss Hennig ended her recollections with a tribute to the family she lived with:

The Hinderer family, with whom I stayed those two years, were God's blessing to me. While wiping dishes for Grandma Hinderer, I could unload my frustrations and always receive comfort and

A photo of District 66 teacher and students from about 1927. Doris Lafere was the smallest student and stood alone in front. Source: From the Doris Schlichting collection. Edited by author.

inspiration. They were the best-hearted Christian people I had ever known, and I needed them during those trying times.

High School

Photographs and stories indicate that none of the Hinderer children attended high school. This was not unusual for farm children early in the 20th century. Granddaughter Doris Lafere completed eighth grade in the spring of 1933. She said she wanted to become a teacher like Miss Anderson in District 66. This meant Doris would have to complete high school and one year of normal school training.

Doris's friend and neighbor, Katherine Gritmacher, graduated from eighth grade with Doris. Katherine Gritmacher's parents allowed her to enroll in high school that fall. Cousin Johnny Krug, the same age as Doris, was also permitted to begin high school in Canby. Doris's grandparents, however, would not allow her to attend high school. Doris said "when it came right down to it, the answer was no, girls don't need to go to high school. They just get married anyway."

Doris's high school wishes were contrary to the beliefs of her grandparents. If she were a boy, there was a chance they might have agreed to send her to high school. More likely, she would have stayed home to work on the farm like John and Carl. In 1933, Doris had just turned 14. Her protestation was no match for her grandparents' firm beliefs.

Doris did not attend high school in the fall of 1933. Nevertheless, she did not give up hope. She continued to plead her case for two years. Katharine and Gottlieb finally relented. In the summer of 1935, Doris left the Hinderer farm to live with her mother Emma in Canby. That fall she began her freshman year at Canby High School. She was two years older than her classmates, but she had finally been granted her wish.

Doris believed the 1935 death of Martin Krug played a role in her grandparents' change of heart. As will be detailed later, Martin did not have a good relationship with his oldest son Johnny. Martin's poor health meant Johnny did most of the work on their rental farm located on the outskirts of Canby. Johnny had to split his work time. On weekdays he first did morning chores at home and then walked to high school. After school, he did afternoon chores, which left little time for schoolwork. Predictably, he did not do well in high school.

When Martin died, Johnny's stepmother Emma moved into Canby. Johnny took this opportunity to leave high school in order to work in a local hardware store. Doris believed that Johnny's decision was very disappointing to his grandmother Katharine, and his stepmother Emma. After Johnny dropped out of school, Katharine allowed Doris to begin high school but stipulated she must live in Canby with her mother Emma.

The story of Doris's high school education reveals how quickly attitudes and practices were changing in rural America. Being raised by loving grandparents on their farm had delighted Doris. However, it also meant that the viewpoints controlling her life were those of late 1800s Germany rather than 1930s America.

Leisure Time

Travel and Hunting. Despite a demanding work schedule, the Hinderers did set aside time for travel. Photographs show family members visiting relatives in Michigan and friends who had moved away from Lac qui Parle County. However, the entire family did not travel together. Two realities accounted for this. First, the children's ages were widely separated. By the time the youngest children were old enough to take summer trips, the older children had married and left the home farm. Second, caring for their farm animals meant daily chores. Someone always had to remain home to do the chores.

George Monson recalled that his grandmother Katharine Hinderer would occasionally visit his family in Kanabec County, Minnesota. Their farm was a few hours' drive north of the Twin Cities near Mora, Minnesota. Katharine never drove a car, so either Carl or John took the wheel. For the visiting Hinderers, the drive from their home in southwestern Minnesota took most of a day. During these visits, George remembered that Katharine and his mother Tena would chatter away for hours in their native German. Neither George nor his two younger siblings could understand more than a few words of German. The ladies' conversation was their way of catching up on family events in a private way. German was their first language and therefore the most comfortable.

John and Katharine's visit to the Monson farm often coincided with fall deer hunting season. By John's admission, hunting was the main reason behind his visits. In the 1930s, the Monson farm in Kanabec County was near prime Minnesota deer hunting land. John and several companions usually hunted in the less-settled areas north of the Monson farm. On occasion, they would hunt for deer in the wooded country near Mille Lacs Lake. John said it was a "men-only" outing with primitive overnight camping and hunting during the day. The photographic evidence indicates their hunting trips were successful.

John's hunting companions were often members of the extended family. Don Engstrand, John's nephew, liked to hunt and fish with his Uncle John. Don recalled driving to the Monson farm so he could hunt deer with these men. He said the hunting party usually included himself, John Hinderer, George Monson, George's father John, and one of George's uncles. The gatherings in Kanabec County were satisfying for everyone. Katharine and her oldest daughter Tena had their private time together, and the men hunted deer together.

Bette (Krug) Weber recalled that the Hinderers did make a few driving trips to visit friends and stay

A photo of a successful fall deer hunt. Snow is falling. John Hinderer is seated second from the left. John Monson is believed to be the hunter seated in the middle. Source: From the Doris Schlichting collection. Edited by author.

overnight. She stated that a family named Joslyn were friends of the Hinderers and had previously lived near the Hinderer farm. Later, the Joslyns moved near Mankato, Minnesota, leading to visits by the Hinderers. This type of overnight stay was unusual for the Hinderers. More commonly, the Hinderers exchanged Sunday afternoon social visits with nearby neighbors.

Sunday Family Visits. During the 1920s and 1930s, the most common Sunday visitors to the Hinderer farm were members of the extended family. By the mid-1920s, sisters Sophie, Emma, and Mary were married and had had their first child. The practice of Sunday family visits began with this new Hinderer generation.

The close relationship between sisters Sophie and Emma continued after they married. Sophie Hinderer married Martin Krug in January of 1918. Her younger sister Emma married Ralph Lafere eight months later in September of 1918. Their first children, Johnny in Sophie's case and Doris in Emma's case, were born only four months apart. Sophie and Martin lived on a rental farm a mile west of the Hinderer farm when Johnny was born. Ralph Lafere deserted Emma and infant daughter Doris shortly after her birth. Emma returned home with Doris to live on her parents' farm. These events meant that by May of 1919, Emma and Sophie lived within a mile of one another. Their families visited one another on an almost daily basis.

Sophie died in 1926, leaving Martin Krug a widower with three young children. Emma (Hinderer) Lafere married Martin Krug less than a year later. Emma and Martin then had children of their own. They lived on several rental farms, first near the Hinderers, and then closer to Canby. Martin's death in 1935 left Emma caring for both her own and Sophie's children. This combined family of Sophie and Emma's children made regular Sunday visits to the Hinderer farm throughout the 1920s and 1930s. Just as Sophie and Emma were together during their own childhood, their children were raised together as one family.

Mary (Hinderer) Engstrand lived on a farm about 10 miles east of the Hinderers. Her first son Ray was born in May of 1920. The three cousins, Johnny (Sophie), Doris (Emma), and Ray (Mary) were born within a year of one another.

Don Engstrand and his sister Norma (Engstrand) Sandrock said the Engstrands and Hinderers spent many Sundays together. Occasionally, Don said, the Hinderers would travel to visit the Engstrands. More commonly, the Engstrands traveled the 10 miles to gather with their extended family at the Hinderer farm.

The storytellers who attended these Sunday gatherings all had fond memories of their time together. Doris, who lived with her grandparents until the mid-1930s, recalled how these weekend gatherings unfolded.

Doris said that Saturday was food preparation day. Her Grandma Hinderer baked bread, rolls, coffee cakes, and desserts like pies, cakes, and

A Sunday gathering in 1932. Left to right front row: Maurine Krug, Deloris Krug, Leonard Krug, Mabel Monson, Ruth Engstrand and George Monson. Behind: Gottlieb H., Emma Krug, Katharine H., Martin Krug, Norma Engstrand, Carl H., Tena Monson, William K., Johnny K., Mary Engstrand, Doris Lafere, Ray Engstrand, Martha H., Don Engstrand, John H. Source: From the Doris Schlichting collection. Edited by author.

cookies. In winter, instead of selling their fresh cream to the creamery, the Hinderers reserved enough to make ice cream for the extended family visits on Sunday.

The Sunday family gathering meant at least one and often two full meals were prepared for the entire family. Chickens were butchered on Saturday and baked or fried on Sunday. On Thanksgiving and Christmas, a baked goose made the holiday meal more special. In the summer, fresh garden vegetables were harvested from the garden. If fresh produce was unavailable, preserved vegetables and fruits were brought upstairs from the cellar. All the food preparation was accomplished by Katharine. Doris said that the visiting family members were always treated to the bounty of the Hinderer farm. Norma (Engstrand) Sandrock recalled the abundance of food placed before the children. She said Grandma Hinderer would stand next to her grandchildren admonishing them to: "eat up, eat up." Maurine (Krug) Gjovig said she felt guilty if she did not accept a second helping on her plate. She said she often ate to the point of feeling uncomfortable. Maurine declared that there was no allowance for picky eaters at Grandma Hinderer's table.

Don Engstrand retold his memories of Sunday visits in summertime after the crops were planted. His memory was from after Martin Krug's death in 1935. Don said his family would drive to the Hinderer farm in their Model-T auto. He agreed with other storytellers that Grandma Hinderer always cooked a big meal for the extended family, adults and children. After the meal, Don said the men and older boys would take a leisurely drive around the countryside. The women, he said, would do the dishes and then gather in the living room for conversation and coffee. Don said the men's automobile ride would start with nearby farms. Sometimes they drove farther west to Burr, still on the Minnesota side of the border with South Dakota.[10] In Burr, the older men would stop for a beer and then drive on, observing the crops. When they returned to the Hinderer farm, there would be more visiting and often another full meal.

Don Engstrand noted one difference between his Engstrand family and the Hinderers. In his own Swedish family, Don said he rarely saw an alcoholic beverage in the house. The German Hinderers, however, always had beer at home. In fact, Don said John and Carl made their own beer for a few years. During this time, Don was too young to sample the home brew, but John and Carl always offered their

Katharine

A photo from 1924 or 1925. The adults are, left to right: Carl H., Martin Krug, John H., John Monson, Tena H., Martha H., and Sophie Krug. The children are Doris Lafere, William Krug, and Johnny Krug. William and Johnny were the sons of Sophie and Martin Krug. Source: The Doris Schlichting collection. Edited by author.

From the summer of 1920. Left to Right: Sophie with Johnny (10 months), Mary with Ray (3 months), and Emma with Doris (15 months). The children's ages are approximate. Source: The Doris Schlichting collection. Edited by author.

A photo of cousins from 1927 shortly after Sophie Krug's death. Left to Right back row: William Krug, Doris Lafere holding George Monson, Don Engstrand, Johnny Krug, Ray Engstrand, and Anna Engstrand (grandmother). Front row: Norma Engstrand and Katharine Hinderer with Maurine Krug. Source: The Doris Schlichting collection. Edited by author.

beer to the older men. For the German Hinderers, drinking beer was acceptable and even expected on social occasions.

Retelling the stories of Sunday family gatherings suggests a purpose behind these visits. Katharine and Gottlieb, poor as they were, found a way to nurture the families of their daughters. The Sunday visits to the Hinderer farm meant supportive conversation for the adults and group playtime for their grandchildren. Food was prepared in abundance and shared with everyone. Farm products were sent home with Emma, and to a lesser degree, Mary. If you were a grandchild, Sunday visits exposed you to the expectations of your grandparents, particularly Katharine, but you also experienced their love and generosity. Most of the storytellers were these grandchildren. The pleasurable memories these storytellers savored is a measure of the success of their grandparents.

Bette (Krug) Weber recalled an annual event that brought children, grandchildren and great grandchildren together. In earlier years, July 4th meant families returned to the Hinderer farm for food, conversation, and a celebration of the holiday. In later years, July 4th evolved into a family reunion held in nearby Canby, usually at a public park. Several reunions were also held in Dawson near the Engstrand farm. Potluck dishes were shared, and an official committee organized the event. No matter the venue, dozens of extended family members traveled back to southwestern Minnesota to enjoy their time together. Eventually, the Hinderer-Krug reunion became biennial. It was often held near the Twin Cities where many Hinderer descendants made their homes. Time spent together was a practice handed down from Katharine and Gottlieb through the later family generations.

Any number of grandchildren and great grandchildren could share stories about July 4th celebrations. One such memory dated from the 1950s. By this time, Gottlieb had passed on, and Katharine was physically frail. Nevertheless, great grandchildren from several families returned to the farm for this holiday.

In the 1950s, Minnesota did not allow selling fireworks or sparklers. However, most forms of fireworks were legal in South Dakota. John Hinderer drove his young nephews to Gary, South Dakota, about ten miles west of the Hinderer farm.[11] John allowed the boys to select from a merchant's cache of fireworks and sparklers. The boys, of course, had no money, but John did. The remainder of the day was spent back on the farm exploding Black Cats and cherry bombs under tin cans, sending them high into the air. In the evening, the sparklers were paraded around the yard by the children. In the memory of one participant, no serious injuries ever occurred, and no fires were started. On the contrary, it was yet another example of the Hinderer elders' dedication to creating wonderful family memories.

Neighborly Sunday Visits. Sunday visits were not exclusively for Hinderer family members. If the Hinderers were at home and alone, a neighbor family might show up for a few hours of conversation. These visits were usually in the afternoon or early evening. Toward the end of the visit, there was always time for coffee, possibly sandwiches, and a dessert Katharine had baked.

Bette (Krug) Weber pointed out that these neighborly Sunday visits were unannounced. In the early years, not all the neighbors had phones, so they had no means of calling before visiting. If a neighbor was driving by and could see that the Hinderers were alone at home, they would simply stop by to socialize. Doris agreed with Bette. She said that neighbors essentially invited themselves to stop by for a visit.

Bette recalled that card games were a common form of entertainment for the men during these visits. She said that Carl and John loved to play cards, and Whist was their favorite game. Doris said that in her earliest recollection, Katharine would not allow her sons to play card games. Eventually, she changed her mind and decided it was not a sinful pastime. Doris explained that Katharine's attitude about card games was a carry-over from her childhood in Germany. In her Deininger family, no card playing was allowed. Doris added that although Katharine later changed her mind, she still maintained strict rules: "I don't want any swearing or arguing" she stated. This admonishment was directed mainly at Carl, Doris said. He had a habit of getting excited and would cuss in the heat of card games. Doris remembered that her Grandfather Gottlieb would sit with the men and enjoy the flow of the card game, but he did not play.

On occasion, the Hinderers might visit their neighbors on a Sunday afternoon or evening. Doris said the nearby Hacker farm was a favorite destination. Doris recalled one Sunday evening when the Hinderers were invited to visit the Hackers. When they arrived, Doris said, a deck of cards came out immediately and the men played their games. Later, when coffee and food were typically served, Doris realized that Mrs. Hacker had neglected to prepare sandwiches or a dessert for her guests. Nevertheless, Mrs. Hacker recovered from her error with aplomb. She spread powdered sugar frosting on graham crackers and served them to her guests. It was embarrassing for the hostess but within the bounds of social forgiveness between friendly neighbors.

When neighbors visited, the men and women gathered in separate rooms. Doris recalled that on the Hinderer farm, the men played cards at the dining room table while the women conversed in the living room. The rooms were close enough that Katharine could easily monitor the level of Carl's excitement during a card game.

The separation of men and women also happened during family visits away from the farm. In the 1950s, Emma (Hinderer) Krug lived on Lac qui Parle Avenue in Canby. When the extended family visited, the men and women always gathered in separate rooms. In this case, the women tended to sit around Emma's dining room table while the men talked in the living room.

Music on the Farm. John's earliest memory of hearing music in the Hinderer farmhouse came near the end of World War I. The United States entered that war in 1917. John said the U.S. government was practically forcing people to buy Liberty Bonds in support of the war effort. The Hinderers bought some of these bonds. In 1918,

The Hinderer's Victrola was purchased in 1918. The standard price at the time was $200. The Hinderer's traded in their WWI Liberty bonds to cover the purchase price. Source: Photographed and edited by author.

they traded their bonds for a Victrola record player. John said it was purchased from a furniture store in Canby. At first, John said, their Victrola used wooden needles which would quickly wear down. Later, steel needles improved the durability, but could permanently damage a record if the tip was slightly bent. As a child in the early 1920s, Doris recalled listening to records played on the Victrola. She said it was one of her favorite pastimes.

Doris said she began taking organ lessons from a neighbor, Louise Arneson, in the late 1920s. Doris first played on a pump organ. She said you had to use both feet to pump air into the instrument. There were stops she pushed in or pulled out to control the tone of the sound. For Doris, taking lessons and practicing on the pump organ was fun.

The 1929 purchase contract for the Hinderer's Baldwin "Monarch" style piano. The price was $350. The Hinderers made a down payment followed by quarterly installments with interest. Source: The Doris Schlichting collection. Edited by author.

Doris said that after several years playing the pump organ, Louise Arneson talked to Gottlieb and Katharine about buying a piano for Doris. It was a serious discussion because the Hinderers could not pay cash for such an expensive purchase. They decided to buy a piano from the Baldwin Piano Company of Chicago. The $350 price was paid with a $50 down payment and $30 quarterly installments which included interest.

Louise Arneson also recommended that Doris should take lessons on the new piano. As a result, Doris became a pupil of Violet Sundeen who traveled to area farms and to homes in Canby. Her fee was 50 cents per lesson.

For Doris, playing the piano and singing allowed her to attend social events. The Hinderer brothers belonged to the Farmer's Union, which held monthly meetings in farmer's homes. If the homes owned a piano, Doris went with her uncles to play the piano and sing. Doris said that at the meeting, the members first recited the pledge of allegiance, and then she would play and sing the national anthem. A few years later, Sigvald Arneson, the brother of Louise Arneson, formed a men's singing quartet. They were invited to sing at area churches and social events. Their engagements were mostly in the Providence Valley area of Lac qui Parle County, near where the Engstrands lived. Doris became their piano accompanist, which meant she practiced with the quartet and traveled to their events. If events were in the evening, Doris might not be home until 10:30 p.m. She said her Grandma Hinderer would always be awake waiting for her. For young Doris, playing the piano was a means of gaining confidence in her skills, both musical and social.

Depression Followed by Wars

The Great Depression, which began in 1929, weighed down families across America, including the Hinderers. Times were hard for everyone, John said, but by this time the Hinderer quarter section of farmland was debt-free. Other farm families were not so fortunate. John said, "Our family didn't have a lot of problems from the Depression, but there were foreclosures going on around us." He recalled one event in particular:

One time our neighbors the Labbs came by and picked me up to try to stop a [foreclosure] sale. We *went up to the courthouse in Madison and they did stop the sale. There were some farmers who didn't give a darn, but others had almost finished paying off their loans when they got foreclosed. Those were the ones we tried to stop. I know Charlie Schoephoerster who lived a mile north of us only had about $500 left to pay. They were going to foreclose on him, but that got stopped. It was fair enough in a way.*

The actions of John and his neighbors typified this era of small towns and small farms. The farmers worked with each other, with town bankers, and with their public officials. Not only was it "fair enough" as John stated, but it also kept both families and communities financially solvent for everyone's benefit.

World War II was the economic catalyst that lifted the country out of the Great Depression. American factories were a production hub for wartime materials several years before the 1941 attack on Pearl Harbor.

Several Hinderer family members joined the armed forces during World War II and later during the Korean War. John Hinderer was the only member of the first American-born generation to serve. In the second American-born generation, Johnny Krug, Don Engstrand, Leonard Krug, George Monson, and brother-in-law Bill Gjovig all served. Some family members enlisted, while others were drafted. The World War II service records of four Hinderer men will be detailed in a later chapter.

Photos from the World War II years show uniformed family members who were home on leave. Their visits were sufficient reason to celebrate with a family gathering and a photo. The service members missing from these photos were likely at their active duty stations. Each visit home carried with it the chance it would be his last. World War II Hinderer servicemen experienced close calls, but not one of them died while on active duty.

After the War

By 1950, John Hinderer had been back home for five years. The Hinderer farmhouse and outbuildings now had electric outlets, electric lights, and running water. Electricity also provided power for their wells, various tools in the machine shed, and household appliances. The basement cellar was still used for food storage, but refrigerators had become the primary means of preserving food. John and Carl handled the field work using tractor-powered machinery and new labor-saving farm implements. Their beef cattle and hogs were

The 1940 U.S. Census listed Gottlieb, Katharine, and sons Carl and John. Martha had not yet returned home from Michigan and John was drafted into the army later that year. Source: Year: "1940; Census Place: Freeland, Lac Qui Parle, Minnesota; Roll: m-t0627-01932; Page: 4B; Enumeration District: 37-10" (Provo, UT: Ancestry.com), accessed August 2022. Edited by author.

A photo of Gottlieb and Katharine Hinderer taken in the early 1940s. They are wearing their "Sunday" suit and dress. They are standing in front of their porch. Source: From the Doris Schlichting collection. Edited by author.

raised exclusively for cash sale. The Hinderer farm, like most others, had become a market-oriented operation. Home-produced soap and butchered pork were unnecessary. In fact, buying store-bought merchandise for farm and household use saved both time and money.

While Katharine still maintained a presence in the kitchen after 1945, the daily cooking and cleaning duties increasingly rested on Martha's shoulders. Whether it was what Martha wanted to do was never asked. She was needed at home. During the 1950s, caring for her aging parents was added to her list of daily duties.

By the end of the 1940s, Gottlieb's health was failing, particularly his mental capabilities. Regardless, he remained living on the same farm he had purchased from the railroad in 1899. Other than aging, his physical appearance had not noticeably changed. His now-white moustache was still bushy, and most often he wore his everyday bib overalls.

In February of 1951, Gottlieb and Katharine celebrated their wedding anniversary. It was billed as their 60th but was actually their 59th. The difference was unimportant. The occasion was marked by flower arrangements, a corsage for Katharine and a flower in Gottlieb's lapel. Many family members gathered once again at the Hinderer farmhouse. Many photos were taken including one showing five generations. The timing was good. Gottlieb Hinderer died six months later, August 25, 1951, less than a month short of his 85th birthday.

Katharine died in 1964 at age 91. During the 13 years after Gottlieb's death, she remained living on the home farm. Near the end of her life, her energy diminished, and she could no longer climb the stairway to her bedroom. Instead, she slept on a daybed in the small room off the living room.[13] Katharine lamented her failing eyesight and hearing. Nevertheless, she continued writing letters in her adopted English language to family members including Doris (Lafere) Schlichting. Doris received the last letter from her grandmother in 1962. Katharine wrote of the weather, the crops, and her failing health. After composing two pages in pencil, she was forced to rest from her writing. Martha later found the unfinished letter, added a few lines, and mailed it to Doris.

Katharine and Gottlieb lived uncommonly long lives.[14] From their youthful meeting in Brend, Germany, they defied the odds. They abandoned their birth families and their country, choosing instead to trust each other and the opportunity in America. They found a temporary home on rental farms in Iowa, where they began their family. Their ambition to own farmland brought them to southwestern Minnesota. There, they bought unbroken prairie land in Lac qui Parle County. They built a farmhouse step-by-step and expanded

Katharine

A photo of the extended family from the early 1940s. Left to right, top: Deloris Krug, Bette K., Florence K. Middle adults: Gottlieb Hinderer, Emma K., Martha H., Tena Monson, Mary Engstrand, Norma E., Mabel Monson, John H., William Krug, Ruth E., Ray E. Lowest: Jeanette Krug, Leonard K., Bob Monson, Katharine H., John Monson, Carl H., Arthur Engstrand. Source: The Martha Hinderer collection. Edited by author.

This 1942 photo included servicemen Johnny Krug and John Hinderer. Left to right: Carl H., Emma Krug, Leonard Krug, Johnny Krug, Deloris Krug, Katharine H., John H., and Gottlieb H. Source: The Martha Hinderer collection. Edited by author.

This wintertime 1943 photo included no uniformed servicemen. Left to right: Katharine Hinderer, Carl H., Gottlieb H., William Krug, Bette K., Maurine K., Florence K., Martha H., Jeanette K., Deloris K. Source: The Martha Hinderer collection. Edited by author

The Hinderer Farm: Through the Years

1950 Census

The 1950 U.S. Census listed 83-year-old Gottlieb as the senior household member and his wife "Kathrine" (Katharine), age 77. Siblings Carl, John and Martha lived with them. Source: "Seventeenth Census of the United States, 1950; Record Group: Records of the Bureau of the Census, 1790-2007; Record Group Number: 29; Residence Date: 1950; Home in 1950: Freeland, Lac qui Parle, Minnesota" online database (Lehi, UT: Ancestry.com), accessed August 2022. Edited by author.

A photo of Gottlieb and Katharine on their wedding anniversary in 1951. They dressed up for this special occasion. Note their Victrola record player in the background. Source: The Doris Schlichting collection. Edited by author.

Katharine

> 1962
>
> Embry, Minn. Tue. June 26.
>
> Dear Doris Hans & Children,
>
> Guess I will try and write as long as I can see yet, how are you all, hope you are all well as we are, anyway we can not complain, of course I can not hear nor see much but can be up and around.

Katharine's last letter to Doris was written in 1962 when she was 90 years old. She wrote in pencil and commented on her failing eyesight. She did not finish the letter, but it was found by Martha who mailed it to Doris. Source: The Doris Schlichting Collection. Edited by author.

Form No. 1-M—WARRANTY DEED — Minnesota Uniform Conveyancing Blanks (1978)
Individual(s) to Individual(s)

193222

No delinquent taxes and transfer entered; Certificate of Real Estate Value (✓) filed ( ) not required
Certificate of Real Estate Value No. 89-300
DEC 28 1989 , 19____

Raymond J. Olsen
County Auditor

by_____ Deputy

Office of County Recorder
STATE OF MINNESOTA
County of LAC QUI PARLE
I hereby certify that the within document was filed in this office for record on DEC 28 1989, at 11:00 o'clock A.M., and was duly recorded in Book 151 of Deeds on pages 618-619
was duly recorded as Doc. No. 193222

Doris Farmer
By_____ Deputy

STATE DEED TAX DUE HEREON: $ 330.00

Date: November 6 , 19 89

FOR VALUABLE CONSIDERATION, John William David Hinderer, a single man
_____ , Grantor(s),
(marital status)

hereby convey(s) and warrant(s) to Dennis E. Koenig
_____ , Grantee(s),

real property in Lac qui Parle County, Minnesota, described as follows:

The North Half of the Northeast Quarter (N 1/2 NE 1/4) of Section Thirty-five (35), and the South Half of the Southwest Quarter (S 1/2 SW 1/4) of Section Twenty-five (25), all in Township One Hundred Sixteen (116), Range Forty-five (45), excepting therefrom the following described tract:

A portion of the Hinderer farm sale document. John sold the farm late in 1989 to Dennis Koenig. Source: Lac qui Parle County Recorder's Office. Edited by author.

their farm operation as they were financially able. Resolve and a relentless work ethic sustained them through two world wars and the Great Depression. They lived out their entire lives on this farm.

Their children, the first American-born generation, saw times of great success, and times of failure. It did not matter. Katharine, in particular, remained intent on nurturing each child and each grandchild. Her rules were strict and her expectations were high, but when faced with failure or need, her response was to nurture and share.

After Katharine died in 1964, her three unmarried children, Carl, John, and Martha, continued living on the farm. Carl died in 1979, leaving twins John and Martha to handle the work of farming the land, raising animals for sale, and keeping up with household duties. By this time, John and Martha were in their 70s and there was no successor to continue the work of farming.

When Carl died, John inherited sole title to the farm. He sold the Hinderer farm in 1989 when he and Martha were 83 years old. They purchased a comfortable home on the northeast edge of Canby along the main roadway, Highway 75.[15] John and Martha lived in their Canby home for five years. By 1994, they were in their late 80s and Martha was having difficulty mentally. John sold their Canby home and both he and Martha moved into an apartment at Sylvan Place, a care facility in Canby.[16] At Sylvan Place, they received the assistance they required for the remainder of their lives. John and Martha died in April and July respectively in 2003. In December, they would have been 97 years old. John, Martha, their parents, and most of their siblings are all buried in the Canby City Cemetery.[17]

Family Recipes

Martha's recipes (Appendix C) are reproduced as recalled or recorded by family members.

Notes

1. Bette, Florence, and Leonard were all children of Emma Hinderer (Krug) and Martin Krug.

2. Sandwiches were made using Katharine's home baked buns. The bun recipe is detailed in Appendix C.

3. To her children, Katharine was known as "Ma."

4. When John used this phrase, his "golly" was pronounced "gully."

5. Lye has a basic pH. Lye burns were treated with a neutralizing dilute acid such as vinegar and/or large amounts of water.

6. Doris was uncertain why she was told to bang pans together. Most likely, Katharine's request was simply meant to summon John.

7. In the 1960s, the Zacchaeus German Lutheran Church congregation joined Our Saviors Lutheran Church in Canby. Their old building on Haarfager Avenue was taken over by a different religious denomination.

8. Doris did not pursue a teaching career. She did complete high school, but married Henry Schlichting soon after.

9. The stove jacket contained water which was heated by the fire. The hot water could be used to wash hands. It also allowed residual heat to radiate from the stove after the fire had burned out.

10. To locate Burr, in Google Maps insert coordinates 44.749195, -96.359294 in the search box and click the search button. Today, Burr only has grain storage buildings and a few homes.

11. To locate Gary, South Dakota, in Google Maps insert coordinates 44.793535, -96.456106 in the search box and click the search button.

12. In addition to Whist, the men enjoyed playing Hearts and Michigan Rummy.

13. In the Chapter 8 photos showing the sequence of rooms added to the farmhouse, the room with Katharine's daybed was numbered 3.

14. The average life expectancy for someone born in the U.S. in 1870 was about 45 years.

Katharine

15. To locate John and Martha's Canby home, in Google Maps insert coordinates 44.717083, -96.264371 in the search box and click the search button.

16. The use of the Sylvan Place building has changed. It is now known as Sanford Cardiovascular Institute.

17. As will be detailed later, siblings Tena and Mary are buried elsewhere. To locate the Canby cemetery, in Google Maps insert coordinates 44.703808, -96.275718 in the search box and click the search button.

Chapter 10

The Monson Family

Timeline

1862 – Mary McRae was born in Ontario, Canada

1865 – William Monson was born in Ireland

1884 – William Monson emigrated to America

1891 – William Monson married Mary McRae

1892 – Christine "Tena" Hinderer was born in Iowa

1893 – John Monson was born in Redwood Co., Minnesota

1898 – The Hinderers moved to Minnesota

1902 – The Monsons moved to Kanabec Co., Minnesota

1904 – Tena Hinderer began working away from home

1906 – Twins John and Martha Hinderer were born

1918 – World War I ended

1923 – Mary (McRae) Monson died

1923 – William Monson gave farmland to John Monson

1925 – Tena Hinderer married John Monson

1926 – George Ellsworth Monson was born

1929 - The Great Depression began

1929 – Mabel Evelyn Monson was born

1934 – Robert John Monson was born

1941 – The U.S. entered WWII

1948 – William Monson died

1956 – John Monson died

1981 – Tena (Hinderer) Monson died

1994 – The Monson farm was sold

TENA HINDERER

Throughout her life, Christine Hinderer was known as Tena.[1] She was seven years old when the first construction stage of the Hinderer's Lac qui Parle County farmhouse was completed in 1899. Her sisters Sophie and Emma were only a few years younger than Tena. By 1904, Sophie and Emma were old enough to help their mother Katharine with household work. This allowed twelve-year old Tena to leave home and work as a domestic helper for other families. Tena's confirmation photo was taken in 1906 when she was 14 years old. In December of that year, her youngest siblings, twins John and Martha, were born on the Hinderer farm.

Despite Tena's early departure from home, she maintained a close connection to her birth family. In 1917, Tena wrote a postcard to her little brother John Hinderer. At the time, Tena was almost 25 and John was 10 years old. This and several other postcards were postmarked from Dawson, a small town in Lac qui Parle County. The postcards depicted sites of the town including Dawson Surgical Hospital, a three-story brick building billed as "Absolutely Fireproof, Strictly Modern." Tena's postcards suggested that she was working at the hospital. Her exact job at the hospital is unknown, but it would have been in an unskilled service capacity. Her work in Dawson prevented Tena from seeing John regularly, but the postcards and letters kept her in touch with her Hinderer family.

Tena's message to ten-year-old "Johnnie" revealed an affection for her much-younger sibling. She asked how he was doing in school and encouraged him to write a "big letter" back to her. The composition of the postcard message

Katharine

The confirmation picture of Tena Hinderer, age 14, circa 1906. By the time of her confirmation, Tena was working away from home as a domestic helper. Source: The Doris Schlichting collection. Edited by author.

An affectionate postcard message from Tena Hinderer to her ten-year-old brother "Johnnie." Source: The Doris Schlichting Collection. Edited by author.

A postcard image of the Dawson Surgical Hospital, circa 1917. Source: The Doris Schlichting collection. Edited by author.

confirmed what later surprised Tena's children. Despite her infrequent attendance at District 66 school, Tena Hinderer expressed herself well in English, even though it was her second language.

Three years after that postcard from Dawson, the 1920 U.S. Census identified Tena Hinderer working in Canby, Minnesota, for the family of Dr. H. Tillisch. The census listed 28-year-old Christina Hinderer as the Tillisch family's "servant." In later years, Tena told her children that she was quite fond of this family.

Soon after the 1920 census was published, Tena moved from Canby to Northfield, Minnesota, 35 miles south of the Twin Cities. The town of Northfield was the location of a care facility called the Odd Fellows Home.[2] Family members recalled that Tena worked in the laundry of the Odd Fellows Home.

The 1920 U.S. Census listed 28-year-old Christina Hinderer working as a "servant" for the family of Dr. H. and Maude Tillisch in Canby, Minnesota. She also cared for the two Tillisch sons. Source: "1920 United States Federal Census" online database (Provo, UT: Ancestry.com), accessed September 2022. Edited by author.

Workers at the Northfield Odd Fellows Home included Tena Hinderer, back row far right. Source: The Doris Schlichting Collection. Edited by author.

John Monson's Family

In 1925, Tena Hinderer married John Monson. Their marriage introduced both Irish and Scottish ancestry into the extended Hinderer family. John's father's family was entirely Irish, while his mother's family was entirely Scottish.

William Monson,[3] the father of Tena's husband John, was born in Ireland on January 15, 1865, near Boyle, in County Roscommon.[4] William's father was Edward Monson, and his mother was Ellen Rourke Monson. Neither of William's parents ever left Ireland. According to family information, William was one of eleven children.

William left Ireland before he was 20 years old. A search of passenger records discovered a "Wm. Monson" who arrived in New York aboard the vessel *Republic* on April 19, 1884. The *Republic* took on passengers in Queenstown, Ireland, and Liverpool, England, before crossing the Atlantic. No other Monsons were listed, indicating that this Wm. Monson traveled alone. This passenger listing is consistent with the family story of William's emigration to America.

William Monson first worked in southern Indiana on a farm and in a sawmill. He then moved to Minnesota where he worked for several years as a lumberman. By 1888, William had settled in Redwood County, Minnesota,[5] where he worked as a farm laborer. Redwood County lies near the bend of the Minnesota River where the rich soil is well suited for farming.

William's future wife, Mary McRae, was born in Ontario, Canada on February 2, 1862.[6] Mary's parents were both born in Scotland. Her father's name was Donald McRae. No further information is known about Donald. Mary's mother was Jennet (sometimes spelled Jenn, Jane, or Jeanette) Matheson McRae. Jennet emigrated from Scotland to Canada as a young child.

The McRae family moved from Ontario, Canada to Sleepy Eye, Minnesota, in 1886.[7] Sleepy Eye is in Brown County a few miles east of the Redwood County line. By 1891, Mary's family had moved from Sleepy Eye to the village of Morgan in neighboring Redwood County. At this same time, William Monson was working as a farm laborer in Redwood County.

Minnesota state records document that William Monson married Mary McRae on January 8, 1891, in Redwood County, Minnesota. The details of how William met Mary prior to their 1891 marriage are unknown.

The first document listing the family of William and Mary Monson was the 1895 Minnesota State census. At the time of this census, they lived in Three Lakes Township of Redwood County and had three children. Their second child, Tena Hinderer's future husband "Robert," was two years old. His name was officially John Robert Monson, but he was sometimes listed as simply John, Johnie, John R, John Rob, or as in this case, Robert.

Five years later, the 1900 U.S. Census listed William and Mary still living in Three Lakes Township, Redwood County, Minnesota. In 1900, they had five children. Their second child, seven-year-old Johnie, was the only male child. John's sister Ethel was four years younger. Two nephews of William Monson also lived with this family. Both young men were Irish immigrants. William was described as a farmer who rented rather than owned his farmland. His two Ireland-born nephews were farm laborers, most likely working for William on his rental land.

William Monson wanted to own farmland. His problem was that he could not afford to buy the high quality farmland where he lived in Redwood County. His situation was similar to what the Hinderers faced at about this same time in Iowa. Like the Hinderers, William Monson had to look for land he could afford near the edges of agricultural development.

Kanabec County

William Monson found untilled land for sale in Kanabec County, Minnesota.[8] He was not alone in purchasing potential farmland in this more

Ancestors of John R. Monson

William MONSON
b: 15 Jan 1865 in County Roscommon, Ireland
m: 08 Jan 1891 in Morgan, Redwood Co., Minnesota, USA
d: 29 Sep 1948 in Kanabec Co., Minnesota, USA

- **Edward MONSON**
  b: Abt 1823 in County Roscommon, Ireland
  m: 10 Nov 1851 in Killukin, County Roscommon, Ireland
  d: 11 Feb 1908 in Boyle, County Roscommon, Ireland

- **Elinor OROURKE**
  b: 1832
  d: 28 Jul 1914 in Boyle, County Roscommon, Ireland

John R. MONSON
b: 04 Feb 1893 in Three Lakes Township, Redwood Co., Minnesota, USA
m: 11 Nov 1925 in Lac qui Parle Co., Minnesota, USA
d: 23 Apr 1956 in Mora, Kanabec Co., Minnesota, USA

Mary MCRAE
b: 02 Feb 1862 in Ontario, Canada
d: 21 Mar 1923 in Kanabec Co., Minnesota, USA

- **Donald MCRAE**
  b: 1829 in Scotland

- **Jennet MATHESON**
  b: 06 Jan 1838 in Scotland
  d: 1921 in Regina, Saskatchewan, Canada

John R. Monson's paternal ancestors were Irish, and his father was the immigrant. His maternal ancestors were Scottish, and his mother's parents were the immigrants. Source: Compiled by author.

The 1900 U.S. Census listed William and Mary Monson and their five children. "Johnie" (John Robert) was their second child and only son at that time. Ethel was three years old. William was born in Ireland and Mary was born in Canada. William rented his farmland. Two of William's Ireland-born nephews lived with them. Source: "1900 United States Federal Census" online database (Provo, UT: Ancestry.com), accessed September 2022. Edited by author.

remote region. Located north of the Twin Cities, the county had doubled in population in the ten years between 1890 and 1900.[9] Kanabec County land was affordable, but it presented a considerable challenge to convert it into productive farmland.

Kanabec County had gently rolling terrain with native woodlands mixed in with marshy lowlands. Like most of northern Minnesota, retreating glaciers thousands of years earlier left a mix of soil types. The higher ground tended to be sandy and lent itself to successful farming. Low-lying areas were wet with poorly productive clay soil. The greatest challenge to farmers, however, was clearing rocks and boulders from the land after the trees were removed.[10]

Storyteller Bob Monson is Tena and John Monson's youngest son and William's grandson. Bob described the land his grandfather purchased as one of the rockiest quarter sections in Kanabec County. He pointed out the contrast between the rich and easily farmable soils of Redwood County and the more labor-intensive requirements of Kanabec County land. Bob generously offered that William made his first land purchase in wintertime when, perhaps, snow obscured the underlying rocky terrain.

In February 1902, William Monson bought 78 acres of uncleared land in section 19, Comfort Township, Kanabec County. The purchase document stated he paid $1,170.00 for his land. The seller was a single woman who lived in Goodhue County, Minnesota.

A 1902 personal property assessment for Comfort Township listed all of William's possessions and assigned each of them a dollar value. William's property assessment stated that he owned two horses, six cows, and one hog. He also owned a wagon, a sewing machine, and one clock. The value of his entire estate was $195.[11]

Despite William's meager possessions in 1902, his land holdings increased quickly. He added to his initial 78 acres with the purchase of adjacent land. By 1905, he owned 200 acres of land in section 19 of Comfort Township, Kanabec County.

A 1905 plat map of the county documented his land ownership.

In that same year, the 1905 Minnesota State Census listed William and Mary together with eight children. The census confirmed they lived in Section 19 of Comfort Township. Their oldest son was John R., 12 years old. Their two youngest children, sons Edward (usually referred to as Ned) and Duke (Dan) were both born in Kanabec County. Williams's two Irish nephews no longer lived with his family.

The 1910 U.S. Census listed William and Mary's family with no changes from 1905. They lived in the same location and their eight children still lived with them in Comfort Township.

By 1920, William and Mary's family had changed. Tena Hinderer's future husband John Monson was 27 years old and still living at home with his parents. However, three Monson daughters, including 23-year-old Ethel, no longer lived with William and Mary. The 1920 U.S. Census also added a new family member, Grace Marcy, described as an adopted daughter who was born in Iowa.

Soon after that U.S. Census was conducted in January 1920, William Monson began another series of land transactions. His method was the same as he used in 1902. He first bought a small acreage and then purchased adjacent land parcels. In the end, he owned another quarter section, 160 acres.

William's new land purchase was in Section 13 of Whited Township, Kanabec County. It was about ten miles northeast of his home farm in Comfort Township. He bought the first 40 acres in May 1920. He bought the adjacent 120 acres in January 1923. William and his wife Mary continued to live on their original farm in Comfort Township.

Subsequent events revealed William's long-term intention. In November 1923, ten months after he bought the final 120 acres in Whited Township, William deeded the original 40 acres to his oldest son John Robert for one dollar. Five years later in 1928, he deeded another 40 acres to him, also for one dollar. Finally in 1939, he deeded the last 80

The Monson Family

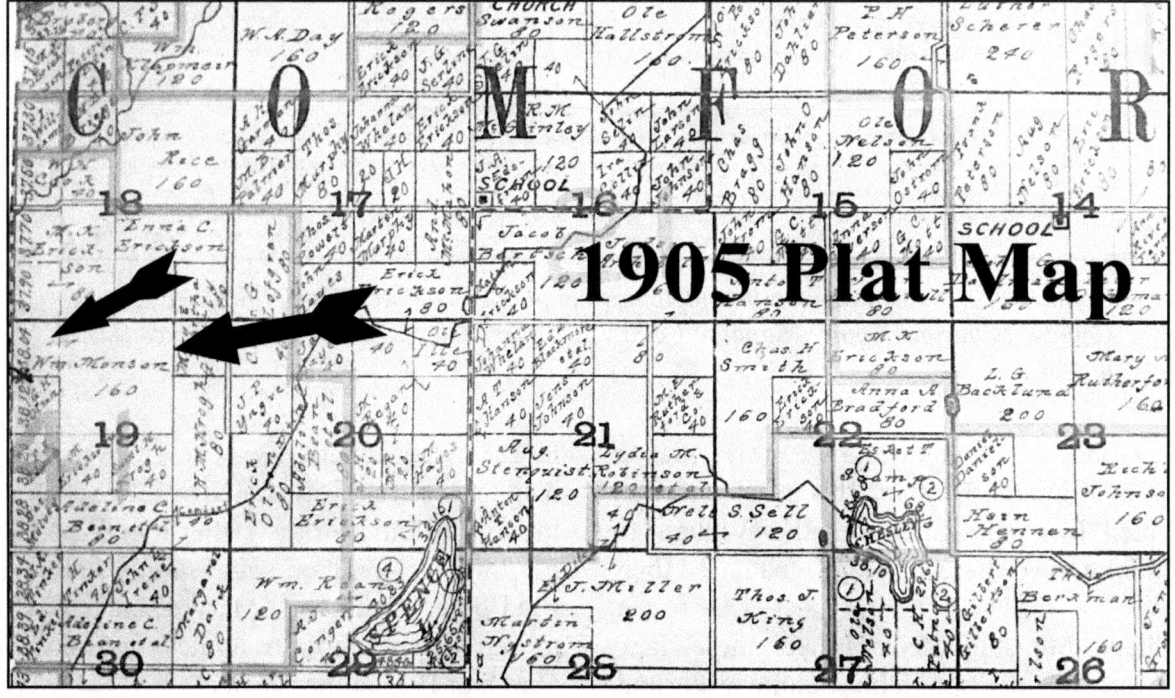

In 1902, William Monson purchased 78 acres in Section 19 of Comfort Township, Kanabec County. He paid $1,170 for his land. Source: Kanabec County Recorder's Office. Photographed and edited by author.

A 1905 plat map of Comfort Township documented Wm. Monson owner of 200 acres (160 + 40) in section 19. Source: Access courtesy of Kanabec County Historical Society. Photographed and edited by author.

The 1905 Minnesota Census listed William, Mary, and their eight children. Their oldest son, John R., was 12 years old. The two youngest children were born in Kanabec County. Source: "1905 United States Federal Census" online database (Provo, UT: Ancestry.com), accessed September 2022. Edited by author.

In May 1920, William Monson bought 40 acres of untilled land in Whited Township, Kanabec County, Minnesota. Source: Kanabec County Recorder's Office. Photographed and edited by author.

acres to John, who then owned the entire quarter section in Whited Township. This quarter section in Whited Township, gifted by father William to his son John, was where John and Tena raised their family.

William Monson accomplished these land maneuvers for his son John despite a serious problem in his immediate family. His wife Mary struggled with a debilitating illness beginning in 1921. Her affliction was never given a specific diagnosis, but she was treated by a "nerve specialist" in a sanitorium near the Twin Cities. When she did not improve, William sought other opinions and tried other treatments. Mary ultimately returned to her Kanabec County home where she died in March of 1923 at the age of 61.[12]

John Monson knew that his father intended to give him the farmland in Whited Township.

> **364**   DEED RECORD NO. 18
>
> Filed for record this **26th** day of **Jan.** A. D. 192**3**, at **4** o'clock **P.** M.
> .... Register of Deeds.
> By .... Deputy.
>
> **This Indenture,** Made this **15th** day of **January** in the year of our Lord one thousand nine hundred and **twenty-three** between **Viola F. Beall and Philip Beall, her husband,**
>
> of the County of **Ramsey** and State of **Minnesota** part**ies** of the first part, and **William Monson,**
>
> of the County of **Kanabec** and State of **Minnesota** part **y** of the second part;
>
> **Witnesseth,** That the said part**ies** of the first part, for and in consideration of the sum of **Three thousand Eight Hundred Forty and no/100 ($3,840.00)** DOLLARS, to **them** in hand paid by the said part**y** of the second part, the receipt whereof is hereby acknowledged, do hereby Grant, Bargain, Sell and Convey unto the said part**y** of the second part, **his** heirs and assigns, Forever, all **that** tract or parcel of land lying and being in the County of Kanabec and State of Minnesota, described as follows, to-wit:
>
> The East half of the Southeast quarter (E½ of SE¼) and the Southwest quarter of the Southeast quarter (SW¼ of SE¼) of Section Thirteen (13) in Township Forty (40) North of Range Twenty three (23), and containing 120 acres be the same more or less according to the U. S. Government survey thereof:

In January 1923, William Monson added 120 acres to his original 40 acres in the same quarter section of Whited Township. He now owned the full quarter section, 160 acres. Source: Kanabec County Recorder's Office. Photographed and edited by author.

> **466**   DEED RECORD NO. 18
>
> Filed for record this **24th** day of **Nov.** A. D. 192**3**, at **2** o'clock **P.** M.
> .... Register of Deeds.
> By .... Deputy.
>
> **This Indenture,** Made this **22nd** day of **November** in the year of our Lord one thousand nine hundred and **Twenty-three** between **William Monson, a widower**
>
> of the County of **Kanabec** and State of **Minnesota** part **y** of the first part, and **John R. Monson,**
>
> of the County of **Kanabec** and State of **Minnesota** part **y** of the second part;
>
> **Witnesseth,** That the said part **y** of the first part, for and in consideration of the sum of **One Dollar and other valuable consideration** ~~DOLLARS,~~ to **him** in hand paid by the said part**y** of the second part, the receipt whereof is hereby acknowledged, do hereby Grant, Bargain, Sell and Convey unto the said part **y** of the second part, **his** heirs and assigns, Forever, all **that** tract or parcel of land lying and being in the County of Kanabec and State of Minnesota, described as follows, to-wit:
>
> The Northwest quarter of the Southeast quarter (NW¼ of SE¼) of Section Thirteen (13), of Township Forty (40) Range Twenty three (23) containing 40 acres be the same more or less, according to the U. S. Government survey thereof:

Within months of his land purchase, William Monson began a series of "sales" (for one dollar) of his Whited Township land to his son John. Source: Kanabec County Recorder's Office. Photographed and edited by author.

Storytellers George and Mabel Monson said that from the start, their father was tasked with "opening up" this land. They said,

When he had raw land, first he burned it, then he dynamited out stumps, picked up rocks, and finally broke the ground for farming.

George and Mabel added that their father's quarter section,

varied a lot. Some parts were good for farming while others were too wet or too rocky to ever be farmable. On the higher ground there was some sandy loam, but by and large it was more clay.

By 1923, John Monson was the farmer responsible for the entire quarter section in Whited Township. Importantly, this land included 40 acres adjacent to a roadway where he built his house and outbuildings.[13] One of the first buildings John constructed was a granary. George and Mabel Monson said their father lived in this granary while he constructed their house.

TENA AND JOHN

Tena Hinderer and John Monson were older than average when they married. By 1925, John was 32 and Tena was 33. They were introduced to one another by John's younger sister Ethel. Both Tena Hinderer and Ethel Monson worked at the Odd Fellows Home in Northfield, Minnesota. How Ethel Monson introduced Tena to her brother John is unknown. Regardless, Ethel's shy-appearing older brother and similarly reserved Tena were a perfect match. A photo from the summer of 1925 included siblings John and Ethel Monson visiting the Hinderer and Krug families in Lac qui Parle County.

Tena and John were married on November 11, 1925, at the home of Tena's parents, Katharine and Gottlieb Hinderer. It was a fitting tribute to her parents and a statement of Tena's affection for her birth family. She had been living away from home since 1904, over 20 years. Nevertheless, she chose to be married in the house that, as a child, she watched being built.

In 1925, John Monson and his sister Ethel visited the Sophie and Martin Krug family. The photo was taken at the Krug rental farm a mile west of the Hinderer farm. Left to right: Sophie (Hinderer) Krug holding Maurine, Ethel Monson, John Monson. Front: Martin Krug, Doris Lafere, and Johnny Krug. Source: The Doris Schlichting collection. Edited by author.

Tena Hinderer and John R. Monson were married on November 11, 1925, at "Home of [the] bride near Canby." The two witnesses were Ethel Monson and Carl Hinderer. Source: Lac qui Parle County Recorder's Office, Reprinted in July 2017. Edited by author.

Tena and John on their wedding day in November 1925. They were married at the Hinderer farmhouse. The Hinderer's porch is in the background. Source: The Doris Schlichting collection. Edited by author.

LIFE ON TENA AND JOHN'S FARM

The terrain of John Monson's farmland and the Kanabec County climate dictated the crops that he grew. At first, John "opened up" the sandy-loam areas on higher ground where he planted corn. The entire process of cutting trees, dynamiting and grubbing out stumps, removing rocks, and tilling soil was completed acre by acre prior to planting. George Monson added,

> *Because of the poor soil quality and the less favorable weather, we did not raise much corn except as was used for silage.[14] We grew a lot of hay and had dairy cattle, as well as hogs and chickens.*

Grasses and legumes like clover also grew well on the low-quality Kanabec County soils. These were harvested as hay to feed the cattle during the winter. The least fertile areas became pastureland for cattle. George observed that,

> *At first, most families had some of each type of farm animal and several types of crops. As time went on, there seemed to be more specialization into one type of livestock and crop.*

For John Monson, the quality of his land and the climate of Kanabec County meant dairy farming would become the mainstay of his farming career.

The woodlands on John Monson's quarter section were a fuel resource for the family. Bob Monson recalled,

My chores included filling the wood box for my mother. We used this wood to heat the house during the winter. My mother also cooked and canned on a wood-burning cookstove in the kitchen.

Tena and John had three children. George was born in 1926, Mabel in 1929, and Bob in 1934. The three Monson children were raised during the height of the Great Depression. Like their cousins in Lac qui Parle County, each of them was assigned work duties at home. From an early age, George helped his father with fieldwork and cared for their livestock. Bob, who was eight years younger, did the same in later years. Bob added,

My parents supervised me to make certain my jobs were done right. The wood was to be piled straight and the calves [feeding them was also his job] were to be fed, not played with.

Mabel noted that she also did some outside chores, but mainly helped her mother Tena with housework.

English was the language spoken in the Monson home. George and Mabel recalled that their mother Tena was more comfortable speaking German. However, their father John Monson, raised by Irish and Scottish parents, did not understand German. Consequently, unlike the prior generation of German-speaking Hinderer children, the Monson children all spoke English from their earliest years.

John Monson's three children grew up near their father's birth family, including their grandfather William. George, Mabel, and Bob Monson never knew their father's mother Mary (McRae) Monson. She had died in 1923, two years before Tena married John. With the two farms only a few miles apart, Tena and John's three children commonly visited and were, in turn, visited by their father's Monson family

Bob Monson said he enjoyed visiting his grandfather William's farm in Comfort Township. "It was larger than ours with more machinery, which fascinated me." Bob explained that when he was a boy, his uncles Bill (William) and Ned (Edward) farmed his grandfather's land.

John Monson's younger sister Ethel married Herman Weidendorf in 1928. By the late 1930s they lived near Mora, Minnesota, the largest town in Kanabec County. Ethel had a son Jerry. Bob Monson said, "I was about Jerry's age, and we were close friends. I would stay with their family and be with my cousin Jerry."

Visits by the Monson children to their Hinderer grandparents in Lac qui Parle County were less frequent. George and Mabel said

Our family would get to visit the Hinderer farm maybe every year or two. We were always milking cows, so our father John and one of the boys would usually stay home to do the chores. Once in a while we would stay at the Engstrand farm or maybe for a night with Emma Krug in Canby.

Bob added,

Uncle John [Hinderer] was my favorite. He was younger and put up with us kids. We were treated well by everyone in this family. I loved the special treats and rides through the country. The scenery there was different from our home area. It was better farming land than ours and they had more machinery.

George Monson recalled that their first car was a 1926 Model T, and later a Model A. He added,

The Model T had a gearshift that was worked with your feet on the floorboard, but the Model A came with a hand gear shift. My father would go around the field practicing driving with the hand shift.

The 1940 U.S. Census listed John and Christina Monson with their three children: George age 13, Mabel age 10, and Robert age 5. Source: "1940 United States Federal Census" online database (Provo, UT: Ancestry.com), accessed September 2022. Edited by author.

George suggested that his father was never comfortable driving their autos away from home. His mother Tena never learned to drive a car. When he was old enough, George drove his family to visit their Lac qui Parle County relatives.

A 1948 snapshot of the Monson family. Left to right: George age 22, Tena, John, Mabel age 19, and Bob age 14. Source: The Doris Schlichting collection. Edited by author.

John Monson was late in converting horsepower to tractor power. In the mid-1940s he bought a used "International" brand tractor with lugs on the rear wheels and steel front wheels.[15] George said, "He bought it from one of his brothers who was looking to upgrade to a rubber-tired tractor." Like his Uncle John in western Minnesota, George Monson wanted to update their farm equipment. He replaced his father's original tractor and implements with more modern models. George added that they always bought used rather than new machinery. Bob agreed that his father was never at ease driving their tractors. This was fine with Bob who always liked working with machinery. In the end, George and Bob used modern machinery in the fields while their father tended to their farm animals.

The Monsons did not install electricity until the mid-1940s. Bob Monson recalled he was

at church practicing for Christmas, and when we arrived back home, the electricity was on. What a Christmas! It made a big difference to our life on the farm. We did not have to carry lanterns all the time.

. . . we [later] installed a motor on the pump jack on the well. My mother bought an electric motor for her washing machine. [The electric motor] saved many frustrating days trying to

Another photo from 1948 included three Monson siblings, their adopted "sister," and their father William. Left to right: oldest brother John Monson, likely adopted "sister" Grace Marcy, father William Monson, sister Ethel (Monson) Weidendorf, and brother Ned (Edward) Monson. Source: From the Martha Hinderer collection. Edited by author.

start the old gas engine that powered the clothes washer. We later bought a milking machine for the barn, a refrigerator for the house, and we added an [indoor] bathroom with running water.

The three Monson children attended grade school in nearby Quamba, Minnesota. George and Mabel said, "there were eight grades, with grades one through four in one room, and the last four grades in another room." Bob added,

> These were some of the best years of my life although I didn't realize it at the time. . . . we played football and softball. We had good teams and played against neighboring schools.

After grade school, the three Monson children attended high school in Mora.[16] Bob said they walked about ¾ mile to meet the school bus. His walking buddies were neighbors Sheldon and Darrell. Their school bus stop was on an open country corner subject to wind and storms. In bad weather, the boys could walk a little farther and wait for the bus at a nearby farmhouse. Bob said Sheldon and Darrell were tough kids, "They never wore winter underwear or winter caps even when it was very cold."

George, Mabel, and Bob

George, b. 1926. During his early years, George Monson was his father's primary source of extra manpower doing field work and chores at home. He graduated from Mora High School in 1944. That same summer, his Uncle Ned (Edward) Monson was helping a neighbor with thrashing when a rubber-tired wagon blew a tire. The explosion spooked the team of horses and they bolted, throwing Ned off the wagon. Ned was run over by the rear wheel of the wagon and suffered serious injuries. Having graduated from high school only a few months earlier, George was now tasked with doing all of the work on his Uncle Ned's farm.

Two years later in 1946, Ned had fully recovered, and George returned home for a few months to help his father on their own farm. He later worked on construction projects around Kanabec County. Because of these events, George mostly lived away from home between 1944 and 1950. During these years, George's teenage brother Bob was their father's only assistant on their home farm.

In 1950, George was drafted into the Army and served during the Korean War. After serving in Korea, George did not return directly to his family's farm. For 18 months, he was enrolled at the Dunwoody College of Technology learning to be an auto mechanic.[17] Following this vocational schooling, he worked as an auto mechanic until 1956 when his father John died unexpectedly.

After his father's death, George returned home to help Bob on their family farm. George retired from farming in 1993. He never married but continued to live in Kanabec County for the remainder of his life. George Ellsworth Monson died in 2017 at age 90.

George Monson's 1944 high school graduation photo. Source: The Doris Schlichting collection. Edited by author.

Mabel, b. 1929. Mabel Monson was born in 1929, the onset year of the Great Depression. From an early age, she was Tena's helper in the Monson farmhouse. While her brothers were tasked with outdoor farm work, Mabel learned domestic duties. These early years at home were before electricity was installed in their farmhouse, so all housework was manual.

Mabel's long-term goal, however, was not working at home. She was a good student and achieved academic success in Quamba grade school and Mora High School. Like her parents and older brother George, Mabel had a quiet disposition. Nevertheless, her ambition and scholarly aptitude directed her to a vocation away from the farm.

Mabel found her career in nursing. She pursued her initial training at General Hospital in Minneapolis. After graduation, she worked for several years in area hospitals as a registered nurse. She then returned for specialized training at both the University of Minnesota and in the state of Colorado where she was awarded a master's degree in public health nursing.

Mabel's career in public health took her to several locations in Minnesota and as far away as Washington D.C. Her career path then evolved from being a practitioner of public health nursing to teaching these skills to younger nurses.

In 1979, Mabel's mother Tena's health was in decline. Consequently, Mabel resigned her teaching post at Gustavus Adolphus College in St. Peter, Minnesota, to care for her mother at home. Following Tena's death in 1981, Mabel continued to live on the Monson farm. When the farm was sold out of the family in 1994, she retired to a small home in Mora. Mabel Monson died in Mora on January 8, 2011.

A photo of Mabel Monson during her graduate nurse training in the late 1940s. Source: The Martha Hinderer collection. Edited by author.

Katharine

Bob, b. 1934. Bob Monson was born September 9, 1934, at the height of the Great Depression. Bob said that like his older siblings, he was born at home. From the beginning, Bob stood in contrast to his older brother and sister. He was more talkative, at ease in a crowd, and laughed often. He was physically proportioned more like his father with a lanky frame, eventually growing taller than his older brother George. His cousin Bette (Krug) Weber said Bob had the longest and loudest laugh in the family, and she loved him for it.

Bob confessed that his easy-going nature did not make him a good student. Like George and Mabel, he first attended Quamba grade school and then completed high school in Mora. He said

> *I found it odd that I never studied agriculture in school but was a farmer my entire life. I figured the best use I had from schooling was bookkeeping, which helped me keep track of my farming business.*

Bob graduated from high school in 1952. His older brother George had been drafted into the Army in 1950 at the onset of the Korean War. At this same time, Mabel was away from home studying for a nursing degree. This meant that in 1952, the farm and household chores rested on parents John and Tena, and their 18-year-old son Bob.

The death of John Monson in 1956 brought Bob's brother George back to the home farm to help with the fieldwork and caring for the dairy cattle. Bob said that from then on, he and his brother worked together.

Bob said that modernizing their farm was paramount in the late 1950s and 1960s. They bought machinery and added cattle to their dairy herd. They installed a milking parlor in their barn and bought a hay baling system that reduced their manpower needs. Bob said neighbors helped each other,

> *We had a good neighbor named Ernest who lived across the road. He was a bachelor. We worked*

Bob Monson's 1952 high school graduation photo. Source: The Doris Schlichting collection. Edited by author.

> *well together and helped each other out by sharing machinery. We had another neighbor, Vylan, who was handy and helped us with carpentry.*

The brother's farming enterprise was not always successful. Bob explained,

> *We first sold our milk cows so that George could help our mother as she became less capable. We did not milk cows for two years, instead raising young cattle. We discovered this was not profitable because the sale price of cattle was poor. [So] we decided to start milking again.*

Apart from farming, Bob and George enjoyed socializing with their neighbors. Bob developed an interest in a local bowling league. He once bowled a perfect score of 300. Bob said that George had taken up square dancing. The brothers worked out a schedule so each of them could be away from the farm for several days at a time. Bob's favorite vacations were exploring the north shore of Lake Superior.

Bob entered politics in the 1970s and was elected to a township board. It meant attendance at meetings, taking care of township business, and running for re-election. Bob said, "we were fortunate to have a peaceful township even when we put in new zoning. Everyone was willing to work together."

During the early 1990s, Bob supplemented his farm income by doing maintenance work at a senior health care facility in Mora. He said he enjoyed working with the older residents but retired after five years due to stiffness in his knees.

Bob, at age 59, married Edna Wolf in September 1993. Edna owned a farm in Hinckley, Pine County, Minnesota, a few miles east of the Monson farm. Bob and Edna attended the same church. Bob explained their meeting,

I bought her some chocolates for Christmas the prior year. We had been sitting together in church for some time, so it [our marriage] *was not a surprise to other members.*

Bob and Edna first lived on her farm in Hinkley. Within a year of their marriage, the Monson home farm was sold out of the family. In retirement, Bob and Edna moved away from her farm and bought a comfortable home in Brook Park, also in Kanabec County. Bob said he and Edna have had a good life together.

The Later Years

John Monson's death in 1956 was sudden, but not entirely unexpected. Bob said his father's heart attack was preceded by visits to a doctor who advised him of his heart condition. Regardless, his death brought George home to begin the years of farming with his brother Bob, who was only 22 years old when his father died.

John Monson's obituary was simple and stated the facts. He was born in Morgan, Minnesota, and arrived in Kanabec County with his parents when he was eight years old. As a young man, he fought the odds and gradually carved out a living on land seemingly too poor to farm. His dairy farm supported his wife and three children until he died at age 63.

Following her husband John's death, Tena continued her household duties while her sons did the fieldwork and tended the animals. By the early 1970s, Tena's physical abilities had diminished. George regularly helped with household work, and Mabel took vacations at home during the busiest farming months in the summer.

In July of 1975, Tena fell at church and fractured her pelvis. After she returned home, George continued to do most of the household duties. However, in addition to Tena's physical disabilities, she suffered from a decline in her mental health.

The 1950 U.S. Census was the last to include the entire Monson family. Source: "1950 United States Federal Census" online database (Lehi, UT: Ancestry.com), accessed October 2022. Edited by author.

Katharine

The onset of her dementia was gradual, but in the end, it became the overriding factor. She was initially cared for in a local nursing facility but did not do well. In 1979, Mabel resigned her teaching position to return home. She cared for Tena and also accomplished many of the daily household duties. It was an overwhelming assignment even for a nursing-trained person like Mabel. Due to the combined efforts of all three of her children, Tena was able to remain at home until her death in 1981.

By 1994, Bob had married and both George and Mabel were in their late 60s. Without a new generation to take over operation of the farm, the Monson siblings decided to sell their quarter section. They sold their home and farmland in December 1994.

Deceased Monson family members are all buried in one section of the Oakwood Cemetery in Mora, Minnesota.[18]

Family Recipes

Tena's recipes (Appendix C) are reproduced as recalled or recorded by family members.

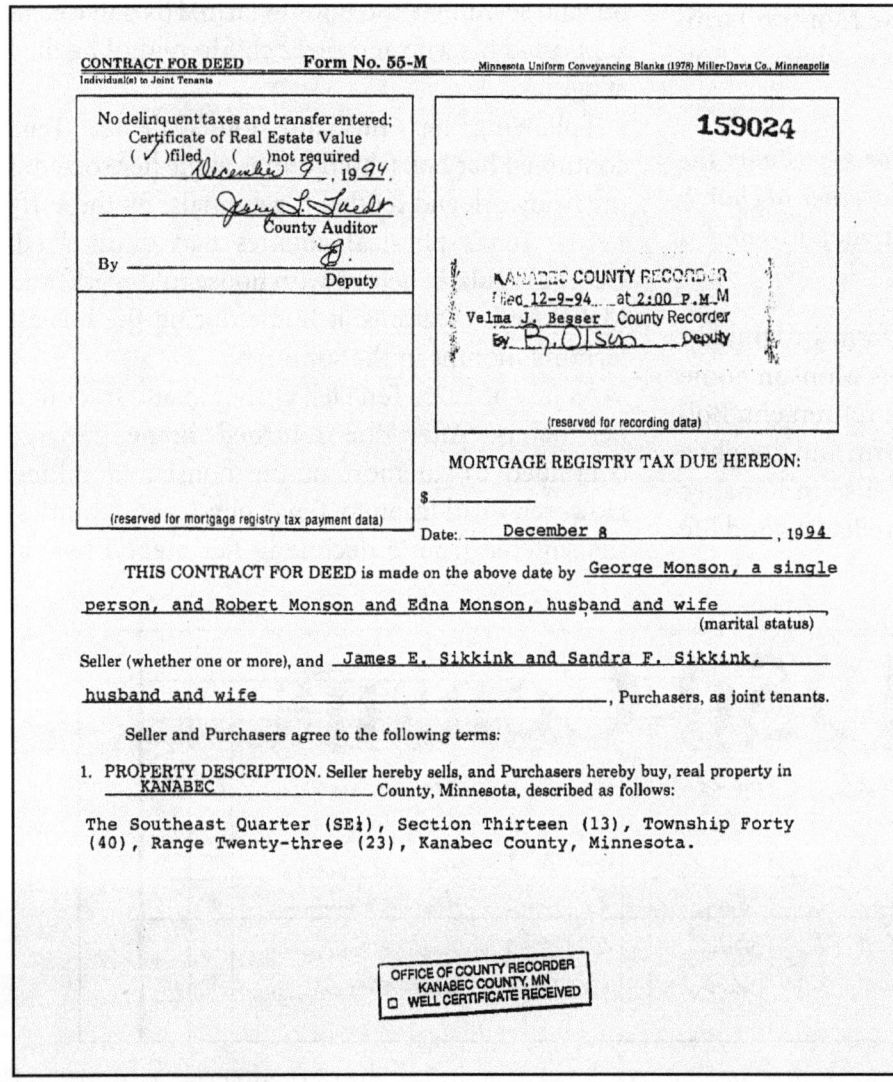

Part of the 1994 sale record of the Monson's farm in Kanabec County. Source: Kanabec County Recorder's Office. Photography and editing by author.

Notes

1. Merlin Schlichting observed that in German, Christine is pronounced "Chris-TEE-neh" with three syllables. In English, Christine is pronounced "Chris- TEEN" with two syllables. The Hinderers may have shortened her name but preserved the German sound by calling her Tena.

2. The 120-acre Northfield, Minnesota, Odd Fellows Home had a children's building and an old folks building. The Odd Fellows was a cooperative organization of workers. Their Northfield home was meant to care for orphans, widows, or elderly members who were unable to care for themselves. In later years, the number of residents at the home decreased as government support programs increased.

3. The ancestry of John Monson was derived from official documents and from family information. The family information was sent in a 1981 letter from Jane Strating to her cousin Mabel Monson. In turn, Mabel shared it with this author.

4. To find Boyle, in Google Maps insert coordinates 53.975452, -8.297415 in the search box and click the search button.

5. To locate Redwood County, in Google Maps insert coordinates 44.403886, -95.238403 in the search box and click the search button.

6. The date (February 2, 1862) of Mary's birth was derived from family information. Mary's obituary stated she was born on February 9, 1862.

7. This information comes from Mary McRae's obituary.

8. Kanabec (pronounced kah-NAY-bic) is derived from the Ojibwe word for snake. The Snake River courses diagonally through the county.

9. Wikipedia s.v. "Kanabec County, Minnesota," last modified August 24, 2022, 01:56 (UTC), https://en.wikipedia.org/w/index.php?title=Kanabec_County,_Minnesota&oldid=1106311665.

10. The mix of rocks, boulders, and various soils left by glaciers is known as glacial till.

11. Access to William Monson's personal property record courtesy of Kanabec County Historical Society.

12. Mary's end-of-life health information was taken from her obituary. The author of this book speculates that Mary suffered from an unnamed mental illness.

13. To locate John and Tena's house, in Google Maps insert coordinates 45.948788, -93.149391 in the search box and click the search button.

14. Silage preparation meant cutting and chopping the corn before the ears matured. When stored and aged, it underwent fermentation which aided preservation. Silage provided a nourishing mix fed to the cattle throughout the winter months.

15. John Hinderer bought his first tractor in the mid-1930s, about 10 years earlier.

16. To locate Mora, Minnesota, in Google Maps insert coordinates 45.876864, -93.293074 in the search box and click the search button.

17. The Dunwoody College of Technology in Minneapolis was a leader in vocational instruction for most of the 20th century. Today, it still offers degrees in many technical fields, including construction and electronics.

18. To locate the Monson burial site, in Google Maps insert coordinates 45.885201, -93.305574 in the search box and click the search button.

Katharine

Ancestors of Martin John Krug (1893-1935)

1 Martin John Krug
b. 6 Oct 1893, Gardner, Ill.
m. 16 Jan 1918 to Sophie Hinderer in Canby, Minn.
m. 2 Dec 1926 to Emma Anna Lafere in Canby, Minn.
d. 4 Jan 1935, Canby, Minn.

2 John George Krug
b. 23 Mar 1867, Grundy Co., Ill
m. 13 Nov 1892, Grundy Co., Ill.
d. 26 Sep 1895, Grundy Co., Ill.

3 Anna Magdalena Hansen
b. 7 Nov 1873, Grundy Co., Ill.
d. 2 Dec 1950, Canby, Minn.

4 Johann Konrad Krug
b. 27 Oct 1840, Bavaria, Germany
m. 15 Apr 1866, Will Co., Ill.
d. 18 May 1923, Grundy Co., Ill.

5 Anna Margaretha Elizabeth Schaller
b. 28 Feb 1846, Bavaria, Germany
d. 21 Sep 1919, Dwight, Ill.

6 Andreas Boysen Hansen
b. 26 Mar 1852, Rejsby, Tønder, Denmark[1]
m. 25 Mar 1873, Gardner, Ill.
d. 2 Jun 1938, Canby, Minn.

7 Marie 'Mary' Perschnick[2]
b. 12 Apr 1855, Lindchen, Brandenburg,[3] Germany
d. 9 Jan 1933, Canby, Minn.

8 Johann Christoph Krug
b. 3 Jan 1797, Niederoberbach, Bavaria, Germany
m. 28 Jan 1821, Neuendettelsau, Bavaria, Germany
d. 12 Apr 1860, Grundy Co., Ill.

9 Anna Barbara Deuerlein
b. 16 Sep 1802, Neuendettelsau, Bavaria, Germany
d. 8 Sep 1855, Illinois

12 Hans Peter Hansen
b. 17 Jun 1812, Guldager, Ribe, Denmark
m. 30 Mar 1839 Rejsby, Tønder, Denmark
d. 25 May 1871, Rejsby, Tønder, Denmark

13 Ingeborg Kirstine Jensdatter
b. 3 Dec 1812, Rejsby, Tønder, Denmark
d. 1 Jul 1899, Illinois

14 Johann Perschnick[2]
b. ca. 1809, Brandenburg, Germany
m. 5 May 1833, Drebkau, Brandenburg,[3] Germany
d. 9 Feb 1889, Grundy Co., Illinois

15 Christiane Kubla[4]
b. 1809, Brandenburg, Germany

16 Johann Matthias Krug
b. 1750, Bavaria, Germany
m. 16 Nov 1790, Niederoberbach, Bavaria, Germany
d. before 1821, Niederoberbach, Bavaria, Germany

17 Anna Marie Barbara Schmidt
b. 1762, Niederoberbach, Bavaria, Germany

18 Johann Peter Deuerlein
b. 8 Jan 1776, Neuendettelsau, Bavaria, Germany
m. 17 May 1797, Neuendettelsau, Bavaria, Germany
d. 10 Apr 1821, Neuendettelsau, Bavaria, Germany

19 Katherina Reiter

28 Hanns Perschnick[2]
b. 24 Sept 1775, Brandenburg,[3] Germany
m.
d. 6 Mar 1849, Lubochow, Brandenburg,[3] Germany

29 Elisabeth Poreschack
b. 1773, Brandenburg,[3] Germany
d. 3 Apr 1852, Lubochow, Brandenburg, Germany

30 Matthes Kubla
b. Brandenburg, Germany

31 Maria Noack

Sources
> United States Federal Censuses, Ancestry.com, Provo, UT.
> Illinois, Marriage Index, 1860-1920, Ancestry.com, Provo, UT.
> U.S., Find A Grave Index, 1600s-Current, Ancestry.com, Provo, UT.
> Baden, Germany, Lutheran Baptisms, Marriages, and Burials, Ancestry.com, Lehi, UT.
> Ansbach, Germany, Lutheran Parish Register Extracts, 1526-1940, Ancestry.com, Provo, UT.
> Minnesota, Territorial and State Censuses, 1849-1905, Ancestry.com, Provo, UT.
> Germany, Prussia, Brandenburg and Posen, Select Church Book Duplicates, 1794-1874, Ancestry.com, Provo, UT.
> Trinity Lutheran Ch. Register, Grundy Co, Ill.

Notes
[1] Some records list his birth year as 1854, but all U.S. records indicate 1852.
[2] In some records the name is "Perschnig."
[3] Brandenburg is one of the federal states of present-day Germany. During the years included in this chart, the region was known as Lusatia (in German "Lausitz") and was part of the Kingdom of Prussia. For more information, see https://www.britannica.com/place/Lusatia.
[4] Christiane Kubla might not have been mother to all of Johann Perschnick's children. The record is incomplete.

Chapter 11

The Illinois Krug Family

Timeline

1818 – Illinois became the 21st state

1852 – Johann Christoph Krug's family arrived in America

1854 – Trinity Lutheran Church was built

1858 – Margaret (Margaretha) Schaller arrived in America

1861 – The American Civil War began

1865 – The American Civil War ended; Lincoln assassinated

1866 – Johann Konrad Krug married Margaret Schaller in Illinois

1867 – Martin's father, John George Krug, was born in Illinois

1869 – The first transcontinental railroad was completed

1871 – The German Empire was formed

1871 – Andrew (Andreas) Hansen arrived in Illinois

1872 – Mary (Marie) Perschnick arrived in Illinois

1873 – Railroad speculation in the U.S. led to economic depression

1873 – Andrew Hansen married Mary Perschnick in Illinois

1873 – Martin's mother, Anna Magdalena Hansen, was born in Illinois

1879 – Edison invented the electric light bulb

1892 – Martin Krug's parents were married in Illinois

1893 – Martin Krug was born in Illinois

1893 – The Panic of 1893 led to four years of economic depression

1895 – Martin's father John George Krug died in Illinois

1896 – Martin's mother was remarried to Nels Hansen

1898 – The Spanish-American War

1903 – Martin's maternal grandparents moved to Minnesota

1904 – Martin, his mother, his stepfather, and his half siblings moved to Minnesota

This chapter traces the lives of Martin Krug's ancestors. It identifies their European origins and their early life in Illinois. It follows them as their farmland passes through younger family generations and ultimately takes Martin and his parents to Yellow Medicine County, Minnesota.

Martin Krug was born in 1893 in Illinois, but lived most of his life in Minnesota. His parents, John George Krug and Anna Magdalena Hansen, were also born in Illinois. A generation earlier, Martin's four grandparents were all born in Europe and emigrated to America as children or young adults. His father's Krug family came from Bavaria in southeastern Germany. His mother's Hansen family came from Brandenburg in northeastern Germany and also from Denmark.

The immigration years of Martin Krug's grandparent's straddled great events in Germany and in America. His paternal Krug ancestors left their homeland for America in the 1850s before Germany was united as a country. Their arrival was also nearly a decade before Americans fought a civil war over slavery. Martin's maternal Hansen ancestors left their European homelands in the early 1870s. By this time, independent German states had united to form the German Empire. In America, the civil war had ended, and slavery had been abolished.

Martin's ancestors settled in northeastern Illinois. Most of them had been farmers in Europe and they continued to work as farmers in Illinois. When they arrived in America, the Midwest had newly available and affordable farmland.

The diagram of Martin Krug's ancestors at the beginning of this chapter lists his direct line ancestors. Each person is preceded by a number, with Martin as #1. Martin's father is #2, his mother is #3, and so on back in time. While the diagram is incomplete, all of the direct line ancestors discussed in this chapter are listed on the ancestor chart.[1]

In the narrative that follows, Martin's ancestors are named and also identified by their number in the diagram. Some ancestors also have underlined given names. These are the names they were commonly known by during their lifetime. Readers are encouraged to refer to the diagram to identify the ancestor being discussed.

The Krug Immigrants - Adults

Martin's paternal Krug ancestors emigrated from Germany to Illinois in 1852. These ancestors all came from the modern state of Bavaria. When they emigrated in 1852, Germany was not yet a nation,[2] and their Bavarian homeland was an independent country.

Martin's great grandfather Johann Christoph Krug (#8) was born in a small rural area known as Niederoberbach.[3] Johann Christoph's future wife, Anna Barbara Deuerlein (#9), lived in the nearby town of Neuendettelsau.[4] Both Niederoberbach and Neuendettelsau were located in a region known as Franconia. After the German Empire was formed in 1871, Franconia became part of the German state of Bavaria. Johann Christoph and Anna Barbara were married in 1821 in her hometown, Neuendettelsau.

Church records indicate that after their marriage, Johann Christoph and Anna Barbara remained in Neuendettelsau where he worked as a farmer. Their children were born over the ensuing years including a son, Johann Konrad (#4), born in 1840. In all, they had 14 children including four who died in childhood while they lived in Neuendettelsau.

Johann Christoph and Anna Barbara moved away from Neuendettelsau soon after their son Johann Konrad (#4) was born in 1840. By the early 1850s, family documents identified them living in the town of Kanndorf[5] about 50 miles northeast of Neuendettelsau.

In 1839, Johann Christoph "registered" to leave Bavaria.[6] Registration to emigrate did not require an immediate departure. It did, however, reveal his intention to leave his homeland. His emigration from Franconia to America occurred more than a decade later and is well documented.

The family of Johann Christoph Krug departed from the port city of Hamburg on April 17, 1852 aboard the sailing ship *Harburg*.[7] Like most poor immigrants, they traveled in the steerage quarters between ship decks. Their arrival date in America is unknown, but sailing ships usually took four to twelve weeks to make the crossing. Documents from America indicate they had settled in Grundy County, Illinois, later that same year, 1852.

The emigration of this Krug family from Franconia occurred at the same time as a religious leader in the village of Neuendettelsau achieved prominence. Johann Konrad William Loehe[8] never left his pastorate in Neuendettelsau, but his influence was felt widely in the American Midwestern states of Illinois and Iowa.

Pastor Loehe was visited by church missionaries who had returned to Franconia after traveling through the sparsely settled American Midwest. They wanted Loehe to sponsor new religious enclaves in America. Sponsorship often meant Loehe would pay the one-way trans-Atlantic fare for families willing to emigrate to America. These families were expected to form new church congregations wherever they settled. The result was a number of new "Franconian" congregations in the American Midwest.

In 1854, with Pastor Loehe's sponsorship, a new church was established in Goodfarm Township, Grundy County, Illinois. For decades, its name, "Frankenkirche" (Franconian Church) reflected the Bavarian origin of its membership.[9] In the later 1800s, the name of the church was officially changed to Trinity Lutheran Church.[10]

Johann Christoph and Anna Barbara Krug (#8 & #9) were early members of the Franconian congregation in Goodfarm Township. The timing of the Krug family's emigration and their early

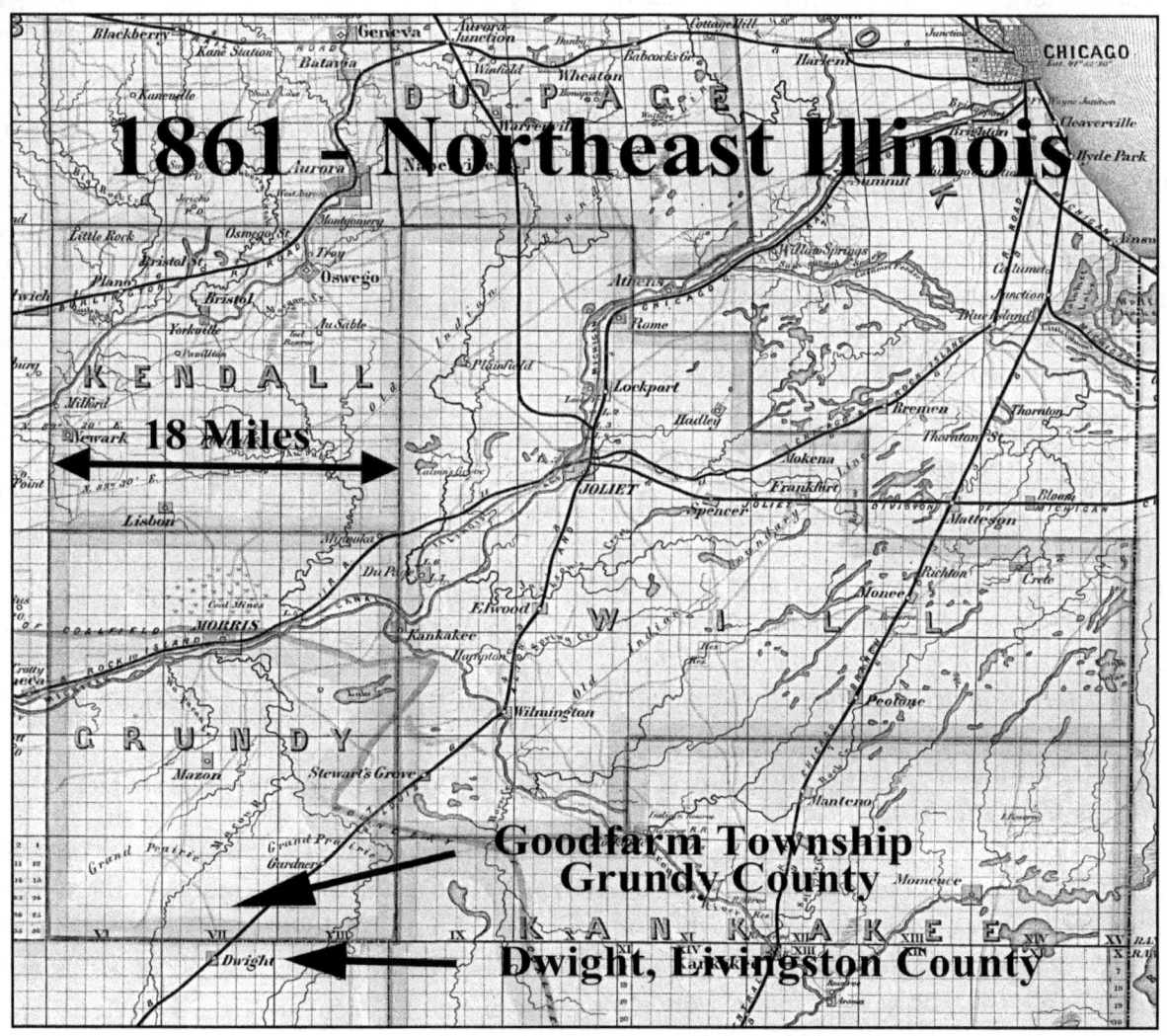

An 1861 map of northeastern Illinois. The Krug family settled in Goodfarm Township in the southern part of Grundy County. The town of Dwight in neighboring Livingston County was nearby. Note the close proximity to Chicago on Lake Michigan. Source: Leopold Richter, "Sectional Map of the State of Illinois: Especially Exhibiting the Exact Boundaries of Counties as Established by Law and the General Topography of the State as Towns, Streams, Lakes, Ponds, Bluffs, Railroads, State-& Common-Roads & etc. Also the Main Coal Field, Mineral Districts, Outcrops of Coalbanks, Mines & etc, scale 1:380,160; two parts, 163 x 53 cm each (Springfield, IL: L. Richter and L. East, Bro. & Co., 1861), Library of Congress, accessed December 18, 2022, https://www.loc.gov/item/98688466/. Edited by author.

church membership suggests they may have been a part of this "Franconian" movement sponsored by Pastor Loehe.

Like other Midwestern Franconian churches, Trinity Lutheran Church was isolationist in its practices. Rather than trying to convert neighbors to their own religious beliefs, the goal of the membership was to remain separate from American society. They only permitted their native German language to be spoken in church and in the schools their children attended. Their attempts at isolation ultimately failed, but for decades the early church members remained apart from their neighbors and from American society.

In the 1850s, Grundy County was an increasingly popular German immigrant destination. The early settlers were faced with a sparsely populated prairie that was unfenced and unbroken. In the book *History: Grundy County Illinois* published in 1882, life in 1850s Goodfarm Township was described:

> *About 1850 a tide of German emigration began to flow into the township [Goodfarm], which continues until this nationality constitutes fully one-half of the population.... In a country without continuous fences, and few landmarks save the groves [of trees], it required some considerable skill and an intimate knowledge of the country to successfully cross even a small prairie in broad daylight. Crossing the uncultivated prairie at night was a very uncertain venture even to the most expert. Each family had its signal light which was readily recognized by its members. It was a frequent practice to erect a pole by the chimney of the cabin and place a lighted [kerosene] lantern at the top. Others had a light in the window, which often saved a dreary night's experience on the prairie.*[11]

Johann Christoph and Anna Barbara Krug lived in Goodfarm Township for less than a decade. Three years after her arrival, Anna Barbara (#9) died on September 8, 1855. Her death occurred a few days before her 53rd birthdate. Her husband Johann Christoph (#8) died on April 12, 1860 at the age of 63. Johann and Anna Barbara are buried in Goodfarm Cemetery across the roadway from Trinity Lutheran Church.

The tall cemetery marker for Johann Christoph Krug (#8) and Anna Barbara (Deuerlein) Krug (#9) has a metal plate with their death dates. The lower two names include one son, George Bernhard, "b. 1839." (Most sources list George Bernhard's birth year as 1838). Source: Photographed and edited by author.

KRUG IMMIGRANTS - CHILDREN

Johann Christoph and Anna Barbara Krug's three youngest sons were Georg Bernhard (b.1838), Johann Konrad (b.1840) (#4), and Georg Leonhard (b.1844). Only Johann Konrad (#4) was a direct line ancestor of Martin Krug. Therefore, he is the only brother included on the ancestor chart. This Krug generation, including Martin Krug's paternal grandfather Johann Konrad Krug (#4), arrived in America as children or teenagers. The three Krug brothers were close in age and remained close to one another throughout their adult lives. All three became farmers in Goodfarm Township, Grundy County, Illinois.

The Illinois Krug Family

One of three January 1866 land purchase/sale documents. Martin Krug's grandfather Johann Konrad Krug (#4) bought 80 acres of inherited farmland from his two brothers, Bernhard and Leonhard. Source: Recorders Office, Grundy County, Morris, Illinois. Edited by author.

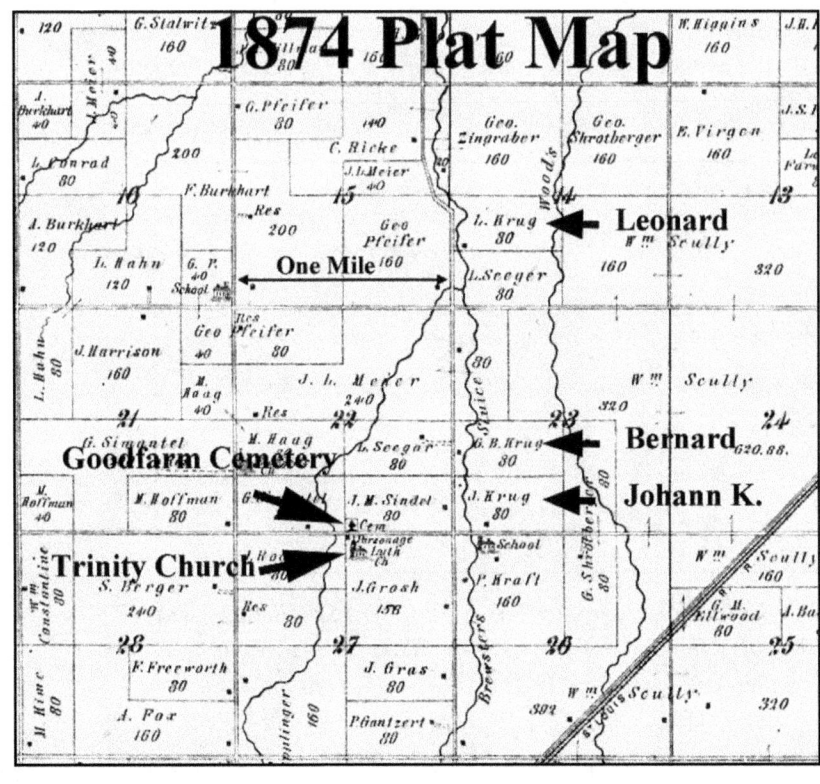

An 1874 plat map located the three 80-acre parcels owned by the three Krug brothers. Two of the parcels are less than a mile from Trinity Lutheran Church. Source: "Atlas of Grundy Co. and the State of Illinois" (Chicago, IL: Warner & Beers, 1874), University of Illinois at Urbana-Champaign Library, accessed December 18, 2022, https://digital.library.illinois.edu/items/2d2bc3f0-fe25-0139-7ab5-02d0d7bfd6e4-3. Edited by author

Katharine

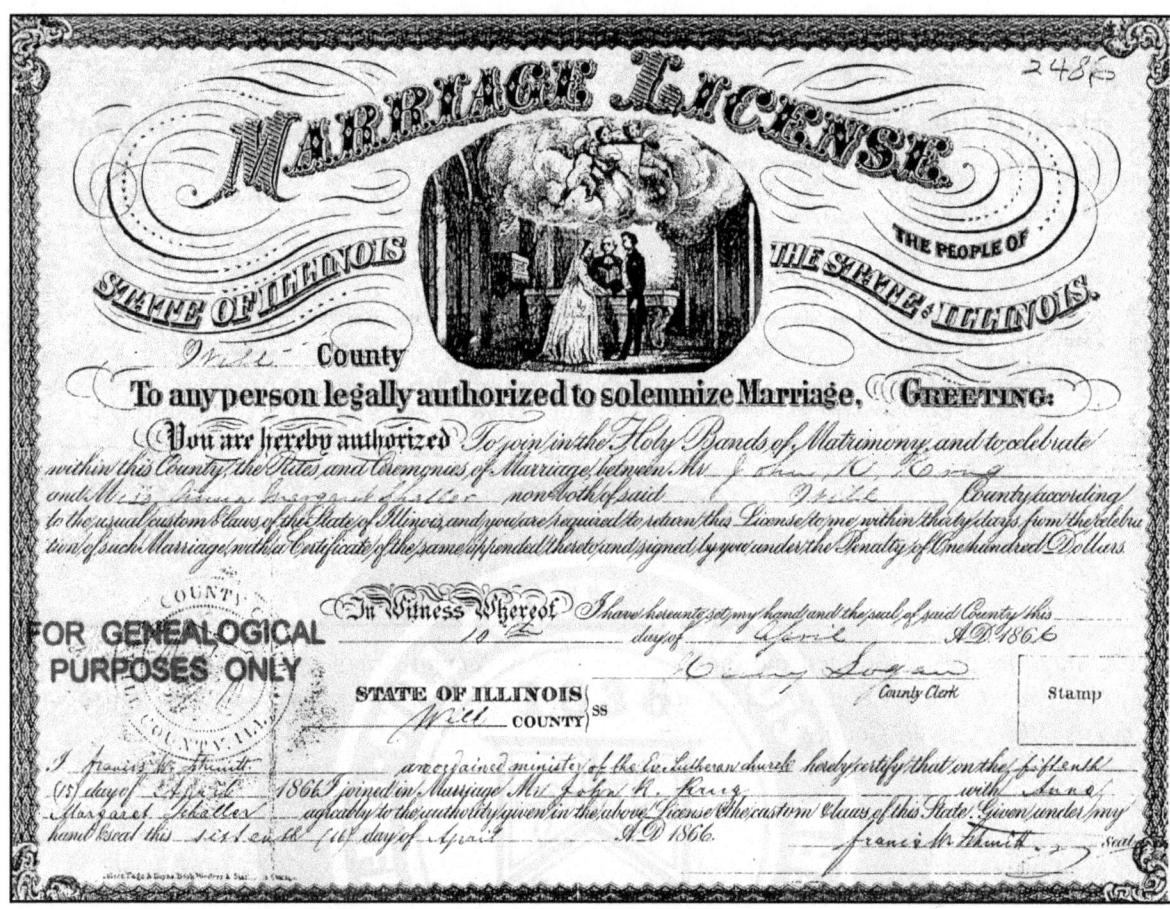

The April 15, 1866 marriage certificate of Martin Krug's paternal grandparents Johann Konrad Krug (#4) and Anna Margaret Schaller (#5). They were married in Will County, Illinois, Margaret's home county. Source: Will County, Illinois Recorders Office. Edited by author

The family of Johann "Conrad" Krug and Anna Margaret Elisabeth (born) Schaller as listed in the Trinity Lutheran Church Register. The parent's names were followed by three of their children including Martin Krug's father Johann George b. 1867. The right column listed the person's birthplace and date. Note that as late as the 1880s, church entries were in German. Source: Trinity Lutheran Church Register. Photographed and edited by author.

Grundy County land records do not include land purchase documents for immigrant Johann Christoph Krug (#8). Nevertheless, the location of the farmland he owned can be deduced from subsequent land purchase and sale records between his three farmer sons, Bernhard, Johann, and Leonhard (in English - Bernard, John, and Leonard).

When Johann Christoph died in 1860, he owned three 80-acre land parcels. His three sons jointly inherited the ownership of this land. All three parcels were located close to Trinity Lutheran Church in Goodfarm Township. In January of 1866, the three brothers split the ownership of the parcels so each brother separately owned 80 acres of farmland. Each brother paid $500 to his two other brothers (total $1,000) for his 80 acres. The net result of these three transactions was that no money was gained or lost by any brother. They had evenly split the three land parcels they inherited from their father.

Johann Konrad Krug (#4) & Anna Margaret (Margaretha) Elizabeth Schaller (#5)

Twelve-year-old Margaret (Anna Margaretha Elizabeth) Schaller (#5) arrived in New York harbor with her mother and four sisters in July 1858. It was six years after the Krug family arrived in America. The Schaller passenger listing stated they were bound for Illinois. No other information is known about this family or their connection to Illinois.

In 1866, Margaret Schaller (#5) was living in Will County, Illinois, which is adjacent to Grundy County where the Krug family lived. In April 1866, three months after Johann Konrad Krug (#4) gained sole ownership of his 80 acres of farmland, he married Margaret Schaller (#5).

The families of the three Krug brothers are included in the record book of Trinity Lutheran Church.[12] The page listing the Krug brothers was compiled shortly after 1884. Johann Konrad (#4) and Margaret (#5) (Schaller) Krug's family eventually included six children. At the time the record book was compiled, the list of their children began with John George Krug (b.1867) (#2), Martin Krug's father. He was their first child and would be their only son. This child, John George, was a member of the first American-born generation in the Krug family.

The 1900 U.S. Census found Johann Konrad (#4) and Margaret (#5) Krug still living in Goodfarm Township, Grundy County, Illinois. A year later in 1901, Johann Konrad purchased two city lots in the nearby town of Dwight, a few miles south in Livingston County. By the time of the 1910 U.S. Census, the couple had moved away from Goodfarm Township to their retirement home in Dwight. At the time of this 1910 census, Johann Konrad Krug was 69 years old and Margaret was 65.

Margaret Krug (#5) died September 21, 1919 in Dwight, Illinois. Johann Konrad died four years later in 1923, also in Dwight, Illinois. They are buried in Goodfarm Cemetery across the roadway from Trinity Lutheran Church.[13]

The burial marker for Johann Konrad Krug (#4) and his wife Margaret (#5) is located in Goodfarm Cemetery across the roadway from Trinity Lutheran Church. See text and endnote for exact location. Source: Photographed and edited by author.

Hansen Immigrants

The Hansen family came from the southern part of Denmark, about 20 miles north of the Prussian (now German) border.[14] An 1860 Danish census listed the family members. The parents were Hans Peter Hansen (#12) and his wife Ingeborg (#13). They had four children at the time of this census. Martin Krug's maternal grandfather, Andrew (Andreas) Hansen (#6), was eight years old in 1860.

Martin Krug's Hansen ancestors arrived in America nearly 20 years after his paternal Krug ancestors. His maternal grandfather, Andrew (Andreas) Boysen Hansen (#6), emigrated from Denmark to Quebec, Canada. He arrived in the fall of 1871. The passenger list indicated Andrew was 20 years old. He was accompanied by his widowed mother Ingeborg Kirstine (Jensdetter) Hansen (#13). Andrew's father, Hans Peter Hansen (#12), had died in Denmark earlier in 1871. The reason for Andrew and his mother's entry via Quebec, Canada is unknown. Nevertheless, they soon made their way to Grundy County, Illinois.

Nine years after her immigration, widow Ingeborg Hansen (#13) was listed in the 1880 U.S. Census. She was 70 years old and lived in Greenfield, Grundy County, Illinois. She was described as a "boarder" living on a farm with part of her extended family. This census listing indicated that immigrant Ingeborg Hansen (#13) joined family members already settled in Grundy County when she arrived in 1871. Ingeborg Hansen died July 1, 1899 and is buried in nearby Dwight, Livingston County, Illinois.[15]

Perschnick Immigrants

Martin Krug's maternal grandmother was Mary (or Marie) Perschnick (b.1855) (#7). The Perschnick family came from today's German state of Brandenburg. Brandenburg was part of Prussia prior to 1871 when the German Empire was formed. Their home in Lindchen, Brandenburg, was about 30 miles west of today's border between Germany and Poland.[16]

The Perschnick family members didn't all arrive in America at the same time. A timeline for this family highlights the dates of their immigration. Despite arrivals spanning the course of 22 years, the family all settled in Goodfarm Township, Grundy County, Illinois.

Hanna (Johanna) (b.1840) Perschnick was the first in her family to arrive in America. Hanna was not a direct-line ancestor of Martin Krug, so she does not appear on his ancestor chart. Her importance is that her Illinois arrival in 1855 led the way for the other Perschnick family members to join her in Goodfarm Township, Grundy County, Illinois.

Hanna Perschnick left her Brandenburg homeland in May 1855 when she was only 14 years old. She traveled alone, but she was berthed in a first class ship's cabin rather than in steerage. This meant either her family in Brandenburg or her contact in America paid a higher fare for her Atlantic Ocean transit. Hanna first lived with relatives in Chicago, Illinois.[17] The identity of these relatives is unknown.

The immigration record for Andrew (Andreas) B Hansen (#6) age 20 and his widowed mother (incorrectly listed as his wife) Ingeborg Hansen (#13) age 60. They arrived in Quebec, Canada on 27 Oct 1871 aboard the steamer Caspian. Source: "Canada, Incoming Passenger Lists, 1865-1935" online database (Provo, UT: Ancestry.com), accessed August 27, 2019. Edited by author.

1860 Census

Year:	FT-1860	Source reference:	S. 119
Cadastre/Address:	Et Huus		
Household No:	250		
Name:	Hans Peter Hansen	Gender:	M
Age:	49	Civil status:	Gift
Birth place:	Guldager Sogn Ribe Amt		
Position in household:	Daglønner. Huusfader		
Parish:	Ballum	District:	Tønder, Højer og Lø
Shire:	Tønder	Place name:	Reisby
Source entry No:	D6391	Record No.:	1408

All members of the household

Name:	Age:	Married?:	Pos. in household:	Occupation:	BirTD place:
Hans Peter Hansen	49	Gift	Daglønner. Huusfader		Guldager Sogn Ribe Amt
Ingeborg Kirstine Jensen	50	Gift	hans Kone. Almisselem		Her i Sognet
Jens Peder Hansen	21	Ugift	deres Børn. Væver		Her i Sognet
Cilla Margretha Hansen	13	Ugift	deres Børn		Her i Sognet
Peder Hansen	11	Ugift	deres Børn		Her i Sognet
Andreas Boysen Hansen	8	Ugift	deres Børn		Her i Sognet

Source: Dansk Demografisk Database

The 1860 Danish census listed the family of Hans Peter Hansen (#12) and his wife Ingeborg (#13). They had four children including Andrew (Andreas) (#6) age 8. Source: Dansk Demografisk Database, accessed August 27, 2019, https://www.rigsarkivet.dk/udforsk/rigsarkivets-soegedatabaser/ddd-dansk-demografisk-database/. Edited by author.

Perschnick Family Timeline – Arrows mark arrival dates

5 May 1833 – Johann Perschnick (#14) m. Khristiane Kubla (#15) in Drebkau, Brandenburg

20 May 1838 – Gottlieb Perschnick b. in Lindchen, Brandenburg

19 Oct 1840[1] – Hanna[2] (Johanna) Perschnick b. in Lindchen, Brandenburg

23 Mar 1850 – Wilhelmine Perschnick b. in Lindchen, Brandenburg

7 Mar 1851 – Christiane (Johana) Perschnick[3] b. in Lindchen, Brandenburg

12 Apr 1855 – Mary (Marie) Perschnick (#7) b. in Lindchen

15 May 1855 – Hanna Perschnick, age 14, departed (solo) from Hamburg aboard *Copernicus*

➤ 23 Jun 1855 – Hanna Perschnick arrived in New York aboard *Copernicus*[4]

24 Jun 1860 – Hanna Perschnick married G. Bernhard Krug[5] in Grundy Co., Illinois

➤ 5 Jun 1869 – Gottlieb (b.1838), Wilhelmine (b.1850), and Christiane (b.1851) Perschnick arrived

6 Feb 1870 – Christiane (b.1851) Perschnick married G. Leonhard Krug in Illinois[6]

Jul 1870 – Gottlieb Perschnick, age 32, was working on Hanna and G. Bernhard Krug's farm[7]

➤ 8 Jun 1872 – Mary (b.1855) (#7), and Caroline Perschnick (b.1857) arrived

25 Mar 1873 – Mary Perschnick (#7) married Andrew (Andreas) Hansen (#6) in Illinois

7 Nov 1873 – Anna Magdalena Hansen (#3) was born in Illinois

10 May 1875 – Gottlieb Perschnick, age 36, arrived in N.Y. with Eleanor Forster, age 22[8]

31 May 1875 – Gottlieb Perschnick married Eleonore Forster in Illinois

➤ 2 Jun 1877 – Widower Johann Perschnick (#14) arrived in N.Y. He traveled in 2nd cabin

9 Feb 1889 – Widower Johann Perschnick (#14) died in Illinois

---

[1] The Trinity Lutheran Church register states Hanna was b. 15 Oct 1840. Her baptismal record states it was 19 Oct 1840. Hanna Perschnick was first in her family to emigrate to America. She later married G. Bernhard Krug.
[2] The underlined names are the names they were known by.
[3] Christiane Perschnick later married G. Leonhard Krug.
[4] Hanna's obituary states she first lived with "relatives" near Blue Island (Chicago area), Illinois.
[5] This date comes from Hanna's obituary.
[6] This date comes from the Illinois marriage index.
[7] This information comes from the 1870 U.S. Census.
[8] Gottlieb had returned to Germany in order to bring his future wife Eleanor to America.

The Perschnick family timeline illustrates four arrival dates spanning 22 years. They all settled in Goodfarm Township, Grundy County, Illinois. Source: Compiled by author.

The 1855 transit record of Hanna (Johanna) Perschnick age 14. She traveled alone in a first class cabin aboard the sailing ship Copernicus. Source: "Hamburg Passenger Lists, 1850-1934, Staatsarchiv Hamburg" online database (Provo, UT: Ancestry.com), accessed December 15, 2019. Edited by author.

Hanna's transatlantic voyage is one of the few that documents both a departure date and a New York arrival date. In all, her transit time was five weeks. She was a passenger on the *Bark Copernicus*. The ship's description indicates it was most likely a three-masted sailing ship. Five weeks was an excellent transit time for a sailing ship.

The next documented event for Hanna Perschnick was her marriage. On June 24, 1860, five years after her immigration, Hanna Perschnick married Georg Bernard Krug.[18] Hanna's marriage into the Krug family was a pivotal event. It brought together these two families in Goodfarm Township, Grundy County. Georg Bernard Krug (b.1838) was the older brother of both Johann Konrad Krug (b.1840) (#4) and Georg Leonard Krug (b.1844). These are the same three Krug brothers discussed earlier in this chapter. Hanna's marriage to Bernard Krug was the beginning of a very close relationship between the Krug and Perschnick families.

Hanna's older brother Gottlieb Perschnick arrived in Illinois in 1869. He was accompanied by two of Hanna's younger sisters, Wilhelmine and Christiane. One year later, the 1870 U.S. Census

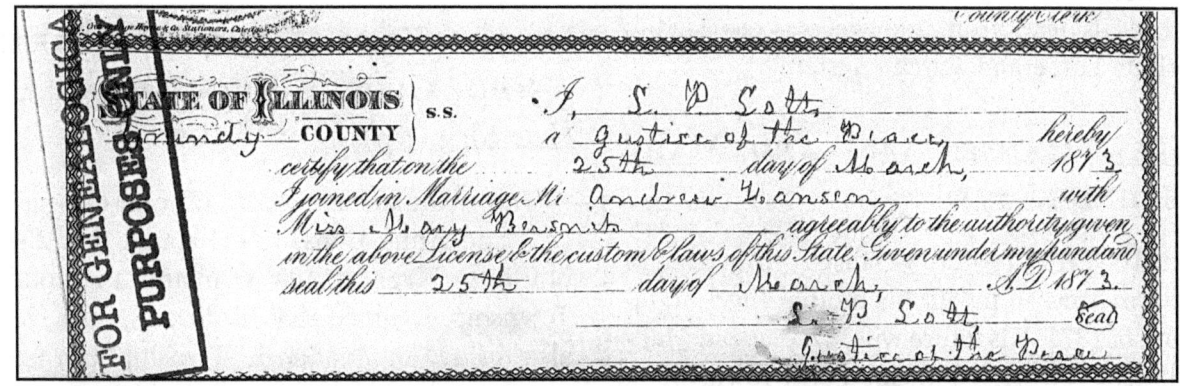

The marriage record of Andrew Hansen (#6) and Mary Perschnick (#7). They were married by a Grundy County, Illinois, Justice of the Peace on March 25, 1873. Source: Copy of license courtesy of Grundy County Recorder's Office. Edited by author.

listed Hanna's immediate family as well as her older brother Gottlieb living together. Gottlieb was working as a hired man on Bernard and Hanna Krug's farm.

In June of 1872, two more siblings of Hanna (Perschnick) Krug arrived in America. Mary Perschnick (b.1855) (#7) was 17 years old, and her sister Caroline was 15. They were among the over 700 passengers aboard the steamer *Weser*. By 1872, steamships had replaced sailing ships for most Atlantic crossings. These two Perschnick sisters traveled in the less-costly steerage section of the steamer. Although Mary Perschnick (#7) was only 17 when she arrived, less than one year later, she married Danish immigrant Andrew Hansen (#6). His arrival with his mother Ingeborg was discussed earlier.

Mary (Perschnick) Hansen (#7) was Martin Krug's maternal grandmother. However, Mary was not the only Perschnick woman to marry into the Krug family. In Martin's extended Krug family, two of Mary's Perschnick sisters married Krug brothers. As a result, Perschnick sisters were Martin Krug's relatives on both sides of his family.

In June of 1877, the final Perschnick family member arrived in America. Widower Johann Perschnick (#14), the father of the Perschnick siblings, joined his children in Goodfarm Township, Grundy County, Illinois. He was 68 years old. Johann died in February of 1889, twelve years after his arrival and shortly before his 90th birthday. His death from "old age" was recorded in the Trinity Lutheran Church register.

Andrew Hansen (#6) and Mary Perschnick (#7)

Twenty-year-old Andrew Hansen (#6) arrived in Goodfarm Township with his mother Ingeborg in October of 1871. His future wife, 17-year-old Mary Perschnick (#7), arrived in Goodfarm Township in June of 1872 less than a year later. The details of their meeting are unknown, but in Mary's obituary it is stated that her husband Andrew was a "young farmer" living near Gardner, Illinois.[19] Andrew and Mary were married by a Grundy County Justice of the Peace on March 25, 1873. Andrew was 21 years old, and Mary was a month shy of her 18th birthday.

Andrew and Mary Hansen's first child was Martin Krug's mother, Anna Magdalena Hansen (#3), born in November 1873. They had four more children, all born on their farm in Grundy County. For unknown reasons, Andrew and Mary left their Illinois farm in 1895. By this time, however, their oldest daughter Anna Magdalena (#3) was 22 years old and no longer living with her parents. Andrew and Mary Hansen lived for a few months in Hyram, Utah, and then homesteaded for several months in Missouri. In the late summer of 1895, less than a year after leaving, they returned to Goodfarm Township in Grundy County, Illinois.[20]

At the time of the 1900 U.S. Census, Andrew and Mary were still living in rural Goodfarm Township with their three youngest children. However, in June of 1905, a Minnesota State Census recorded them living in Oshkosh Township near Canby in Yellow Medicine County, Minnesota. This information matches obituary records for Andrew and Mary which state they moved to Minnesota in 1903. Their move to Minnesota in 1903 is significant because it soon attracted their daughter Anna Magdalena and her family to follow them.

Martin Krug (#1) and His Parents – John George Krug (#2) & Anna Hansen (#3)

The civil marriage record of John George Krug (#2) and Anna Hansen (#3) stated that 25-year-old John Krug rented farmland in Goodfarm Township. It added that his bride, Anna Hansen, also resided in Goodfarm Township. Her age was not stated, but she had just turned 19 years old.

John and Anna grew up on farms close to one another in Goodfarm Township, but how they met

The civil marriage record of John George Krug (#2) and Anna Hansen (#3). They were married on November 13, 1892. They both lived in Goodfarm township prior to their marriage. John rented his farmland. Source: A copy of this record was supplied by the Grundy County Recorder's Office. Edited by author.

is unknown. Their 1892 marriage was recorded in the Trinity Lutheran Church register. As noted earlier, John's parents and his two Krug uncles were all members of Trinity Lutheran Church. John and Anna's marriage in Trinity Lutheran Church suggests that the bride's Hansen family were church members as well.

Martin John Krug (#1) was born on October 6, 1893 in Goodfarm Township, Grundy County, Illinois. He was the first and only child of John and Anna Krug. His civil birth record in Grundy County did not include his given name. This suggests that when this civil birth record was completed in late October, his parents had not yet decided on a given name. This civil record documented his birth date, his birthplace in Goodfarm Township, his parent's names, and his father's occupation as a farmer.

The Trinity Lutheran Church record of Martin's baptism sheds light on his given name. He was baptized on November 5, 1893, one month after his birth. By this time, his parents had given him the name Johann Andreas Martin Krug. The first two names, Johann and Andreas, were meant to honor his two grandfathers: Johann Konrad Krug (#4) and Andreas (Andrew) Hansen (#6). However, Martin was the given name he was always known by.

There are no additional records from Martin's birth family until the death of his father, John George Krug (#2), on September 26, 1895. At the time of his death, John George was 28 years old. He died less than three years after his marriage to Anna. His son Martin had not yet reached his second birthday. The death of John George Krug

Katharine

The poorly preserved Trinity Lutheran Church marriage record of John Krug (#2) age 25 and Anna Hansen (#3) age 19. They were married on November 13, 1892. Source: Trinity Lutheran Church Register. Photographed and edited by author.

The Grundy County civil birth record of Martin Krug (#1). His name was not listed. His birthdate was October 6, 1893. He and both of his parents were born in Goodfarm Township. His father was a farmer. Source: A copy of this record was supplied by the Grundy County Recorder's office. Edited by author.

The Trinity Lutheran Church baptismal record for Martin Krug. His first two given names, Johann and Andreas, honored his two grandfathers. They were also listed as his sponsors in the far right column. Martin was born October 6th and baptized one month later on November 5th in 1893. Source: Trinity Lutheran Church Register. Photographed and edited by author.

The Trinity Lutheran Church death record of John George Krug (#2). He died of diphtheria on September 26, 1895, and was buried the same day. See text for an English translation of the far right column. Source: Trinity Lutheran Church Register. Translated by Merlin Schlichting. Photographed and edited by author.

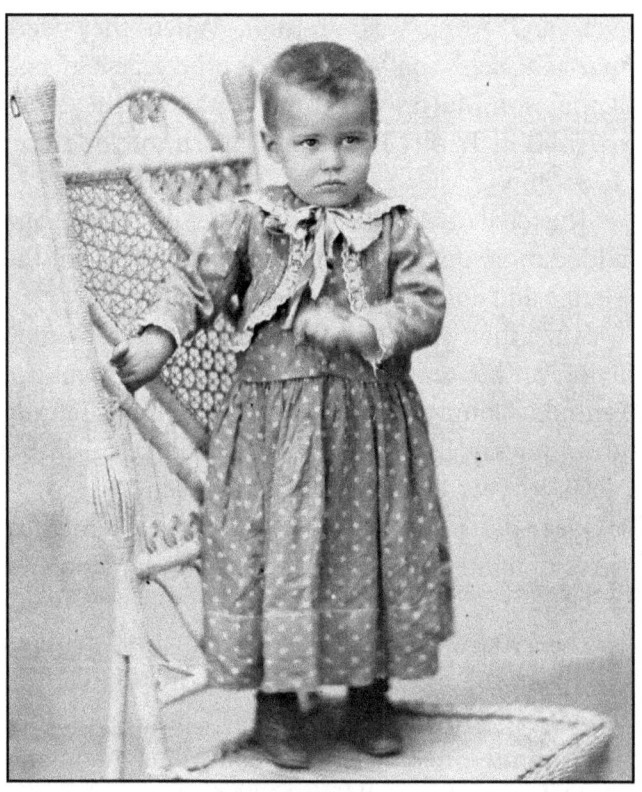

An undated studio photograph of Martin Krug, estimated to be two years old (late 1895 or early 1896). Martin is "unbreeched," a custom of dressing small boys in frocks (e.g., dresses).[22] The photo was taken in Gardner, Illinois. Source: Brenda (Weber) Lamb. Edited by author.

was recorded in the Trinity Lutheran Church registry. It stated that he died and was buried on the same day. The cause of his death was diphtheria. The far right column states, in German, that he left behind a widow, one little son, his parents, his wife's parents, his siblings, and his brothers-in-law. The last part of this entry correctly indicates that John George was the only son his parents had.

Diphtheria is still a dreaded contagious disease that kills children and young adults by suffocation. At the time of John George's death in the mid-1890s, the bacterial cause of diphtheria had been established. However, there were no U.S. public health preventative measures in place until the 1920s. Diphtheria spreads quickly by airborne material. Quite likely, John George's burial on the same day he died was meant to minimize exposure of others to the infection that had killed him. Today, infant DPT (Diphtheria, Pertussis [whooping cough], and Tetanus) vaccination protocols have nearly eliminated the risk of exposure to diphtheria in the U.S.[21]

The death of John George Krug left his widow Anna in a dire situation. She was not yet 22 years old, had a two-year-old child, and had no means to support herself and her child. John George had been renting the land he farmed, so Anna did not inherit any land. She was left with only their few personal possessions. Her parents, Andrew and Mary Hansen, had returned to Illinois in August of 1895, only a month prior to John George's death. There is no record stating the reason for their return, and if it had any relation to John George Krug's illness and death.

The home where Anna (Hansen) Krug (#3) and two-year old Martin lived after her husband's death is unknown. Most likely, she and Martin moved in with her parents and younger siblings who still lived in Goodfarm Township. At the time, her parents had three children still living at home. They ranged in age from six to 14 years.

An often-repeated family story suggested that following her husband's death, Anna (Hansen) Krug (#3) was strongly encouraged to find another husband. This was the pragmatic solution often taken by a young widow with no means of financial support. The difficulty Anna faced was finding such a man in a sparsely populated rural part of Illinois where families were poor. The solution for Anna came by way of a considerably older man who, like Anna, had lost a spouse.

Nels Hansen

Anna's second husband brought with him a confusion of surnames. Anna's birth surname was Hansen and her father was the Danish immigrant Andrew Hansen (#6). Her second husband, Nels Hansen, was also born in Denmark. Hansen is a very common surname in Denmark. As far as is known, these two Danish-born Hansens were unrelated.

Nels Hansen (b.1859) left his Danish home as a 15-year-old. He became a ship's crew member and for ten years sailed to many Atlantic Ocean seaports. His first marriage was to Nellie Rees, a resident of the port town of Swansea in South Wales, United Kingdom. Nels and Nellie had one son, William James Hansen, who was born in 1887.

By the year 1888, Nels was living in the U.S. where he worked for several years as a laborer in Eastern Seaboard factories. However, by 1893 Nels had relocated to Grundy County, Illinois. He rented farmland in Greenfield Township, located immediately east of Goodfarm Township.

In late 1893, Nels Hansen returned briefly to South Wales where his wife and child were still living. Subsequent U.S. immigration documents identify Nels, his wife Nellie, and son William. They arrived at the port of Philadelphia on January 25, 1894 and then made their way to Grundy County, Illinois. Nellie died less than three months later on April 10, 1894.[23] Her death left 35-year-old Nels caring for their seven-year-old son William while farming rented land in Greenfield Township, Grundy County, Illinois.

The loss of their spouses brought Nels Hansen and Anna (Hansen) Krug (#3) together. Anna's husband John George Krug (#2) had died in September 1895, about 18 months after the death of Nels Hansen's wife Nellie. There is no record of how widow Anna and widower Nels met one another. Regardless, the timing of their spouse's deaths and the proximity of their homes eventually led to a second marriage for Nels Hansen and Anna (Hansen) Krug.

NELS HANSEN AND ANNA (HANSEN) KRUG

Thirty-seven-year-old Nels Hansen married 22-year-old Anna (Hansen) Krug (#3) on October 22, 1896. The 15-year age difference between Nels and Anna was unusual. When they were married, Nels's son William was nine years old, and Anna's son Martin was three years old. They were married in Trinity Lutheran Church in Goodfarm Township.

The civil marriage record of Nels and Anna added more details. It listed information about the couple and about both of their parents.

After their marriage, Nels and Anna remained living on his rental farm in Greenfield Township, Grundy County, Illinois. Their combined family grew quickly. By the time of the 1900 U.S. Census, Nels's 15-year-old son William Hansen and Anna's six-year-old son Martin Krug had been joined by three daughters ages two years, one year, and two months.

The 1900 U.S. Census also listed Anna's parents Andrew (#6) and Mary (#7) Hansen still living in Goodfarm Township, Grundy County, Illinois. Their family included two teenage daughters and an 11-year-old son all living at home.

THE TWO HANSEN FAMILIES MOVE TO MINNESOTA

The Andrew (#6) and Mary (#7) Hansen family were first to move from Illinois to Minnesota. They arrived in March 1903 and purchased a farm five miles east of Canby in Oshkosh Township, Yellow Medicine County.[24] They lived on this farm for the remainder of their working lives. They moved into the town of Canby when they retired from active farming.[25]

Nels and Anna (#3) Hansen were still farming in Illinois when Andrew and Mary moved to Minnesota. By 1903, Nels and Anna had added a fourth daughter, Emma Helene Hansen (b. June 20, 1902), to their family. Emma was Martin Krug's half-sister. Later in her life, she would become "storyteller" Emma (Hansen) Swenson. During Martin's adult lifetime, his younger half-sister Emma was an important link between the Hansen and Krug families.

The October 22, 1896 marriage record of Anna Krug and Nels Hansen in Trinity Lutheran Church. Nels lived in Greenfield Township and had been born in Denmark. Anna Krug's unmarried name was Hansen. The witness column on the right names Anna's parents, <u>Andrew</u> (Andreas) and <u>Mary</u> (Marie) Hansen. Source: Trinity Lutheran Church Register. Photographed and edited by author.

The 1896 civil marriage record of Anna (Hansen) Krug (#3) and Nels Hansen. Their ages and their parent's names were recorded, and their homes were located. It was the second marriage for both Anna and Nels. Source: Copy courtesy of Grundy County, Illinois, Recorder's Office. Edited by author.

Storyteller Emma (Hansen) Swenson made it clear that her birth family's (Nels and Anna) move to Minnesota was at the behest of her grandmother <u>Mary</u> Hansen (#7). Emma Swenson stated, "Grandma said to come, so they did. You see, what Grandma said, went."

Information in the 1905 Minnesota State Census allowed calculation of the date Nels and Anna (#3) Hansen moved from Illinois to Minnesota. It was March of 1904. This census listed their entire family including the two older boys, William Hansen and Martin Krug, and four younger daughters. Youngest daughter Clara was born one month after their arrival in Minnesota.

Storyteller Emma (Hansen) Swenson remembered her family's move from Illinois to Minnesota. She recalled their travel,

The 1900 U.S. Census identified the combined family of Nels and Annie (Anna) Hansen in Greenfield Township, Grundy County, Illinois. Nels was a farmer born in Denmark in 1859. He emigrated to America in 1888. "Annie" was born in Illinois in 1874. Nels's son William Hansen was born in England in 1885, while his stepson Martin Krug was born in Illinois in 1893. Nels and Anna's daughters were Nellie, Lydia, and Alvina. Source: "1900 United States Federal Census" online database (Provo, UT: Ancestry.com), accessed December 24, 2022. Edited by author.

We moved to Minnesota from Illinois before I was two years old. This was either the last part of 1903 or the first part of 1904 [it was March of 1904]. *I remember coming by train with my parents, my older half-brother Martin, and* [my] *three older sisters. My mother's mother* [Mary] *and father* [Andrew Hansen] *had already moved to Minnesota and were living near Canby.*

This recollection by Emma was unusually accurate for an event she experienced as a two-year-old child.

For several years, Nels and Anna rented farmland in Fortier Township west of Canby, Minnesota. By 1910, however, they had purchased farmland in Oshkosh Township, Yellow Medicine County. This was the same township where Anna's parents, <u>Andrew</u> and <u>Mary</u> Hansen (#6 & #7), owned farmland.

By the time of the 1910 U.S. Census, Nels's son William was no longer living with the family. Anna's son, 16-year-old Martin (Krug), however, was still living at home. Nels and Anna had seven children of their own — six daughters and one son. Nels and Anna's Oshkosh Township farm would be their home for many years.

Martin Krug was eight years old when he first arrived in Minnesota in 1904. He was the only member of his paternal Krug family to leave Illinois. By 1910, he was a teenager living in Oshkosh Township east of Canby, Minnesota, being raised by his mother Anna and his stepfather Nels. His mixed parentage, however, set him apart from the other Hansen children. This sense of not fully belonging was built into his personality, and it generated an edge to his character.

By 1910, sisters Sophie and Emma Hinderer were teenagers as well. Sophie turned 15 that year and Emma thirteen. With their sister Mary Hinderer able to care for their younger twin siblings John and Martha, Sophie and Emma were periodically sent out from the Hinderer farm to work as domestic helpers for other families. They would live with these families for months at a time. One or several of these employer families lived in the town of Canby, Minnesota.

Taken altogether, these circumstances brought Martin Krug into the same Canby, Minnesota, social circle as the two Hinderer sisters.

■ ■ ■

Notes

1. This type of ancestor chart is known as an "Ahnentafel." The only people listed are parents, also known as "direct line" ancestors. Siblings are not included on this type of chart.

2. The German Empire was formed in 1871.

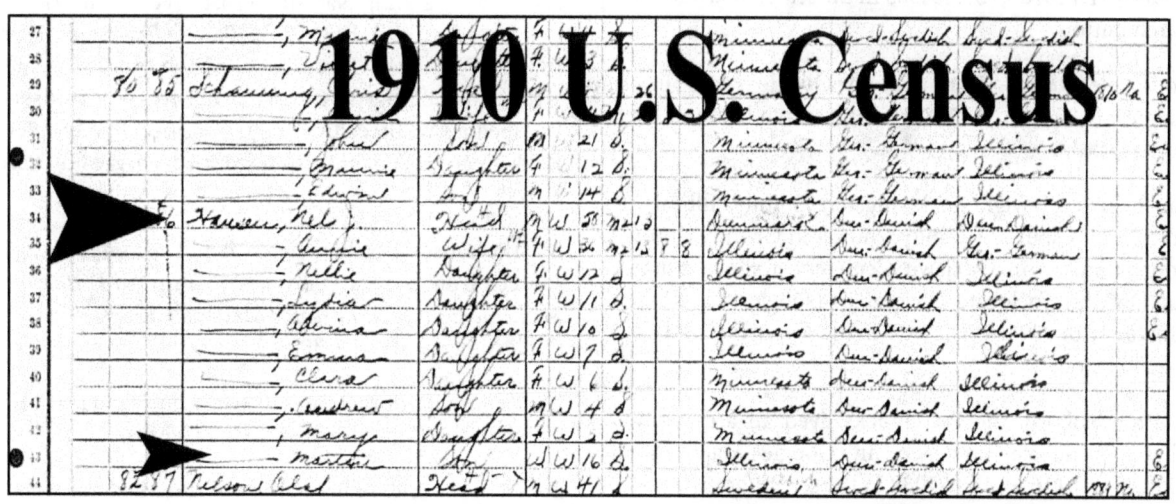

1905 Minnesota Census

The 1905 Minnesota State Census located the family of Nels and "Annie" (Anna) Hansen living west of Canby in Fortier Township, Yellow Medicine County, Minnesota. Their children included 11-year-old Martin Krug. When this census was taken in June of 1905, they had lived there one year and three months (far right columns). By calculation, this means they moved to Minnesota in March 1904. Source: "Minnesota, Territorial and State Censuses, 1849-1905" online database (Provo, UT: Ancestry.com), accessed December 24, 2022. Edited by author.

1910 U.S. Census

The 1910 U.S. Census listed the Nels and "Annie" (Anna) Hansen family living in Oshkosh Township, Yellow Medicine County, Minnesota. Their seven children and Anna's first-born son, 16-year-old Martin Krug (his Krug surname was omitted), were also listed. Source: "1910 United States Federal Census" online database (Provo, UT: Ancestry.com), accessed December 24, 2022. Edited by author.

3. To locate Niederoberbach, in Google Maps insert coordinates 49.228463, 10.588078 in the search box and click the search button.

4. To locate Neuendettelsau, in Google Maps insert coordinates 49.286334, 10.7877981 in the search box and click the search button.

5. To locate Kanndorf, in Google Maps insert coordinates 49.779265, 11.247856 in the search box and click the search button.

6. Registration to emigrate was voluntary and not binding. Like the Hinderers in Brend, Johann Christoph Krug registered to emigrate years before he actually emigrated.

7. "Hamburg Passenger Lists, 1850-1934" (online database), *Ancestry.com* (Provo, UT: Ancestry.com, 2008), accessed November 2022. Original source information: Staatsarchiv Hamburg; Hamburg, Deutschland; *Hamburger Passagierlisten*; Volume: 741-2, GS Band 152; Page 1.

8. Wikipedia s.v. "Johann Konrad Wilhelm Löhe," last modified July 3, 2022, 17:59 (UTC), https://en.wikipedia.org/w/index.php?title=Johann_Konrad_Wilhelm_L%C3%B6he&oldid=1096316229.

9. Early church information was sourced from a 1954 church centennial booklet.

10. To locate Trinity Lutheran Church, in Google Maps insert coordinates 41.139652, -88.404415 in the search box and click the search button.

11. *History of Grundy County, Illinois* (O. L. Baskin & Co., 1882), 355, 356, https://archive.org/details/historyofgrundyc00chica/page/n3/mode/2up .

12. Access to Trinity Lutheran Church documents was graciously provided by former pastor William Mitschke.

13. To locate Goodfarm Cemetery, in Google Maps insert coordinates 41.140186, -88.404583 in the search box and click the search button.

14. To locate Rejsby, Denmark, in Google Maps insert coordinates 55.254246, 8.726801 in the search box and click the search button.

15. The town of Dwight in Livingston County, Illinois, is only a few miles south of Trinity Church in Grundy County. Ingeborg is buried in Oaklawn Cemetery a short distance west of Dwight. To locate Dwight, in Google Maps insert coordinates 41.092994, -88.428919 in the search box and click the search button.

16. In Brandenburg, the Perschnicks lived an area named Lindchen. To locate Lindchen, in Google Maps insert coordinates 51.611616, 14.087088 in the search box and click the search button.

17. The information on Hanna's settlement in Chicago comes from her newspaper obituary.

18. Hanna's marriage information comes from her obituary.

19. The town of Gardner is also in Grundy County, a few miles east of Goodfarm Township.

20. This unusual series of moves was recorded in both Andrew and Mary's obituaries.

21. Elimination of disease risk depends entirely on vaccination. In countries without near-universal vaccination, diphtheria remains a lethal disease.

22. Unbreeching, the custom of dressing small boys in frocks (e.g., dresses, gowns), started in the mid-16th century and continued until the very early 20th century. The reasons were 1) economics (clothes were expensive so it made sense to dress young very children in outfits that allowed for their growth or in hand-me-downs of both sexes), and 2) practicality (changing diapers and toilet training was much faster and easier without having to deal with the complicated buttons and fastening of regular children's clothes).

Breeching was the first time a little boy began wearing short trousers (or breeches), which still allowed for growth and were cheaper than long trousers. In the 19th century, this usually occurred between the ages of four and six. It was a very special occasion celebrated by friends and families because the change in dress signified that the little boy was now a young man. (Jane Ashelford, *The Art of Dress: Clothing and Society, 1500-1914* (New York NY: Abrams, 1996); Linda Baumgarten, *What Clothes Reveal: The Language of Clothing in Colonial and Federal America* (Yale University Press, New Haven CT, 2002); Natasha Frost, "For Centuries, People Celebrated a Little Boy's First Pair of Trousers," September 18, 2017, Atlas Obscura, https://www.atlasobscura.com/articles/breeching-party-first-pants-regency-trousers-boys; Wikipedia s.v. "Breeching (boys)," last modified September 5, 2024, 23:46 (UTC), https://en.wikipedia.org/wiki/Breeching_(boys).

23. The cause of Nellie's death is not recorded. Information sourced from Arthur P. Rose, *An Illustrated History of Yellow Medicine County Minnesota* (Marshall MN: Northern History Publishing, 1914), 529-30.

24. The month of their arrival has been calculated from their listing in the 1905 Minnesota State Census.

25. The obituaries of both Andrew and Mary corroborate this information.

Chapter 12

Sophie and Martin Krug

Timeline

1892 – Gottlieb and Katharine Hinderer were married in Iowa

1892 – Martin Krug's parents were married in Illinois

1893 – The Panic of 1893 led to four years of economic depression

1893, Oct. – Martin Krug was born in Illinois

1895, Sep. – Martin's father John George Krug died in Illinois

1895, Nov. – Sophie Karoline Hinderer was born in Iowa

1896, Oct. – Martin Krug's mother married Nels Hansen in Illinois

1897, Feb. – Emma Hinderer was born in Iowa

1898, autumn – The Hinderers arrived in Minnesota

1901 – McKinley assassinated; Theodore Roosevelt became president

1904 – Martin, his mother, his stepfather, and his half siblings arrived in Minnesota

1908 – Henry Ford introduced the Model T

1914 – WWI began in Europe

1917, Apr. – The U.S. entered WWI

1918, Jan. – Sophie Hinderer married Martin Krug

1918, Sep. – Emma Hinderer married Ralph Lafere

1918, Nov. 11 – World War I ended

1919, Apr. – Doris Lafere was born to Emma (Hinderer) Lafere

1919, Aug. – Johnny Krug was born to Sophie and Martin

1919, Nov. – Mary Hinderer married Albert Engstrand

1920 – National Prohibition of alcohol began

1922 – William Krug was born to Sophie and Martin

1923, Dec. – Louise Marie Krug was born to Sophie and Martin.

1924, Jan. – Louise Marie Krug died

1925, Jan. – Maurine Krug was born to Sophie and Martin

1926, Mar. – Sophie Hinderer died

1926, Dec. – Martin Krug married Emma (Hinderer) Lafere

In several respects, Martin Krug and Sophie Hinderer had similar childhoods. They were both born in Midwestern states, and their families moved to Minnesota at the turn of the 20th century. Their parents were farmers, and they grew up in large families. Neither family was wealthy, but the children were provided with adequate food and shelter. In both families, the children were encouraged to attend school unless the workload at home required their labor.

Martin and Sophie's childhood also had differences. Sophie Hinderer's family moved to Minnesota to buy affordable farmland. Once the land was purchased, year-to-year economic success was achieved through wise crop selection and timely farm management. They raised animals and garden produce to provide food for the family. Hard work was required from all family members, adults and children. The Hinderer family was characterized by strong bonds, an intense work ethic, and a sense of shared purpose.

Martin Krug's childhood was disrupted by the death of his father when he was only two years old. Martin had no personal memory of his father. His family's move to Minnesota followed a summons from his maternal grandparents rather than a self-directed search for new farmland. In the Nels Hansen family, Martin felt different from other family members. He lacked a sense of family bonding and a shared purpose. Martin was always provided for, but he did not fit comfortably into the Nels Hansen family.

Sophie Hinderer

Sophie Karoline Hinderer was born November 15, 1895 on her parent's farm in Fayette County, Iowa. She was the third child and second daughter in the Hinderer family. When she was three years old, her family moved to Lac qui Parle County, Minnesota. The farmland her father purchased was unplowed prairie with no housing. Her Hinderer family spent the winter of 1898 in a primitive sod house. When the weather warmed the next spring, Sophie observed the first steps of the room-by-room construction of the Hinderer farmhouse.

Life on the Minnesota Hinderer farm was austere. The chores assigned to Sophie and her siblings were essential to the family's success. When her older sister Tena began working away from home in 1904, nine-year-old Sophie became her mother's primary helper. For the next several years, Sophie and her younger sister Emma shared household duties. When their younger sister Mary was old enough, she was tasked with caring for the two youngest Hinderer children, twins Martha and John. This allowed either Sophie or Emma to be assigned work away from the Hinderer farm. One of them usually remained at home to help their mother Katharine, while the other worked for other families. The wages they earned were added to the Hinderer farm income. Storyteller and brother John Hinderer recalled that Sophie was more likely to be the sister helping Katharine at home, while Emma worked away.

The impression given by John Hinderer and others was that both Sophie and Emma were easy to be around and had calming personalities. Although they worked hard, both at household chores and in the fields, their heavy workload did not lead to anger or a resentful disposition. Either sister could be trusted to finish their assigned chores, whether at their own home or in the homes of their employers. In spite of frequent times of separation, Sophie and Emma clearly enjoyed each other's company. This sisterly bonding was both a refuge and a source of happiness in their early life.

Sisters Sophie and Emma Hinderer seemed inseparable from the start. In 1897, they were baptized on the same day in Postville, Iowa. In 1911, they were confirmed on the same day in Canby, Minnesota. As young women, they attended social events together and, according to

The 1900 U.S. Census included the Hinderer family shortly after their arrival in Minnesota. All of the children were born in Iowa including four-year-old Sophie and three-year-old Emma. (Children John and Martha were not born until late in 1906) Source: "Year: 1900; Census Place: Freeland, Lac Qui Parle, Minnesota" (Family History Library Microfilm: 1240772; Page 10; Enumeration District: 0126), accessed November 2021. Edited by author.

Martin Krug

If Sophie Hinderer's early life was one of bonding with a sibling, Martin Krug's early life was one of isolation. His household included Nels Hansen's son William from Nels' first marriage as well as much younger half-siblings. Martin did not form a close bond with any of these family members. His mother Anna loved Martin dearly, but he remained emotionally apart from and even resentful of his stepfather, Nels Hansen.

Martin's family moved from Illinois to Minnesota in 1904 when he was eight years old. They first lived on rented land but later purchased a farm in Oshkosh Township near his maternal grandparents. The 1910 U.S. Census listed 16-year-old Martin living with his stepfather Nels Hansen, his mother Anna, six half-sisters, and one half-brother. Nels's son William from his first marriage no longer lived at home.

Martin's half-sister and storyteller Emma (Hansen) Swenson offered one insight,

> *My folks talked German to us kids, but talked Danish* [Nels Hansen's native language] *to each other. My sisters never learned Danish, but I could understand quite a bit more than the rest of them.*

Speaking in a language Martin did not understand further isolated Martin from his mother and his stepfather.

A circa 1910 studio photo of sisters Sophie (seated), age 15, and Emma age 13. Source: Image courtesy of Becci Fischer. Edited by author.

family stories, they shared the attention of young men. Their lives took separate pathways at the time of their marriages, but only for a short time. In the end, it was as if their two lives blended into one.

The 1910 U.S. Census listed the Nels and "Annie" (Anna) Hansen family living in Oshkosh Township, Yellow Medicine County, Minnesota. Their seven children and Anna's son, 16-year-old Martin Krug (his Krug surname was omitted) were also listed. Source: "1910 United States Federal Census" online database (Provo, UT: Ancestry.com), accessed December 24, 2022. Edited by author.

The divide between Martin and his stepfather was widened by Martin's strong-willed maternal grandmother, Mary (Perschnick) Hansen. Her farm was within walking distance of the Nels Hansen farm where Martin lived. Emma Swenson explained how this family dynamic played out:

With my Grandma Hansen, everything had to be in German, which made it bad. Martin figured he didn't have to do anything my dad [Nels Hansen] said. If Martin didn't get his way, he knew he could run off to Grandma Hansen and stay with her. She spoiled Martin so bad, and he didn't have to listen to his stepfather.

Emma Swenson believed Martin's rebellious nature stemmed from a fractured family relationship and an overly indulgent grandmother.

Sophie Hinderer Meets Martin Krug

By early 1917, World War I had come to a murderous stalemate in the heartland of Europe. In the war years before 1917, the U.S. had shipped supplies to the allies, but a strong isolationist sentiment in America made a declaration of war on Germany politically untenable. However, when German U-boat activity and political subterfuge ramped up in early 1917, public opinion in America became more hawkish.

The United States declared war on Germany on April 6, 1917. At the time, the U.S. had virtually no standing army. Consequently, the Selective Service Act was passed by congress allowing conscription of young men. The first of three draft registrations began on June 5, 1917. It required all men between the ages of 21 and 31 to be registered for military service. Martin Krug, age 23, and his best friend Alfred Anderson, age 21, dutifully filled out their draft forms. The date of Martin's registration was June 5, 1917.

Martin Krug was described as medium height and weight with brown eyes and brown hair. He was employed as a farm hand working for his stepfather Nels Hansen in Oshkosh Township, Yellow Medicine County, Minnesota. He was

Martin Krug completed a draft registration form in the summer or fall of 1917. He worked as a farm hand for his stepfather Nels Hansen. See text for further details. Source: "United States World War I Draft Registration Cards, 1917-1918: Martin Krug, 1917-1918," FamilySearch, accessed January 20, 2023, https://www.familysearch.org/ark:/61903/1:1:K8W9-CS9.

The January 16, 1918 civil marriage license of Martin Krug and Sophie Hinderer. The witnesses were Sophie's siblings Marie (Mary) and Carl Hinderer. Source: License copy courtesy of the Yellow Medicine County Recorder's Office. Edited by author.

unmarried, and he was a natural-born U.S. citizen. Alfred Anderson's registration form was similarly completed. Martin Krug was never drafted into the military, but his friend Alfred Anderson was not as fortunate.

There is no record of the date or place Sophie Hinderer met Martin Krug. When they were married in January 1918, Martin was 24 years old and Sophie was 22. Emma Swensen again provided some clues about their meeting,

> *He [Martin] was gone a lot of the time. He and his friend Alfred Anderson ran around a lot. Emma [Hinderer] used to talk about them. This Alfred Anderson got killed in World War I, but I can remember him coming over to our place [the Nels Hansen farm] to stay with Martin all the time. They were at dances a lot because they both played instruments. Martin played the guitar. Now about that time, the Hinderer girls [Sophie and Emma] were working in Canby, so I figure that may be how they met.*

Emma Swensen later added that she believed Martin dated younger sister Emma Hinderer before he dated Sophie.

Sophie's marriage to Martin Krug was the first marriage for the American-born generation of Hinderers. Their January 16, 1918 wedding was recorded in Yellow Medicine County.

Storyteller John Hinderer, who was 12 years old at the time, recalled that Sophie and Martin were married in the Hinderer's farmhouse. An official studio photograph showed the young couple.

The January 1918 marriage photograph of Sophie Hinderer and Martin Krug. Source: From the Doris Schlichting collection. Edited by author.

Sophie and Martin – Early Times

After their marriage, Sophie and Martin lived on a farm near the Hinderers in Lac qui Parle County. How they came to rent this farm is not recorded. However, the close proximity of the two farms meant Martin had easy access to Hinderer farm equipment and expertise. This was important because at that point in his life, Martin was not an experienced farmer.

Martin and Sophie's rented farm consisted of two parcels (160 + 80 acres) of land including outbuildings and a house. Their farmhouse was located only one mile from the Hinderer farmhouse. Martin and Sophie's farm was owned by the Arneson family who were long-time friends of the Hinderers.

Two hundred and forty acres would have been an impossibly large acreage for one inexperienced farmer to manage. At this same time, it took two Hinderer men, Gottlieb and Carl, along with help from young John Hinderer, to farm their own 160 acres. Most likely, Martin actively farmed only a part of the 240-acre Arneson property shown on the 1916 plat map.

When Martin and Sophie lived on the Arneson farm, their long driveway led from a gravel road up a slight incline into a grove of trees. The farmhouse and outbuildings were located in the grove of trees. Today, the driveway is overgrown with vegetation and the grove of trees contains only metal storage structures. No farmhouse remains. The gravel road at the beginning of the old driveway is now named 195th Ave. N.[1]

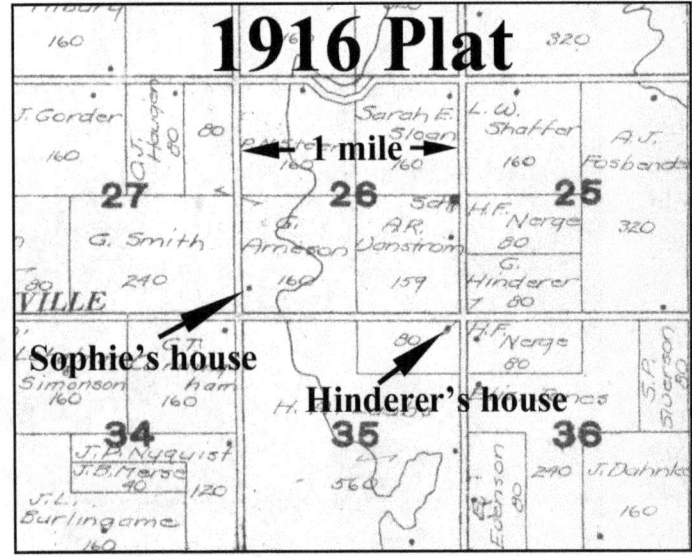

A plat map drawn in 1916 located the Arneson farm where Sophie and Martin lived. An arrow connected the 160 and the 80 acre parcels. The small black boxes marked the location of Sophie's house and that of the Hinderers. The two houses were only a mile apart. Source: Image access courtesy of Lac qui Parle County Museum. Photographed and edited by author.

A 2017 photo of Martin and Sophie's rental farm building site. The camera was pointed northeastward. The now-overgrown driveway ended in a grove of trees where only metal grain bins remained. Source: Photographed and edited by author.

Family Complications

In 1919, the Hinderer family was involved in a turmoil that directly affected Sophie and Martin. Sophie's younger sister Emma married her first husband, Ralph Lafere, in September 1918. This occurred eight months after Sophie had married Martin Krug. Emma's marriage was not approved of by her parents and it did not end well. In late April of 1919, Emma's first child was born. At this same time, Ralph Lafere abandoned Emma and her newborn child, Doris. These events will be detailed in a later chapter.

Without a means of support, Emma and her newborn daughter returned home to live on the Hinderer farm. During the summer of 1919, Emma and her infant were living only a mile away from Sophie and Martin. The renewed proximity of sisters Sophie and Emma changed the lives of both families.

John Hinderer remembered when Emma and her daughter Doris returned to live with the Hinderers. He said that at first, Emma helped Katharine with household chores and also worked in the fields with the men. After a short time, she began working away from home as a domestic helper. When Emma worked away from home, her infant Doris was cared for by grandmother Katharine and teenagers John and Martha.

Sophie and Martin's first child Johnny (John Martin) Krug was born in late August of 1919. As with all of Sophie's children, Johnny was born at home on the Arneson farm. Cousins Johnny and Doris lived their early childhood years within a mile of one another.

Yet another event added to the complexity of 1919 for the Hinderer family. In November of 1919, sister Mary Hinderer married World War I veteran Albert Engstrand. Therefore, by the end of that year, there were three important events in the lives of these three Hinderer sisters: Sophie and Martin Krug had their first son Johnny, Emma and her daughter Doris were living on the Hinderer farm, and Mary and Albert Engstrand were newly married.

The 1920 U.S. Census for Freeland Township, Lac qui Parle County, Minnesota, was recorded in January that year. The census taker interviewed Martin and Sophie Krug on January 23, 1920. In his recording, Sophie was listed as "Sophia" and their son, known as Johnny throughout his life, was listed as "John."

The same census taker interviewed the Hinderer family one week later on January 30, 1920. In this recording, he misspelled Gottlieb's given name and spelled Katharine's name as "Catherine." Nevertheless, he correctly listed the Hinderer "children" living at home in birth order. This sequence included 22-year-old married daughter Emma (Hinderer) Lafere. The last person listed in the Hinderer household was granddaughter Doris. Her surname (Lafere) was not stated, and she was less than a year old.

Sophie and Martin – Family Years

There is little direct information about the day-to-day lives of Martin and Sophie on the rented Arneson farm. Storyteller John Hinderer was a young teenager in 1920. He said Sophie often brought her son Johnny to visit the Hinderer farm. The Hinderers, in turn, took fresh produce and other food to Sophie's house.

A picture emerges of Sophie and Martin's daily routine. The fieldwork and care of animals would have been a full-time job for any farmer, including young Martin Krug. Sophie managed all of the household chores and cared for their young son Johnny. For both of them, summers were a time of maximum workload and winters a time of surviving the harsh elements. Neither of them was experienced or necessarily proficient at their tasks, but they had nearby assistance from the Hinderers. In particular, Sophie's years as Katharine's primary helper gave her the knowledge of how a family could survive in spite of little income from their farm.

The U.S. Census recorded on January 23, 1920 listed the family of Martin and "Sophia" (Sophie) Krug. Their son John (Johnny) was less than a year old. Source: "Year: 1920; Census Place: Freeland, Lac Qui Parle, Minnesota," Roll: T625_842; Page: 8A; Enumeration District: 91 (Provo, UT: Ancestry.com), accessed January 7, 2023. Edited by author.

The U.S. Census recorded on January 30, 1920 listed the family of "Gotleib" (Gottlieb) and "Catherine" (Katharine) Hinderer. Their children living at home were Carl, Emma Lafere, "Johnny" (John), and Martha. Granddaughter Doris (no surname listed) also lived with them. Source: "Year: 1920; Census Place: Freeland, Lac Qui Parle, Minnesota," Roll: T625_842; Page: 11A; Enumeration District: 91 (Provo, UT: Ancestry.com), accessed January 7, 2023. Edited by author.

Following the birth of Johnny Krug in August of 1919, Martin and Sophie had three more children. Their second son, William Andrew Krug, was born on May 14, 1922. Eighteen months later, a daughter Louise Marie was born December 21, 1923. Storyteller John Hinderer said that at the time Louise Marie was born, Sophie was ill with an infection. Within days of her birth, the baby developed pneumonia. Louise Marie died January 27, 1924, only a few days past one month of age.

Sophie and Martin's last child was a daughter, Maurine LaRayne, born January 24, 1925. Maurine later said that the spelling of her given names always tested her patience. She pointed out that even her baptismal certificate misspelled both Maurine and LaRayne. In fact, her given names were spelled yet another way on her birth certificate, and again they were wrong.

Maurine recalled that she later asked her Aunt Martha Hinderer about the many spelling errors. Martha explained that when a child was born at home, the birth was telephoned to a pastor or official. Martha said their own Pastor Hennig would spell the names however he wished. This resulted in frequent spelling differences between the family's version and the official birth documents. Maurine said that in her own case, family members learned to spell Maurine correctly, but she avoided using LaRayne. It was an uncommon name and nearly always misspelled.

By the summer of 1925, Sophie and Martin's family was complete. They had three young children, a farm to tend, and Hinderer relatives nearby able to lend them a hand when needed. Sophie's older sister Tena visited the Krug farm during that summer. Tena introduced her husband-to-be, John Monson, and his sister Ethel Monson to the Hinderer and Krug families. The photo of the Monson's visit to the Krug rental farm was previously shown. John and Ethel Monson are seated on the front porch of the Krug farmhouse. Sophie is holding her child Maurine. Martin is wearing his work boots and overalls, and the two young cousins, Johnny Krug and Doris Lafere, are seated on the porch steps. It is an image that reflects the hard work of farming, the mix of Hinderer and Krug family generations, and a hope for the future of the Monson clan. Sophie Krug's appearance, however, suggests an older and less robust woman than was seen in earlier photos. It may have simply been a tired moment, or it may have been a sign of the disease that was already sapping her strength.

A circa 1920 snapshot of Sophie Krug holding her child, most likely son Johnny. Source: The Doris Schlichting collection. Edited by author.

In 1925, John Monson and his sister Ethel visited the Sophie and Martin Krug family. The photo was taken at the Krug rental farm a mile west of the Hinderer farm. Left to right: Sophie (Hinderer) Krug holding Maurine, Ethel Monson, John Monson. Front: Martin Krug, Doris Lafere, and Johnny Krug. Source: The Doris Schlichting collection. Edited by author.

Sophie Krug's Death and the Aftermath

The tragic events that began in late 1925 and persisted into 1926 profoundly affected the Krug, Hinderer, and Hansen families. In the 1920s, young adults died mainly from infectious diseases like TB, typhoid, or pneumonia. Sophie's death from cancer on March 25, 1926, would have been outside of the experience of family members.

Storyteller Maurine (Krug) Gjovig said she was too young to remember her mother, but she was always curious to learn what sort of person her mother was. When she was a young adult, she asked others in the family about Sophie. Maurine reported,

> It seemed to me that that disease [cancer] was considered almost a disgrace in those days. At first, I really couldn't get much information about my mother. People didn't seem very willing to talk about it. I finally asked Aunt Mary [Hinderer] Engstrand, and she said my mother was a wonderful person. Later on, the Hansens, who were my father's family, would always talk about her. They all thought the world began and ended with Sophie.

At the time of Sophie's death, her older sister Tena had been married to John Monson for only five months. On the day of Sophie's death, Katharine Hinderer sent a brief telegram to Tena and John. Her single sentence conveyed the news of Sophie's death and the plans for her funeral.

Sophie's obituary was published in the local newspaper the same week as her death and funeral. The general format of the obituary was conventional. In addition, it stated that Sophie had been in the hospital for more than two weeks before she died from a "tumor."[2]

The community's love for Sophie and the sympathy expressed toward her family were overwhelming. Friends and neighbors demonstrated their support at her funeral. The service was held at Zacchaeus Lutheran Church in Canby. The unprecedented attendance was described in a second article in the *Canby News*. As was noted in her obituary, Sophie was buried in the Canby Cemetery.[3]

On the day of Sophie's death, Katharine Hinderer sent this telegram to her oldest daughter Tena and her husband John Monson living in Brook Park, Kanabec County, Minnesota. Source: From the Doris Schlichting collection. Edited by author.

Following the funeral service, a reception was held at the Hinderer farm. Storyteller Doris (Lafere) Schlichting said she knew something was wrong with her Aunt Sophie, but she was not told how serious it was. On the day of the funeral and reception, six-year-old Doris was sent to stay at a neighbor's home. Doris said she walked out to the roadway that day and recalled seeing the many cars parked in the Hinderer's yard and along the roadside.

At the time of his mother's death, Johnny Krug was six years old, William was not yet four, and Maurine had just turned one. Considering the relentless decline of Sophie's health, caring for her three children was beyond her physical capabilities. She was severely ill for months prior to her final hospitalization.

Storyteller Emma (Hansen) Swenson was 24 years old in 1926. She said she moved in with

DEATH OF YOUNG MRS. MARTIN KRUG

Daughter of Mr. and Mrs. Gotlieb Hinderer Dies at Canby Hospital Thursday Morning—Leaves Husband and Three Small Children.

Sophia Krug, wife of Martin Krug, passed away this Thursday morning at 7:30 o'clock at the Canby City Hospital, where she was taken fifteen days ago for treatment for tumor.

The deceased was a daughter of Mr and Mrs. Gotlieb Hinderer of Freeland township, and was born at Pottsville, Alamakee county, Iowa, Nov. 15, 1896. At the age of three years she came with her parents to this community 27 years ago and on Jan. 16, 1918, she was united in mariage to Martin Krug. To them were born four children, of whom three survive, namely: Johnnie 6, Wiliam 3, and Maurine 1 year old. One small daughter preceded her mother 2 years ago.

Besides her husband and children and parents, the deceased is survived by her brothers, Carl and John, and sisters, Tena, Emma, Mary and Martha.

The funeral services will be hold Saturday, March 27, at the German Lutheran church in Canby at 2 o'clock p. m., and burial will take place at the Canby city cemetery.

—o—

Sophie Krug's obituary stated that she died of a "tumor" after being hospitalized more than two weeks. It summarized her life story and identified the family she left behind. She was to be buried in the Canby Cemetery. Source: Canby News. In the public domain. Edited by author.

A LARGE FUNERAL

A gentleman attending the last sad rites of the late Mrs. Martin Krug at the local German Lutheran church, March 27th, said it was the largest funeral ever held in that church, between three and four hundred people being present, many of whom could not get inside of the church. The floral tributes were many and beautiful, four flower girls being appointed to take charge of them.

A second article published by the Canby News *described the unprecedented attendance at Sophie Krug's funeral. Source:* Canby News. *In the public domain. Edited by author.*

Martin and Sophie in the months before Sophie's death. She confirmed that Sophie was too sick to do the household chores and care for the three young children. After Sophie died, Emma Swenson said she remained on the Arneson farm and helped Martin through the summer of 1926.

Katharine Hinderer also provided much-needed help after Sophie died. All three of Sophie and Martin's children were initially taken in to live with the Hinderers. The boys, although still very young, knew the way to their own home a mile away. Emma Swenson said that during the late spring of 1926, Johnny and William regularly walked along the gravel road back to their own farmhouse. For the boys, these walks were an important connection to their home and their father. After their visits, they walked back to the Hinderer farm where their Grandmother Katharine kept them well fed. In the face of the loss of their mother, the young boys were given comfort and love on both farms.

After a few months of living with the Hinderers, Johnny and William were sent to live with the Nels and Anna Hansen family near Canby. Maurine, who would have been only 18 months old at the time, remained living with the Hinderers throughout the summer and fall of 1926.

Sophie Krug was buried in the Canby Cemetery. Source: Photographed and edited by author.

A photograph circa 1940 of Sophie and Martin Krug's three children. Left to right, Johnny, Maurine, and William. Source: From the Doris Schlichting collection. Edited by author.

A Perspective

Sophie Hinderer and Martin Krug were married for only eight years. Theirs was a union of two different personalities and experiences. Sophie grew up with close family connections and a sisterly bond. Martin grew up estranged from nearly everyone in his family. Yet, their differences were somehow complementary. After their marriage, Sophie settled into the rigors of managing a household and Martin settled into the work of farming. Their three young children were the beginning of what surely would have been a larger family. Their home was near relatives who were supportive and could offer both helpful advice and experienced labor. The promise was there, but it was not to be.

As the months after Sophie's death went by, what emerged was a new relationship between Martin Krug and Sophie's sister Emma (Hinderer) Lafere. When Martin married Emma in December of 1926, Sophie's three children returned to live on the Arneson farm. They spent the remainder of their childhood years with their father and their stepmother Emma. The children did not embark on their separate pathways until late in their teen years.

The next several chapters tell the story of Emma Hinderer's married life. It was Emma who, after a failed first marriage, chose to become Martin's wife and a mother to Sophie's children. For Emma, it was a second chance at marriage and family life. Her sisterly bond with Sophie held an obligation for her to raise their combined families. Emma's Hinderer family, particularly her mother Katharine, would provide the resolve and the means to support the growing Krug family.

Notes

1. To locate the building site, in Google Maps insert coordinates 44.824574, -96.253331 in the search box and click the search button.

2. The death certificate for Sophie Krug stated she died of carcinoma of the left ovary with bowel obstruction and secondary anemia present for five months. Ovarian carcinoma was and is uncommon in general.

3. To locate the Canby Cemetery, in Google Maps insert coordinates 44.704014, -96.276522 in the search box and click the search button.

Chapter 13

Emma Hinderer, Ralph Lafere, and Doris Lafere

Timeline

1881 – Ralph Lafere was born, possibly in Canada

1897, Feb. – Emma Hinderer was born in Iowa

1898 – The Hinderers arrived in Minnesota

1914 – World War I began in Europe

1917, Apr. – The U.S. entered WWI

1918, Jan. – Sophie Hinderer married Martin Krug

1918, Sep. – Emma Hinderer married Ralph Lafere

1918, Nov. – Germany Surrendered; World War I ended

1919, Apr. – Doris Lafere was born in Sioux Falls, South Dakota

1919, May – Emma and Doris moved back to the Hinderer farm

1919, Sep. – Johnny Krug was born

1919, Nov. – Mary Hinderer married Albert Engstrand

1920, Jan. – National Prohibition of Alcohol began

1920, Jan. – Ralph Lafere was imprisoned in Illinois

1920, Jul. – Ralph Lafere married Lillie DeGrush

1920, Aug. – Women achieved voting rights in the U.S.

1921, Sep. – Ralph Lafere was arrested in Minnesota

1926, Mar. – Sophie Hinderer died

1926, Dec. – Emma Lafere married Martin Krug

1918 – A Dangerous World

Near the end of 1917, American troops were on their way to the trenches of northern France. The arrival of American soldiers eventually shifted the balance of power in favor of the Allies. In November of 1918, Germany surrendered, and World War I came to an end.

In early 1919, U.S. troops were returning home. Some of them were unscathed, and some would never recover. The trauma to American soldiers and their families was great. World War I was responsible for an estimated 15 to 22 million military and civilian deaths worldwide.[1]

One year earlier in March 1918, the world became aware of what would prove to be an even deadlier threat. The first U.S. case of what was later called "Spanish Flu" was documented at a military camp in the state of Kansas. Within two years, nearly a third of the world's population had been infected by successive waves of this pandemic. Wartime censorship in America as well as other combatant countries banned news stories about this flu. However, the press in neutral Spain wrote freely about the spreading contagion. The news stories coming from Spain led to the misconception that the flu began in Spain. In America, "Spanish Flu" was the misnomer applied to the new disease. Without a vaccine, there was no means of limiting the at-risk population. Without antiviral drugs, there was no way to treat the infection. Two years after it began, the pandemic was finally reduced to sporadic cases in more remote areas of the world. Overall, an estimated 50 million people died worldwide from this pandemic.[2] This was more than twice the number of deaths due to combat in World War I.

A world war followed by an unpreventable and untreatable pandemic was the backdrop to fundamental changes in America. In world affairs, American isolationism was no longer an option. On the domestic front, two long-simmering legislative issues were resolved.

AT HOME IN AMERICA – WOMEN'S SUFFRAGE AND PROHIBITION

During most of the 1800s, the law of the land did not permit women to vote. By the 1890s, several states in the western part of the U.S. allowed women to vote, but only in local elections. More commonly, American women did not have voting rights in any election.

By the end of World War I, there was political momentum to prohibit gender-based voting restrictions in federal and state elections. It would be the final resolution to an issue that had been argued about since before the Civil War. Throughout those years, women's suffrage had been linked to multiple other issues like the abolition of slavery, inheritance laws, and alcohol prohibition. These alignments sometimes helped the cause of women's suffrage, but more often harmed it.

World War I had proven that American women were necessary, capable, and successful at doing "men's work." When women produced munitions in factories and labored alone on farms while their husbands were away in the war, the "men's work" argument was silenced.

During the war years, President Woodrow Wilson, a Democrat, split from his party's opposition to suffrage to gain support at home for the war effort in Europe. With President Wilson's added backing, congress voted in favor of women's suffrage during the summer of 1919. By August of 1920, the amendment had been ratified by three fourths of the states and was formally added to the U.S. constitution. It had taken 132 years for women to be granted the same constitutional voting rights as men.

One of the movements that was sometimes tied to women's suffrage was the prohibition of alcohol consumption. Common sense dictated that these two issues were unrelated. Women's suffrage granted voting rights to half of the adult population, while prohibition was meant to regulate the behavior of all citizens. Nevertheless, the two issues often appeared side by side in newspaper headlines. Both were resolved at about the same time.

During most of the 1800s, consumption of alcoholic beverages was a common practice throughout the world. Alcoholic drinks accompanied most meals. One reason for this practice was sanitation. In those days, drinking a beverage containing alcohol was far safer than drinking water that was often contaminated.

In the early 1900s, prohibition of alcohol became the dominant theme for movements wanting to "clean-up" America. Conservative Christian groups joined with political progressives to correct our "nation of drunkards."

The Anti-Saloon League wielded enormous political power in the early 1900s. Politicians who dared oppose its anti-alcohol and the underlying anti-immigration sentiment were at risk of losing their careers. The Main Street saloon had become a symbol of evil. The more civilized reformers conducted protest marches and walked picket lines. Others were not so orderly. A self-righteous woman named Carrie Nation wielded a hatchet and personally destroyed the wooden bars inside saloons across her native state of Kansas. She then proudly served multiple prison terms for these attacks. For like-minded vigilantes, their violence was justified by the certitude of their beliefs.

• • • • • • •

Nothing so needs reforming as other people's habits. It is the prohibition that makes anything precious. ~ Mark Twain

• • • • • • •

During the 19th century, a federal tax on the sale of alcoholic beverages had generated much-needed revenue for the U.S. treasury. The advent of a permanent federal income tax in 1913 diminished the government's need for tax revenue from alcohol sales.

Prejudice against Americans viewed as undesirable also played a role in the prohibition movement. Recent immigrants were the main groups that were targeted. The great influx of Irish and German immigrants arriving in the 1800s brought with them a cultural practice of beer consumption.

In World War I, the German enemy provided a powerful link between the anti-immigration and anti-alcohol movements. Anti-German war rhetoric quickly expanded into a condemnation of the drinking habits of American citizens with German heritage. Anti-immigration and anti-alcohol motives were easily disguised as wartime patriotism. It all played into the hands of the prohibition movement.

It was important to the prohibition promoters that a congressional vote take place prior to the 1920 census. The U.S. population was increasing rapidly, and large urban centers were heavily populated by immigrants. The political sense was that mandatory redistricting after 1920 might swing the popular vote away from the prohibitionist's cause.

The 18th Amendment on prohibition was passed in August of 1917. Within a year, it was ratified by three fourths of the states. The amendment was aimed not at the consumption of alcohol, but on the production, distribution, and sale of intoxicating beverages. According to the terms of the amendment, enforcement of the law was delayed until January of 1920. As a result, Americans had more than a year to stock up on their favorite alcoholic beverages.

The Volstead Act, passed by Congress in 1919, established how prohibition laws were to be enforced. Minnesota representative Andrew Volstead chaired the congressional committee that wrote this law. Federal prohibition agents were tasked with enforcing the new amendment to the U.S. Constitution.

After prohibition went into effect, early surveys suggested that alcohol consumption had gone down. This early success was welcomed by the reformers, but it did not last. The robust economic times of the 1920s gave way to widespread poverty with the Great Depression. Out-of-work citizens used the transport and sale of alcohol to make money. Gangsters in cities like Chicago skimmed money from victimized business owners. As a result, "moonshine" brewed in home stills was distributed in mason jars and tin cans throughout America. Prohibition created a new money-making infrastructure exploited by criminals and ordinary citizens alike. "It was meant to eradicate an evil. Instead, it turned millions of law-abiding Americans into lawbreakers."[3]

Americans were not alone in the movement to correct societal ills blamed on alcohol. In the early 1900s, Canada allowed individual provinces to establish laws regarding alcohol production and sales. During World War I, however, this temporarily changed into nation-wide alcohol regulation. Canadian prohibition advocates used the war to promote abstinence. The Canadian version of prohibition differed from the U.S. in that Canadians could legally manufacture the alcohol, but they could only sell it outside of Canada.[4]

The difference between the American and Canadian prohibition laws created local "rumrunners."[5] Alcohol was legally produced in Canada and then transported to the northern U.S. border. Once inside the U.S., it was illegally hidden in vehicles and transported south to be profitably sold throughout the United States. Western Minnesota was in the crosshairs of this alcohol traffic. Today's Highway 75, extending from the Canadian border through Canby, Minnesota, was a newly built roadway in the 1920s. This road led southward through Minnesota, Iowa, Nebraska, and all the way to Texas. It became known as the "king of trails," a favorite for rumrunners. A Minnesota historian wrote:

> *this [Highway 75] was the rum-runner's favorite route. . . . It was on this road near Canby that a rum-runner was killed in an accident while driving a booze-laden Cadillac. The guard "riding shotgun," escaped with injuries.*[6]

While the anti-alcohol and anti-immigration movements merged across the U.S., only the issue of prohibition impacted the Hinderer family. For immediate family members, abstinence from consumption of alcohol was a minor inconvenience at most. It was bootlegging that directly affected the life of at least one family member. During her marriage to Martin Krug, Emma Hinderer was forced to live outside of the laws set down by the 18th Amendment and the Volstead Act. Emma and Martin's story will be told in a later chapter.

The anti-immigrant rhetoric of the early 1900s did not extend to the farming country of southwestern Minnesota. The Hinderer family did not personally experience the anti-German fervor of World War I. Storyteller John Hinderer said he felt no such discrimination.

During these years, churches near the Hinderers still carried the names and spoke the languages of the countries from which their members emigrated. A Norwegian church was located a few miles west of the Hinderer farm. Several miles to the east, a Swedish congregation was conducting services in Providence Township. The Hinderers themselves were members of the German Lutheran Church in Canby. In this sparsely populated rural area, a variety of languages were spoken in homes and during religious services.

Plat maps from the early 1900s reveal why there was no anti-German discrimination. On those maps, most of the landowners living near the Hinderers had either German or Scandinavian names. With neighboring families who were first and second generation immigrants, ethnic tolerance was the day-to-day practice in this part of rural Minnesota.

Emma and Her Hinderer Family

In 1917, Gottlieb Hinderer had help with chores as well as fieldwork. His oldest son Carl was a young man of 23 and capable of all the farm work he was assigned. In June 1917, Carl registered for military service; however, he was never called into active duty.

Mother Katharine had less predictable help at home from her daughters. Storyteller John Hinderer said that his sister Sophie was the one who helped Katharine at home most of the time. Younger sisters Emma and Mary mainly worked and lived away from home. Together, though, these three sisters were Katharine's source of help at home. Twins John and Martha were only eleven years old.

When they worked away from home, Emma and Sophie Hinderer worked as domestic helpers for families in the Canby area. In 1917, Emma was 20 years old, and Sophie turned 22 that November. Their older sister Tena had been working away from home for over a decade.

At this same time in 1917, 24-year-old Martin Krug lived with his mother and stepfather on a farm near Canby. He was also required to register for military service. Like Carl Hinderer, Martin Krug was never called into active duty. Martin's half-sister and storyteller Emma Swenson said Martin often played a musical instrument at dances in Canby. These dances in 1917 were where Martin Krug met sisters Emma and Sophie Hinderer.

Storyteller Emma Swenson added that during 1917, Martin Krug first dated Emma Hinderer, but later began dating her sister Sophie. Emma Hinderer's thoughts and feelings about this turn of events were not recorded. However, her lost relationship with Martin Krug likely distanced Emma from what had been a close friendship with Sophie.

After Sophie and Martin's marriage in January 1918, Emma occasionally helped her mother Katharine at home on the farm. More often, 21-year-old Emma lived and worked in Canby. For the first time, Emma was truly on her own, and the months after Sophie's marriage proved to be a lonely and difficult time in her life.

EMMA AND RALPH LAFERE

Ralph Leon Lafere[7] became a part of Emma Hinderer's life during the summer of 1918, and perhaps even earlier. Records from his life are sparse. Ralph's claims and statements were inconsistent and at times untruthful. Only a few documents are available from his days in Canby. In reviewing these documents, Ralph's tendency to be deceptive must be kept in mind.

Ralph Lafere claimed he was born January 9, 1881, making him 37 years old in 1918. He also claimed he was a naturalized citizen. U.S. naturalization records have been archived and can be readily searched. These records do not contain a listing for Ralph Lafere.

On September 12, 1918, Ralph Lafere registered for military service. Two months later, Germany surrendered, and World War I was over. Although he was never drafted, his registration document listed information about him. His physical description indicated he was tall with a medium build, brown eyes, and dark hair. He claimed he had no living relatives. Ralph contradicted this last statement in a subsequent document.

Ralph Lafere stated he worked as a flour packer at the G.W. Van Dusen Company in Canby. This was plausible. G. W. Van Dusen Co. operated grain storage elevators built next to railway lines across Minnesota and into the Dakotas. The grain elevators were a necessary hub where farmers brought wagon loads of grain to be shipped eastward. Most grain elevators also had a flour mill on the same property. Farmers reserved some of their harvested wheat to be milled into flour for use back at home. Ralph claimed he worked at the flour mill in Canby.

There is no information about how Ralph and Emma met in 1918. Ralph's September 1918 registration for military service was followed two

An undated studio photograph of Emma Hinderer. She was likely in her early 20s. Source: Image courtesy of Becci Fischer. Edited by author.

weeks later by his marriage to Emma Hinderer. Their 16-year age difference was unusual.

The location where Emma and Ralph's marriage took place is puzzling. They were married on September 23, 1918 at a Lutheran church parsonage in Madison, Minnesota. Madison is located on Highway 75 in Lac qui Parle County about 20 miles north of Canby. At this time, Emma and Ralph both lived in Canby. So far as is known, they did not attend church in Madison. The Hinderer family lived near Madison, but they were members of the German Lutheran church in Canby. Nevertheless, the Madison church parsonage was where Emma and Ralph chose to be married.

The front side of Ralph Lafere's military registration form. His birthdate was listed as well as his claimed naturalized citizenship and his employment. He signed the document as LaFere rather than Lafere. Source: "U.S., World War I Draft Registration Cards, 1917-1918" online database (Provo, UT: Ancestry.com), accessed April 7, 2023. Edited by author.

The reverse side of Ralph Lafere's military registration form. His physical description and the date of his registration were listed. Source: "U.S., World War I Draft Registration Cards, 1917-1918" online database (Provo, UT: Ancestry.com), accessed April 7, 2023. Edited by author.

The marriage of Emma Hinderer and Ralph Lafere took place in the parsonage of a Lutheran Church in Madison, Minnesota. Both Emma and Ralph lived in Yellow Medicine County. No Hinderer family members were listed on the marriage document. Source: Yellow Medicine County Recorder's Office. Edited by author.

The two witnesses to the marriage were the Madison pastor's wife and a woman with an unfamiliar name. No member of the Hinderer family was listed on the marriage document. The unexpected marriage location and the absence of family members suggests the marriage did not have the approval of Emma's parents. Possibly, the Hinderers were unaware of the marriage.

Storyteller Doris (Lafere) Schlichting was Emma's first child. She speculated that Emma and Ralph's marriage may have occurred without the knowledge of the Hinderer family. Doris noted that her mother Emma was two months pregnant at the time of her September 1918 marriage to Ralph Lafere. Doris thought that in Emma's mind, her mother Katharine's likely disapproval would make an out-of-the-way marriage the path of least resistance.

Doris went on to describe several visits to the Hinderer farm by Emma and Ralph after their marriage. She learned about these visits later in her life. Doris was told that Ralph Lafere came to the Hinderer farm to ask them for money. Doris added that her grandmother Katharine was suspicious of Ralph and refused to loan him any money. These disagreeable encounters further separated Emma from her Hinderer family. Doris thought that her mother had no choice but to side with her new husband. A few months after their marriage, Emma and Ralph left Canby and moved southward along Highway 75 to Sioux Falls, South Dakota.

SIOUX FALLS, SOUTH DAKOTA

By the end of 1918 or early 1919, Emma and Ralph were living in Sioux Falls, South Dakota. Ralph had left his employment at the Canby flour mill, and Emma had left her job as a domestic worker. Years later, Doris was told by her grandmother Katharine that Ralph and Emma lived in a small rental apartment in Sioux Falls.

Storyteller John Hinderer added information concerning Emma and Ralph. John was only 12 years old in early 1919, but he had a clear memory of how events unfolded. John characterized Ralph Lafere as "kind of a stinker." For John Hinderer, this was as unkind a description as he ever used. John said that after Ralph took Emma to Sioux Falls, he wrote a letter to the Hinderers which again asked them to send him money. John said,

> *Of course, my mother [Katharine] could tell right away that something was wrong. So, she called down to the police in Sioux Falls to find out what was going on. Well, I guess that scared him [Ralph], so he beat it.*

Doris Lafere was born on April 28, 1919 in Sioux Falls, South Dakota. Grandmother Katharine later told Doris that her father Ralph had abandoned Emma shortly before Doris was born. Katharine added that the landlady in the apartment where Emma lived, a woman named Alice, acted as a midwife when Emma went into labor. Doris was told that a physician also attended her home birth and later signed her birth certificate. However, it was the landlady, Alice, who gave personal care to Emma before and after Doris was born.

Later in her life, Doris discovered that her original birth name was Alice Marguerite Lafere rather than Doris Catherine Lafere. Doris made this discovery when she needed her birth certificate to obtain a passport. Through clever research, the South Dakota authorities found her original birth certificate, which included her birth name, Alice Marguerite. Emma must have been so grateful to her landlady that she named her newborn daughter after her.

Emma Lafere faced serious problems in Sioux Falls. She was living in a rental apartment with a newborn child. She had no husband, and she had no means of earning a living. John Hinderer said that in her distress, Emma called home in May of 1919 to ask her mother Katharine for help. John added that his older brother Carl was dispatched in their Model-T to drive to Sioux Falls, 110 miles south of the Hinderer farm.

Carl together with Emma and her baby immediately left Sioux Falls and returned home to

Doris Lafere's birth certificate revealed that she was originally named Alice Marguerite Lafere (spelled LaFere). The birthplace of her father Ralph Lafere was listed as Canada. Source: The Doris Schlichting collection. Edited by author.

252

the Hinderer farm. Emma's departure from Sioux Falls left her seven-month marriage forever in the past. She never learned the whereabouts of her husband, Ralph Lafere.

When Emma returned home in the summer of 1919, her younger sister Mary Hinderer was working as a domestic in Canby. Doris was later told that her Aunt Mary said the name Alice did not seem right for Emma's baby daughter. Mary proposed, and Emma agreed, that the baby should be named Doris Catherine instead of Alice Marguerite. Once the decision was made, the Hinderer family simply began calling Emma's baby Doris. No official name change was ever documented in any civil record. Throughout most of her life, Doris was unaware she had a different birth name.

EMMA ON THE FARM; 1919-1926

During the first seven years following Emma's return to the Hinderer farm, she worked both at home and as a domestic helper living with other families. These years are reviewed in other chapters. For most of these seven years, Emma lived with her employer families. Her daughter Doris, however, always remained with the Hinderers and was raised by her grandmother Katharine.

In late January of 1920, the U.S. Census recorded residents living in Lac qui Parle County. This census included the Hinderer family in Freeland Township. Gottlieb and Katharine were listed together with their children Carl, John, and Martha. Their daughter Emma Lafere was also listed as was their granddaughter, Doris.

RALPH LAFERE – AFTER SIOUX FALLS

Ralph Lafere abandoned his wife Emma prior to the birth of Doris Lafere on April 28, 1919. The exact date he left Emma in Sioux Falls was not recorded. His travel route from Sioux Falls and his destination are also unknown.

The U.S. Census dated January 2, 1920, revealed Ralph Lafere's whereabouts. He was one of six prisoners incarcerated in the town of Wheaton in DuPage County, Illinois.[8] The reason for his imprisonment was not given. This census was taken about nine months after he abandoned his wife Emma in Sioux Falls, South Dakota.

The 1920 Census provided additional information about prisoner Ralph Lafere. He repeated his claim that he was born in Canada and, in contrast to later statements, acknowledged he was married. He added that both of his parents were Canadian born. He claimed his father's native language was English while his mother's native language was French. With a French surname like Lafere, this is the opposite of what would have been expected.

The 1920 U.S. Census recorded on January 30th included the family members who lived on the Hinderer farm. Daughter Emma Lafere and granddaughter Doris (Lafere) were listed. Source: "1920 United States Federal Census" online database (Provo, UT: Ancestry.com), accessed March 28, 2023. Edited by author.

The 1920 U.S. Census recorded on January 2nd listed Ralph Lafere in a jail in DuPage County, Illinois. See text for details. Source: "1920 United States Federal Census" online database (Provo, UT: Ancestry.com), accessed March 28, 2023. Edited by author.

The same 1920 U.S. Census identified a woman working near the jail where Ralph Lafere was incarcerated. Lillie DeGrush[9] worked as a cook at a home for the feeble minded. Lillie was born and raised in neighboring Indiana. She was 52 years old in 1920 making her about 14 years older than Ralph Lafere. The jail where Ralph was imprisoned and the home for the feeble minded where Lillie worked were within a few blocks of one another in Wheaton, Illinois.

In some way, Ralph Lafere met Lillie DeGrush prior to the summer of 1920. They were married on July 29, 1920. At the time of this marriage, Ralph was no longer in jail. He listed his occupation as a laborer living in Chesterton, Indiana.[10]

Ralph and Lillie were married by a Justice of the Peace in Chesterton, Porter County, Indiana. In their marriage record, Ralph claimed he was born in Canada on July 9, 1891. On his World War I registration card, he had listed his birthdate as January 9, 1891.[11] The marriage record stated that Ralph's father was deceased but had been a farmer born in Canada. It added that his mother had also been born in Canada, but she currently lived in Minnesota. This contradicted his military registration two years earlier, which stated that both of his parents were deceased. Furthermore, Ralph claimed on this 1920 marriage document that he had never been married. This was a false statement. It raises the question whether Lillie DeGrush was ever aware of Ralph's 1918 marriage to Emma Hinderer.

Ralph Lafere's marriage to Lillie DeGrush is the only known document that listed the two of them together. By the time of the next U.S. Census in 1930, Lillie DeGrush was listed as a widow who worked at a grocery store in Porter County, Indiana. By using her former DeGrush surname, Lillie had chosen to ignore her 1920 marriage to Ralph Lafere.

A person going by the name of Ralph Lafere was located one final time. Newspaper articles and court records from September 1921 found Ralph Lafere in trouble with the law once again. This was only 14 months after his marriage to Lillie DeGrush. Ralph must have left Lillie and was traveling once again.

On September 11, 1921, three men were involved in a fight and robbery while aboard a train boxcar near Northfield, Minnesota. The three indicted men were identified as John Lafere, Ralph Lafere, and a man named Louis Antelope. The story of these "boxcar bandits" was published in several local newspapers. At a subsequent sentencing, John Lafere declared that he alone was involved in the fight, while the other two men, including his "brother" Ralph Lafere, played no role in the altercation. The alleged victim sustained injuries when he fell or was pushed from the moving train. For his admission of guilt, John Lafere was sentenced to five years in the state penitentiary in

Ralph Lafere married Lillie DeGrush on July 29, 1920 in Porter County, Indiana. Ralph's claim about his parents conflicts with a prior document. His statement that he had no prior marriage was false. Source: "Porter County (Indiana) Clerk of the Circuit Court, Marriage Record," 1920-1921, p. 330, Ralph L. Lafere and Lillie May DeGrush, married 29 July 1920; FamilySearch Library Digital Collection 5014501, accessed January 2023, http://www.familysearch.org. Edited by author.

Stillwater, Minnesota. The other two men, Ralph Lafere and Louis Antelope, were freed.

This incident of the "boxcar bandits" was the last time a man using the name Ralph Lafere was uncovered. Searches for later census documents as well as death records revealed no mention of Ralph.

A professional genealogy team was also engaged to search for records listing a man named Ralph Lafere. Their search of U.S. and Canadian archives did not reveal any birth or death records for him. A complete absence of these vital statistics is rare for people living in the early 1900s. It raises the question of whether Ralph Lafere was this man's real name.

Ralph Lafere has remained an enigmatic character in the Hinderer story. The documents that have been presented are the only ones discovered. These few pages contain both contradictory and outright false statements. Clearly, whoever Ralph Lafere was, he did not want to be identified or tracked. The most logical conclusion is that Ralph Lafere was a fictitious name meant to conceal his true identity.

John LaFere Gets Five Years; Brother and Antelope Freed

John LaFere, indicted by a Rice county grand jury for the robbery of Tony Yes, a Bosnian, in a box-car south of Northfield, plead guilty to the charge in the district court last week and was sentenced by Judge A. B. Childress to five years in the state penitentiary at Stillwater. His two companions, Louis Antelope and Ralph LaFere, indicted on the same charge, were freed, Antelope being acquitted by the jury, and the case against LaFere being dismissed.

County Attorney Lucius Smith of Faribault conducted the prosecution, and C. P. Carpenter, who was appointed by Judge Childress, represented the defendants.

John LaFre, who was given the five year prison term, plead guilty to the charge when arraigned before the court, but denied that either his brother or Antelope were implicated in the affair. He also declared that Yes was the first to attempt a hold-up, testifying, "he tried to stick me up, and I beat him to it."

Yes testified that he had entered a boxcar at Albert Lea on the night of September 10, and there found three other men whom he said were the three men charged with robbing him. With the three men he rode in the car to Northfield where he said he was held up and badly beaten with a board. He also alleges that he was thrown bodily from the car after being struck with the board, sustaining severe injuries which necessitated his confinement for a week in the Northfield hospital.

The elder LaFere contradicted Yes' testimony. He said that the others were sleeping when the affair occurred and no loud noise was made. During the struggle that ensued he said he and Yes, locked together, fell from the car and it was then that Yes sustained the injuries about his head. He also declared that he took no money from Yes but admitted having taken the watch.

Local police officials, including Chief W. D. Smith, Ben Way, and Paul Skauge, were called to testify in the case. They testified to finding Yes and the subsequent arrest of the three men, two at the depot here and the other at Randolph.

One of several local newspaper articles described the indictment of three "boxcar bandits," including Ralph Lafere. His "brother" John Lafere testified that he alone was involved in the fight and was sentenced to a five-year prison term. The case against Ralph Lafere was then dismissed. Source: Northfield (Minnesota) News, *December 2, 1921, p. 12, col. 2, accessed January 2023, https://newspapers.mnhs.org (Minnesota Historical Society). Edited by author.*

Using DNA to Search for Ancestors

In the past, this would have been the endpoint to identifying Doris Lafere's father and his extended family. Today, however, DNA analysis provides a new tool for discovering ancestors. This growing field of inquiry requires a professional team schooled in the nuances of biologic inheritance. An expert team was engaged to look for Doris's father using DNA technology.

Several avenues of DNA research have been developed over recent decades. While some DNA studies identify only maternal or paternal ancestors, autosomal DNA reveals ancestry along both lines. Analysis of autosomal DNA is also capable of suggesting the closeness of a relationship. Privacy of information is a legitimate concern in this research, and the permission of those involved is always obtained.

The use of autosomal DNA begins with an analysis of a member of Doris's immediate family, in this case using her son David Schlichting's DNA.[12] The first step is to restrict the study to the subject's maternal (Doris's) side of the family. The next step requires eliminating the DNA matches Doris inherited from her mother, Emma Hinderer. The DNA matches that remain are segments of DNA that Doris inherited from her biologic father. These paternal DNA segments are then compared to DNA segments from other individuals in a large databank. If a significant amount of shared DNA is found, those people are biologically related to Doris. The amount of shared autosomal DNA predicts the closeness of the relationship. Siblings share the most DNA while more distant relatives share less. Although the closeness of the relationship is approximate, there is no doubt they are biologically related.

Analysis of the DNA Doris inherited from her biologic father produced unexpected results. She shared a significant amount of DNA with descendants of a family who, in 1920, lived in Tracy, Lyon County, Minnesota.[13] Lyon County is adjacent to and southeast of Yellow Medicine County and Canby where Emma Hinderer lived and worked. This Lyon County family included four sons. In the summer of 1918, these sons ranged in age from 17 to 34. Biologically, any one of these sons would have been capable of fathering a child.

An initial consideration was that Ralph Lafere might have been one of these sons who was using a false name. This idea was disproven by the 1920 U.S. Census. In January of 1920, Ralph was incarcerated in Wheaton, Illinois. That same month, the census documented all four brothers living in Lyon County, Minnesota. Ralph Lafere could not have been a member of the Lyon County family.

The 1920 U.S. Census added that the four brothers from Lyon County all worked for the railroad line that ran northwestward through Lyon County. This same line then continued through Canby in Yellow Medicine County, and on into South Dakota. Because of their employment with the railroad, any one of the four brothers could have traveled to Canby as part of their work. At this same time during the summer of 1918, Emma Hinderer was working as a domestic in Canby, Minnesota.

Following the initial discovery of shared DNA, descendants of the four Lyon County brothers were contacted. These descendants were all made aware of the search objectives and several of them volunteered to have their DNA analyzed. In theory, this process might have identified which one of the four brothers was Doris's biologic father. The result of this limited analysis was inconclusive. Nevertheless, it is correct to conclude that one of the four brothers was Doris's biologic father.

The search for Doris's biologic father fell short of an exact identification of one individual. However, the DNA analysis was able to trace her father back to one family and a specific time.

The DNA studies also allow construction of a timeline for Emma Hinderer during 1918. Her older sister and best friend Sophie had married Martin Krug in January 1918. Emma was left working at home or in Canby during that spring and summer.

In late July, she had an encounter with a man from Lyon County who worked for the railway line that ran through Canby. This encounter resulted in her pregnancy. Two months later, Emma married Ralph Lafere, a man who worked at a Canby flour mill.

Was Ralph Lafere aware of Emma's pregnancy at the time of their marriage? The answer to this question is unknown. It is possible that even Emma was unaware or at least unsure of her pregnancy when she married Ralph.

The convoluted story of Doris Lafere's father can be viewed from many perspectives. Emma's pregnancy was not unusual for that time. As a young woman in 1918, she had no means of preventing this pregnancy. Similar outcomes were experienced by several young women in the Hinderer family. Her mother Katharine was pregnant when she arrived in America. In Katharine's time, childbearing before formal marriage was normal. It was only later that moral judgements against such a common occurrence took hold.

For Emma Hinderer, the years 1918 and 1919 marked the beginning of her adult life. Her marriage to Ralph Lafere had resulted in estrangement from her birth family. When she was abandoned by Ralph at a time of great vulnerability, the kindness of her landlady Alice steadied her through the birth of her first child. Her call to the Hinderers brought her back home to live with her birth family. The strength of the Hinderers allowed Emma time to recover and rebuild a sense of who she might become. Furthermore, the strength of this Hinderer family was sufficient to embrace Emma's first child Doris, who they raised as their own.

■ ■ ■

Notes

1. Wikipedia s.v. "World War I Casualties," last modified May 21, 2024, 09:08 (UTC), https://en.wikipedia.org/wiki/World_War_I_casualties.

2. Centers for Disease Control and Prevention, "1918 Pandemic (H1N1 Virus)," *CDC Archive*, accessed April 2, 2023, www.cdc.gov/flu/pandemic-resources/1918-pandemic-h1n1.html.

3. This quote and other prohibition information is sourced from *Prohibition*, episode 1, "A Nation of Drunkards," directed by Ken Burns and Lynn Novick, aired on October 2, 2011, on PBS, https://www.pbs.org/kenburns/prohibition/.

4. Gerald Hallowell, "Prohibition in Canada," in *The Canadian Encyclopedia*, last modified November 13, 2020, https://www.thecanadianencyclopedia.ca/en/article/prohibition.

5. The term "rumrunning" or "rum running" (formerly spelled rum-running) was usually applied to illegal movement of alcohol by sea, while bootlegging referred to illegal movement over land. However, the two terms are often used interchangeably.

6. Carl and Amy Narvestad, *A History of Yellow Medicine County*, Minnesota: 1872 –1972 (Granite Falls, MN: Yellow Medicine County Historical Society, 1972), 118.

7. Ralph's surname was variably spelled Lafere, LaFere, or La Fere.

8. DuPage County, Illinois, is a suburb of Chicago. To locate DuPage County, in Google Maps insert coordinates 41.861838, -88.082986 in the search box and click the search button.

9. Lillie's surname is variably spelled DeGrush, DeGrosh, or DeGroush.

10. Chesterton is in Porter County, Indiana, where Lillie DeGrush lived. It lies along the southern edge of Lake Michigan. It is 70 miles east of Wheaton, Illinois, where Lillie had worked and Ralph had been imprisoned.

11. This error, January vs. July, may have been a typographical error made by the person recording the marriage.

12. David Schlichting is the son of Doris (Lafere) Schlichting. All of Doris's children would have similar autosomal DNA findings.

13. To locate Tracy in Lyon County, Minnesota, in Google Maps insert coordinates 44.232024, -95.621111 in the search box and click the search button.

Chapter 14

Emma Lafere and Martin Krug

Timeline

1893 – Martin Krug was born in Illinois

1897 – Emma Hinderer was born in Iowa

1918, Jan. – Sophie Hinderer married Martin Krug

1918, Sep. – Emma Hinderer married Ralph Lafere

1918, Nov. – World War I ended; Germany surrendered

1919, May – Emma and her infant Doris returned to the Hinderer farm

1920 – Prohibition began in the U.S.

1926, Mar. – Sophie Krug died

1926, Dec. – Emma Lafere married Martin Krug

1927 – 1935 – Emma and Martin lived on four rental farms

1928 – Deloris Krug was born

1929 – Leonard Krug was born

1931 – Elizabeth (Bette) Krug was born

1932 – Florence Krug was born

1933, Dec. – Prohibition was repealed in the U.S.

1934 – Jeanette Krug was born

1935, Jan. – Martin Krug died

1935, Mar. – Emma and the children moved into Canby

Doris – Her Childhood

Storyteller Doris Lafere was Emma Hinderer's only child by her 1918 marriage to Ralph Lafere. When Ralph abandoned Emma in April of 1919, Emma called home and asked her parents for help. Her brother Carl drove to Sioux Falls, South Dakota and brought Emma and her newborn daughter home to live on the Hinderer farm. Later in her life, Doris was told that after living with the Hinderers for a short time, her mother Emma began working for other families. With Emma working away from home, Doris was increasingly under the care of her Grandmother Katharine Hinderer. Doris said that in her child's view, this was a happy arrangement. It was as if she had two mothers.

Reflecting back on her childhood, Doris later questioned her grandmother about her upbringing. Katharine revealed that she and Emma had an agreement. With Emma working away from the farm, Katharine would raise Doris. It was an informal arrangement, and no adoption papers were ever filed. Doris added that she was never told of this during her childhood. Katharine and Emma's agreement held throughout the early 1920s. Events in the year 1926, however, brought the Hinderer, Lafere, and Krug families into an even more intertwined relationship.

1926

In early 1926, Katharine Hinderer became focused on the rapidly failing health of her daughter Sophie Krug. Sophie had weakened and eventually became bedridden. Katharine stepped in to provide comfort and care to Sophie and Martin's three little children. Likewise, Martin

Krug's Hansen family helped out during what was a bleak time for everyone. Martin's half-sister Emma Swenson moved in with Martin to help with daily chores as well as caring for Sophie. The relentless progression of Sophie's cancer ended with her death on March 25, 1926.

After Sophie died, her three children were lovingly taken in by their Hinderer and Hansen grandparents. The two boys, Johnny and William, stayed with their Hansen grandparents who lived near Canby, Minnesota. Maurine, who was a very young toddler, was cared for by Katharine Hinderer. This arrangement continued through most of 1926. Both granddaughters, Doris Lafere and Maurine Krug, lived on the Hinderer farm.

As the months after Sophie's death passed, seven-year-old Doris said she realized that her mother Emma was spending time with widower Martin Krug.[1] She said Martin would visit the Hinderer farm on Sundays and would stay to have a meal with the family. Martin often brought his two sons Johnny and William with him. Doris recalled these as happy family occasions when she and her three Krug cousins spent afternoons playing together.

A studio portrait of Martin Krug likely from the early 1920s. Source: Image courtesy of Becci Fischer. Edited by author.

The December 2, 1926 marriage of Martin Krug and Emma Lafere took place at the Lutheran Church in Canby, Minnesota. The witnesses were family members Martha Hinderer and Andrew Hansen. Source: Marriage certificate copy courtesy of the Yellow Medicine County Recorder's Office. Edited by author.

By the fall of 1926, Martin Krug's visits to the Hinderer farm had evolved into a courtship of Emma Lafere. Their eventual marriage in early December provided a resolution to the many difficulties brought about by Sophie Krug's death. This is not meant to diminish the real affection Martin had for Emma. However, as noted earlier, in sparsely populated rural areas, the death of a spouse was often followed by a remarriage. A new marriage was a pragmatic way for a surviving parent to continue raising children from an earlier marriage.

Martin and Emma's marriage certificate indicated they were married in Canby, Yellow Medicine County. The officiant was the pastor of the Canby Lutheran church the Hinderers regularly attended. Emma's first marriage to Ralph Lafere had not included any family members as witnesses. In contrast, her marriage to Martin Krug was witnessed by members of both families. Emma's younger sister Martha and Martin's half-brother Andrew Hansen were the official witnesses to Emma and Martin's 1926 marriage.

A September 2000 photo of the driveway entrance to the Nessett farm three miles west of Canby at 1618 230th Avenue. The long gravel driveway curves to the left, bridges a seasonal creek, and ends at the farm buildings in the background. Source: Photographed and edited by author.

A 2017 photo of Martin and Emma's Walters rental farm at the north edge of Canby. The house had been remodeled prior to this photo. The current street address is 2232 190th St. Source: Photographed and edited by author.

The Rental Farms

Storytellers Emma (Hansen) Swenson and Maurine (Krug) Gjovig both recalled that Martin and Emma Krug lived on four different rental farms during their eight years of marriage. Martin never owned a home or farmland during his lifetime. His frequent moves from one rental farm to another were unusual. Emma Swenson and Maurine both speculated this was due to Martin's inability to make his rental payments. In truth, Martin Krug was neither a dedicated nor a successful farmer. Because this was during the early part of the Great Depression, Martin deserves some leniency in this judgement. Nevertheless, income he gained from farming was insufficient to support his family's basic needs.

The exact dates that Martin and Emma moved from one farm to another were not recorded, but the sequence and approximate dates are known. In the year 2000, storyteller John Hinderer identified the location of Martin and Emma's four rental farms.

After their marriage in December of 1926, Emma and Martin remained on the rental farm where he and Sophie had lived. It was located one mile west and a half mile north of the Hinderer farm in Lac qui Parle County.[2] Doris (Lafere) Schlichting recalled walking from the Hinderer farm to visit her mother Emma on the Arneson farm. This indicates that Martin and Emma continued to live on this farm at least through the spring of 1927.

According to Minnesota state birth records, Martin and Emma's first child was a boy they named Virgil. He was born in Yellow Medicine County in June of 1927. Sadly, this newborn infant lived for only about six weeks. His birth date and location indicate that Martin and Emma had moved to a second rental farm near Canby, Yellow Medicine County by June of 1927. John Hinderer identified this second rental as the Hendricks farm. He pointed out the farm's location on 230th Ave., about a mile north of Canby.[3] Infant Virgil Krug was born and died while his parents lived on this property.

John Hinderer and other storytellers called Martin and Emma's third rental farm the Nessett farm. This farm was located at the western edge of Hammer Township, also in Yellow Medicine County. Once again, John was able to identify the farm and, in the year 2000, knew the family who lived there.[4] The Nessett farm was located three miles west of Canby, Minnesota, at 1618 230th Ave.[5] Most of Martin and Emma's children were born on this farm. Their oldest daughter Deloris[6] was born in April 1928 on this farm. Their second child Leonard was also born on this farm in August 1929.

After Leonard's birth in 1929, Martin and Emma had three more children, all daughters. Elizabeth (Bette) was born in 1931, Florence in 1932, and Jeanette in 1934. Bette and Florence were both born on the Nesset farm. Jeanette was born on Martin's fourth and final rental farm. This fourth and last farm was known as the Walters farm. It was located at the north edge of Canby.[7] Martin Krug died in January of 1935 while he and his family were living on the Walters farm.

A Complicated Family

Throughout the time Martin and Emma moved from one farm to another, all of Martin's children lived with them. His three children by Sophie and his five children with Emma were raised together. Emma's first child, Doris Lafere, spent a week or two with her cousins and half-siblings during the summer, but her permanent residence during these years was with her grandparents Katharine and Gottlieb on the Hinderer farm.

Martin's oldest son by his first wife Sophie was Johnny Krug. Johnny always had a contentious relationship with his father. He often bore the brunt of the fieldwork as well as the daily chores caring for their animals. Johnny was more accepting and less resentful towards his stepmother Emma. Even so, Johnny was old enough to have a clear memory of his mother Sophie, and he suffered greatly from her absence.

Johnny's sister and storyteller Maurine (Krug) Gjovig felt sorry for him. She said, "My Dad always seemed to hold Johnny responsible and would take it out on him." She said her father was sick a lot, even as early as when they lived on the Nessett farm. Maurine said,

Johnny had to take over the chores and hardly ever got to go to school because of working on the farm. Even so, he passed eighth grade...I can remember one day he went out to get the mail and I could hear him running back to the house yelling that he passed.

Maurine added,

at night he [Johnny] would just beat the heck out of his pillow. It used to make me so mad, but we didn't really talk about it back then. I've asked him about it a bit since, and he seemed to be brainwashed to believe his dad had to whip him in order to make him good.

In Johnny's view, it was more acceptable for him to take out his anger on himself than to vilify his father.

Those who remembered these years stated that Martin and Sophie's second son William used other means to cope with his father's demands. Like his older brother Johnny, he was often told to help with the outside work. More often than not, William was able to escape his father's demands, relying on his older brother Johnny to shoulder the workload. Maurine believed it was not that William was intentionally mean to his brother. Rather, he used a more circuitous way to avoid the hard labor Martin demanded. Considering their ages when their mother Sophie died, Johnny and William were both significantly affected by her death. William simply expressed his loss differently.

Maurine was too young to have any memory of her mother Sophie. She was raised by her Aunt Emma after her father and Emma married. Maurine said that in her earliest memory, Emma was the mother in her family and Martin was the father. She naturally assumed she was Emma's daughter. Reflecting back, Maurine believed her true relationship to Emma was not a secret that was deliberately hidden from her. The Hinderer and Hansen families simply did not discuss her mother Sophie's death.

Maurine's enlightenment came by way of her brothers Johnny and William. Maurine said she was about three years old when:

> Mom [Emma] *must have gotten after them* [Johnny and William] *for something, and they were talking between the two of them, and I was there, all ears.*

One of her brothers said, "We don't have to listen to her [Emma], she isn't our mother." I [Maurine] said, 'What!'" As she told this story, Maurine said she could remember her outburst as if it were only yesterday. She said, "It was like the world went someplace without me; I felt awful. To think I didn't have my own mother." As time went on, Maurine said she pieced together the complicated family she belonged to. She said,

> *By the time I started school I had everyone categorized. Doris was from one family, Johnny, William, and I were another family, and the younger kids were a third family.*

The Parents

Although Martin Krug lived on a farm his entire life, he never wanted to be a farmer. It is not surprising that he was unable to financially support his large family by farming alone. Of the many recollections by Martin's children, none of them described their father working long days in the fields or spending late hours caring for his animals. Many reasons were recited for Martin's failure at farming: he was often sick, he drank too much, he smoked too much, he had asthma, and so on. His half-sister Emma (Hansen) Swenson said,

> *Although Martin wasn't really sick when they lived on that Nessett farm, he drank pretty heavily, and I think that hurt him. They say he had asthma, but he also did all of that blamed smoking. I'm against both drinking and smoking. Nobody better try to smoke around me.*

Martin's many problems, whether due to outside causes or self-induced, meant income from farming could not support his family. In the end, what most defined Martin Krug was his attempt to make money outside of farming.

Martin's interest in playing the guitar was described in an earlier chapter. He and his boyhood friend often traveled to Canby to play their instruments at dances and parties. This was, however, a social pastime for Martin rather than an attempt to develop a money-making career.

Following his marriage to Sophie Hinderer, Martin studied at home to become a detective. Martin's daughter, Maurine (Krug) Gjovig, saved a certificate her father achieved from a detective training correspondence course. The certificate was dated March 30, 1918. At that time, Martin was 24 years old and had been married to Sophie for only two months. Martin was, in theory, farming at this time, but his aspirations were clearly elsewhere. Martin kept this detective certificate hanging on the home walls of all four of his rental farms. It was displayed on the wall of the Walters farm when he died there in January 1935. It would seem that Martin took particular pride in this achievement. There is speculation, but no documentation, about whether Martin ever used his detective training skills.

Martin Krug's most talked about "side hustle" was buying and selling moonshine. Hinderer family members and his older children were all aware of this activity. Prohibition in the U.S. made liquor trafficking illegal from 1920 through 1934. Nevertheless, during most, if not all of the years he was married to Emma, Martin made money brokering liquor.

Prohibition was officially repealed in December of 1933. However, Yellow Medicine County, where Martin and Emma lived, remained "dry" another year. Throughout 1934, Martin Krug could buy liquor legally in nearby "wet" counties and then return home to sell it illegally in Yellow Medicine County. Nevertheless, the writing was on the wall. The end of Martin's income stream from alcohol sales was imminent.

In some ways, Emma (Lafere) Krug is more difficult to characterize than Martin Krug. In 1919, Emma was abandoned by her first husband, Ralph Lafere. Undoubtedly this left her both humbled and humiliated. Her return home to the Hinderer farm was likely accompanied by neighborhood gossip. Emma was by nature a quiet and even a somewhat shy young woman. Photographs of Emma from these early years tend to show Emma looking downward.

Regardless of how low she felt in 1919, Emma Lafere began to work as a domestic helper away from home. For Emma, these working years helped to rebuild her confidence and allowed her to mature as a woman. In the seven years between her return home in 1919 and her marriage to Martin Krug in 1926, Emma regained her sense of self-worth. By the time she married Martin Krug, she was 29 years old with the skills and the temperament needed to be in charge of a large household.

Maurine (Krug) Gjovig characterized her stepmother Emma as a perfectionist but not a strict disciplinarian. Maurine was the oldest girl living in Emma's household. Although still only a child, Maurine said she felt like her job was to mind the younger children. She explained,

Emma had so much work with the house that she didn't have time for minding the kids, so I was their mother. She [Emma] *cleaned, cooked, baked and worked out in the field. My father Martin*

A photograph from 1919 after Emma and her infant Doris had returned to live on the Hinderer farm. Emma, age 22, looked downward shyly. Left to right: Katharine, Sophie, two friends, Emma, and Martha holding Doris. Source: from the Doris Schlichting collection. Edited by author.

needed the help and was sick a lot already on the Nessett farm.

Maurine was correct in her assessment of Emma's workload. The years of Emma's marriage to Martin were long before any farms had electricity. Emma's cooking, washing clothes, and cleaning house were all done without the convenience of electricity or indoor running water. With a family eventually totaling eight children, her daily workload was endless.

Other storytellers agreed with Maurine. Emma loved all of the children she raised but tended to allow them to settle their own disputes. Maurine added that Emma was "soft" when it came to discipline and said the kids could talk her into anything. To Maurine, this added to her own job as disciplinarian. She said, "Johnny would occasionally help me out with the kids, but he worked in the field most of the time." She added, "William was no help because he was a character and he needed discipline too." On reflection, it could be postulated that Emma's soft and easy-going style was a simple necessity. As the number of children under her care grew, Emma's workdays became even more difficult. She had all she could do to keep up with household chores as well as helping Martin in the fields and caring for their farm animals. There was no time in Emma's life for closely monitoring her children.

In the final analysis, a characterization of Emma Krug as a wife and mother can be framed by what she accomplished. She worked hard both at home and in the fields. At home, she picked her battles knowing she could not personally oversee every moment of her children's lives. The children she raised were adequately provided for, even during the times when their father was too sick to work. When Martin was indisposed, Emma helped Johnny with fieldwork and cared for their animals. Through all of this, Emma remained a kind and soft-spoken woman with an easy smile. Emma Krug became a 38-year-old widow when Martin died in 1935. By this time, she had developed many of the self-assured attributes of her mother, Katharine Hinderer.

FARM STORIES – RECOLLECTIONS OF CHILDHOOD

Several of Martin Krug's children were old enough to have memories about growing up on the rental farms. The oldest of these storytellers was Maurine, Sophie's youngest child. The others were Leonard, Bette, and Florence Krug. These three younger siblings added their own recollections from very early in their childhood. Martin's half-sister Emma (Hansen) Swenson lived for weeks and occasionally months with the Krug family. The children's memories and Emma Swenson's recollections paint a more complete picture of family life on the Krug farms.

Maurine (Krug) Gjovig's earliest farm stories date back to when Martin and Emma lived on the Nessett farm three miles west of Canby, Minnesota. She said Leonard Krug was born on that farm toward the end of 1929 when Maurine was not yet five years old. Maurine characterized Leonard as taking after his mischievous half-brother William. She said Leonard's antics were never malicious, but he could challenge her in many ways.

Maurine said she appreciated the times when her cousin Doris Lafere came to stay with them during the summer. She explained,

She [Doris] was six years older than me. I always enjoyed it when she came because it took some of the pressure off me. Then she was the disciplinarian, and I could breathe easier.

Maurine's assumed role as chief disciplinarian had a lasting effect on her. She said,

It seemed like when we lived there [the Nessett farm], I had a kid on my hip all the time. They were only about a year and a half apart. I took care of their diapers, combed their hair, and everything. I said I wasn't going to have children when I got married because I already raised a family.

Maurine also recalled occasional times of leisure. She said,

For fun, we would visit some friends who lived a ways off. It was far enough that we had to drive the old Whippet.[8]

Our farm [the Nessett farm] was at the base of a hill and the driveway was a long ways from the road. We would have to drive up that driveway in the mud. That old car was piled full of kids and we probably would have gotten up the hill faster if my dad had told us all to walk.

During the years of living on the Nessett farm, the older children walked to a country school. The shortest route to their school followed a railroad track that ran east to west. However, according to Maurine, the children were not allowed to use this route because there were two railroad bridges they had to walk across. Mother Emma feared the children might fall from a bridge and be seriously hurt. The safer pathway along the roads meant they had to walk an extra half mile.

Maurine added a story about the railroad tracks near the Nessett farm. One morning Deloris and Leonard were out playing in a field near the farmhouse. Maurine said,

I heard the train whistle and right away, I just knew that those two kids were on the tracks even though I couldn't see them. I went tearing down that back road a half mile and jerked those kids off the tracks when the train was almost on them. I don't know how I knew those kids were on the tracks, but I did.

Even though he was very young, Leonard Krug said he remembered Maurine pulling him and Deloris off the tracks. He added, "she always reminds me that she saved my skin."

A photo of Martin Krug and his children taken on the Nessett farm in early 1930. Left to right: Maurine age 5 is standing behind Deloris age 2. Martin is holding baby Leonard, then William age 8 and Johnny age 10. Source: Photo courtesy of Becci Fischer. Edited by author.

Katharine

The 1930 U.S. Census was recorded in April. This was about the same time as the family photo displayed previously. It listed Martin Krug's family in birth order. They were living on the Nessett farm. Source: "1930 United States Federal Census" online database (Provo, UT: Ancestry.com), accessed May 26, 2023. Edited by author.

A blurry photo from about 1930 labeled "Ma and the Kids" taken on the Nessett farm. Emma held baby Leonard with Maurine in front of her, then Johnny, Deloris, and William. Note in the background their Whippet sedan with wooden-spoked wheels and chains to help them drive up the long muddy driveway. Source: Photo courtesy of Becci Fischer. Edited by author.

Deloris and Leonard were later involved in a more humorous episode. Maurine recalled,

Those same two got into the wine once. It was in the summertime of course, and Mom [Emma] noticed they were acting sort of funny. They were outside and walking zigzag all over. Mom went into the pantry and discovered they had gotten into the wine. It was homemade wine and they were both drunk, wobbling all over. She [Emma] was so scared that the preacher might come and find them. She just let them wobble around and sleep it off. I'll never forget that.

Daughter Florence (Krug) Rousseau retold how Maurine comforted her when they lived on the Walters farm. Florence said that one day she decided to walk along the roadway toward Canby. Florence pointed out that she was very young, only two or three years old, at the time. Maurine later told Florence that she heard a semi-truck blasting its air horn over and over. All of the children were accounted for except Florence. Maurine looked out the window and saw this huge truck slowly moving toward the farmhouse sounding its horn. In front of the truck was little Florence running toward home crying.

Maurine added that she often worried about what her family would eat for their next meal. She said,

If it was not for the Hinderers, we would have been sunk. They would haul in food for us all of the time. They brought potatoes and vegetables from their farm plus milk and meat. They really kept us afloat.

Looking back, Maurine said

I had a difficult childhood. I remember on the Nessett farm mom [Emma] had a washboard with a hand wringer next to it mounted on top of some tubs. We didn't have a real washer [with a mechanical agitator] until we moved into Canby. I hated wash day. I would come home from school for dinner at noon and there would be clothes hanging in every room. There was so much moisture in the air that our hair would go all flat and we would have to go back to school looking like that.

Maurine added details about their last rental farm. She said,

I suppose we moved from the Nesset place because my dad was sick and he couldn't handle the farming. We moved to the Walters place in March of 1934 and Jeanette was born there in May. My father died there the next January when she [Jeanette] was a little over six months old.

When we moved there we thought we were in heaven because it [the Walters farm] had electricity. I'll never forget how exciting it was to push a button and the light would come on. We only lived there one summer so there wasn't much farming done there. Any outside work was done mainly by Ma and Johnny.

Maurine's account revealed information about the Walters rental: the family lived there less than one year, Martin was sick and unable to work for essentially all of that time, and this farm had electricity.

Emma Swenson said her relationship with Martin and Emma Krug's family was really a continuation of her helping Martin after Sophie died. She said it was difficult for a woman to find a salaried job in those days, so she worked in the homes of different family members. She said her mother (Anna Hansen) talked to Martin about having his half-sister live with his family. Martin agreed to have her help sew and care for the children. Emma Swenson said, "I stayed there for several months at a time." In particular, Emma Swenson lived with Martin's family when Emma Krug had a newborn to care for. Emma Swenson said, "I know I was there at least when Leonard and Bette were born."

A family gathering on the Hinderer farm in 1932. Children in front row left to right: Maurine K., Deloris K., Leonard K., Mabel Monson, Ruth Engstrand, and George Monson. Behind them left to right: Gottlieb Hinderer, Emma K., Katharine H., Martin K., Norma E., Carl H., Tena Monson, William K., Johnny K., Mary Engstrand, Doris Lafere, Ray E., Martha H., Donald E., John Hinderer. Source: From the Doris Schlichting collection. Edited by author.

Emma Swenson said she always got along well with Emma Krug. She added,

Now Sophie and I didn't always get along...[but] Emma and I got along awfully good. Even when I lived in Canby and Emma was in a nursing home, we would spend quite a bit of time together. Everybody would say—here come the two Emmas.

Both Maurine and Emma Swenson recalled another episode of mischief caused by Leonard. This happened on the Walters farm when Martin was sick and not working. As Maurine described it,

The kids were outside playing with some little ducks. We [Maurine and Emma Swenson] looked out the window and there was Leonard burying a little duck alive! Aunt Emma [Swenson] ran out the door yelling at him and he took off with his little feet going like wheels. They ran around that big house until all of a sudden he jumped into the rain barrel and put the cover back on. When she saw he was gone, she knew what he had done and went to that barrel and pulled him out. He was probably only about four years old and I make sure I kid him about it every time I see him. I've mentioned it to Aunt Emma too, and we laugh about it.

Emma Swenson said:

I always got along pretty well with the Krug kids. I still talk to Deloris and Maurine, and with Johnny and William when they were alive. I think the

world of Leonard. I was around when he was born and was with the family for quite some time.

Storytellers Bette (Krug) Weber and Leonard Krug accurately summed up the years on the rental farms and those that soon followed. Bette pointed out that Martin Krug's children by both Sophie and Emma were raised together as one family. There was never a sense of any difference or rivalry between the children of the two mothers. To be sure, the children had their own personalities and many squabbles, but they all belonged to one family. Leonard reflected back on his childhood and teenage years. He said,

What really sticks in my mind was how, in our family, people really cared about you a lot, even if you were just a kid. I know I couldn't have been treated any better whether I was living at home with Ma,[9] or out on the Hinderer farm.

Martin Krug and Prohibition

Throughout most of Martin Krug's married life, prohibition of the production, distribution and sale of alcohol was the law of the land. As noted in chapter 13, the law that detailed the enforcement of this 18th Amendment was known as the Volstead Act. Andrew Volstead was a U.S. Representative from Minnesota. His name was attached to this act simply because he was the chairman of the committee that created it. Andrew Volstead's home was in Granite Falls, Minnesota. Ironically, Granite Falls was the county seat for Yellow Medicine County where bootlegger Martin Krug lived.

Martin Krug did not let the proximity of Andrew Volstead's home interfere with his illegal activity brokering moonshine. In fact, neither did many residents of Volstead's hometown of Granite Falls, Minnesota. At one time, the town had its own speakeasy that masqueraded as a gas station with an attached dance hall. The dance hall served liquor to a select clientele while they had their autos serviced. A nearby drug store was allowed to dispense alcohol, but by prescription only. It was said that on Saturdays, the line of people waiting to fill prescriptions was so long it extended out the front door.[10]

Maurine added more detailed information about her father's alcohol trade. She said,

He was a bootlegger you know. I know that was going on when we lived on the Nessett farm and maybe even before that. I would hear him talking about it. He was getting the liquor in Vesta which was southeast of Canby.[11] He and a bachelor neighbor would drive to Vesta to get it. They would bring it back and resell it. I never saw any transactions, but I knew it came home and my dad would hide it. It came in tin cans that looked like turpentine cans.

Leonard Krug said he knew where his father hid the liquor. He recalled,

Ma [Emma] told me my father had a hiding place for the liquor he bootlegged. She said there was a hidden storage place underneath the kids' play area. He [Martin] first dug a hole in the ground and then placed a metal plate over the pit. Then he covered the plate with dirt and kid's play sand. I think the federal guys came out a couple of times looking for it, but they never found it.

Maurine said she remembered the sheriff coming to the Walters farm looking for Martin's stash of bootlegged alcohol but could not find it.

As a young child, Maurine had a personal reaction to her father's illegal alcohol trade.

I told Ma that I was so ashamed to think my dad was doing that. She [Emma] said that was the only way we had food on the table during the depression. She said he wasn't well and couldn't work.

Maurine recalled that even her Uncle John Hinderer drove with Martin to buy moonshine in Vesta on one occasion. John later told Maurine that there were many people doing what Martin did. These explanations from her stepmother Emma and Uncle John allowed Maurine to accept her father's illegal bootlegging business.

Martin Krug's half-sister Emma Swenson had her own point of view. From her many months of living with Martin and Emma, she was well aware of Martin's bootlegging and his trouble making ends meet. She said,

> Now the Nessetts, they were good Christians. I say that because, you know, Martin sold liquor. Some say that was wrong. Well, I said, I don't know if it was or not. The Nessetts were uppity Christians, but when Martin had hard times, they came out to the farm and took everything of his they could find. That was when we had that dry weather and he couldn't pay his bills. They even took his chickens. So, I said, which is the bigger sin? Should he not sell liquor and let his kids starve to death? I figure you can look at it two ways.

Emma Swenson's plain logic was aimed directly on an age-old dilemma: what is truly right when acting legally conflicts with caring for others in need?

The Death of Martin Krug

Martin Krug was not a well man for years prior to his death at the age of 41. Much of his health decline can be blamed on bad habits: he smoked and drank too much. His daughter Maurine said he was a chain smoker and his half-sister Emma Swenson said his drinking hurt him. Others in the family spoke of Martin's failure to correct these increasingly serious problems affecting his health. Martin's years of living on the Nessett farm included repeated times when he was unable to do any physical work.

Maurine thought the family's move to the Walters farm was meant to reduce the daily workload. During this time, Martin's wife Emma and son Johnny had to do all of the outside chores themselves. When they moved to the Walters farm, Emma was seven months pregnant with their last daughter Jeanette.

Maurine added more detail and her own opinion,

> I think my father was bedridden for weeks or months before he died. The word they used was asthma, but I think it was emphysema because he was a chain smoker. He was sick at home the whole time [they lived on the Walters farm] and died there.

Martin Krug died on January 4, 1935 at home on the Walters farm. His death certificate stated that the cause of death was long-standing bronchial asthma complicated by recent pneumonia and finally cardiac (heart) failure. In 1935, there was no effective treatment for asthma, and there were no antibiotics to treat pneumonia. At that time, the course of Martin's illness and his death was neither unusual nor unexpected.

Martin and Emma's children had various memories about his death. Leonard said he was told his father's death was due to pneumonia or asthma, or maybe both. Leonard also said his only recollection was an image of his father in a casket in either their parlor or living room. Bette said she was told her father died of an asthma attack, but she had no personal memory of his death or funeral. The children's Uncle John Hinderer said, "I think it was the asthma that got him. He would get coughing spells a lot."

Martin's half-sister Emma Swenson offered her own opinion. She clarified that she was not present at any time during Martin's final days or at the time of his death. Emma said her information came from a conversation she later had with Emma Krug. Emma Swenson said,

> We heard he had pneumonia, but you know there were bootleggers there when he died. They were the people Martin was getting his liquor from. Emma Krug told me later that these guys were

MARTIN KRUG IS VICTIM OF TWO DAYS OF ILLNESS

Canby Farmer, 41, Leaves Wife and Eight Children to Mourn.

JOSEPH KACK, SR., DIES IN WABASSO

Mrs. John P. Olson of Newhall, Iowa, Nee Amalia Dyrland, Passes.

Martin Krug

Martin Krug, well known Canby farmer, died Friday morning at his home one mile north of Canby, after being ill two days.

Mr. Krug had not been enjoying good health for a number of years, and at times had to stay in bed for several weeks at a time. That being the case, the family was not alarmed when he took sick last week with what seemed to be an old ailment, about two days before his death. On Friday morning at 4:30 his soul took its flight. When Mrs. Krug went to care for him, after having spent nearly all night at his bedside, he lay pale and still with no sign of life left in him.

Funeral services were held Tuesday, Jan. 8, at one o'clock in the home and at one-thirty in Zachaeus, Ev. Lutheran church, with Rev. Wm. Hennig officiating. The

Martin Krug's obituary was published in the Canby newspaper shortly after his death. Source: As published in the Canby News. *In the public domain. Edited by author.*

at the farm and told her she could rest and they would keep an eye on Martin. I think they had given him a drink.

Another thing was that at one time Martin had worked as a cop to arrest people who had liquor. He had a diploma on the wall in the bedroom that was from a detective school. I think these bootleggers saw the diploma and I am afraid they may have given him something. Yes, I really think so. Emma [Krug] said that when she woke up, the men were gone and Martin was dead.

Florence (Krug) Rousseau said she was told this same story by Emma Swenson. Florence added that her mother, Emma Krug, never talked to her about any men in the house when her father died. Florence said, "My mother never said anything to me about it. She just accepted things as they happened and moved on."

Emma Swenson's speculation opened up a line of conjecture that has been repeated by other family members. Her statement that Martin had worked as a cop and arrested people who trafficked in liquor has never been verified. It may have simply been Emma Swenson's speculation based on seeing Martin's detective correspondence course diploma. What is certain is that Martin made money from bootlegging moonshine. Emma Swenson's speculation cast Martin as a secret agent who turned over his liquor suppliers to law enforcement. While this is not impossible, it does seem unlikely. In the end, the identity of the men Emma Krug spoke of and any connection they may have had to Martin's death remains speculation.

AFTER MARTIN KRUG'S DEATH

At the time of Martin's death, Emma Krug was caring for eight children. The oldest son Johnny was 15 years old and had been the primary farm laborer for years. Emma's youngest, Jeanette, was only eight months old. With Martin gone, Emma had no source of income and a large family to care for. It was a situation that could not last.

Because it was January when Martin died, the Hinderer farmers would have had little daily field work. Storyteller John Hinderer said,

After Martin died, Emma and the kids didn't stay on the Walters place more than a few months. They had a sale of some of her things, and then they all moved into the town of Canby. I often went to the Walters place and did chores for them. They had the four horses and some cows. I don't know if Johnny and William were still going to school, but the younger ones were.

In the spring of 1935, Emma Krug made a decision that would set the course of the rest of her own life and that of her children. She alone was now responsible for raising all of the children. Without a husband, farming was not possible. The solution for Emma was to leave the Walters farm, find an affordable home to rent in Canby, and look for income-producing work. Within two months of Martin's death, she sold their farm animals and farm equipment. For Emma Krug and her eight children, it was the beginning of a new chapter in their lives.

■ ■ ■

Notes

1. Martin knew Emma (Hinderer) Lafere from earlier times in Canby. Storyteller Emma Swenson said Martin dated Emma before he began to date and eventually marry Sophie Hinderer.

2. To locate the building site on the Arneson farm, in Google Maps insert coordinates 44.824574, -96.253331 in the search box and click the search button.

3. To locate the Hendricks rental property, in Google Maps insert coordinates 44.733120, -96.280608 in the search box and click the search button.

4. In the year 2000, John and the author drove down the long driveway to this farmhouse. John introduced the author to the residents during a pleasant conversation.

5. To locate the Nessett farm, in Google Maps insert coordinates 44.736977, -96.337308 in the search box and click the search button

6. Deloris Krug's given name was usually spelled this way by the family. In documents, the spelling is variable: Doloris, Delores, Deloris, and Dolores.

7. The Walters farm was at the northern edge of Canby at 2232 190th St. To locate this farm, in Google Maps insert coordinates 44.723044, -96.276559 in the search box and click the search button.

8. The Whippet was an auto marketed by the Willys-Overland company from 1926 to 1931. It was priced to compete with the Ford Model T and the Ford Model A. It went out of production shortly after the start of the Great Depression.

9. All of Emma and Sophie's children called Emma "Ma." It was a term of endearment.

10. These and other anecdotes were printed in "Our Prohibition Story, Granite Falls, MN., January 17, 1919." (Access courtesy of the Yellow Medicine County Historical Society, July 2017).

11. Vesta, Minnesota is east of Yellow Medicine County in neighboring Redwood County. To locate Vesta, in Google Maps insert coordinates 44.507757, -95.415198 in the search box and click the search button.

Chapter 15

Emma Krug—Single Parent

Timeline

1935, Jan. – Martin Krug died on the Walters rental farm

1935, Mar. – Widow Emma Krug and the children moved into Canby

1935, summer – Johnny Krug dropped out of high school but still lived at home

1935, fall – Doris Lafere moved in with Emma's family and began high school

1938, Dec. – Johnny Krug enlisted in the Navy and moved away

1939 – World War II began in Europe

1939, Nov. – Doris Lafere was married and moved away

1941, Jun. – William Krug finished high school and continued to live at home

1941, Oct. – John and Carl Hinderer bought a house at 409 Lac qui Parle Avenue for Emma

1941, Dec. – Pearl Harbor was attacked. The U.S. declared war

1942 – Emma and the children moved to Lac qui Parle Avenue

1942 or earlier – William Krug worked at a CCC camp in northern Minnesota

1942, Sep. – John Hinderer was drafted into the Army

1943, Jun. – Maurine Krug finished high school and moved away

1945, May – World War II V.E. day. Germany surrendered

1945, Jul. – Deloris Krug married and likely moved away

1945, Sep. – World War II V.J. day. Japan surrendered

1947 – Leonard Krug enlisted in the Navy and moved away

1949, Jun. – Bette Krug finished high school and moved to Montevideo

1951, Jun. – Florence Krug finished high school

1952, Mar. – Florence married and moved away

1952 – Jeanette Krug finished high school

1955 – Jeanette Krug married and lived away

1969 – Carl Hinderer sold his half of the Lac qui Parle Avenue home to William Krug

1978 – The Lac qui Parle Avenue home was sold out of the family

1990 – Emma Krug died

EMMA KRUG'S CANBY HOMES

When Emma Krug's husband Martin died in January of 1935, she was left with a few farm animals, some small farm implements, and household goods. The Walters farm she lived on was rental property, so Emma did not own the land. Within a few months, Emma had sold all of her farm-related possessions. The cash she earned from this sale provided temporary support for Emma and the eight children she was raising.

Emma and her children[1] moved to the town of Canby, Minnesota, in March 1935.[2] She rented a house on the corner of Oscar Ave. and 2nd Street.[3] John Hinderer and others called this home the Lund rental house. When Emma moved into this house, Johnny Krug, age 15, was the oldest child living at home, and one-year-old Jeanette was the youngest. From March of 1935 until late 1941, Emma and her children lived in the Lund house.

The 1940 U.S. Census located Emma Krug and her children living on Oscar Avenue in the Lund house. By 1940, Johnny was in the Navy and Doris had married and moved away. The census stated that Emma rented this house and was unemployed. Source: "1940 United States Federal Census" online database (Provo, UT: Ancestry.com), accessed April 17, 2023. Edited by author.

Maurine (Krug) Gjovig thought that Emma did not work away from home during the early years they lived in the Lund house. Maurine pointed out, however, that the agencies paying Emma support money wanted her to find outside work. With children less than five years old at home, this was out of the question. Even after her children were all in school, Emma's work away from home was only part time. Over the years, the great majority of Emma's income came from one form of assistance or another.

Maurine said that in 1941, the Lund house was sold to new owners who wanted to live in the home. This forced Emma to look for a new house to rent. In the fall of 1941, John and Carl Hinderer bought a house located at 409 Lac qui Parle Avenue in Canby.[4] Their purchase document was recorded in early November 1941. Emma's two brothers bought this home explicitly for her and her children as a rental. John said,

Carl and I bought the house on Lac qui Parle Avenue and they [Emma and her children] *moved there. I think we didn't pay too much for it, but it was good enough and they lived there a long time. We charged them $25 a month rent and that went for them to buy the house. So finally, toward the last, they bought that house with those $25 rent payments.*

Maurine recalled that she and her siblings were not entirely happy to move away from the Lund rental. This was because the Lund house was located in the central part of Canby very close to their school. In contrast, the Lac qui Parle rental was on the northeastern edge of Canby. A small creek marked the eastern edge of this property, and only farms and open land lay beyond the creek. Eventually, the children became accustomed to their new house and its more rural neighborhood. In particular, Florence and her younger sister Jeanette made friends with one of their neighbors who were farmers. This family kept horses, which the two sisters loved to ride.

Maurine described the Lac qui Parle Ave. house as lacking some of the modern features of the Lund house. Although it had electricity, the only source of water was a small hand pump located in an entry room beside the back door. This water, however, was only used for washing hands and was not safe to drink. Maurine added that the older children had to fetch buckets of drinking water from a neighbor's well.

The house on Lac qui Parle Avenue included a single car garage near the rear of the property. A room with an outdoor toilet was attached to one side of this garage. With no running water, there was no bathroom inside the house itself.

> **DEED RECORD No. 69, YELLOW MEDICINE COUNTY, MINN.**
>
> Instrument No. 104969   Form No. 1   WARRANTY DEED, Individual to Individual
>
> E. W. Peterson and wife
>
> To
>
> Carl J. Hinderer and John Hinderer,
>
> Filed for record the 4 day of November A. D. 1941, at 1:15 o'clock P. M.
>
> S. A. Haugland, Register of Deeds
>
> By .... Deputy
>
> **This Indenture,** Made this 29 day of October, 19 41 between E. W. Peterson and Mabel Peterson, his wife,
>
> of the County of Yellow Medicine and State of Minnesota part ies of the first part, and Carl J. Hinderer and John Hinderer,
>
> of the County of Lac Qui Parle and State of Minnesota part ies of the second part,
>
> WITNESSETH, That the said part ies of the first part, in consideration of the sum of Twenty two hundred and no/100 — — — — — — — — — — — — — — DOLLARS, to them in hand paid by the said part ies of the second part, the receipt whereof is hereby acknowledged, do hereby Grant, Bargain, Sell, and Convey unto the said part ies of the second part their heirs and assigns, Forever, all the tract or parcel of land lying and being in the County of Yellow Medicine and State of Minnesota, described as follows, to-wit:
>
> The Lot Three (3) and the Southwesterly fifteen (15) feet of Lot Two (2) of Block Forty-three (43) of the Sixth (6) Railroad Addition to Canby, Minn.

John and Carl Hinderer purchased the house at 409 Lac qui Parle Avenue for $2200. The purchase document was recorded on November 4, 1941. Source: Copy courtesy of the Yellow Medicine County Recorder's Office. Edited by author.

Florence (Krug) Rousseau said that years before their move from the Lund house, John and Carl Hinderer had installed a gas-burning kitchen stove. Before the family moved, the brothers removed this stove and reinstalled it in the Lac qui Parle Ave. house. The stove was used both for cooking and for heating the kitchen. An oil-burning room heater was already located in the dining room adjacent to the kitchen. These were the only two sources of heat in the house.

According to Florence, the Lac qui Parle Ave. house needed work when they first moved in. The stairway to the second story bedrooms required structural repair and the basement was infested with vermin. She said,

I know mother and William had to smear some poison stuff on slices of bread and lay them around in the basement. At first, this basement had a dirt floor. I don't know how they did it, but John and Carl put in a concrete floor eventually. I can remember them leveling the fresh concrete by using a big grain shovel. You can imagine that the floor wasn't really smooth. I think finishing off the floor also helped get rid of the rats. There were rats in the garage as well and that always bothered me. That is where our outdoor toilet was located, and I was always afraid one of them would climb up and bite my bottom.

The children learned they had to be respectful of their new neighbor, an older couple named Sneigowski. Florence recalled,

They were very particular about their house and yard, so we had to be careful. One time when mother was up to the cities [Minneapolis and St. Paul], I was taking the wash water out and threw it on the ground under their hedge. You see, we

This photo from the early 1940s pictured Emma Krug standing in front of the 409 Lac qui Parle Ave. house. In these early years, the house had an open front porch. Source: From the Doris Schlichting collection. Edited by author.

didn't have sewer or anything, so you had to throw the water somewhere. Well, old lady Sneigowski told me right away not to throw the water on the hedge because it might kill it.

EMMA'S CHILDREN – LEAVING HOME

The world in which Emma's children grew up shaped the decisions they made later in life. The 10 years from 1935 to 1945 were uncertain times for young Americans. The financial hardships of the Great Depression were immediately followed by World War II and the loss of many lives. Both of these events had the effect of shortening the time horizon for teenagers and young adults. Their future planning was, of necessity, focused on more immediate goals. Most young women married soon after high school and many young men volunteered or were drafted into the military.

In the Krug household with its lack of financial resources, the children did not look toward a college-level education. Most of them graduated from high school, but some did not. Each one made their own decision and Emma, true to her child-rearing philosophy, allowed them to map their own pathway.

A 2001 photo of the house at 409 Lac qui Parle Ave. In this photo the front porch had been converted into an enclosed room. The garage that originally had an attached outhouse can be seen in the background. Source: Photographed and edited by author.

Each of the nine children Emma raised, from oldest to youngest, is profiled below. The information presented includes the timing of their departure from Emma's household. The timeline at the beginning of this chapter also includes the dates Emma's children left home.

Doris Catherine Lafere, b.1919. Doris Lafere's early childhood has been chronicled in earlier chapters. She was raised on the Hinderer farm by her grandparents, Katharine and Gottlieb. She enjoyed the frequent company of cousins Johnny Krug and Raymond Engstrand who lived on nearby farms. Photos from these years frequently show Doris visiting these families, or her cousins visiting her on the Hinderer farm.

In 1935, three factors allowed Doris to leave the Hinderer farm and live in Canby with her mother Emma. First, although Doris had been out of school for two years, she continued to ask her grandmother Katharine to allow her to begin high school. Second, Martin Krug's death led to Emma's move into Canby where a high school was located. Finally, her cousin Johnny Krug dropped out of high school in order to work at a hardware store in Canby. Johnny's decision was disappointing to his stepmother Emma and grandmother Katharine. In combination, these circumstances resulted in a change of heart for Grandmother Katharine. She agreed Doris could move into Canby to begin high school as long as she lived with her mother Emma.

Emma Krug moved into the Lund rental house in March of 1935. Doris Lafere joined her mother during the same summer and began high school that fall. Doris was 16 years old when she began her freshman year in high school, two years older than her classmates.

Two years later in 1937, Doris decided to spend her summer months working as a domestic helper for a pastor's family in rural Mower County, Minnesota.[6] This occurred after her sophomore year in high school. At the time, she was as old as

A studio photo of Emma Krug's family from about 1945. Left to right standing: Bette b.1931, Deloris b.1928, Florence b.1932, Johnny (Sophie's) b.1919, Jeanette b.1934, William (Sophie's) b.1922, Leonard b.1929. Seated: Doris b.1919, Maurine (Sophie's) b.1925, and Emma. Source: The Doris Schlichting collection. Edited by author.

most high school graduates. Doris explained her departure that summer. She said she simply wanted to experience living away from home.

During that summer of 1937, Doris was introduced to her future husband Hank (Henry) Schlichting. Hank's family lived next door to the church parsonage where Doris worked. Hank had been working for an uncle in Oregon but had come home to visit his family during the summer. When the summer ended, Doris returned to Canby to continue high school, and Hank returned to Oregon. A long-distance relationship ensued with letters passing between Oregon and Canby, Minnesota. Hank and Doris were married in November of 1939, six months after Doris graduated from high school.

Following her marriage in 1939, Doris moved from the Lund house in Canby to Austin, Minnesota, where Hank was employed as a barber. As noted earlier, John and Carl Hinderer did not buy the 409 Lac qui Parle Avenue property until late 1941. Doris only lived in the Lund rental house during the years she attended high school.

John Martin Krug, b.1919. Johnny Krug was born in August 1919, four months after the birth of his cousin Doris Lafere. Until he was seven years old, he lived within walking distance of Doris who lived with the Hinderers. These two cousins spent time with one another on a weekly and sometimes daily basis. Even after Johnny's mother Sophie died and his father married Emma, Johnny and his cousin Doris remained close. Johnny's contentious relationship with his father also tended to ally him more closely with his cousin and younger siblings.

Although they were the same age, Johnny and Doris never attended Canby high school together. Johnny's work on his father's rental farms resulted in poor school attendance and consequently poor performance in high school. Maurine said that Johnny dropped out of high school in 1935, the same year his father died and Emma moved into Canby. Johnny found work at Gamble's Hardware Store in Canby, but he still lived at home with his stepmother Emma. During that summer, Doris moved from the Hinderer farm into Canby, so she could start high school in September. The result of these choices was that cousins Johnny and Doris lived in the Lund house at the same time, but they never attended high school together.

Johnny Krug continued to work in Canby living with Emma until he enlisted in the Navy in 1938. His military oath of allegiance was dated December 6, 1938. Johnny left Emma's home in Canby in late 1938 or early 1939. His first listing on a Naval muster roll was dated April 30, 1939 aboard the USS *Utah*.[7] World War II was not declared in Europe until nearly a year after Johnny's enlistment. This suggests Johnny's enlistment was driven by a desire

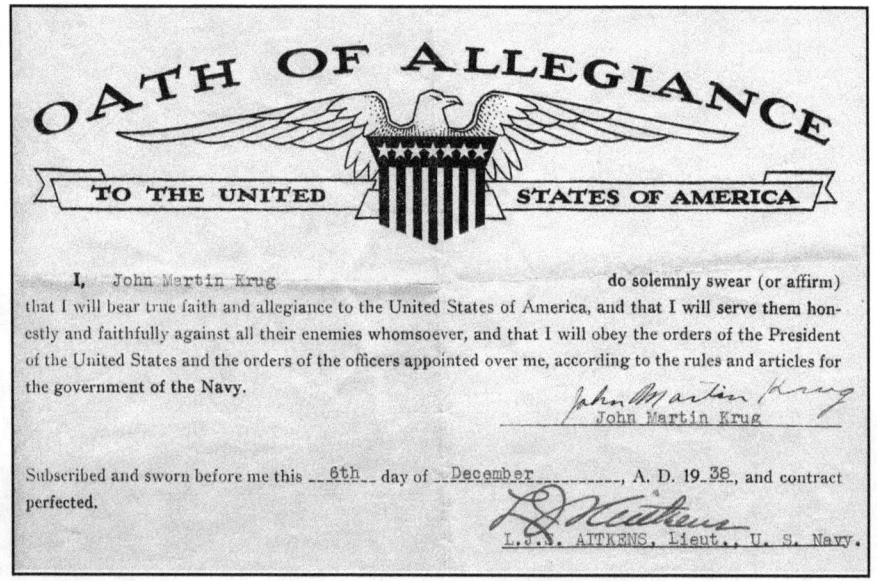

Johnny Krug enlisted in the U.S. Navy on December 6, 1938. The first record of Johnny aboard a navy ship was dated April 30, 1939. Source: the Doris Schlichting collection. Edited by author.

In 1935, Doris Lafere and Johnny Krug posed in front of Emma Krug's Whippet automobile. They both lived at the Lund rental house. Doris was about to begin high school and Johnny had just dropped out of high school after his sophomore year. Source: the Doris Schlichting collection. Edited by author.

to move past his painful early life. Johnny's years in the Navy during World War II will be detailed in a later chapter.

Johnny's sister Maurine and his half-sister Florence agreed that soon after World War II ended in 1945, Johnny returned home to Canby. By this time, Emma and her children were living in the Lac qui Parle Avenue house. Florence said that Johnny was a "wreck" when he first came home. Her opinion was that his experience at Pearl Harbor left him psychologically damaged. She said he was always very quiet around the house and constantly paced the floor or walked up and down the stairs. The younger children felt sorry for him, but his agitated behavior also made them uncomfortable.

Florence added that Johnny soon left Canby for California. Later, he returned to Canby with a young woman named Lela Pankow. Lela was born in Missouri but had moved to California where she met Johnny. Johnny and Lela were married in Canby in September of 1945. Maurine recalled that for a short time after their marriage, they lived in a room in Emma's house on Lac qui Parle Avenue. Near the end of 1945, they found their own rental apartment and Johnny found a job with the local utility company. Johnny never lived with his stepmother Emma again.

Maurine said both Lela and Johnny became dissatisfied with their lives in Canby. They moved back to California where Johnny and Lela eventually separated. Johnny continued living in California and years later married Mildred Scott. Like Lela, Mildred was originally from Missouri, but later had moved to Southern California. Johnny and Mildred periodically returned to visit his family in Canby, but their permanent residence remained in Southern California. After Mildred's death, Johnny married for a third time and continued to reside in Southern California.

William Andrew Krug, b.1922. William Krug lived with his stepmother Emma throughout his life. He did, however, leave home for a short time to work at a Civilian Conservation Corps (CCC) camp in northern Minnesota. These camps were intended to employ out-of-work young men during the Great Depression. The men living in the camps worked on projects considered beneficial to the public. William's half-brother Leonard Krug said that William sent his CCC earnings back home to help Emma make ends meet. Florence believed there may have been a medical reason that William went to the CCC camp rather than being drafted into the military. The CCC program ended in 1942, so William's months at camp were prior to that time.

After working at the CCC camp, William found employment with a feed company baling flax straw in the Dakotas. According to Leonard Krug, William worked for this feed company for more than a year. Later, William worked in the repair shop of a farm implement dealer in Canby. Repairing farm machinery was William's true calling. Both Leonard Krug and Florence Krug's husband Gerald Rousseau said William was a top-notch mechanic. They said he would be sent from

William Krug's high school graduation photo. He graduated from Canby High School in the spring of 1941. Source: The Doris Schlichting collection. Edited by author.

Canby to as far away as South Dakota to repair farm equipment that had broken down in the field. Leonard remarked that for years, William was the best mechanic in the shop.

With his steady income and mechanical skills, William was a natural for becoming a chauffeur for family members. Florence recalled that before she and Gerald could afford their own vehicle, William drove them everywhere. Early on, William drove Emma's old Whippet automobile. By this time, Whippets were no longer being produced, but William had the skills to keep their car running. When Emma and the children visited the Hinderer farm on Sundays, William was the usual driver.

William eventually bought a Studebaker sedan that he carefully maintained throughout the 1950s and well into the 1960s. He parked his Studebaker in the single car garage behind Emma's Lac qui Parle Avenue house.

Carl Hinderer and his younger brother John purchased the Lac qui Parle Avenue house in 1941 for $2200. In November of 1969, 75-year-old Carl sold his half of that property to William Krug for $1000. It was clearly a favorable purchase for William. This meant he was co-owner of the house along with his Uncle John Hinderer. By this time, Emma had been paying (possibly with William's help) her $25 per month rent for nearly 30 years. John Hinderer said these rent payments went toward Emma's eventual ownership. The details of the agreement leading to this transaction between Carl and William were never revealed, but it proved satisfactory to everyone involved.

William Krug died in May of 1978. He is buried in the Canby City Cemetery. On behalf of his estate, his stepmother Emma Krug sold his interest in the Lac qui Parle Avenue home. This transaction was accompanied by John Hinderer selling his ownership interest as well. As a result, the Lac qui Parle Avenue home was sold out of the family in October of 1978.

Maurine LaRayne Krug, b.1925. Maurine was an important source of information concerning her stepmother Emma. She was only ten years old when her father Martin died, but she had already taken on the role as Emma's primary assistant at home. Many of the details about daily life in Emma's home were learned thanks to Maurine.

Unlike their older brother Johnny, both Maurine and William attended and graduated from Canby High School. Maurine said she loved the sports teams at school and played basketball, volleyball and softball. She said there was a rivalry between herself and the daughter of her father Martin's half-brother. Maurine said, "We were both in the same class and both of us were darned good pitchers." Maurine added,

I did have one kind of serious boyfriend in high school, but mostly a bunch of us kids would just tear around together going to dances.

In November of 1969, 75-year-old Carl Hinderer sold his half interest in the Lac qui Parle Avenue house to 47-year-old William Krug. William paid Carl $1,000 for this half interest. Source: The Yellow Medicine County Recorder's Office. Edited by author.

Maurine graduated from high school in the spring of 1943. That same summer, she moved from Canby to Austin, Minnesota. She had decided to earn money by working at the Hormel Meat Packing Plant in Austin. During these summer months, Maurine lived with the family of her married cousin, Doris (Lafere) Schlichting. Maurine explained that this was during the war and many women and younger girls were needed to make canned foods that were shipped overseas to feed the troops. Maurine said she walked to and from work so she could save every cent she earned. She said she paid Doris rent during the summer, but when it was time for her to return to Canby, Doris gave it all back.

When Maurine returned home in the fall of 1943, she began a year of Normal School training in Canby. The purpose of this year was to prepare a person to teach in a country school. In 1944, Maurine began her first teaching year at a district school eight miles east of Canby. She had to buy a car to drive to and from the school while she continued living with her stepmother Emma.

Maurine married Bill Gjovig in May of 1944. They had met while Maurine was in high school and were engaged in 1942. Maurine said she was only a junior in high school at the time of their engagement. Bill had joined the Navy in 1942, and he was away from home during nearly all of their engagement. After their marriage, Bill was shipped out again and did not return to Canby until late 1945. During Bill's absence, Maurine continued living with Emma in the Lac qui Parle Avenue house.

Maurine said that after the war, it was something of a scramble for rooms in Emma's house. Johnny Krug and his first wife Lela had returned to Canby and initially lived with Emma on Lac qui Parle Avenue. When Johnny and Lela moved in with Emma, Maurine found a small apartment to rent

Maurine Krug's 1943 Canby High School graduation picture. Source: The Doris Schlichting collection. Edited by author.

An early 1940s photo of Deloris Krug standing on the open front porch of the Lac qui Parle Avenue house. It likely dates from between 1942 and 1944. Source: The Doris Schlichting collection. Edited by author.

in Canby. After husband Bill was discharged home in December of 1945, he and Maurine continued to live in her apartment. By the end of 1945, Maurine no longer lived with Emma on Lac qui Parle Avenue.

Deloris Mae Krug b.1928. Deloris was the oldest of Emma and Martin Krug's children who survived into adulthood. She was born while her parents lived on the Nessett rental farm west of Canby. Deloris was not interviewed, so information about her came indirectly from her siblings and from public documents.

Deloris's half-sister Maurine was only three years old when Deloris was born. Maurine considered herself responsible for Deloris and the younger children. Episodes involving Deloris and Leonard were described in a previous chapter. By nature, Deloris was adventurous and would often test the patience of her elders, including Maurine.

The 1930 U.S. Census identified two-year-old Deloris living with her family on the Nessett farm in Hammer Township west of Canby. A decade later, the 1940 U.S. Census identified 11-year-old Deloris and her family living on Oscar Avenue in the Lund rental house. Maurine said that Deloris went to Canby High School but did not graduate. However, Maurine added that Deloris completed high school graduation requirements later in her life when she lived in Minneapolis.

Minnesota marriage records indicated that Deloris Mae Krug married Kenneth Richard Johnson on July 22, 1945. The marriage took place in Yellow Medicine County where Deloris lived. At the time, Deloris was 17 years old. There is no information regarding her husband or where he and Deloris lived. The date this first marriage ended is unknown. Most likely Deloris left Emma's home on Lac qui Parle Avenue shortly after her marriage in 1945.

Deloris spent the majority of her adult life living in the Twin Cities area of Minnesota. Although she later had sons, these years are not chronicled, and search attempts yielded no additional information about Deloris. Public documents identified her death on February 10, 2002 in Minneapolis, Minnesota, at the age of 72.

Leonard Ray Krug b.1929. Like his older sister Deloris, Leonard was born while his parents lived on the Nessett rental farm west of Canby, Minnesota. Leonard's hijinks as a child have been described in earlier chapters. He was six years old in 1935, the year his father Martin died and his mother Emma moved into Canby.

Leonard's family memories were mainly from the years Emma and the children lived in the two Canby rental homes. From childhood on, Leonard lived in Canby during the school year, but spent summer months on the Hinderer farm. He said that when he was younger, the summers on the Hinderer farm were really more of a vacation. Later on, however, his Uncle John Hinderer put him to work painting the outbuildings on the farm. By the time he was a young teenager, he had learned to drive the Hinderer's John Deere tractor and was able to help with field work.

Before finishing high school, Leonard decided to leave home and work in North Dakota. He said he drove a truck a bit and then worked in a warehouse lifting 100-pound sacks of potatoes into railroad boxcars. He was only 16 years old at the time. The next fall he returned home and wanted to restart high school. This turned out to be a problem, he said, because he could never seem to catch up with the class subjects. As a result, he dropped out of high school again. Leonard said the high school superintendent even came to their house and encouraged him to remain in class, "but like a dummy I didn't go back." Instead, he worked as a manual laborer at a building project in Canby. Leonard said he was 17 when that project was completed. This was in 1946 and World War II was over. He continued, "I just decided to enlist in the

Leonard Krug pictured in 1943 in front of the Lac qui Parle Avenue house. The event was likely his confirmation. Note the lack of an enclosed porch in early 1943. Source: From the Doris Schlichting collection. Edited by author.

Navy. Uncle John took me to Montevideo, and I left from there." Leonard's story indicated that he no longer lived at the family home on Lac qui Parle Avenue after 1946.

Elizabeth Anna (Bette) Krug, b.1931. Bette Krug was born on the Nessett rental farm west of Canby. She was a few months shy of her fourth birthday when her father Martin died in January of 1935. Bette said she did not have a memory of her father. Bette did have a vague memory of living in the Lund house, but said nearly all of her childhood recollections dated from when the family lived on Lac qui Parle Avenue.

Bette said she always liked to read and loved school. History was her favorite subject. It was an eight-block walk from the Lac qui Parle Avenue house to school. Bette said she did not mind the walk and even went to school when classes were cancelled due to snow. The students were allowed to study or read inside the school on those days and that was what she would do.

Bette's love of school was at its peak when she took World History and English in 10th grade. She said both of these teachers were excellent. Her enjoyment diminished in her junior year. She said both the history and English teachers were not good and the classes were boring. Of all of Emma's children, Bette was the most academically oriented.

Bette said she made money during high school by working as a waitress in two downtown Canby cafes. She did not earn much money, but the owners allowed her to do homework between customers. She used what money she made to buy her own clothes. Considering her mother's precarious financial situation, Bette's work during high school was surely beneficial to Emma and the family.

During the years the family lived on Lac qui Parle Avenue, Bette and others recalled that Emma worked away from home. Several storytellers recalled Emma's part time work as a cook in the school cafeteria. Bette said that her mother also took in ironing from other families. She worked on it when she was at home, and it added a little cash income.

Like her siblings, Bette also remembered spending time on the Hinderer farm during summers. For their mother, it was one less mouth to feed, and the children learned valuable skills. Bette recalled helping in the Hinderer kitchen and washing dishes when a threshing crew was working on the farm. During these days, Bette said there was non-stop cooking in the kitchen. She said that although Grandma Katharine was the one in charge, Bette's usual assignment was helping Martha. She added that during most of the summer, the Hinderer family ate meals in the kitchen. Everyone, including Bette, was seated around the small kitchen table.

Bette added another fond memory,

Bette Krug's 1949 high school graduation picture. Source: The Doris Schlichting collection. Edited by author.

Grandma Hinderer would always save pennies and put them in a jar. When the jar was full, she would dump it out and divide out the pennies for us kids. It didn't amount to a large sum, but as kids we didn't often have any money at all in our pocket, so this was important. A nickel would buy a lot in those days.

It is interesting that with only a few exceptions, the children's stories about summer days living with the Hinderers referred only to themselves. It was as if only one of the Krug children at a time stayed on the farm. This may have often been true, or perhaps their memories of those summers were very personal and singularly pleasing.

In addition to working in Canby, Bette said she spent the summer of 1946 helping her older half-sister Doris who lived in Austin, Minnesota. Doris and her husband Hank were raising three children. Doris's third child was sickly, so Bette volunteered to help during her summer vacation months. When high school began in September, Bette returned home to Canby.

Following her high school graduation in 1949, Bette took a job at the hospital in Montevideo. It was far enough from Canby that she had to live in Montevideo.[8] Her work in the hospital began with helping in the hospital kitchen but evolved into a nurse's aide position. Her nurse's aide training in Montevideo led to a similar hospital position in Austin, Minnesota, where Doris and Hank lived. After Bette left home in 1949, only Emma, William, Florence, and Jeanette lived on Lac qui Parle Avenue.

Florence Marie Krug, b. 1932. Florence was the last of Emma and Martin's children born on the Nessett farm west of Canby. Florence said she did not have a memory of living on the rental farms or of her father Martin's death in 1935.

Florence did recall several events while living in the Lund rental. She said there was an old man named Schoephoerster who lived in a small apartment next to their house. She said he was a kind man, and he always sat in a rocking chair smoking a pipe. Florence said

He had these big smoking pipes, and we [Florence and Jeanette] *would sit on the floor in front of him watching him rock back and forth puffing on his pipe. We finally talked him into letting us try the pipe, of course, so we would all sit there and smoke pipes.*

Florence said her mother Emma was always gentle with the children and would not raise her voice when she corrected them. Her discipline never included angry words or spanking. Florence also remembered that Emma received compliments about her children's appearance. The compliments said, in effect, that the children always wore neat and clean clothes when they were out in public. Florence said Emma's insistence on her children being neat and clean began when they were quite young. She summarized, "mother's formula was that you should train your kids before they are three and not try to make up for it later."

Florence also recalled that she and her sisters were given regular household jobs while they lived on Lac qui Parle Avenue. The children cleaned rooms once a week, but there was no regular allowance or pay for their work. Instead, Emma's method was to occasionally give the children a nickel or so and tell them to go downtown and buy a treat for themselves. These trips were unexpected and recalled by the children as fun afternoon excursions. Emma found a way to give the children enjoyment even though she could not afford to pay them a regular weekly allowance.

Florence graduated from Canby High School in the spring of 1951 and married Gerald Rousseau

The 1950 U.S. Census listed 52-year-old Emma Krug as the head of the family. She worked as a cook at school and lived on Lac qui Parle Avenue. William was 28 years old and was incorrectly listed as Emma's son. Daughter Florence was 17 years old. Jeanette was listed at the top of the next page of the census. Source: "1950 United States Federal Census" online database (Provo, UT: Ancestry.com), accessed April 17, 2023. Edited by author.

Katharine

Florence Krug's graduation picture. She graduated from Canby High School in the spring of 1951. Source: The Doris Schlichting collection. Edited by author.

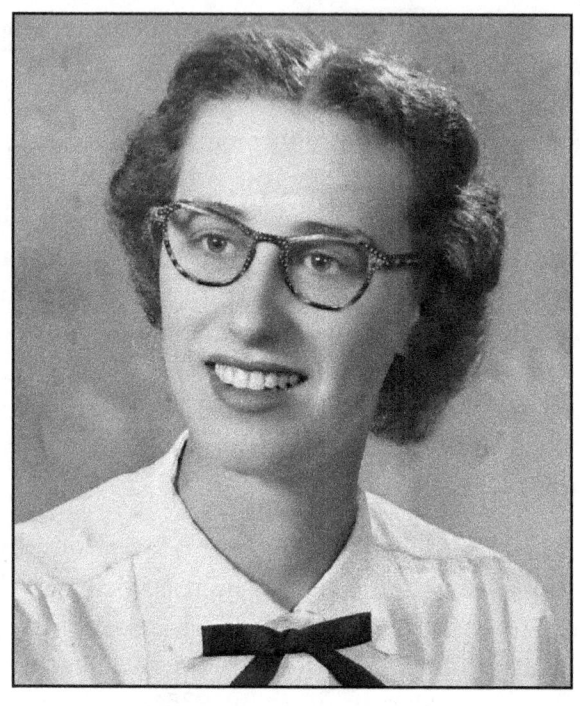

Jeanette Krug graduated from Canby High School in the spring of 1952. Source: The Doris Schlichting collection. Edited by author.

in early 1952. Florence explained that these were difficult times economically for many people and for them as well. Her husband Gerald worked during most of the year but was often out of work during the winter months. At about this same time, her mother Emma wanted more work hours in order to be eligible for Social Security. The resolution was that Emma moved to the Twin Cities to work for her daughter Jeanette's young family. William Krug also moved to the Twin Cities and secured a job there. This left the Lac qui Parle Avenue house vacant, so Florence, Gerald, and their first child moved in. This agreeable arrangement continued for several years after which Emma and William returned, and Florence and Gerald purchased their own home in Canby.

Jeanette Marlene Krug, b. 1934. Jeanette Krug was the only child born on the Walters rental farm and was less than a year old when her father Martin died in January 1935. Jeanette died at the relatively young age of 59 and was not interviewed.

Jeanette's older sister Florence said the two of them were always together as children and characterized them both as "tomboys." Florence said she and Jeanette mostly found things they both enjoyed doing at home. These things ranged from riding their neighbor's horses to "made up" games. Their relationship remained close throughout their school years. Their teamwork often placed them at odds with their older sister Bette. Both Florence and Bette agreed that the three of them often did not see eye to eye and that Bette was the sister who was usually excluded. Their differences were in both personality and the activities they enjoyed. Bette enjoyed reading and schoolwork while her two younger sisters were more outgoing and preferred their "tomboy" games.

Jeanette graduated from Canby High School in the spring of 1952. This was about the same time her older sister Florence was married. The date when Jeanette left home is not documented; however, Jeanette married Jerry McDaniel in April of 1955. Their marriage took place in the Twin Cities rather than Canby. This suggests Jeanette had moved away from Canby and established a residence in the Twin Cities shortly after her high school graduation in 1952.

Family Stories – The Hinderers

The quiet hand of Katharine Hinderer can be recognized behind the generosity of the Hinderers toward Emma and her children. Every storyteller positioned her as the driving influence behind the Hinderer's interaction with the Krug family. Her leadership was later assumed, in part, by John Hinderer who carried it forward into the 1940s. John became a big brother or father figure to the Krug children, and from all appearances, he enjoyed this role.

Maurine Krug said that when she lived on the rental farms, her family would not have had enough food to eat without the Hinderers. When widow Emma Krug moved into Canby, her financial situation was even more grim. This sharing of food by the Hinderers covered a span of more than 25 years. John Hinderer said,

We would always take stuff into town for them. We would take a gallon of skim milk with us. Also, Johnny and William would go up to the creamery with a gallon pail and get some buttermilk almost every day. The guy at the creamery who churned the butter always had some buttermilk left over, so he gave it to them for about ten cents. Sometimes they just drank it. Usually, Emma would [use the buttermilk to] *bake pancakes every morning. That would work good you know.*

Leonard Krug spent many summers on the Hinderer farm. His Uncle John allowed him to drive the Hinderer's first tractor, a John Deere Model B. Leonard recalled,

That old Model B had steel [rear] *wheels with metal lugs. It also had a tall hand lever for a clutch. The first time John let me drive the tractor through the gate, he got off and opened the gate and told me to bring the tractor through. So, I pushed the clutch lever forward and very slowly went through. Then he said to stop, but I panicked and kept looking for a clutch pedal. He kept yelling whoa, but eventually he just jumped on and pulled the clutch lever back. It was kind of funny afterwards.*

The tractor's hand clutch came into play later when it was grain cutting time. Leonard said,

That same tractor was used to pull the binder. When I was eleven or twelve, I would drive the tractor and Carl would be riding on the binder. The binder would cut the grain and bundle it up with a twine tie around it, and then kick it out. We had a rope rigged up from Carl's seat on the binder forward and attached to the clutch lever on the tractor. He could stop it [the tractor] *if he wanted* [by pulling the rope]. *That way, John was freed from driving and could go do the shocking.*

Leonard recalled the time his Uncle John Hinderer was drafted into the Army and had to leave home. This would have been in 1942. He said this saddened everyone in the family including himself. He said John was like a father to him.

After John left, 13-year-old Leonard worked with his Uncle Carl. Leonard said John's absence meant he had to be the one to help Carl with fieldwork. He said that when his Uncle Carl worked away from home on a threshing crew, he was the only one left to do the fieldwork at home. Leonard said,

Carl would ride a few times around to show me how to open up the field with a plow, and then I would finish it up myself.[9] I would use the old John Deere B with a two-bottom plow. One time, I must have hit something because it killed the dang tractor. So, I got down and started to turn the flywheel to restart it, but it wouldn't fire. I suppose it was too hot. You should have seen the blisters on my hand from spinning that old flywheel. I had to walk all the way home and told Marty

[Martha] *that the tractor killed on me. I thought I would catch hell, but she said don't worry about it. Anyway, we had lunch and about mid-afternoon I walked back to the field and turned it over once, and it started right off. So, I just went back to plowing the field like nothing had happened.*

Bette Krug recalled that her mother Emma always had a backyard garden on Lac qui Parle Avenue, and she canned the vegetables for winter meals. She added,

We also got a lot of food from Grandma and Grandpa Hinderer on the farm. Much of this was fruit that mother canned for winter use. If we hadn't gotten extra food from them, I don't think we would have had enough to live on. Mother's garden and the things given to us by the Hinderers were the main sources of food for our family."

Bette's summers on the Hinderer farm were limited to her grade school years. She said she only stayed on the farm for a few weeks rather than all summer. She said,

Mostly I would be with Martha outside taking care of her chickens or taking lunches out to the men working in the fields. The women did almost all of the work in the garden as well. I know that washing dishes was one of my jobs. Although I always got along well with Martha, we didn't ever have what you might call sisterly conversations or small talk.

Bette added,

Martha loved her coffee, and it seemed like she always had a cup of hot coffee handy when she was in the kitchen. She made her coffee using an old pot on the stove, and you know by the end of the morning, that pot would be dark and strong.

It was the late 1930s and early 1940s when Florence spent summertime on the Hinderer farm. Her "tomboy" style fit perfectly into life on the farm. She explained it this way,

If you look at [my mother] Emma's family, first there was a girl [Deloris], then a boy [Leonard], then a girl [Bette] and then me. It was as if I really should have been a boy.

A snapshot of Jeanette, Florence and Leonard from about 1937 when they lived at the Lund rental house in Canby. Source: The Doris Schlichting collection. Edited by author.

She said her sister Jeanette would come out to the farm for Sunday visits, but she didn't want to stay during the week. Florence said one of her jobs was to help Martha with the house cleaning and she loved the balcony over the screen porch. She said, "We would take all the rugs out on the balcony and shake them out." Florence added,

I would mostly sleep with Grandma [Katharine] in the upstairs bedroom by that front balcony. Martha's bedroom was behind Grandma's and occasionally I would sleep there with her. The men slept on the other side upstairs. That upstairs seemed nice to me. The ladies' rooms were larger than the men's, and all of the floors were covered with linoleum.

Florence was not interested in traditional homemaker skills. She said,

I think Grandma wanted to teach me some of the things she could do [like] embroider, but she gave up on that. I wasn't interested in cooking either. Mostly I liked to be outside with John and Carl, running around barefoot in the barnyard. I did help Martha take out the mid-morning and mid-afternoon lunch to the men in the fields. That was always a treat for me. The lunch was in a basket or a cardboard box. We would fix a sandwich and maybe a piece of cake with coffee. They would never go without their coffee.

The main meals on the farm always included meat from the animals the Hinderers raised. Florence recalled,

If there was going to be chicken for supper, usually John would grab a big rooster and take care of it. Then it would be soaked in scalding water, and we would pluck off the feathers. We would have our fresh chicken that evening for supper. They also would cook and can chicken in jars during the good weather and use it for winter meals. Grandma had canned chicken, beef, and pork in addition to all of her canned fruits and vegetables.

She brought it out in the winter, especially when company was there. They worked like dogs compared to what we have to do today.

Florence continued,

On Saturdays my job was to shine shoes. Mainly it was John's shoes, but sometimes I did Carl's too. They would slip me a little change for that. By the time I was a teenager, John and Carl had gotten rid of their horse named Queen, and only King was left. I really got attached to King. He was their work horse and I think they may have kept King around because I liked to ride him. I was a little scared of him because [as a child,] he seemed big to me. I would ride him bareback around the barnyard and even out into the fields.

Like Bette, Florence spent much of her time with her Aunt Martha. She said,

Martha and I had a lot of fun together. She was my buddy. She would take me with her in the black

A photo from about 1939 taken at the Lund rental house. Emma was standing behind her daughters Jeanette on the left and Florence. Source: From the Doris Schlichting collection. Edited by author.

Dodge when she went to Gary, South Dakota, to get her teeth fixed. Once, I snuck a cat along that I hid in the back seat. Along the way, the cat let out a meow and Martha's eyes got big. I think I had to stay in the car with the cat when Martha went into the dental office.

Another story from Florence helped to characterize her "buddy" Martha.

Both Grandpa [Gottlieb] and Carl used chewing tobacco. I don't recall Martha complaining about Carl, but she would get mad at Grandpa. He would spit out the juice on the sidewalk [by the house], and Martha would have to get out there and clean it off. It couldn't have been much worse than chicken poop, but it just bothered her I guess. Martha was a person who wanted things clean.

Like others in the family, Florence relished the holidays when the extended family visited the Hinderer farm. In her words,

On all of the major holidays, especially the Fourth of July, the entire family would gather at the Hinderer farm. It was just expected that you would come. It was so much work for Grandma and Martha to cook for everyone, but they seemed to love it. They had turkey for Thanksgiving and dessert was homemade suet pudding. To me, everything they made was good. When you think about it, you wonder how those women ever had time to get anything else done. They were always cooking, washing dishes, baking, or washing clothes. How did they find extra time for things like spring cleaning? They did it, but you wonder how.

These stories about the Krug and the Hinderer families confirm their close relationship. From the Krug's perspective, the Hinderers were a lifeline, supplying food for Emma and the many children under her care. The Hinderer brothers even purchased the Lac qui Parle Avenue house so the Krug family could continue living together.

From the Hinderer's perspective, Emma and the children were always a part of their responsibility, regardless of what was needed. The bond between these families was so close that in practice, they merged together. It was as if they saw one another as members of a single family.

A photo of the family from about 1939. Siblings William, Johnny (in uniform), and Maurine stand in the rear. Martin and Emma's children Leonard, Jeanette, Deloris, Florence, and Bette stand in front of them. Source: From the Becci Fischer collection. Edited by author.

Family Stories – Emma

Both Bette and Florence recalled their mother Emma's tendency to believe in omens and superstitious events. Bette said she remembered them because they scared her. One story her mother told was about *hearing a strange sound at night, like someone was walking through the house dragging their leg. Then, someone they knew would die a day or two later.*

Both Florence and Bette recounted another of Emma's superstitions. This one said that someone would be going about their usual work at home when a large dog would appear outside a screen door. The dog just sat there, and then it disappeared. Again, a few days later, someone known to that family died.[10] Bette added,

I think my mother would talk about this sort of thing quite a lot. Sometimes it would be with my sisters, or maybe with William. She didn't claim to have any special ability to see into the future, but I think people tended to believe in that sort of thing back in those days.

Bette and Florence both enjoyed a much lighter side of their mother's personality. They said that Emma always enjoyed music. Florence recalled that she was once told her mother played the accordion, but she had no personal memory of it.

When the girls were growing up, both of their Canby homes had a single radio.[11] Emma could not afford to buy a phonograph, so the radio was how the family listened to music.

Bette's memory of music at home centered on dancing. She recalled,

Mother always loved music, and I remember all of us girls and mother dancing in the living room. We would push the rug to one side of the room, and dance around the floor.

Early on, I remember lying on the couch and watching my older sisters and mother dancing around. My mother was quite a dancer. I don't think my brothers joined in. This would have been in the middle or late 1930s. It was during those years that I formed my favorite things to do like reading, music, and dancing.[12]

Florence added her recollections,

A photo from about 1939. The location is uncertain. The adults are Gottlieb, Emma, Katharine, William, and two relatives from Michigan, Carl and Elsa Brenner. The children are Florence, Leonard, Jeanette, and Bette with Deloris behind her. Source: From the Doris Schlichting collection. Edited by author.

Mother loved music. She always came to Jan [Jeanette] and my high school choir concerts. I wanted to learn to play the piano, but there wasn't money for any instruments or pianos in our house. So, we sang in the choir at school. Leonard was the only one of us who played in the high school band, and he played the tuba. Of course, we didn't own the instrument, but I can recall him bringing his tuba home to practice.

The radio in Emma's living room served a second entertainment purpose. Both Florence and Bette said they and their siblings spent evenings listening to broadcasts of weekly series. Their favorites were the ones with scary music like "The Squeaking Door," "The Shadow," and "The Inner Sanctum."

The children all characterized their mother as a very good cook. Bette said one of her favorite meals was a beef stew with biscuits on top baked in the oven. She said,

> *I think we lived on hot dishes and casseroles of various sorts. That type of food could be made cheaply, and it filled us kids up. The main ingredient would be some starch like noodles or macaroni. She also baked a lot of bread at home and that would always be a main part of our meals. Then there was skim milk from the Hinderer farm. We drank skim milk before it became fashionable.*

Doris added her memory of bread baking saying her mother baked at least ten loaves of bread at a time and then repeated the process when they were all eaten. Bette said her mother nearly always baked a sweet treat for dessert. In her words,

> *Mother also baked cookies and cakes for us kids. Her pies were delicious; especially the lemon meringue, but cookies were my favorites. Most of her pies were fruit pies because she could get the fruit for nothing from her own or Grandma Hinderer's garden. The Hinderers had apple trees on their farm, and that was what we had most of the time.*

Bette also recalled that her mother would not fall asleep at night if one of the children was out late. Bette said if she was out late,

> *I would usually go into her bedroom and talk to her when I got home. She was the type of person who didn't seem to need much sleep at night anyway. She would sleep hard when she first went to bed, and then she would wake up and just doze through most of the rest of the night.*

Beginning with the departure of Johnny and Doris in the late 1930s, the number of children under Emma's care slowly dwindled. After Florence and Jeanette graduated from high school in the early 1950s, Emma's household settled into its eventual companionship of Emma and Sophie's second son William.

More Children's Stories

Emma Krug's storyteller children related many memories from their childhood. Their shared stories described life in Emma's large, blended family in mid-1900s Canby, Minnesota. Their memories are too valuable to omit. Here are more of those stories.

After World War II, **Johnny Krug** lived in Southern California. Bette (Krug) Weber said she moved to that same area shortly after her marriage in 1953. Bette's husband Ray had found a job with Douglas Aircraft, and often had to work on Saturdays. Bette said,

> *If Ray was working, Johnny would come over to our little apartment, and we would sit around and visit. It would usually be about current events. Johnny had problems after his years in the service, but he really seemed good when he was with Ray and me. We never talked about his years in the military or what he saw at Pearl Harbor. Mildred [Johnny's second wife] and I would talk on our own and she said Johnny would sometimes lapse into a kind of depression. It was really sad because when we were together, he seemed as normal as anyone.*

In retirement, Bette and Ray and Johnny and Mildred both had motor homes and would sometimes rendezvous. Bette said these were always pleasant occasions and she felt closer to Johnny than anyone else in the family. She said she marveled at Mildred and how she remained with Johnny regardless of his moods and depression.

Johnny also renewed his early childhood friendship with his cousin Doris (Lafere) Schlichting. By the mid-1960s, Doris and her family were living in San Diego County. The two families visited one another while Johnny worked for the U.S. Post Office and lived in the Los Angeles area.

In retirement, Johnny and Mildred moved to the outskirts of San Bernardino in the eastern part of the Los Angeles basin. They also owned a cabin in Big Bear, a community in the San Gabriel mountains north of his home. Johnny died in 1999 at the age of 79.

William Krug's younger half-sister Florence married Gerald Rousseau in 1952. After their marriage, they lived in or near Canby where William lived with Emma. William was always known as "William" with one exception. Gerald and Florence called him "Willy" and Gerald said Willy was his favorite brother-in-law. Gerald recalled many exploits with William and described a few of their lighter moments together. Both Gerald and Florence said it seemed like Willy was always a part of their family. They had fun together and their two daughters loved him.

Florence said that Willy often came out to their farm in the evenings after supper. At the time, she and Gerald's farm was near the outskirts of Canby. She said they even bought an extra tractor so William could help with field work. Gerald said Willy would not always do a perfect job, but he just liked having him around. Gerald and William also hunted together. Sometimes it was for rabbits and sometimes deer. Gerald said they did not always follow the rules for hunting seasons, but when times were hard, game animals were a valuable addition to their food supply. Florence added,

A lot of times both mother and William would come out to the farm late in the afternoon, and we would sit outside at the picnic table and have our supper. It wasn't anything fancy, but our girls just loved being with them.

A May 1942 photo of Emma and Johnny Krug taken at Emma's Lac qui Parle Avenue home. Source: From the Doris Schlichting collection. Edited by author.

Another photo from May of 1942 taken at Emma's Lac qui Parle Avenue home. Deloris, Johnny, and Maurine are in the rear with Jeanette and Florence in front of them. Source: The Doris Schlichting collection. Edited by author.

Katharine

A photo taken in late 1942 on the Hinderer farm. Left to right: Florence, Norma Engstrand, William, Deloris, Leonard, and Maurine. Source: From the Doris Schlichting collection. Edited by author.

Leonard said he and William were good buddies.

He was seven or eight years older than me, but we did quite a few things together. We would go hunting together in our old Whippet auto. We went out at daybreak during pheasant season, and William would use a .22 rifle.[13] *In those days, the area was just lousy with pheasants, and the roosters would come out to the road in the early morning. William could pick them off with that .22 without even getting out of the car. He was a good shot!*

William or Willy lived with his stepmother Emma on Lac qui Parle Avenue until his death in 1978. He was 56 years old when he died. William is buried in the Canby City Cemetery.

Maurine Krug shared wonderful details about the summer after her high school graduation. This was the summer she lived with her cousin Doris in Austin, Minnesota.[14] As noted earlier, Maurine's goal was to earn as much money as possible so she could attend teacher training school in Canby.

Maurine said that Hormel's in Austin was considered a war plant because they canned food for servicemen.[15] Maurine and her girlfriend applied for work at the plant and were hired immediately. Maurine said,

My first job was peeling onions. We [Maurine and her friend] cried our eyes out for at least a week. Then they sent us down to where they labeled boxes of food. It was a dungeon-like place, but there were the two of us together. Then they took my friend away, and I was scared. Next, they sent me to an assembly line where they were canning some kind of relish for the Russians. But this is what is good: I came down with the hog itch, and all ten fingers had blisters all over.[16] *When that happened, I would go to the plant Doctor before work and he would apply salve and bandage all of my fingers. Then I would have to pick up this pork and put it in cans. I kept thinking that those Russians were going to die, but I didn't say anything.*

Maurine continued,

Then a few weeks later this guy who sat in the back was missing. When he returned, he was white as a sheet and looked like a skeleton. I asked him what happened, and he said he had yellow jaundice [most likely hepatitis]. He said the plant police came to his home and hauled him in to work even though he could hardly sit up. They said this was a war plant and everyone had to work even if they were sick. Then one day an inspector came in and looked at me with my bandaged fingers. I explained that I had the hog itch and zoom, I was out of there and over to the supervisor's office. They next moved me to this place where they processed the cold pork. We had to put these big chunks of meat into a machine that had big knives going around. We stood on stools to get high enough to throw the meat in. Of course, everything was full of grease and slippery. The gal across from me and I thought one of us might fall in.

Maurine's saga continued,

Then I started feeling really sick and I had yellow jaundice. My supervisor got nasty to me because he thought I was sick from being pregnant. Even though I was sick, I wouldn't stay home because I didn't want the plant police to haul me in to work. Doris was so worried about me being sick that she wrote to Grandma Hinderer who wrote back that I should quit that job. Of course, I didn't pay attention to anyone and dragged myself to work and back home every day. I was sick for three weeks and the only thing I could keep down was Pepsi Cola. That is what I lived on. When I started to feel better, that is when I turned yellow. Then my supervisor came over and saw I was really sick. The best part is that this supervisor got it [jaundice] too, and I was kind of glad. When I started to eat again, it scared Doris half to death because I gained and gained weight. She thought I was pregnant. When I went back home, I stayed on the Hinderer farm for a while, and Grandma Hinderer thought I was pregnant too. I was fat! I weighed 148 pounds.[17]

Leonard Krug said that he enjoyed the summers he spent on the Hinderer farm. In his words, "Grandma [Katharine] Hinderer was a petite little lady, but I think she was boss." Leonard continued,

Mostly I remember that when I stayed there, I couldn't wait for Saturday night. Either grandma or Uncle John would give me fifty cents and we would go to town. Now that was a lot of money in those days. I would go to the show and have my popcorn too. After the show, I would go get a double dip ice cream cone for a nickel and I would probably still have about fifteen cents left. I knew that John and Carl would go to a restaurant or the pool hall to have something to eat before we went home. I would make a beeline to every one of them to find my uncles so they would pay for my lunch too, and I could keep whatever money I had leftover.

Leonard recalled that the family moved (from the Lund house) to the house on Lac qui Parle Avenue when he was in seventh or eighth grade. He said

In that house I would be in trouble with my sisters all the time. They would chase me around the table until I would have to bolt out that back screen door and out across the creek to hide on the other side. Ma would always be yelling at us to not slam the screen door. At that age, I didn't want to have anything to do with my sisters." Leonard pointed out that, *"We did always have meals together as a family, and there was always a prayer to start with.*

Bette Krug explained some of the children's duties when they lived on Lac qui Parle Avenue. She said,

As kids, we all had jobs or duties. These tended to get switched around so we didn't have to do the same job all the time. One of the jobs was to clean the upstairs bedrooms. I was always a reader, and if the upstairs cleaning was my duty, I might slough off a bit and lie across the bed and read for some time. Occasionally, Mom would have to come upstairs and get me going again. We also took turns doing dishes, and I seem to recall that we even had to do the [breakfast] dishes before we went to school in the morning.

Bette suggested that the children's sleeping arrangements were somewhat variable.

A photo of family members taken in January of 1943. Adults left to right: Gottlieb, Martha, Katharine, Deloris peeking over Maurine, Carl, William (rear). The children are Bette, Jeanette, and Florence. Source: The Doris Schlichting collection. Edited by author.

Another rule was that we had to have our beds made before we could go to school. Of course, I slept with my two younger sisters [Florence and Jeanette], *so with three of us, making the bed didn't take long. Sometimes I would sneak in and sleep with mother, but usually one of my older sisters* [Deloris or Maurine] *would be sleeping in her bed. I recall that someone slept on the front porch too.*

Florence agreed with Bette that the three girls all slept together upstairs in what she called the "big bedroom." She added that mother Emma and sister Deloris were in a second upstairs bedroom, while William and Leonard were in a third bedroom. She did not recall where Maurine slept. She wondered if Maurine might have slept on the old hide-a-bed on the front porch after it was enclosed. Although the two boys had their own room, the girls' sleeping arrangements were more flexible.

Bette's disputes with her two younger sisters carried over into clothing. She said she was usually eager to get to school early in the morning. Her sister Florence, however, would tend to arrive later, sometimes wearing Bette's clothes. Bette said this upset her because, particularly in high school, she bought her own clothing with the money she earned as a waitress. Clothing problems were also recalled by Maurine. She said,

When we moved into Canby, Deloris would go downtown to the shoe store and try on shoes and then wear them home. I was helping Mom with the budget at the time and she didn't know what to do. After this happened a second time, I went down to the shoe store and told them Deloris was never to wear another pair of shoes home or they would be the ones to pay for them. That was the end of the problem.

Bette said,

I was always a tea drinker and I think that came from my mother. I would get home from school and make a little pot of tea before starting my homework. My mother and possibly some of the

A group photo from 1945 taken in front of the Lac qui Parle Avenue house. Left to right standing: John H., Carl H, Don Engstrand, Gottlieb H., Johnny Krug, Katharine H., Arthur Engstrand, Mary Engstrand, William Krug, Deloris Krug, Maurine Krug, Ruth Engstrand. Seated: Martha H., Florence Krug, Norma Engstrand with David and Sharon Schlichting, Doris Schlichting. Source: From the Doris Schlichting collection. Edited by author.

older ones at home would always have tea after the evening supper. She [Emma] would never have coffee at that time of day. I know William always had his coffee in the morning. Mother had a sensitive stomach, and I think tea agreed with her better. I still have my little teapot that I used back then.

On Lac qui Parle Avenue, Christmas was celebrated at home. Bette recalled,

On Christmas Eve there was a program at the church. After that, we would come home for hot chocolate and snacks. I don't think we paid much attention to things like Santa Claus. There might be a few presents, but we never got very many. I have a vague memory of William staying behind when we all went to our Christmas Eve program and then showing up at church later. I suspect that had something to do with getting a few presents out for us kids.

The children's stories from when Emma was a single parent were very personal and yet uncomplicated. This blended family had its ups and downs. There were disputes, but there were also close bonds. Despite the depression and the war that followed, they all navigated their childhood and teenage years to become responsible adults.

Emma – The Later Years

By the mid to late 1950s, Emma and William were the only family members living on Lac qui Parle Avenue. Families who returned for summer vacations or July 4th reunions would think of these two as the family members living in Canby. To a new generation, the life of Emma and William may have appeared plain and simple. The storytellers in Emma's family, however, have revealed as rich and vibrant a family history as could be imagined.

By 1978, Emma and William had been living in the Lac qui Parle Avenue house for about 37 years. Emma was 81 years old and William was 56. William had already been in poor health for some years. His death in May of 1978 led to a decision to sell the house. At the time of his death, William was part owner of the home along with John Hinderer. Emma's ownership interest is unknown, but John said she had used her rent payments to establish ownership in the house.

After the house was sold, Emma rented a small apartment in St. Leo, Minnesota, a few miles east of Canby. In later years, she moved into Sylvan Place, a retirement and care facility in Canby. Emma Krug died on October 8, 1990. She was 93 years old. Emma and other family members are buried in Canby City Cemetery.[18]

Family Recipes

Emma's recipes (Appendix C) are reproduced as recalled or recorded by family members.

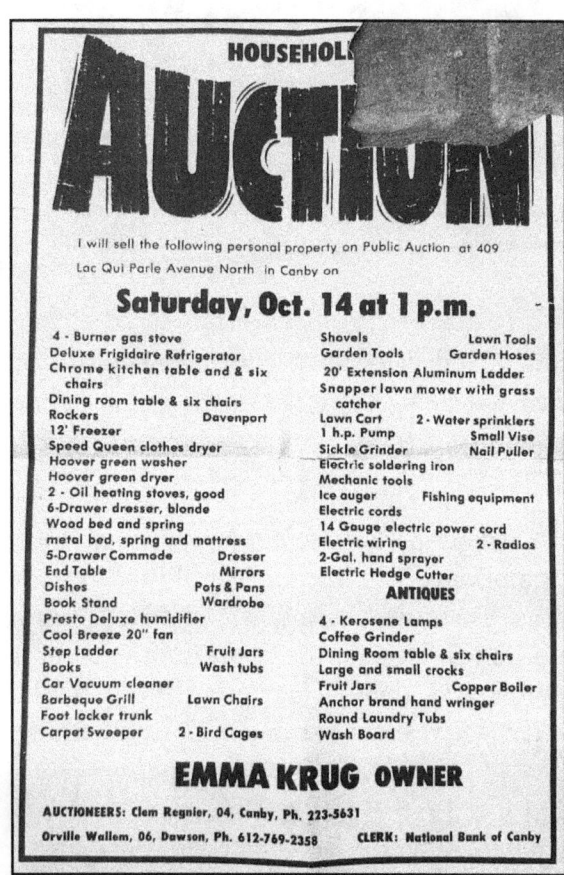

Emma Krug auctioned off much of her personal property in October of 1978. Source: From the Doris Schlichting collection. Edited by author.

The gravestone of Emma Krug in Canby City Cemetery. Source: Photographed and edited by author.

Notes

1. The phrase "her children" refers to all of the children Emma was raising. This includes her sister Sophie's three children: Johnny, William, and Maurine, as well as her oldest child Doris Lafere.

2. Source: Maurine (Krug) Gjovig said the family moved into Canby in March 1935.

3. To view this location, in Google Maps insert coordinates 44.708736, -96.274061 in the search box and click the search button. The exact street address of the Lund rental house is unknown, but it was located on the corner of this intersection.

4. To view this location, in Google Maps insert coordinates 44.709955, -96.269527 in the search box and click the search button.

5. According to Florence, the hand pump drew non-potable water from an underground cistern.

6. To view the location of the parsonage where Doris worked, in Google Maps insert coordinates 43.797293, -92.906915 in the search box and click the search button.

7. Muster rolls list the men aboard a certain Navy ship. They were recorded as often as monthly and can be used to track sailors as they were transferred between vessels.

8. To view Montevideo, in Google Maps insert coordinates 44.953234, -95.716188 in the search box and click the search button. Montevideo is located across the Minnesota River in Chippewa County, Minnesota, about 35 miles northeast of Canby.

9. Opening up a field with a moldboard plow meant making initial passes that could be repeated until the field was entirely turned over. The method used depended on the shape of the field and the farmer's preference.

10. Variations of this "door dog" superstition appear in a number of cultures. In Emma's example, the dog's unexpected appearance was an omen of the future death of someone known to the person who saw the dog.

11. In later years, William bought a small radio he listened to in the kitchen of the Lac qui Parle Avenue house.

12. Bette's recollection from the 1930s would have been while they lived in the Lund rental house.

13. A .22-caliber rifle is a small rifle with a bore diameter of 0.22 inches. Most bird hunters use a shotgun, but William was accurate enough to use a rifle that fired a single small projectile.

14. This was the summer of 1943 at the height of World War II. Maurine roomed with Doris, her husband Hank, and their daughter Sharon during this summer.

15. In 1943, this company was known as George A. Hormel & Company. Consumption of their canned products like Spam, Chili, and Dinty Moore Beef Stew grew rapidly during World War II. The company is now named Hormel Foods.

16. The so-called "hog itch" was due to a skin parasite common in pigs and transferred to the humans who handle them or their byproducts. Maurine's blisters and itching were her reaction to this parasite. Her story indicates that the workers used their bare hands when handling the food products.

17. The jaundice Maurine and others experienced was most likely infectious hepatitis.

18. To locate Canby City Cemetery, in Google Maps insert coordinates 44.703788, -96.276455 in the search box and click the search button.

Chapter 16

Mary and Albert Engstrand

Timeline

1844 – John Erlandson Engstrand was born in Sweden

1852 – Anna Christina Johnson (Jonasson) was born in Sweden

1870 – John Engstrand and Anna Johnson emigrated separately to Minnesota

1873-1878 – Locusts plagued Minnesota crops

1876 – John Engstrand homesteaded in Lac qui Parle County

1876 – The town of Canby was founded

1880 – John Engstrand married Anna Johnson

1880/81 – Severe winter storms isolated Midwest settlers

1881 – Arthur Engstrand was born

1884 – The town of Dawson was founded

1896 – Albert Engstrand was born

1898, May – Mary Hinderer was born in Iowa

1898, Autumn – The Hinderers arrived in Minnesota

1909 – Arthur Engstrand began farming his father's land

1914 – WWI began in Europe.

1917, Apr. – The U.S. declared war on Germany

1918, Jun. – Albert Engstrand was shipped to France

1918, Nov. – Germany surrendered

1919, Mar. – Albert Engstrand was discharged home disabled

1919, Nov. – Albert Engstrand married Mary Hinderer

1920 – Raymond Engstrand was born in Minneapolis

1922 – Donald Engstrand was born in Minneapolis

1924, Aug. – Norma Engstrand was born in Minneapolis

1924, late Aug. or Sep. – Albert and Mary returned to the Engstrand farm

1924, Oct. – John Engstrand died

1927, Aug. – Anna Engstrand died

1927, Nov. – Ruth Engstrand was born in Lac qui Parle County

1930 – Albert Engstrand lived at a Veteran's Hospital

1932 – Albert Engstrand died

1949 – Don Engstrand took control of the Engstrand farm

1981 – Mary (Hinderer) Engstrand died

Emigration from Scandinavian countries and from Germany peaked between 1870 and 1890. The number of immigrant Scandinavian farmers was far less than Germans, but the primary push driving both groups from their homeland was similar. These countries experienced a dramatic increase in population in the late 1800s, but there was no increase in farmable land. Without more land, young farmers could not support their families. The availability of affordable farmland was what brought them to America.

Half of the Scandinavian immigrants were Swedish, followed in numbers by the Norwegians, and then the Danes. For the Swedes, 98% of those who left their homeland came to America rather than any other destination.[1] The new arrivals clustered in regions where earlier Swedish immigrants were already living. In these select settlements, they spoke their native language and established churches similar to the ones they attended in Sweden. Those immigrants who were merchants opened businesses with Swedish names and served a clientele of fellow immigrants.

John Engstrand – The Early Years

John Engstrand was born in 1844 and his future wife Anna Johnson was born in 1852. During their childhood years in Sweden, they did not know one another. U.S. Census documents and family stories agree that John and Anna both emigrated to America in 1870.[2] They settled in separate locations within Carver County, Minnesota. This particular county southwest of the Twin Cities was populated by many Swedish immigrants.[3]

John Engstrand was 25 years old when he arrived in 1870. For six years, he lived near the town of Belle Plaine[4] at the southern edge of Carver County, Minnesota.

In April 1876, John joined a Swedish immigrant family and traveled by covered wagon westward across the state to Lac qui Parle County. His grandson, Don Engstrand, wrote that John first stopped at Benson, Minnesota,[5] 45 miles northeast of Lac qui Parle County. At that time, Benson was a regional land office. Here, farmers wishing to settle on "free" homestead land could file their land claims. Don Engstrand added that his grandfather John walked the final 45 miles from Benson to his eventual land claim location in Section 12 of Providence Township, Lac qui Parle County.

Two years later, John Engstrand returned to Carver County, Minnesota. His goal was to persuade fellow Swedes to move west to Lac qui Parle County. According to one account,

> He was well-rewarded. When he returned to Lac qui Parle, 40 people formed an oxen train and accompanied him. The [Swedish] people who were already settled there were eager to add more people of their own nationality and religious faith.

They hoped that with more arrivals, a Swedish church might be established.[6]

When John Engstrand arrived in Lac qui Parle County in 1876, this region of southwestern Minnesota was relatively unsettled by European immigrants, but that was changing quickly. Fourteen years earlier in 1862, the Minnesota Sioux Indians had been expelled from their lands along the Minnesota River, including land in Lac qui Parle County. The U.S. government then offered this former Sioux land to homesteaders. By the time John Engstrand arrived, there was a sense of urgency for farmers who wanted to claim homestead land. Unclaimed parcels were still available, but the land best suited for farming was fast disappearing.

Historically, the Homestead Act of 1862 had allowed settlers to claim a maximum of 160 acres (a quarter section) of government-owned land. Gaining full title to their homestead took claimants at least five years. They were required to build a livable structure, improve (plow and plant) some acreage, and remain living on their claim for five years. Don Engstrand said his grandfather built a "shanty" and made the required land improvements on his northeast quarter of Section 12. The official recording of his homestead was written several years after he first made his claim at the Benson land office.

A summarization document for John Engstrand's 160-acre homestead was compiled in March of 1883. It specified that John had used the land office in Benson, Minnesota, to file his original claim.

Several years later, John Engstrand claimed another 80-acre parcel adjacent to his homestead claim. Don Engstrand called this his grandfather's tree claim. John Engstrand was able to claim the additional 80 acres by using the Timber Culture Act of 1873. This legislation was meant to encourage farmers to plant trees on the open prairie. In theory, the trees would be a source of timber for constructing houses, farm buildings, and towns. The Timber Culture Act was widely abused, and it was eventually repealed in 1891. Nevertheless, farmers like John Engstrand used this 18-year window of time to add to their property. The summarization document for John's tree claim was dated 1890.

The record of John Engstrand's homestead claim. It was recorded July 1, 1882, and it indicated that John paid four dollars to file his homestead claim. Source: The Lac qui Parle County Recorder's Office, Madison, Minnesota. Photographed and edited by author.

The summarization document for John Engstrand's 160 acre homestead claim. The land office he used was in Benson, Minnesota. The "authority" line lists the 1862 Homestead Act that granted eligibility to individuals like John to claim land. Source: U.S. Department of the Interior, Bureau of Land Management, General Land Office Records, "Land Patents," accessed February 3, 2023, https://glorecords.blm.gov/. Edited by author.

John Engstrand and Anna Johnson – Family Years

Anna Johnson's 1870 arrival in America was confirmed by the 1870 U.S. Census. It documented 18-year-old Anna living in Carver County, Minnesota, with her 45-year-old mother Johanna and two younger sisters. This family of four was living with a Swedish-speaking couple. Anna worked as a servant for this couple.

Katharine

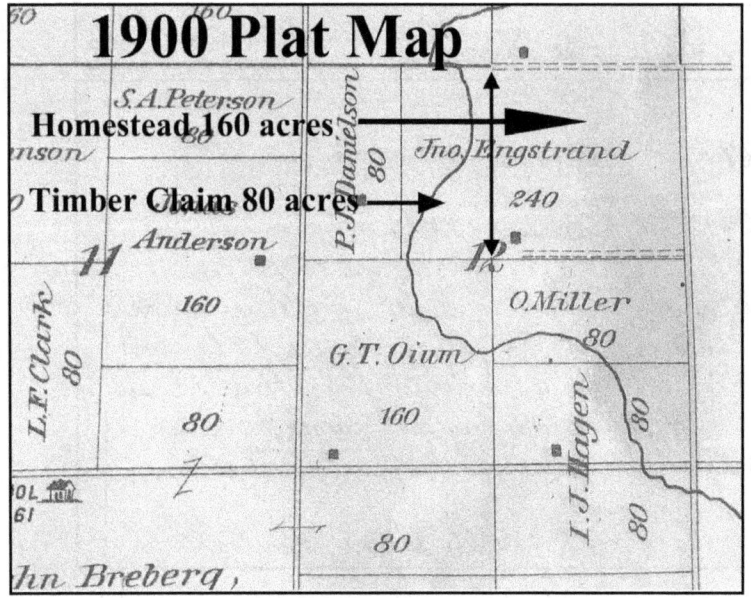

A 1900 Plat map included section 12 of Providence Township. Jno. (John) Engstrand owned a total of 240 acres in the northeast corner of section 12 of Providence Township. The vertical line with double arrows approximates the divide between his 160 acre homestead and his 80 acre tree claim. The Lac qui Parle River winds northward through his tree claim land. The Engstrand farmhouse is indicated by the black square, almost a half mile from the roadway. Source: The Lac qui Parle County History Museum, Madison, Minnesota. Photographed and edited by author.

John Engstrand first met Anna Johnson sometime between his 1878 return to Lac qui Parle County and early 1880. It is even possible that Anna Johnson was in the wagon train of 40 people John Engstrand brought from Carver County. John and Anna were married on April 30, 1880. Don Engstrand said their marriage took place in his grandfather's claim shanty.

The 1880 U.S. Census was taken in June, two months after John and Anna's marriage. It located the newlyweds living on their homestead in Providence Township, Lac qui Parle County. It documented that 35-year old John, 28-year-old Annie (Anna), and both of their parents had all been born in Sweden.

The marriage of John Engstrand and Anna Johnson took place on April 13, 1880. Both John and Anna were living in Lac qui Parle County at the time of their marriage. Source: The Lac qui Parle County Recorder's office, Madison, Minnesota. Edited by author.

The severe winter that followed John and Anna's 1880 marriage was previously described in Chapter 7. The newlywed couple were isolated in their claim shanty throughout that long winter. Don Engstrand wrote about the first snowstorm that struck on October 16, 1880,

For four days they [John and Anna] *dared not go outside of the shanty even to take care of the livestock. Hay was burned for fuel, flour was ground in a coffee mill, and roasted wheat was used for coffee.*

The one favorable outcome of that harsh winter was the birth of their first child, Arthur, in February of 1881.

Before the town of Dawson, Minnesota, was founded in 1884, the only reliable wagon trail from Providence Township led to Benson, 45 miles away. For the first four years of their marriage, the town of Benson was where John and Anna sold their farm crops and bought supplies. According to grandson Don Engstrand,

His [John's] *means of transportation was an ox team. With these slow-going but sure-footed animals, he traveled everywhere for some years; going to church, to market, to wedding parties, visiting* [neighbors], *and tilling the soil.*

Stories from the past were handed down to Don Engstrand. One such story spoke of what Don called his grandfather's "act of bravery." Don wrote:

One of the first years John lived on his homestead he was chopping willows for stove fuel below a fifty-foot bank along the Lac qui Parle River. It was getting dark and [when] *he looked up, he saw a pack of wolves lined up on top of the bank watching him. Having to go past them to get home, he took an armful of sticks and charged the wolves throwing sticks at them. The wolves scattered and he walked home safely.*

The early Swedish settlers in Providence Township wanted to reestablish their old-country church practices. At first, they met in private homes for Sunday services. Most settlers who lived near the Engstrands later joined the "Nordahl" Swedish congregation located south of the Engstrand homestead. John and Anna Engstrand's first two children were baptized in the Nordahl Swedish church.

The 1900 U.S. Census listed the Engstrand family. The six children ranged in age from Arthur age 19 to Albert H. age 3. Note that John Engstrand himself was the census enumerator and he began the township listing with his own family. Source: "1900 United States Federal Census" online database (Provo, UT: Ancestry.com), accessed January 31, 2023. Edited by author.

Katharine

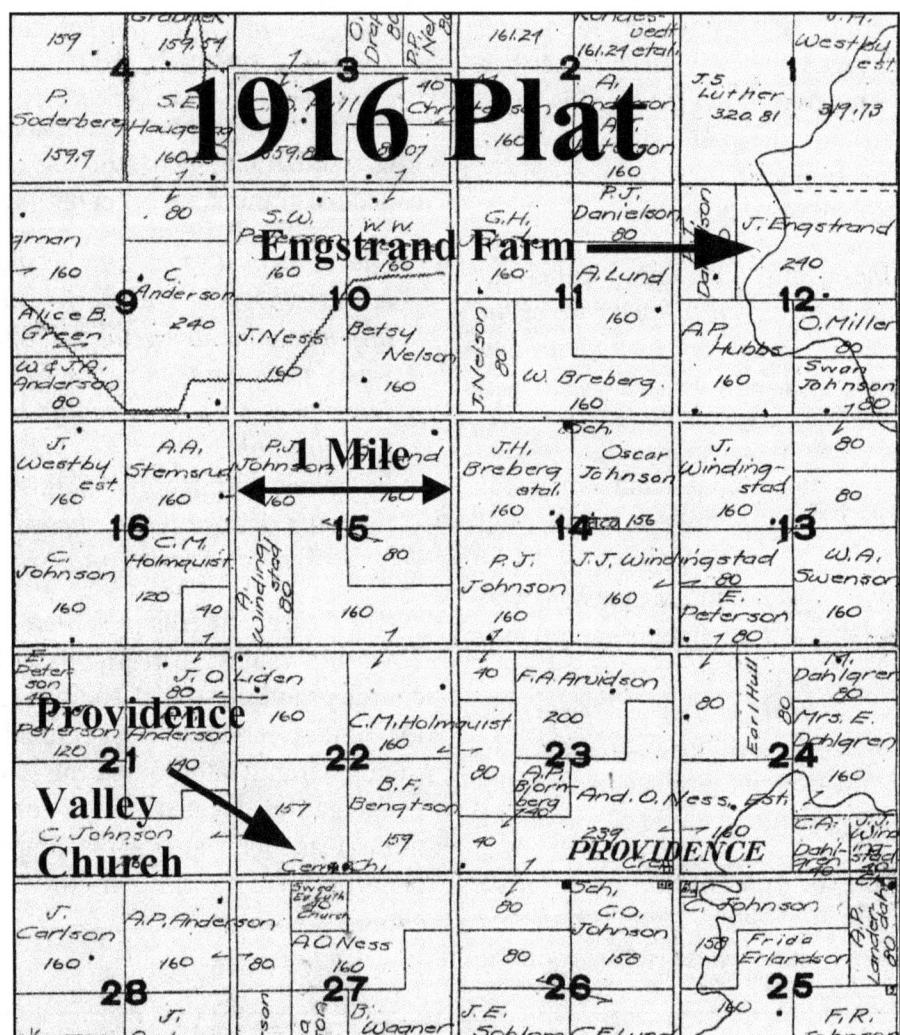

This plat map from 1916 illustrates the relationship between the Engstrand farm and Providence Valley Lutheran Church and cemetery. Source: Access to this map courtesy of the Lac qui Parle County History Museum, Madison, Minnesota. Photographed and edited by author.

The family of John and Anna Engstrand as listed in the Swedish American Church Records. The titles above the columns have been added for clarification. Source: "U.S., Evangelical Lutheran Church in America, Swedish American Church Records, 1800-1947" online database (Lehi, UT: Ancestry.com), accessed January 31, 2023. Edited by author.

A snapshot quality photo from the early 1920s of Anna and John Engstrand. Source: Original photo courtesy of Norma (Engstrand) Sandrock. Edited by author.

Providence Valley Lutheran Church was organized in 1892. The church building and cemetery were located in Section 22, several miles southwest of John and Anna's farm. Once it was completed, this was the church John and Anna's family attended for the remainder of their lives. Many Engstrand family members have been buried in the Providence Valley Lutheran Church cemetery.[7]

Don Engstrand wrote about his Engstrand grandparents:

Twelve children were born to John and Anna Engstrand. In addition to the six children who died in infancy, there was: Arthur, the oldest, who [later] *farmed the Engstrand farm; Agnes and Esther who were registered nurses; Dr. Oscar who was a medical doctor; Adolph who was a farmer near Granite Falls; and Albert H. who was in combat in World War I,* [was] *wounded three times, and discharged totally disabled.*

By 1897, John and Anna's family was complete. Their last child, Albert H., later married Mary Hinderer. Albert and Mary were the parents of Don Engstrand.

Don Engstrand was proud of his grandfather John Engstrand's civic achievements,

[He] *was one of a committee who organized and named Providence Township. ...he was the clerk of School District 61 for many years, town clerk, and county commissioner for four years. He was* [one of] *the county commissioners who signed the papers when Dawson was incorporated as a town.*

John Engstrand was also intent on improving his own farm. As his family grew, he added a new farmhouse to his original claim shanty. He built barns to house his animals and sheds to protect his machinery from the elements. Storyteller Don Engstrand added,

In 1903, he drilled a 139 ft. deep well which produced soft water. The water was pumped by a windmill to the house, the barn, and the hog house. [In the house] *he had a bathtub, and sewer pipes* [that drained wastewater] *from the house.*

John Engstrand installed these "modern" plumbing features decades before his neighbors and long before electricity was available. John and Anna Engstrand lived the remainder of their long lives on their home farm in Lac qui Parle County, Minnesota.

Arthur Engstrand – Dutiful Farmer and Civic Leader

Arthur Engstrand was born in John and Anna's claim shanty in February 1881. He was their first child, making him the oldest of the six Engstrand children who survived into adulthood. Arthur's close relationship with the Hinderer family was secured when his youngest brother Albert married Mary Hinderer in late 1919. At the time, Arthur was living on the Engstrand home farm with his parents.

Arthur had a naturally quiet demeanor and, early in his life, pursued an academic career. He graduated from Dawson High School in 1904 and then received normal school training in nearby Madison, Minnesota. His first teaching assignment was at District 66 school where the Hinderer children, including Mary Hinderer, were students.

The 1900 U.S. Census listed 19-year-old Arthur living on his parent's farm and working as a farm laborer. In the 1905 Minnesota State Census, Arthur still lived on the Engstrand farm, but he was working away from home as a teacher. Arthur continued teaching for only a few years after the 1905 census. Storyteller Don Engstrand was Arthur's nephew. Don said that around 1909, John Engstrand asked his oldest son Arthur to assume primary control of the family farm operation. At the time, Arthur was 28 years old and his father was 65. His father's summons to manage the family farm ended Arthur's teaching career.

Arthur's management of the farm was similar to his father's progressive style. The farmhouse was modernized and outbuildings were improved to accommodate greater numbers of livestock.

Arthur Engstrand was required to register for possible military service during World War I. When the first cycle of conscription began in 1917, Arthur was 36 years old and beyond the registration age limit. However, in the subsequent 1918 cycle, 37-year-old Arthur was required to register. He was listed as native-born and

A 1941 family photo included Carl Hinderer on the left, and Arthur Engstrand. Source: The Martha Hinderer collection. Edited by author.

worked as a farmer in rural Lac qui Parle County, Minnesota. His physical description was listed as tall and slender with blue eyes and light-colored hair. Surprisingly, Arthur was also required to register for conscription during World War II. By that time, he was 61 years old and still lived on his home farm. Arthur was not drafted into military service during either world war.

Arthur's nephew Don Engstrand lauded his uncle's civic achievements. Don said,

> he was always active in local affairs. For [the] 27 years between 1913 and 1940, he was the [Dawson] town clerk. He also succeeded his father, John, as clerk for District 61 school in Providence Township. . . . In his later years he served as the township assessor.

Arthur's success at farming and his participation in civic affairs were not his only achievements. By the late 1920s, he had also become an important stabilizing influence on his brother Albert, his sister-in-law Mary (Hinderer), and their young family.

Mary Hinderer

Mary Clara Hinderer was born on May 12, 1898. At that time, her birth family still lived on their Iowa farm. Later that year, the Hinderers moved to Minnesota. Mary was an infant when her family moved into the sod house during the winter of 1898, and when they began building their farmhouse in 1899.

Twins John and Martha Hinderer were born in December of 1906 when Mary was eight years old. Mother Katharine cared for her twins during their infancy in 1907. Soon thereafter, Mary was given the assignment of caring for her twin siblings. Mary's daughter and storyteller Norma (Engstrand) Sandrock said that she did not believe her mother (Mary) had to work in the fields like the older Hinderer sisters. Instead, Mary was given domestic tasks like sewing and mending clothes in addition to caring for John and Martha.

During the school year, Mary attended District 66 school north of the Hinderer farmhouse. In the Hinderer family, the youngest children were able to attend more years of school than their older siblings. Mary completed six years of schooling at District 66 school. Her future brother-in-law, Arthur Engstrand, was one of her teachers. Mary's daughter and storyteller Norma (Engstrand) Sandrock observed that in spite of only six grades of formal schooling, her mother had excellent penmanship and was very good at spelling.

Like her older siblings, Mary was given religious instruction at Zacchaeus Lutheran Church in Canby. Her confirmation photo is undated, but it was likely taken in 1912 when she was 14 years old.

Late in her teenage years, Mary left the Hinderer farm to work in the homes of other families. By doing so, she followed the pattern set by her three older sisters. Storyteller Norma (Engstrand) Sandrock said that one of her mother's work assignments was in the Canby home of Esther (Engstrand) Severson. Esther was a sister to Engstrand brothers Arthur and Albert. She was 10 years older than her youngest sibling Albert.

Mary Hinderer's confirmation photo was undated, but was likely taken in 1912 when she was 14 years old. Source: Photo courtesy of Becci Fischer. Edited by author.

An undated photo of the students attending District 66 school a short distance north of the Hinderer farm. Mary Hinderer is the tall girl in the back row on the far right. Source: From the Doris Schlichting collection. Edited by author.

Katharine

In 1919, Mary Hinderer was working for Esther's family in Canby, Minnesota.

ALBERT ENGSTRAND

Albert Henning Engstrand was born on September 19, 1896. He was the youngest of John and Mary Engstrand's children. Albert was 13 years old in 1909 when his father requested his oldest brother Arthur to return home and manage the Engstrand farm. In 1915, Albert graduated from high school in nearby Dawson, Minnesota.[8] After high school, Albert attended Gustavus Adolphus college in St. Peter, Minnesota for two years.[9] Gustavus Adolphus was (and remains) a well-regarded liberal arts college with deep roots in the Swedish-American community.

The completion of Albert's second year of college coincided with America's entry into World War I. The first in a series of U.S. draft registration laws went into effect on June 5, 1917. All young men between the ages of 21 and 31 were required to register. Albert Engstrand registered on June 14, 1917, a few months before his 21st birthday.[10]

Within months of his registration, Albert Engstrand was conscripted into military service. Along with his fellow army inductees, he was sent to Camp Cody, New Mexico for basic training. Camp Cody was a hastily organized encampment meant to train new recruits. The first inductees arrived at Camp Cody in October 1917.

Albert Engstrand was a newly trained private in the 42nd or "Rainbow Division" of the U.S. Army. This division was composed of troops from many states, including Minnesota. It was nicknamed the "Rainbow Division" because the troop's homes spread "like a rainbow" across the country. Once the division troops were trained at Camp Cody, they were sent to the east coast where they boarded ships headed for France. Albert was a member of Company 10 in the 42nd Division. He and his fellow company members departed for France from Brooklyn, New York on June 18, 1918.[11]

Storyteller Don Engstrand summarized his father's experience in World War I,

Albert Engstrand's official army photograph taken in 1918. The arched emblem on his left shoulder identified the "Rainbow Division" he joined. Source: From the Doris Schlichting collection. Edited by author.

My father Albert was in France during World War I and was wounded three times. One of these injuries was due to a shell or some shrapnel that cut through his helmet and gashed his head. This was a serious wound and affected him for the rest of his life. Later, he was discharged from the service totally disabled.

Don said he was given this information by his uncle, Dr. Olson. He was Don's uncle by way of his marriage to Albert's sister Agnes. Don said Dr. Olson had been a soldier in France at the same time as his father Albert.

Albert's obituary, written years later, stated,

In several instances he was placed in the front line trenches and is one of the few survivors of those going "over the top." He was listed as wounded four times, the last time on Oct. 15, 1918, seriously by a large shrapnel shell. He spent four months in hospitals after which he was sent home, crippled. On March 18, 1919 he was discharged, permanently and totally disabled.[12]

Considering the dates listed in these sources, Albert Engstrand spent between three and four months in the frontline trenches of northern France. His most serious wound in mid-October of 1918 was one month before Germany surrendered and World War I ended. The multiple wounds and subsequent lengthy hospitalization speak to the intensity of the trench warfare he experienced. It would be expected that his disabling wounds were both physical and psychological.

Albert and fellow wounded soldiers sailed home from Bordeaux, France in late January 1919. They arrived in Brooklyn, New York on February 25, 1919.[13] He was discharged to his Minnesota home three weeks later on March 18, 1919.

Albert's graduation from college, military experience, and married life can be arranged in a timeline. It lists the key events during the last 15 years of his life.

Albert Engstrand was among the soldiers returning on the S.S. West Eagle. They departed from Bordeaux France on January 31, 1919 and arrived in Brooklyn on February 25, 1919. The soldiers were sent to Camp Merritt for out-processing. Source: "U.S. Army Transport Service Arriving and Departing Passenger Lists, 1910-1939" online database (Provo, UT: Ancestry.com, 2011), accessed January 31, 2023. Edited by author.

ALBERT ENGSTRAND AND MARY HINDERER

In January of 1919, Hinderer family members lived in both Minnesota and South Dakota. Sophie (Hinderer) and Martin Krug had been married for a year and were living on the Arneson farm a mile from the Hinderer's home. Sophie was pregnant with their first child. Emma (Hinderer) and Ralph Lafere were living in Sioux Falls, South Dakota, and Emma was pregnant with her first child (Doris). Tena, the oldest Hinderer daughter, had been working away from home for more than a decade. Twins John and Martha were 13-year-old teenagers and, together with older brother Carl, lived at home with their parents Katharine and Gottlieb Hinderer.

In Providence Township, by early 1919 Arthur Engstrand had been managing the home farm for ten years. His father John was 74 years old and no longer capable of the heavy labor of farming. Arthur's mother Anna kept house for her husband and son. Arthur's younger siblings had all moved away from the home farm.

The November of 1919 wedding portrait of Mary Hinderer and Albert Engstrand. Source: From the Doris Schlichting collection. Edited by author.

The marriage certificate for Mary Hinderer and Albert Engstrand. The date and location of their marriage was stated as well as the two witnesses. Source: Courtesy of the Lac qui Parle County Recorder's Office. Accessed in July of 2017. Edited by author.

ALBERT and MARY ENGSTRAND – TIMELINE

1917, April – U.S. declared war on Germany

1917, May or June – Albert completed his 2nd year at Gustavus Adolphus college

1917, June 14 – Albert registered for military service

1917, Oct. 1-15 – First inducted men arrived at Camp Cody, New Mexico for basic training, including men from Minnesota

1918, June 28 – Pvt. Albert Engstrand sailed from Brooklyn, New York to France

1919, Feb. 29 – Pvt. Albert Engstrand returned to the U.S. from Bordeaux, France. He was sent to Camp Merritt New Jersey. He was then discharged home, fully disabled

1919, Nov. 12 – Albert Engstrand married Mary Hinderer

1920, Jan. – Albert and Mary lived with a family in Ramsey Co., MN. He was unemployed

1920, later – Albert was a student at a "tech school," and they lived in Minneapolis

1920, May 26 – Raymond Engstrand was born

1921 – Albert and Mary lived at the same Minneapolis address. Albert was a metal worker

1922 – Albert was listed as a student. He and his family lived at a second address in Minneapolis

1922, July 26 – Donald Engstrand was born

1924, Aug. 9 – Norma Engstrand was born. The family lived at a third address in Minneapolis. Albert was listed as a salesman

1924 – After Norma's birth in August, Albert's family moved to the Engstrand farm

1924, Oct. 8 – Albert's father John died on the Engstrand farm

1925, Summer – the Monsons visited the Engstrand farm. Albert was pictured with the family

1926 – Mary's sister Sophie died in March. Sister Emma married Martin Krug in December

1927, Aug. 27 – Albert's mother Anna died on the Engstrand farm

1927, Nov. 10 – Ruth Engstrand was born to Albert and Mary on the Engstrand farm

1930, April – Albert lived at the Veteran's Hospital in St. Cloud, Minnesota. Mary and the four children remained on the Engstrand farm

1932, Mar. 18 – Albert died in Wayne County, Indiana

A 15-year timeline from 1917 to 1932 lists the sequence of key events in the lives of Albert and Mary Engstrand. Source: Compiled by author.

Into this set of family circumstances, a disabled Albert Engstrand arrived home in late March of 1919. His future wife Mary Hinderer was working for the family of Albert's sister Esther in Canby. Storyteller Don Engstrand said, "After the war, my father stayed with his sister Esther in Canby." Esther was the person who introduced disabled war veteran Albert Engstrand to his future wife Mary Hinderer.

Albert and Mary were married on November 12, 1919 in Lac qui Parle County. Storyteller John Hinderer said the marriage ceremony took place in the Hinderer home. He added that Albert's oldest brother Arthur was his best man. John said the weather that day was "kind of nasty." Best man Arthur had to make his way to the Hinderer farm in a horse-drawn wagon. The marriage certificate confirmed the wedding location as Freeland Township where the Hinderers lived. Albert's oldest brother Arthur was listed as one witness, and Mary's oldest sister Tena was the second witness. At the time of their marriage, Albert was 23 years old and Mary was 21.

Within a few weeks of their marriage, Albert and Mary left Lac qui Parle County and moved to the Twin Cities. Don Engstrand said that his parents moved there so his father Albert could attend a technical school. The 1920 U.S. Census conducted that January, two months after their marriage, located Albert and Mary Engstrand in St. Paul, Minnesota. They were living with another couple who were ten years older and had five children of their own living at home. Albert Engstrand was listed as unemployed.

Within a few months, Albert and Mary moved from St. Paul to Minneapolis. A 1920 city directory identified their Minneapolis address and stated that Albert was a student. This confirmed storyteller Don Engstrand's understanding about his father attending a technical school. Their first child, son Raymond Albert, was born in Minneapolis on May 26, 1920. One year later in 1921, Albert Engstrand was listed in the city directory as a metalworker. This indicated that his technical schooling had resulted in his first regular job.

In 1922, Albert and Mary were living at a different address in Minneapolis, and Albert was, once again, listed as a student. Their second child, son and storyteller Donald Clayton Engstrand, was born on July 26, 1922 at this second Minneapolis address.

The 1924 Minneapolis City Directory found Albert and Mary's family residing at a third address in that city. Albert's occupation was said to

The 1920 U.S. Census conducted on January 10th identified Albert and Mary Engstrand living with another family in St. Paul, Ramsey County, Minnesota. Albert was unemployed. Source: "1920 United States Federal Census" online database (Provo, UT: Ancestry.com), accessed February 28, 2023. Edited by author.

be a salesman. Their third child, daughter Norma Marie, was born in Minneapolis on August 9, 1924. Within weeks of Norma's birth, Albert and Mary's young family left the Twin Cities and moved back to the Engstrand home farm in Lac qui Parle County.

The picture that emerges from Albert's four years of living in the Twin Cities is one of an inability to sustain a job capable of supporting his family. His wartime experience in France likely contributed to the unrewarding outcome of his attempts at a trade school education and employment.

Albert and Mary returned to live on the Engstrand farm in late August or early September of 1924. Within a few months of their return, Albert's father, John Engstrand, died on this same farm he first homesteaded. At the time of his death on October 8, 1924, he was one month shy of his 80th birthday. His wife Anna continued living on the farm until her death three years later in 1927 when she was 75 years old.

During the summer of 1925, Mary's oldest sister Tena visited the Engstrand farm with her husband-to-be John Monson and his sister Ethel. It was the same summer the Monsons were photographed at the Arneson farm where Martin and Sophie Krug lived. The photo taken at the Engstrand farm showed Albert's family, the Monsons, and one cousin, Doris Lafere. It was one of the very few photos showing Albert with his family while they lived together on the Engstrand farm.

After Anna Engstrand died in August of 1927, there were no remaining members of the immigrant Engstrand generation in Lac qui Parle County. Three months after Anna's death, Albert and Mary's last child, Ruth Georgiana Engstrand, was born on November 10, 1927.

Albert Engstrand worked on the home farm with his brother Arthur for several years. By the late 1920s, however, Albert's mental decline due to his war injuries had become increasingly apparent. Storytellers Don and Norma both recalled that at one point their father Albert wanted to move his family away from the farm. However, his wife Mary would not leave. As Don stated, "My mother knew that this was not going to work, and she wouldn't leave the farm . . . she was more secure staying on the farm." Don added, "My father did leave but would return from time to time to see us on the farm and to see his sister Esther [in Canby]."

Albert's unpredictable presence on the farm had an unsettling effect on his older children. Don

A photo taken in the summer of 1925 when Tena Hinderer together with Ethel and John Monson visited the Engstrand farm. Left to right standing: Ethel Monson, Mary holding Norma, Albert Engstrand, Tena Hinderer, and John Monson. Seated L. to R. are Raymond Engstrand, cousin Doris Lafere, and Don Engstrand. Source: From the Doris Schlichting collection. Edited by author.

said his father became elusive and was sometimes a shadowy figure seen around the farm buildings. His progressive decline eventually led to a decision to admit him to an institution. At the time of the 1930 U.S. Census, Albert lived at the Veteran's Hospital in St. Cloud, Minnesota. Both Norma and Don recalled family visits to see their father at the hospital. However, documents from both 1931 and 1932 indicate that Albert had left the Veteran's Hospital. He was first located in Washington State and then in the state of Indiana. Albert Engstrand died on March 18, 1932 in Wayne County, Indiana.[14]

During those final years of his life, Albert Engstrand suffered from a severe psychological disturbance. The term "shellshock" was first applied during and after World War I to describe what we now call PTSD, post-traumatic stress disorder. At the time of Albert's return home after the war, there was no treatment for this illness. Families of veterans were left to cope, as best they could, with the damage caused by combat.

Albert Engstrand was given a full military funeral service and was buried at Providence Valley Lutheran Church cemetery. It was the same church his parents helped found, and that he attended. Albert's service to his country was also honored by a front page story in the local newspaper, the *Dawson Sentinel*.

During the last five years of Albert Engstrand's life, his wife Mary and brother Arthur were the strength of the family. Mary's two sons, Raymond and Don, were old enough to recognize their father's deterioration. Her two daughters, Norma and Ruth, were too young to fully understand Albert's decline and eventual absence. Norma said she was aware her father did not live at home, but as a child did not think about why he was absent. Each child viewed their father's absence from their own life perspective. In spite of Albert's gradual decline and his eventual death, Mary and her brother-in-law Arthur kept the family together.

In the extended Hinderer family, Albert Engstrand's decline and death was not discussed. The Hinderer's response to Albert's death in 1932 was similar to their response to Sophie's death in 1926. Their efforts were directed toward helping with everyday duties and nurturing the surviving family members. In spite of family configurations that may have seemed strange to outsiders, the Hinderers simply accepted, without judgment, the difficult circumstances they were given.

A low-quality photo from about 1928 taken at the Engstrand farm. Back row left to right: John Hinderer, Arthur Engstrand, Gottlieb Hinderer, Emma Krug holding Maurine Krug, Albert Engstrand, Mary Engstrand holding Norma Engstrand. Front row: cousins Johnny Krug, Doris Lafere, William Krug, Raymond Engstrand and Don Engstrand. Source: From the Norma (Engstrand) Sandrock collection. Edited by author.

Mary and Albert Engstrand

ON SENT

Lac qui Parle County's Newsiest Newspaper

C QUI PARLE COUNTY, MINNESOTA, THURSDAY, MARCH

A. ENGSTRAND, WAR VETERAN, DIES ON FRIDAY

Was Seriously Wounded While on Active Duty in France; Given a Military Funeral.

Albert Hening Engstrand, disabled World War veteran, passed away Friday, March 18. The funeral, at which military rites were conducted, was held Monday at the Providence Valley Lutheran church. Rev. P. O. Wee

MUSIC FESTIVA TO BE GIVEN RURAL SCH

Lac qui Parle Coun in State To Spo Extensive Progr of Music.

The teachers of the elementary rural school qui Parle County have undertaken a program which will culminate formance by the county over one hundred juven

The March 24, 1932, edition of the Dawson Sentinel *headlined the life history of local war veteran Albert Engstrand. See full transcription that follows. Source: Courtesy of the Dawson Public Library, as published in the* Dawson Sentinel. *In the public domain. Edited by author.*

This gravestone in Providence Lutheran Church cemetery marks the burial site of World War I veteran Albert Engstrand.[15] Source: Photographed and edited by author.

A. ENGSTRAND, WAR VETERAN, DIES ON FRIDAY

Was Seriously Wounded While on Active Duty in France; Given a Military Funeral.

Albert Hening Engstrand, disabled World War veteran, passed away Friday, March 18. The funeral, at which military rites were conducted, was held Monday at the Providence Valley Lutheran church, Rev. P.O. Wee officiating. Burial was made in the Providence Valley church cemetery. Pallbearers were Arnold Mahlum, Chester Hill, Walter Bergman, Jalmer Olson, Henry Bolstad and Obert Thompson.

Albert Engstrand enlisted in the U.S. Army on June 14, 1917 and was immediately sent to a camp in New Mexico where he remained for a short time before being transferred to the 166th Infantry, Rainbow Division and was sent overseas where he saw active duty. In several instances he was placed in the front line trenches and is one of the few survivors of those going "over the top." He was listed as wounded four times, the last time on Oct. 15, 1918, seriously by a large shrapnel shell. He spent four months in the hospitals after which he was sent home, crippled. On March 18, 1919 he was discharged, permanently and totally disabled.

Albert Engstrand was born on Sept. 19, 1896 at Dawson where he grew to young manhood on the home farm. After finishing his common school education, he went two years to Gustavus Adolphus college at St. Peter after which he enlisted in the army.

On November 12, 1919 Mr. Engstrand was united in marriage to Mary Hinderer of Canby. He spent the next four years in Minneapolis but later moved back to Dawson and established his residence at the home and place of his birth. Four children were born to Mr. and Mrs. Engstrand, all of whom survive him: They are: Raymond, Donald, Norma and Ruth. Besides his widow and children, two brothers and two sisters also survive him. They are Arthur of Dawson, Mrs. R. G. Olson of Minneapolis, Mrs. P. H. Severson of Canby and Oscar Engstrand of Warren. Mr. Engstrand's father and mother preceded him in death.

(March 24, 1932, article in the *Dawson Sentinel* transcription by author)

Life on the Engstrand Farm

Daily life on the Engstrand farm reflected the heritage of the adults living there. Norma (Engstrand) Sandrock explained why she and her siblings grew up speaking only English. She said her father was from a Swedish-speaking family, and her mother grew up speaking German. Without a common native language, both parents and children always spoke English at home.

Norma said her mixed Swedish and German ancestry also influenced daily food preparation. She said her mother prepared some German meals, but not as frequently as her grandmother Katharine Hinderer. When the Engstrands visited the Hinderer farm, meals based on German recipes were always a part of the children's experience. Norma added that her grandmother Anna Engstrand often prepared Swedish dishes for the family. As a result, the children were treated to a cultural mix of home-cooked meals.

Both Norma and Don used kind words to describe their Uncle Arthur. Norma said her uncle was naturally calm and soft-spoken. To the Engstrand children, he was a steadying influence. Don said that during his childhood and school years, the Engstrand farm was technically owned by Arthur. Nevertheless, his uncle did not give Don or his older brother Ray orders about what chores they were expected to do. As Don put it, "he was pretty easy-going."

Norma added that her Uncle Arthur never interfered with Mary's ideas about child-rearing. This included disciplining the children. Don agreed that it was his mother who decided what chores the children should do. She would also reprimand them if their jobs were not done correctly. He said she "did not have the push and leadership of Grandma [Katharine] Hinderer, but she was the one who ran the Engstrand household."

Norma recalled that her mother Mary would usually take her two daughters with her when she visited friends or neighbors. Norma said

In general, she was very good to us children. [However] *she was critical if we went somewhere and didn't say or do the right thing.* [If we made a mistake,] *we would hear about that when we got home.*

Norma analyzed her mother's motive,

I would say my mother was not very talkative herself or comfortable at conversation. Having another person [her daughters] *present made conversation easier for her.*

Norma and Don also agreed that there was a clear division between the jobs given to the two older boys and the two younger girls. The Engstrand sisters helped their mother with household chores while their brothers helped with the field work and animal care.

Norma listed the jobs she and Ruth were expected to accomplish. Mary taught her two daughters how to sew and cook. During their childhood, the farm did not have electricity, so all cooking was done on their cookstove. Mostly, the girls learned to bake cakes as well as other desserts. Norma said a work assignment she did not enjoy was cleaning the soot from the glass chimneys of the kerosene lamps. It was dirty and tedious work, and it had to be done nearly every day.

As children, the list of duties for the two girls rarely extended beyond household chores. However, one outside job they always enjoyed was a walk on summer evenings to drive the cattle home from the pasture. The girls walked along a pathway near the river to reach the cattle. When driving the cattle home in the evening, they were facing east. Norma said she liked to watch the long shadows from the setting sun preceding them along the pathway. To her it was a kind of dreamy procession.

Norma admitted that when she was outdoors, she was easily distracted by nature. Before bedtime, she and Ruth always made a necessary visit to the outhouse in the backyard. In summer, Norma said, these visits were often prolonged by viewing the stars in the crystal-clear night sky. In springtime, Norma said she also enjoyed picking bouquets of wildflowers. As she put it, "When you are a kid, most things become some sort of play."

Other types of work and fun also blended together for Norma. She said,

> *In the spring we would go to the edge of a grove of trees and pick wild asparagus. It grew among the trees and grass, but was tasty when it was fresh.*

Like the Hinderers, the Engstrand's main source of produce was from their garden. According to Norma,

> *I recall helping to weed it. That was not my favorite job, and it seemed like I had to do a lot of it. We always canned a lot, maybe [a total of] 200 one and two-quart jars of vegetables [each summer]. My mother also canned chicken and pork.*

Also like the Hinderers, the Engstrands butchered a hog in the winter. The freshly cut meat was stored outside of the main house on the porch. The cold winter temperature quickly froze and preserved the meat.

The Lac qui Parle River flowed northward through the Engstrand's western-most 80 acres. This was part of their grandfather's tree claim land. The river provided summer fun and an attractive diversion for the children. Norma said their summer swimming hole was about a quarter mile from the farmhouse. Norma admitted that even during the school year she and Ruth often took a detour so they could walk on steppingstones across the river. She said,

> *The stones were not easy to stay on, and I would often end up falling in and getting wet. Of course, mother would bawl me out when I got home and tell me not to do that again, but I would anyway. We loved to do it.*

The same river was the scene of an accident for Norma. She recalled,

> *It was in the winter and we were riding on a sled down a hill nearby. On one ride, I ran into a barbed wire fence. There were two of us girls on the sled, but I was in the front. [It left me with] bad cuts on my face. [Somehow] mother heard of my accident and walked with me the half mile back home. Then Uncle Arthur drove me to town for help.*

Norma said the stitching done in Dawson did not heal well and left her with unsightly scars. Norma had two uncles in the Twin Cities who were physicians. They encouraged Mary to have Norma's scars repaired by a specialist, which she did. Norma said this resulted in better healing and a much-improved appearance.

Norma related that adults in their family were allowed to have fun as well.

> *In the winters, we used to have dances at people's houses. Usually, someone played the accordion and the rest of us danced. We did it at our home too. There would be a lot of neighbors attending. I think we pulled the rugs back to make a dance floor. This was adults too, not just kids. It was good winter entertainment.*

Both Don and Norma said that alcohol was an uncommon indulgence in their home. Don contrasted the Engstrand's abstinence with the Hinderer home where drinking beer socially was more commonplace. Norma said one exception was when their Engstrand relatives from the Twin Cities visited. She recalled her Uncle Arthur "served them a mixed drink, so he did have a bottle somewhere."

Don Engstrand told of his own childhood days working on the farm. He said,

> *Ray [his brother] was two years older than I was, so he had more and heavier jobs than I did. One time the two of us as boys took the place of one man during thrashing. We were part of a bundle team and I remember that was pretty hard work and I*

got tired. Ray was stronger and lasted longer. Ray did the harder jobs like shocking. I would drive a little F-12 International tractor pulling the binder. My Uncle Arthur would ride the binder and Ray and the hired man would do the shocking.[16] *My other jobs were chopping and hauling wood as well as [corn] cobs for burning in the cookstove.*

One harvest event stood out in Don's memory:

. . . one time we had a bunch of neighbors over on a Sunday afternoon, and there must have been at least four of us boys. We were pretty young yet, but we were walking down to where they had just finished cutting down a big field of flax. It was all laying on the ground and hadn't been shocked yet. We decided we would have a race and see who could shock a row of flax the fastest. I tell you; we got a lot of work done for just playing.

The difference in the ages of the four siblings and their job separation had a downside according to Norma. Most of her childhood contact was with her mother and her younger sister Ruth. In particular, she said she had little contact with her brother Ray who was four years older than Norma. She said,

By the time I was ready for high school, he had already left home. I often think now that I really didn't know Ray well, but I liked him back then. He was intelligent and was always interested in learning things. I think I would have enjoyed having conversations with him or learning from him.

The dustbowl years of the 1930s affected all farmers and their families. Storyteller Norma (Engstrand) Sandrock, however, recalled little change in her own life. Her explanation was simple,

I don't think that we as kids were even aware of it. We never had very much to begin with. It may have been during that time that some of our

A 1937 photo of the Hinderers visiting the Engstrands. Left to right: Gottlieb Hinderer, Don Engstrand, Carl Brenner (a Michigan Hinderer relative), Norma E., Ruth E. in front of Mary E., Katharine, and Martha Hinderer. Note the metal framework of the windmill behind Martha. Source: From the Martha Hinderer collection. Edited by author.

Katharine

relatives in the Twin Cities would send clothes out for us to wear. We had our own [garden and livestock] sources of food, so when I see the pictures of the long lines of people waiting for food, it was not something I experienced. ...there was no discussion about our family suffering either.

Don Engstrand's recollection differed in the detail of how farming changed during those depression years.

In those days, there was a lot more wheat grown around here, but that turned out to be a bad deal. In 1935 there was a big rust infestation and whole fields [of wheat] had to be burned up.[17] The previous year had been a drought year and only the wet slough bottoms had any crop at all. I think we got by because my uncle [Arthur] borrowed some money to buy feed. I know one time we got a semi-load of corn bundles from around Lac qui Parle Lake just to feed the cows. During that drought of 1934, my uncle [Arthur] decided our oats would never form a mature crop. To get something out of it, Ray and I were [told] to rake up the mowed oats and save it for feed. We did this by hand and part of my job was to be in the hayrack to stomp down [barefoot] the dry fluffy oats. The problem was that there was a lot of Russian thistle in there and they were already starting to get a little sharp so that was not a pleasant job. What we did save was fed to the animals. It wasn't good, but it was something.

THE ENGSTRAND'S FARMHOUSE

Storyteller Norma (Engstrand) Sandrock described the Engstrand farmhouse in detail.

Downstairs you entered through the [original] shanty into the kitchen. There was a pantry with a milk separator by the kitchen. [There was also] a cellar below with a dirt floor. I think there were rats in the cellar and poor mother had to go down

A photograph of the Engstrand house taken in about 1925. Source: Original photo courtesy of Norma (Engstrand) Sandrock. Edited by author.

there. We kept potatoes on a big pile on the dirt floor, and carrots too. There were also shelves for all the home-canned goods.

Norma continued:

After the kitchen there was a dining room followed by the living room. The stairway up to the bedrooms started in the living room. There was no central heating in that house. There was only one [fuel-burning heating] stove in the dining room and it was cold upstairs. You could see your breath. We had a windmill that pumped water from a well into [an elevated] tank and then into the house. So, we had running water in the house without electricity. Upstairs we had all of the bedrooms. We girls were in the same bedroom as my mother. There was another bedroom for my two brothers and another for the hired man. My uncle Arthur had his own bedroom.

Norma recalled that harvest time presented a need to hire extra labor.

During harvest season, the men went into town to get a hobo to come out and help with the work. The hobos would ride into Dawson on the train, and we would hire them to help with grain shocking and things like that. The hobos always had bedbugs, so we would always be looking for bugs when we changed the bedding. We would watch for them in the sheets and we lifted the mattress to look too. Mother and I worked together. I think she had a sprayer, or just picked them off. I don't think we had a bedbug problem in any other room, just the one for the hired help.

SCHOOL DAYS

The Engstrand children all attended the district school located about a mile from their farmhouse. Norma said,

We would cut across the fields and walk over the river to get there. Our usual path was through a neighbor's field. Our group would be myself and my brothers plus my friend Helen and her brother. They lived another mile from us, so they walked farther. In the winter when it was so cold, maybe thirty below, my Uncle Arthur would hitch up the horses to a sleigh. The neighbor [Helen's father] would come along to help with the horses. We kids were in the sleigh, all covered up. Our teacher lived at a neighbor's house and she would already be at school with the stove going.

Norma said their district school, like most, had eight grades. However, the students were often mixed with several grades working together. Norma revealed that she was often teamed with children in older grades, so she was more advanced than other students her age. One consequence of this was that her mother Mary decided to keep Norma at home a year before sending her to high school. Norma used that year to learn to play the piano. She said,

I got interested in piano because of my cousin Doris Lafere who lived on the Hinderer farm. Whenever we went there, I would ask Doris to play the piano for me. I begged and begged until my mother finally got me a piano. Our piano was in the living room, but there was no stove in there. It was so cold that I got my coat on and stayed in the room as long as I could. I was teaching myself to play. . . . when I got cold, I would come out and warm myself by the stove and then go back to the piano. . . . I think my fingering technique was not good because I [was self-taught and] did not realize how important it was. I might have done better, but at least I was good enough to play at my girlfriend's wedding.

The Engstrand children all graduated from Dawson High School. Norma said her oldest brother Ray rode a bus to the high school in Canby during his freshman year because there was no bus service to Dawson. After that first year, local bus service was provided and Ray was able to attend Dawson High School. When Norma was ready for high school, she rode the bus most days. She added that her brother Don sometimes drove her

Don Engstrand's 1940 Dawson High School graduation picture. Source: From the Doris Schlichting collection. Edited by author.

to school in their family car. Although she was capable of driving, Norma said she did not drive to school because she was too embarrassed. She said her family only had one car, and the other kids drove much nicer cars than the one that the Engstrands owned.

Like her older siblings, Ruth Engstrand attended and graduated from Dawson High School. Her graduation year was likely 1944. Regrettably, her high school graduation photo was not found in any family albums.

In April 1944, Mary Engstrand and her four children were pictured in a studio photograph. Mary Engstrand was 46 years old; Ray was 24, and Don was a few months shy of his 22nd birthday. Daughter Norma was not quite 20 years old and Ruth was 17.

Their Separate Ways

Ray b.1920. Ray Engstrand graduated from high school in 1938, near the end of the Great Depression.

Ray Engstrand's 1938 Dawson High School graduation picture. Source: From the Doris Schlichting collection. Edited by author.

Norma Engstrand's Dawson High School graduation picture believed to be from 1942. Source: From the Doris Schlichting collection. Edited by author.

Following graduation, Ray left home to attend the University of Minnesota in the Twin Cities. Don Engstrand recalled that while attending the university, Ray became ill with a blood infection. Don visited his older brother in the hospital. He believed that a newly available drug called sulfa was likely what saved Ray's life. Don said Ray's blood infection occurred just before the start of World War II and sulfa was the only available antibiotic. Ray's brush with death resulted in a heart murmur that persisted for the rest of his life.[18]

In the early 1940s, Ray completed his college studies and in 1950 was working in Minneapolis as a purchasing agent for the Cargill Company. In the 1950 U.S. Census, 30-year-old Ray Engstrand was living in Minneapolis with his aunt, Agnes Olson. Her career had been in nursing. She became a widow when her husband died in 1947.

In November of 1950, Ray Engstrand married Alice Krueger. Ray continued working for the Cargill Company until 1960 when he and his family moved to Sioux City, Iowa. He held managerial and sales positions for several companies in Sioux City during the remainder of his working years. Ray died in Sioux City in 1996.[19]

Don b.1922. Storyteller Don Engstrand graduated from Dawson High School in 1940. His graduation was about 18 months before America entered World War II. In April 1940, the U.S. Census listed 17-year-old Don living with his mother, his siblings, and his Uncle Arthur on the Engstrand farm. As required by law, Don registered for military service two years later at age 19. His enlistment date in the Army Air Corps was February 24, 1943.[20] Don's wartime experience will be explored in a later chapter.

Like his older brother Ray, Don completed a college education. After his service in World War II, he attended the St. Paul campus of the University of Minnesota. He graduated with a Bachelor of Science degree in 1948. Don was interested in farming and wanted to pursue the latest developments in agriculture. He worked in St. Peter, Minnesota, for Cargill, the same company his older brother Ray was working for in Minneapolis. Don's specialty interest was hybrid seed development.

Don said that around 1949, his Uncle Arthur sustained a serious injury while working on the Engstrand farm. Arthur requested that Don should come back home to manage the farm. It is interesting to note that Arthur's request to Don was similar to John Engstrand's request to Arthur many years earlier. As a result of Arthur's injury, Don moved from St. Peter back to his childhood home in Lac qui Parle County.

Don related that prior to agreeing to return home, he came to an understanding with his Uncle Arthur. He wished to modernize their farm and wanted Arthur to allow him to make those changes. Don said that Arthur offered no objection and happily gave him full control of the farm.

After Don was back home managing the farm, he began teaching a class in nearby Madison, Minnesota. The subject of his class was modern agricultural methods. His students were veterans like himself who had returned home at the conclusion of World War II. Don said he enjoyed giving back to his community and to the veterans he served with during the war years.

Don Engstrand married Lillian (Lysholm) Davidson in October 1982. Don was 60 years old and Lillian was 71. It was late in their lives, but they found years of enjoyment during their retirement. When Don formally retired from farming, he and Lillian lived in both Minnesota and Arizona. During the winter, they lived in the warmer climate of Mesa, Arizona. In summers, they lived in Dawson or at their cabin on Lake Miltona, five miles north of Alexandria, Minnesota.[21] Storyteller and veteran Don Engstrand died in Dawson, Minnesota, in April 2007. He is buried in the Dawson Cemetery.

Norma b.1924. Storyteller Norma (Engstrand) Sandrock graduated from Dawson High School with the intention of attending college like her two older brothers. However, her wishes were contrary to what her mother Mary could afford. Norma explained that most of the money her mother lived on came from government benefits following her husband Albert's death. As a compromise, Mary agreed to send Norma to a business school in Minneapolis.

While Norma was home from business school for the Christmas holidays, she had an attack of acute appendicitis. The surgical procedure was successful, but she developed phlebitis after the operation. Norma explained that she was told to remain still after the operation, and she followed those instructions "too" literally. The lack of movement caused blood clots to form in her legs. She was transferred to the Mayo Clinic where the phlebitis was diagnosed and treated correctly.

Even with appropriate treatment, Norma said she suffered from lingering leg problems and had to remain at home for two more years.

Norma said that after her medical problems resolved, she enrolled in an airline school in Kansas City. She estimated that she was about 21 or 22 years old at the time. When she graduated from airline school, she was hired by Northwest Airlines and moved back to Minneapolis to work for them. She said she ended up working as a Northwest travel representative for nearly 40 years. Her place of work was in a prominent hotel in downtown Minneapolis.

In the early 1960s, Norma's future husband, Milt Sandrock, came to see a friend who worked in the hotel where Norma was working. Norma and Milt

An April, 1944 studio photograph of Mary Engstrand and her four children. Rear – Norma on the left and Ray on the right. Seated – Mary, Ruth, and Don. Son Don was home on leave while serving in the Army Air Corps. See text for their ages. Source: From the Doris Schlichting collection. Edited by author.

were introduced to one another and then dated for several years. They were married on April 10, 1965. Following their marriage, Norma continued working for Northwest Airlines while Milt sold insurance and real estate. They lived in the Twin Cities area throughout their working years. Milt died in 2007. Norma (Engstrand) Sandrock died in 2021. She and Milt are both buried at Ft. Snelling National Cemetery in Minneapolis, Minnesota.

Ruth b.1927. Ruth was the youngest of the Engstrand siblings and the only child born to Mary and Albert after they returned to live on the Engstrand farm. Like her older siblings, Ruth attended the local district school followed by high school in Dawson. Her older sister Norma believed that Ruth had more difficult teenage years than her siblings. Regardless, Ruth graduated from high school in 1945.

Following high school, Ruth graduated from a beauty training school in 1947. She worked in that field most of her adult life. Ruth married Frank Motyka Sr. in Los Angeles, California, in 1953. Six years later, a 1959 city directory located Ruth and Frank living in Butte, Montana. Ruth eventually separated from her husband and relocated to the Twin Cities. In later years, she worked as a beautician in Madison, Minnesota. Ruth spent her retirement years living in Tucson, Arizona. She died in April 2017 in Dawson, Minnesota. Ruth is buried in Providence Valley Lutheran Church cemetery where she and her family attended church.[22]

Arthur, Mary, and the Engstrand Farm – The Later Years

When Don Engstrand took over management of the Engstrand farm in 1949, he inherited a productive business that had remained solvent during the Great Depression and subsequent war years. According to Don, this was no small feat.

Commodity prices were so low [during the depression] *that ear corn was often burned in place of corn cobs or wood in the kitchen stove.*

As economic conditions improved, Don recalled, "the farm buildings were remodeled and modernized. The farm looked good again." Don's Uncle Arthur had managed to save the family farm and had restored it to a respectable appearance.

Don said his Uncle Arthur knew the value of modernizing his farm business. For example, Arthur installed electricity as soon as it was available. Don said that during the summer of 1940, the local electrical company completed a spur line from Dawson along the roadway at the end of the Engstrand's driveway. When the spur line was completed, Arthur immediately tapped into the electrical system. As Don noted,

This was the beginning of great changes in rural family living. The instant lights, refrigerators, freezers, electric stoves, and electric irons were the first great benefits.

After Don assumed responsibility for the farm, his Uncle Arthur continued to live with the family in his retirement years. In fact, Arthur always lived in the home where he was born and raised. Arthur Engstrand died in early 1960, a few months before his 80th birthday. He is buried alongside other family members in Providence Valley Lutheran Church cemetery.

Mary Engstrand had moved with her family from Minneapolis to the Engstrand farm in 1924. During the later years of her disabled husband's life, Mary's sense of reality dictated that she must raise her children on this same farm. She accomplished this during a severe economic depression followed by World War II. Mary's decisions were often dictated by her limited financial resources. Considering the obstacles she faced, her achievements and those of her children were a tribute to her single-minded determination.

Mary Engstrand died June 10, 1981 on the Engstrand farm. She was 83 years old. Mary is buried with other family members in the Providence Valley Lutheran Church cemetery.

The burial marker of Mary (Hinderer) Engstrand in the Providence Valley Lutheran Church cemetery. Source: Photographed and edited by author.

Like his grandfather John and Uncle Arthur, Don Engstrand initiated many changes in the Engstrand farm business. He said that greater specialization was the trend in the 1950s. He built a mechanical feeding system, some silos, and enough feeders to raise up to 300 beef cattle at a time. Don said he also bought and rented additional land to supply the grains and silage needed to feed his cattle. Don, like his Uncle Arthur, was very active in his local community and farming affairs. He was a civic leader and served on the boards of multiple agriculture-related businesses in Lac qui Parle County, Minnesota.

Don was managing the Engstrand farm when it gained "Century Farm" status in 1976. For him, it was a proud achievement for the Engstrand family. He rightfully acknowledged the hard work and foresight of his grandfather John and his Uncle Arthur Engstrand. Don should have added his own name to the series of forward-thinking farmers who worked on this land for more than 100 years.

Don Engstrand said he retired from farming in 1978. During his retirement he was involved with several international agricultural development projects. His favorite study project was located at a farmer cooperative in Jamaica.[23]

In retirement, Don also continued to do maintenance work on the Engstrand farm. He had numerous hobbies including gathering and polishing agates found in nearby fields. He called himself a rockhound. Don did not have children of his own. Nevertheless, he was a role model to other family members and cared for his sister Ruth's son from childhood until he was an adult. Don also personally organized family gatherings that included several reunions of the Hinderer clan in his hometown of Dawson.

On a personal level, storytellers Norma and Don were extremely helpful and willing to share their family history. They were candid and thoughtful about their own lives during the depression and post-war years. Intelligence and noteworthy achievements were the hallmarks of the Engstrand branch of the Hinderer family.

Family Recipes

Emma's recipes (Appendix C) are reproduced as recalled or recorded by family members.

■ ■ ■

Notes

1. Roger Daniels, *Coming to America: A History of Immigration and Ethnicity in American Life*, 2nd ed. (New York: HarperCollins, 2002), 165.

2. Two writings contributed to this historical information. In 1984, Don Engstrand, son of Mary (Hinderer) Engstrand, wrote about his Engstrand grandparents' early years. Similarly, *Lac qui Parle County Pioneer Stories: 1871-1958* discussed the arrival of John Engstrand.

Statehood Centennial Committee, *Lac qui Parle County Pioneer Stories: 1871-1958* (Lac qui Parle County Schools, MN, 1958), https://archive.org/details/lacquiparlecount00unse/page/n5/mode/2up.

3. To locate Carver County, Minnesota, in Google Maps insert coordinates 44.814377, -93.788335 in the search box and click the search button.

4. To locate Belle Plaine, Minnesota, in Google Maps insert coordinates 44.625416, -93.766901 in the search box and click the search button.

5. To locate Benson, Minnesota, in Google Maps insert coordinates 45.316234, -95.608351 in the search box and click the search button.

6. Statehood Centennial Committee, *Lac qui Parle County Pioneer Stories: 1871-1958* (Lac qui Parle County Schools, MN, 1958), https://archive.org/details/lacquiparlecount00unse/page/n5/mode/2up.

7. To locate Providence Valley Church and cemetery, in Google Maps insert coordinates 44.834856, -96.144580 in the search box and click the search button.

8. To locate Dawson, Minnesota, in Google Maps insert coordinates 44.931162, -96.054495 in the search box and click the search button.

9. To locate Gustavus Adolphus college, in Google Maps insert coordinates 44.324800, -93.975996 in the search box and click the search button.

10. "U.S. Adjutant General Military Records, 1631-1976" (online database), *Ancestry.com* (Provo, UT: Ancestry.com, 2011), accessed February 28, 2023.

11. "U.S. Army Transport Service Arriving and Departing Passenger Lists, 1910-1939" (online database), *Ancestry.com* (Provo, UT: Ancestry.com, 2011), accessed January 31, 2023.

12. Albert's obituary appeared in the *Dawson Sentinel* on March 24, 1932. Access courtesy of the Dawson Public Library. In the public domain.

13. "U.S. Army Transport Service," *Ancestry.com*.

14. Albert Engstrand's death certificate listed the manner of his death as suicide.

15. See note 7 for mapping coordinates of Providence Lutheran Church and cemetery.

16. The Engstrand's binder cut the grain, moved it on a belt to one side, and tied it into bundles. These bundles were then piled together to form large shocks—larger stacks of bundles—that were later hauled to a threshing machine. Don's job was to drive the tractor that pulled the binder. Arthur rode atop the binder to assure it was cutting and binding correctly. Ray and the hired man stacked the bundles into shocks. It was a four man operation.

17. Wheat and other grain rust is a fungal disease that spreads by wind-blown spores. Control is difficult and burning fields was used to prevent the fungus from maturing and spreading the spores.

18. Prior to the availability of a wide spectrum of antibiotics, bacterial blood infection (sepsis) was often fatal. Those who survived frequently had heart abnormalities due to the bacteria forming colonies on a heart valve. The bacteria deformed the valve, thus leading to an audible heart murmur.

19. Information on Ray Engstrand's working years came from his Obituary.

20. "U.S. Department of Veterans Affairs BIRLS Death File, 1850-2010," *Ancestry.com*, iBeneficiary Identification Records Locator Subsystem (BIRLS) Death File/i. (Washington, D.C.: U.S. Department of Veterans Affairs; Provo, UT: Ancestry.com, 2011), accessed March 15, 2023.

21. To locate Lake Miltona, in Google Maps insert coordinates 46.042994, -95.367911 in the search box and click the search button.

22. Information about Ruth came from her sister Norma and from Ruth's obituary as published by Hansen and Dahl Funeral Home in Dawson, Minnesota, 2017. Accessed March 16, 2023.

23. Information about Don Engstrand and the farm were gleaned from Don's 1984 writing about the Engstrand Century Farm. This partially autobiographical work was sent by Don to the author. It is gratefully acknowledged.

CHAPTER 17

Our Greatest Generation—Hinderer Family Members in World War II

Timeline

1933 – Hitler seized political power in Germany

1935 – Mussolini's army invaded Ethiopia

1936 – Germany, Italy, and Japan formed an Axis agreement

1938, Dec. – Johnny Krug enlisted in the Navy

1939, Sep. – Germany invaded Poland. England and France declared war

1941, Dec. – Japan bombed Pearl Harbor. The U.S. declared war

1942, Jun. – Japan occupied two Aleutian Islands off Alaska

1942, Aug. – 1943, Feb. – The Battle of Guadalcanal

1942, Sep. – John Hinderer entered the Army

1942, Oct. – Bill Gjovig entered the Navy

1942, Nov. – U.S. forces landed in North Africa

1943, Feb. – Don Engstrand entered the Army Air Corps

1943, Jul. – Allied forces took control of Sicily

1943, Sep. – Italy surrendered; then German forces occupied Italy

1944, Jun. – D-Day landing in Normandy, France

1944, Aug. – Allied forces landed on the French Mediterranean coast

1945, Mar. – Allied forces crossed the Rhine River into Germany

1945, May – Germany surrendered

1945, Aug. – Japan surrendered

1945, Aug. – Johnny Krug was discharged from the Navy

1945, Sep. – John Hinderer was discharged from the Army

1945, Nov. – Don Engstrand was discharged from the Army Air Corps

1945, Dec. – Bill Gjovig was discharged from the Navy

1946 – Leonard Krug enlisted in the Navy

1950, Dec. – Bill Gjovig was recalled to active duty

1952, Feb. – Bill Gjovig was discharged from the Navy

FOUR HINDERER MEN

Four members of the Hinderer family fought in World War II. In the order of their military entry date, they were Johnny Krug, John Hinderer, Bill Gjovig,[1] and Don Engstrand. John Hinderer and Don Engstrand fought in the European war theater while Johnny Krug and Bill Gjovig were in the Pacific theater.

The dates these men began and ended their military service are included in the timeline at the beginning of this chapter. With the exception of Johnny Krug, they entered military service after the Japanese attack on Pearl Harbor in December 1941.[2]

JOHNNY KRUG, U.S. NAVY

Johnny Krug attended Canby High School through the end of his sophomore year. When school was out in the spring of 1935, 16-year-old Johnny began working at a hardware store in

Canby. He did not return to school that fall, and he never completed his high school education. Johnny enlisted in the Navy in early December 1938.

At age 19, Johnny left his home in Canby and traveled to Minneapolis, Minnesota. He wanted to join the U.S. Navy. He was first sent to the Naval Training Station at Great Lakes, Illinois, for basic training.[3] After he completed this boot camp, he was given the entry rank of Seaman 2nd Class.

Martha Hinderer, who was 32 years old in 1938, kept a handwritten log of her nephew Johnny Krug's years in the Navy. Martha listed some service dates and named the ships on which Johnny served. She guessed at other details such as when and where Johnny was at specific times. Her log was generally accurate, but it revealed how exact locations and dates were kept secret from soldiers' families.

In April 1939, Johnny received his first duty assignment aboard the USS *Utah*. The *Utah* was an aging battleship built in the World War I era. It was well beyond its battle-worthy years and had been converted into a ship used for training young seamen. A photo from 1940 showed the *Utah* equipped with small caliber deck guns that were used for training.

Navy muster lists tracked crewmembers on board specific ships and their job classification. Most were simple personnel lists, but some identified changes in rank or transfers to another vessel or duty station. Navy muster lists from late 1939 into early 1941 indicated that Johnny Krug

Martha Hinderer kept a hand-written log of her nephew Johnny Krug's location before and during World War II. Her note is generally accurate. Source: From the Martha Hinderer collection. Edited by author.

progressed through the enlisted ranks while aboard the USS *Utah*. In May 1941, Johnny was newly classified as a machinist's mate. This meant he had been trained to maintain and repair the ship's propulsion system.

On May 12, 1941, seven months before the attack on Pearl Harbor, Hawaii, Johnny was transferred from the USS *Utah* to the USS *Argonne*. The *Argonne* was classified as a supply ship. The

	of U.S.S. UTAH for the month ending 30th day of April, 1939,				
	1 NAMES (Alphabetically arranged without regard to ratings, with surname to the left and the first name written in full)	2 SERVICE NUMBER (The service number must under no condition be omitted)	3 Rating at Date of Last Report	4 Date of Enlistment	5 Place of Enlistment
1	JOYCE, Paul	337 11 75	A.S.	24 Jan 39	St. Louis, Mo.
2	KAMMAN, Harry A.	243 51 13	F1c	18 Feb. 36	Philadelphia, Pa
3	KAISER, Earl R.	337 11 70	A.S.	17 Jan 39	St. Louis, Mo.
4	KEGERREIS, Jarry N.	372 07 71	A.S.	24 Jan 39	Denver, Colo.
5	KIRKPATRICK, Dean E.	321 29 51	A.S.	25 Jan 39	DesMoines, Iowa
6	KISH, Alexander J.	102 60 10	MM2c	8 Apr 39	GuantanamoBay Cu
7	KNUTSON, Francis K.	321 13 96	F2c	16 Feb. 37	DesMoines, Iowa
8	KRUG, John M.	328 55 65	Sea2c	6 Dec 38	Minneapolis, Minn
9	KUNTZ, Phillip J.	328 56 53	A.S.	24 Jan 39	Minneapolis, Minn
10	LANHAM, Shelby R.	337 11 76	A.S.	24 Jan 39	St. Louis, Mo.
11	LA RUE, George W.	372 07 77	A.S.	24 Jan 39	Denver, Colo.
12	LEBER, William G.	321 29 36	A.S.	25 Jan 39	DesMoines, Iowa
13	LEMERT, Richard H.	321 29 49	A.S.	25 Jan 39	DesMoines, Iowa
14	LINK, Lee J.	321 20 52	F2c	12 Oct 37	DesMoines, Iowa
15	MC CLUNG, Robert H.	368 05 62	MM2c	12 Oct 38	MareIsland, Cal.
	6 Branch of service	7 Received, transferred, deserted, discharged, change of rating, death, or any other change of status	8 Date of occurrence in column 7	9 Vessel or station from which received, to what vessel or station transferred, where discharged and character of discharge, where deserted, and amount due or overpaid. Where died, cause of death and where and when buried. If raised and authority for same. If disrated, give cause; if on detached duty, give place of duty. If passenger, give purpose of travel and final disposition.	
1	USN	REC.	4/29/39	from USNTS Great Lakes, Ill. for duty.	
2	USN	TRAN	4/26/39	to Nav. Hosp San Diego, Cal for treatment.	
3	USN	REC.	4/29/39	from USNTS Great Lakes, Ill. for duty.	
4	USN	REC.	4/29/39	from USNTS Great Lakes Ill. for duty.	
5	USN	REC.	4/29/39	from USNTS Great Lakes, Ill. for duty.	
6	USN	TRAN	4/26/39	to USS DORSEY FFT USS PENSACOLA for duty.	
7	USN	TRAN	4/29/39	to USS OKLAHOMA for duty.	
8	USN	REC.	4/29/39	from USNTS, Great Lakes, Ill. for duty.	
9	USN	REC.	4/29/39	from USNTS, Great Lakes, Ill. for duty.	
10	USN	REC.	4/29/39	from USNTS, Great Lakes, Ill. for duty.	

This U.S. Navy record indicated Johnny Krug (#8 in the upper and lower sections of the page) was sent from the training center at Great Lakes, Illinois, for duty aboard the USS Utah on April 29, 1939. Source: "U.S., World War II Navy Muster Rolls, 1938-1949" online database (Lehi, UT: Ancestry.com), accessed August 31, 2023. Edited by author.

A 1940 photo of the aging battleship USS Utah. *The original large deck gun batteries had been replaced by smaller caliber guns used for training new seamen. Source: "80-G-547671 USS* Utah *(AG-16)," Naval History and Heritage Command, accessed August 30, 2023, https://www.history.navy.mil/our-collections/photography/us-navy-ships/battleships/utah-bb-31/80-G-457671.html. Edited by author.*

Argonne arrived in Pearl Harbor on the island of Oahu, Hawaii in August 1941. Machinist's mate Johnny Krug was aboard the *Argonne*. By chance, Johnny's old training ship, the USS *Utah*, was already docked at Pearl Harbor. Although both ships had small caliber guns mounted on their decks, neither of them was equipped for combat.

Several minutes before 8 o'clock on the morning of December 7, 1941, waves of Japanese warplanes began their raid on U.S. Navy ships and airfields near Pearl Harbor. There is no personal account of Johnny's whereabouts, but he was likely aboard the USS *Argonne*. In a written report following the raid, the *Argonne's* commander stated that there were no fatalities on his ship. He also claimed that sailors manning the *Argonne's* small caliber guns had shot down one Japanese aircraft.[4]

At the time of the air raid, the USS *Argonne* was berthed at a repair dock. The dock was across a narrow bay of water from Ford Island where the Japanese warplanes inflicted the most catastrophic damage. Those aboard the *Argonne* could clearly

A 1920s photo of the supply ship USS Argonne. *Source: "NH 58095 USS* Argonne *(AS-10) (EX-AP-4)," Naval History and Heritage Command, accessed August 30, 2023, https://www.history.navy.mil/content/history/nhhc/our-collections/photography/numerical-list-of-images/nhhc-series/nh-series/NH-58000/NH-58095.html. Edited by author.*

see the fiery destruction and loss of life across the bay.

Johnny Krug's former ship, the USS *Utah*, was berthed on the opposite side of Ford Island from the prime targets of the Japanese planes. According to later reports from the Japanese command, the USS *Utah* was never on their list of targets. However, the *Utah* was berthed at a location normally occupied by a combat-ready American aircraft carrier. The leading Japanese pilots recognized the defenseless *Utah* and did not release their torpedoes. However, six trailing planes attacked the *Utah* with full force. Two of their torpedoes struck the *Utah* causing it to list sharply and capsize. The attack on the USS *Utah* took the lives of 58 men, both officers and enlisted men.[5] Most likely, some of those who died were former shipmates known to Johnny Krug. In the aftermath of the destruction and loss of life at Pearl Harbor, the United States declared war on Japan and Germany.

After the attack on Pearl Harbor, Johnny Krug remained aboard the undamaged USS *Argonne* for four months. In early April 1942, Johnny was re-assigned to duty on a newly commissioned destroyer, the USS *Fletcher* (DD-445). Johnny and some of his *Argonne* shipmates left Pearl Harbor as passengers on a heavy cruiser, the USS *Indianapolis*. The cruiser's destination was New York harbor where the USS *Fletcher* was awaiting the arrival of its new crewmembers.

Records for the USS *Fletcher* indicate that it was built in a New Jersey shipyard and commissioned for duty on June 30, 1942.[6] Naval muster rolls from later that year stated that Johnny Krug began his duty on the *Fletcher* the same day it was commissioned.

The USS *Fletcher* was the lead *Fletcher*-class destroyer, and it served throughout the Pacific theater during the remainder of the war. It received 15 battle stars during World War II and later saw additional service during the Korean War.[7] From June 30, 1942 until his discharge in August of 1945, Johnny Krug was assigned to duty aboard the *Fletcher*.

From the east coast of the United States, the *Fletcher* sailed in a formation of war ships into the Pacific Ocean toward the Solomon Islands and the Philippines. By the summer of 1942, Japanese forces had already occupied the Philippines and were threatening to attack Australia. When the *Fletcher* arrived, it saw action at Guadalcanal, the largest of the Solomon Islands. Guadalcanal was an important steppingstone for the Japanese on their pathway to Australia. The eventual victory of

A snapshot-quality photo of the partly capsized USS Utah. *It was the ship Johnny Krug had previously served on. Fifty eight men aboard the* Utah *died during the December 7, 1941 air raid. Source: "80-G-266626 USS* Utah *(AG-16)," Naval History and Heritage Command, accessed August 30, 2023, https://www.history.navy.mil/content/history/nhhc/our-collections/photography/wars-and-events/world-war-ii/pearl-harbor-raid/attacks-off-the-west-side-of-ford-island/80-G-266626.html. Edited by author.*

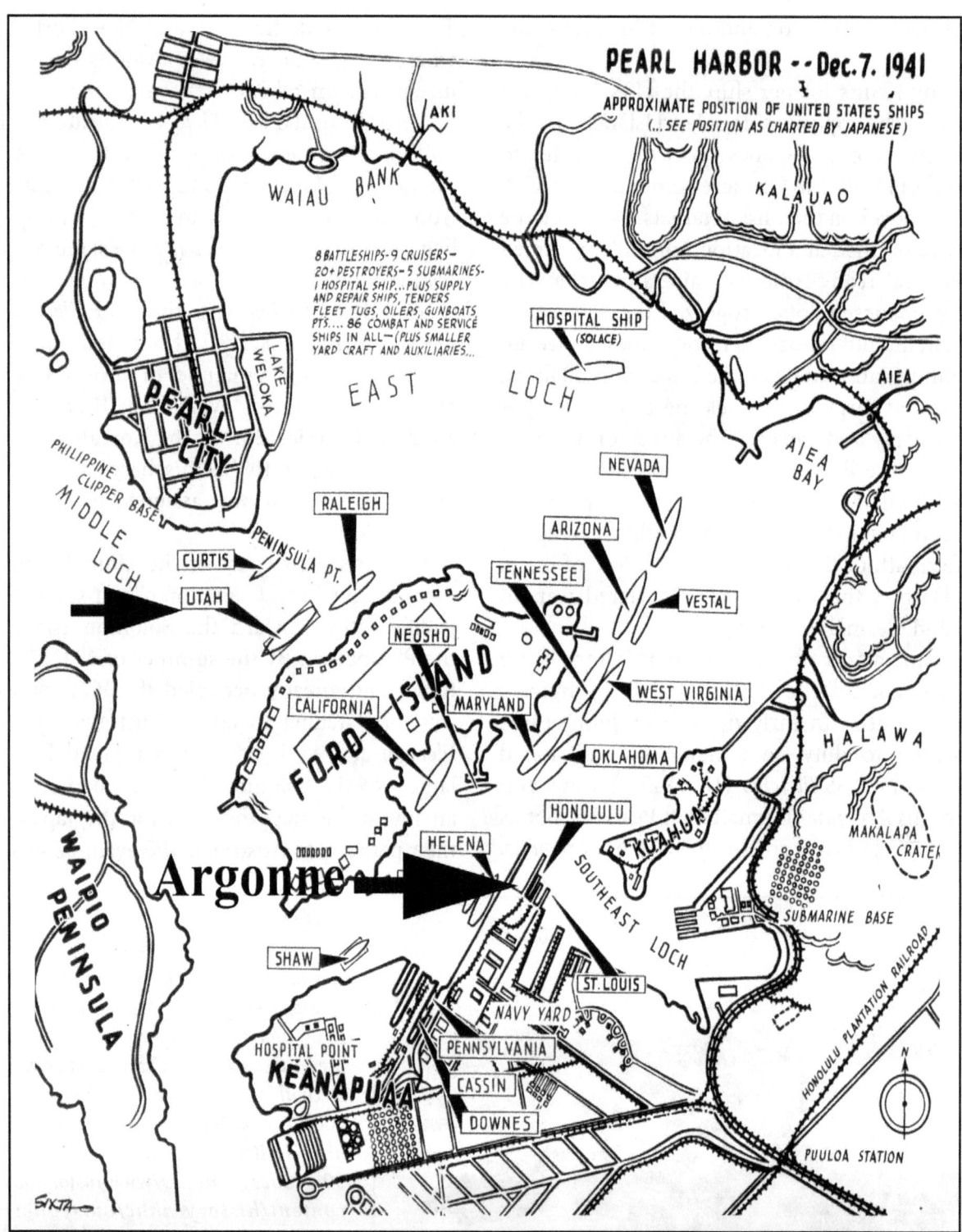

An illustration of the American ship positions in Pearl Harbor on December 7, 1941. A small arrow identifies Johnny Krug's former training ship, the USS Utah. The larger arrow identifies the location of Johnny's duty ship on that day, the USS Argonne. Source: "Map of Pearl Harbor, Hawaii, With Approximate Position of Ships on 7 December 1941," National Archives and Records Administration, public domain, accessed August 31, 2023, https://catalog.archives.gov/id/12009088. Edited by author.

Our Greatest Generation — Hinderer Family Members in World War II

A photo of the destroyer USS Fletcher *taken in July of 1942. It was commissioned on June 30, 1942. Johnny Krug was among the sailors assigned to duty on the same day it was commissioned. Source: "19-N-31243 USS* Fletcher *(DD-445)," Naval History and Heritage Command, accessed August 30, 2023, https://www.history.navy.mil/content/history/nhhc/our-collections/photography/numerical-list-of-images/nara-series/19-n/19-N-30000/19-n-31243-uss-fletcher--dd-445-.html. Edited by author.*

The December 31, 1942 muster record for the USS Fletcher. *Johnny Krug's listing indicated that he had boarded the* Fletcher *on June 30, 1942. The arrow identifies this date. Source: "U.S., World War II Navy Muster Rolls, 1938-1949" online database (Lehi, UT: Ancestry.com), accessed August 31, 2023. Edited by author.*

Katharine

Johnny Krug was number 26 in the upper section of his final service record. The lower section stated that on August 22, 1945, he was transferred from the Fletcher *to Camp Elliott north of San Diego for discharge processing. The day after Johnny's transfer, the USS* Fletcher *sailed out to sea. Source: "U.S., World War II Navy Muster Rolls, 1938-1949" online database (Lehi, UT: Ancestry.com), accessed August 31, 2023. Edited by author.*

A June 1945 photo of Johnny Krug taken in Canby when he was home on leave. Source: From the Doris Schlichting collection. Edited by author.

the Americans on Guadalcanal was considered a major turning point in the Pacific war effort.

During the remainder of World War II, the USS *Fletcher* took part in numerous naval battles and provided firepower support for shore invasions. It saw action in other Solomon Islands, in New Guinea, and in the Philippines. In late May 1945, the *Fletcher* returned to the Naval port in San Diego, California, for repairs. While the ship was being repaired, many of the sailors on the *Fletcher* were given leave. Johnny Krug used his leave time to return home to Canby. By the time the Japanese surrendered on August 15, 1945, Johnny had returned to the USS *Fletcher* docked in San Diego. On August 22, 1945, he was transferred from the USS *Fletcher* to Camp Elliott north of San Diego for discharge processing.

John Hinderer, Pvt. U.S. Army

On October 16, 1940, President Franklin Delano Roosevelt signed into law a peacetime military registration for males ranging in age from 21 to 35. John Hinderer was 33 years old and complied with the new selective service requirement. John's registration was dated the day the law went into effect.

John was conscripted into active military duty on September 14, 1942, nine months after the attack on Pearl Harbor and the U.S. declaration of war. John and other new recruits from western Minnesota traveled by bus to Ft. Snelling in the Twin Cities where they were officially inducted. John wrote his first letter home that evening, September 14, 1942:

Dear Folks,

We got here at about 10:30, that is to the bus station. Had dinner there, beef roast and blueberry pie. Then an Army truck took us out here to the Fort [Snelling]. Had a lecture and a little examination and then had more talking. After that we had supper. Here they call it chow.

Then we got our bunks. Then more talking on how to make our beds and what all we had to do, what officers we had to salute and all kinds of things. Then had to make up our beds. It won't be so hard after we get used to it.

Don't send any mail here yet as we may get moved in a couple of days. . . . Will write more later.

With love, John

Three days later, John and fellow inductees were on a troop train destined for Ft. Bliss in El Paso, Texas. Ft. Bliss was the training facility for a newly organized anti-aircraft gunnery unit. John wrote that his train arrived in El Paso on September 20, 1942. His letter home described the train ride from Minneapolis to Ft. Bliss:

Fort Bliss, Tex.
Sep. 20, 1942

Dear Mother & all,

We got on the train in Mpls. at about 5 Thurs. evening and really got started at six. Got about 50 miles or so out of Mpls. and had to stop for a washout. Did not get started again until 1:30 that night. ...there were 160 of us, had 5 cars for the men, all Pullman cars. There were 34 in our car. Then they had cooks car, supply car and another car. We had our mess kits and canteen cups and they would bring the eats right to our seats. After eating they had hot water at the end of the car where we could wash our dishes. We ran short of bread, but at Kansas City 6 cars of men got on and so we traded sugar for their bread.

We were not allowed to leave the car or go into the next car all the way down, and we had to have either the windows or screens down. Lights out at 9 o'clock. This was a troop train.

After Kansas City I was in No. 1 car right behind the engine. Didn't get much sleep after we got started.

The country kept getting worse the farther we came out. Western Kansas is nothing but hills,

The front side of John Hinderer's military registration card. Source: "U.S., WWII Draft Cards Young Men, 1940-1947" online database (Lehi, UT: Ancestry.com), accessed September 12, 2023. Edited by author.

The reverse side of John Hinderer's military registration card. It listed his physical description and was dated the day the registration law went into effect, Oct. 16, 1940. Source: "U.S., WWII Draft Cards Young Men, 1940-1947" online database (Lehi, UT: Ancestry.com), accessed September 12, 2023. Edited by author.

sand, rocks, sage brush and a little grass. About 4 PM we got to Trinidad Colorado. From there we crossed a ridge of mountains to Raton New Mexico. Going to the top there were 3 big engines in front and one behind. Sure was nice going through there. On top we went through a tunnel, quite a long one. . . . New Mexico seems to be just plains and hills what I saw of it.

Got to El Paso at about 8 o'clock. El Paso is a pretty town. There are about 30,000 people in it. It is a half mile from the Mexican border and Ft. Bliss is 5 miles north of El Paso. This all lays sort of in the Rio Grande valley which is maybe 10 miles wide.

. . . We are in a new camp. There had been only 19 men here before we came. [We were assigned] new bunk houses, they are 14' by 14'. When we got here this morning there was just a little gas heat stove and four locker trunks in each house. One fellow is from Echo and one from Kenyon [both in Minnesota] that are with me. We were together on the train too. They slept in the lower berth and I in the upper on the train. Then there is another fellow that was in the same car. All are nice men. Well, we each got new cots, new mattresses, sheets, pillow and case, 1 blanket and 1 comforts.[8] This is everything new. The commander said the guns we will use will have to be made yet.

When I get these letters all straight I can tell you exactly what each means. My new address is: [first] *put my name, Btry B 533 Sep. CA Bn, Fort Bliss, Texas. Sep stands for special CA,* [coast artillery], *Bn I don't know.*[9] . . . *He mentioned the different guns, but I don't remember them all.*

The eats here are not as good as they were at [Ft.] *Snelling.*

With love, John
Pvt. John Hinderer
Btry B 533 Sep CA Bn
Fort Bliss, Texas

When it was fully manned, the 533rd Anti-aircraft Battalion had 755 enlisted men and a cadre of 39 officers. It consisted of four firing batteries identified by the letters A, B, C, and D. John was in B battery. The 533rd Battalion was deliberately unattached to any larger Army group. This allowed the entire battalion or any one of the four batteries to be deployed to wherever they were needed in the war theater.

Each of the four firing batteries was eventually equipped with eight "Bofors" 40mm guns and eight machine guns.[10] These weapons were designed to be mobile and could be moved to a new location within 15 minutes. The guns used by the 533rd were intended to destroy enemy aircraft, but they could also be used against ground forces.

By late October 1942, John's unit had received their newly manufactured weapons and had begun field training in the New Mexico desert north of Ft. Bliss. He wrote home describing his experience:

Fort Bliss
Oct. 24, 1942

Dear Martha & all,

This is Saturday evening, 6:45 now. We go by mountain time here.

Well, we got back from out in the field, or I should say desert yesterday evening about 4:30. Last Monday morning the battalion left about seven o'clock. There were between seven and eight hundred men all together. We had to carry our canteen with water, cartridge belt and rifle, field bag with raincoat, towel and a few extra mess kit things. They hauled [by vehicle] *our barracks bags with blankets, tents and extras,* [such] *as coats and underwear and socks. I wore one pair you sent down and they were just fine. I had them and another light pair over the white ones yesterday on the way back.*

Walked 26 miles from seven in the morning until four thirty. We stopped ¾ hour at noon and 10 minutes of every hour [to] *rest. Some fellows get blisters on their feet but mine were fine.* [I] *get a little tired. All the men from B btry. walked all the way.*

On Monday we walked out [into the desert] *ten miles.* [We] *got there at noon and stayed that night. Tuesday morning, we were ready to go to the firing range at six o'clock. That was 26 miles from where we were. Our gun section got to shoot a while. An airplane pulled a canvas along behind it and that is what we would shoot at. Sounded loud at first but we soon got used to it.*[11] *Wednesday we walked 16 miles. Thursday we went to the target range for a while and had field practice and Friday walked back.*

I slept [in a two-man tent] *with the fellow from N. Dakota named Rassing. The first night was quite cool but after that it was fine. We each had 2 wool blankets and a comfort and then we put the raincoat over the front so it was quite warm. It is quite a thing to get dressed, take down the tent and roll up the bedding and get everything ready to move, also get in line to get the eats and to wash mess kits and do it all in the dark, at least in the morning. We sometimes build fires.*

. . . Today we got four new machine guns and we had to clean them up and get them ready. Tomorrow morning 32 of us [will] *have breakfast at six and leave for the rifle range again at 6:30. This is 4 miles out. Will be back at noon. Two of the fellows that were with me in the other hutment*[12] *went to the canteen and brought some*

ice cream so our bunch, the five of us, talked and ate. It is 9:15 now. Was going to write to Emma [John's sister Emma Krug] but guess I better go to bed tonight.

They brought mail out once a day. We still have no table, am writing on a chair now. Will close now. Write when you can.

With love, John

John wrote letters to his mother Katharine or twin sister Martha at least once a week and twice some weeks.[13] He mentioned receiving letters as well as boxes of food and clothing from the Hinderer farm, from his siblings, and from other family members. He wrote that he also received both letters and cash from Hinderer relatives living in Michigan.

The urgency of the war effort impacted everyone in America. People who lived comfortably at home were told to forget differences, reject rumors, and expect hard labor every day of the week. In his "Fireside Chat" two days after the attack on Pearl Harbor, President Franklin Delano Roosevelt said it plainly,

We are now in this war. We are all in it—all the way. Every single man, woman, and child is a partner in the most tremendous undertaking of our American history. We must share together the bad news and the good news, the defeats and the victories… Every citizen, in every walk of life, shares this same responsibility. The lives of our soldiers and sailors—the whole future of this nation—depend upon the manner in which each and every one of us fulfills his obligation to our country.

Roosevelt's words were taken to heart by members of the Hinderer family.

In early December 1942, one year after the attack on Pearl Harbor, John speculated about coming home on leave for Christmas. For him, at least, this did not happen. Instead, he spent the holiday at Ft. Bliss where he was taught how to drive and maintain an Army truck. His B battery was then sent into the New Mexico desert for shooting practice using both the 40mm Bofors anti-aircraft guns and their machine guns.

In the early months of 1943, some of the men who were over 38 years of age were discharged home. John was 36, so he remained with his batterymates at Ft. Bliss. His letters home included snapshots of himself and his friends. In these letters, you can sense some boredom with the everyday tasks but

John Hinderer sent this photo home in late 1942. The two-man tents and the troops preparing for their training maneuvers were shown. Source: The John Hinderer collection. Edited by author.

John Hinderer (far right) and his Ft. Bliss training buddies in the New Mexico desert. The photo was dated November 26, 1942. Source: The John Hinderer collection. Edited by author.

Fortunately, the movement of John's 533rd Battalion was methodically archived in military records. Although these files were classified as "secret" for many years after World War II, they were eventually made available to the public.[14]

On February 18, 1943, three days after John's final letter from Ft. Bliss, the entire 533rd Battalion left Texas in three troop trains headed to the east coast. The colonel in command later wrote that it was supposed to have been a secret departure and journey. However, a band from town played farewell marches and people along the route gave the troops magazines and sandwiches. The country was united behind the young troops on their way to Africa and Europe.

The 533rd Battalion left Brooklyn harbor on February 28, 1943 aboard the R.M.S. *Andes*, a also some anxiety. The soldiers in the 533rd knew they would soon be shipped overseas, but they could not know when it would be.

John's letters from Ft. Bliss also included references to a few fellow recruits living in the small buildings they called hutments. The command at Ft. Bliss gave each soldier a booklet so fellow soldiers could enter their names, where they came from, and make a few comments. It became a memento of their months at Ft. Bliss. John saved his own booklet which contained several pages of entries listing his new friends. Most of the soldiers in John's booklet were from the upper Midwest and, like John, many had been farmers.

John's final letter from Ft. Bliss was dated February 15, 1943. It contained only routine information without a hint of when his battalion might be sent overseas. His next letter was dated November 15, 1944, 21 months later. No doubt John wrote many letters home during this time, but they were either lost or destroyed.

John Hinderer's official military portrait taken at Ft. Bliss, Texas. Source: From the Doris Schlichting collection. Edited by author.

Katharine

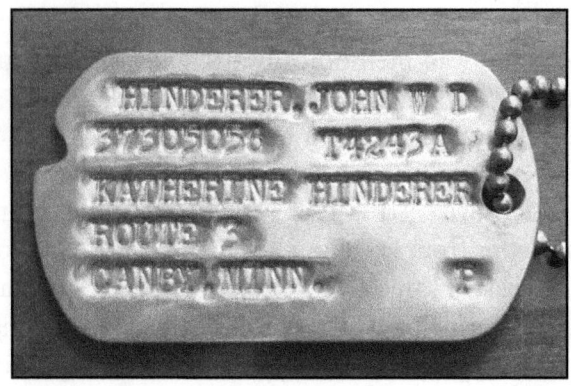

John Hinderer's "dog tag" identification was worn at all times. The name and address of his next-of-kin (his mother Katharine) was stamped below his military service number. Source: From the Doris Schlichting collection. Photographed and edited by author.

British ocean liner that had been converted into a troop carrier. Officially, there were 4000 troops on board, but John's estimate was double that number. Despite having no escort ships, the ocean liner made the trans-Atlantic voyage without incident.

John described conditions aboard the R.M.S. *Andes*. He said,

There were five decks, and we were lucky because it was a passenger [cruise] ship, so it was better. Of course, they had changed it so all the fancy places like the dance hall were filled with three-high bunks. We had been out about two days when the guy [bunked] above me woke me up and said the ship had started to first go one way, then another way, then it would slack up or go faster. I guess they were afraid of submarines. We had started by going 600 miles straight south to get out of the main danger area. It took nine days to get across.

Official military records agreed with John's story. The R.M.S. *Andes* landed in Casablanca, French Morocco on March 9, 1943. The 533rd Battalion was then split into its four batteries and assigned guard duty near Casablanca. John estimated he spent at least two months in and around Casablanca. The battalion could not be deployed to more distant locations until their anti-aircraft guns

A page from John Hinderer's memento booklet of Ft. Bliss friends. Source: From the John Hinderer collection saved by Doris Schlichting. Photographed and edited by author.

Our Greatest Generation — Hinderer Family Members in World War II

A snapshot of John Hinderer and three of his buddies in dress uniforms at Ft. Bliss. Left to right: John Hinderer, Iverson, Rassing, and Mehrens. Iverson was later stationed with John on Sardinia. Source: From the Doris Schlichting collection. Edited by author.

arrived. According to camp rumor, the ship carrying their guns across the Atlantic had been sunk. When they finally received guns, the 533rd was deployed to guard port areas along the Atlantic coast of French Morocco. Next, the battalion was shipped eastward to locations along the Mediterranean coast of Africa including Tunisia, Algeria, and as far east as Iran. Their anti-aircraft guns were deployed to guard strategic facilities such as airports and seaports. John added, "Most of the time, we didn't know where they were sending us." Their last African deployment was guarding the port at Bizerte, Tunisia, the northernmost city along the Mediterranean coast of Africa.[15]

The Army's original plan was for the 533rd Battalion to become part of the

John purchased this 1944 picture postcard in La Maddalena, Sardinia where he was stationed. The deep water harbor is in view with the island of St. Stephano across the harbor. Source: From the John Hinderer collection. Edited by author.

mid-1943 campaign to retake Sicily. However, the battalion commander later recorded that the fighting in Sicily was completed so quickly that his unit was never needed there.[16] Instead, they remained in Bizerte, Tunisia where unit records indicated they defended the port against numerous strafing attacks by enemy aircraft.

The four batteries of the 533rd departed Africa in November 1943. John's B battery was deployed to guard the deep-water harbor at La Maddalena, a city located on an island off the northern tip of Sardinia.[17] John described this deployment,

La Maddalena [harbor] had deep water about two miles [long] by a half mile [wide] and our ships would come in there with supplies. It was deep enough for the big ships and it was protected from the wind. There were usually five or six of those big ships in the harbor unloading supplies and we were the protection for them. . . . Mostly the Germans would be flying over taking pictures at night so we couldn't see them. You could hear them come in real low by the water and then you could see them take flash pictures. They were probably only four or five hundred feet up. We were right by the water with our guns.

John wrote that B battery set up camp near the La Maddalena waterfront. John's unit included 200 men, their anti-aircraft weaponry, and all of their support systems. Altogether, B battery's encampment required a substantial physical space. John said their waterfront location was within walking distance of the town of La Maddalena.

The soldiers were housed in large tents that had wooden planks for flooring. John wrote that the camp amenities were meager. The men strung a few electric lights inside their tent and were issued a small stove that gave off a little heat. Weather permitting, the soldiers ate chow outside the tents. John said that when they first set up the tents, there were no army cots to sleep on. He wrote "... there isn't any straw here for our bed sacks so I rigged up a bed out of [paper] sacks, it's softer than boards anyway." When the weather warmed and the mosquitoes hatched in the spring, the men all slept under nets and took daily medication to prevent malaria.

John's letters to his sister Martha often contained a list of specific items he needed. It was Martha's task to buy them, if she could find them, and ship them to John. The lists included sundries such as razor blades, toothpaste, hand cream, soap, and shaving cream. John also asked for hometown newspapers and magazines. The boxes sent to John took one to two months to reach B battery in La Maddalena. Edibles like candy, gum, homemade sweets, and even cheese were shipped to John by many family members.

In early 1944 while stationed at La Maddalena, John's B battery received instructions on how to identify newer enemy aircraft. They were also taught how to use updated sighting systems for their anti-aircraft weapons. The military records connected to B battery listed only occasional episodes of enemy plane alerts. With so little combat activity, the troops organized intramural sporting events to pass the time.

John spent one year stationed in Sardinia. He wrote at least 75 letters home during that year.[18] His letters described the island and the Italians living there. In an April 1944 letter he wrote, "The land here is mostly mountains and rock with small patches [in some valleys] where they farm." He added,

Most of the work is done with oxen or by hand . . . the farm women chop wood if they have some, and they wear square wool cloths on their heads [for sun protection].

He said the people in the countryside were poor and traveled along the roads in carts pulled by donkeys. John noted,

The buildings here are all made of stone or brick with heavy plaster. The roofs are all tile and most

of the floors are stone. That's about all there is here is stone anyway.

As the spring changed into summer, John's letters described the many seasonal fruits grown on the island. The troops could buy ripened fruit at local markets to supplement the mostly dreary military rations. With La Maddalena located at seaside, fish provided a large part of the local diet. The soldiers could buy fish to cook back at camp, or they could order the day's catch in local cafes.

During his many months in La Maddalena, John became friends with a family named Spillo. He said,

They [the Spillo family] had something like a wine joint and we would go into town for some wine. It was just a little place no bigger than one room. This [Spillo] family lived a couple of blocks away in a tiny little place. They had two kids in there too. . . . I got pretty well acquainted with them. If it got dark before I left, I would have to walk back to the tents through the dark narrow streets. There was always a blackout, so there was no light at all. I would have a knife or something like that, but toward the last I got a Berretta.[19] The fatigue pants I wore were wide and I sewed a little patch of cloth on the side so the little gun would just slip inside. I never had to use it. There were no Germans there, but the Italians were hurting for clothes and they might just want to get your clothes.

John spent most of his time in Sardinia at La Maddalena. However, in early April 1944, B battery traded duty locations with another anti-aircraft battery. They moved to the town of Sassari, an inland city 60 miles southwest of La Maddalena.[20] This temporary switch lasted only one month.

The June 1944 Allied D-Day invasion along the beaches of Normandy, France brought a tidal shift in the western European war theater. Despite a great loss of life, Allied forces secured the Normandy beachhead and inched eastward. It was the beginning of recapturing France from German occupation. Two months later, combined Allied forces assaulted German-controlled cities along the French Mediterranean coast. This created yet another front for the German army to defend. The Mediterranean coast of France would become the landing site for Allied supplies and troops such as John's unit.

In early August 1944, John was given a week of leave from his daily duty. He was sent to Cagliari, Sardinia, a coastal city at the southern tip of the island.[21] He sent a letter home on August 5th,

I'm really taking it easy. Having a week off with nothing to do but eat, sleep, and bum around. There is a nice beach here where we can swim ... can take in three [movies] a day but usually see only one or two. We drive to town for a while most every day.

John Hinderer kept this snapshot photo of the Spillo family he befriended while stationed in La Maddalena, Sardinia. On the back was written: "Signora Spillo, Emanuelita, gigi. Sep44." Source: From the John Hinderer collection. Edited by author.

Katharine

The slow pace and relative safety of John's duty at La Maddalena ended in early October, 1944. B battery broke camp at La Maddalena and boarded a military transport ship to Cagliari, Sardinia. This was the same city where John had been on leave only a few months earlier. John was not allowed to disclose his unit's movement to a new location. However, in a letter written before leaving La Maddalena, he described his duty as "cleaning up" [the camp]. This vague wording passed the censor's inspection. Whether Katharine and Martha understood John's meaning is unknown.

By November 15, 1944, B battery had boarded a transport ship once again. They sailed north along the coast of Sardinia and temporarily returned to La Maddalena harbor. John wrote about their return,

We stopped for a day at La M. [La Maddalena], could not get off the boat but quite a few from the town rowed out with small boats to the ship, was pretty good to see those again that we were with for about a year. When we [had] left the first time [a month earlier in October], I didn't think we would ever get back that close again.

John's many letters from Sardinia revealed a deep discontent with Army life. In his letters to his mother and Martha, he compulsively identified every letter he had received since he last wrote. He also listed family members who had not written. In one letter, John revealed that he liked to write return letters immediately after he received new mail. The natural outcome of this practice was that John was always waiting for letters from family members.

John's many questions to both Martha and his mother were centered on news about neighbors at home, the weather there, and the status of the crops. His mind was clearly focused on the home farm. In part, this could be attributed to avoiding subjects the censors would not allow. However, the wording he used suggested some degree of jealousy toward those who had not been conscripted or were serving stateside. John was older than nearly all of his fellow draftees, and he did not write about a close relationship with soldiers in his unit. In 75 letters, the only soldier's name he mentioned was "Iverson," who was a friend from his training days at Ft. Bliss.

Katharine Hinderer wrote several carefully worded letters to her son John inquiring how she might help him obtain a release from military service. John instructed her to have a local attorney compose a letter to John's superiors requesting his release. Katharine sent such a letter to John which he delivered to his commanding officer. The Captain of John's unit explained to him the nearly impossible process of achieving an early release during wartime. He said it would require testimonial letters from neighbors at home documenting extreme family hardship due to John's absence. The request would then be bumped up the chain of command and eventually to Washington D.C. for final approval. The Captain's explanation of this elaborate procedure extinguished any further discussion of an early discharge.

In late 1944, all four batteries of the 533rd Battalion landed in the city of Marseilles along the French Mediterranean coast. Their anti-aircraft guns were needed for the Allied push northward through France and eventually into Germany.

Once they landed in Marseilles, John's 533rd Battalion became attached to the Seventh United States Army. Originally under the command of General George S. Patton, the Seventh Army had defeated German General Rommel in North Africa. They had then taken Sicily in the summer of 1943 and drove the Italian army northward out of southern and central Italy.

The re-vitalized French resistance fighters also joined the Allied soldiers in the south of France. These combined forces slowly pushed the German army northward from Marseilles. By mid-October 1944, the Seventh Army had advanced 400 miles northward and joined the Allied forces fighting from Normandy eastward. It was one month later, in mid-November of 1944, that John and the 533rd anti-aircraft battalion landed in recently recaptured Marseilles, France.

John's letters home pick up the narrative after he landed in Marseilles. Most of these letters were inside small envelopes, but a few arrived home by what was known as V-Mail (Victory Mail).[22] The soldier's letters were always screened by military censors looking to remove any reference to specific locations or strategic war activities.[23]

15 November 1944 France

John sent this letter to his mother by V-Mail a few days after landing in Marseilles, France. The return address, the date, and the general location are in the upper right. The censor's stamped approval is in the upper left. Source: Courtesy of Becci Fischer. Edited by author.

After they landed in Marseilles, John's 533rd Battalion was transported via convoy to the front lines in northeastern France. The Allied forces were pushing eastward toward the Rhine River border between France and Germany. German aircraft were strafing the highways used by the Allies to supply their front lines. The 533rd had the task of engaging these airplanes so supplies could get through to the frontline troops of the Seventh Army.

In mid-December 1944, the Allies reached the Rhine River. John's 533rd Battalion was split into its four batteries which were then reattached to the Allied frontline ground units. The placement of the four batteries stretched for 20 miles along the Rhine River border.[24] John later recalled that his battery first guarded supply roadways and communications lines near Haguenau[25] on the French side of the Rhine River.

During the winter of 1944/1945, what became known as the Battle of the Bulge was fought on the French side of the Rhine River. A surprise German counter-attack first punched through the thinly deployed Allied forces. This initial German attack was followed by weeks of intense fighting and a great loss of life.

John said his anti-aircraft group was positioned behind the frontlines and rarely engaged in ground combat. Nevertheless, both Allied and German forces occasionally occupied parts of the same town. John said the two armies usually did not engage one another. As he put it, "It was more like if you stay on your side, then I'll stay on mine."

John wrote home to his twin sister Martha on February 10, 1945. He could not disclose his exact location in France, but he described his daily routine:

Feb 10, 1945
France
Miss Martha Hinderer
Rt. 3. Canby Minnesota

Dear Martha and All,

... Well, how is everyone there now? Am OK here. Got your letter of 23 and 27 yesterday and today the News from Aug and Sep. Most is old but a lot of it is new to me...

I have been working in the kitchen since the first of the year. Liked it alright during the winter when it was so cold as it's not very nice to have to stay on [manning] the gun at that time. The other fellow that helps me and I get up at five in the morning and are on the gun until seven, then start breakfast. This other fellow, he is from Texas, does a lot of trucking so isn't here so very much. It's quite a job when we move, packing everything up, putting tents up and down, especially if the weather is bad.

It's pretty hard to buy anything here, potatoes is about all there is quite a lot of. Am staying upstairs in a house, a family below with 4 kids. Also, some chickens and rabbits [are in] the barn with the house along the side. I don't go to town very often, the most [of them] are not much of towns. It's where all the farmers live with a church and probably a few stores or so in it, depending on how big it is. Most all their names have a "heim" or something like that on the end of them.

Will close for now, may go to church in the morning. Write when you can.

With Love To All, John.

The fighting back and forth across the Rhine River continued until March 1945 when, for the final time, the German Army was driven out of northeastern France. John said that once his unit crossed the Rhine, they moved quickly through southwestern Germany. With their constant movement and reassignments, even a 200-man unit like John's B battery was spread thinly over many miles of German countryside.

Back in the U.S., a hometown newspaper ran a story about Lac qui Parle County men assigned to the 533rd Battalion. The somewhat boastful tone of the newspaper story contrasted with the official records of enemy airplanes damaged or destroyed. The original battlefield records were lengthy and meticulously detailed. Each claim of a destroyed or even damaged airplane was accompanied by many pages of testimony. Soldiers who witnessed the event were required to submit a written account of what they saw and the reason they believed the enemy plane was destroyed or damaged. Some claims even included hand-drawn illustrations of the anti-aircraft gun positions, the pathway of the airplane(s), and the location of any visualized crash. Unlike newspaper stories, battlefield records were detailed factual documents.

Battlefield records also listed casualties for the 533rd Battalion. Even though their anti-aircraft gun positions were some distance from frontline combat, they did suffer casualties. From March 1943 through May 1945, two battalion soldiers were killed, three were seriously wounded and 16 were listed as "lightly wounded in action."

John's letters home during this time continued to dwell on mundane topics such as his kitchen duty, clothing needs, and questions about life back on the Hinderer farm. He was not allowed to write about war activities, and he did not often cross that line. Only rare letters had a word or two cut out by the censors who screened every sentence he wrote.

The area of southwestern Germany that John and the 533rd Battalion entered was well known to John's parents. His letters to his mother Katharine could not reveal his exact location, but he later recalled that he saw road signs for Ulm, a city only 30 miles southeast of the Hinderer family's former home in Brend.

> **BRILLIANT 533rd INCLUDES LOCAL MEN**
>
> Sixth Army Group, Germany— The thrill that comes with sinking the first shot in the bulls-eye is shared by four Lac qui Parle boys, members of the 533rd anti aircraft battalion. They are Cpl. Albert A. Ohm, Nassau; Pvt. Thomas O. Olson and Pfc. Orville L. Moe of Madison; and Pfc. John W. Heiner of Canby.
>
> While standing a recent "watch on the Rhine" in support of the U. S. Seventh army in General Jacob L. Devers' 6th army group, a section of one of the battalion's batteries fired a single round and bagged an ME-109.
>
> The single-shot action is hardly routine for these ack-ack men. In numerous other engagements, their 40-mm. Bofors and multiple-mount 50-cal. machine-guns have poured a withering fire from deep-dug camouflaged emplacements at enemy aircraft.
>
> With organization streamlined to match the unit's mobility and speed, the 533rd, commanded by Lt. Col. Claude A. Dance, Shreveport, La., has acted in various roles of anti-aircraft defense and anti-tank defense.
>
> "Assignments have included protection of bridges and headquarters and support of infantry and field artillery," said Col. Dance. "Accustomed to fighting in forward areas, my men recently began protecting one bridge before the engineers even built it."
>
> Activated in 1942 at Fort Bliss, Texas, the 533rd began foreign service February 28, 1943, landing at Casablanca. At Bizerte, gun crews fought off as many as 100 attacking planes in four raids. The battalion spent almost a year on Sardinia, protecting airfields and harbor installations, before entering southern France last November.

In early 1945, a hometown newspaper carried this story about soldiers in the 533rd Battalion who were from Lac qui Parle County, Minnesota. In the first paragraph, John Hinderer's name was misspelled as John W "Heiner." Otherwise, the article is accurate in recounting the places John's battalion had been deployed. Source: From the John Hinderer collection. The person who originally cut out this article and the newspaper it appeared in were not identified. Edited by author.

John's fluency with the dialect spoken in southwestern Germany served him well.[26] He said,

We weren't supposed to talk with [the German farmers], but I could speak German, so what the heck, I did. They were all pretty decent. We could buy wine from them.

He went on to recall,

One time we were camped a good mile out of town. Some of the guys took their dirty clothes in to town for women to wash. That night about 8 o'clock we got notice that we had to move because the Germans were making a drive toward us. So, we got our stuff ready fast, but then [we] thought about the clothes in town. The sergeant said I should go along [go with the soldier to retrieve his clothes because John could speak the language] and by the time we got there it was after midnight. The woman [who did the washing] was upstairs and looked out the window. She dropped the bags [of clean clothes] down to us. We beat it back to camp, but our group had already left. We didn't know what to do, so we just started walking. Pretty soon some other [U.S.] soldiers picked us up and took us over to our guys. So, we almost lost our outfit, but we were just lucky.

John later recalled,

Once in a while we would find a German soldier that had stayed behind and was hiding out. We had dogs to sniff out any [enemy] soldiers. When we found them, we would send them back to our prisoner of war camps.

The 533rd Battalion records documented encounters with enemy airplanes in northeastern France as early as December of 1944. However, the frequency of these encounters increased dramatically in March and early April of 1945 when the battalion pushed deeper into southwestern Germany.

In a letter to his sister, Martha, dated March 5, 1945, John wrote that he had been sent back into

France for rest and recuperation. It was the first time he had been apart from B battery since he first arrived at Ft. Bliss, Oklahoma two and a half years earlier. He wrote about how odd it seemed being away from the intensity of the war:

Dear Martha,

Am going to write a few lines now before the movie starts. It's going to be the first for me while over here. I wrote in my other letter that I was getting off for a little rest and here I am. It is really nice. I'll write more about it later. This was the first time I've sat at a table and eaten with waiters bringing the food for a long time. Seems sort of funny. Had a shower this afternoon … and a complete set of new clothes, need a haircut yet and I'm all set. Will do that tomorrow. Rather quiet back here but guess we'll [I will] get used to that too.

Hope you are all well there, will write when I get back up [to his B battery] *if not before. Hope the boys will have some mail stacked up for me when I get back. All for now.*

With Love, John

John returned to B battery in southwestern Germany in mid-March 1945. During his final weeks of combat, most of the attacking airplanes his battery saw were the workhorse propeller-driven ME-109 fighters (Messerschmitt Bf 109). Some, however, were identified in battlefield reports as the much faster ME-262s (Messerschmitt 262). These were the first jet-powered fighter airplanes used in World War II. The sighting systems and the training of the Allied anti-aircraft gunners left them unprepared for these newer and more advanced enemy aircraft.

John later recalled,

In April 1945 they came and told me I could go home. Hurry up, they said, you have to get your stuff [out] *before it gets dark. They didn't want to drive at night because there were Germans* [soldiers] *around there. I was the only one sent back right then. That was the way it happened. All of a sudden they would tell one guy to pack up and go.*

The exact date John left B battery in Germany was not recorded in his unit's journal or later recalled by John. Considering the weeks it took for him to return home, the best estimate is that he left the 533rd Battalion in mid-April 1945.

After John left the front lines, the 533rd Battalion continued their drive eastward through southern Germany, nearly to Munich. In those last few weeks before Germany surrendered, the 533rd Battalion's journal recited the capture of many German officers and enlisted men. These German soldiers wished to surrender to the Americans who treated them better than the soldiers from other Allied armies.[27]

John's journey home retraced the same path the 533rd Battalion had taken months earlier. He said,

I worked my way back into France and then south to Marseilles. A couple of weeks later we went back to Africa [French Morocco] *and stayed another week.*

John was then booked aboard a merchant marine ship along with 34 other American soldiers and 500 German POWs.[28]

John said it took the slow-paced "Liberty Ship" 24 days to cross the Atlantic. The main job for John and the other American soldiers was to feed the prisoners. Those prisoners who were familiar with kitchen duty also helped with the cooking and baking. In theory, the Americans on board were also supposed to be guarding the prisoners. John, however, said that he could speak their language and got along well with the German prisoners.

One American officer took issue with John's fraternization with the German POWs. John described this Captain as "kind of a stinker." The Captain reported what he considered to be John's misbehavior to the Major in command. John said that the Major, however, always supported the

American troops returning home. In the end, nothing came of the Captain's report. John stood his ground, "I was over there long enough that I didn't take any BS from those guys either."

Germany's surrender on May 8, 1945 occurred while John was in transit back to the U.S. When he arrived stateside, John was first sent to Ft. Snelling in the Twin Cities and then home for two weeks of leave. As he recalled, "this was the end of May, just before Decoration [Memorial] Day."

John was not immediately discharged from the Army. After two weeks at home, he was sent to San Antonio, Texas for temporary duty. His next and final assignment was Ft. Sill, Oklahoma. As a now-experienced anti-aircraft gun operator, John was tasked with training new officers in the proper operation and maintenance of these weapons. He was finally discharged from active duty on September 24, 1945. In total, it had been three years and ten days since he was first conscripted. John's only comment about returning home was, "They were filling silos about that time." For John Hinderer, the war was over, and he was, once again, a farmer from Minnesota.

Don Engstrand, Lt. U.S. Army Air Corps

In 1984, Don Engstrand wrote a history of his family's farm in Providence Township, Lac qui Parle County, Minnesota. He included a short reference to his experience during World War II:

After graduating from Dawson High School in 1940, he [Don] *entered the University of Minnesota, St. Paul campus, where he graduated in 1948 with a Bachelor of Science degree. Before graduating,* [his college education was interrupted when] *he joined the Army Air Corps where he became a pilot with a Second Lieutenant rating. He spent three years in the service and flew twenty-three missions as a pilot of B-24 bombers in the 464th Squadron [Bomb Group], 55th Wing of the 15th Air Force in Italy. He received an honorable discharge with a rank of First Lieutenant.*

In a later interview, Don chose not to elaborate on his wartime experience. Consequently, nearly all of Don's wartime information was gathered from publicly available military records.

Don registered for military service on June 30, 1942, six months after the Japanese attack on Pearl Harbor and the U.S. declaration of war. He listed his mother Mary as his next of kin and his Uncle Arthur as his employer.

By the time Don began active duty on February 24, 1943, he had completed at least one and possibly two years of college at the St. Paul campus of the University of Minnesota.[29] Like other new recruits, he was first sent through basic training or boot camp.

When Don began basic training in the spring of 1943, his Uncle John Hinderer's anti-aircraft unit was already stationed in French Morocco. John's unit would soon be sent to guard allied facilities along the Mediterranean coast of Africa. In the Pacific war theater, Don's cousin Johnny Krug had been aboard the destroyer USS *Fletcher* for more than a year. The battles to retake control of many Pacific islands with unfamiliar names continued for two more years.

Don Engstrand ultimately joined the 464th Bombardment Group, but he was not part of the original unit when it was formed. The first members of the 464th began stateside training in B-24 bombers in October 1943. Don was still a student pilot learning to fly two-seater aircraft at this time.[30] Don's training trailed that of the first members of the 464th by about six months.

The records from Don's military career suggest that he wanted to become a pilot from the beginning. Don progressed through three levels of student pilot training first using single and then twin engine aircraft. Don had to transfer to separate bases in California as he moved through the flight training sequence. By the end of March 1944,

Katharine

The front side of Don Engstrand's selective service registration card included his birthdate and his next of kin contact information. Source: "U.S., WWII Draft Cards Young Men, 1940-1947" online database (Lehi, UT: Ancestry.com), accessed September 26, 2023. Edited by author.

The reverse side of Don Engstrand's selective service registration card included his physical description and the date of his registration – June 30, 1942. Source: "U.S., WWII Draft Cards Young Men, 1940-1947" online database (Lehi, UT: Ancestry.com), accessed September 26, 2023. Edited by author.

Don Engstrand's official dress uniform photo was taken in 1944. Source: From the Doris Schlichting collection. Edited by author.

The first IFR (Individual Flight Record) for 21-year-old student pilot Don Engstrand. In December 1943 he transferred to a training base in Taft, California, for training in a two-seat T-22 single prop airplane. Source: Access to Don Engstrand's flight log pages was achieved with the help of World War II researcher Bill Beigel: Bill.Beigel@WW2Research.com. Edited by author.

2nd Lieutenant Don Engstrand had successfully achieved a pilot rating. At this same time, his future unit, the 464th Bomb Group, had already crossed the Atlantic and was flying out of a new Allied bomber base in southeastern Italy.

In early May 1944, Don Engstrand was transferred to an air base near Las Vegas, Nevada, to begin pilot training in B-17 bombers. His training included daytime flights where he was listed as a co-pilot, and nighttime flights using only instruments. The B-17 was the standard American heavy bomber used during the early years of the war. It had solid attributes but also had a more limited flight range and smaller payload capacity. In its favor, it could fly above most German flak explosions, it had a leak-proof fuel system, and it was relatively easy to maneuver during combat.

By the spring of 1944, the Italian arm of the Axis power structure had ceased to exist. Mussolini had been deposed and replaced by a pro-Allies government in middle and southern Italy. The northern section of the country, however, remained under German control. Those Italian regions supporting the Allies then declared war on Germany. This change of allegiance allowed the Allies to construct long-range bomber bases in southern Italy. The 464th Bomb Group in Italy flew out of a newly constructed air base known as Pantanella.³¹

The June 1944 D-Day landing on the beaches of Normandy, France, occurred while Don Engstrand was learning to fly B-17s over the desert near Las Vegas. At the same time, members of the 464th Bomb Group in southeastern Italy had begun flying bombing missions throughout Europe. Their assigned aircraft, the B-24 Liberator, had sufficient range to target industrial facilities in Germany and Axis-controlled regions of eastern Europe. Their mission targets included railroad marshalling yards, oil refineries, fuel storage facilities, aircraft factories, and chemical plants.³²

Don was fortunate that he did not participate in these early combat flights out of Pantanella. The initial bombing missions achieved success, but it was at a great cost in both aircraft and personnel. In May 1944, the 464th's first full month of combat, 18 missions were flown; however, 16 B-24s and their aircrews had been destroyed.

In early June 1944, the battered 464th was ordered to stand down, meaning they could no longer fly any combat missions. The down time gave the ground crews time to address the frequent mechanical problems of their B-24s. It also gave the operations managers time to rethink how the

A formation of B-24 Liberators (Fifteenth Air Force) on a bomb run over an Axis-controlled oil refinery. Flack bursts are seen throughout the sky and plumes of black smoke rise from the damaged refinery. Source: Richard R. Ganczak, "Bombing of Concordia Vega Oil Refinery in Ploesti [Romania] by USAAF B-24s, 31 May 1944," Library of Congress, public domain, accessed September 25, 2023, https://loc.gov/pictures/resource/cph.3b43591/. Edited by author.

squadrons were configured. Their decision was to tighten the flight formation known as the "box." In theory, tightening the box would improve their ability to ward off attacks by German fighter aircraft.

The mission routine the 464th used, and Don later experienced, had a strictly controlled sequence. It began with the B-24s lifting off from their Pantanella base one by one until an entire box was airborne. One or several of these box units then headed to a pre-determined point, usually

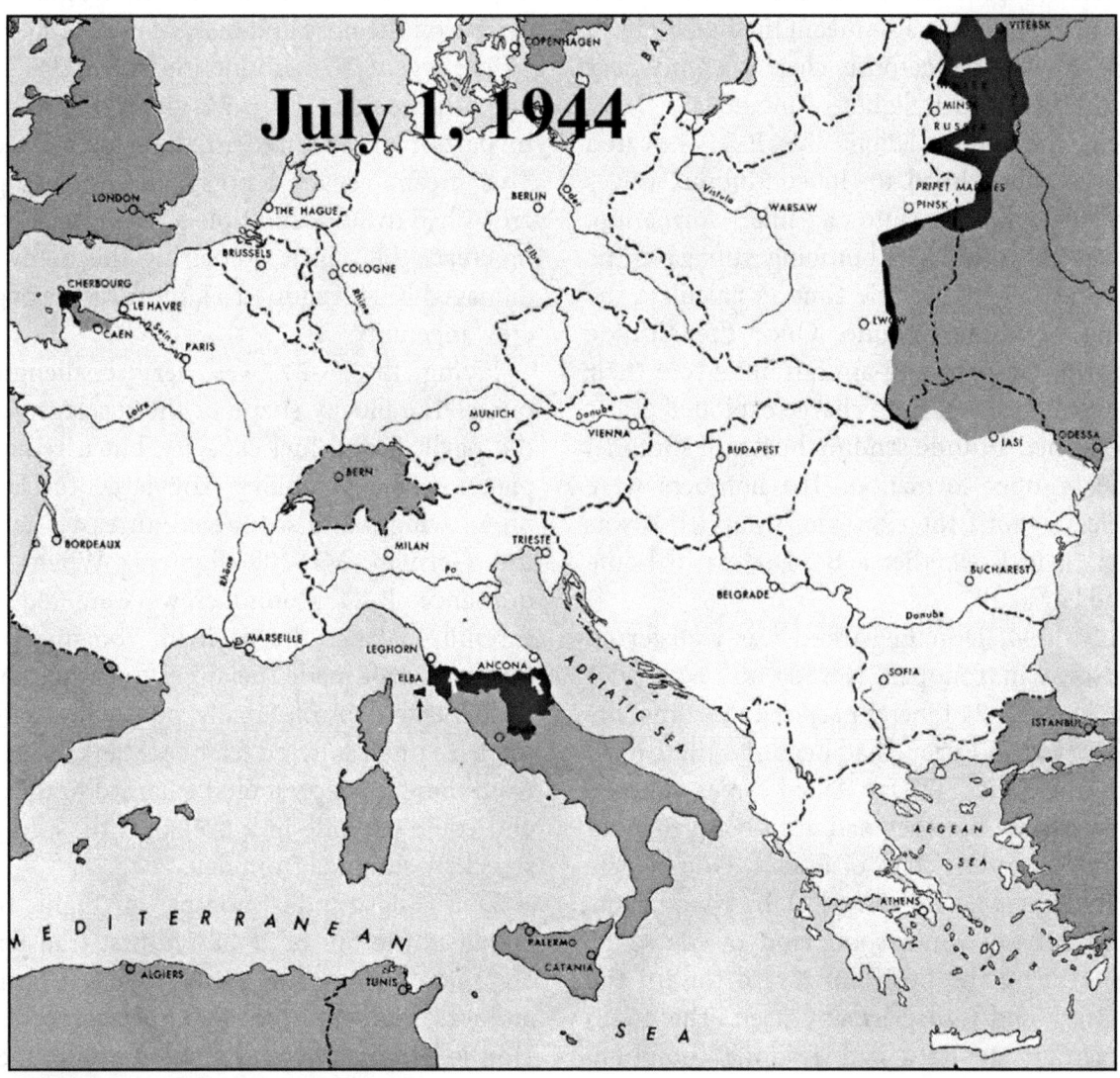

The European war map on July 1, 1944. Axis-controlled territory is white, Allied-controlled territory is grey and active battle areas are black. White arrows are allied attack zones. The 464th Bomb Group was based in Allied-controlled southeastern Italy. The Normandy attack in northwest France had given the Allies a small toehold, but Axis powers still controlled nearly all of Europe. Source: "1944-07-01GerWW2BattlefrontAtlas," in Atlas of the World Battle Fronts in Semimonthly Phases to August 15th 1945: Supplement to The Biennial report of the Chief of Staff of the United States Army July 1, 1943 to June 30 1945 to the Secretary of War, *last modified April 5, 2023, 14:22 UTC, public domain, accessed October 12, 2023, https://commons.wikimedia.org/w/index.php?curid=3272640. Edited by author.*

over the Adriatic Sea. At this precise location, they would rendezvous with bomber groups from other bases. The entire mass of bombers then proceeded in formation toward that day's target. This rendezvous procedure was a highly complex series of maneuvers requiring precise calculations and hours of practice. High fuel consumption during the rendezvous also meant the fuel tanks of some B-24s were dangerously close to empty near the end of their return flight to Pantanella.[33]

When the entire flight of B-24s neared their target, they lined up in continuous waves of airplanes locked into a final formation. Unfortunately, this rigid bombing run gave the German radar crews ample time to calculate the incoming bomber's altitude. Once the altitude was known, German anti-aircraft units sent their flak charges skyward. Each charge exploded at the predetermined altitude sending bursts of shrapnel into the bomber formation. The bombers were defenseless against the clouds of shrapnel. It was a matter of luck whether a B-24 returned home unscathed or at all.

In July 1944, Don Engstrand was transferred to an airbase in Tonopah, Nevada, to begin pilot training in the B-24 Liberator. About this time, the tide of the war in Europe had begun to tilt toward gains by the Allies. D-Day Allied forces suffered heavy casualties, but they had achieved a toehold on the northwestern coast of France. Don's Uncle John Hinderer was still based at La Maddalena, Sardinia, but he would soon land in Marseille, France to begin the push northward toward the Rhine River and into Germany itself. The 464th Bomb Group in Italy had resumed bombing missions targeting German-controlled industrial infrastructure throughout Europe.

Don's first days flying a B-24 introduced him to the aircraft that had been chosen for long-range bombing missions over Europe. Production numbers of the B-24 Liberator exceeded any other heavy bomber ever built in America. Over 18,000 B-24s were built in five different factories across the country. They were flown by every branch of the American military and by other Allied nations as well.[34] Their spacious fuselage earned them the nickname "flying boxcar." During World War II, numerous variations of the B-24 were built. The later models that Don Engstrand flew had improved protection from additional machine gun turrets on the nose and belly of the bomber.

The urgent B-24 production by five U.S. factories had a downside. The B-24s often differed slightly in parts manufactured in the separate factories. This meant repair depots and overseas ground crews had to stock multiple versions of these parts or create their own. Repairing the many battle-damaged B-24s required a large measure of ground crew ingenuity.

Flying the B-24 was very challenging for pilots. The blocky shape of the fuselage added to the payload and fuel capacity, but it reduced the plane's maneuverability. The large fuselage and broad wingspan also offered an easier target for the German ME-109 fighters. When loading ordnance, B-24 ground crews were required to carefully balance the payload. Too much weight forward or aft made the aircraft nearly impossible for pilots to control. Finally, production models of the B-24 often suffered from fuel tank leaks. Fumes from these leaks presented a hazard to the aircrew and could explode in a fireball if the aircraft was struck by shrapnel from flak.

Don Engstrand's months of flight training ended in the fall of 1944. He first transferred to Hamilton Field north of San Francisco, California, and was then sent overseas. On December 2, 1944, Don joined his assigned combat group, the 776th Squadron of the 464th Bomb Group, already stationed at Pantanella Italy. It was only one year earlier that Don Engstrand had taken his first flight in a single engine training airplane. Now, he was a combat pilot in the long-range bomber designed to destroy the industrial heart of Nazi Germany.

When Don arrived at Pantanella in December 1944, the 464th Bomb Group had only been flying

Our Greatest Generation — Hinderer Family Members in World War II

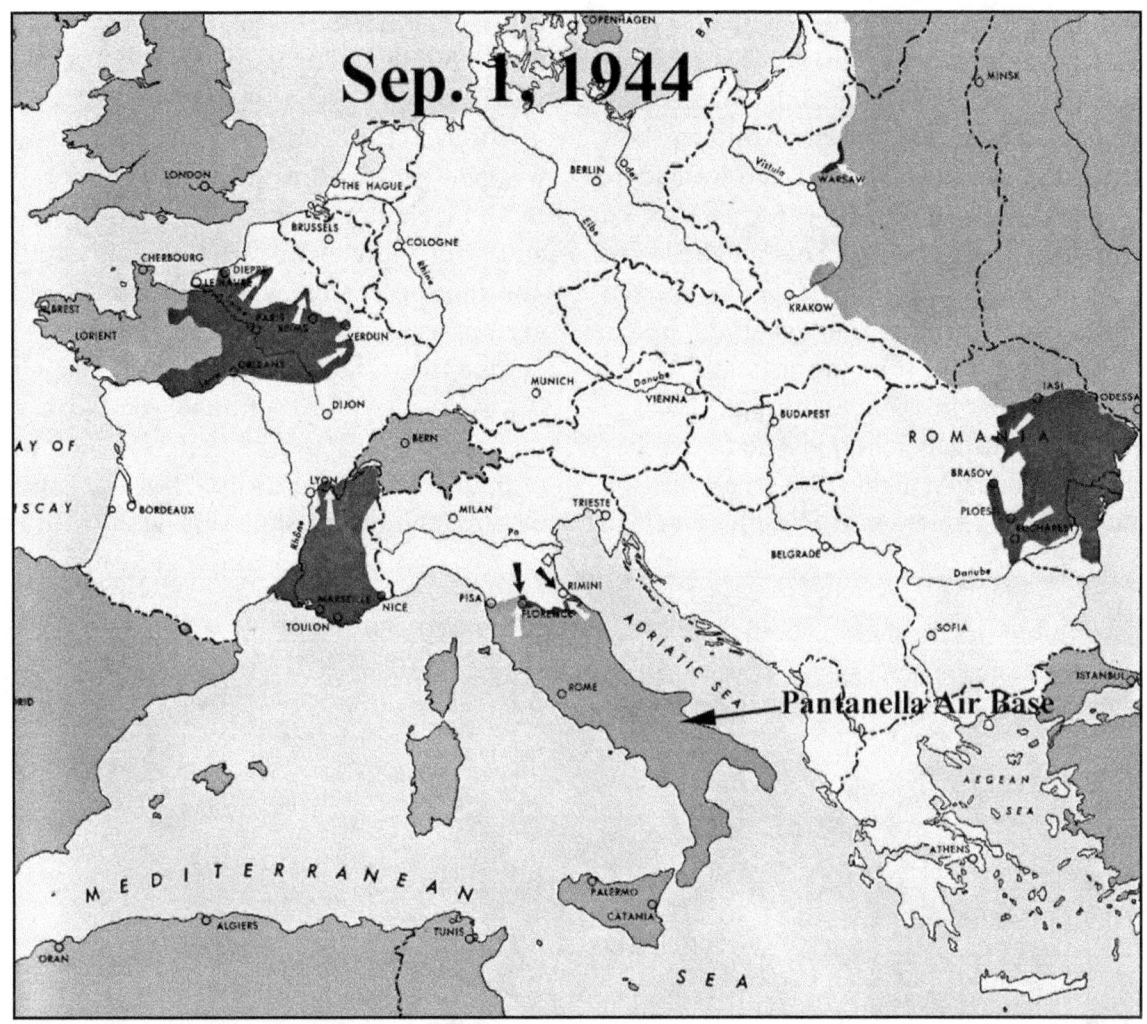

The European War Map as of September 1, 1944. Axis-controlled territory is white, Allied-controlled territory is grey and active battle areas are black. White arrows are allied attack zones. The 464th Bomb group was based in allied-controlled southeastern Italy. By this time shortly before Don's arrival, the Allies were advancing eastward from Normandy, France and northward from the French Mediterranean coast. Source: "1944-07-01GerWW2BattlefrontAtlas," in Atlas of the World Battle Fronts in Semimonthly Phases to August 15th 1945: Supplement to The Biennial report of the Chief of Staff of the United States Army July 1, 1943 to June 30 1945 to the Secretary of War, *last modified April 5, 2023, 14:22 UTC, public domain, accessed October 12, 2023, https://commons.wikimedia.org/w/index.php?curid=3272640. Edited by author.*

combat missions for seven months. Nevertheless, the group had already lost two of its lead officer-pilots and numerous aircraft.[35]

At Pantanella, every ground crew was assigned an individual airplane. These crews were responsible for loading ordnance, repairing damage, and returning their bomber to flight-ready status. The pilots and other air crew members could be re-assigned to another bomber, but the ground crew "owned" their airplane. These ground crews were a tight-knit group with remarkable repair and fabrication skills. As the bombers returned from

Katharine

a mission, the ground crew would watch for their airplane. The first question always was whether their aircraft had survived the mission. If their airplane was spotted, the question became how much damage had been sustained, and were there injuries or casualties on board.

Don's first combat mission out of Pantanella was on December 18, 1944. His individual flight record stated that this flight lasted almost eight hours. The extended length of time meant that this was a completed combat mission. Short flight times of one or two hours usually reflected a flight that had been aborted. Don's first flight was a repeat mission that targeted oil refineries at Blechhammer in central Germany. The following day, Don and the 464th Bomb Group targeted these oil refineries once again.[36]

Toward the end of December, 1944, foul weather settled over Pantanella grounding the B-24 Liberators. There were many days of rain and even snow in this part of southeastern Italy. The unexpected break allowed both the air and ground crews to celebrate the Christmas holiday despite their long distance from home. Chow for Christmas Day was traditional roast turkey and all the trimmings.[37] January 1945 was another month of poor weather in Europe. Don was only able to fly three combat missions during the entire month.

Don Engstrand's flight record for his first month in Italy; December, 1944. His first combat mission was on the 18th. The short flight time on the 21st meant it was an aborted mission. Don was the co-pilot on all of these missions. Source: Access to Don Engstrand's flight log pages was accomplished with the help of World War II researcher Bill Beigel: Bill.Beigel@WW2Research.com. Edited by author.

While Don's bomb group was grounded by the foul weather, his Uncle John Hinderer's anti-aircraft unit was aiding Allied advances in northeastern France near the Rhine River border with Germany. At the time, these two Hinderer family members did not know how close their combat units were to one another.

At Pantanella, the early morning air crew briefings always included a secondary target. If weather or visibility conditions over the primary target were poor, the group leader could redirect all of the B-24s to the secondary target. Flying the added miles to a secondary target, however, presented yet another challenge. The first aircraft into the skies consumed the most fuel while waiting for other planes and then waiting again at the rendezvous point. Redirecting to a secondary target meant still more fuel was consumed. On the flight home, crews often had to pitch any extra weight out of their airplane hoping to make it back to Pantanella. Even with extreme measures, some planes ran out of fuel before reaching their home base. There was an emergency refueling airstrip on the Island of Vis, off the coast of Yugoslavia (Croatia today) near the city of Split. Refueling at the Island of Vis was better than ditching the B-24 in the ocean or bailing out over enemy-controlled land.[38]

February 1945 provided more favorable weather, and Don's IFR (Individual Flight Record) noted seven completed missions. On six other days, his flight crew took off from Pantanella, but then aborted their mission. Either bad weather or mechanical problems were likely to blame.

2nd Lt. Don Engstrand's IFR (Individual Flight Record) from February 1945 indicated he flew seven combat missions. The "C" in the right column indicated a completed combat mission. It is unclear if Don was the co-pilot or first pilot. Source: Access to Don Engstrand's flight log pages was accomplished with the help of World War II researcher Bill Beigel: Bill.Beigel@WW2Research.com. Edited by author.

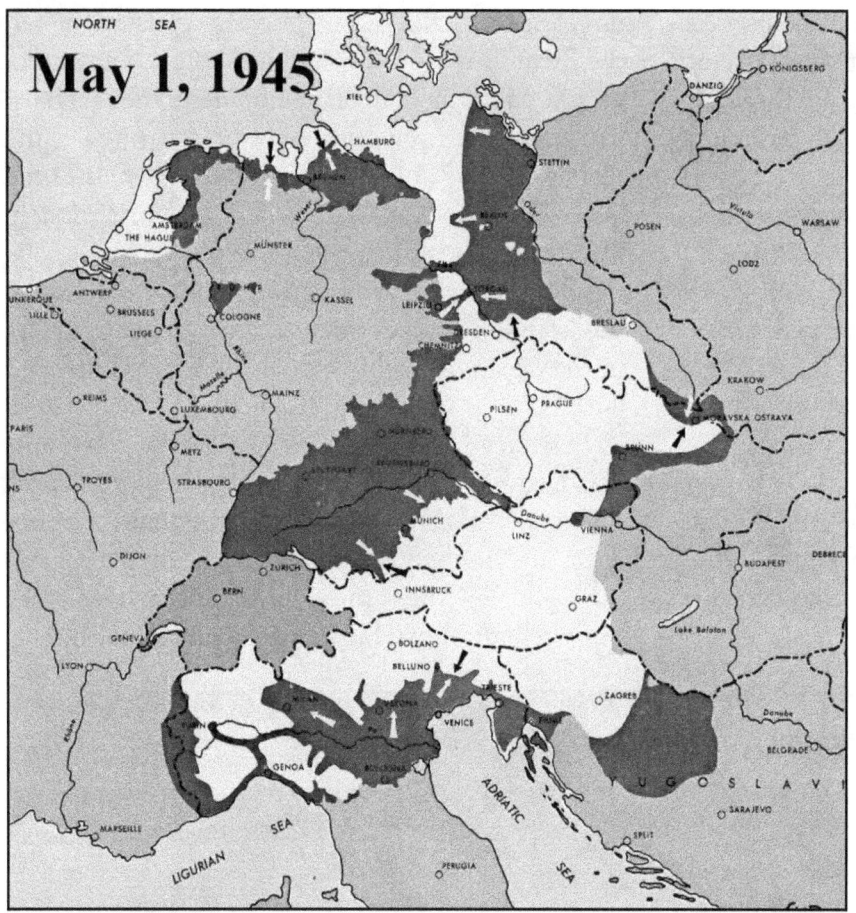

The European War Map as of May 1, 1945. Axis-controlled territory is white, Allied-controlled territory is grey and active battle areas are black. White arrows are allied attack zones. Northern Italy was the scene of intense fighting along the Po River. By this time, the Russians had overrun Berlin, and the Allies controlled the industrial heartland of Germany. Source: "1944-07-01GerWW2BattlefrontAtlas," in Atlas of the World Battle Fronts in Semimonthly Phases to August 15th 1945: Supplement to The Biennial report of the Chief of Staff of the United States Army July 1, 1943 to June 30 1945 to the Secretary of War, *last modified April 5, 2023, 14:22 UTC, public domain, accessed October 12, 2023, https://commons.wikimedia.org/w/index.php?curid=3272640. Edited by author.*

The February missions targeted oil refineries and railroad marshalling yards in Austria, and railroad bridges and marshalling yards in northern Italy. During these flights, Don was listed as both Co-Pilot and First Pilot.[39]

April 1945 was a decisive month for both Hinderer family members fighting in the European war theater. By early April, John Hinderer's unit had crossed the Rhine River and was advancing eastward in southern Germany. About mid-month, John was ordered to leave his unit. He then began his trek back to North Africa and then home to the U.S. At the same time, his nephew Don Engstrand had been promoted from 2nd Lieutenant to 1st Lieutenant. In April 1945, Don completed what would be his final month flying combat missions out of Pantanella. Only five of these missions were recorded as completed.

Don's five completed missions in April 1945 were all directed at targets in northern Italy. Winston Churchill had called the Mediterranean theater the "soft underbelly" of the Axis power, but it proved to be anything but soft.

One month before Germany's surrender, their defenses remained entrenched in the mountainous regions of northern Italy. The 464th Bomb Group joined a multi-national Allied force pushing the battle-hardened German military northward. The B-24 Liberators from Pantanella targeted bridges, airfields, and German troop concentrations in northern Italy. This was the final Allied push through the Po River valley northward toward the Italian Alps.

As the fierce fighting in northern Italy neared its end, secret negotiations were underway to finally end the war in Europe. Adolph Hitler died by suicide in his Berlin bunker on April 30, 1945. One by one, German commanders across Europe signed letters of unconditional surrender. V-E

(Victory Europe) day was officially celebrated on May 8, 1945.

Don's last day flying out of Pantanella was a two-hour non-combat flight on May 6, 1945. As he later wrote in his life story, Don flew 23 combat missions in B-24s out of Pantanella, Italy.

Like his Uncle John Hinderer, Don Engstrand was not immediately discharged from military service when the war ended. By the end of May 1945, Don was back in the U.S. and stationed at Sioux Falls, South Dakota. He was given leave to return home in June 1945. In August, he was sent to Galveston, Texas, where he logged in a few hours flying aging B-17 bombers. In early September 1945, his IFR (Individual Flight Record) stated, "CLOSED: SUBJECT OFFICER RELIEVED FROM ACTIVE DUTY." Don was transferred from Galveston to Camp McCoy, Wisconsin, for final out-processing. His last day of active duty was November 7, 1945.

Bill Gjovig, U.S. Navy

Bill (William Edward) Gjovig was born on July 4, 1922. Bill's paternal grandparents were Norwegian immigrants who homesteaded in Yellow Medicine County, Minnesota. Bill's father, Erik Larsen Gjovig, inherited his parents' farm. Erik's first wife died in 1902, and he then married Bill's mother in 1911. Altogether, Erik had seven children, and Bill was the youngest.

Bill first attended a nearby country school and later completed four years at Canby High School. In early April 1940, the U.S. Census listed 17-year-old Bill Gjovig living at home with his parents and two of his siblings. He was described as a farm laborer working for his father. The census stated he had completed four years of high school, but he actually graduated later that spring.

On June 30, 1942, two years after his high school graduation, Bill complied with draft regulations by registering for possible military service. This was six months after the attack on Pearl Harbor and America's declaration of war on Japan and Germany. At the time, Bill was about to turn 20 and was working for his older half-brother, Herman Gjovig, at a grain company in Canby.

On October 2, 1942, three months after his military registration, Bill Gjovig enlisted in the U.S. Navy. His entry document stated he had enlisted for a three-year tour of duty. In his case, enlistment was clearly voluntary. Like Johnny Krug, Bill signed his enlistment papers at the U.S. Navy Recruitment Center in Minneapolis.

Bill went through basic training at the Naval Training Station, Great Lakes, Illinois, training center. He arrived there on October 4, 1942 and had completed his training by November 5th. It was a relatively short boot camp, but soldiers were urgently needed.

A June, 1945 photo of 1st Lt. Don Engstrand after he returned home from Italy. He is standing in front of Emma Krug's Lac qui Parle Ave. house in Canby. Source: From the Doris Schlichting collection. Edited by author.

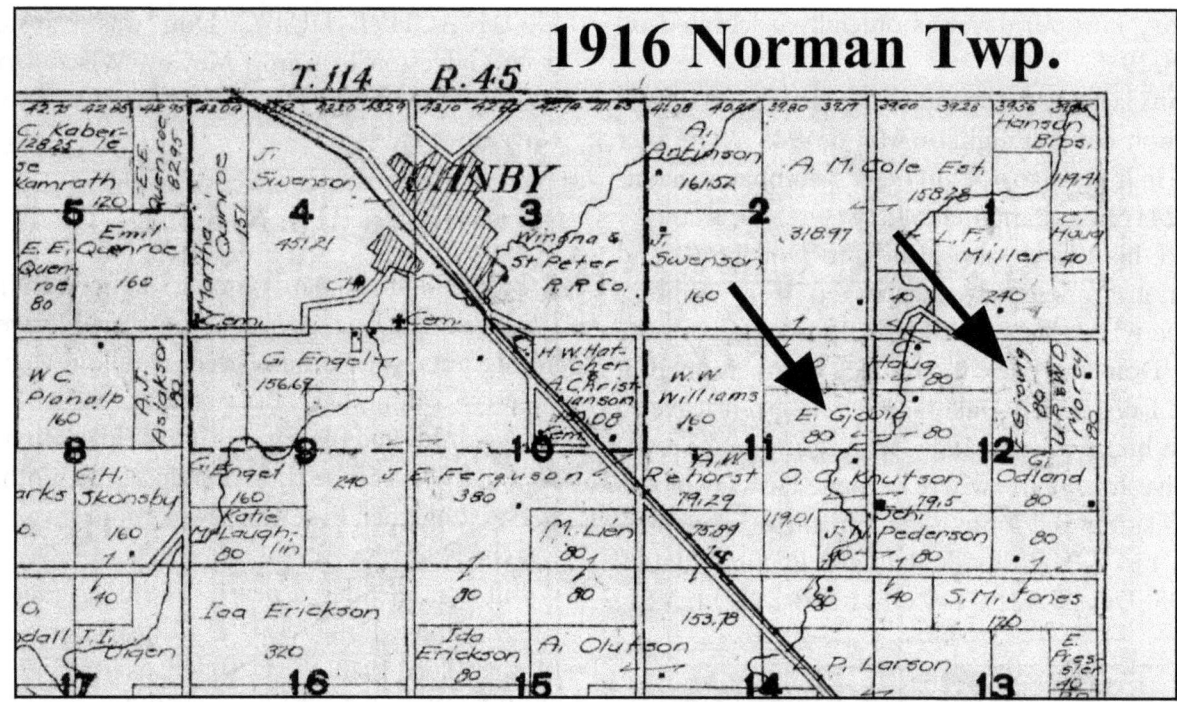

A 1916 plat map of Norman Township, Yellow Medicine County, Minnesota. Each bold-numbered section is one mile square. Erik Gjovig's three 80-acre land parcels were about two miles southeast of Canby. Bill Gjovig was born and raised on this farm. Source: "Yellow Medicine County Minn.," University of Minnesota, accessed October 27, 2023, http://geo.lib.umn.edu/plat_books/stateofmn1916/counties/yellow_medicine.htm. Edited by author.

After basic training, Bill was sent to Norman, Oklahoma to train as an Aviation Ordnanceman (AOM).[41] This Oklahoma training camp had been commissioned only two months earlier. Ultimately, it became the largest center for ordnance training during World War II.[42] By March 20, 1943, Bill had completed the 12-week training course. Among his classmates, Bill received high marks. His service school record indicated he received the 8th highest total score out of 151 trainees.

Following AOM training, Bill was transferred to a second training school in Purcell, Oklahoma. This school was located ten miles south of Norman and about 20 miles south of Oklahoma City. Like the camp at Norman, the gunner's school in Purcell was a hastily constructed training center. Farmland near Purcell was condemned by the U.S. government and converted to suit the needs of the war effort. By early May 1943, Bill Gjovig had completed his more specialized training as a naval aircraft gunner.

Bill's first duty assignment was to FAW (Fleet Air Wing) 6 based on Whidbey Island near Seattle, Washington. He spent May and June of 1943 working on ordnance maintenance and repair. In early July 1943, Bill became a bombardier and gunner on a PBY amphibious airplane. Small numbers of PBY airplanes were grouped into what were known as patrol units. Bill was assigned to the patrol unit VP-43 that had recently returned from Alaska.

The PBY designation of Bill's aircraft stood for Patrol Bomber with the "Y" a code letter for the American factory where it was built. The PBY saw extensive action during World War II. Its slow air speed, 100–125 mph, meant air-to-air combat was to be avoided. Its main attribute was versatility. It had an exceptionally long flight range with an

The front side of Bill Gjovig's military registration card completed four days prior to his 20th birthday. He worked for his older half-brother Herman Gjovig at a grain company in Canby. Source: "U.S., WWII Draft Cards Young Men, 1940-1947," online database (Lehi, UT: Ancestry.com), accessed October 27, 2023. Edited by author.

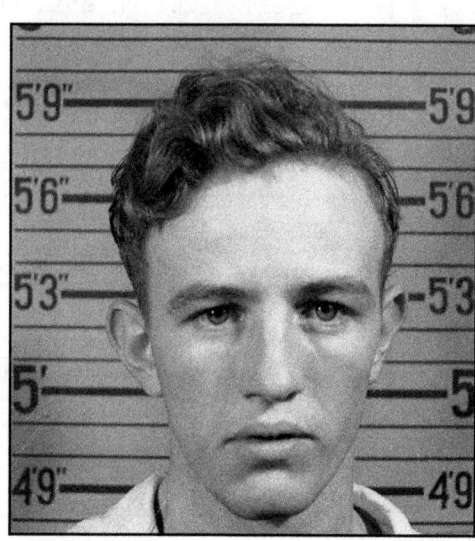

Bill Gjovig as photographed when he enlisted in the U.S. Navy. Source: Bill's enlistment photo was shared by WWII researcher Bill Beigel.[40]

The reverse side of Bill Gjovig's military registration card dated June 30, 1942. His physical description and the date of his registration were listed. Source: "U.S., WWII Draft Cards Young Men, 1940-1947" online database (Lehi, UT: Ancestry.com), accessed October 27, 2023. Edited by author.

On October 2, 1942, Bill Gjovig enlisted in the Navy for three years of active duty. He was to be paid $50.00 per month. He was transferred to Great Lakes, Illinois, for basic training. His original next of kin was his father Erik Gjovig. This was later overwritten as Maurine Gjovig when she and Bill were married in 1944. Source: Bill Gjovig's service record was accessed with the help of World War II researcher Bill Beigel Bill.Beigel@WW2Research.com. Edited by author.

ability to land on either water or land. It was capable of carrying a small payload of torpedoes, bombs, or depth charges, and it had machine gun "blisters" on either side of the fuselage. A third machine gun was mounted in the nose of the aircraft. The airspeed of the PBY was slow enough that the nose gunner could poke his head outside of the gun mount during flight. He became another set of eyes on missions shadowing enemy ships. Bill Gjovig's usual position on combat missions was in one of the fuselage blisters or manning the machine gun in the nose of the PBY.

When Bill joined VP-43 in July 1943, this unit had recently returned from what became known as the Aleutian campaign of World War II. The Aleutians are an American-owned chain of islands

Our Greatest Generation — Hinderer Family Members in World War II

that extend over 1000 miles westward from mainland Alaska toward Russia. The Aleutian campaign began in the summer of 1942, only six months after Pearl Harbor. Japanese forces attacked and occupied the western-most Aleutian Islands. In all of World War II, these captured islands were the only American-owned territories occupied by enemy forces.

It had taken from the summer of 1942 until late 1943 for Allied forces to recapture the windswept Aleutian Islands. Of the almost 100,000 Allied soldiers who fought in the Aleutian campaign, several thousand lost their lives.[43]

When Bill Gjovig joined VP-43 in July 1943, the Aleutian campaign had already been underway for one year. The original members of VP-43 had rotated back to Washington State where new members, like Bill, were added. While stateside, VP-43 was assigned an improved model of the PBY. The unit then spent two months in Oregon and Washington training new crew members and flight-testing the new aircraft. Bill participated in this training prior to facing combat missions.

In early October 1943, Bill and the other members of VP-43 flew north to a base on Attu, the westernmost island in the Aleutian chain.[44] After their arrival, however, they came under repeated strafing attacks by Japanese aircraft. These attacks forced VP-43 to abandon their Attu air base. They retreated to a protected airbase closer to the mainland of Alaska. The battle to reclaim Attu continued for two more months. Bill Gjovig was a member of a flight crew involved in these battles. It was not until mid-December 1943 that Allied forces, including VP-43, were able to regain control of the airbase on Attu Island.

Once the base on Attu was back under American control, the PBY airplanes stationed there began nighttime reconnaissance and bombing missions to the Kuril Islands.[45] These barren islands stretch from Japan northward to the tip of the Russian Kamchatka peninsula. From December 1943 through April 1944, PBY flight crews from the

Bill Gjovig graduated from Norman, Oklahoma, AOM school on March 20, 1943. He scored 8th highest in his class of 151 trainees. Source: Bill Gjovig's service record was accessed with the help of World War II researcher Bill Beigel Bill.Beigel@ WW2Research.com. Edited by author.

369

Katharine

This PBY with wheels retracted was photographed over the Aleutian Islands of Alaska in March 1943. The photo has been edited. The arrow identifies the machine gun blister along the fuselage. Source: Horace Bristol, "A PBY-5A Catalina Patrol Bomber over the Aleutian Islands (1943)," National Archives and Records Administration, accessed December 19, 2023, https://catalog.archives.gov/id/520976. Edited by author.

A closeup view of the fuselage gun blister of a PBY aircraft. The pictured crew member carried a machine gun up a ladder into his seated position inside the blister. Source: Howard R. Hollem, "Installing a 30-Calibre Machine Gun Port Side Gun Blister in a Navy PBY Plane (1942)," Library of Congress, public domain, accessed December 19, 2023, https://www.loc.gov/pictures/item/2017878256/. Edited by author.

Aleutians flew long-range bombing missions from Attu to the Kurils. On these flights, they faced Japanese forces and had to fly through some of the worst winter weather in the Northern Hemisphere. In later years, Bill Gjovig confided to his wife Maurine that these were the missions when he most feared he might not survive. For his part on these flights, Bill received two stars, one for each of his two exceptionally dangerous Kuril Island missions.[46]

In late April 1944, VP-43 squadron was relieved of their duty in Alaska and sent back to the continental U.S. After months of harrowing flights and bitter cold, all members of the squadron were given passes to go home.

Bill's home leave in May 1944 had a very personal outcome. His fiancé Maurine Krug had just finished her first year of teaching at a country school. Bill Gjovig married Maurine Krug on May 18, 1944 in Canby, Minnesota. Their marriage took place at St. Stephen's Lutheran Church in Canby. The civil record from Yellow Medicine County included the name Deloris Krug, Maurine's oldest half-sister. She was a witness to their marriage.

At the time Bill and Maurine were married, Maurine's stepmother Emma Krug was living in her rental house on Lac qui Parle Avenue in Canby. A photo of the newlyweds was taken in front of Emma's home. Maurine was wearing a traditional bride's dress and Bill wore his formal Navy uniform.

Bill Gjovig returned to active duty on June 7, 1944. He was still assigned to FAW (Fleet Air Wing) 6 based on Whidbey Island in Puget Sound northwest of Seattle.[47] His duty description was general ordnance maintenance and repair of the same PBY aircraft he was familiar with. There is no indication that Bill and his unit ever returned to the Aleutian Islands.

With Bill away on active duty, Maurine resumed teaching at a country school near Canby. At first, she continued to live on Lac qui Parle Avenue with her stepmother Emma Krug. Later on, she moved to a small apartment in Canby.

In late April 1945, Bill was reassigned to the western Pacific war theater. His service record indicated he was first sent to Rec Ship (Receiving ship) USS *San Francisco* based at Naval Air Station Kaneohe on the east side of Oahu, Hawaii.[48]

Bill Gjovig received two stars to be placed on his air crew insignia. They reflected his two dangerous missions from Attu Island to the Kuril (Kurile) Islands north of the Japanese homeland. Source: Bill Gjovig's service record was accessed with the help of World War II researcher Bill Beigel Bill.Beigel@WW2Research.com. Edited by author.

Although the Kaneohe base was home to Bill's patrol unit, their PBY aircraft usually flew missions westward into distant regions of the war theater. The exceptional fuel capacity of the PBY made them the only aircraft capable of roundtrip flights of over 1,500 miles.

Bill's final assignment in mid-June 1945 was to Patrol Bomber Unit 23 (VPB-23). Once again, he was a flight crew member on PBY amphibious aircraft. This assignment began only two months prior to the Japanese surrender.

VPB-23 was based on various islands in the Micronesia subregion of the western Pacific. Their aircraft were occasionally assigned bombing runs but were more commonly sent on either reconnaissance operations or "Dumbo" missions.

On reconnaissance missions, the PBY air crews located and shadowed fleets of enemy ships in the western Pacific. The slow-flying PBYs used nighttime flights and cloud cover to remain hidden from the enemy. Some PBY units painted their airplanes black to enhance their concealment.[49]

The term "Dumbo" was a code word used by the United States Navy for air-sea rescue missions. Bill's amphibious PBY airplane was perfectly suited for these rescue efforts. It could land in the ocean and pull men directly from the water. No inflatable rafts were needed. PBY air crews were credited with saving the lives of thousands of ditched pilots and shipwrecked seamen during World War II.

The formal Japanese surrender in early September 1945 signaled the final few months of Bill Gjovig's World War II duty. On October 31, 1945, his unit was sent to Saipan in the western Pacific Mariana Islands. Several weeks later, the entire squadron flew back to Naval Air Station Kaneohe on Oahu, Hawaii. The unit's final flight was from Kaneohe to the Naval Air Station in San Diego where VPB-23 was disestablished.[50] Bill was discharged from active duty on December 20, 1945.

A PBY floating at sea. A crew member stood on the wing holding a fire extinguisher while the engine was started. This 1943 photo was taken at Attu, Aleutian Islands. Source: Horace Bristol, "80-G-475771: PBY-5 "Catalina" Patrol Bomber, July 1943," National Museum of the U.S. Navy, public domain, accessed December 28, 2023, https://www.history.navy.mil/content/history/museums/nmusn/explore/photography/aircraft-us/aircraft-usn-p/pby-catalina-aircraft/80-g-475771.html. Edited by author.

The civil marriage record for Bill Gjovig and Maurine Krug was archived at the Recorder's Office in Yellow Medicine County, Minnesota. They were married on May 18, 1944 at St. Stephen's Lutheran Church in Canby, Minnesota. Deloris Krug was a witness to the marriage. Source: Access to this record courtesy of the Yellow Medicine County Recorder's Office. Photographed and edited by author.

Maurine (Krug) Gjovig said that after Bill returned to Canby, they continued to live in her small apartment. She added that Bill was rehired by the same grain elevator where he had worked prior to entering the Navy.[51] When they had saved enough money, they bought their first home in Canby.

Bill's military service might have ended when he returned home in late 1945. However, as Maurine described it,

> *He [Bill] and his best friend got talked into joining the inactive reserves for the Navy. They were told they wouldn't have to worry about getting called up, but when Korea [the Korean War] started in 1950, they were the first to be called up.*

Bill's Korean War active duty dated from December 1950 through February 1952.

ON REFLECTION

> It is, I believe, the greatest generation any society has ever produced.
>
> Tom Brokaw
> *The Greatest Generation*

The four Hinderer family members who served in World War II returned to their Minnesota homes when the war ended. Johnny Krug was discharged in August 1945 and John Hinderer in September.

A photo of Maurine Krug and Bill Gjovig on their wedding day, May 18, 1944. They posed in front of Emma Krug's home on Lac qui Parle Avenue in Canby, Minnesota. Source: From the Martha Hinderer collection. Edited by author.

Katharine

This June 1945 family photo included three servicemen home on leave. Standing left rear: John Hinderer, Don Engstrand, and Johnny Krug. Bill Gjovig was still in the western Pacific. Others standing left to right: Carl Hinderer, Gottlieb Hinderer, Katharine Hinderer, Arthur Engstrand, Mary Engstrand, William Krug, Deloris Krug, Maurine (Krug) Gjovig, and Ruth Engstrand. Seated left to right: Martha Hinderer, Florence Krug, Sharon Schlichting, Norma Engstrand holding David Schlichting, and Doris (Lafere) Schlichting, mother of Sharon and David. Source: The Doris Schlichting collection. Edited by author.

Don Engstrand came home in November and Bill Gjovig returned to Canby that December. By year's end, they had all stepped away from combat zones around the world and returned to their lives as ordinary citizens.

The enormity of World War II events can only be grasped by considering the six years of deadly combat in Africa, Europe, Asia, Alaska, and throughout the Pacific. It was the largest and most destructive conflict in world history. The horror of this war was personally experienced by the men who volunteered or were conscripted into military service.

The four Hinderer family members who served their country during World War II did not spontaneously discuss their wartime experience. It was never a topic of conversation during family discussions or later family reunions. Memories were revealed only when they were asked about their personal experiences. Even then, some declined to discuss the subject. Most of the stories they told were limited to generalizations about everyday military life. The fear they experienced and the destruction of the war were never mentioned. Any bravado-laced stories were left for wartime newsreels and later Hollywood productions. The four Hinderer men who participated in World War II understood what war correspondent Ernie Pyle meant. They felt gratitude the war was over rather than pride in anything they had accomplished.

We won this war because our men are brave . . .and the passage of time and the gift of nature's materials. We did not win it because destiny created us better than all other people. I hope that in victory we are more grateful than proud.

~ Ernie Pyle, WWII correspondent

■ ■ ■

Notes

1. Maurine Krug said she and Bill Gjovig became engaged in 1942 when she was a junior in high school. Bill's World War II military service is included due to his eventual marriage to Maurine.

2. The word "enlistment" was the term used in the military records for these men. At least for John Hinderer, his "enlistment" was not voluntary. Today, we would say he was drafted or conscripted into military service.

3. To locate the Naval training station, in Google Maps insert coordinates 42.312354, -87.834008 in the search box and click the search button.

4. "USS *Argonne*, Report for Pearl Harbor Attack" (January 28, 1942), Naval History and Heritage Command, accessed August 20, 2023, https://www.history.navy.mil/research/archives/digital-exhibits-highlights/action-reports/wwii-pearl-harbor-attack/ships-a-c/uss-argonne-ag-31-action-report.html.

5. Wikipedia s.v. "USS *Utah* (BB-31), last modified June 27, 2024, 12:27 (UTC), https://en.wikipedia.org/wiki/USS_Utah_(BB-31).

6. The date a ship was commissioned was the date it officially began duty. An earlier cruise would have been conducted to assure that the vessel was seaworthy and ready for battle.

7. The term lead destroyer meant it was the first ship commissioned in this class of destroyers.

8. Each soldier was issued one wool blanket and, as John wrote, one "comforts." Comforts were a bed covering like today's comforter.

9. John's unit was the 533rd Battalion (Bn). The 533rd had four batteries: A, B, C, and D. John was in B battery.

10. Bofors guns were Swedish-built and were the best mid-range anti-aircraft guns available at the time. They were deployed by most of the Allies during World War II. The Bofors and the smaller caliber machine guns were built and mounted so they could be quickly moved in the field.

11. Later in his life, John suffered from severe hearing loss. No doubt, his many months firing anti-aircraft guns contributed to his eventual loss of hearing.

12. Hutments were the small buildings where the men slept. John said his hutment measured 14 X 14 feet.

13. John's letters home and their original envelopes were saved by the Hinderers. After John died, the letters were found in his room in the Canby care facility where he lived. Florence Rousseau saved the letters and passed them on to her daughter Becci Fischer. Becci, in turn, gave them to the author. Becci's generosity is gratefully acknowledged.

14. The historical files of John's 533rd Battalion were copied and sent to the author. This assistance by the Dwight D. Eisenhower Presidential Library & Museum in Abilene, Kansas, is gratefully acknowledged.

15. To locate Bizerte, Tunisia, in Google Maps insert coordinates 37.278470, 9.864593 in the search box and click the search button.

16. The British part of the battle to retake Sicily was known as "Operation Mincemeat." It was an unusually successful effort including a carefully planned deception dramatized by the 1950s film "The Man Who Never Was." A second British dramatization released in 2021 was titled "Operation Mincemeat."

17. To locate La Maddalena at the northern tip of the island of Sardinia, in Google Maps insert coordinates 41.216321, 9.408413 in the search box and click the search button.

18. These 75 letters were sent to his mother Katharine and sister Martha. They were shared with the author by Sharon (Schlichting) Halverson.

19. John's Berretta was an Italian-built semi-automatic handgun. These pistols were used as service revolvers by several countries during World War II.

20. To locate Sassari, in Google Maps insert coordinates 40.725683, 8.552228 in the search box and click the search button.

21. To locate Cagliari, in Google Maps insert coordinates 39.225936, 9.1224654 in the search box and click the search button.

22. The V-mail process entailed photographing the letter and then transmitting it as a thumbnail-sized microfilm negative. Once in the U.S., it was reprinted as a small letter inside a small envelope and delivered by regular mail.

23. Several of John's letters have words or phrases cut out by a censor's scissors. It was important that these letters home did not identify the location of the soldiers or reveal strategic information.

24. In this area, the Rhine River runs south to north and is the border between France on the west and Germany on the east.

25. To locate Haguenau, France, in Google Maps insert coordinates 48.812941, 7.790370 in the search box and click the search button.

26. John grew up speaking the dialect of this particular part of southwestern Germany where his parents had been born.

27. In one incident, an older biplane landed near the 533rd. The German pilot said they flew there from Russian-occupied territory so they could surrender to the Americans. The Russians were known for brutal treatment of German prisoners of war.

28. German POWs were shipped back to the U.S. for economic reasons. It was less expensive to feed and house them in U.S. camps than to ship supplies to POW camps in Europe.

29. February 24, 1943 was Don's enlistment date according to the U.S. Department of Veteran Affairs files.

30. Access to Don Engstrand's individual flight record pages was accomplished with the help of World War II researcher Bill Beigel: Bill.Beigel@WW2Research.com Mr. Beigel's assistance is gratefully acknowledged.

31. The Pantanella air base was located near the town of Canosa, less than 10 miles from the Adriatic Sea. In Google Maps insert coordinates 41.223632, 16.067079 in the search box and click the search button.

32. "464th Bombardment Group," Army Air Corps Museum, accessed May 3, 2023, https://www.armyaircorpsmuseum.org/464th_bombardment_group.cfm.

33. Michael Hill and Bette Karle, *The 464th Bomb Group in World War II* (Atglen, PA: Schiffer Publishing, 2001), 48.

34. Wikipedia s.v. "Consolidated B-24 Liberator," last modified June 21, 2024, 20:48 (UTC), https://en.wikipedia.org/wiki/Consolidated_B-24_Liberator.

35. The Pantanella base was led by commanding officers who were also pilots and flew combat missions.

36. "464th BG Missions," The 464th Bombardment Group (H), accessed October 22, 2023, https://the464th.org/PDFs/Missions.pdf.

37. Hill and Bette, *The 464th Bomb Group*, 140.

38. To locate the Island of Vis, in Google Maps insert coordinates 43.047094, 16.154820 in the search box and click the search button.

39. IFR (Individual Flight Records) were not completed uniformly. Don's entry is unclear about whether he was the first pilot (left seat) or the co-pilot.

40. This photo and Bill Gjovig's service record were accessed courtesy of World War II researcher Bill Beigel: Bill.Beigel@WW2Research.com. Mr. Beigel's assistance is gratefully acknowledged.

41. Aviation Ordnanceman is the term used for men trained in the maintenance and operation of Naval aircraft weapons. These weapons included machine guns, torpedoes, depth charges, and bombs.

42. "Naval Air Technical Training Center: Norman, Oklahoma 1942-1946 and 1952-1959," Oklahoma Naval Air History, accessed December 19, 2023, https://www.oklahomanavalairhistory.com/nattc.php.

43. "Battle of the Aleutian Islands," History.com Editors/A&E Television Networks, accessed December 21, 2023, https://www.history.com/topics/world-war-ii/battle-of-the-aleutian-islands.

44. To locate Attu island in the Aleutians, in Google Maps insert coordinates 52.902242, 172.901722 in the search box and click the search button.

45. To locate the Kuril (or Kurile) island chain, in Google Maps insert coordinates 47.331456, 150.917133 in the search box and click the search button.

46. Michael Roberts, "VPB-43," in *Dictionary of American Naval Aviation Squadrons, Volume 2: The History of VP, VPB, VP(HL), and VP(AM) Squadrons* (Washington, D.C.: Naval Historical Center, Department of the Navy, 2000), 458-461, https://www.history.navy.mil/content/dam/nhhc/research/histories/naval-aviation/dictionary-of-american-naval-aviation-squadrons-volume-2/pdfs/DictionaryAmericanNavalAviationSquadronsVol2.pdf.

47. To locate Naval Air Station 6 on Whidbey Island, in Google Maps insert coordinates 48.342658, -122.661894 in the search box and click the search button.

48. To locate Naval Air Station Kaneohe, in Google Maps insert coordinates 21.444774, -157.751194 in the search box and click the search button.

49. The black-painted aircraft were known as "black cats." The "cat" stood for Catalina. PBY Catalina was the common name of the airplane.

50. The term "disestablished" meant the unit was permanently shut down. In contrast, "deactivated" meant the unit was no longer active, but could be reactivated.

51. Maurine's term "grain elevator" meant the grain company owned by Bill's older half-brother Herman Gjovig.

Chapter 18

Katharine—A Tribute

Every life meets obstacles and setbacks, some more difficult than others and some more unjust. But there is always some scope of self-determination, no matter how narrow. In that space, we are on our own.

~ David Von Drehle, *The Book of Charlie*

• • • • • • •

"You want to grow up to be a lady, don't you?" I said not particularly.

~ Harper Lee, *To Kill a Mockingbird*

In the old country, Katharine Deininger followed the custom for daughters during that period of time. In her birth family, she was the oldest child to survive into adulthood, but she would never be the one to inherit the family's home or land. Meager though they were, these family possessions would all be inherited by a son. A daughter was expected to find employment away from home and then marry.

Her early life was an accommodation to what was expected in late-19th century Germany. She was not one to protest loudly or wave a banner proclaiming the injustice of cultural rules for women. Her young life was about achievement despite societal constraints.

Katharine found employment working as a domestic for the Hinderer family in Brend, Germany. She soon began a relationship with the Hinderer's oldest son Gottlieb. In time, their relationship resulted in Katharine's pregnancy. By itself, this was not uncommon. The norm for couples was to live with either of their parents, have children, and then formally marry once the man was earning a sufficient income to support his young family.

Despite this ordinary beginning, Katharine and Gottlieb decided to leave their families in Germany and emigrate to America. Gottlieb's cousin in Iowa was their contact and destination. Once they settled on an Iowa rental farm, they formalized their marriage. It was a statement of their resolve to live independently without family support. The birth of five children was followed by a move to southwestern Minnesota where they bought farmland on credit. They spent their first winter living in a dirt-floor sod house. After this hardship, they began to build their farmhouse step-by-step. It would be their one and only home.

Nothing came easily during those early years in Minnesota. They plowed what land was tillable, pastured the rest, and raised a mix of animals meant to feed their family. From early childhood, their children were expected to work at home. This was often accomplished at the expense of their schooling. Each year required a strategic plan to keep the family going one more cycle of seasons.

Katharine carried with her the old world values she was born into. Whether it was the choice of which church to attend or what behavior was permitted at home, she had a sense of what was right and what mattered. The character of the church members took precedent over the theology behind the denomination. Children were respectful and were raised to be self-reliant. Years later, all the storytellers recognized that Katharine was the primary force in the Hinderer family.

Within Katharine's old world values, there was room for change. At first, she would not allow her children to play card games. Later, these games were tolerated, as long as the players maintained a measured demeanor. She had first believed that high school was not necessary for a girl. Later, family events proved it could be beneficial for everyone, so she accepted and even promoted the idea. Katharine was able to navigate a fine line between her old world values and new world circumstances.

Throughout her life, Katharine recognized superficiality and disingenuous behavior. When action was required, she took the lead. She tolerated neither fools nor villains. As the family matriarch, she responded to bad behavior with a calm determination to help the victims. This approach was her strength. Punishment was for others to mete out. Her role was to engage and support family members who might otherwise have sunk into self-pity or depression.

Two World Wars and the Great Depression directly affected the Hinderer family. Despite difficult times, this family, and especially the young children, all survived. How was this possible? In part, they were fortunate, but the extended Hinderer family also had an uncommon bond. It was a resilience borne of their strength of character. The credit goes to Katharine for instilling that character into this family.

You can see Katharine's influence in all her children's lives. The oldest children worked an unending life of hard labor. Tena and Carl were child laborers by necessity. At home or working away, a self-directed childhood was never a possibility for them. Nevertheless, they lived full lives. Work became its own reward. Neither Tena nor Carl expressed regret for what they were required to do during their childhood.

The middle children each had their own crushing challenges. Sophie's young family was left motherless by her early death, yet her sister and best friend Emma stepped in to raise her three children. Emma herself made relationship choices that later required decades of support from her birth family. As a child, Mary was tasked with caring for her younger twin siblings. Later, she married a man forever doomed by the aftermath of World War I. How did she raise their four children? She relied on the strength of family. Her brother-in-law Arthur became a reliable father figure. The extended Hinderer family provided the substance of what every child needs: love and support. Martha Hinderer wished to have a life of her own away from the farm. Nevertheless, when her twin brother John was conscripted into World War II, she diligently returned to help out at home.

Finally, it was John Hinderer who most embodied the legacy of his mother Katharine. Although he never married, he was a father figure in the early lives of his many nieces and nephews. Every one of the storytellers spoke of John with a near-reverence. The very worst John would say about someone was that they were "kind of a stinker." Like his mother Katharine, he did not dwell on accusations, condemnations, or vengeful behavior. What was important to him was caring for the family. Regardless of whether they were victims of bad luck or bad behavior, he was always there. John led a long and full life, and this was reflected in the memories of those he touched. John Hinderer was a mirror image of his mother Katharine carried forward into the next generation.

The lessons Katharine taught her family are not restricted to the past. Life is not so different today. If you are fortunate, you are born into a life that offers broad choices. And if you are not fortunate, there remains some measure of self-determination, no matter how small. In her time, Katharine was not one of the fortunate. It did not matter. Her family was the focus and purpose of her life. Strength of character was the gift she gave to her children and later generations. She became an example and a teacher to those willing to work thoughtfully toward contentment in their own lives. As she neared the end of her long life, Katharine did not dwell on some dreamy past. Rather, she found solace in what simple choices remained. In her last letter she wrote, "I cannot see nor hear much, but [I] can be up and around."

• • • • • • •

The essential drama of life is the drama to construct character, which is an engraved set of disciplined habits, a settled disposition to do good.

~ David Brooks, *The Road to Character*

Appendices

■ ■ ■

Appendix A: Ancestor Families

Appendix B: A Tour of St. Stephan Church, Aldorf

Appendix C: Family Recipes
- Katharine Hinderer
- Martha Hinderer
- Tene Monson
- Emma Krug
- Mary Engstrand

Appendix A

Ancestor Families

Introduction

Ancestor families for both Gottlieb Hinderer and Katharine Deininger were briefly outlined at the beginning of Chapters 2 and 3. Both of their family lines have been expanded in this appendix.

Each family is described using a type of ancestor chart known as an Ahnentafel. This is a numbering scheme where the index ancestor (Gottlieb or Katharine) is given the number 1. Prior generations include only a person's father and mother (direct line ancestors). The father is given the next highest number and the mother is given the subsequent number. The result is that all fathers have an even number and the mothers have an odd number. For example, Gottlieb Hinderer is #1, so his father is #2 and his mother is #3. The resulting chart is a predictable ancestor tree. Each ancestor's number describes where to locate them on the chart and where they fit in the direct ancestor line.

In these charts, some ancestors are missing. Generally, the farther back in time a person lived, the greater the likelihood that their information could not be found.

In former times, local churches kept register volumes listing family events. The information listed in the Ahnentafel primarily comes from these archived church registers. The archived church records were found in two locations. Some were discovered at the Württemberg Regional Archive Center in Stuttgart Germany. Other church records were discovered using genealogy websites, mainly Ancestry.com and Familysearch.org.

These Ahnentafel charts were researched and compiled in 2018 and 2019. Merlin Schlichting evaluated the original records and translated the listings first into modern German and then into English. He also corresponded with personnel working at the Stuttgart archive. The author, David Schlichting, researched and evaluated the information that came from genealogy websites.

With rare exception, ancestor names and dates have been included only if an original church document was viewed and translated. If a date or name was only claimed by another genealogist, it was not included unless an original document provided corroborating information.

Katharine

Ancestors of Gottlieb Hinderer (1866-1951)

1 Gottlieb Hinderer
b. 15 Sept 1866 in Germany
m. 5 Feb 1892 to Katharine Deininger
d. 25 Aug 1951 rural Canby MN

2 Johannes Hinderer
b. 20 Aug 1842
m. 3 Sept 1865
d. 18 Aug 1923

3 Sophie Weller
b. 9 May 1844
d. 9 Dec 1903

4 Gottfried Hinderer
b. 15 Oct 1804
m. 4 Jun 1833
d. 21 Nov 1874

5 Rosine Bareiss
b. 23 Nov 1810
d. 22 May 1870

6 Jacob Weller
b. 25 Nov 1804
m. 12 May 1829
d. 22 Apr 1873

7 Anna Maria Schäfer
b. 16 Mar 1810
d. 15 Jan 1891

8 Matthäus Hinderer
b. 5 Feb 1770
m. 5 Jun 1798
d. 25 Oct 1851

9 Anna Maria Bareiss
b. 1 Feb 1781
d. 25 Dec 1842

10 Johann Georg Bareiss
b. 8 Oct 1778
m. 14 Jul 1807
d. 31 Jul 1852

11 Rosine Majer
b. 29 Nov 1782
d. 25 Nov 1836

12 Matthäus Weller
b. 18 Jan 1765
m. 8 Feb 1791
d. 27 Jan 1832

13 Christine Häffner
b. 18 Feb 1770
d. 1 Jan 1824

14 Johann Wilhelm Heinrich Schäfer
b. 6 Aug 1780
m. 16 Oct 1804
d. 4 Dec 1842

15 Anna Maria Ziegler
b. 10 Jul 1779
d. 3 Jan 1848

16 Andreas Hinderer
b. 13 Oct 1730
m. 26 May 1767
d. 2 Aug 1786

17 Maria Schöllhammer
b. 29 Jul 1741
d. 10 Feb 1824

18 Johann Georg Bareiss
b. 13 Apr 1760
d. 1816

19 Katharina Maria Kühnlin
d. 1813

20 Matthäus Bareiss
b. 27 Nov 1740
m. 7 May 1771
d. 21 Nov 1812

21 Anna Maria Majer
b. 19 Jan 1752
d. 13 Sept 1819

22 Johann Georg Majer
b. 7 Jun 1756
m. 10 Jul 1781
d. 26 Jan 1785

23 Anna Maria Weller
b. 18 Jun 1765
d. 24 Aug 1837

24 Johann Jacob Weller
b. 14 Oct 1724
m. 20 May 1754
d. 13 May 1800

25 Veronica Stieffel *
b. 16 Sept 1730
d. 15 Jan 1766

26 Johann Michael Häffner
m. 2 May 1769 to
27 Anna Maria Ebertin

28 Johann Albrecht Gottlieb Schäfer and
29 Margaretha Sÿbilla Schäfer

30 Michael Ziegler and
31 Ursula Stolch

Appendix A: Ancestors of Gottlieb Hinderer, 1866-1951

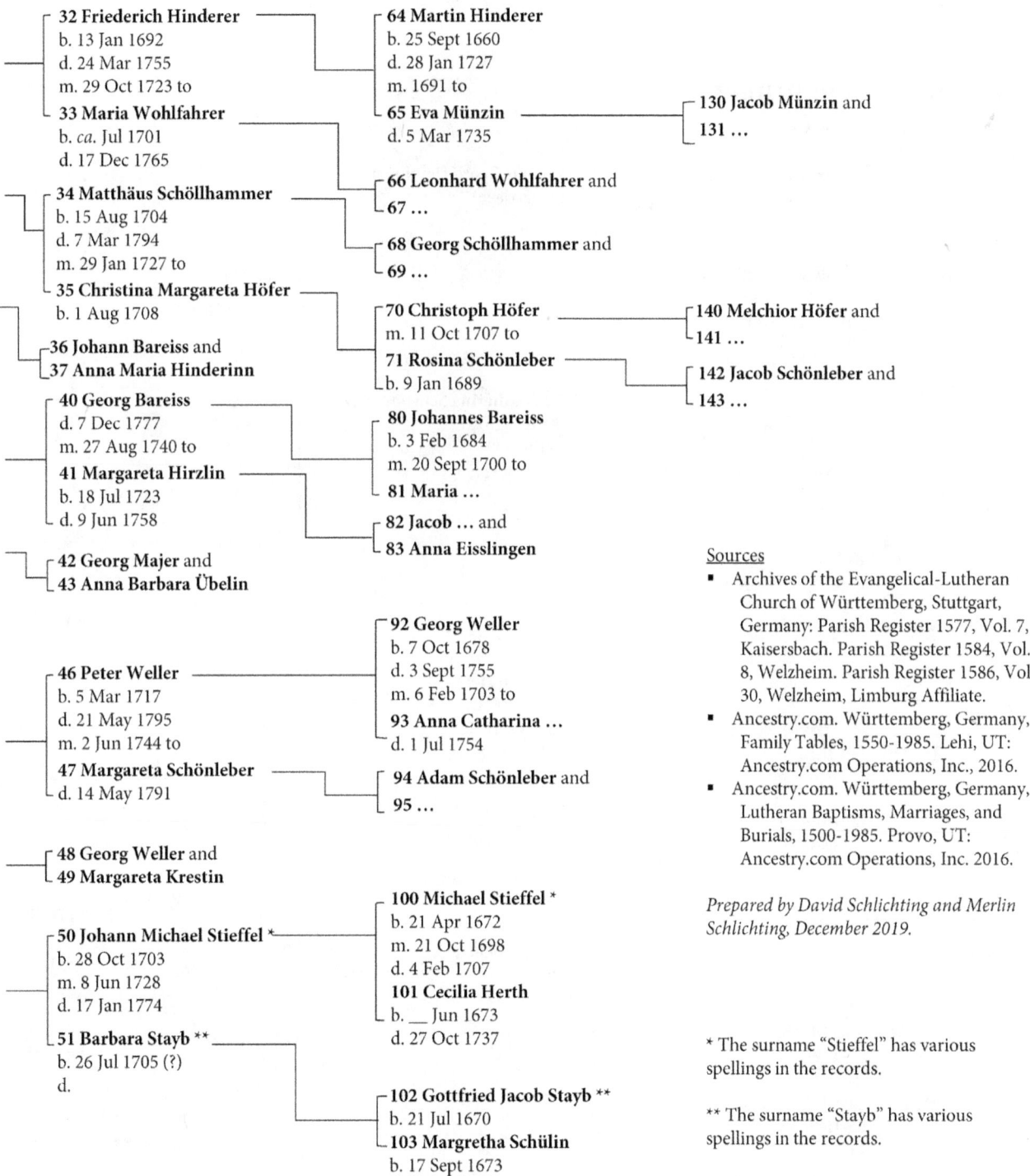

Sources
- Archives of the Evangelical-Lutheran Church of Württemberg, Stuttgart, Germany: Parish Register 1577, Vol. 7, Kaisersbach. Parish Register 1584, Vol. 8, Welzheim. Parish Register 1586, Vol. 30, Welzheim, Limburg Affiliate.
- Ancestry.com. Württemberg, Germany, Family Tables, 1550-1985. Lehi, UT: Ancestry.com Operations, Inc., 2016.
- Ancestry.com. Württemberg, Germany, Lutheran Baptisms, Marriages, and Burials, 1500-1985. Provo, UT: Ancestry.com Operations, Inc. 2016.

Prepared by David Schlichting and Merlin Schlichting, December 2019.

* The surname "Stieffel" has various spellings in the records.

** The surname "Stayb" has various spellings in the records.

Katharine

Ancestors of Katharine Deininger Hinderer 1872-1964

1 Katharine Deininger
b. 14 Oct 1872, Gehren, Württemberg, Germany
m. 5 Feb 1892 to Gottlieb Hinderer
d. 19 Mar 1964, rural Canby, MN

2 Johann Gottlieb Deininger
b. 13 May 1840
m. 25 Jan 1874
d. 22 Feb 1927

3 Karoline Heinz
b. 16 Dec 1851
d. 11 July 1934

4 Johann Georg Deininger
(no marriage)

5 Eva Catharina Schwinger
b. 21 Apr 1817
d. 9 Feb 1902

6 Gottlieb Heinz
b. 3 Aug 1810
m. 19 Jun 1842
d. 1 Jun 1867

7 Rosine Weller
b. 3 May 1827
d. 25 Dec 1877

10 Jacob Schwinger
(no marriage)

11 Rosina Heinz
b. 25 May 1790
d. 12 Apr 1854

12 Johann Georg Heinz
b. 17 Jan 1776
m. 6 Mar 1794
d. 21 Aug 1851

13 Catharina Müller
b. 31 May 1777
d. 25 Aug 1844

14 Christian Weller
b. 21 Jan 1796
m. 17 Jun 1823
d. 18 Nov 1867

15 Catharina Weller
b. 17 Dec 1805
d. 31 Jan 1861

Sources
1. Archives of the Evangelical-Lutheran Church of Württemberg, Stuttgart, Germany: Parish Register 1577, Vol. 7, Kaisersbach; Parish Register 1584, Vol. 8, Welzheim; Parish Register 1586, Vol. 30, Welzheim, Limburg Affiliate.
2. Ancestry.com. Württemberg, Germany, Family Tables, 1550-1985. Lehi, UT: Ancestry.com Operations, Inc., 2016.
3. Ancestry.com. Württemberg, Germany, Lutheran Baptisms, Marriages, and Burials, 1500-1985. Provo, UT: Ancestry.com Operations, Inc. 2016.

Prepared by David Schlichting and Merlin Schlichting December 2018

Appendix A: Ancestors of Katharine Deininger Hinderer, 1872-1964

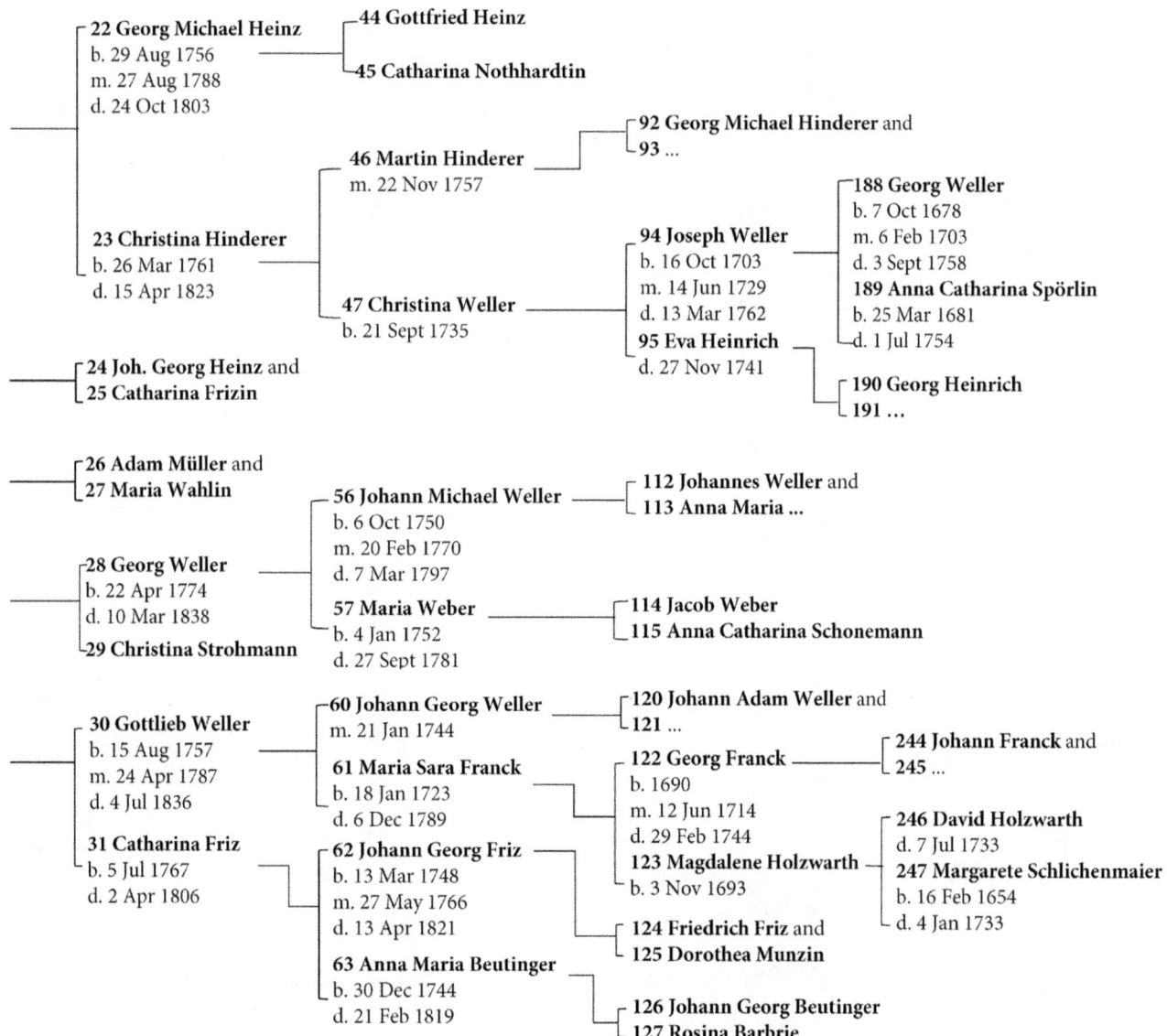

387

Appendix B

A Tour of St. Stephan Church, Aldorf

Tour Conducted on October 6, 2019 by Pastor Friedmar Probst

On October 6, 2019, Pastor Friedmar Probst conducted a tour of St. Stephan Church (*Stephanuskirche*) in Alfdorf. During the tour, Pastor Probst offered comments on the history of Alfdorf, its relation to surrounding villages, and the history of the church itself. Pastor Probst had been at St. Stephan Church for 19 years and planned to retire in 2020. The Sunday afternoon tour included his own perspective on the church and the community.

During the morning service earlier that day, Pastor Probst had announced to the congregation that my brother Merlin, my son Ryan, and I were attending their harvest festival service while exploring the ties between our Hinderer family and the Alfdorf community. That afternoon, Pastor Probst conducted our tour in English. It was not his native language, but it reflected his knowledge that two in our group would not understand a tour conducted in German. His time and consideration were greatly appreciated.

The Tour Begins: Historic Alfdorf and Its People

Until about 150 years ago, towns like Alfdorf had one or two land-owning noble families. The other residents were mostly poor and lived along narrow streets in tiny houses closely compacted side by side. During daylight hours they worked on distant large farms, returning to their homes in the evening.

The homes of the poor surrounded the town center. Any farmable land they owned stretched in narrow ribbons behind their compacted houses. These narrow strips of land were used to grow vegetables and other food crops meant to feed their families. Most of the residents also owned a few animals that were housed under the same roof as the family. The animals were another source of food. In former times, animal waste was piled in front of the house by the street. Today, no houses with farm animals remain in Alfdorf.

The Alfdorf church was constructed to be a large church because it was intended to be a regional church. People living in villages near Alfdorf would walk or use horses to attend church each Sunday. Churches created close ties between towns and nearby villages.

In this part of Germany, the villages and towns are close together, often a mile or less apart. For example, the village of Brend, where the Hinderer family lived, was and still is connected to Alfdorf by a walking path. It takes only 30 minutes to complete the one-way walk from Brend to St. Stephen Church in Alfdorf.

A regional church was where citizens could expand their range of friendships. In their own small villages they might know 100 or fewer people. On Sundays, however, they could meet many people from a large region. In particular, it served to broaden the marital prospects for the young residents of small villages. In this way, church attendance functioned as both a religious and a social experience.

St. Stephan Church of Alfdorf

As early as 1297, church records identified a chapel at the current site of St. Stephan Church.

Over the next two centuries, the old records noted that the chapel was periodically enlarged, and a bell tower was constructed.

The Protestant Reformation, which began in 1517, brought conflict to Alfdorf and other towns in Wuerttemberg. Catholic leaders and their aligned civil authorities struggled against the emerging Protestant leaders with their own aligned civil authorities. The control of Alfdorf vacillated between religious leaders. After 1639, however, Protestantism prevailed.

A Protestant nobleman, Baron Georg Friedrich vom Holtz, became the first patron of St. Stephan Church. As patron, Baron vom Holtz was required to maintain and repair the church. If a church could not be repaired, the patron was responsible for rebuilding the church. Because of their status as patrons, members of the vom Holtz family were buried in an exclusive burial plot within the main cemetery. The original spelling of the patron's surname was "vom Holtz," but a more recent spelling is "vom Holst."

In the 1770s, at the same time of the American Revolution, the vom Holtz patron responsible for St. Stephan church proposed several plans to modify the existing church structure. After months of consideration, he decided instead to tear down the old church and build a new one.

In 1773, this vom Holtz patron hired a well-known builder, Johann Michael Keller, from the nearby town of Schwäbisch Gmünd. Keller had designed many Baroque-style buildings which remain today in Schwäbisch Gmünd.

Keller proposed to rebuild the church using a transverse orientation. He had built a similarly designed church in the nearby town of Aalen. Historically, churches were built with the altar at the east end and the bell tower and main entrance at the west end. The Keller transverse design placed the altar along the long north wall and the main entrance centered on the opposite south wall. The bell tower remained at the west end and the east end had only a small service door. The pews were angled in a half circle facing the altar. The idea was to focus the congregation's attention toward the central altar.

The crucifix above the new St. Stephan altar was originally sculpted in 1687-88 and was salvaged from an earlier church. The corpus (body of Christ) was carved from Italian marble. The cross itself was carved from leiss-graphite limestone; a rock form common in the Alfdorf area. It was unusual for Protestant churches built after the Reformation to feature a cross with the corpus. The prevailing belief was that because of the second commandment, no corpus (body) or pictures of God or saints should be seen in the church. The St. Stephan patron and the congregation, however, did not agree with that restriction.

During Sunday church services, the vom Holtz family sat in a separate glassed-off room in the balcony. Their room was centered above the main entrance to the church, so they had a direct view of the altar. The heater in Baron vom Holtz's room was forged in 1721 in a village about 35 miles from Alfdorf. Originally, it was the only source of heat in the church, and it only warmed the patron family's room. The wood fuel for the heater was stoked from outside of the patron's room. Any ashes were removed from outside of the room as well. Throughout Europe, room heaters such as these separated the messy part of wood-fired heating from the privileged residents inside of the rooms. The vom Holtz coat of arms was also painted on the wall of this private room. Members of the vom Holtz family still reside in the Alfdorf area and attend services at St. Stephan Church.

The wall painting behind the church altar was completed in 1951. The story of the painting was troubling for Pastor Probst to discuss. Two-hundred-seventeen soldiers from the Alfdorf area had been killed in WWII. These young men were husbands, brothers, and sons of congregation members. When a church family learned of a death, they crafted a memorial wreath of branches and flowers to be hung from the church balcony

Appendix B: A Tour of St. Stephan Church, Aldorf

A picture of the south side of St. Stephan Church. The onion-shaped bell tower at the west end of the church can also be seen. The main entrance doorway is centered along the south side. Source: Photographed and edited by author.

railing. When the wreaths dried out, the wealthier families could afford to replace them, but the poor families could not.

The congregation's minister at the time suggested replacing the wreaths with a painted wall mural as a memorial to all of the lost men. A painter from northern Germany, Rudolph Schäfer, was hired to do the artwork. Schäfer was born in 1878, so in the year 1951, he was 73 years old. The theme of his wall painting was the idea of sacrifice.

The congregation's minister in 1951 had been a decorated WWII Nazi officer. It troubled Pastor Probst that Bible stories of religious sacrifice were linked to the Nazi code of glorifying the sacrifice of one's life for their political cause.

One area of the painting showed Abraham telling his son that although they had no lamb to sacrifice, God would provide. The terrible truth was that later, Abraham slayed this son as the sacrifice. Another painting represented a Bible story alluding to the coming death of Jesus, another sacrifice of a life. Above these two Bible stories, Schäfer painted the souls of the children killed by Herod rising toward the heavens: again a reference to death and sacrifice.

Schäfer also painted two hilltops in the background. These two hilltops can be seen in the distance by people in Alfdorf. Their addition was Schäfer's effort to personalize the painting for the congregation.

Katharine

The wall-mounted heater in the patron's room was originally forged in 1721. Source: Photographed and edited by author.

Pastor Probst reflect more deeply on the painting. To him, the Schäfer mural promoted the sacrifice of life for a political cause as if it were a religious cause. He concluded that personal religious beliefs and war themes were separate ideas and should not be mixed. For this reason, the 1951 paintings were troubling to Pastor Probst.

David Schlichting

Following WWII, people would come from up to 30 miles away to see this painting. For these people, the war with its death and destruction had been a personal experience. Today, the painting is not as meaningful according to Pastor Probst. The people who lived through that war have all passed away.

Pastor Probst noted that his own father had recently died in February 2019. His father was born in the 1920s, and had been in the German army during WWII. This family experience made

Appendix B: A Tour of St. Stephan Church, Aldorf

The 1951 wall painting behind the altar depicts Biblical scenes of sacrifice. The altar with the stone cross and corpus are in the foreground. The pulpit was built above and behind the cross. Source: Photographed and edited by author.

A photo from October 2019. Left to right: Merlin Schlichting, Pastor Friedmar Probst, and David Schlichting. Source: Photographed by Ryan Schlichting and edited by the author.

Appendix C

Family Recipes

Katharine Hinderer
Sandwich Buns
Wax Bean Pickles
Spaetzle
Pfeffer Nuesse (Pepper Nut) Cookies

Martha Hinderer
Martha's Overnight Cookies
Overnight Salad

Tene Monson
Doughnuts
Berlinerkranz Knots
Sour Cream Raisin Bars

Emma Krug
Emma Krug's Cookies
Honey Cookies
Scotch Date Cookies
Suet Pudding
Gingerbread Cake
Sour Cream Pie
Carrot Cookies
Pinwheel Cookies

Mary Engstrand
Noodle Surpice Casserole
Banana Nut Bread

Katharine Hinderer

Sandwich Buns

2 dry yeast cakes & 1 tsp. sugar dissolved in 1 c. warm water
3 c. warm water   1 tsp. salt
11 to 12 c. flour   1 c. lard
1 c. sugar   4 c. butter

Crumble and dissolve the yeast cakes into 1 cup of warm water into which 1 teaspoon of sugar has been added. Allow this to stand for five minutes.

Place the 3 cups of warm water in a separate bowl and add some flour. Beat the flour into the water. Add the sugar, salt and more flour to this mixture. Now add the yeast mixture, followed by more flour. Add the lard, butter, and any remaining flour. Mix with spoon until it is too thick, and then use hands. Mix to soft dough.

Cover the dough with a lid or with towels, and let it rise until it doubles in size. Knead the dough by punching in one side, and then folding the edges over the hole created by the punching. You can add more lard if needed.

Cover the dough and let it rise until it is about half again larger. Pinch off dough, and bake.

Source: Katharine's basic recipe was saved by Bette (Krug) Weber. Doris (Lafere) Schlichting recalled that when she was a child living on the Hinderer farm, Katharine Hinderer would bake these buns in the cookstove oven. She used a black baking pan that was so large it just fit into the oven. It was at least three times the size of a standard 9 X 13 cake pan. Doris said wood was used to fire the stove when it was used for baking. (Corncobs were used when the cookstove was being used for heating the kitchen.) The baked buns were cut in half and used to make "lunch" (mid-morning and mid-afternoon) sandwiches taken to the men working in the fields.

Wax Bean Pickles (makes 1 quart)

1 qt. yellow wax beans cut at a slant
⅔ c. vinegar
⅓ c. water
1 c. sugar
1 stick cinnamon

Heat the vinegar, water, sugar, and cinnamon to boiling. Add the cut beans and cook until they are slightly softened. Can and seal in a one quart jar.

Source: Doris (Lafere) Schlichting recalled that this version of wax bean pickles was prepared by her grandmother Katharine in the 1920s. When Doris later married Henry Schlichting, she discovered that his mother, who was also of German heritage, canned wax bean pickles using a similar recipe.

Appendix C: Family Recipes

Spaetzle

2 c. sifted flour
2 eggs
1 egg yolk
½ tsp. salt

⅔ c. cold water
¼ c. butter, melted
½ c. breadcrumbs

Mix together the flour, eggs, egg yolk, salt, and cold water. Stir this well. The texture should be runny. Heat a large kettle of salted water to high boil. Pour the runny dough slowly into the boiling water while stirring the water vigorously. Boil for 5 minutes. Drain the spaetzle and rinse it with cold water. Heat the butter and breadcrumbs until slightly browned, and then pour it over the spaetzle.

Note: Spaetzle was used instead of potatoes and was most often served with some form of pork and sauerkraut.

Special Note: This recipe was tested, and the outcome suggests that modifications are necessary.

Source: Katharine Hinderer prepared spaetzle on the Hinderer farm. Most likely it was a recipe recalled from her early life in Wuerttemberg Germany.

Pfeffer Nuesse (Pepper Nut) Cookies

4 c. flour
2 c. white sugar
1 Tbsp. each: cinnamon, cloves, and nutmeg
1 tsp. baking powder
5 eggs
½ c. citron (candied cherries and/or canned pineapple chunks were often used instead of citron)

Sift the dry ingredients together. Add the fruit and then the well-beaten eggs. Mix this thoroughly together. With buttered hands, shape the dough into hickory nut-sized cookies. Bake on waxed paper at 325°. Do not over bake. This recipe makes 70 cookies.

Note: Pfeffer Nuesse cookies should be baked a month prior to eating and placed in a tight container to slowly blend the flavors. They are usually brittle and nearly hard when eaten. If they become too hard, place half a raw apple or a slice of fresh bread with the cookies in a sealed container. Sprinkle powdered sugar over the cookies before eating.

Source: Katharine did not state the exact source, but the recipe likely came from her family in Germany. Pfeffer Nuesse cookies are traditionally served in Germany during the Christmas season.

Martha Hinderer

Martha's Overnight Cookies

6 c. flour	½ c. dark Karo syrup
2 c. white sugar	1 c. chopped nuts or coconut
2 eggs	1 Tbsp. soda in ¼ c. hot water
1 c. shortening	Dash of salt

Stir all of the ingredients together. Shape the dough into two rolls, and chill them in the refrigerator overnight. Slice the dough into about ¼ inch thick cookies, and bake at 350°. Do not over bake.

Source: Doris Schlichting supplied this recipe. In her memory, only Martha made these overnight cookies.

Overnight Salad

Night before
1 three oz. can crushed pineapple with juice
1 pt. whipping cream
1 pkg. dry lime Jell-O
1 ten oz. pkg. miniature marshmallows

Next day
1 tsp. vanilla
1 seven oz. pkg. buttermint candy

Mix the pineapple with juice, the dry Jell-O, and the marshmallows together. Let this mixture stand overnight in the refrigerator.

The next day, whip the cream, and add the vanilla. Mix this with the overnight mixture and fold in the candies at the end. Keep cool until served. This salad can be preserved frozen for up to a month if desired.

Source: Bette (Krug) Weber provided this recipe from Martha.

Tena Monson

Doughnuts

3 ¼ c. flour
1 tsp. salt
2 tsp. baking powder
1 tsp. baking soda
1 c. white sugar

2 eggs, beaten
1 c. sour milk
2 Tbsp. cream
1 tsp. nutmeg

Add the salt, baking powder, and baking soda to the flour and sift them together. Blend in the sugar, beaten eggs, sour milk, cream, and nutmeg. Do not mix more than necessary. Cook in hot oil until golden brown.

Source: George and Mabel Monson believed this was their mother Tena's recipe. She made these doughnuts often, and it was a favorite family recipe. Cousin Jerry Weidendorf was quoted as saying that Tena's doughnuts were the best. George recalled that when he was young, Jerry's first words of greeting would be to ask if Tena had any doughnuts.

Berlinerkranz Knots

4 c. flour
1 c. sugar
1 tsp. baking soda
½ c. butter

½ c. lard
5 eggs, separated
½ c. sweet cream

Add the sugar and baking soda to the flour and sift them together. Mix the butter and lard into the flour mixture as you would for a piecrust. Beat the five egg yolks, and then add them to the dough mixture. Add the sweet cream to the mixture. Mix this dough thoroughly.

Roll the dough into a long rope about the diameter of your little finger. Cut the dough into about six-inch long ropes. With each rope, cross the two ends over one another leaving a bit of each end beyond the crossover point. Whip the egg whites and then dip the wreaths into the egg whites first, and then some granulated or coarse sugar. Bake on a greased cookie sheet at 350° for 10 to 15 minutes, until golden.

Source: George Monson recalled that his mother prepared these occasionally while he was growing up. As is traditional in Europe, these were mainly a Christmas treat. The source of this particular recipe is unknown. These wreath-shaped cookies have been holiday specialties in Germanic and Scandinavian cultures. The term "knots" in the recipe name refers to the local practice of crossing the ends, rather than making a circular wreath shape.

Sour Cream Raisin Bars

Crumb Base
1 ¾ c. flour
1 c. brown sugar
1 ¾ c. quick oats
1 tsp. baking soda
1 c. oleo (margarine), melted

Filling
2 eggs, whole
1 ½ c. white sugar
3 Tbsp. cornstarch
2 c. sour cream
2 c. raisins

Crumb Base: Preheat the oven to 350°. Combine the flour, brown sugar, quick oats, and baking soda. Blend these well. Add the melted oleo and mix thoroughly. Place ⅔ of this mixture in a 9 X 13 baking pan. Bake at 350° for 15 minutes. Allow it to cool.

Filling: In a saucepan, combine the eggs, white sugar, cornstarch, sour cream, and raisins. Carefully bring this mixture to a boil, then reduce the heat and boil slowly for 10 to 15 minutes. Stir often to avoid scorching. Pour the filling over the baked crumb base. Cover the filling with the remaining crumb base and bake at 350° for 20 minutes.

Note: The recipe states that "Old Home" regular sour cream and "Promise" margarine work well for these bars.

Source: George Monson recalled that his mother made these while he was growing up. He enjoyed them and later made these bars himself. There is a note on the recipe stating it came from a Mrs. Honabel in Minot, North Dakota. George did not know if his mother knew Mrs. Honabel personally.

Emma Krug

Emma Krug's Cookies
Makes 3 dozen

1 egg
2 c. oatmeal
nuts
pinch salt
1 c. flour

½ c. coconut
1 c. brown sugar
½ c. melted shortening
¼ tsp. soda in 2 Tbsp. hot water

Heat at 375°

Note: The above ingredients and directions are exactly as Emma wrote them. See the photo below.

Source: This recipe was written in pencil by Emma on the inside front cover of a small book titled "A Calendar of Dinners with 615 Recipes." The book's introductory chapter was titled "The Story of Crisco." The book was published in 1916 as a promotion for Crisco.

Emma wrote this cookie recipe on the inside front cover of a book promoting Crisco. She did not give these cookies a name. Source: The Doris Schlichting collection. Edited by author.

Honey Cookies

Night Before
3 eggs
1 c. sugar
1 c. light clover honey
1 tsp. vanilla
1 c. flour
2 tsp. baking soda
Pinch of salt

Next Morning
4 c. flour (possibly more)

Night Before: Beat the eggs well, and then beat in the sugar, honey, and vanilla. Sift the flour into a separate bowl. Measure the flour again, add the soda and salt to it, and sift it again. Stir the flour mix and eggs together. Chill the mixture overnight in the refrigerator.

Next Morning: Stir about 3 ½ cups of the flour into the chilled mixture. The consistency should be sticky. Spread the last ½ cup of flour (or more if needed) onto a board. Roll out the dough to about ¼ inch thick. Cut out the cookies with a doughnut cutter. Bake at 350° until golden brown. Watch them closely because they bake quickly.

Source: Emma Krug, her mother Katharine Hinderer, and her sister Martha Hinderer made variations of honey cookies. With John Hinderer tending beehives, the family had a ready source of honey. By the late 1950s, it was mainly Emma who baked these cookies for her grandchildren. They were chewy, sweet, and loved by the children.

Scotch Date Cookies
Emma Krug

Cookie Dough
2 c. flour
2 c. oatmeal
1 c. brown sugar
¾ c. shortening
½ c. milk
1 tsp. baking soda

Date Filling
1 lb. pitted dates*
1 c. sugar
½ c. or slightly less water
1 Tbsp. lemon juice

Cookie Dough: Mix all of the ingredients together.

Filling: Place the dates, sugar and water in a saucepan. Heat the mixture to boiling, and then simmer it until the dates are soft. Add the lemon juice.

Roll the dough onto a floured board. The dough should be thin, just over 1/8 inch thick. Cut out small circles of dough the size of Oreos (Emma used a Calumet baking powder can). Bake at 350° for 8 – 10 minutes. Do not over bake. Take the cookies from the oven and spread some filling between two warm cookies.

*Emma often substituted a pound of ground up raisins instead of dates.
Source: Doris recalled only her mother Emma baking these cookies.

Suet Pudding

Pudding
1 c. suet, ground
1 ½ c. raisins, chopped
1 c. brown sugar
1 c. sour milk (buttermilk)
1 tsp. baking soda
2 ½ c. flour

Sauce
1 ¼ Tbsp. (about) cornstarch
2 c. cream or half and half
⅔ c. white sugar (or to taste)
1 tsp. vanilla

Pudding: Place the suet and raisins in a mixing bowl. In a separate bowl, add the soda to the milk and mix it well. Add a little of the milk mixture to the suet and raisins. Mix this well so there are no suet lumps. Add the brown sugar and the rest of the milk mixture.

Cook the pudding about 2 hours in a steamer using a circular greased metal pan at least 2 ½ inches deep. Tie two sheets of waxed paper over the tin so no steam gets inside of it. Cool the pudding, and then store it in the refrigerator, or freeze it for longer storage.

Sauce: In a small bowl, add enough water to the cornstarch to dissolve it and allow it to flow easily. In a heavy saucepan, add the sugar to the cream, and heat it carefully. Stir it constantly until it boils. Remove it from the heat.

Add about 2 tablespoons of the hot cream to the cornstarch mixture, stirring it quickly to avoid lumps. Place the remaining cream mix on the stove and reheat to near boiling. Add the cornstarch mixture slowly to the heated cream, stirring it constantly. Bring this to a boil. This mixture should be like very thin gravy. Remove the sauce from the heat and stir in the vanilla. Store the sauce in the refrigerator.

Serving: Serve the pudding and sauce hot. Re-steam the pudding to heat it. Separately reheat the sauce. Cut small pieces of pudding onto a serving plate and pour the hot sauce over the top. Serve immediately.

Source: Doris Schlichting provided this recipe. It is elaborate and was only prepared for holidays, especially Christmas. Katharine Hinderer, Emma Krug, Doris Schlichting, and possibly others in the family made suet pudding. The Hinderers had their own suet from the hogs they butchered. Doris recalled that her mother Emma bought her suet in Canby.

Gingerbread Cake

⅓ c. shortening
½ c. white sugar
1 egg
½ c. molasses
1 ½ c. flour
1 tsp. baking soda
¼ tsp. salt
1 tsp. ginger
¾ c. boiling water

Cream the shortening and sugar together. Add the egg and then the molasses. Mix well. In a separate bowl, mix the flour, soda, salt, and ginger together. Gradually add the flour mixture to the other mixture. Stir in the boiling water. Bake in a greased and floured cake pan at 350°. Serve the cake with a mashed banana and whipped cream on top.

Source: Doris Schlichting supplied this recipe written by her mother Emma Krug. It is not known if Emma copied the recipe or made it up herself.

Sour Cream Raisin Pie

9-inch Pie shell previously baked

Filling
1 ½ c. raisins
½ tsp. cinnamon
½ tsp. nutmeg
¾ c. sugar
1 ½ Tbsp. flour
½ tsp. salt
1 ½ c. sour cream
4 egg yolks, beaten

Meringue
3 egg whites
¼ tsp. cream of tartar
6 Tbsp. sugar
½ tsp. vanilla

Filling: In a saucepan, cook the raisins, cinnamon, and nutmeg with enough water to cover for 15 minutes, or until the water is gone. In a separate bowl, blend the sugar, flour, salt, and sour cream together, and then blend in the egg yolks. Pour this mixture into the raisins in the saucepan. Cook this slowly, stirring gently until it thickens. Use care, as it will scorch easily. Pour the thickened filling into the baked pie shell.

Meringue: Beat the egg whites and cream of tartar until it becomes foamy. Beat in the sugar, one tablespoon at a time, until it is stiff and glossy. Beat in the vanilla.

Spread the meringue over the pie and bake it at 400° until the meringue is light brown on the surface.

Source: Doris (Lafere) Schlichting recalled that only her mother Emma made this pie.

Carrot Cookies

Cookie Dough
2 c. flour
2 tsp. baking powder
1 c. "spry" (shortening)
1 egg, beaten
¾ c. white sugar
1 tsp. vanilla
1 tsp. lemon flavoring
1 c. mashed carrots

Frosting
1 c. powdered sugar
1 tsp. melted butter
1 – 2 Tbsp. orange juice

Cookie Dough: Add the baking powder to the flour and sift them together. Cut the shortening into the flour. Mix in the beaten egg and gradually mix in the sugar. Add the vanilla and lemon flavorings and mix thoroughly. Mix in the mashed carrots. Roll out the dough on a floured board and cut out the cookies. Bake at 350° until done. Do not over bake.

Frosting: Stir the melted butter into the powdered sugar. Add the orange juice and mix thoroughly. Spread the frosting over the cookies when they have cooled.

Source: Bette (Krug) Weber provided this unusual recipe from her mother.

Pinwheel Cookies

Dough
1 c. shortening
2 c. brown sugar
3 eggs
1 tsp. baking soda
4 c. flour
½ tsp. cinnamon
1 tsp. salt

Filling
1 lb. pitted dates (may substitute ground raisins)
½ c. white sugar
½ c. water
½ c. finely chopped nuts

Dough: Cream the shortening and sugar together. Mix in the eggs, one at a time. Dissolve the soda into a little water and add this to the mixture. In a separate bowl, sift the flour, then measure and sift it again with the cinnamon and salt added. Add the flour mixture to the shortening, sugar and egg mixture. Mix these thoroughly and place the dough in a refrigerator until chilled through.

Filling: Cook the fruit, sugar, and water until it is thick and soft. Mix this well, and then add the nuts. Cool the filling.

Roll out the chilled dough to ¼ inch thickness. Spread the cooled filling evenly over the dough. Roll the dough up like a jellyroll and chill it until it is cold enough to slice thinly—about ¼ inch thick.

Bake the cookies at 375°. Do not over bake.

Source: Doris Schlichting recalled that only her mother Emma made these cookies. They took considerable time to prepare. Dates were an exceptional fruit to find in Canby grocery stores, so raisins were often substituted.

Mary Engstrand

Noodle Surprise Casserole

3 qt. boiling water with 1 Tbsp. salt added
4 oz. noodles
1 c. cooked chicken, cut up
1 c. whole kernel corn
1 c. cooked peas
½ c. mushrooms
½ c. chopped green peppers
2 tsp. salt
1 ½ c. top milk (likely means cream)

Typically, "noodles" were elbow macaroni. Boil the noodles in the salted water until they are tender. Drain the noodles. Combine the chicken, corn, peas, mushrooms, and peppers with the noodles in a casserole dish. Mix the salt and milk, and add this to the casserole. Bake for about 30 minutes.

Source: Mary placed this recipe in a cookbook titled "620 Favorite Recipes from Providence Valley." The Engstrand's church was named Providence Valley Lutheran Church, and was located several miles southwest of the Engstrand farm. The church Ladies Aid published this cookbook in 1949.

Banana Nut Bread

½ c. shortening
¾ c. white sugar
2 c. sifted flour
½ tsp. salt
1 tsp. baking soda
1 Tbsp. lemon juice
1 c. mashed bananas
1 c. chopped nuts

Blend the shortening and sugar together until creamy. In a separate bowl, add the salt and soda to the flour, and sift them together. Stir the flour mixture into the shortening and sugar mixture. Stir in the bananas, lemon juice, and nuts. Use 3 well-greased number 2 cans (about 4 inches diameter) for baking; filling each can about ½ full of dough. Bake in a moderate (350°) oven for about 50 min.

Mary's note: Baking in the tin cans makes ideal sized loaves for tea sandwiches.

Source: Mary also placed this recipe in the cookbook titled "620 Favorite Recipes from Providence Valley." The Engstrand's church was named Providence Valley Lutheran Church, and was located several miles southwest of the Engstrand farm. The church Ladies Aid published this cookbook in 1949.

- Page numbers in *italics* indicates a photograph
- Endnotes (n) appear in **bold** with the page number first followed by n for "note" and the note number if there is one. For example, **25n3** means an index topic is found on page 25 in endnote number 3.

Index

A

Aladdin lamp *155*, **162n10**
Alfdorf 11, *12*, 19, *21*, 389
    1831 map *20*
America 104
American Civil War 6, 7
Arnold Boninger 79
    Michael Weller *78*
Aviation Ordnanceman **376n41**

B

B-24 Liberator *358*, 359–360
    "flying boxcars" 360
Bareis
    Albert C. (brother) 92
    Rosa (sister) *90*, *91*
        marriage to Gottlob Hinderer 89
Bareiss, Rosina
    marriage to Gottfried Hinderer, b. 1804 21
Barge Office in Battery Park 53, 64, *65*
Battle of the Bulge 351
Battle of the Little Bighorn 122
Baum, L. Frank
    The Wonderful Wizard of Oz 116
Berretta **375n19**
binder (grain) **331n16**
"birds of passage" 54
black cat (PBY Catalina) **377n49**
Bofors gun **375n10**
Brandenburg 220
breeching (unbreeching) **232n22**
Brend *12*, 22–24, 26
    1831 map *23*

Brenner, Carl and Elsa *293*, *323*
Brenner, Elizabeth 79
    married to Michael Weller 79. *See also under* Weller: Michael

C

Canby, Minnesota 127, 129–130, *131*, *132*
    1881 panorama *130–131*
    1893 fire 130
    John Lund 129, 130
    John Swenson 127
        store *127*
Columbia 87
comforts (bed covering) **375n8**
commission date (ship) **375n6**
Custer, George Armstrong 122

D

Dakota War of 1862 121–122
Dawson Surgical Hospital (Minnesota) *194*
deactivated unit (vs. disestablished) **377n50**
Deininger
    children
        Fritz (Friedrich) 36, *37*
        Karl *36*
        Katharine (*see* Hinderer, Katharine)
        Marie (Anna Maria) 36, *37*
            Christine Luise (daughter) 36. *See also under* Frey; Schmid
        Pauline *37*
    family table *34–35*
    farm 39, *40*, *41*
        Frey family 38
        Marie Deininger 38
        Pauline Deininger 38
        pencil sketch *38*
        Schmid family 38
    Gehren 33
    Johann Gottlieb 1, 33
        Eva Catharine Schwinger (mother) 36
        Huettenbuehl 33
        Johann Georg (father) 36
    Karoline (*née* Heinz) 1, *33*
    marriage 44

Katharine

diphtheria 227
    vaccination **232n21**
disestablished unit (vs. deactivated) **377n50**
District 66 176, *178*, *311*
Donau 79
door dog **301n**
DPT (Diphtheria, Pertussis [whooping cough], and Tetanus 227
Dumbo 372
Dunwoody College of Technology, Minnesota **211n17**

E

electricity 153
Ellis Island 53, 64, 83
Engstrand
    Albert 239, *312*, 312–313, *317*, *318*
        death 318, *319*
        Don (Donald Clayton) (son) 138, *181*, *182*, *270*, *299*, 309, 316, *317*, *318*, *323*, *326*, 327, *328*, 374
            464th Bombardment Group 355
            B-17 pilot training 357
            B-24 Liberator pilot training 360
            military service 355, 356, 357–365, *365*
            Pantanella, Italy 360–365
        marriage *314*, 316
        Mary (Maria Clara Caroline) (*née* Hinderer) *181*, *182*, *188*, 239, *270*, *299*, *317*, *318*, *323*, *328*, 374. *See also under* Hinderer, Katharine (*née* Deininger): children
            death 330
            Raymond Albert (son) *182*
        Norma Marie (daughter) 138, *181*, *182*, *188*, *270*, *296*, *317*, *318*, *323*, *326*, 327–329, *328*, 374
        Raymond Albert (son) *181*, *182*, *188*, *270*, 316, *317*, *318*, *326*, 326–327, *328*
        Ruth Georgiana (daughter) *181*, *188*, *270*, *299*, *317*, *323*, *328*, 329, 374
    Arthur *188*, *299*, 310, *318*, 374
    "Century Farm" 330
    home *324*
    John (father) 140, 304–305, *309*
        Anna (*née* Johnson) *182*, 304, 305–306, *309*
            death 317
            death 317
            marriage 306
    enlistment **375n2**

F

Freeland township **161n3**
Frey
    Christine Luise (Marie Deininger's daughter) 38
    Gotthilf 38
    Marlies (daughter) 38. *See also under* Schmid

G

Gehren 29, *30*
German Confederation of 1815 3, 4, 5, 6
German Empire of 1871 5, 7, 33
German POWs 354, **376n28**
German Revolution of 1848 5
"German Triangle" 57
Gilded Age 8
Gjovig
    Bill (William Edward)
        marriage 371, *373*, **375n1**
        Maurine LaRayne (*née* Krug) 137–138, 374. *See also under* Krug, Martin John: Sophie (*née* Hinderer)
        World War II
            Aleutian Campaign 369, 371
            Aviation Ordnanceman 366
            Fleet Air Wing (FAW) 366
            Japanese surrender 372
            military service 365–366, *367*, 368–369, 371–373
            Naval Training Station, Great Lakes, Illinois 365
            Navy enlistment 365
            Patrol Bomber Unit 23 (VPB-23) 372
            Patrol Bomber Unit 43 (VPB-43 366–368
            USS San Francisco 371
    Herman (Bill's half brother) 365
glacial till **211n10**
Great Depression 185–186
gunny sack **162n13**

H

half-timbered construction **27n10**
Hansen, Andrew (Andreas) Boyson 220, 224
   Anna Magdalena (daughter) 224
      first marriage to John George Krug 224–225. *See also under* Krug: John George
      second marriage to Nels Hansen 227 (*see* Hansen, Nels)
   emigrating to America 220
   Hans Peter (father) 220
      Ingeborg Kirstine (*née* Jensdetter) 220
         emigrating to America 220
   Mary Marie (*née* Perschnick) 224. *See also under* Perschnick
   Minnesota 228
Hansen, Nels 228
   Anna Magdalena (*née* Hansen). *See also under* Hansen, Andrew (Andreas) Boyson
      John George Krug (first husband) (*see* Krug: John George)
      Nels (second husband) 227, 228
   Emma Helene (daughter) 138, 228
   Minnesota 229–230
Harburg 214
Haug, Gottlieb 76
   death 76
   marriage to Rosine (*née* Weller) Koeder 76. *See also under* Weller: Jacob
Havel 53, 54, *61*
   Gottlieb Hinderer 63, *64*
   Katharine Deininger 63–64, *64*
Heinz 41, 44
   book of sermons 44–48, *45–47*
      Gottlieb 44
      Karoline 45
   family table *42–43*
   Freiderich (son) 44
   Gottlieb 41
   Karl August (son) 44
   Karoline (daughter and Katharine Hinderer's mother) 1, 44
   Rosine (b. 1827, *née* Weller) 41

Hinderer 15, 21–22
   Carl Jacob. *See also under* Hinderer, Katharine (*née* Deininger): children
   Christian (b. 1804) 103
      Rosina (*née* Weller) 103
   Emma Anna. *See also under* Hinderer, Katharine (*née* Deininger): children
   Gottfried (b. 1804, Johannes Hinderer's father) 1, 22, 23, 103
      family table *22*
      Rosina (*née* Bareiss) 21
   Gottfried (b. 1857, Gottlieb Hinderer's cousin) 102–108
      Carolina Rosina (daughter) 104
      Christian and Rosina (parents) 104
      emigrating to America 104
      Emma Christine Elisa (daughter) 107
      family table 108
      Ida (daughter) 107
      Iowa 104, 105
      Lena Catherine (Katie) 107
         marriage to Clarence Tebelman 107
      Minnesota 107
      Rosine (*née* Nise) 104
   Gottlieb (b. 1866, Johannes Hinderer's son) 1, 5, 7, 19, 82, *93*, 109, 147, *181*, *187*, *188*, *189*, 270, *293*, *298*, *299*, *318*, *323*, *374*
      ancestor list 384–385
      birth 1
      children (*see* Hinderer, Katharine (*née* Deininger): children)
      death 187
      emigrating to America 24, 54, 59, 61
         Havel 63
      family table 111
      Iowa 66, 94, 101–102, 109
      Katharine (*née* Deininger) (*see* Hinderer, Katharine)
      Michigan 66, 94
      Minnesota 165–166 (*see* Hinderer, Katharine (*née* Deininger): Minnesota)
   Johannes 1, 22, 23, 82–84, *86*, 91
      August (son) *86*, *89*, *91*, 92, 92–93, *93*

Hinderer, Johannes (*continued*)
- Tina (*née* Walz) 92, 93
- Walter 93
- Christine Catharine (daughter) 66, 86–89
  - Elsa 94
  - marriage to William Weber 86, 88. *See also* *under* Weber, William
- emigrating to America 24, 82, 83
- family table 16, 85
- Gottlieb (son) (*see* Hinderer: Gottlieb, b. 1866)
- Gottlob (son) 86, 89, 89–92, *90*, *91*, 93
  - Edna *91*
  - Elmer *91*
  - family table 91
  - marriage 89
  - Rosa (*née* Bareis) *90*, *91*
- Johann (John) Georg (son) 85–86, *86*, *91*
- marriage 1
- Michigan 19, 70, 83–84
- Sophie (*née* Weller) 19, 70. *See also* *under* Weller: Jacob
  - death 84
- John (*see* Hinderer, Katharine (*née* Deininger): children)
- Martha (*see* Hinderer, Katharine (*née* Deininger): children)
- Mary (Maria Clara Caroline) (*see* Hinderer, Katharine (*née* Deininger): children)
- Matthäus (grandfather of Johannes Hinderer) 22, 24
- Sophie Karoline (*see* Hinderer, Katharine (*née* Deininger): children)
- Tena (Christine Katharine) (*see* Hinderer, Katharine (*née* Deininger): children)

Hinderer, Katharine (*née* Deininger) 1, 7, 29, 33, 109, *146*, *147*, *181*, *182*, 187, 188, 189, 265, 270, 293, 298, 299, 323, 374, 379–380
- ancestor list 386
- birth 2
- children
  - Carl Jacob 110, *146*, *147*, 167–169, *181*, *182*, 188, 270, 298, 299, 310, 374, 380
    - death 191
  - Emma Anna 110–111, 114, *146*, *147*, 169, *170*, *182*, 234–235, *235*, 249, 265, 380
    - marriage to Ralph Lafere 239. *See also* *under* Lafere
    - remarriage to Martin John Krug 244. *See also* *under* Krug, Martin John
  - John 137, 139, *146*, *147*, *157*, *158*, 167–169, *171*, *180*, *181*, *182*, 188, 270, 299, *318*, 380
    - 533rd Anti-Aircraft Battalion 343
    - Battle of the Bulge 351–352
    - death 191
    - discharge 355
    - German POWs 354
    - induction 341
    - military service 341–355, *345*, *346*, *347*
    - North Africa 346–347
    - R.M.S. *Andes* 345–346
    - Sardinia 348–350
    - Seventh United States Army 350
  - Martha *146*, *147*, 149, 170, *171*, *181*, *182*, 188, *265*, 270, 298, 299, 323, 374, 380
    - death 191
  - Mary (Maria Clara Caroline) 114, 139, *146*, *147*, 169–170, *311*, 311–312, 311–312, 380
    - marriage to Albert Engstrand 239. *See also* *under* Engstrand: Albert
  - Sophie Karoline 110, *147*, 169, *170*, 234–235, *235*, *237*, 380
    - marriage to Martin John Krug 237. *See also* *under* Krug, Martin John
  - Tena (Christine Katharine) 109–110, *147*, 169, *181*, *182*, 193, 194, 195, *317*, 380
    - marriage to John Robert Monson 202, *203*. *See also under* Monson: John Robert
- death 187
- emigrating to America 24, 36, 54, 59, 61
  - *Havel* 63–64
- family table 111
- Gehren 29
- Gottlieb (b. 1866, husband) 379 (*see* Hinderer: Gottlieb, b. 1866)
- hymnal 114, *115*
- Iowa 66, 101–102, 109, 379
- Johann (father) 1
- Karoline (mother) 1
- Michigan 66

Hinderer, Katharine (*née* Deininger) (*continued*)
   Minnesota 133, 139–140, 166–167, 379
      church 175
      crops 155–158
      education
         District 66 *176, 178*
         elementary 175–178
         high school 178–179
      electricity 153
      farm animals 161
      farmhouse 145–150, *147, 148, 149, 153*
      food 172–173, 174–175
         storage 152
      heat 152
      hunting 179–180
      lighting 153
         Aladdin lamp *155*
         Aladdin lamp **162n10**
      Model T 154–155
      music 184–185
         Victrola *184*
      soap 173
      sod house 140
      telephone 153, *155*
      The Great Depression 185–186
      transportation 154–155
      travel/visits 179, 180–181, 183–184
      washing clothes 173
      water 150–152
   working as a domestic for the Hinderer family 60–61
hog itch **301n16**
Holtz, Baron Goerg Friedrich (vom Holst) 13, 390
Holy Roman Empire 2, *3*
Homestead Act of 1862 58, 121, 304
Hormel Foods (George A. Hormel & Co.) **301n15**
hutment **375n12**

I

immigration 54, 56
   by ship 59–60
   German immigration statistics 54
   "German Triangle" 57
   Homestead Act of 1862 58
   to America 57–59
   Wuerttemberg 61, 70
      Wuerttemberg Emigration Index 63
Industrial Revolution 4, 6, 59
Iowa 95–97
   Postville 101
      St. Paul's Evangelical Lutheran Church 101

J

Jacobson, "King Jake" 125, *126*
Jacobson Party 125

K

Kader, Godfrey 76–77. *See also under* Koeder
Kanabec County 196–197, **211n8**
Keller, Johann Michael
   Schwäbisch Gmünd 390
Koeder 18, 71–78
   emigrating to America 19, 71–72
   family table *73*, 76
   Friederich (son) 19, 70, 71
   Godfrey [sometimes spelled Kader] (son) 76–77
   last name spelling variations 18
   marriage 18, 71
   Michigan 19, 70
   Rosine (*née* Weller) 70, 76–78. *See also under* Weller: Jacob
   Ulrich
      death 76
Krug
   Johann Christoph 214, 219
      Anna Barbara (*née* Deuerlein) 214, 216
         death 216
      children
         Georg Bernhard 216,
            marriage to Hanna Perschnick, 223
         Georg Leonhard 216
         Johann Konrad 214, 216
      death *216*
      emigrating to America 214
   Johann Konrad (Johann Christoph's son) 219
      death 219

Krug, Johann Konrad (*continued*)
    Margaret (Anna Margaretha Elizabeth, *née* Schaller) 219
        death 219
    John George (Martin Krug's father) 219
        Anna Magdalena (*née* Hansen) 224–225. See also under Hansen, Andrew (Andreas) Boyson; Hansen, Nels
        diphtheria death 225, 227
        Martin John (son) 225 (see Krug, Martin John)
Krug, Martin John (John George's son) *181*, *182*, *202*, 213–214, 235–236, *237*, *241*, *260*, *267*, *270*
    birth 225
    death 266, 272
    detective training correspondence course certificate 264
    Emma Anna Lafere (*née* Hinderer) *181*, *188*, *268*, *270*, *278*, *279*, *291*, *293*, *295*, *318*. See also under Lafere; Hinderer, Katharine (*née* Deininger): children
        Bette (Elizabeth Anna) (daughter) 138, *188*, *263*, *279*, 285–287, *286*, *292*, *293*, *298*
        death 300
        Deloris Mae (daughter) *181*, *188*, *263*, *267*, *268*, *270*, *279*, *284*, 284–285, *292*, *293*, *295*, *296*, *298*, *299*, *374*
        Florence Marie (daughter) 138, *160*, *188*, *263*, *279*, 287–288, *288*, *290*, *291*, *292*, *293*, *296*, *298*, *299*, *374*
            marriage to Gerald Rousseau 295
        Jeanette Marlene (daughter) *160*, *188*, *263*, *279*, *288*, 288–289, *290*, *291*, *292*, *293*, *298*
        Leonard Ray (son) 138, *181*, *188*, *263*, *267*, *268*, *270*, *279*, *285*, *290*, *292*, *293*, *296*
    marriage 244, 261
    widowhood 273
    Prohibition 265, 271–272
    Sophie (*née* Hinderer) *182*, *202*, *237*, *241*, *244*. See also under Hinderer, Katharine (*née* Deininger): children
    illness and death 242–243, 259–260
        Johnny (John Martin) (son) *181*, *182*, *188*, *202*, *239*, *241*, *244*, *263*, *267*, *268*, *270*, *279*, 280–281, *281*, *292*, *295*, *299*, *318*, *374*
    military service (WWII) 333–334, 336–337, *340*, 341
    Naval Training Station, Great Lakes, Illinois 334
    Navy enlistment 334
    Pearl Harbor 336–337
    USS *Argonne* 334, 336, 337
    USS *Fletcher* 337–338
    USS *Indianapolis* 337
    USS *Utah* 334, 337
    marriage 237
    Maurine LaRayne (daughter) *181*, *182*, *188*, *202*, 240, *241*, *244*, *264*, *267*, *268*, *270*, *279*, 282–284, *284*, *292*, *295*, *296*, *298*, *299*, *318*, *374*
        marriage to Bill Gjovig *371*, *373*. See also under Gjovig: Bill (William Edward)
    William Andrew (son) *181*, *182*, *188*, 240, *244*, 263–264, *267*, *268*, *270*, *279*, 281–282, *282*, *292*, *293*, *296*, *298*, *299*, *318*, *374*
unbreeched 227

L

Lafere
    DNA 257
    Emma Anna (*née* Hinderer). See also under Hinderer, Katharine (*née* Deininger): children
        Doris Catherine (daughter) *149*, 170–172, *178*, *182*, *202*, *241*, *265*, *270*, *279*, 279–280, *281*, *317*, *318*. See also under Schlichting: Doris (Lafere)
        birth 252, **161n6**
        marriage to Henry Schlichting **191n8**
    first marriage to Ralph Lafere 249, 251
    second marriage to Martin John Krug 261. See also under Krug, Martin John
    Lillie DeGrush 254
    Ralph 239, 249–250, 251, 253–255
        "boxcar bandits" 254
        Sioux Falls, South Dakota 251–252
La Grande Armée 6
Lake Agassiz 119
lead destroyer **375n37**

life expectancy in 1870 **191n14**
Loehe, Johann Konrad William 214–215
Long Depression 7
Lund-Hoel House **133n23**
Lund, John 129, 130, 145
    Lund-Hoel House **133n23**
lye **191n5**

M

Manifest Destiny 58
Marcy, Grace *206*
McRae
    Donald 196
    Jennet Matheson 196
    Mary (daughter) 196
Messerschmitt
    ME-109 354
    ME-262 354
Michigan 69–70
    Washtenaw County 70
Milwaukee Road 97, 99
Minnesota 119–124
    Canby 127, 129–130, *131*, *132*
        1881 panorama *130–131*
        1893 fire 130
        fire 130
        John Lund 129, 130
        John Swenson 127
            store *127*
    Hinderer family life (*see* Hinderer, Katharine (*née* Deininger): Minnesota
    Indian land 120–122
    Lac Qui Parle County 125–127
    Lake Agassiz 119
    Ojibwe 120
    Sioux 122–123
    St. Peter Railroad Company 127
    water 123–124
    Yellow Medicine County 125–127
moldboard plow **301n9**
Monson
    John Robert 180, *182*, *188*, *202*, *205*, *206*, *241*, *317*
        children
            Bob 137, *160*, *181*, *182*, *188*, *198*, 204, *205*, *208*, 208–209
            George Ellsworth 137, *181*, *182*, 204, *205*, 206–207, *207*, *270*
            Mabel 137, *181*, *188*, 204, *205*, 207, *270*
        death 209
        farm 203–206, 210
        marriage 202, *203*
        Tena (*née* Hinderer) *188*, 202, *205*, 209–210, *270*. *See also under* Hinderer, Katharine (*née* Deininger): children
        death 210
    William (b. 1865) 196, 198, 200, *206*
        children
            Duke (Dan) 198
            Edward (Ned) 198, 206
            Ethel 169, 196, *202*, *206*, *241*, *317*
            John Robert (*see* Monson: John Robert)
        Edward (father) 196
        Ellen Rourke (mother) 196
        Mary (*née* McRae) 196
            death 200

N

Neckar 104, 105
Nise
    Johann (brother) 104
    Rosine (sister)
        married to Gottfried Hinderer, b. 1857 104. *See also under* Hinderer: Gottlfried, b. 1857

O

Odd Fellows **211n2**
Ojibwe 120
    Chippewa **133n4**
Operation Mincemeat **375n16**
    The Man Who Never Was **375n16**

P

Pacific Railroad Act 58
Panic of 1873 7
Panic of 1893 114, 116
PBY Catalina **377n49**
Pearl Harbor 336–337

Pearl Harbor (*continued*)
    Franklin Delano Roosevelt 344
    map *338*
    USS *Utah* 337
Perschnick
    Caroline 224
    Christiane 223
    Gottlieb 223
    Hanna (Johanna) 220
        emigrating to America 220, 223
        marriage to Georg Bernard Krug 223
    Johann 224
    Mary (Marie) 220
        marriage to Andrew Hansen 224. *See also under* Hansen, Andrew (Andreas) Boyson
    Wilhelmine 223
Probst, Friedmar (Pastor) 389, *393*
Prohibition 246–248
Protestant Church of Kaisersbach 31–33, *32*

R

Recipes
    Banana Nut Bread 406
    Berlinerkranz Knots 399
    Carrot Cookies 404
    Doughnuts 399
    Emma Krug's Cookies 401
    Gingerbread Cake 403
    Honey Cookies 402
    Martha's Overnight Cookies 398
    Noodle Surprise Casserole 406
    Overnight Salad 398
    Pfeffer Nuesse (Pepper Nut) Cookies 397
    Pinwheel Cookies 405
    Sandwich Buns 396
    Scotch Date Cookies 402
    Sour Cream Raisin Bars 400
    Sour Cream Raisin Pie 404
    Spaetzle 397
    Suet Pudding 403
    Wax Bean Pickles 396
Republic 196
R.M.S. *Andes* 345, 346
Roosevelt, Franklin Delano 344
Rosenberg, Gottlieb (shoemaker) 76
Rousseau
    Florence (*née* Krug) 138
    Gerald 295
    marriage 295
Rufname 33
rum running (rumrunning) **258n5**
rust (grain) **331n17**

S

Saale 82, 83, 85, 89, 92
Sandrock, Norma (*née* Engstrand) 138. *See also under* Engstrand: Albert
Schaffer, Anna Maria
    marriage to Jacob Weller 18. *See also under* Weller: Jacob
    Rehnenmuehle 18
Schaller
    Margaret (Anna Margaretha Elizabeth) 219
Schlichting *51*
    David 38, *51*, *299*, *374*, *393*, **258n12**
    Doris (Lafere) 137, *149*, *299*, *374*
        marriage to Henry Schlichting **191n8**
    Merlin 38, *51*, 393
    Ryan 38
    Sharon *299*, *374*
Schmid
    Heinz 38
    Marlies (*née* Frey) 38. *See also under* Frey
    Wolfgang (son) 38, *51*
        Max *51*
        Ursula 38, *51*
Schwinger, Eva Catharine 36
Second Reich. *See* German Empire of 1871
sepsis **331n18**
Seventh United States Army 350
Seven Weeks War of 1866 5
silage **211n14**
Sioux
    Battle of the Little Bighorn 122
    Dakota War of 1862 121–122
    Great Plains 122–123
    Minnesota 120–122
Sitting Bull 122

sod house (soddies) 141–142, *142*
Spanish Flu 245–246
Statue of Liberty 53
stove jacket **191n9**
St. Paul's Evangelical Lutheran Church (Postville, Iowa) 101
St. Stephan Church (Aldorf) *13*, 13–14, *14*, 15, 389–392
    altar *393*
    Johann Michael Keller 390
    Pastor Friedmar Probst 389, *393*
    pencil sketch *15*
Swenson, Emma Helene (*née* Hansen, Martin Krug's half sister) 138. *See also under* Hansen, Nels
Swenson, John 127
    store *127*
Sylvan Place **192n16**

T

Tebelman
    Clarence 107
    Donald (son) 107
    Lena Catherine (Katie) (*née* Hinderer) 107
telephones 153–154, *155*
The Long Winter 124
The Man Who Never Was **375n16**
The Wonderful Wizard of Oz 116
Trinity Lutheran Church (Grundy County, Illinois) 215, 216

U

unbreeching (breeching) **232n22**
USS *Argonne* 334, *336*, 337
USS *Fletcher* 337, *339*, 341
    commissioned 337
USS *Indianapolis* 337
USS *San Francisco* 371
USS *Utah* 280, 334, *336*, 337

V

Vereine 5
V-Mail (Victory Mail) 351, **375n22**
Vom **27n3**

W

Walz, Tina 93
    marriage to August Hinderer 93. *See also under* Hinderer: Johannes: August
water
    artesian **162n9**
    hard **162n8**
    soft (rainwater) 150
water dowser 152
Weber, Bette (*née* Krug) 138. *See* Krug, Martin John: Emma Anna Lafere (*née* Hinderer)
Weber, William 86–89
    Elsa (daughter) 94
    emigrating to America 87
    family table 88
    Maria Funk (mother) 87
    marriage to Christine Catharine (*née* Hinderer) 86, 88. *See also under* Hinderer: Johannes
    Michigan 87
Weidendorf, Ethel (*née* Monson) *206*
Weller 15, 17–19
    Jacob 1, 18
        Anna Marie (daughter) 18, 19
        Anna Marie (*née* Schaffer) 18, 83
        family table *72*
        Katherine (daughter) 18, 19
        Rosine (daughter, b. 1830) 18, 71
            first marriage to Ulrich Koeder (*see* Koeder)
            second marriage to Gottlieb Haug (*see* Haug)
        Sophie (daughter) 17, 18, 19
            marriage to Johannes Hinderer 1. *See also under* Hinderer: Johannes
    Johann Georg (Katharine Deininger ancestor) 41
    Johann Jakob (Sophie Weller's grandfather) 18
    Michael 18, 19, 70, 76, 78–82
        Anna (daughter) 79
        Elizabeth (*née* Brenner) 79
        emigrating to America 78–79
        family table *80*
        Fred (son) 79
        Gottlieb (son) 79
        marriage *80*

Weller, Michael (*continued*)
    Mary (daughter) 79
    Michigan 19
    Theodore Carl (son) 79
Weller, Rosina (married to Christian Hinderer, b. 1804) 103
Weser 224
Whippet *268, 281*, **274n8**
Wilder, Laura Ingalls 124
    The Long Winter 124
Wilhelm II, Kaiser 7, 8
Winona & St. Peter Railroad Company 127, 145, **133n18**
Women's Suffrage 246
World War I 236, 245–246
World War II 186
    Aleutian Campaign 369–370
    Aviation Ordnanceman **376n41**
    B-24 Liberator *358*, 359–360
        "flying boxcars" 360
    Battle of the Bulge 351
    Berretta **375n19**
    black cat (PBY Catalina) **377n49**
    Bofors gun **375n10**
    comforts (bed covering) **375n8**
    commission date (ship) **375n6**
    deactivated unit **377n50**
    disestablished unit **377n50**
    Dumbo 372
    enlistment **375n2**
    Franklin Delano Roosevelt 344
    German POWs 354, **376n28**
    hutment **375n12**
    lead destroyer **375n37**
    Messerschmitt
        ME-109 354
        ME-262 354
    Operation Mincemeat **375n16**
        The Man Who Never Was **375n16**
    PBY Catalina **377n49**
    Pearl Harbor 336–337
        USS *Utah* 337
    selective service 341
    Seventh United States Army 350
    V-Mail (Victory Mail) 351, **375n22**

Wuerttemberg 3
    Emigration Index 63
    farms 17
    marriage rules 48–50

Z

Zacchaeus German Lutheran Church *175*, **191n7**

www.ingramcontent.com/pod-product-compliance
Lightning Source LLC
Chambersburg PA
CBHW081124170426
43197CB00017B/2746